*JEAN-JACQUES ROUSSEAU*

# JEAN-JACQUES
# ROUSSEAU

## THE PROPHETIC VOICE
## (1758-1778)

BY

## Lester G. Crocker

*VOLUME II*

*The Macmillan Company, New York*
*Collier-Macmillan Publishers, London*

*The Macmillan Company*
*866 Third Avenue, New York, N.Y. 10022*
*Collier-Macmillan Canada Ltd., Toronto, Ontario*

Library of Congress Catalog Card Number: 68-22818

FIRST PRINTING 1973

Printed in the United States of America

*. . . toi qui n'as pas pris le triste emploi de dire
la vérité aux hommes. . . .*

*Emile,* BOOK V

My task is to bear witness to the truth. For this I
was born, for this I came into the world, and all
who are not deaf to truth listen to my voice.

JOHN 18:37

# Contents

*JEAN-JACQUES ROUSSEAU*

# I. Fruits of Solitude

### 1. LOOKING BACK—AND FORWARD

ON December 15, 1757, Jean-Jacques had moved, with Thérèse, to a small house in the park of Mont-Louis, at Montmorency, not far from the Hermitage. The unwanted mother-in-law had been shipped off to Paris, where Grimm took care of her, settling her in an artisan's house. For this Rousseau had no feeling of gratitude. On the contrary, still embroiled in the great quarrel with Diderot and his group, he suspected that Grimm's solicitude had only one motive, keeping in touch with his movements. That affair, and the sorry denouement of his friendship with Mme. d'Houdetot, were not his sole preoccupation during 1758.

We now go back to the agitated wintry day when Jean-Jacques closed the door of his cottage at the Hermitage, with a bitter anguish that must have made him think of another time, some fifteen years before, when he had closed the door of Les Charmettes. Some men shrug off the past. Rousseau carried the past, still living, with him. Looking back was part of his nature, even though he longed to escape from time. And before Les Charmettes there had been Bossey, and before that, his home in Geneva. Each a closed world *"selon mon coeur,"* secure and insulated. But there was no permanence for him. Each home was but a temporary resting place, and each had come to an end with a brutal expulsion and flight toward a new refuge where some of his dreams might come true. They never did. Yet with Jean-Jacques, more than with most men, it is the imponderables in human conduct, the dreams, desires, and fantasies, that matter most, for they infuse and transform whatever happens in his life.

Each comfortable enclosure he had known had been replaced by an uncertain, seemingly hostile world, giving him the desperate feeling of having lost control of his life. He had not forgotten the fears and rejections, the isolation and homelessness, the feeling of being different from

all others and a misfit. It was bad enough that he could not get along
with men. Why did they all turn against him? But the two women, who
should have been more understanding, had also rejected him. How
could this be, when, as he said, "to be loved by all who approached me
was my keenest desire"?

How could he understand what separated him from other men? His
strangeness, the obsessional, paranoid traits, the guilt and inferiority
feelings that made him uncomfortable with others and led him to react
in abnormal, compensating ways—he could fathom none of all that. He
lost himself in fantasy, yet he was oddly deficient in imagination, blind
to the real world of people, while at the same time anxious, self-defeat-
ingly anxious, for its acceptance—and, much more, for its admiration. He
was rebellious to its demands, but dependent in his proud independence. No wonder he experienced fear and trembling before a world he
saw as one of hostile masks, each peering into him, judging him, stirring
up the dregs of his past sins and weaknesses. But Maman, and then
Sophie, they had understood him. With them (he thought) there were
no masks, and they had seen his heart. If they had misunderstood and
misinterpreted, if they had not recognized his purity and his worth, then
human nature must be very corrupt indeed. He had mistaken his ability
to vent his emotions freely with Maman and Sophie for an act of truly
giving himself. But a defining characteristic of the neurotic, especially
the obsessional, is precisely that he is unable to give himself. He is the
prisoner of his self-centeredness.

Much in Rousseau's vision of the world and of himself was distorted.
That he was unaware of it, convinced of his total rightness, was the very
sign of his illness. The tramp and adventurer had won fame, after all.
That was enough to confirm his subjective certainty. But the split with
the social order had only widened, because he had founded his fame,
and his identity, on that split. The voluntary exile to the Hermitage,
the long quarrel with its complex intrigues, bickering, suspicions, and
deceptions had heightened his neuroticism, so that he saw himself the
target of a conspiracy to destroy him and the truths he bore within him.
No one was to be trusted, save a few friends who remained, mainly in
Geneva. More and more, the "plot" was to become his great obsession.
Diderot himself, Casini reminds us, had "glimpsed the morbid aspect of
his personality when he pointed out in all his apostasies—[from Protestantism to Catholicism], from Catholicism to Protestantism, from *philosophie* to natural religion—the sign of his psychic anomaly. These apostasies were the lucid delirium of a neurotic." He had left behind him
not only a long-time friend, Diderot, "but the whole Age of Reason.
The sentimental pathos of the epistolary novel, the sickly narcissism of
the *Confessions*, the deep religious and nature feelings of the *Rêveries*,
the lucid madness of the dialogues, *Rousseau juge de Jean-Jacques*, no
longer have any common measure with the Encyclopedic culture."[1]

That is why we must feel what Rousseau felt if we are to understand what he thought.

It is the intensely personal, subjective tone of his writings that lends them their force and that sparked the enthusiastic response they received. Regarding himself as both unique and universally human, Rousseau drew all his ideas from his subjective experience. . . . Weak, sick in body and mind, perverted, unfit for society, he knew all the distress of the human condition. . . . Contemplating him from the vantage point of our own time, we see the gigantic and tortured figure of the prophet of modern man's predicament.[2]

Reality was not acceptable, and it had refused to accept him. All his life, he had rebelled against it. And his escape from it, into fantasy, pure sensation, or vague mysticism, seemed to him the discovery of a new and better reality. Reality was his guilt: his mother and his father, sexuality, petty thefts, the infamy of the ribbon, exhibitionism and masochism, ingratitude toward the Gouvons and Lemaître, his relationship with Maman and his failure to help her, the abandonment of his children, and now the sordid affair with Saint-Lambert and Mme. d'Houdetot. The fantasy was his aspiration to innocence: Bossey, the Maman he made up, Mlle. Galley and Mlle. Graffenried, his communings with nature.

As Rousseau wandered in the little garden at Mont-Louis, it must have seemed that in his personal life everything had failed him—his recourse to childhood and innocence, love, friendship, society, and now even solitude. We know that it was in these failures that he found his greatness. No one can explain a man's greatness. It is in him. But one can try to explain its growth in him and the form it takes. If Rousseau had not failed in his struggles to find identity and self-esteem, he would not have embraced his alienation and his role as the prophetic voice. He would not have asked himself what it means to be someone—"someone among others and somebody *else*."[3] What does it matter if he distorted his role, identified himself with Socrates, Cato, Moses, Lycurgus, or Jesus Christ? His dreams and fantasies were to be sublimated into his works. They were to be his true destiny and reality, the road to his freedom. Through the creative act he fought "the dark forces of destruction" that endangered his psychic existence, but unfortunately his victory was not to be complete.

Now, as during much of his life, the past was a burden of regret and longing, the future cloudy and threatening, the present oppressive. Here at Mont-Louis he wanted only to retreat into a world bounded by his own self. Within that circumference, he felt his own presence with intensity and delight. Other, hostile, realities disappeared. The experiencing of his existence sufficed for an exquisite narcissistic pleasure and became the sole reality in his consciousness.

Peace of mind was not possible at first, but he gradually recovered his self-possession, and the final break with Diderot, in the spring of 1758, brought him a great sense of relief.

Since I had shaken off the yoke of my tyrants, I led a rather calm and peaceful life. Freed from the spell of too keen attachments, I was also released from their chains. Disenchanted with protective friends who wanted to control my fate completely and enslave me to their supposed favors despite myself, I was resolved to limit myself in the future to relationships of simple good will which, without hindering freedom, and based on equality, make life pleasant. I had enough of those to enjoy the sweet savor of freedom without suffering dependency (*Confessions*, Book X).

In fact, Rousseau had been able to work even during the crisis, and that had been an invaluable catharsis and therapy. The great work was *La Nouvelle Héloïse*. The novel had been "completed" in four parts in October 1757. He informed Mme. d'Houdetot on February 13 that he was about to do a fifth part. There were to be six in all, and their completion took until the middle of September. We shall see how the emotions of their love affair were transmuted into his love novel, and how they changed it.

That task was intertwined with much else. For Mme. d'Houdetot he wrote his "Lettres à Sophie" (or "Lettres morales") during the harsh winter days. For her, too, he recopied large parts of *La Nouvelle Héloïse*. She was never far from his mind. There was also another work, shorter, but intellectually and psychologically valuable to him, which he was to entitle *Lettre à d'Alembert sur les spectacles* (*Letter to d'Alembert on the Theater*). Like all else he wrote, it was, or became, intimately connected with his life and his problems. To see how it developed, we must go back.

The seventh volume of the *Encyclopédie* had come off the presses on October 10, 1757. It contained a long article by d'Alembert, "Genève," in the course of which he proposed the establishment of a theater in Rousseau's native city. In making this suggestion, d'Alembert was undoubtedly acting on behalf of his close friend Voltaire. The latter was not only France's leading writer of tragedies. He had set up his private stage at Les Délices, his home on the edge of Geneva, and spent much time putting on performances, often taking a role in them. The other performers were usually his guests, among them, at one time, his favorite actor, Lekain. Despite the ban on theater in Geneva, many of the city's patricians attended these performances. Voltaire was extremely vexed when the Grand Council of the republic bade him put an end to them. His reaction, quite typical, was to mount a covert campaign to establish a theater in Geneva.

There was danger in this. The controversy over the morality of the theater, and of actors in particular, was an old one in Christian countries. In Geneva, the quarrel had become political at the turn of the century.[4] The struggle among the classes was involved.* Calvin, who wanted to control men's thoughts as well as their conduct—as Rousseau was to plan on doing—had used the theater for his purposes. When the sumptuary laws of 1617 closed the theaters, the aristocracy, and the civil powers they controlled, resisted. In the 1730's the controversy became a part of the political struggle that led to foreign intervention in 1737. Under the protection of the French envoy, the Gherardi troupe came from Lyons to put on performances. This aroused the opponents of the oppressive governing classes, whom they now accused of being under the royalist and papist French influence. When the troupe departed, the Consistory condemned those Genevans who had taken part in performances. Another troupe came in 1739. The scandalous behavior of the actors on this occasion convinced the people that the Consistory had been right. Once again, all performances were banned. Infractions by amateurs continued to occur, and to be punished.

In August 1756, d'Alembert arrived in Geneva to gather material for his article. Voltaire had moved to Monrepos, in the Vaud canton. There he was free to indulge his passion for the stage, and there he was visited by his friend.

D'Alembert's article "Genève" is a model of his usual prudence. He hits at the "philosophic" party's foe, but always indirectly, with vague and elusive argumentation. He supports the stage, but admits that the behavior of actors requires "regulation." He urges that the republic "permit comedy," and lets it go at that, not specifying whether he means a permanent theater (as Rousseau and others were to interpret him) or occasional visiting companies.

All this might have passed without much fuss, had d'Alembert not added a second part to his article—innocently, Green thinks, but with clever design according to Fuchs' more plausible judgment.[5] D'Alembert, with the *Encyclopédie* in mind, eulogized the Genevan pastors for their broadmindedness and for the "perfect Socinianism" (i.e., Unitarianism) professed by some. How could such a "philosophical" clergy oppose the theater? "Theatrical performances would form the taste of the citizens and would give them a *finesse de tact*, a delicacy of feeling which it is very difficult to acquire without help." He obviously did not have a high opinion of Genevan culture.

D'Alembert could not have anticipated the violent reaction—further inflamed by satirical barbs at the city—his words were to arouse. He had done no less than to cast heavy doubt on the orthodoxy of the Calvinist ministers. In truth, there was reason for this doubt. The Genevan clergy, moreover, was largely on the side of Les Représentants, the popular party opposed to the oligarchy. They supported sumptuary laws and condemned the theater, while the aristocrats wanted to imitate the Pa-

* See Lester G. Crocker, *Jean-Jacques Rousseau: The Quest (1712–1758)*, Ch. 1.

risian aristocracy. Now patriotic Genevans rallied to the cause. Dr. Tronchin asked d'Alembert for clarifications, and got none. The canny *philosophe* counted on dividing the foe. The Vénérable Compagnie des Pasteurs et Professeurs de l'Académie de Genève, after six weeks of arduous debate, put out a fighting "Déclaration" which both rejected the accusation and condemned the Encyclopedists for their "licentious and sophistical philosophy." The question of the theater was not mentioned. The vagueness of the defense showed that d'Alembert had been right in suspecting a deep division of opinion.

The only riposte to d'Alembert's proposal for a theater was an ineffectual tract put out in April 1758 by an anonymous lay citizen. The Genevans did not suspect that an eloquent voice was even then polishing off a powerful counterattack that would make the affair a *cause célèbre* and turn the tables on d'Alembert and the Encyclopedists. The *Lettre à d'Alembert* was, in fact, completed. It was written in a fury of concentration that, in Rousseau's own words, "saved my life and distracted me from moments of anguish in which, without it, I should have died of despair."[6] The *Lettre* had been composed in the space of three weeks, between the early part of February and March 9, with two brief interruptions: one caused by illness, the other by a correspondence with Vernes, the Genevan pastor, in defense of his religious beliefs.

Rousseau did not know of d'Alembert's article when it first appeared. Ironically, it was Diderot who first told him about it in the course of his famous last visit of December 5. Rousseau's immediate reaction was a wave of indignation at this underhanded effort to corrupt his country; but he said nothing, having other matters to argue about. When he finally read the piece shortly after moving to Mont-Louis, he was too depressed to summon up the energy to reply. Not until February did he go daily to the open lodge that looked out over the valley of Montmorency toward Paris, in the distance. There, in the intense cold, he was warmed by the fire of his indignation as he wrote what he considered to be his most "virile" work and one of his chief titles to glory. His recollection of the experience is keen and revealing:

The injustices which I had only witnessed had irritated me; those I had suffered saddened me. My sadness was without bitterness. It was the sadness of a heart which was too loving, too tender, a heart which, deceived by those it had taken to be of the same stamp, had been forced to withdraw within itself. Filled with everything that had just happened to me, still shaken by such violent emotions, my heart mingled the feeling of its sorrows with the meditation born of the subject; I painted Grimm, Mme. d'Epinay, Mme. d'Houdetot, Saint-Lambert, myself. How many sweet tears I shed while writing it! Alas, it is only too evident that love, the *amour fatal* from which I was striving to recover, had not left my heart. All that was tinctured with a certain self-pity. I felt that I was dying, and that I was saying my last goodbye to the public. Far from fearing death, its approach filled me with joy. But I regretted leaving my fellow-men before they realized all I was worth, without their knowing how I deserved to have been loved by them, if they had known me better (*Confessions*, Book X).

The refutation of d'Alembert might be called an inevitable event, one that had in the moral realm (to use a favorite phrase of Rousseau's) the necessity of physical law. He who proudly signed himself "Citoyen de Genève" and lauded patriotism had to take up the cudgels in his country's defense. R. A. Leigh describes the *Lettre à d'Alembert* as partly an act of love, but also a political act. The position Rousseau takes aligns him "more sharply even than the 1754 visit and the *Discourse on Inequality* with the popular party."[7]

Personal pique could not have been entirely absent. Why hadn't Diderot asked *him* to do the article on Geneva? Who was better qualified, he or d'Alembert? When he finally read the article, the suspicion of an Encyclopedist plot against his native city surely occurred to him, and he fancied himself to be one of its targets. And then, the occasion fitted so well with the direction of his thought and his work. All during his life his attitude toward France was ambivalent. He loved his host country secretly, he admits in the fifth book of the *Confessions*, even when he scolded it. He admired its culture and could not get along without it. Indeed, he could live nowhere else but in France. Yet he was always criticizing its effeteness, its hypocrisy, class exploitation, and moral corruption. What better example than the theater? The way of life of actors and actresses was in itself *prima facie* evidence; but far more important was the very nature of comedy and tragedy. It was not a question of his reviving the old, old censure of the Church. He himself had demonstrated that society (with the resplendent exception of Sparta) led inevitably to moral degeneracy. But if civilization brought such evils in its wake, he had argued, the arts and sciences were largely responsible. And if the arts were pernicious, then the theater was surely the most civilized, corrupt, and harmful form of all the arts. Disguise, deception, insincerity, artificiality—these evils in social men are epitomized in the theater.

Already, in the second part of *La Nouvelle Héloïse*, he had drawn "a parallel between the stage and Paris society at large, to the effect that both use highly artificial speech to disguise the absence of genuine feeling and convincing deeds."[8] Now, having taken his stance as moral conscience of his age, it would serve his purposes to draw up a general and systematic indictment. This applied especially to the passions. In the final moralizing shape he had given his novel, after the debacle of his love affair, he had portrayed the world of the passions as false, with its deformations and the perturbations it introduced into the authentic rhythm of things. Love was a dangerous phenomenon of culture, and it was the very substance of theater. Finally, here was the opportunity to give to the world (it was always "the world" that was watching him, and that always concerned him) open evidence of his break with the *philoso-phes*, combined with an insidious thrust against them. In the final revision the thrust became, in the famous footnote we earlier referred to, a harsh accusation of betrayal against Diderot and a public announcement that their friendship was at an end.

On March 9 the *Lettre à d'Alembert* was completed, and Rousseau offered it to Rey, his publisher in Holland, for thirty louis. He imposed two conditions: the manuscript must be published with his name on the title page; but until then, "profound secrecy" must be observed. In fact, he told only Mme. d'Houdetot about his work. D'Alembert knew nothing of it until June, when it was in press. His Genevan friend Jacob Vernes had suggested in January that he undertake a refutation of the infamous article, but Rousseau said nothing about it even to him until he proudly announced its forthcoming appearance: "Dear Vernes, let us be men and citizens until our last breath. Let us dare to speak for the good of all, even if it is detrimental to our friends and to ourselves."[9] The reason seems clear. Instead of taking this opportunity of giving his compatriots proofs of his orthodoxy, he wanted only to avoid any involvement in the theological controversy. He had in mind a more important end than futile doctrinal disputes, for which he felt only scorn. So strongly did he feel about this that in answering Vernes, on February 18, he expressed views that must have seemed scandalous to the Genevan because of their similarity to the ones d'Alembert had attributed to the clergy of that city.

I believe in God, and God would not be just if my soul were not immortal. That, it seems to me, is all there is to religion that is essential and useful. Let's leave the rest to the argufiers. As for eternal punishment, it is not in harmony with man's weakness and God's justice, and so I reject it.

Their exchanges became heated. Rousseau, vexed by Vernes' criticism, sounds more and more like Diderot: "What do you expect me to think of the author of a remedy that cures nothing?"

Secrecy was necessary, then, not only because he wanted d'Alembert to be caught unawares, but because he wanted no advice and no interference. On March 20 the Preface was dated, the revision finished on April 15, the manuscript sent off to Rey on May 14. About June 20, Rousseau effectuated important modifications in his Preface. These included the famous condemnation of Diderot and other rhetorical changes prompted by Diderot's betrayal of his secret love and by the ensuing rupture with Mme. d'Houdetot. He presents himself simultaneously as a courageous, virile polemist and as an unhappy man on the point of death (an old trick of his), "the victim of the wicked man who had just dealt him the final blow." His rhetoric is designed to make him sound like a voice from beyond the grave "which, from the depths of eternity, rises implacably against the criminal friend, to confound him forever and to deliver his hateful falsehoods to the just scorn of decent people."[10]

On June 25, Rousseau finally told d'Alembert about his refutation. D'Alembert wrote back that he was flattered, eager to read it and profit from it. Ironically, it was d'Alembert, acting as royal censor, who had to give the *imprimatur*. This he did on July 22. Rousseau, ever suspicious of a plot against him, feared that distribution of the books in France would be forbidden. "I cannot doubt," he writes to Rey on September 6, "that I have many irreconcilable enemies [in Paris], all the more dangerous because they hide under a disguise of friendship in order to harm me and because they will never forgive me the harm they have done me; they betray me secretly; I despise them openly, and that is not the way to be spared." His apprehensions were groundless. Early in October, publication was official. But in September the *Lettre* was already in the avid hands of some Parisian readers, and the scandal had broken.

## 2. THE *Lettre à d'Alembert*

Quickly, Rousseau proceeds to dispose of the theological question. The accusation of Socinianism is unjust, because no one can know what another person's faith is, unless he admits it. But then the *philosophe* creeps right into Rousseau's lines, as he goes on to assert that any religion is good if it is peaceful and reasonable. We cannot ask a man to believe what his reason finds absurd, and God will surely not punish him for following his God-given reason. This "defense" was not to be to the liking of the pastors of Geneva! But Rousseau was not in a mood to compromise his stand on anything.

Now the shafts fly at the target. The theater is a form of amusement. Amusements without a constructive purpose are a waste of time in a life in which time is short. The need for them springs from idleness and the loss of simple, natural tastes. The touchstone of entertainments, then, can only be their effect on the people. What good can theater be, when under the guise of public assembly each spectator really isolates himself? Unity is destroyed. Whereas passions and natural inclinations need to be subdued, the theater excites them. Following Plato closely, Rousseau declares catharsis a fallacy; the inverse is the case, for one passion opens the door to all, and only reason can purge.[11]

Another myth (propagated by Diderot) is that the theater can be a school for morals, by making virtue attractive and vice odious. Nonsense! The only way to shape conduct is by laws, public opinion, and the bait of pleasure. The first of these is extraneous to the theater, the second governs it instead of being corrected by it, and the third only brings us back for more corruption. Man, Rousseau insists, is born good, and so he already prefers virtue before going to the show. That is not the point. A man prefers virtue—the modification is essential—whenever his own interest is not at stake. Honesty, as the world goes, is a trap.

The evildoer profits both from his own villainy and from the just man's goodness. We all love virtue in other people, and that, precisely, is what happens at the theater. The spectator applauds other men who are virtuous and goes away smugly self-satisfied because nothing has been required of him. Thus, the pity evoked by tragedy is a pseudoemotion which undermines the real pity that is the source of moral action. There can be no genuine involvement, because the theater is an *imitation* of real emotions, and the actor is not himself.[12]

In plays where vice is punished and virtue rewarded, the means are usually extraordinary and unconvincing. In tragedy, the reverse is often true. We see good men perish and admire monsters because of their greatness. Thus, the common people are accustomed to horrors of which they should be kept in ignorance. Comedy is even more pernicious; the more perfect, the worse it is. Take Molière. What is his work but "a school of vices and immorality, more dangerous even than books in which they are openly inculcated"?[13] The whole art of Molière is "to ridicule goodness and simplicity, and to make us take sides with trickery and lying." His plays can be summarized in a phrase: "The fools are the victims of the villains." Of course that's the way of the world. But should the theater put it on for our approbation? Anticipating the modern idea of empathy, Rousseau asks: "To be interested in someone [in a play], what is it but to put yourself in his place? And when that identification occurs, we become accomplices in villainy."[14]

With this Rousseau embarks on a scathing, implacable analysis which it would be hard, at least from the viewpoint of moral rigor, to rebut. It reaches a paroxysmal climax with a twenty-four-page blast at *Le Misanthrope*.

From its lack of usefulness, it follows that the theater, which can do nothing to improve morals, can do much to spoil them. By favoring all our inclinations, it gives new ascendancy to those which rule us. The continuous emotions we feel enervate us, weaken us, make us more unable to resist our passions; and the sterile interest we feel for virtue serves only to soothe our vanity without forcing us to practice virtue.[15]

Condemnation of the morals of actors and actresses must follow. Always original, always personal, Rousseau gives a new turn to the traditional censure. More reprehensible to him than the actor's disorderly life is the very nature of his art. Rousseau's critique goes right back to the core of his social criticism: the wearing of masks, the split between appearance and reality. Acting is

a trade in which [the actor] displays himself for money . . . and publicly puts up his person for sale. . . . What is, at bottom, the character which the actor receives from his profession? A mixture of baseness, falsity, ridiculous pride, vile degradation, which makes him fit for all kinds of roles except the noblest of all, that of a man, which he renounces.[16]

The actor cultivates the talent of deceiving the public, in a society whose very stamp is false appearance and deceit.

We need not follow Rousseau in his exposition of the revolutionary and harmful effects on Genevan mores that the introduction of theater would bring about, destroying the simple, innocent social life of the *cercles* (social clubs—not so innocent according to the complaints of the Consistory, which charged them with drunkenness, disorderly conduct and neglect of family duties).[17] But it leads us into another aspect of the *Lettre*, the most interesting of all. Rousseau's personality forms and infuses his philosophy, and his philosophy always lays bare his personality. Can we wonder who is his model for the true genius?

Such is the simplicity of the true genius: he is neither an intriguer nor an activist; he does not know the path to honors and fortune and never thinks of seeking it out; he does not compare himself to anyone; he needs no one outside of himself; impervious to insults, heedless of praise, if he knows himself, he does not try to judge his place and enjoys himself without evaluating himself.[18]

We have no trouble in recognizing the ideal Jean-Jacques into which Rousseau projected himself.

Grimsley recalls that the ruling oligarchy looked on the *cercles* with disfavor as centers of subversive discussion and criticism. The Geneva Rousseau so often extols was in part an idealization, in part a turning back to older cultural values (Geneva, Sparta, the Roman republic) about which he had read so avidly during his early years, "as a means of obtaining moral and emotional security in a hostile society. . . . Such an attitude helped Jean-Jacques to gain momentary protection against the dangers of isolation, for, by identifying himself with these older and simpler cultures, he was able to feel independent of and superior to his immediate surroundings."[19] This vision of Geneva was a distant shelter. He knew it did not correspond to present reality. He himself tells us what Geneva meant to him:

I have never seen the walls of that happy city without being overcome with a sudden weakness which came from an excess of tenderness. The noble image of liberty, the images of equality, of union, of gentle ways of life moved me to tears. How wrong I was, but how natural that error! I thought I saw all that, because I bore it in my heart (*Confessions*, Book IV).

By what right did d'Alembert, this spokesman for the jealous animosity of Rousseau's enemies, try to shatter whatever basis was left for this illusion? Proudly, he added "Citoyen de Genève" to his name on the title page.

While the *Lettre à d'Alembert* reflects the fierce hatred for an ego-centered, competitive society which inspires Rousseau's early writings, now we encounter a new emphasis on puritanism. Women and sexuality were continuing problems for him. We have seen his perversions and frustrations, his ineradicable shame and guilt. Women and sexuality were to be feared and loathed, more perhaps for Jean-Jacques than for a Calvinist puritan or a medieval ascetic, even though he needed and craved them—or more exactly, because he did. These conscious or unconscious feelings permeate the *Lettre à d'Alembert* and form one of a number of themes he borrowed from *La Nouvelle Héloïse*. The sexes must live in separation, he cries; nature and social good both demand it. Occasional mixed gatherings, well, yes. But the danger is great—for men. Women have only their morals to lose (a loss they welcome); men also lose their natural character, if they do not control women severely: "for this weaker sex, unable to take up our harder way of life, makes us adopt its way, which is too soft for us; unwilling to tolerate separation, women, lacking the power to become men, turn us into women."[20] A slap at the effete Parisians Rousseau had met in the salons? Yes, but more deeply a protective reaction to his own admitted passivity and feminine tendencies. If he felt that men had to wage a perpetual fight to keep their "natural" superior position, it was because he really feared the potential superiority and domination of women.* Men have to use their greater power to keep women down, while women constantly use their ruses to subvert that power. He sees that disaster already occurring to the French.

. . . cowards consecrated to the whims of the sex that we should protect and not serve, we have learned to despise it by obeying it, to offend it by our mocking attentions; and every woman in Paris assembles in her apartment a harem of men more womanly than herself, who know how to pay beauty every kind of homage except the one she deserves, that of the heart. . . . Imagine the quality of soul of a man who is uniquely occupied by the important business of entertaining women, and who spends his life doing for them what they were meant to do for us, when, exhausted by labors they cannot perform, our minds call for relaxation.[21]

Therefore it is true that nature intended the two sexes to live apart, each in its own way.† Concluding that the separate *cercles* in Geneva should be continued, he makes a significant remark, one that he never explicitly applied to society in general, although it will be the basis of his thinking: the "faults are not in the *cercles*, but in the men who compose them."[22]

Again and again Rousseau tilts lances with love. It is "a dangerous passion," the realm where women rule because men can overcome their

* He assures us that women "love no art, are expert in none, and have no genius." They learn rapidly, but lack creativity. They cannot even describe love, the thing that matters most to them. And Rousseau shrewdly guesses that the well-known *Lettres portugaises* were written by a man—a fact that has been confirmed only recently (*Lettre à d'Alembert*, ed. M. Fuchs, pp. 138–9).

† In a footnote, Rousseau informs the reader that this principle is developed in a more extensive fashion "in a manuscript which has been deposited with me." He is referring to his own novel *La Nouvelle Héloïse* (*Ibid.*, p. 144).

resistance only at the cost of their freedom. On the stage even innocent
love is as seductive as a criminal passion. "No matter how you depict
love: it seduces, or it is not love."[23] This is contrary to public interest. It
transfers to love (an egocentric or personal emotion) the zeal that
should be given to virtue (socially directed emotion).

Standing firmly against the license of his time, Rousseau stoutly declares that it is woman's duty to remain at home and to avoid the looks
of men. Then he cries out against the expected wave of criticism: "Immediately there will be raised against me that ephemeral philosophy,
which is born and dies in the corner of a large city [the home of vices]
and which seeks to stifle the cry of Nature and the unanimous voice of
mankind."[24] Social order is at stake, nothing less. How infamous are the
philosophes who (like Diderot) tell us not to be ashamed of natural
needs, not to expect women to resist their desires any more than men do,
not to expect us to be different from other animals! Is not shame as
natural as desire? retorts Rousseau. Is not modesty the natural source of
a woman's power to lure men? For the rest, "Man is neither a dog nor a
wolf. As soon as the first social relationships are established in the species, its feelings acquire a moral dimension forever unknown to
beasts."[25] Even if this were not true and if sexual restriction imposed on
women were a social invention, that is justification enough. "A house
from which the mistress is absent is a body without a soul that soon
deteriorates."

Although Rousseau appears at the last to be hedging his bets, there is
no doubt about the real significance of his position. We are no longer
"in nature." Rousseau does not want men to be divided between nature
and culture. If we are to "make man one," as he had so eloquently
urged, we must "give him all to society," which has superseded nature.
In an "artificial world" nature is a disturbing factor, and its laws must
give way to artificial laws. Sexual mores are a matter for governmental
control.

So it is with the arts. They should serve the desired political ends.
Rousseau does not conceive of them as self-justified or existing to satisfy
aesthetic needs, but as part of a social apparatus. He would have said,
with Anthony Comstock, "morals, not art or literature"; or with the
twentieth-century totalitarian, that literature and the arts must serve the
purposes of the State and help to make "the new man." Art is not
necessarily excluded, but it is subordinate to a civic end. The theater of
ancient Greece won his approval.

Censorship, it follows, is justified. Luxury and a taste for idleness,
both fostered by the theater, are corroding. The former accelerates the
"natural trend" toward inequality, for the rich can easily put themselves
above the law.[26] But Rousseau goes further. A simple, agricultural people can be trusted to have healthy amusements. But in the corrupt
society of a city, the police, or censorial arm of government, must control

all forms of entertainment; for in the city each easily conceals "his conduct from the public eye."[27] Here Rousseau anticipates his later dicta about limiting or abolishing privacy. In smaller towns, this is less urgent, for in them "individuals always under public observation are born censors of each other and the Police easily exercise surveillance over all." Why is this so imperative? Rousseau makes it clear that the effectiveness of laws in the control of behavior is limited. In the first place, laws must be in a delicate and accurate counterbalance to the vices of a people. More important, laws can influence mores only "when they draw their strength from them."[28] Therefore, it is behavior that must be controlled.

How then can the government get a hold on behavior? I reply, through public opinion. If our habits are born from our own feelings when we are isolated, in society they are born from others' opinions. When we do not live within ourselves, but in others, their judgments rule everything. Nothing seems good or desirable to individuals except what the public has judged to be such, and the only happiness most men know is to be thought to be happy.[29]

In a good society there can, then, be no laissez-faire, no possible trust. "Whatever is bad in morals is also bad in politics."[30] Freedom was fine in the hypothetical state of nature. But in society, where freedom breeds vices and wickedness, discipline is the only recourse. "Opinion," the object of Rousseau's denunciation as a corrupting force in corrupt societies, is the most powerful weapon for social good, if those who govern would only realize it and utilize it. Rousseau did not possess the phrase "thought control," but "censorship" and "surveillance" are part of his vocabulary. He implies that he will elsewhere outline the means to this end and limits himself here to affirming that they are not laws, punishments, persuasion, nor overt coercion. There is an "art" to changing "opinion." It is most difficult to accomplish, and the real job to be done is preventive.

Rousseau does specify one activity, a form of entertainment he considers useful. The people should be assembled on given occasions for public festivals. These are no longer "spectacles," because everyone will take part, "do it so that each sees himself and loves himself in all the others, so that all may be better united."[31] What Rousseau is seeking, in addition to order, is immediacy, "transparency," unity. These require spontaneity, but the *occasions* for spontaneity must be prepared and arranged. A footnote throws more light on Rousseau's ends: "Do you want to make a people energetic and hard-working? Give them festivals and offer them amusements which make them love their condition and prevent them from desiring a better one." When all are equally overworked, none feels sorry for himself. The essential for a healthy state is for each to feel in his place and, being satisfied or not looking for better, to work in harmony with all others for the public weal, rather than for himself. A "sweet and precious ignorance" is best for the people. The spirit of Sparta, the martial spirit, is a good guideline. The spirit of commerce and profit-making is antithetical to an organic community. Two ideas are constantly combined in Rousseau's political thought: manipulation or regimentation, and deception.

Looking back to his own childhood, Rousseau describes a public festival at which he had been present. In the torchlight the people danced gaily in the public square; then five hundred soldiers formed a serpentine chain to the sound of fife and drum. Women and children flowed out of their houses, everyone joined in toasts, laughter, and embraces.

There followed a general emotion I could not describe. . . . My father, hugging me, was seized with a shudder I still feel and share. "Jean-Jacques," he said to me, "love your country. Do you see these good Genevans? They are all friends, they are all brothers; joy and harmony reign amongst them. You are a Genevan. Some day you will see other peoples; but even if you travel as much as your father, you will never see their like."

In such festivals there are genuine emotions, and the people are both spectators *and* actors.

Rousseau's own emotion, throbbing and sincere, echoes again in the final lines of the *Lettre*, when he apostrophizes the youth of his native city:

May they always feel how solid happiness is preferable to the hollow pleasures which destroy it! May they transmit to their descendants the virtues, the liberty, the peace which they have gotten from their fathers! This is the last wish with which I end my writings, it is the wish with which my life will end.[32]

He goes on to sketch rapidly the ideal community he had known in the environs of Neuchâtel. There the farmers are well-to-do landowners, hard-working because the fruits of their labor belong to them. Independent, they use their leisure to make themselves all they need. When winter isolates them, they know no boredom. Snow becomes the equivalent of water, the mountaineers' wooden houses the analogue of the island fastness that was one of Rousseau's archetypal fixations. Comfortable in their warm homes, joyful in their family life, these happy men are carpenters, locksmiths, glaziers, woodworkers, ironmongers all at once, each for himself.[33] Rousseau's political plans will always embody this regressive economic theory, so opposed to the nascent capitalism and division of labor that Adam Smith was to defend in *The Wealth of Nations* (1776). Rousseau, as Jouvenel puts it, was "the anti-progressive philosopher *par excellence*."[34] His ideal has been well described as one of "stagnant, closed little collectivities."[35]

It would be a mistake to see in these political speculations only abstract theory. Rousseau, it has been said, was a *"subjectif."* He is constantly plumbing and analyzing himself, a self "to which he relates the entire world."[36] His ideas express his longing for a purer state of harmony and social unity, such as he imagined his beloved Geneva had once enjoyed. In the world as it is, his deep need for love and communion were frustrated. It is useless to ask whether it was his fault or the world's; in his own mind there was no doubt about the matter, and that was all that ever counted for him. "The truth that I know or that I take to be such," he wrote (June 25, 1761) to the anarchistic monk Dom Deschamps "is very pleasing; it puts me into a very sweet state and I cannot conceive how I could change it without a loss." His subjective truth led to political schemes that were the analogues of his amatory reveries, except that they struck rich veins of inspiration. He was beginning to tell the world what a better society would be like and how it would operate. Order and social orientation ("virtue"), values lacking in himself, are the values he proclaims. But he tells us that *men* have never attained them, and never can if they are left to their own contrivings. As he again wrote to Dom Deschamps (August 12, 1761): "If all men were virtuous they would be happy; but the real and temporal advantage of being good among wicked men, that is the philosopher's stone yet to be found." He meant that it could not be found. Men must be "formed" into social beings. Such a society would achieve his personal objectives and make unnecessary his revolt against the world's injustice.

Rousseau's polemic against the theater is, we can see, no mere intellectual exercise. It had the deepest roots in his personal problems and in his attitude toward life. He constantly comes back to himself, overtly or unknowingly.

Nowhere is this more dramatically in evidence than in the long denunciation of Molière's *Le Misanthrope*. The savagery of his diatribe—the most remarkable part of this remarkable tract—is the expression of Rousseau's complete empathy and identification with its hero, Alceste.

What then is this Misanthrope of Molière? A good man who detests the morals of his age and the wickedness of his contemporaries; who, precisely because he loves his fellow-men, hates in them the wrongs they inflict on each other and the vices of which those wrongs are the products. . . . If there were neither knaves nor flatterers, he would love everyone.[37]

Molière's sin is to make such a man as Alceste (*mutatis mutandis*, Jean-Jacques) the object of ridicule instead of the highest esteem. Only "a great and noble soul" could be so "embittered by the continual spectacle of human wickedness" or feel such a "burning love of virtue." But ridicule is "the favorite weapon of vice," one that undermines respect for virtue; it can be answered only by a crushing scorn.[38] Philinte, the foil to Alceste, Rousseau identified with Grimm or d'Holbach or possibly Diderot. He is anathematized as a "moderate," one of those who are

satisfied to leave things as they are, "because it is to their interest that
they should not be any better." Thinking still of himself, Rousseau
asserts that Molière has falsified Alceste's character by making him respond so irritably when he himself is the target:

For, having declared war on the wicked, he expects them to make war on him.
If he had not foreseen the harm that his frankness would bring to him, it
would be rashness and not a virtue. Let a false woman betray him; let unworthy friends dishonor him; let weak friends abandon him: he must suffer all
that without complaint.[39]

Had that not been Jean-Jacques' lot? Rousseau is enraged not only
because of his strong self-identification with Alceste. He also, one would
suspect (whether or not he suspected it), is furious at being unmasked.
"Alceste's explosion against Oronte stirs the suspicion that his rejection
of the code of *politesse* has less to do with abstract moral principles than
with a personal, constitutional [in]capacity to enact its rituals."[40] Both
Jean-Jacques and Alceste wish to achieve self-glorification, admiration,
and distinctiveness. After attempting to cope with life's problems, they
withdraw. Ostensibly committed to exalted principles (which Jean-
Jacques all too often was unable to follow), each presumes "to sit in
judgment on a society which he will or can not join."[41] Unskilled in the
rituals, they reject them; refusing to play the game, they still covet the
prizes. Their disdain springs from failure or a deep-seated fear of failure
and a sense of personal inadequacy, and they turn to moral superiority
as a shortcut to distinctiveness. They seek invulnerability to the dangers
of the human arena in a posture from which "they may cavil, rant, and
rage against it." Both Alceste and Rousseau, finally, object to a society
in which "breaches of virtue and morality can be tolerated; [whereas]
infringements on elegance, decorum, place, pleasure, and harmony must
be ruthlessly prosecuted."
   The rigor, the need for absolutes, the separation into black and white
that characterize this interlude are typical of the authoritarian mind.
Molière's error, proclaims Rousseau, was in falling short of the mark, in
not making Alceste uncompromising *enough*. He should not have tried
to spare the feelings of Oronte, the ridiculous sonnet-maker. "It is not
worthwhile to be a misanthrope if you go only halfway; for, if you allow
yourself the least compromise or alteration of the truth, what is the
justification for stopping before you become as false as a courtier?"[42]
   Molière was against Alceste because he thought that a society of Al-
cestes would not be possible. He felt it necessary to respect human
limitations. Rousseau wants a society of complete sincerity, where everyone could be an Alceste—or rather, where no one would have to be. In
our society, Alceste–Jean-Jacques is unique, and he must suffer for it.
With this development in the *Lettre* we must couple the apologia Rousseau puts toward the end.

If my writings give me some pride, it is because of the purity of intention which inspires them and the disinterestedness of which few writers have given me an example and which very few will wish to imitate. Never has a private purpose sullied the desire to be useful to others which caused me to take pen in hand, and I have almost always written in a way contrary to my own interest. *Vitam impendere vero*: that is the motto I have chosen and of which I feel myself worthy. . . . The love of the public good is the only passion which makes me speak to the public; I know then how to forget myself, and if someone offends me, I do not answer him for fear that anger will make me unjust. This maxim is advantageous to my enemies. . . . Holy and pure truth to which I have consecrated my life, never will my passions sully the sincere love I have for you; neither self-interest nor fear will be able to alter the homage I love to offer you![43]

The rhetorical posturing of this passage and of the closing lines already cited should not blind us to the deep and fervid sincerity of the unhappy man who wrote them. Sincerity, however, masks the unconscious, all that one does not admit to oneself. Rousseau was serving himself, to be sure, in assuming the role of the biblical prophet; but that lay buried deeply within him, and he saw himself only in his heroic guise as the willing sacramental offering. He belonged, he was sure, to a different species of man; he was the only true man, the natural man, in the sense that all others were corrupted by the artificialities of society. Dominated by *amour-propre*, the others lived outside of themselves and based their existence on the "opinion" of others. Slaves of "opinion," constantly role-playing, they sought appearance only, not reality. With them the "relative self" has replaced the "absolute self." Jean-Jacques knew he could speak to them as no one else had ever done, or could.

### 3. REVERBERATIONS

Once again, Rousseau had achieved a *succès de scandale*. As with the two *Discourses* and the *Lettre sur la musique française*, he had stung the literary "establishment" into a fury. The number of pamphlets or articles hurled against his *Lettre à d'Alembert* went beyond four hundred. D'Alembert himself put out a "Lettre à M. Rousseau, citoyen de Genève," a polite but firm and intelligent refutation which included a spirited defense of women. ("The women," Mme. de Créqui wrote to Jean-Jacques on January 12, "are somewhat furious.") The longest rejoinder was that of the *philosophe* Marmontel; his series of articles in the *Mercure de France* (November 1758 to January 1759) were also published early that year as a volume in Geneva (*Réponse de M. Marmontel*). Their tone was set in the opening lines: "He who has considered belles-lettres as a cause of the corruption of morals; he who, for our good, would put us out to pasture, had to disapprove of sending his fellow-citizens to a school of urbanity and good taste."[44] Marmontel had grasped the inmost direction of Rousseau's thought. His critique of Rousseau is devastating, and nowhere more so than in his defense of Molière. Like d'Alembert, Marmontel is aroused by the attack on women. "M. Rousseau is unable to believe that a woman can be his equal." But surely when he says that "man is born good," he must include women in that statement: D'Alembert, for his part, equally perceptive, hinted that Rousseau's severity toward women covered a weakness for them and perhaps fear.

Rousseau's critics pay no heed to the general political implications of his tract. (Only d'Alembert points out his scorn for the common people.) As Rousseau himself said, he was thinking beyond the political comprehension of his contemporaries, beyond what was "thinkable" to them. The *philosophes* fixed their anger on the aggression against the theater, literature, and culture in general, as well as on the implicit attack on Diderot and the *Encyclopédie*. The theater, as Rousseau understood so well, was the spearhead of literature's social influence; but in their minds it was a school for virtue and, equally important, a medium for propaganda that could outflank the censorship. Rousseau's dogmatic, provocatively offensive tone outraged the *philosophes*. He was Alceste, and they were a group of Philintes. This antithesis they were quite willing to accept and turn against him.

Voltaire was infuriated by this lowborn upstart who, not content with trying to turn the clock back, had thwarted his pet project. Most recently, on September 12, 1756, he had still communicated with Jean-Jacques in terms of faintly condescending civility. Rousseau's "Lettre sur la Providence" had surely vexed him, but he sought to avoid a hostile debate or quarrel. *"Mon cher philosophe,"* he began—surely an ill-chosen word!—"You and I can, in the intervals between our illnesses, reason in verse and in prose; but allow me, at the present juncture, to lay aside all those philosophic discussions, which are only amusements." Inviting his antagonist to visit him at Les Délices, he assures him that "of all those who have read you, none esteems you more than I, in spite of my bad jokes, and that, of all those who will see you, none is more disposed to love you tenderly." In September 1758 word of Rousseau's forthcoming *Lettre* against the theater spread rapidly. Voltaire, quite accurately, saw it as a second gauntlet. "Is it true," he asked d'Alembert (September 12, 1758), "that Jean-Jacques is writing against you, and that he is reviving the quarrel over the article 'Geneva'? They are saying even more, they are saying that he carries sacrilege to the point of bursting forth against the theater, which is becoming the third sacrament in Geneva. They're mad about the stage in the land of Calvin." The angry *philosophe* finds it hard to stop. Rousseau is a Diogenes, "barking at us from within his barrel." Why, this man was himself writing plays and operettas (and was an ardent theatergoer, Voltaire might have added). As if this ingratitude were not enough, he dares to lift his pen against d'Alembert, who had covered him with praise. Indeed, the world is full of madmen. "Ah, what a century! Poor century!"

A year later, Voltaire cheered d'Alembert for his reply to Rousseau. "You have deigned," he writes, on October 15, 1759, "to demolish that madman, Jean-Jacques, with reasoned arguments. As for me, I do like the man who responds to arguments against movement by walking. Jean-Jacques proves that a theater is unsuited· to Geneva; I build one." Voltaire was still containing his wrath within the limits of private correspondence.

Diderot, deeply wounded, held his fire. Rousseau's *Lettre* was more ammunition for his charge that Jean-Jacques was "the dupe of his own sophistries," that his life was a standing contradiction of his principles, and for all the other accusations of the *Tablettes*, which he wrote at about this time, and which he put aside for future use. Meanwhile, he had only to let the letter speak for itself and play the injured party, anathematized by his own friend at the very time when persecution of the *Encyclopédie* had backed him against the wall. Rousseau had in fact chosen an inopportune moment, and his thrust seemed like the stiletto of a coward administering the *coup de grâce*.* Saint-Lambert was, as we saw earlier, only too glad to seize the pretext of this "atrocity" to break off with Rousseau, though he soon found it convenient to go to dinner with him.[45] Darkly, Diderot told his friends that he could say nothing because the honor of others was at stake—as if he resigned himself to being a martyr.[46]

Grimm, on the other hand, who had criticized Rousseau's earlier writings in measured terms in his secret *Correspondance littéraire*, pulled off his gloves and clawed at his enemy:

M. Rousseau was born with all the talents of a sophist. Specious arguments, a mass of deceitful reasonings, of art and artifice, joined to a vigorous, simple, and touching eloquence, will make him a redoubtable adversary in anything he attacks. But despite the magic and enchantment of his brilliant style, he will not persuade you, because only truth persuades. One is always tempted to say: that is very beautiful and very false.[47]

As for the work at hand, "it is prolix, languid, and even flat." Its arguments destroy each other. Rousseau writes "in bad faith," which makes it difficult for him "to avoid being absurd and ridiculous."

Rousseau did not know of these hidden dagger thrusts. He would have expected them, perhaps even welcomed them. They would have confirmed his conviction about the "plot" and testified to the separation of the ways. He had dedicated his life to the truth, to moral purity, to the denunciation of corruption. "They" stood for sophistry and the

---

* Besides, what could Diderot have said? (See Crocker, *Jean-Jacques Rousseau*, Vol. I, Ch. 8, especially pp. 334–6.) Diderot's own stiletto had been the false propaganda letter of December 5.

triumph of corruption, and d'Alembert was only their most respectable spokesman. They had to reduce him to impotence. It was to be an unrelenting, no-quarter battle, and he had joined it with no thought of retreat or crying for mercy. *Vitam impendere vero*! That motto was now inscribed on his shield, and he would raise it high for all to see, so that none could doubt that Jean-Jacques meant and lived the principles he proclaimed. His plan was made. In the solitude of Montmorency, he was trying to recover his serenity, his inner equilibrium, so that he could fathom *his* truth. Displaying it to the world, he would display his real self to the world. It would know him, and he, too, would at last know who he was.

That is why, in his only rebuttal to the numerous refutations of his *Lettre à d'Alembert*, the brief "Réponse à une lettre anonyme," he declares, "I am not an enlightened citizen"—the *philosophes* were "enlightened"—"but only a zealous citizen. . . . I don't know what philosophers are made for, and I do not care to know." The Encyclopedists are not his *"confrères,"* as his adversary claimed: "The friends of truth are all my *confrères*."[48] Geneva had welcomed his book, *that* counted most. He had a letter from Jean Sarrasin (November 4). "You have just rendered a signal service to our common fatherland," wrote the minister, adding that all who thought soundly acknowledged it.[49] And his friend Moultou joined in praise (November 10): "Your book has rallied all the good citizens here, frightened and shamed the wicked, and now the measure of love that each has for his country can be judged by the degree of esteem he gives to your work. In a word, if Geneva is able to keep its former manners or recover them, she will owe that to you."[50]

What more did Jean-Jacques need, when the testimony of his own conscience was confirmed by that of his beloved fellow-citizens?

### 4. A QUIET TIME

This sense of mission gave Rousseau the energy and determination to plunge into his work; and it was his work that enabled him to recover his equilibrium after the long months of intrigues, quarrels, and self-destructive emotions. The year 1758 was an essentially laborious and fruitful time, despite the unhappiness of the last bitter éclat against Diderot and the depressing, drawn-out end of the affair with Mme. d'Houdetot. "I was sick and unhappy," he admits in the Preface to the *Lettre à d'Alembert*, but "solitude calms the soul and lulls the passions to which the disorder of society gives birth. . . . Now that I no longer see men, I have almost stopped hating the wicked."

For the most part, solitude was to fail him as much as "independence" from "opinion." He needed others and their esteem; protesting against both, he constantly sought them. The concept of self is interpersonal and is elaborated out of the appraisals of other persons. Even when we are alone, our thinking relates to other people, real or imaginary. Jean-Jacques' whole life illustrates this truth. The search for self-respect was a never-ending task for him. But the world was against him, that was his firm conviction. He wrote to Mme. d'Houdetot (February 13, 1758), about Diderot:

He hasn't even deigned to answer me and so he abandons in his adversity the friend who so keenly shared his. That's enough from him; this desertion tells me more than all the rest. I cannot stop loving him; but I shall never see him again as long as I live. I have only you left in all the world; but you will abandon me in your turn when it suits you, I know people too well not to expect it.

With a pretense of modesty, Rousseau confided to the reader of his *Lettre* that "an instant of momentary ferment produced a flash of talent in me." But it will never recur, he adds, and anyhow his death will scarcely await publication of the book. Jean-Jacques was carrying on a good deal of work for a dying man. In addition to his refutation of d'Alembert, the "Lettres morales" and *La Nouvelle Héloïse* were on his desk, *Emile* was very much on his mind, as was *The Social Contract*. R. A. Leigh justly writes of "this complex soul, lazy to the point of delight, and yet endowed with an astonishing capacity for work."[51] He was even then about to set down his religious beliefs, with calm intellectual lucidity, in his letter of February 18 to Jacob Vernes—a sign that he was already working on the *Profession de foi* which was to be so influential a part of *Emile*. It was a step in his itinerary and a needed self-reassurance. "If virtue does not always make man happy, at least he cannot be happy without it; the afflictions of the just are not without compensation and even the tears of innocence are sweeter to the heart than the prosperity of the wicked."* He had heard from Deleyre in Paris about the malicious gossip being circulated against him. The famous, eloquent letter he was to write to Diderot on March 2 was brewing in his mind.

Spring arrived early, and the fine weather renewed Jean-Jacques' spirits. Proudly he rejected an offer of six louis from his old Genevan friend Deluc. Such well-meaning generosity is not appropriate with a man whose custom is "not to take from another man's purse no matter what the reason." These proud words were accompanied by a sermon on the evil of money and the blessedness of true virtue. "Open your heart and close your purse—those are the friends for me."[52] With the shame of years of parasitism behind him, how could he help speaking out like that?

He kept pushing away an insistent admirer and would-be friend, François Coindet, an ardent young man of twenty-three. "If you wish to be occasionally welcomed, don't make a pest of yourself."[53] A Genevan,

---

* The last phrase is the subtitle of *Juliette*, one of Sade's major works. It is a central theme throughout eighteenth-century thought and fiction.

Coindet was working in Paris as a bank clerk. He was not put off by rebuffs and made himself so useful by acting as an intermediary between Rousseau and his publisher, Rey, that Jean-Jacques had to accept him.

Leigh reproaches Rousseau for lack of frankness and for exploiting his admirer.[54] To a degree the reproach is merited, but on one occasion at least Jean-Jacques bluntly refused to give him the title of friend. "Do you think you can agree to take that name as you do that of partner or associate? It does not work that way, believe me. Friendship comes without your thinking about it. It is formed gradually, grows strong with the years. True friends have been friends a long while before thinking of taking the name."[55] But he agrees to be Coindet's father confessor and moral guide. If he did give Coindet moral instructions, they produced scant effect. Coindet was known as a rake and censured for his inattentiveness to his job. In later years he could read Rousseau's judgment of him: "I had a young Genevan called Coindet, a good lad, I believed, thoughtful, serviceable, zealous; but ignorant, cocksure, gluttonous, self-seeking, who had come to see me as soon as I went to reside at the Hermitage and who, with no introduction save his own, soon established himself in the household despite me."[56] Rousseau goes on to call him a tricky scalawag, "pushing to the point of effrontery."

At this time Rousseau also renewed old friendships, neglected in the heat of love and of strife, with the Dupins, Mme. de Créqui, Lenieps. The friendly controversy with Jacob Vernes continued through several exchanges. Rousseau stoutly maintained his deism (though he never called it that).

"No, my worthy friend, it is not on some scattered sheets of paper that we should look for God's law, but in the heart of man, where His hand deigned to write it. Oh, man, whoever you are, learn to consult your conscience and your natural faculties, and you will be just, good and virtuous, you will bow before your master and you will share in eternal happiness in his heaven."[57]

We know of no correspondence with Mme. de Warens in 1758, and she is not mentioned in the *Confessions*. From another document we learn of Maman's pathetic situation and of her courage or persistence; we see her still trying to borrow money to set up a small porcelain factory. "If God grants me this mercy, through the succor of my friends I will be able to operate this little establishment. It is my daily bread, which will shelter me from many uncertainties, for the future, that is certain, and I beg you to stretch your hand out ot me, so that I may succeed. God will pay you back."[58] Did she ever think of her youth, her secret adventures, the brooding and sickly Jean-Jacques who had loved her so desperately, in his own strange way, and whom she had cast aside for the virile and faithless Wintzenried?

In May there were two setbacks for Rousseau. At the same time that Mme. d'Houdetot put a brusque end to their strained epistolary friendship, a hernia manifested itself. He describes its appearance and his pains with clinical precision. "This swelling is in a straight line and in an oblique direction. You would take it for a prolongation of the penis. It disappears when I lie down and reappears when I get up."[59] After May, there is no further mention of it.

It was probably on May 11 that Rousseau received a visit from another great adventurer and lover, another Jean-Jacques by name, but of a quite different species. Casanova relates how he went to Montmorency with Mme. d'Urfé, who, like so many aristocrats, was attracted by the eloquent and scandalous *solitaire*. The pretext used was to give him some music to copy, a job for which he charged double the going rate, but which he performed with meticulous perfection. Jean-Jacques did not impress Casanova.

We found a man who reasoned well, who had a simple and modest bearing, but who was quite undistinguished in his person and in his mind. We did not find what is called a likeable man. He struck us as rather boorish, and Mme. d'Urfé needed no more to judge him a rude fellow. We saw a woman [Thérèse] whom we had heard about. She scarcely glanced at us. We went back to Paris laughing at this queer philosopher.

Casanova also relates what the Prince de Conti had told him about his own visit to Rousseau. The prince, eager to talk with the famous philosopher, made the trip alone. He came upon Jean-Jacques walking in the park and straightway told him he had come to take dinner with him.

"Your Highness will have poor fare. I'll have another place set." He goes out, comes back, and after spending two or three hours strolling with the prince, takes him into the parlor, where they were to dine. The prince, seeing three settings, says:
"Who is the third person with whom you want me to dine? I had thought we should dine tête-a-tête."
"That third person, Milord, is my other self (*est un autre moi-même*). She is a being who is neither my wife, nor my mistress, nor my servant, nor my mother, nor my daughter; she is all of that at once."
"I believe it, my friend, but having come here only to dine with you, I shall leave you to dine with your everything. Adieu."[60]

And Casanova comments: "Such is the stupidity of philosophers when they seek distinction through singularity." The episode is apocryphal. We do not know of any visit that Conti made to Rousseau by himself. But the pride, the ego-defensiveness, is authentic.

Rousseau's paranoid tendencies always lurked in the background, ready to be aroused at the slightest suspicion, just as he was ever ready to raise his guard against the chance shaft that might pierce his vulnerable ego-defenses. He had the strong feeling of isolation that characterizes the severely neurotic, maladjusted individual who feels he is rejected. In a

letter to Lenieps (April 5), he clearly expresses his belief that his enemies, under the cloak of friendship, carried a hidden dagger, and that
their animosity was inspired by the knowledge that they had wronged
him. Once he was convinced of this, the net of suspicion would gradually be spread wider and wider. On May 14, not having had news from
Rey in a month, he began to fear that his publisher had betrayed him or
was planning to do so. He made no direct accusation, but his letter to
Rey concluded, "After having waited the time necessary for your answer
to reach me, if I have received none, I shall consider myself freed of any
engagement with you, and shall console myself for the time you have
made me waste by sacrificing it to my word and to honesty." The suspicion was, of course, baseless, and Rey hastened to reassure his author.

Jean-Jacques was entering into a brief depression, from which he was
saved by friends, new and old, who did not want to "enslave" him and
govern his life. His favorite was Loiseau de Mauléon, a thirty-year-old
barrister at the Paris Parlement. He was to win fame as the defender of
the martyred Jean Calas, whose memory it was Voltaire's glory to reha-
bilitate. Rousseau later took some retrospective credit, claiming that he
had predicted a brilliant career for Mauléon if he defended only justice
and virtue. "He took my advice and the results followed."[61] Mauléon
died in 1771, broken by an unhappy love affair. A Paris bookseller,
Hippolyte-Lucas Guérin, was among the chosen friends, and he put
Rousseau in touch with a well-known publisher in Amsterdam, Jean
Néaulme. Several ecclesiastics were admitted to Jean-Jacques' friendship.
Antoine Maltor was the elderly curate of nearby Groslay. From his
acquaintance with Rousseau's homonym, the then-illustrious poet Jean-
Baptiste Rousseau, and other celebrities, the curate had a store of anecdotes with which to beguile his morose friend. Father Bertier was a
lively physics professor who achieved momentary notoriety by publishing a book in which he affirmed that the only way to understand *Genesis*
was to read everything backwards.

In Paris Jean-Jacques maintained his relations with Deleyre, though
he was suspicious of his friend's earlier defense of the *philosophes*.
Among the group, he deems worthy only Duclos, the *littérateur*, although he later tells of continuing to see Condillac and Mably. Among
his compatriots living in Paris were the elderly Daniel Roguin, "le bon
Lenieps," and Coindet. The Dupins still received him warmly and
understood his need for independence. But his favorite *grande dame*
was Mme. de Créqui. Her literary salon had been one of the most brilliant in Paris. Now she had turned to piety and no longer received
*philosophes* and men of letters. She felt a warm regard for Rousseau and
was to play a part in later events. An unexpected visit from Jean-
Jacques' old Spanish friend, Carrión, who had been appointed to Paris,
brought the pleasurable hope of reviving that idyll. It was to be frustrated, Rousseau tells us, by the officious Coindet, who took advantage

of his being outside of Paris "to insinuate himself in my place." We have seen that excuse before.

Another neighbor from the past was Le Blond, who had shared Jean-Jacques' trials in Venice. By a coincidence that Rousseau later interpreted as part of the "plot," he had rented a house at La Briche, near Montmorency. Apologizing to the world and his own conscience for not calling on Le Blond, Rousseau wrote: "But indolence, neglect, and delay in carrying out small duties have always done me more harm than great vices. My worst faults have been of omission. I have rarely done what I should not have done, and unfortunately I have done still more rarely what I should have done."[62] On this purported *mea culpa* the editors of the *Confessions* justly comment: "We know this psychology: the intention, the desire to act as he should are sufficient for Jean-Jacques; he enjoys this good feeling without reservation. He forgets to carry out his desire to manifest it to others except in his imagination. Or else he gives way to passivity."[63]

As Rousseau set down his recollections, the mention of Le Blond reminded him of his quarrel with another friend from Italian days, Jonville, the envoy to Genoa with whom he claims to have stayed during part of his quarantine in that seaport. He had enjoyed Jonville, after the latter's return to Paris in 1745, especially because the envoy had a fund of nasty stories about Rousseau's enemy Montaigu. Suddenly, in 1755, he found Jonville glacial and never returned to his house again. Racking his mind for an explanation, Rousseau comes up with an odd story. He had gone with Jonville and some others to a gay supper party with some *filles de joie*. Rousseau swears—and we may believe him—that his only share in the fun was to "meditate rather sadly the unhappy fate of those creatures."[64] For the same reason he left nothing for the girls, and this he thought, was the motive for Jonville's hostility. People generally explain others' behavior in accordance with their own self-projections, and for Jean-Jacques money was a constant preoccupation. He was undeniably a penny pincher. The farfetched explanation seemed plausible to him. Jonville himself, however, told the Abbé Trublet that the estrangement resulted from his aversion to Jean-Jacques' antireligious talk and to his conversions, of which Trublet had taken malicious delight in telling him.[65] Rousseau never learned of this.

The year 1758 slipped into 1759. It was a quiet time for Jean-Jacques, but not for his former friends. While he was submitting a mémoire to M. and Mme. Dupin, doubtless his *Extrait du projet de paix perpétuelle* of their late protégé, the idealistic Abbé de Saint-Pierre, a deadly blow against the "philosophic party" was being prepared by the combined forces of Church and State. On January 23 the King's attorney, Omer Joly de Fleury, denounced to the Parlement of Paris both the scandalous *De l'Esprit* of Helvétius and the subversive enterprise known as the *Encyclopédie*, of which Diderot and d'Alembert were the editors, along with some other impious writings. On March 8 the license for the *Encyclopédie* was revoked. Helvétius' book was publicly burnt. Frightened despite his wealth and position, he retracted and ate humble pie, leaving his even more daring *De l'Homme* for posthumous publication. Diderot, however, persisted in his enterprise, and the *Encyclopédie* was finally completed and distributed in 1766.[66]

Rousseau read Helvétius with great interest and not a little annoyance. His marginal notes take issue with the basic themes of *De l'Esprit:* that judgment is passive and inheres in sensation, that recollection is only an attenuated sensation. The "activity" of the mind was important to Rousseau's defense of free will and his belief that the materialists were wrong when they argued that everything in the mind derives from sensation. He agrees with Helvétius' contention that men are evil and willingly hurt each other. When Rousseau sold his library to Louis Dutens in 1766, for some reason he stipulated that his notes not be printed until after his death.

On February 9, 1759, Voltaire acquired the property of Ferney, just outside the Swiss border. There, safe from both the French and the Swiss, he would spend the two decades that remained to him, ruling his peasants like a benevolent philosopher-king, entertaining celebrities from everywhere, indulging in his love for theater, working steadily to *écraser l'infâme*, fighting intolerance and injustice. But the Patriarch of Ferney was not a forgiving man. He was to be very unjust toward the "madman and traitor," Jean-Jacques. *Candide*, which came out that month, was taken by Rousseau as a reply to his own polemical "Lettre sur la Providence," and in part, at least, it was.

Rousseau was diligently toiling on a masterpiece of his own, in addition to making copies of *La Nouvelle Héloïse* and negotiating with Rey for its publication. The new work was *Emile*. Beginning in January, he completed the draft of a 430-page manuscript in five months. For a long time he had been thinking about the problems of bringing up children. It was not, as he claimed in 1761 in a letter to Mme. de Luxembourg,[67] remorse about his own children that prompted him to write *Emile*. The stimulus came from the family problems of two of his noble lady friends, the intelligent and sensitive Mme. de Créqui and Mme. de Chenonceaux.[68] But remorse overtook him as he wrote his treatise, and he was moved to pen the dramatic outcry quoted earlier.[69] This first version of *Emile* (the Favre manuscript) was to be thoroughly reworked. What was begun as an abstract treatise was turned into a kind of pedagogical novel, with a well-characterized hero, Emile, and a heroine, Sophie. Other changes of major importance profoundly altered the meaning and value of the work.[70]

As usual, there was some unpleasant incident to interrupt Jean-Jacques' tranquillity. The Opéra, without consulting him, had decided to put on *Le Devin du village* again. When the news reached him, he balked. This was his property, and "they" were arrogantly disposing of it, as if it were theirs. Promptly he sent out a batch of heated letters of protest. The impenetrable wall of the "establishment" registered no reaction—at least no direct notice was forthcoming. The Opéra made a gesture, restoring Rousseau's free admission privileges. It was laughable. He no longer went to the opera or the theater, now that he had condemned them and changed his way of life. He shot off a scornful letter to his friend Duclos, who had arranged the move.[71] The fruitlessness of further complaints led to the crescendo of the long letter of April 2 to Lenieps, who had also tried to help. Written with a sustained biting fury spiced by sardonic black humor, this letter shows Rousseau's mood as completely uncompromising, even though he knows his powerlessness. "I am the weakest of beings; everybody can wrong me with impunity, I see they know it, and the Opéra Directors' insults are the ass's kick in the pants to me."[72]

Surprisingly, that quarrel was patched up a few years before the end of Rousseau's life. In Bachaumont's *Mémoires secrets* the following entry occurs for April 24, 1774: "M. Rousseau of Geneva has been reconciled with the directors of the Opéra, through the intervention of the *chevalier* Gluck. The latter made them realize the wrongs they had done this great man; he has persuaded them to make reparations on various financial matters." The Opéra had uninterruptedly kept *Le Devin* as a regular part of its repertoire; in March 1772 it had even added Rousseau's *Pygmalion*. It must have been a fair windfall for the aging prophet.

Rousseau's obdurate belligerence in this matter reflects both his passion for justice (we recall how doggedly he sought for what he felt to be justice against Montaigu after his return from Venice) and a hardening toward society and his own adversaries. He was not prepared to compromise on any issue. Did he realize how he haunted his adversaries? They could not put him out of their minds. Diderot and his group frequently referred to him, with acid-dipped pens. Voltaire wrote to a lady friend that March: "You are of that sex which has civilized ours, and without whom we should have been only savages, as Jean-Jacques wants us to be."[73]

Rousseau did try to reestablish his connection with Tronchin, whom he did not yet consider an enemy. Seizing a convenient pretext, he wrote the renowned Genevan doctor a flattering letter on March 23. The reply was courteous, but Tronchin went out of his way to put in a remark that was at the very least challenging. "But tell me," he asks, "how is it, or rather how is it possible that the friend of mankind is no longer the friend of men, or hardly so? Can the whole, which after all is only the sum of the parts, derive from its parts a value they do not have? We shall never love a gang of thieves each of whom deserves to be hanged."[74] Rousseau meditated a while, then sent back one of those eloquent pleas that always made him his own best lawyer, even as he was always his own betrayer.

Monsieur, in order to answer you I must ask you in turn, on what grounds do you judge me? Your manner of proceeding with me bears considerable resemblance to the interrogation of the wretches who are handed over to the Inquisition. If I have been denounced by secret accusers, tell me who they are, and then I shall be able to answer you. Meanwhile, of what shall I accuse myself? If from my birth I have done the least harm to anyone in the world, let that harm fall on my own head! . . . May it please God to cover the earth with enemies of men who can, each for himself, call down the same curse with as clear a heart. I ask you again, on what grounds do you judge me? . . . You say we shall never love thieves worthy to be hanged. I beg your pardon, Monsieur, their father or brother may love them, be unhappy about them, and cry to them wrathfully: "Leave your base trade, wretches!" [Rousseau goes on to say that the true misanthrope is he who encourages them to continue what they are doing.] I am the friend of mankind, and men are everywhere. The friend of truth also finds malevolent men everywhere, and I do not need to go very far.

To Tronchin's invitation to return to Geneva, Rousseau replies that he prefers not to witness the decadence of his native city.[75] So effective was this outcry that Tronchin replied with a disclaimer and an apology. Rousseau, however, did not find the explanation satisfactory, and doubtless was highly annoyed by Tronchin's pointed remarks about his living among the French rather than among his fellow-citizens.[76] "I have told you honest truths in harsh terms," he wrote back. "You had done the opposite. Which of us had a better right to complain?"[77]

Voltaire was not so easily put off. On May 16 he asked Tronchin to send him Rousseau's letter—"personal" letters were mostly public in the eighteenth century—and word of it quickly spread. "Send me, I beg you, the letter from the descendant of Diogenes' dog. Extreme insolence is extreme stupidity, and nothing is more stupid for a Jean-Jacques than to say 'mankind and I.'"

On March 14, Rousseau felt his *Nouvelle Héloïse* was ready except for recopying and sent Rey his preliminary conditions. Despite previous bickering over petty matters, frequently the product of Jean-Jacques' suspicious imagination, their negotiations went smoothly. Among his demands were a promise to print the novel beautifully on fine paper, to duplicate his manuscript exactly (including all errors), and to send no copies to Geneva. Curiously, he affirms that the first parts of the novel are "weak and bad," an opinion repeated in the *Confessions* but not shared by most readers. The publisher had the first part in his hands in April, the second in May, at the same time that Rousseau was working on the fifth book of *Emile* and copying *La Nouvelle Héloïse* for Mme. d'Houdetot. In June the author had his first payment of 400 livres on the agreed total of 2060. Royalties did not yet exist.

Jean-Jacques was too busy to be seriously disturbed when at the Foire Saint-Germain a parody by Favart, the popular composer who wrote for the Opéra Comique, made him the butt of some gibes, picturing him as Diogenes in his barrel. The *Parodie de Parnasse*, as it was called, took off against the *philosophes* in general, "but Rousseau's eccentricities of character and person," as one scholar puts it, "lent themselves especially to such treatment and he became a stock figure in these comedies."[78] Palissot was the most notorious of the mockers of *"philosophie."* In his first such farce, *Le Cercle, ou les originaux (The Group, or the Eccentrics,* 1755), Rousseau had been represented as a hypocritical maker of paradoxes interested only in getting into the limelight. The following year Patu's *Les Adieux du goût* gibed at Rousseau as "the maddest of wise men" (*"un sage des plus fous"*). There were others, and the most stinging blast, Palissot's *Les Philosophes,* was only then being readied.

In this way, one public image of Rousseau was created or confirmed. Paradoxically, it was the same image that the Encyclopedists and Voltaire were also fostering, even though the Encyclopedists were, more than Rousseau, the principal targets of the outrageous caricatures. In general, it was still held that Rousseau's writings were not meant as serious philosophical discourses. Even the well-disposed were puzzled by the contrast between his moral seriousness and his paradoxes, which seemed a cynical disregard for truth. Thus, the magistrate de Brosses wrote to a friend about the *Lettre à d'Alembert* that it was badly received in Geneva, and that Rousseau misinterpreted his own country. This judgment was confirmed by the Swiss philosopher-naturalist Charles Bonnet, who termed the *cercles* admired by Rousseau "a political evil."[79] All that Rousseau says about Switzerland, declares de Brosses, "is exactly the opposite of the truth. On the other hand, he writes admirably and with great strength of mind. What a pity that he uses such a head and such a style to wear himself out with paradoxes and make the greatest possible abuse of his mind. Fortunately he writes in bad faith and doesn't believe a word of what he says."[80]

Another public image was to emerge following the publication of *La Nouvelle Héloïse.* Already he rivaled Voltaire as one of the two great personalities that everyone of importance desired to meet. Already strangers were writing to him, showering him with encomiums and, better still, declaring themselves his disciples, a word that had a particular connotation to him. Watelet, the artist and landscape architect, would write (February 24, 1759) that he would be happy if the poem he was sending him "brings me the esteem and friendship of a virtuous man." A few days later Loyseau de Béranger assured him that "the reading of your works, your conversation, have inspired in me, toward you, all the respect and admiration that a well-born soul owes to genius and virtue." A lofty spirit, Lamoignon de Malesherbes, was moved to beg him not to stop writing. "It would be a double misfortune if public clamor stilled the voice of those whose works have never breathed anything but virtue and humanity" (June 30, 1760). Margency, on January 21, 1760, thanked Rousseau for the consolation he had found in his writings. "I have felt what you say, that to be happy I had to stop asking others what I was, and ask myself." Remarks like these were a long-needed nourishment to his ego.

Although the first reputation "was a ghost that was never quite laid,"[81] and persisted as a weapon against Rousseau and against the *philosophes*, it was the second image that was destined to triumph and become a legend at the end of his life and during the French Revolution. Although his reputation was to have its ups and downs in the succeeding decades, during that period, at least, he triumphed over his enemies.

Presumably Rousseau did not know that the pastor Vernes, in whom he confided, was also corresponding with his enemies. On January 9, Diderot denounced him to Vernes, for his aggression in the *Lettre à d'Alembert*.

I do not write to you; rather I converse with you, as formerly I used to converse with that man who has buried himself in a forest where his heart has become embittered and his way of living perverted. How I pity him! Just imagine that I loved him, that I remember it, and that I see him alone between crime and remorse, with deep waters beside him. He will often torment my thoughts. Our mutual friends have judged between him and me. I have kept them all, he has none left.[82]

Only one day later, Palissot sent Vernes his opinion of Rousseau's latest work: "This man is a great painter. He is full of vigor, feeling, energy. 'Tis a great pity he is mad."[83]

### 5. MADAME LA MARÉCHALE

Because of the peculiar nature of his fame, Jean-Jacques' dream of a peaceful, retired life within a small circle of intimate, unpretentious friends was not destined to last. The worldly great were knocking or about to knock on his rustic door. It was the fashion for the highest aristocracy, and for those who aspired to that station, to patronize men of letters and to boast of at least one domesticated *philosophe*. Rousseau was particularly attractive because of his unsocial posturing, his scandalous quarrels, and the notoriety of his outlandish ways. As often happens, the unwilling swain seemed the most desirable. One cannot, then, go along with Grimm's snide remark, "He has replaced us with people of the highest rank."[84] Those people were his admirers. On the other hand, this man who declared himself the enemy of the great was magnetically attracted to them. We have already examined the psychological roots of his *snobisme*.[85] To see himself sought after and adulated in the intimate insularity of a small circle of men and women who had the magic of power, of possessing everything without doing anything, gave him a deep satisfaction which he intensified by playing the gruff, hard-to-get bear. In some way he could identify himself with that power and transcendence of ordinary life. Jean-Jacques did not really like peasants, although he caressed his illusions about their simple, virtuous, carefree life. He was comfortable among them because he did not feel "looked at," or at least was looked at as a superior being. But admission to the intimate, enchanted circle of the great gave him the precious illusion of having won equality.

In the spring and summer of 1759, Rousseau was "captured" by the illustrious Charles-François-Frédéric de Montmorency, Duc de Luxembourg and Maréchal de France, by his enchanting wife, and by their aristocratic circle. They were to have a significant impact on his life.

The Duchesse (or Maréchale) de Luxembourg was truly a *grande dame*. In her full-length portrait she has a regal air. Her finely drawn features speak of wit and intelligence, of imperiousness combined with graciousness. A magnificent brocaded dress covers rather ample proportions, then in vogue, and uncovers a full-blown bosom that no doubt provoked Jean-Jacques' longing glances. Tall and graceful, she had a radiant, haughty, and imposing beauty. About her another great lady, Mme. du Deffand, wrote:

Her gestures have so much grace, they are so natural and so perfectly in harmony with what she says, that it is difficult not to be swept along to think and feel as she does. She dominates, wherever she is, and she always makes the kind of impression she wants to make. She uses these advantages almost like God, and she lets us believe that we have our free will while she determines us and from the height of her omnipotence makes, like Him, some that are chosen and some that are cast out. . . . Nothing escapes the subtlety of her mind and the delicacy of her taste. . . . She is witty and gay, faithful in her promises, loyal to her friends, sincere, discreet, helpful, generous. In a word, if she were less penetrating, or if men were less ridiculous, they would think her perfect.[86]

She had been born, on October 27, 1707, into an illustrious family, daughter of the Duc de Villeroy and granddaughter of Louis XV's tutor. Her father had a distinguished career in the military and in government. At a time when marriages were a family arrangement with no commitment to conjugal fidelity, she was wed at fourteen to Joseph-Marie, Duc de Boufflers. The new Duchesse de Boufflers and her husband slipped easily into the dissolution that characterized the Regency.* Lascivious by temperament, they were rivals in madcap escapades. The

---

* The Duchesse de Boufflers (later de Luxembourg) is not to be confused with the Comtesse de Boufflers (Marie-Charlotte de Campet de Saujon, Comtesse de Boufflers-Rouverel, 1725–1800), who was soon to become Rousseau's devoted friend. A distant cousin of the duchess, and mistress of another friend of Rousseau's, the Prince de Conti, she was called "the wise Minerva" by Mme. du Deffand. She should also be distinguished from Amélie de Boufflers, her granddaughter and the future Duchesse de Lauzun. Amélie died on the guillotine. There was also a Marquise de Boufflers, mistress of Stanislas at the court of Lunéville (Lorraine) and mother of a well-known writer, the Chevalier de Boufflers; she does not enter into Rousseau's life.

duke was exiled from Court a year after their marriage, following a shameless priapic orgy in the park of Versailles. The licentious gallantry of the Court of Louis XIV had degenerated into open debauchery, and husbands were forced to tolerate what they could not prevent without covering themselves with ridicule. They avoided their wives, and there were no bounds. The duchess once administered a public slap to the Comte de Tressan in payment for a couplet he had turned about her (although it is related that she sang it herself):

> Quand Boufflers parut à la Cour
> On crut voir la mère d'Amour.
> Chacun s'empressait de lui plaire,
> Et chacun l'avait à son tour.[87]

> (When Boufflers came to court
> She seemed to be Cupid's mother.
> Everyone was eager for her favors,
> And everyone had her in turn.)

The duke found favor with no less a personage than Marie Lesczinska, queen of France, who had appointed his wife lady-in-waiting. Apparently he had less endurance than his wife. He left the world, little better than he had found it, in 1747, at the age of forty-one. They had two children (one always gave the father the benefit of the doubt). Both were to die young, the daughter in 1760, the son (and his son as well) in 1761, the same year in which the Duc de Luxembourg also died.

The duchess was now forty, the Queen's favorite and official mistress of the Duc de Luxembourg, whose military feats were to win him a marshal's baton in 1757. She decided that she was of an age to reform. The first step was to regularize her liaison with the duke. His first wife, Marie de Seignelay, one of the outstanding bibliophiles of the time, also died in 1747, a convenient coincidence. The first step, marriage, was accomplished in June 1750. The second was to establish the most elegant salon in Paris, one reputed for its decency and stringent moral tone. Very soon she became known as the mentor to youthful aristocracy and the arbiter of good taste and social success.

No event in the maréchale's life was more important than her encounter with Rousseau. From the time of her marriage to the duke, they spent Easter and a good part of the summer at his estate at Montmorency, which he had acquired after his marriage. The imposing château, set in a large and beautiful park, had a library of one hundred thousand volumes and a *cabinet* of physics and natural history set up by Buffon. Culture was wedded to urbane elegance in the loveliest of settings. "The imposing appearance of that fine building," writes Rousseau, "the terrace on which it is built, the view, unique in the world perhaps, its vast salon decorated with taste, its gardens planted by the celebrated Le Nôtre: all that forms a whole whose striking majesty has nonetheless a certain simplicity which supports and maintains one's admiration."[88] He adds a strange observation. When the château is viewed from the opposing hill, "it absolutely appears to be surrounded by water." Such an impression once more reveals Rousseau's *idée fixe* of isolation and his fondness for small islands.

Rousseau had not been long in the neighborhood before the Luxembourgs, in 1758, sent their valet to extend to him an open dinner invitation. The courtesy was repeated when next they returned. He declined courteously and was proud of himself. "It reminded me of the time when Mme. de Beuzenval sent me to the pantry to have dinner. Times had changed; but I remained the same. I did not want to be sent to the pantry, and I cared little about dining at the table of the great." But he also admits that he was frightened by the idea of being surrounded by courtiers. The Comtesse de Boufflers, who was staying with the maréchale, was sent to court him, in the hope that she would be a more effective emissary, but once more in vain. In April 1759 it was the turn of the Chevalier de Lorenzy. Several visits ensued, but although he and Jean-Jacques became friendly, the chevalier also failed in his mission. Then one day, when Jean-Jacques was least expecting it, the duke arrived in person, accompanied by a half-dozen followers. To this assault he had to surrender. But the visit filled him with embarrassment. His little hut was falling into disrepair. Only a few days earlier (April 13) he had written to Coindet: "My thatched cottage is in bad shape, so that I shall inevitably end up by sleeping in the cellar or the street." The one room, adorned with stacked dirty dishes and broken earthenware, was a poor place to receive nobility. The floor threatened to give way at any moment. Quickly Jean-Jacques persuaded his visitors to walk with him to his "donjon," the open, unheated shack where he did all his writing.

The spell of the Maréchale de Luxembourg's charm immediately ensnared him. He had encountered her years before, when she was still the Duchesse de Boufflers, in the aristocratic milieu he so despised and so eagerly patronized. She was in the prime of her beauty then, but was reputedly *"méchante."* Now, instead of the cutting epigrams and *bons mots* he expected to hear, he found her conversation simple yet exquisitely delicate, sincere above all. She seemed not to notice his shy awkwardness. He would have been her complete captive from the first moment had not her daughter-in-law, the young Duchesse de Montmorency, spoiled its perfection by pretending to flirt with him. Had they come to make fun of him, as Cervantes' duke and duchess had so cruelly mocked Don Quixote?

Fortunately the maréchal was clearly treating him as an equal and wholeheartedly subscribed to the declaration of independence that Jean-Jacques made to him. With rare understanding, he did not and never would offer money or employment. What a difference between this man, the King's closest friend, and the so-called friends of yesteryear!

The Luxembourgs did urge him to move temporarily, while his floor was being repaired, either to their château or to a house called the Petit-Château, on the grounds. Rousseau declined the château, alleging "the extreme distance between you and me." The proper respect for rank involved the danger of falling either into unseemly familiarity or groveling. We can see that the danger was real. "I shall say to myself every day of my life: remember that Monsieur le Maréchal Duc de Luxembourg honored you with his visit, and sat on your wicker chair in the midst of your broken earthenware; it was not because of your name or fortune, but because of some reputation for probity you have acquired, and never make him blush for the honor he did you."[89] Rousseau did accept the offer of the Petit-Château and moved in on May 6. He was enchanted by the beauty of the estate and the simple comfort of his quarters:

It was in this profound and delightful solitude, in the midst of woods and brooks, concerts of all kinds of birds, the perfume of orange flowers, that in a continuous ecstasy I composed the fifth book of *Emile*, whose brilliance of style I owed in large part to the stimulus of the surroundings in which I was writing. With what eagerness I ran to the peristyle each morning at sunrise to breathe in the perfumed air! What good *café au lait* I drank there, tête à tête with my Thérèse! My cat and dog kept us company. With them alone I should have been content all my life, without feeling a moment of boredom. I was in a terrestrial paradise, living in its innocence and enjoying its happiness.[90]

To the Chevalier de Lorenzy he wrote wryly about neglecting his music-copying, an important source of income: "My feet are making me lose the use of my hands, and my trade is none the better for it."[91]

Rousseau's correspondence reveals that his joy was not unclouded. Were these great nobles playing a game, using him for their diversion? He was troubled by the paradox of his being their guest, to the point of telling the duchess their friendship could not last. His principles were involved, and the public image he was cultivating. Opinion, which he affected to despise, meant very much to him. On the day he moved in, he wrote to Mme. Dupin assuring her that he had not become more "reasonable," as she had put it. He still carried high his motto, *Vitam impendere vero*. He warned Lorenzy that he would not pay court to the duke and duchess, nor to anyone. "I have my rules, my tone, my manner which I cannot change."[92]

His sincerity is beyond question; he was not merely posturing. His character contained an important element of fanatical absolutism. But he was also a realist, despite his dreams and fantasies, and sometimes shrewd. His renown hinged on his singularity and the posture he had assumed. "I shall not infringe my maxims," he wrote to the Comtesse de Boufflers (October 7, 1760), "not even for him [the maréchal]. To them I perhaps owe in part the honor he has done me. . . . If I thought like another, would he have deigned to come and see me?" A letter to the maréchal on May 27 shows him to be still agitated and troubled in his prickly pride. "I am aware that my residence here, which is nothing for you, is of the greatest consequence for me. I know that even if I slept only one night here, the public, and posterity perhaps, would hold me to account for that single night." The world, he was sure, was looking at him, in his uniqueness.[93] He is a "*solitaire,*" he goes on, and a romantic. But the maréchal and he may yet be friends, if only His Grace does not try to be his patron, or send him gifts, expect adulation, or make him a showpiece for the curious. And if we think back to some of the supplicating letters of earlier years, which Rousseau would have liked to blot out from being, we can better appreciate his concluding lines: "I do not think I need any excuse for taking the tone which I am taking with you. . . . Monsieur le Maréchal, I might, it is true, speak to you in more respectful terms, but not in more honorable ones." Graciously and gracefully, the maréchal replied, "When you know me you will see that I do not deserve and cannot bear praise; therefore, Monsieur, let us stick to friendship. If I can win yours, I shall be more flattered than by any words or expressions."[94]

Rousseau was not wrong about his public image. On June 5, Diderot dispatched the news to Grimm. "Rousseau has accepted lodgings with M. de Luxembourg. They are saying here that he went to suckle Mme. de Luxembourg in order to improve the acidity of her blood."[95] Ten days earlier he had sent to his beloved Sophie Volland the new work of "the great sophist." "Listen to him," he urged her, "just as if I had no reason to complain about him. One can, then, be eloquent and sensible, without having either principles of honor, nor true friendship, virtue, nor truthfulness!"[96]

The correspondence with Dr. Tronchin came to a fruitless end. With relentless logic, Tronchin threw Rousseau's own words back at him, especially about Diderot and about Geneva. The excellent government of Geneva, he concluded, "makes us pity those who live at Montmorency, where a citizen, lacking all we have here, may fear another citizen and in a moment of need find himself stripped both of the protection of the laws and of means of self-defense."[97] Tronchin's prediction, Rousseau was to discover soon, was unhappily accurate. He could easily match Tronchin's skill in debate, and pitted a bit of sophistry against the doctor's malevolence and hypocrisy. He had not lost any friend, he retorted, because Diderot and the others were not his friends. And even if the charge were true, it would speak well of his love of mankind, since friendship tends to be exclusive and unjustly preferential. As for Geneva, if Tronchin, who also claimed to be his friend, was so harsh to him, what kind of treatment could he expect from the others?[98] Rousseau gave up his attempt to reestablish this link with the "establishment" of Geneva.

Other friends were urging him to return to Geneva. He spiked their efforts in a letter to Vernes. He could not go back while Voltaire was there. "Besides, my dear Genevans . . . you are so elegant, so brilliant, so smooth, what would you do with my bizarre appearance and my gothic maxims? What would I become in your midst, now that you have a *maître en plaisanteries* [Voltaire] who teaches you so well?" He did make one concession. If ever he should be forced to leave France, he would give his country another chance.[99] In fact, Rousseau was too happy where he was to think of uprooting himself. Another Genevan, the pastor Antoine-Jacques Roustan, reproached him for thinking of the treatment he would receive instead of the good he could do to his country; already, thanks to Jean-Jacques' influence, young people were taking up military exercises and developing a martial spirit.

A letter of July 10 to a Genevan friend, Bernard Cartier, a watchmaker living in Paris, is of interest on two counts. Referring to his urinary trouble, Rousseau wrote: "A deformity with which I was born makes it absolutely incurable."[100] Second, his hardened, aggressive attitude, obvious in several letters, is quite marked when he objects to the polite and conventional ending to Cartier's letter. "I am pleased with you and your letter, except the end where you say that you are more devoted to me than to yourself. You lie. There is no point in using the familiar form of address with people and then telling them lies. Goodbye, dear patriot, I greet and embrace you with all my heart. You may be sure that is not a lie."

In the middle of July the duke and duchess returned for their annual sojourn at Montmorency. They petted and pampered him so, Rousseau claimed, that he could scarcely do less than be with them every day. "I went there in the morning to pay my court to Madame la Maréchale; I dined there; I went there in the afternoon to stroll with M. le Maréchal; but I did not sup there, because of the high society and because they supped too late for me."[101]

He tried to keep his distance, but was unable to very long. "I have always been all or nothing. Soon I was all. Seeing myself fêted, spoiled by persons of such lofty rank, I went beyond the limits and began to feel toward them a friendship which one may only have for his equals." He became more familiar, and they remained respectfully polite. That was the way he preferred it.

He felt more comfortable with the duke than with the *grande dame*. He was a little uneasy about her sincerity, and much more so about her well-known mordant judgment of other people's conversation. Women, he knew, would rather be offended than bored—at least aristocratic French women, about whom he was writing such nasty things. He hit upon a way of avoiding embarrassment: if he could not talk wittily, he could read movingly. And so every morning at ten, while she reclined majestically in bed and the maréchal sat attentively at his side, he read from *Julie, ou la Nouvelle Héloïse*. The maréchale, recognizing her own

image in the youthful follies of Julie and her reform, became entranced
by the story and by its author. She embraced him "ten times a day" and
made noble guests move so that he could sit next to her at dinner. His
Venetian memories surely added savor to this gesture, but the worry
lingered. Her infatuation might evaporate and change to distaste. "Unfortunately for me," he remarked, "that fear was only too well
founded."

Rousseau had gone back to his cottage at Mont-Louis shortly after the
Luxembourgs' return. Mathas, his landlord, had thoroughly repaired
and renovated it, and had also installed a glass partition and fireplace in
his "donjon." Jean-Jacques set to work putting in a terrace and a garden. He had kept the key to the park and accepted the right to go back
to the Petit-Château several days a week. But the Luxembourgs' stay was
unexpectedly interrupted. The maréchal was called back to Versailles
after the English and Hanoverian armies defeated the French at Minden
on August 1. A week later they were gone.

The maréchale expressed her devotion by mail, and Rousseau in turn
expressed his anxieties.

You are only playing, while I am becoming attached, and the end of the game
is preparing new regrets for me. How I hate all your titles, and how I pity you
for having them! You seem so worthy to me of enjoying the charms of private
life! Why do you not dwell at Clarens?* I should go there to seek the happiness
of my life. But the château de Montmorency, but the Hôtel de Luxembourg?†
Is that where Jean-Jacques should be seen? . . . In your rank, and way of life,
nothing can make a lasting impression.[102]

The maréchal returned a reassuring note. Somehow his postscript, "My
most cordial regards to Mlle. LeVasseur," strikes one as a bit gro-
tesque.[103] The maréchal had not taken offense when it came out at
table that Rousseau had changed his dog's name from Duke to Turk—a
step he had taken in order to avoid offending him! Knowing that Rousseau was very attached to his dog, he even expressed regrets about an
accident that had befallen him. More ardent, the maréchale wrote back,
"I should like to spend my life with you. . . . I believe in your surperior-
ity, I respect it and love it."[104] To the duke Rousseau finally conceded
that inequality is not, after all, incompatible with friendship, only to
write to the duchess the following day that when she had sent a gift
to Thérèse, she had offended him by evading his prohibition of gifts.
That gesture had reminded him of his inequality. No, friendship between them was not possible.[105]

The Luxembourgs understood Jean-Jacques and knew that his peevishness covered a desire to be accepted, admired, and liked. They
pressed him to visit them in Paris. However, the maréchal's letter of
August 16 reveals that Rousseau had made the suggestion first.[106] He

* The imaginary setting of *La Nouvelle Héloïse*.
† The Luxembourgs' mansion in Paris.

went there rather frequently, always saving his honor and reputation by going directly through the side door into the garden, "so that I could say with the most exact truth that I had not set foot on the pavements of Paris."[107] Rousseau was obviously embarrassed by the fact that he was attracted to the elegant home and company of Parisian aristocrats, when he had covered both aristocrats and Paris with choice invective. There was some ground for his apprehensive behavior in a milieu where people did have their eyes on him and where gossip traveled fast. From Vienna Deleyre wrote to him on May 3: "I've just heard from Paris that you are staying with M. and Mme. de Luxembourg. Although your return to the city cannot give rise to any unfavorable interpretation, I should be surprised if you had left the country after what you have always told me about the charms it had for you."

Rousseau now meets a new friend who will play a role in the impending drama. We must beware of his way of introducing her in the *Confessions*, for his view is distorted by the paranoia of his later years. But he correctly notes that "in the midst of this temporary prosperity the catastrophe that was to mark its end was being prepared."[108] Only it was he who, unwittingly, was preparing it, by writing *Emile*.

The new friend was the Marquise de Verdelin. Born in 1728, Marie-Madeleine de Brémond d'Ars had been married at the age of twenty-two to a relative, the sixty-four-year-old Marquis de Verdelin. The old marquis was peevish and jealous, as well as homely, deaf, harsh, brutal, scarred, one-eyed—all Rousseau's adjectives. The ill-assorted couple had daily scenes; after he had tormented her and made her cry, he would do exactly as she wished, persuaded that it was he who wished it, not she. The marquise, wrote Sainte-Beuve, was a woman of character, "as far from the sentimental illusion and eternal *bergerie* of a d'Houdetot as from the biting and polite dryness of a Luxembourg."[109] She could smile despite her unhappiness. She had sought consolation (after considerable resistance, it is said) in the love of Adrien Cuyret, Seigneur de Margency, whom Rousseau had met at d'Holbach's and at the château of Mme. d'Epinay. No longer frequenting that milieu, he remained Rousseau's friend. But Margency was failing the marquise now. Though only a year older than she, he was turning toward piety and becoming markedly unresponsive to her. It became clear that he was trying to break off, especially after the harrowing death in 1761 of his friend, the poet Desmahis.

In the summer of 1759 the Verdelins went to the house they had bought near Rousseau, at Soisy. Although he had snubbed the marquise on several occasions when he and Mme. d'Houdetot had encountered her on their strolls, she now sought him out. Several fruitless visits—he was out, and made no reply—did not discourage her. She sent him pots of flowers for his terrace. Grudgingly, he called to thank her, and so the friendship began.

"This *liaison* began by being stormy, like all the ones I entered into despite myself. There was never any real calm." Again the *Confessions* are warped by Rousseau's suffering. He is more than unfair to Mme. de Verdelin, who was to be unselfishly devoted to him and tolerate his suspiciousness and incredible rudeness as long as he allowed her. She served him with true generosity and friendship until, in his illness, he drove her away. Jean-Jacques' abnormal suspiciousness, born of count-less hurts and rejections, was quick and ready to misinterpret reality. He would have us believe that she was always directing sly, sharp remarks at him and mocking him in an underhanded way. Their correspondence leads us to think otherwise. He was often gruff and offensive; she was patient, understanding, sincere. "Will you never learn," he once wrote by way of a grudging excuse, "that a man's words must be explained by his character, and not his character by his words?"[110] Referring to her attachment to him, she declared: "It is not your intellectual charms that have made me desire it, but your qualities of soul, and they have linked me to you in an unchangeable way."[111] He responded; "I have always esteemed and respected your conduct; but I have been too severe in judging your character by your intelligence. Be good, Madame, and you will be the best of women, for you have more wit than you need to be the worst, and that excess leads to the opposite extreme."[112] The mar-quise had been hurt, too, and this, despite all their differences, brought them together in mutual confidences and weeping. Whatever he relates, Jean-Jacques reciprocated and enjoyed Mme. de Verdelin's affectionate friendship. "Madame, let us break off this correspondence," he wrote in the playful tone he often took with her; "it is too delightful for me, and so too onerous. I either have to be too punctual or too ungrateful. Punctuality is above my strength and ingratitude has no home in my heart."[113] She was not a fortunate woman. Sensitive and loving, she was trapped among the three men, her husband, crabbed and harsh, her lover, selfish and insensitive, her friend, churlish and suspicious.

At the request of the maréchale, Rousseau promised to make her a copy of *La Nouvelle Héloïse*, and began to transcribe it in November. He was still working on Mme. d'Houdetot's copy and felt harried by the two women, each eager for her manuscript. Still this does not explain his misinterpretation of the maréchale's letter of November 6 (?), in which she thanked him and quoted his own words, to the effect that he would reluctantly accept payment. Rousseau was sure that she had taken umbrage at his suggestion, and remained convinced of it to the end. A letter of apology to her was followed the next day by one of his proud outbursts. "Since my last letter, I have examined the passage in question hundreds of times. I have considered it in its natural and proper sense. I have considered it in every sense that it is possible to give it. And I admit to you, Madame la Maréchale, that I am no longer sure whether it is I who owe you an apology or whether you do not owe me one." Rousseau makes no mention in his *Confessions* of the fact that a week later, not having received a reply, he was panicked by the idea that she might be really angry.

You do not answer me, Madame la Maréchale, your silence frightens me. I must have offended you in some way of which I am not aware, or else I was right, perhaps, to fear you would forget me. Deign to put yourself in my place, and be just. Overwhelmed by so many caresses, should I not have foreseen the end of the illusion which made me feel worthy of them? But what is my fault? What did I do to create that illusion? What have I done to destroy it? . . . If my alarm offended you, did you have to punish me by justifying it? . . . If you were not such a great lady, I should fly to your feet and spare no submissiveness or pleas to efface your displeasure, well founded or not. But given your station, do not expect me to do all that my heart asks of me. I should rather punish myself for having listened to it too well, and if this letter remains unanswered, I shall tell myself to hope no more.[114]

The maréchale sent back a reassuring note, and Jean-Jacques' anxiety subsided. The alternation between pride and self-humiliation prolongs the old pattern, and his failure to mention the letter in the *Confessions* is typical. During this same period, Rousseau's correspondence indicates that Deleyre, Deluc, and other friends were the objects of his suspicion and hostility. Time and again they wrote to "explain," to reassure him, to pledge their loyal friendship. Two Genevan visitors were startled when he exclaimed, pointing to his dog, "There's my best friend. I've sought friends among men and found almost none."[115] It was forbidden to utter the name *Grimm* in his house. They noted also that beneath his consistently expressed aversion to praise, "there enters a little pride in his way of acting and thinking, perhaps without his realizing it, for our vainglory is so clever that it knows how to disguise itself under the wrappings of lofty sentiments."

He was not above useful deception, as when he wrote Mme. de Verdelin about her "good husband," or when he assured Vernes that he had no work in press. "When I have some writing ready to come out, you'll not be the last to know."[116] *La Nouvelle Héloïse*, to which Vernes referred, was being readied for the press. He assured others that he had not written it, but had only edited the manuscript, and he kept the public in doubt. *Vitam impendere vero* did not apply. Although this evasiveness clashes with Jean-Jacques' motto, it follows his own consistent recommendation of the judicious use of duplicity. But there was no duplicity when he wrote Vernes of his moments of self-indulgent emotionalism. "I have become almost a child again. Sometimes I recall my old songs of Geneva and I am filled with emotion. I sing them in a cracked voice, and then I shed tears over my country when I think that I have survived it. Adieu."

Rousseau turned down a new chance for steady employment in November. Malesherbes, the director of publications, had become interested in him. Through Margency, he communicated an offer for Rousseau to become a regular book reviewer for the prestigious *Journal des savants*. Jean-Jacques sent back his refusal within a few hours, averring that he could never work *"sur commande,"* or against deadlines. He knew, he explains in the *Confessions*, "that only the love of the great, the true, and the beautiful could inspire my genius. . . . My indifference would have frozen my pen and dulled my mind."[117] In later years, Malesherbes declared that he would never have made such a proposal after he had met Rousseau.[118]

Imprudence led Jean-Jacques to commit another offense against the Duchesse de Luxembourg—at least he was so persuaded. On December 2 he sent an unprompted letter to Etienne de Silhouette, who had been dismissed as controller of finance, congratulating him for issuing new regulations that corrected some of the abuses in tax-collecting. "You have braved the cries of the moneymakers."[119] Rousseau's letter soon made the rounds. The Luxembourgs, who "made money" from the farming-out of taxes, had taken part in the successful campaign to oust Silhouette. The maréchale asked Rousseau for a copy of his letter. She said not a word to him, and there was no sign of displeasure, but he was filled with dark forebodings.

A new winter came on and brought little change. The year 1760 was one of intense literary activity. On January 18, Rousseau sent out the last part of his novel and the Preface. Intense work lay ahead. He was determined to complete *The Social Contract* and *Emile*, and correction of the proofs of *La Nouvelle Héloïse* was another painstaking task. Throughout the year he was also recopying his novel for the maréchale. In December he sold his *Extrait du projet de paix perpétuelle* of the Abbé de Saint-Pierre for periodical publication. It is, then, somewhat surprising to read that at the very time he was receiving Margency's offer to collaborate on the *Journal des savants*, he was seriously contemplating giving up writing.[120] To this end he invested the tidy proceeds of the *Lettre à d'Alembert* and *La Nouvelle Héloïse* in a small life annuity. He would of course finish *Emile*, but would abandon two grandiose projects, the *Morale sensitive* and the *Institutions politiques*, taking from the latter the materials for *The Social Contract* and burning the rest.

He was fed up with men of letters and also, he claimed, with aristocracy. Always seeking and urging unity, he felt himself as divided as he had ever been, belonging only half to himself and half to groups for whom he "was not made." What bothered him most about frequenting the rich was the obligation, not having servants or a carriage of his own, to be constantly handing out gratuities to domestics. This was a vexation to a man both poor and parsimonious; the distaste for literary endeavors was a deeper matter. He had inveighed against the arts, and had become one of their foremost practitioners. In particular he had condemned love stories and novels of seduction, and he was about to publish the most popular work of that sort in the entire century. His enemies were to seize upon the contradiction, and of course he expected that they would. On November 29, 1760, he informed Jacob Vernes that after having taken up the pen at the age of forty he was going to put it down before the age of fifty, never to take it up again. Neither part of this statement is accurate. To Lenieps he declared on December 11 that after *Emile* "the public will hear no more from me." And on June 25, 1761, he wrote to Dom Deschamps that he was laying down his pen forever, cursing the day when a "foolish pride" made him take it up. He knew, he wrote again to Dom Deschamps on August 12, that his writings had lost him friends and created enemies, "enmeshing me everywhere in the nets of perfidy. . . . When I was obscure and loved, I was happy; now that I have a name I live and shall die the most wretched of all creatures." Rousseau was never to carry out his resolution. He was trapped. Despite what he said about his writings, he had found his identity and his self-esteem through them, and his unhappiness had not sprung into being because of them. In his books he had made an image of himself that he wanted to project to the world and to posterity and that in later years he was irrevocably condemned to defend.

Another episode in the war against the *philosophes* took place on May 2, 1760, when the Comédie Française put on Palissot's *Les Philosophes*. Hitting hard in the manner of Aristophanes, Palissot struck his strongest blow at Diderot, who is portrayed as a villain. Diderot had offended Palissot's patron, the Princesse de Robecq, the daughter of the Duc de Luxembourg by his first marriage. Rousseau got off lightly, doubtless because of his connection with the Luxembourg family. He was presented as a buffoon, who came on stage walking on all fours and munching on a head of lettuce. This portrayal may have been inspired by the famous letter Voltaire had sent Rousseau after reading the *Discourse on Inequality*. Jean-Jacques was not overly offended, especially in view of the fact that Palissot made use of some of his own criticisms of the *philosophes*. Diderot swallowed his rage and avenged himself posthumously in his great satire *Le Neveu de Rameau*. Duchesne, who had published Palissot's *succès de scandale*, sent Rousseau a copy—doubtless, the latter speculated, because Palissot thought he would be delighted to see his erstwhile friend torn to ribbons. But Jean-Jacques still thought Diderot less wicked than weak. He still esteemed him and kept fond memories of their years of friendship. It was Grimm who had been the cruel and jealous calumniator. Rousseau indignantly sent the play back to Duchesne. "I shuddered to see myself praised in it. I do not accept your horrible present. I am persuaded that in sending it to me you did not wish to insult me. But you do not know or have forgotten that I have had the honor of being the friend of a respectable man, who has been reprehensibly blackened and defamed in that libel."[121] The reply does honor to Rousseau. It was published and was even quoted by

Grimm in his *Correspondance littéraire*. According to Rousseau, Diderot was furious at being outdone in generosity, and his wife, "known everywhere as a fishwife"—Rousseau's revenge for Diderot's mockery of Thérèse LeVasseur—went around saying the nastiest things about him.[122] When Duchesne sent an apologetic reply, Jean-Jacques answered, "I am not a *philosophe*, as you call me, but an honest man who tries to harm no one, who loves decent people, who enjoys hearing and saying, when he can, useful truths; but who detests personal satire and cannot without out indignation see merit insulted and his former friend defamed."[123]

The Abbé Morellet, prompted or unprompted, sprang to Diderot's defense in a satirical counterattack, *La Vision de Charles Palissot*. The abbé soon found himself lodged in the Bastille, mainly because of his offensive lines about the Princesse de Robecq, who was at that moment on her deathbed. He had had the cruelty to send her a copy of his *Vision*, in which he committed, in Voltaire's words, the barbarity of informing her that she was incurably ill. D'Alembert quickly asked Rousseau to intervene with the Duchesse de Luxembourg on Morellet's behalf.

The duchess did intervene, at Jean-Jacques' request, and Morellet was released without further penalty on July 30. Rousseau thought, however, that Morellet's letter of thanks was not effusive enough. Probably he winced at one sentence in it: "Besides, after the conversation I have had with Mme. la Maréchale, I well understand how she could be excepted from your renunciation of society and its pomp."[124] He repeated its substance in a letter to her (August 6), implying that he took it as an accusation of acting in contradiction to his professed principles. And yet, at the same time, he was writing to Mme. Dupin: "I have not ceased to consider myself as belonging to your family; and what is certain is that you will never have a more sincere or truly devoted servant than I."[125] Years later, in the *Confessions*, Rousseau accused Morellet and d'Alembert of having taken his place in the maréchale's favor.[126]

Palissot's punishment was not to come until the French Revolution. In 1793 the Commune of Paris refused him a *certificat de civisme* on the grounds that he had attacked Rousseau in *Les Philosophes*. It might have cost him his life, but his humble self-accusation saved him from the guillotine.

During these months Rousseau was developing a valuable relationship with Malesherbes. On March 6 he wrote his first letter to the director of publications, an obvious effort to ingratiate himself with this powerful man who had reportedly been so favorably inclined toward him. It is curious to contrast his brusque tone to some aristocratic friends with the punctilious deference, even bowing and scraping, toward Malesherbes and several others. As in letters to other correspondents, he refers to *La Nouvelle Héloïse* as an "insipid collection of letters"; elsewhere he terms it "that cheap, flat novel" or a "tasteless rag." How proud he really was of this book, into which he had poured so much of his heart and mind, is manifest in the Prefaces and in the *Confessions*, or in his self-flattering reminiscence, "Not a single living man of letters, not even Voltaire, has had more billiant moments than mine."[127] He claims to be superior to Richardson and other more "inspired novelists who make up for the sterility of their ideas by multiplying characters and adventures." Doubtless he has the often-misjudged Abbé Prévost in mind. "What has been least noted and what will always make it a unique work is the simplicity of the subject and the chain of interest which, concentrated on three people, is sustained throughout six volumes, without episodic stories, without romantic adventures, without wickedness of any kind either in the characters or the actions."[128] Later that year, he had an ardent but friendly debate with Malesherbes concerning the laws that permitted a French publisher to reprint Rey's edition of *La Nouvelle Héloïse* without compensation. It is to Rousseau's honor that he stoutly defended Rey's interests and refused to accept any money for the French edition. His letters to Rey show that he had been constantly suspicious that Rey might be trying to evade their agreements or even to betray him, and the Dutch publisher is constantly reassuring, mollifying, and flattering him. Rousseau suspected, for instance, that to economize on shipping, Rey had sent the copies of *La Nouvelle Héloïse* by sea instead of by land and that the ship had been captured by the English. Rey was endlessly patient. He undoubtedly had his own profits in mind, but he obviously understood his author's neurotic genius.

Far more momentous ultimately was Rousseau's deteriorating relationship with Voltaire. Nothing dire had occurred as yet, but he correctly suspected that his intervention in the quarrel over the theater was not to be forgiven. He in turn detested the Patriarch of Ferney. We have seen how convinced he was that he could not return to Geneva while Voltaire was there. In a letter to Moultou (January 29), he cries out, "You speak to me of that Voltaire! Why does the name of that buffoon soil your letters? The wretch has ruined my country. I should hate him more if I despised him less. I see in his great talents only an additional shame which dishonors him by the unworthy use he makes of them."

A fuss arose in June when Abbé Trublet informed Rousseau that he possessed a copy of the long letter of 1756 in which Jean-Jacques had refuted Voltaire's "Poème sur le désastre de Lisbonne" (the "Lettre sur la Providence"), and that Formey had printed it. Agitated by the prospect of Voltaire's wrath, Rousseau inquired of Malesherbes, who assured him that he had no knowledge of the matter.[129] He decided to write to Voltaire the same day. "I never expected, sir," he begins, "ever to be in correspondence with you." He proffers every reassurance of his innocence in this unauthorized publication and throws suspicion for the betrayal, probably correctly, on Grimm. If Voltaire wishes to write a rejoinder, he promises to publish it, together with his own letter, without commentary. Then he concludes this letter of explanation or appeasement with these proud words:

I do not like you, Monsieur. You have inflicted the keenest hurts on me, your disciple and enthusiastic admirer. You have ruined Geneva in return for the shelter you received there. You have alienated my fellow-citizens from me as a reward for the eulogies of you which I spread among them. It is you who make residence in my country unbearable to me. It is you who will make me die in a foreign land, deprived of all the consolations of the dying, and thrown for all honor on a refuse dump, while all the honors that a man can expect will accompany you in my country. I hate you, finally, since you have wished it; but I hate you as a man still worthier of my loving you, if you had wished it. Of all the feelings toward you with which my heart was filled, there remains only the admiration which cannot be denied your fine genius and the love of your writings. If I can honor in you only your talents, that is not my fault. I shall never fail in the respect which is due to them, nor the actions required by that respect (*Confessions*, Book X).

Voltaire had been delighted by Palissot's mockery of Rousseau. "Well served!" he had written Mme. d'Epinay on April 25, "because of his idiosyncrasy, his affectation of putting himself into Diogenes' barrel and rags, and still more because of his ingratitude to the most lovable of benefactresses."* He never replied to Rousseau's stinging letter. To d'Alembert he mentioned it in passing (June 23): "I wish Rousseau were not completely mad, but he is. He has written me a letter for which he should be put into a bath and given refreshing bouillons." His strong personal aversion toward Jean-Jacques was intensified by the latter's betrayal of the cause. A letter of July 24 to Mme. d'Epinay is significant in this regard:

I know better than anyone what is going on in Paris and Versailles in regard to the *philosophes*. If we are divided, if we have small weaknesses, we are lost. The *infâme* and the infamous will triumph. . . . Jean-Jacques might have served in the war; but he has completely gone off the deep end. He has just written me a letter in which he says that I have "ruined Geneva." . . . He says that because of me he will be thrown on the "rubbish heap" when he dies, while I shall be honorably buried. What can I say, madame? He is already dead. But urge the living to stay closely united.

Jean-Jacques was far from dead. In fact he was to prove himself at least Voltaire's equal in invective. To his friend Jacob Vernet he used such choice phrases as "this proclaimer of impiety," "this fine genius and vile soul."[130] For the moment the fire was damped down, but it would break out into savagery.

Rousseau's relations with others were as always uneven and troubled.

* Voltaire's letters may be found, in chronological order, in his *Correspondance*, edited by Theodore Besterman, 107 vols.; Geneva, 1953–65.

Deleyre, who was so attached to him, wrote plaintively (July 30), referring to the time when he had accompanied Jean-Jacques to the Hermitage: "Of all the friends you had then, I am perhaps the only one who
loves you and whom you do not love. You see how unjust you are." To
this Rousseau replied sophistically that since Deleyre did not give himself the name of friend, he had to prefer others to him. Besides, Deleyre
was too fiercely proud and independent![131] What Rousseau was referring to was perhaps Deleyre's charge in an earlier letter (July 7) that he
could not lose Jean-Jacques' friendship, "for you like no one, even if you
are not displeased if certain people like you."

Rousseau frequently complains about being besieged by visitors, even
though he was flattered and did not really desire solitude for more than
brief periods. But his ever-unrealized ideal was an isolated harmony of a
few selected friends, who "interpenetrated" each other with perfect
transparency. "It seems to me," he wrote to Coindet (whom he was later
to dislike), "that if you, dear Carrión and I could form a small exclusive
society, into which no other mortal in the world were admitted, that
would be absolutely delightful. I cannot stop building castles in Spain.
Growing older does no good, I become ever more a child."[132] Sometimes, too, he makes a fuss about his aristocratic friends' gifts of wild
game, which he downed with relish, even though they were against his
"principles." Temptation was too strong. When Mme. de Verdelin sent
him some barley medicine, she fearfully begged him not to be angry
with her. But the principles were always in mind, at least; after receiving two such gifts from the Prince de Conti, he rather rudely informed
Mme. de Boufflers in a letter (October 7, 1760—a letter he later said he
blushed to think about) that he would accept no more. "Nothing one
accepts is without a consequence. When one begins by accepting something, soon one refuses nothing. As soon as one accepts everything, soon
one asks; and whoever reaches the point of asking soon does all he can to
get what he asks for."

The Duchesse de Luxembourg had fallen under the spell of *La
Nouvelle Héloïse* when Rousseau had read it to her. Her enchantment
was renewed as she read the several parts of the manuscript. "I find it
even more beautiful than the first time I heard it. No, never will there
be anything so well written, so touching. I am dying to see you."[133] He,
too, expressed his impatience. "The fine days are nearing," he wrote on
March 5; "they will have arrived only when you are here." To which she
gallantly replied, "Can one be so unfortunate as to have a tender affection for a person one never sees?" More gallantly perhaps than Jean-
Jacques, when he wrote (June 18): "How providence has put you both
in the wrong place when it made you so good, so likeable, so worthy!
Ah! you deserved to have been low-born and free; to have neither masters nor valets; to live for yourselves and your friends. You would have
made them happy, and you would have been happy yourselves." Doubt-

less he did not grasp the irony in Mme. de Luxembourg's reply: "Nothing is more charming than your letter. Each day we feel with delight the worth of a friendship as unusual as yours."[134]

Rousseau, as W. H. Blanchard has adroitly pointed out, both loved and hated the maréchale, but was either unconscious of the negative side of his feelings or could not control it.[135] The unconscious feelings grew out of his dependency, which he resented because of the implicit inferiority; they grew perhaps from envy, and certainly from her very femininity. His experiences with Mme. de Warens, Mme. d'Epinay, and Mme. d'Houdetot could not but infuse his inner picture of her: hatred now mingled with fear in his attitude toward women. He was aware that he was doing things that were straining her very deep and sincere friendship for him; but he did not know why he did them. "There must have been a natural opposition between her mind and my own, since, independently of the endless blundering remarks which at every moment escaped me in conversation, there were even in my letters and when I was getting along best with her, things that vexed her without my understanding why."[136] It was "fated," he said.

Jean-Jacques' attitude toward all his friends, as we have seen, was aggressive and provocative. Blanchard has made a keen analysis of this manifestation:

Rousseau was always setting little traps for people by making them aware that he was living under difficult circumstances. Then he would wait for the victim to offer food or financial assistance so that he could demonstrate his independence by refusing all help. He set similar snares in conversation. By his own derogatory opinion of himself, he encouraged others to be self-effacing. Finally, when he had drawn them out into a long sorry tale, he would suddenly turn on the attack, accusing them of insincerity.[137]

These tactics, according to Blanchard, were intimately connected with his sadomasochism. The desire to submit to physical aggression from the female had become internalized, and he was no longer conscious of its disguised workings,

moving behind the scenes, arranging events for its satisfaction. He knew that he derived a feeling of virtue and happiness from fighting injustice, but his joy would have been short-lived had he realized that he himself provoked others to mistreat him. It was much more satisfactory to perceive fate as the assailant. . . . His frequent episodes of rudeness were simply exhibitions of his attempt to deny what he felt was a weakness in himself. He was never provocative or rude when certain he was loved, but only with his dog, Turk, could he find such an unambivalent relationship.[138]

He had never found any one so difficult to provoke as the maréchale.

The Luxembourgs came and went that Easter and did not return until July. Having exhausted *La Nouvelle Héloïse* as a source of entertaining the duchess, Jean-Jacques turned to *Emile*, which she barely tolerated. But she urged him to entrust its publication to her, instead of letting himself be duped by wily publishers. This led to a heated argument. Rousseau was sure that it would not be safe to print it in France without a "tacit license" for which it would be imprudent even to apply. The maréchale maintained the contrary. She persuaded Malesherbes to write Rousseau a letter, unfortunately lost, assuring him that the exposé of his religious beliefs in the part called *Profession de foi du vicaire savoyard* would be approved "by all mankind," and "also by the Court." To Rousseau it was a curious surprise; this very cautious man had become so easygoing for him. A compromise was eventually struck in August 1761. Néaulme, in Holland, would do the printing, but do it for Duchesne, a Parisian publisher. Nothing could allay Rousseau's suspicions that the French censorship would mutilate his work.

A minor cause for embarrassment became for a while a major one in his mind. The duchess had brought with her Amélie de Boufflers, her young granddaughter by her first marriage. She allowed Jean-Jacques to kiss the child. The trouble came about when he met her alone on the stairway and kissed her because he was embarrassed about what to say. She was not even eleven, just a child, says Rousseau, but very pretty and sweet, "with virginal shyness."[139] The next day he was reading by chance a passage in *Emile* "in which I properly censure what I had done the day before." The maréchale approved, in a way that made him blush and take on a guilty look—when all he really felt was "foolish and embarrassed." He swears that "nothing was more tender and chaste than the feelings she [the little girl] inspired in me," that this "reprehensible kiss" was as pure as the others. These very remarks, however, are rather shocking, when applied to a child who was not, as Rousseau alleges, nearly eleven years old, but (as he well knew) exactly nine, and the emphatic denial indicates at least the presence of the guilty thought. But, of course, it was not the fault of any intention of his:

How is it that a very child can intimidate a man whom the power of kings has not frightened? What can I do? How should I act when I can come up with no quick response? If I force myself to speak to people whom I meet, I inevitably utter some stupidity. If I say nothing, I am a misanthrope, a wild animal, a bear. I'd have been better off to be born a total imbecile; but the social talents I lacked have been the instruments of my ruination because of the talents I had (*Confessions*, Book X).

The Prince de Conti came to visit Rousseau twice. He admits that he was deeply flattered by this attention. Illustrious in war and powerful in politics, Conti was a prince of the blood. Sainte-Beuve quotes a contemporary who said that "he made no distinction of rank in society."[140] Rousseau proudly asserts that he owed the honor of his friendship largely to his own merit. (A later footnote embraces Conti in the all-enfolding plot against him.) He boasts also of twice beating the prince at chess, despite the "signs and grimaces" of Lorenzy and the others who wanted him to lose. When the games were over he said, in a respectful but grave voice, "Monseigneur, I honor your Serene Highness too greatly not to win over you always in chess."[141] The prince, he felt, appreciated his treating him as a man. Although Jean-Jacques deprecated his own ability at chess, the notation of one of the games, taken down by a witness, proves that they were "two classical players well trained in the best principles."[142] When he had first come to Paris he had worked hard to become an expert and frequented the Café de la Régence, where the leading players congregated.

Conti's former mistress, Mme. de Boufflers, frequently came with Lorenzy to see Jean-Jacques. She was twenty-eight and attractive. Her husband had never interested her, and she had become Conti's mistress in 1751.* Even though he now sought his pleasure elsewhere, she remained closely attached to him and retained her influence over him. Her ambition to marry Conti, after her husband's death in 1764, was not to be realized.

Jean-Jacques struggled hard not to fall in love with her. "For once I was wise, and at fifty it was time."[143] A spark was still glowing for Mme. d'Houdetot, and so he "said goodbye to love for the rest of my life." Doubtless he was deterred by Mme. de Boufller's close relationship to Mme. de Luxembourg and by his own blossoming friendship with Conti. It would not do to repeat a bad blunder. It was too much like the situation with Mme. d'Epinay and Saint-Lambert, and potentially worse. But love conquered, he adds darkly, was even more fatal to him that love triumphant. Later he was convinced that his rejection was the motive for her joining in the "plot" against him. He was wrong.

Conti had an extensive property in Paris. There Mme. de Boufflers reigned over an influential salon and through her lover exercised substantial power over public affairs. Brilliant and charming, she was enamored of English literature and particularly interested in England's greatest philosopher, David Hume. Like Rousseau, she was able to delude herself about her activities and cover them with an apparently sincere love of virtue. She condemned infidelity, and seemed to mean it. "She is two women," Horace Walpole said of her, "the upper and the lower." Mme. du Deffand remarked on her austere ethics, adding, "What is amusing, though a little annoying, is that this lofty morality is not perfectly in accord with her conduct; what is even more amusing is that the contrast does not startle her."[144] She began a correspondence with Hume and ended by seducing him. It was not easy. The Scotsman was reluctant, but succumbed when "she showed her claws, telling him she could be cruel as well as charming."[145]

Toward the end of the year, Mme. d'Houdetot asked Rousseau to

* See note on p. 32.

follow the manuscript of *La Nouvelle Héloïse*, which he had completed for her in faithful performance of his pledge, with one of *Emile*. Her letter is written entirely in the third person. Rousseau refused, pleading the forthcoming publication of his treatise.

In all these relationships, Rousseau was struggling to be himself; but his self was divided between the role in which he had fixed his identity (his "principles") and simpler means of satisfying his need for esteem and worth. Living the role involved expressing his independence, the first of his principles; the easier way was to yield to the pleasure of longed-for dependence. And so "he fought strange battles within his mind to establish the independence of his conscience against the blandishments of the aristocratic dream world which beckoned and tempted him."[146] His sudden starts of rudeness were the offspring of this conflict. Besides, frankness was now an essential principle. In *La Nouvelle Héloïse* (Part V, Letter XIII), he wrote: "It is better to act contrarily to one's nobility than to virtue, and a charcoal seller's wife is more respectable than the mistress of a prince." Later he was convinced that this statement was the origin of Mme. de Boufflers' "covert but implacable hatred" and of Mme. de Pompadour's animosity. This, he claims, was only bad luck or poor judgment; he readily acknowledges such minor offenses, since they do not involve intent.

When he sent the maréchale her manuscript copy of *La Nouvelle Héloïse* on October 16, he decided to do something special to distinguish it from other copies. He sent with it a chapter, "Les Amours de Milord Edouard Bomston," which he had excluded from the novel, partly because he knew that the portrait of one of the characters might be applied to the maréchale and that she would have had reason to be highly offended by the *rapprochement*.[147] Nevertheless he sent it, and with it a note assuring her that he had burnt the original, that it was for her alone and would remain her secret unless she chose to divulge it. He admits in retrospect that the note could only confirm her realization that he had the possible applicability of the odious character in mind. Yet he earnestly rejects the blame, placing it anew on the "blind fatality which was carrying me away to my fate." It is difficult not to suspect again the impulse to *provoke* guilt and punishment, in which we have earlier found the roots of his masochism. The maréchale, he adds, never—to his great surprise—mentioned the *cahier* at all, and only later did he recognize the harm he had done himself or, more truly, which he fancied he had done himself.

The old year closed with the publication of *La Nouvelle Héloïse* in London, and the new year opened with its publication in Paris late in January. It is the first part of Rousseau's great trilogy. Its impact on his times was so great, and its frame so enduring, that it behooves us to pause to get a close view of its characters and the drama of their lives.

# II. *La Nouvelle Héloïse:*
# The Problem of Reconstruction

> . . . the history of great men whose lives, uncovered by biographers, reveal
> the curious peculiarities of the acts of their minds.
>
> Balzac, *Louis Lambert*

### 1. HOW *La Nouvelle Héloïse* CAME TO BE

ROUSSEAU, his enemies cried, condemned the arts, and practiced them; excoriated the theater, and wrote plays; warned against novels of love, and wrote the most passionate love story of the century. Perhaps what they were really unhappy about was that he had written the most influential novel of the century. It is a curious book, *La Nouvelle Héloïse,* so tangled in theme and motive that it almost defies classification. It can be dramatic, lyrical, and moving; but parts of it are also tedious and un-novelistic. At times the protagonists sweep us along into empathy with their problems and passions, and we believe in them; at other times they evaporate into disembodied voices preaching interminably, to their century and against it, about morals, politics, and education. They were real enough to their contemporaries.

Rousseau, with a certain *mauvaise foi,* declared in his Preface that his novel could not be popular and would please few readers; but he was proud of it, and did all he could to whet the public's curiosity. "The thing that has been least noticed in it, and that will always make it a unique work," he wrote unblushingly in the *Confessions,* "is the simplicity of the subject and the chain of interest which, concentrated among three persons, is maintained throughout six volumes, without romantic adventure, without villainy of any kind, either in the characters or the action. . . . Richardson's novels, superior in so many other things, could not be compared with mine in this regard."

No other novel was so popular. Daniel Mornet counted seventy-two editions before 1800. The lending libraries were besieged; some doubled their fees and limited borrowers to an hour per volume. Readers snatched it from friends fortunate enough to possess a copy and stayed up all night, weeping over Saint-Preux's anguish. The Romantic generation, sixty years later, liked it almost as well. "Good God," cried Lamartine, "I do not understand how its pages do not catch fire!"

In later generations, imbued with realism or cynicism, *La Nouvelle Héloïse* has inspired mostly boredom or derision. For a long period it was scarcely read, except in extracts in anthologies, but within the last fifteen years interest has been reborn. Never again will *La Nouvelle Héloïse* be a popular work, read by a mass audience; its archaic epistolary form—typical in the eighteenth century after the success of Marivaux and Richardson—its old-fashioned rhetoric, exaggerated romantic lyricism, and drawn-out preaching mark it as a literary monument. Character creation and analysis, as we know them, are sketchy, and there is little plot interest or action after the love affair in the first part. These are barriers the modern reader has to overcome. Nevertheless the *cognoscenti* now see new values in *La Nouvelle Héloïse*, a psychology of remarkable subtlety and daring, an exploration of basic problems of the individual and of society. These elements work themselves out in almost clinical terms, as we follow the emotional and intellectual evolution of the two protagonists in an artificial milieu of great psychological pressure.

*La Nouvelle Héloïse* is many things. For Rousseau it was both the wish fulfillment of his dream of love and the catharsis of guilt for his treacherous liaison with Mme. d'Houdetot. In some parts of it he enters the world of fantasy, intoxicates himself with experiences life had always refused him, weaving into his dream fragments of happy memories. His mind was haunted by the dream of lost Edens. Clarens, the estate where Julie, his heroine, lives, and the surrounding countryside, are precisely those where Maman had spent the happy days of her youth, and which she had so often described to him. The characters he creates come from his own memories, or his own self-projection. If he does not entirely succeed in making his characters live, *he* lives in them.

Rousseau did not love women, but the tender, voluptuous, and false memories of them. The enchanted atmosphere of his novel gave him much more satisfaction than love itself would have done. Eros had always found in Jean-Jacques a sorry standard-bearer. Rousseau himself said, "There is nothing beautiful but that which does not exist." Frustrated in all his dreams, stripped of confidence in his ability ever to make an adjustment between his own needs and real beings,[1] he found salvation by withdrawing into the refuge of an imaginary world. "People could not conceive how excited I can get about imaginary beings."[2] In this world he could expand without hindrance and find surcease from conflict. Art became his true reality, in which he set himself free from unhappiness and the dark forces of destruction.

It is Rousseau's idealized self in an idealized world that fills these rambling pages. But his idealized self, like his real self, was not a simple one. If Jean-Jacques saw himself as the perfect lover, even as the forgivable seducer carried away by a perfect passion, he also saw himself as the moral guide and teacher. Events made it necessary for him to redeem himself in the world's eyes and in his own, to justify the role he had sought to give himself when his rather nasty game had been shown up. But all this did not take place at once. Not only did his intentions change while he was writing, but his fragmented self-projection is infused into several of the contrasting characters of his story.

The idea first came to him near the end of August 1756. He had been at the Hermitage for four unhappy months. The spring and lovely summer had been largely fruitless. Unable to concentrate on his work or to communicate with Thérèse, he was beset by an inner emptiness and a dread solitude. He felt tired and old. To escape from the gloom of the present, he wandered in the fields and forest, while tender memories rushed upon him.[3] The women he had known came back to keep him company—Mlle. Galley and Mlle. de Graffenried, and the ineffable delight of that unforgettable day; the haughty Mlle. de Breil, who had deigned to notice him; the tender, timid Mme. Basile, the lascivious Mme. de Larnage, the fiery Zulietta. He felt like a lovesick shepherd. But could he, at his age, sing as he had once done under the windows of a château, hoping that his fairy princess would appear? There was no salvation in the past—not in a past so filled with humiliation and failure. He could only dream, dream and write.

It began, then, as a pastoral novel, *Les Amours de Claire et de Marcellin*. On August 26, Deleyre inquired about the progress of the work. He had not gotten very far. A bladder attack and the pain of probes had sent him back into reality. Then came the polemical episode of Voltaire's "Poème sur le désastre de Lisbonne."

Only after that exchange was he able to go back to his imaginary world. Once fantasy and escapism take hold, "the withdrawal inevitably aggravates the individual's inability to cope with the external difficulties, which in turn drives him to take ever deeper refuge in the compensatory triumphs of fantasy."[4] But now the novel was no longer to be a pastoral. He imagined two lovely girls, as always a blonde and a brunette. He was in love with the blonde, and the brunette was his tender friend. The first lines of the story were scribbled on the back of a sketch of his letter to Voltaire.

Julie and Claire, he called them, and they took possession of his entire being.[5] When autumn's chill sent him indoors, his obsession with them suffused him with fire. He could do no other work. Lascivious thoughts gripped him, but he blocked his guilt feelings by planning a moral ending. Julie would be redeemed, after he had enjoyed his imaginary ecstasy, and become the model wife and mother. She and he would expiate their sins. But who would be her husband? A new idea flashed upon him, and the whole work was transformed. Wolmar, the husband, would be a kind of mediator between *philosophes* and Christians (just as Rousseau would have liked to be). He would join to the spectacle of a moral home that of civic harmony. But true love must be immortal; the lovers, repentant but not quite redeemed, would be united in death, drowned together in a storm, either a double suicide or an accident. If this plan had been followed, the novel would have concluded at the end of what is now Part IV.

The first two parts were written by the end of that winter. They summoned forth his deepest emotions and he sublimated them into his creation. "His characters live in him, independent of him. He speaks to them. He listens to them."[6] Writing one letter, he noted down answers in advance. When a letter was finished, he would walk in the woods, reading it over, his sense of reality lost, as if it were truly a letter. Satisfied at last, he would recopy it in his best calligraphy on the finest gilt-edged paper. At night, before the hearth, he read it aloud. Thérèse would weep. Mme. LeVasseur could not follow, but kept saying, "Monsieur, it is very beautiful." But Diderot, to whom he sent the manuscript on January 17, 1757, evinced no enthusiasm.

When spring budded a second time at the Hermitage, Rousseau was still focusing his "erotic transports" on Julie. Thérèse was obviously no more than a household convenience and palliative; even in the latter regard he probably required a solitary "supplement." She existed outside the circumference of his private emotional world. Then, in May, occurred the crucial event that was to fuse his dream life with reality, the visit from Mme. d'Houdetot that was destined to produce the dramatic crisis we have related. That long episode had ended in Rousseau's defeat and his decision to show his moral superiority by becoming Mme. d'Houdetot's *"directeur de conscience."*

How did these events influence *La Nouvelle Héloïse?* It was once believed that they determined Rousseau to create the *ménage à trois* situation and set the whole course of Parts III–VI. In fact, he had finished the third part and composed some of the important letters of the fourth part before Mme. d'Houdetot's visit. These include, as his correspondence shows, at least Saint-Preux's voyage, Julie's garden, and the dramatic excursion on the lake. In October 1757 he made what he considered to be a final copy and offered it to Rey, who came from Amsterdam to visit him on November 22. Thus, the novel, as it was conceived before Mme. d'Houdetot's appearance, was completed in four parts. It had grown only indirectly from his life, and directly from his complete absorption into the imaginary world he had created.

What Rousseau had done, after meeting Sophie d'Houdetot, was not to transpose life into fiction, but to attempt to reify his dream life, to live it with Sophie. "I saw Julie in Mme. d'Houdetot," he tells us himself, "and soon I saw only Mme. d'Houdetot." When he tried to think of Julie, he could only see Sophie. In *La Nouvelle Héloïse* there are no love scenes inspired by the tender duets between him and Sophie—they had all been written. They became, in his readings to her, a weapon of seduction. The *ménage à trois* situation was a part of Rousseau's basic psychic make-up, but there is little analogy between the situation in the novel and the one he tried to create in life, since in the latter he encouraged Sophie's love for an absent rival (lover, not husband), and enjoyed a strange, vicarious satisfaction from her passion or, at best, from the excess that she spared for him.

Only after the final break with Mme. d'Houdetot did Rousseau's real sufferings exert a decisive influence on his creation. His unhappiness in the summer of 1757 had already decided him to reinforce Saint-Preux's impulsion to suicide, and he wrote the exchange of letters on that subject. Later, something more profound occurred. He had undertaken the novel as a compensation for life's frustrations and disappointments. Now he was to seek refuge in it as a consolation, a self-justification, and a redress for the wrongs of a harsh fate. On January 28, 1758, in the renewed calm of Mont-Louis, he wrote to Mme. d'Houdetot that he had changed his mind about publishing the novel; and on February 13 he told her that he would write a fifth part for her only, never to be published. But he could no longer control his creation that easily. The work now had its own dynamic. The bruising events of his life and his inner torments forced their way into the act of self-expression. Disappointment led him to show Sophie what perfect harmony in a *ménage à trois* could be like, in famous scenes of artless communion made possible by the "confidence of noble souls." Thus, the supper in "Apollo's Room" redeems the humiliation of the real supper at La Chevrette, when Saint-Lambert had fallen asleep while Rousseau read his novel. If only Saint-Lambert had possessed the confidence and wisdom of Wolmar, Julie's husband! Ironically, the psychological dynamics of the novel make a mockery of all this dreaming.

Much more important was Jean-Jacques' need to expunge his guilt, to justify himself to his former friends and especially to his own conscience. He had to depict sensual love conquered and sublimated into the purest passion for virtue. This was his true self, he was sure. If Sophie came to know it, perhaps she, too, could be swayed, relieved from the abasing bondage of her passion for Saint-Lambert, converted to a Platonic idealism! He began to review a systematic statement of his moral and religious convictions; some of it found its way into *La Nouvelle Héloïse*, a kind of rehearsal for the great chords in *Emile*. The final, painful rupture with Diderot, in June, and the gossip in Paris about his devious behavior made self-justification more urgent. No wonder the last two parts are openly hostile to the *philosophes*.

By September 13, 1758, the opus was finished. We have seen how

Rousseau, to safeguard his independence, determined to have Rey publish it in Amsterdam, despite the delays and difficulties foreign publication would involve. Negotiations with the hardheaded publisher, who finally agreed to pay ninety louis for each of the parts, and a final recopying consumed months. From April 1760, Rousseau was occupied with the proofs, which were transmitted under the special protection of Malesherbes, the director of publication. Not until December, after interminable quarrels about type, corrections, distribution, and payments, did Rey send the first copies to London, where they immediately became a sensation. Word reached Paris, but the impatient French public was kept waiting while Malesherbes prepared an expurgated French edition. A few of the original volumes got out, and the news flashed in all the salons: Jean-Jacques had written a masterpiece. The Duchesse de Luxembourg had already talked about it at court, Mme. d'Houdetot in Paris, and Duclos at the French Academy. Bookstores were besieged with frustrated would-be buyers. Somehow they seemed to know, even before they impatiently opened its covers, that this was to be the great novel of their time.

## 2. THE UNRECONSTRUCTED REBEL

*La Nouvelle Héloïse* is, first of all, a pathetic and romantic tale of frustrated love, and this was undoubtedly its greatest appeal. The story has tragic overtones. The two protagonists, Julie d'Etange and Saint-Preux, are torn between the legitimate natural demands of a passionate love and the rules and norms of society. If it is indeed a tragedy, then Julie is the tragic figure; her lover, Saint-Preux, lacks stature and will. He becomes a pathetic victim, while she takes her fate into her own hands and preserves her integrity until the forces of nature, which she defies, wreak her doom. If we were to combine Racine's Phèdre and Mme. de Lafayette's Princess of Clèves, the amalgam would approach the raging passion and the rational control that characterize Julie.

There is also another level, that of the ideal society, in which Rousseau attempts to forge a synthesis based on a "purified" or moral nature and a non-ego-centered society. Julie, who has been corrupted by nature, condemned and restrained by society, strives to attain this level. *La Nouvelle Héloïse* is more than a model or a microcosm; it embodies a firm conviction: "If there is any reform to be made in public mores," affirms Rousseau in the second Preface to the work, "it is with domestic mores that it must begin."

The character of the personal problem reveals broad social, political, and moral dimensions. Human nature is split between enslavement to the empire of the egoistic instincts and aspiration to the eternal verities, to justice and the moral demands of conscience. In which direction lies happiness, man's deepest and constant demand? How far can the two be reconciled? The conflict is not only between these two natural needs, but between them both conjointly and the artificial conventions or imperatives of culture, which govern their expression in any society. The result is a fierce, almost unlivable tension between the passionate search for self-realization (or independence), and its sublimation in a doctrine of virtue as renunciation. The second alternative is chosen, willingly or unwillingly, by Rousseau's characters.

Although *La Nouvelle Héloïse* has been condemned by Rousseau's enemies, in his own time and since, as the enshrinement of an immoral romantic love ethic, he tells us quite truthfully that his purpose was to teach virtue. At least it was the last of his purposes. More precisely, I think, it was to teach what he considered to be "natural" to a virtuous man living in a virtuous society. Jean-Jacques, passionate, sensuous, and egocentric, will escape from his own faults through his characters, who identify virtue with chastity and abstinence, and whose "human self" is absorbed into a "collective self." (The phrases are his, though they are found in other writings.) He will redeem himself by continuing the role and identity he had already assumed, moral preceptor of mankind.

The basic moral law of the true community is "that each should prefer in everything the greatest good of all." Rousseau knows that this is contrary to the natural law, for it follows from the social contract, an act of will. Consequently, it is necessary to remake society, and to remake man *for* society—to create the social man. This is the great problem Rousseau confronts, from differing perspectives, in all his political writings. *La Nouvelle Héloïse* explores its configuration in the smaller group, to see whether the conflicts can be resolved and the social principle brought into effective being.

In the *Discourse on Inequality* and the article "Political Economy," Rousseau had depicted the vices and misery of men in this present condition, living partly in the state of nature and partly in the social state. These are precisely the vices and the misery of Julie and Saint-Preux in the first parts of the novel. It is only after this episode that we perceive the deeper theme of *La Nouvelle Héloïse:* the socialization of the individual. In Julie it is accomplished by moral redemption and dedication; in Saint-Preux, by the pressures of an intensive process of psychological conditioning. As Rousseau declares in a note, men "are not this or that, they are what you make them."

The first three parts of the novel form the first of its three logical divisions. It might be subtitled "The Love Duet." In the secluded manorial estate of Clarens, a young man has been living for a year as unsalaried tutor to Julie d'Etange. He is nineteen, she is seventeen. Saint-Preux, as he is known (remindful of the romantic pseudonyms Rousseau liked to give himself), is like his creator, a wanderer without home or ties, without fortune or career, a completely alienated individual in search of an identity. Passionate, but weak and insecure, he is the model of that species of Romantic hero who has been called the anti-hero. That such a person should have been put in charge of a romantic, isolated young girl is an idea that aroused the derision of Voltaire, who called her parents idiots. When the story opens, teacher and pupil are, of course, in love.

The first part of the novel consists of Saint-Preux's campaign of seduction. He carries it out in steps that have the character of a military campaign of conquest, somewhat like Stendhal's hero, Julien Sorel. It consists of a series of tactical aggressive moves and tactical retreats, in the course of which he never loses sight of the strategic goal. Saint-Preux's two weapons are his passion and his self-acclaimed love of virtue. They are based on a close knowledge of Julie's character. She has a Cornelian passion for virtue and, if not an ardent sexual temperament, at least a great yearning for love, combined with inexperience and a romantic outlook. The campaign is waged largely by correspondence, which is somewhat incredible to the modern reader, especially since they are living in the same house. However, the lovers are "frozen" in each other's presence and can communicate only through written language. It is noteworthy that Rousseau often said that language disguises and deceives and prevents the transparency of immediate communication. The essence of Saint-Preux's tactics is to combine artfully eloquent dithyrambs in praise of virtue and voluptuous allusions or outbursts that gradually grow more bold and precise.[7] To these he adds an occasional appeal to pity, in the lachrymose style Rousseau had so often used himself.

Despite his fine phrases and noble sentiments, Saint-Preux is completely egoistic. He loves virtue, but in his need for Julie appeals to nature against the demands of virtue and society. In his teachings, too, Saint-Preux stresses individual conscience and independence, opposing them to "opinion." Though ready to sacrifice when it appears advisable or necessary, he really intends to sacrifice nothing. While proclaiming that virtue is the only path to happiness, he remains the slave of his emotions. His tactics result in a total confusion of virtue and passionate love, and much later Julie will admit that in talking of one, they really meant the other. The deception, I believe, is largely calculated, but to a certain extent Saint-Preux–Jean-Jacques may also be deceiving himself.

"Opinion" was always the great unseen enemy for Rousseau, threatening his autonomy and self-esteem, thrusting on him obligations and responsibilities from the outside world. But in *La Nouvelle Héloïse*, where culture and dependency will gain the upper hand, there is a marked ambivalence toward "opinion." Another constant is the equivocality of sex and virtue, not only in this seduction, but in all of Rousseau's *ménage à trois* situations, real or fictitious. Virtue and moral teaching appear as the counterparts of sex, redeeming its sinfulness and guilt, compensating, too, for failures of virility. Ultimately, passion is repressed through virtue, and the perturbed self is supposedly purified and strengthened.

Julie is Rousseau's ideal blonde, a combination of all the lovely girls who had enchanted his imagination. The dramatic struggle is hers. She knows Saint-Preux is seducing her; she both desires this and resists it. "All nature seems to be your accomplice; all my efforts are useless, I adore you in spite of myself. . . . You can make me as unhappy as you wish." Unlike Saint-Preux, she is strongly bound to the moral and conventional norms of her culture. His whole effort is to drag her with him in his revolt against these hostile forces from which he is alienated. The strength of her love is so great that she several times rebels against virtue, under his influence, and might even fall completely under his sway, did not countervailing forces pull her back. Her moral redemption involves the resolution of the confusion between virtue and love, between culture and nature. The separation of each into its proper realm will enable her conduct to be based on a clear estimate of values.

By threatening to leave and by demanding that Julie denounce him to her parents, Saint-Preux forces her to admit her love. She promptly turns the tables on him by throwing herself on the mercy of his proclaimed love of virtue. Openly triumphant, our hero reassures her that it is mainly her virtue he loves. Much maneuvering follows, but he makes little headway until, as a reward for his virtue, Julie takes the initiative. With her cousin Claire's help, she arranges a passionate embrace, in a grove, an embrace from which neither will recover. Saint-Preux's fury is now almost uncontrollable: "I can no longer go on like this; I feel that I must either die at your feet . . . or in your arms." Julie has forgotten Corneille's advice:

> La vertu la plus ferme évite les hasards:
> Qui s'expose au péril veut bien trouver sa perte.[8]

Now their love is eternal and invincible, in the image of Tristan and Isolde, and will last beyond death itself. Fate has willed it.

Frightened, Julie sends her conqueror on a journey into the back country. He obeys grudgingly but submissively. One feels his pleasure in this submissiveness, in giving up the initiative and decision into stronger hands. In fact, the novel's major defect is that we find it difficult to believe in a strong woman's undying love for a weak lover. We accept the first infatuation, but not an "eternal passion." Saint-Preux's appeals take on an increasingly effeminate coloration, flashed with occasional erotic allusions and model descriptions of wild, romantic landscapes. "I have surrendered all my actions to your control. . . . But Julie, alas! a wanderer, without family, almost without country, I have only you on all the earth, and love takes the place of everything else for me." In his dream of a sweet exile with her, far from "the look of men," we recognize Rousseau's own dream.

Now Julie's father returns after a long absence. All of her maneuvers fail to induce this stiff-necked soldier and aristocrat to accept such a person as Saint-Preux into the household, except as paid tutor. This offer Saint-Preux refuses, on the grounds that it would then be dishonorable for him to seduce his employer's daughter.

Julie is brought to the edge of despair by her father's insistence that she marry Wolmar, a fifty-year-old friend of his who has heroically saved his life. Now Saint-Preux castigates her love of virtue—a delirium, he calls it—and her hope of breaking insurmountable barriers. He urges her to come to his arms and run away with him. If she will not, the rocks are high and the water deep.

Torn by her passion, Julie falls sick of a fever and Saint-Preux rushes back. Her father will not be budged. "So my father has sold me," she exclaims to her confidante, Claire. "Barbarous, unnatural father!" Love, resentment, and Saint-Preux's virtuous suffering impel Julie to her downfall. She gives herself to him, and so becomes the victim, ironically, of her own virtue, of her regret for hurting "so submissive and so tender a lover," of her need to be true to her pledge. Saint-Preux has won the game of virtue, but through no action of his own. Like Rousseau, he has wanted to be a seducer, to feel his adequacy as a man, but has not known how to finish what he has begun.

Claire now assumes a more important role. Julie has been consulting her, but Rousseau has the aesthetic good judgment not to break the dramatic intensity of the love duet with many letters to or from her. From here on the exchanges between the lovers will become fewer, and the increasing role of letters written by others conveys aesthetically the breaking up of their isolation by a society that intends to put matters in order. At the same time, by a kind of reverse movement, the letters converge on Julie, and she becomes the center of this little world.

Claire and Julie have been close friends since childhood, such tender friends that there is undoubtedly some sexual ambiguity involved. Neither girl is a lesbian, but eroticism is part of their love. "I love only you perfectly," Claire writes to her, adding that her senses "have no need at all of a lover." Saint-Preux watches them kiss tenderly, "the face of one on the other's bosom." Later, Claire is even willing to give up her own marriage, for Julie; she tells her gentle and colorless fiancé, M. d'Orbe, that she is "a kind of monster," and loves Julie more than him. When he dies, she feels little regret: "As soon as he was no longer, I belonged to you alone." Again we see how Rousseau's unconscious and innermost feelings are catheterized by projection into his created characters. In this instance we have a curious reversal of sex in the representation of his latent homosexuality.

In almost each crisis, Claire is the deciding factor, the one who takes charge and tells Julie or Saint-Preux what to do. Much later, we learn that she is also secretly in love with Saint-Preux. With this knowledge in mind, it becomes even more interesting to observe her words and acts. One of the twelve engravings which were executed under Rousseau's direction, depicting the scene of the kiss, symbolizes their relationship. It shows Claire supporting the swooning Julie and watching expressionless; Julie abandons her lips to Saint-Preux, her hand to Claire.

Claire reassures Julie, after her fall. As long as nobody knows, her reputation is safe. The duplicity of *seeming*, of playing the role of a virtuous *jeune fille*, will be protected at all costs. Saint-Preux, with other motives, also consoles her: "Have you not followed the purest law of nature?"

But the purest laws of nature are not valid in society: this is Rousseau's whole point. Everything will go wrong now, and the rest of this part of the novel is largely anguish, passionate declarations, and disappointments building up to a frightening magnitude. The key words become "catastrophe," "misfortune," "fears," "alarm," "fateful," "despair," "bitter sorrows," and others like them. The lovers have found pleasure, but the happiness of unclouded transparency, the immediacy of two souls that for a brief moment touched each other, are gone. Julie, to boot, has lost tranquillity and acquired a guilty conscience. She knows that their love will be "*la grande affaire de notre vie*," but she is at war within herself. Which is more sacred, her obligation to the man she loves or to father, family, and society? Inner harmony has been destroyed, and the external order has been broken. She is the image of all men living in society. Saint-Preux is at a loss to understand her remorse and self-scorn. The violation of conscience, authority, and social rules means little to this "outsider." And all this does not yet swerve Julie from her purpose. She decides that the remedy for one wrong lies in a greater wrong.

Without letting her naïve lover in on her plot, she carefully plans to become pregnant. Irritated by events that impede their secret rendezvous, she takes a desperate step, dares Saint-Preux to sneak into her room. "Miserable toys of a blind fate, sad victims of mocking hope, shall we always be within reach of pleasure without ever attaining it?" Her letter breathes passion and belies those critics who have denied her sexual ardor. It is followed by the most voluptuous and beautiful letter in the entire novel—and the most absurd—penned by Saint-Preux in her room, describing his emotions as he awaits her entrance. Still another letter recounts the joy and the tenderness of his night of love with her. Never had she been so gratefully loving as during the latter part of that night, when she thought of the child Saint-Preux had just given her.[9]

Meanwhile, Saint-Preux has formed a fast friendship with an English lord, Edward Bomston, whom Rousseau draws along the lines of the eighteenth-century stereotype—quick-tempered, somewhat brusque in manner, but loyal, virtuous, and philosophical. Bomston is a rationalist, but unlike Wolmar, Julie's husband-to-be, he is more of a *philosophe*. He is also a sentimentalist who can fall deeply in love with a prostitute. Rousseau, like the *philosophes* (and contrary to the usual cliché), believed men to be more irrational than rational, motivated by sentiment and passion, by drives for prestige and power.

Bomston almost brings about disaster. One night, when he has drunk too much, he remarks that Julie is not as cold with everyone as she is with him. Saint-Preux springs to her defense, and a duel is in the offing. Julie tries to prevent it, sending her lover a letter against dueling that is a model of rhetoric equaled only by Burke's "Speech on Reconciliation." It, too, fails, for Saint-Preux's vaunted defiance of "opinion" goes only so far and no farther. Desperate, she confesses everything to Bomston, and throws herself on his mercy. He responds like a true English gentleman with a noble public apology that brought tears to eighteenth-century readers' eyes. "Happiness for you," he tells Saint-Preux–Rousseau, "is not on the same road or of the same kind as for other men; they seek only power and the look of others; you need only love and peace."

The well-meaning, bumbling Englishman makes matters worse when he speaks to M. d'Etange in favor of Saint-Preux and is sent packing despite his offer to settle a fortune on the young man. Julie squirms miserably as she listens to her father berate her mother. When she dares to speak, she is answered with a volley of brutal slaps that send her reeling to the ground. They are reconciled, but M. d'Etange says he will be obeyed.

M. d'Etange represents convention, and much as Rousseau despises it, he defends it as necessary to a social order. Order, it becomes clear after the first parts, is his highest value, necessary to all others. He condemns class prejudice and usually favors, within limits, marriages based on love; but until a better social order is evolved, the one we have must be respected. Julie is miserable, for her inner being is split. She yearns to lose her guilt and to be reintegrated into the social order of which the family is the fundamental unit; but she also feels that as a woman she is irrevocably committed, beyond the power of will, convention, or the turns of fate. Thus is formed the dramatic tension, with its swells of repressed emotion, that will subsist in the married, virtuous Julie.

Claire now takes the situation in hand and tells Julie she must choose between the two realms of being. With considerable deception, she organizes a little plot with Bomston to get Saint-Preux out of the way. Rather than tell him that Julie has had a miscarriage, she says that Julie had been mistaken about her pregnancy. She encourages him to keep on hoping, while arranging to break up the love affair. The separation is accomplished with a heavy dose of melodrama, and Bomston carries away the desperate, plaintive, star-crossed lover.

Bomston makes one more try. He writes to Julie, offering them a large estate in York and everything that would bring true their dream of happiness, if she will elope with her lover. The critical decision must now be made. She is called upon to choose between egoistic happiness (what Rousseau calls "the human self") and the happiness that comes from a tranquil conscience, submissive to the law of the community. When Julie rejects Bomston's offer—with Claire's encouragement—we know rebellion is at an end and the lovers' fate decided. She never tells Saint-Preux about his friend's offer. In other ways, too, she is not averse to using duplicity to encourage him to go on hoping. She even promises never to marry another man without his consent. We cannot help suspecting that having controlled and manipulated him so completely, she counts on being able to do so again. Indeed, he responds by pledging never to disobey her and always to be whatever she wishes. And when she urges him to stop being so effeminate, he promises to try to be a man.

By now Saint-Preux has reached Paris. In several long letters, Rousseau has him give a brilliant satirical picture of Parisian society, where men, corrupted by "artificial" values and enslaved to "opinion," do not dare be themselves. Music, the theater, the salons, and loose sexual mores fall under the lashes of his whip. Paris is a vast comedy, in which men and women wear masks and play roles, a sterile comedy and a deadly one. At one wild party, Saint-Preux succumbs to the advances of a licentious woman and wakes up to find himself in bed with her. Julie forgives him, but her sermon is severe.

Julie's temporary tranquillity is shattered when her mother discovers Saint-Preux's love letters. Already ill, Mme. d'Etange now sinks rapidly. Claire urges Saint-Preux to put an end to the harm he is doing. "You lost Julie when you left her," she says, conveniently forgetting that she had led him to separation. Saint-Preux responds with a letter to Mme. d'Etange, saying that he will immolate happiness to duty and die happy if she can find Julie a husband worthy of her. "Oh! let him be found, and let him dare to say, 'I will know how to love her better than you.' " But to Claire he writes, "Insane and cruel virtue! I obey your voice without merit; I hate you while doing everything for you." No, replies Claire, you will learn that virtue is the road to happiness, if happiness is ever to be found; and virtue alone can make up for failure to find it. Unconvinced, Saint-Preux predicts that Julie will never forget him, will always love him.

As he looks back on the ravages of time, he reflects that man can find happiness only outside of time. It is so difficult for him to believe in the reality of that past when he had been at the summit of mortal joy. "Days of pleasure and glory, you did not belong to a mortal; you were too beautiful to be perishable. A sweet ecstasy absorbed your duration, concentrated it in a point like that of eternity. Alas! You have disappeared like a flash of lightning. That eternity of happiness was only an instant of my life." To this Claire replies that the same enemy, time, would have destroyed the perfection of their love. Only by its ending now can it escape inevitable corrosion and remain eternally in its pristine glory.

Julie loses the child, and then her mother dies, two signs from heaven that plans conceived in crime do not prosper.

Scarcely has Bomston rescued Saint-Preux from suicide when the constant lover receives two short notes. In one, Julie asks him to free her from her pledge. "It is time to give up the errors of youth and to abandon a deceptive hope. I will never be yours." In the other, M. d'Etange makes the same demand, but with threats and insults. An eloquent letter, swelling with hatred and bravado, answers the second, and a single sentence the first: "I return to Julie d'Etange the right to dispose of herself and to give her hand without consulting her heart."

But nothing is settled so rapidly. In another note, Julie admits her love and her despair. "Goodbye, dear, sweet friend. If I can no longer live for you, have I not stopped living already?" She falls victim to the smallpox and hopes her husband-to-be will find her too ugly to marry. She is even more shaken when she learns that Saint-Preux has come back during her illness and purposely caught the dread disease in order to share her fate. This unparalleled devotion moves her to the edge of revolt again. She swears that her heart will be his alone until her last breath. "You have earned it too well to lose it, and I am tired of serving the phantom of virtue at the expense of justice." Saint-Preux's romantic ethic recaptures its sway. Love is the most sacred duty of all. "Nature, sweet nature, take back all your rights; I abjure the barbarous virtues that destroy you."

But it is the revolt that is a phantom. What she is planning is to go ahead with the marriage and season it with adultery. At this point the reader becomes fully aware of her egocentricity. She will have husband and lover, and Claire, too. "Let all three of you form my whole existence," she urges. But, in fact, she will defraud both her lover, giving him only her heart, and her husband, giving him only her body.

Rousseau is back to his archetypal pattern of the woman with two lovers. Echoes of his past are evident in the fact that the suggestion comes from Julie, and in Saint-Preux's reaction. At first he is horrified by the thought of sharing her, and then, too weak to give her up, he urges her to consummate her plan. But he makes the error of trying his old tactics: "We shall be guilty," he says, "but we shall always love virtue." Virtue and adultery do not mix. Julie chooses virtue and marries Wolmar. Saint-Preux is cashiered with a letter of farewell in which she vows eternal fidelity to her husband. She would have been his if the human order had not changed the order of nature. But in society the natural order is only disorder; and passion corrupts both nature and society.

In this long letter of confession, Julie tells him all the thoughts and acts, all the deceits she has concealed from him. "I deluded you with a hope I never had." Yet her love had never left her until she entered the church for the marriage ceremony. Then a psychological revolution took place in her, a revelation analogous to Rousseau's experience on the road to Vincennes. Until then she had remained divided between nature and virtue, and each of these had in turn been split between her lover and her family ties. Cleverly maneuvered by Claire, she had submitted to the social order, not out of virtue, but out of sentiment.[10] Her first submission, following her mother's death, had failed because she could not stifle her love. But in the church she is illuminated by an act of grace that enables her to escape reliance on will. She suddenly discovers the way to sublimate her love, to purify nature. Religion offers the emotional substitute that enables her to transpose sexual love into the love of order. "An unknown power seemed suddenly to correct the disorder of my affections. . . . I felt myself being reborn; I felt myself beginning a new life."

Now she will be chaste, because chastity is the primary virtue, the control of egoism; she will be faithful, because the family and society depend on fidelity. The function of marriage is not personal satisfaction, but the accomplishment of a social role. Love is a form of egoism, a private will, a refusal of social dependency. "Lovers see only themselves. . . . and the only thing they know how to do is to love each other." No longer will she place her personal interest above the common interest. "I want everything that is related to order." Forget all else, she urges Saint-Preux, "and be the lover of my soul." She still will not surrender him completely. Instead, she creates an immense illusion within which she will struggle to live until she receives a new revelation in death.

When Saint-Preux answers that her only crime, an unforgivable crime, is against love, she cruelly replies that if she had absolute freedom of choice, she would now prefer Wolmar to him. Wolmar "has given me back to myself." She has overcome the anarchy of passion, regained her inner harmony and harmony with her world. Her alienation, but not Saint-Preux's, is ended, she believes.

Who is Wolmar? Many eighteenth-century readers took him as the villain of the piece, the man who spoiled young lovers' lives and forced the girl to marry him even though he knew about her love affair. That was not Rousseau's intention. When we know him, through Julie's description, we understand why she finds him a pillar of strength. Wolmar is completely rational. He has never experienced passion. The heart is deceptive and obedient to self-interest. Wolmar is reason seeking the pure good. He has been the spectator of life, observer and judge of men, rather than actor. Julie calls him "a living eye." His penetrating eye pierces masks and ferrets out secret motives and feelings. Wolmar is an atheist. He is so godlike in his self-possession and his possession of all around him—objects, bodies, and minds—that one almost wonders whether he cannot believe in God because he thinks himself God. Above all, he stands for order, order within himself and around him. When Wolmar sees the innocent suffer, he feels no pity, only disturbance because his sense of order is disturbed. He has put order into the Clarens household. Julie tells us at once that he has done it in a certain way, with as little outer show of authority or constraint as possible. Everyone obeys submissively, and everyone is "free." This idea lies at the heart of Rousseau's political philosophy and is essential to an understanding of it.

Wolmar is as much a projection of Rousseau as Saint-Preux is. He often projected himself into psychological or ideological opposites. If Saint-Preux is his image, Wolmar, like the Spartans he admired, is his mirror image or anti-image. Thus the man who had been the most neglected child will imagine Emile, every detail of whose upbringing is thought out, supervised, controlled. The passionate, sensuous, unchaste Jean-Jacques will make chastity and abstinence a requisite of the reconstructed society.

More seriously than ever, Saint-Preux is tempted to end his life, and once again Bomston dissuades him. The two letters in which they discuss the right of a person to take his own life are among the most famous in the book. Then Bomston bundles him off as an officer in Lord Anson's expedition to circumnavigate the globe. Six years have passed since Saint-Preux and Julie first set eyes on each other, five years since the beginning of the story, three since they were separated. He now disappears for three more years and is presumed lost at sea.

### 3. WOLMAR'S DOMAIN

The years have worked great changes at Clarens. For Julie de Wolmar love is dead, or so she thinks. She is the happy mother of two children, but her happiness is clouded by her inability to confess her past sins to her husband. This failure is the unconscious disguise of deeper guilt feelings. She is in a state of fragile equilibrium, largely induced by rationalization and by a semihypnosis of self-delusion that enables her to convince herself that she is happy. At one moment she feels far from what she was and confident of what she is. At the next, she is afraid of solitude and cannot free herself from the past. Even as she assures herself that it is not love tormenting her, she cries out to Claire, "Ah, my dear, what a soul was his! How he loved!" We see how empty her life really is. Maternal love has not filled the void, and her husband is unable to give her that "life of the heart" she needs.

Most of all, she is unable to face the truth, for it would at once destroy the structure on which her stability rests. The truth is that her love is merely repressed, or sublimated into the love of order. Her memories are her cherished and guilty refuge—and of these Wolmar (despite their supposedly perfect communion) knows nothing. The slow wings of time bring only regret and boredom, and this she cannot understand, for she is rationally convinced that she is happy.

Then the unexpected (but not to the reader) occurs. A letter written by a well-known hand arrives. Saint-Preux has come back from the ends of the earth, convinced that savages are independent, happy, and virtuous and that culture corrupts. He, too, thinks he is cured—"I want to be what I should be." His imminent return frightens Julie into confessing her past sins to Wolmar. He, however, already knew, and has forgiven what doubtless matters little to him. Claire (now a widow with a small daughter) extends to Saint-Preux an invitation to Clarens and informs him that Wolmar intends to complete his "cure."

What emotion when the lovers see each other again! Wolmar, a shrewd manipulator of men, insists they embrace. He has his reasons. Cruel and sweet memories overwhelm the hapless lover; but at the same instant, he realizes that nothing is the same. Wolmar explains that at Clarens they live in a condition of complete frankness and transparency. Saint-Preux begins to feel Wolmar's ascendency. Julie mistakenly thinks that he has achieved what to Rousseau was the great desideratum for individuals and for societies, the harmony that comes about when virtue and self-interest are identified. She thinks he has also attained the independence that needs only self-esteem, instead of seeking out the *look* of approbation or dependency on "opinion."

Wolmar's determination to "cure" Saint-Preux really means that he intends to socialize him. As Claire puts it, "We are so accustomed to governing him that we have a certain moral responsibility for him." Saint-Preux will be the subject for their experimentation, the model of how the rebellious, ego-centered individual, who has been living in the imperfect social state described in the *Discourse on Inequality*—a state of inner war and war between men—can be remade. For, as we have seen, natural impulses, innocent in the state of nature, are in conflict with the social obligations of "artificial" men. The rule of the "human self" must be replaced by that of the "collective self."

Part of the program is educational—the initiation of Saint-Preux to Wolmar's "system." Wolmar has transformed Clarens into what Rousseau obviously considers a model social group. Its characteristics are important for an understanding of his political and social thought. Saint-Preux cannot be integrated into existing societies, which are represented by Julie's father. They only foster divisiveness and rebellion. It is necessary to create a utopian island, all sincerity, harmony, and transparency (supposedly) in which he will be (in Rousseau's vocabulary) denatured, remade, formed. He must learn to rid himself of the atomistic *independence* of natural man, think of himself only as part of a collective whole, and consider the frustration of his desires as his liberation.

Clarens is a unified organism, a true body, whose integrity depends on its autarchy, economic and spiritual. It must be cut off and protected from the corrupt societies in the shadowy but ever-threatening "outside." Xenophobia is preached and practiced. Since "everything that comes from afar is likely to be disguised or falsified," according to Julie, no Malaga wine may be imported. Instead, she has a secret for making local wine taste (or *seem*) like Malaga. It is hard to believe that this illusion is not recognized as a "disguise" or "falsification," but self-delusion of this kind is typical of the authoritarian mind.

Wolmar is the prototype of the "guide," or "Lawgiver" in *The Social Contract*. He is called an "enlightened despot," and the function of the guide is precisely to be enlightened and to "inform" (or indoctrinate) others. His purpose is dual: the establishment of order in his realm and the maximum utilization of its human resources. Wolmar has created a cooperative society that absorbs all its individual components, harnessing the energy of their natural instincts to the collective enterprise and its indivisible goals. The theoretical principle determining the means to this end is the psychological strategy referred to in the *Confessions* (in Rousseau's plan for his *Morale sensitive*), and again in *Emile*: to give moral prescriptions the same mechanical necessity as that of physical laws. The management of individual behavior—the key to Rousseau's sociopolitical program—will be undertaken by Wolmar throughout the remaining part of the novel. It actually reflects back into the first segment as well, for there we see the disaster caused by unmanaged behavior.

Among the specific techniques used by Wolmar, two are of paramount importance. The first is the cultivation of reflexive behavior by a combination of discipline and what psychologists today call "operant conditioning," the setting-up of stimulus conditions that make it difficult for the desired responses not to occur. This is done by "reinforcement," that is, automatic reward or punishment, just as pigeons are taught to peck at one kind of wafer and not another, until behavior itself becomes automatic. Rousseau had outlined this technique in his plan for the treatise, *La Morale sensitive*. Sensations, he affirmed, are accompanied by feeling, which passes into the memory; there it becomes a part of an association and can be evoked by a sign or signal whose action is involuntary. The second part of Wolmar's technique, necessary to the accomplishment of the first, is the use of deceit and disguise, or what is figuratively called "the hidden hand." The reason for Wolmar–Rousseau's aim of reflexive behavior is both simple and crucial: such behavior bypasses the need for virtue. Virtue (the substitution of the *moi commun* for the *moi humain*) is by definition an antinatural, difficult state of inner tension and victory. Rousseau is convinced that few men are capable of it. This is also why he rejects the "enlightened self-interest" philosophy of his time. In brief, Wolmar will have to make a child of Saint-Preux, in order to infuse in him a new set of conditioned reflexes, or in our terms, to implant in him a strong and properly programmed superego.

Wolmar's society has two sectors; a small elite of fully privileged "citizens" and the servants and workers who are benevolently exploited by them. By ingenious methods, which it would take too long to detail, the helots are induced to put out a maximum of work. Incentive pay, love of gain, and the spirit of competition are among the chief mechanisms. Such motives had been condemned in the second *Discourse*, but Rousseau used them consistently, especially in the form of directed competition and emulation, in his political writings. Competition directed to stimulate rivalry in the service of the community is salutary. In a letter to Ustéri (July 18, 1763) Rousseau declares that only the passions hold society together; "without emulation, without glory, without the urge to advancement, private interest is destroyed and, lacking a proper support, the State falls away." The aggressive, egoistic instincts cannot be extirpated, but they can be manipulated so that the individual works for the collective weal while thinking he is working for his own. "Never have I seen a household," writes Saint-Preux, "where everyone served better and was less aware of serving." The ruse and the delusion are patent and avowed. The main thing is to "form" the workers. "The process is started early in order to have them as they want them." The way to obtain reflexive loyalty is "to form and train your own servants." (Rousseau uses the word *dresser*, which is usually applied to animals.) Among Wolmar's ingenious devices is an increase of wages by one-twentieth each year. It is foreseen, however, that few servants will remain that long, so that the increases "are more apparent than real."

Servants and workers are likened to children and are treated like children, ever in need of guidance, discipline, and deception. The rules are harsh and inflexible. Conformity is absolute. But discipline, without deceit, is never enough. In his second Preface, Rousseau tells us, "Children do not enjoy naked reason any more than badly disguised remedies." He quotes Tasso on the virtues of deceit. Since for Rousseau the end justifies the means, it is right and proper to deceive others for their own good (that is, to make them content or to give them happy illusions) or for the good of the collective whole. The rules are explicit. But the manipulation is hidden. Together, they provide a complete regimentation of private life. In fact, the helots are allowed very little private life. This point is of maximum significance. Everything is kept in full sight, and every act is viewed in the light of the whole. An inflexible, partly hidden "yoke" (Rousseau loves the word) restrains and guides the subjects.

Here as elsewhere Rousseau lays great emphasis on repression and control of the sexual instincts, the most dangerous component of egoism because they are the most aggressive and the most refractory to social discipline. The servants must be largely deprived of sexual life so that they may think of their master's good, or the common good, rather than their own. "To prevent a dangerous familiarity between the sexes, we do not hinder them by positive laws which they would be tempted to evade secretly; but without appearing to be thinking about it, we establish customs that are more powerful than authority itself* . . . we manage it by giving them occupations, habits, tastes, pleasures that are entirely different."

How well Rousseau understood the theory as well as the practice of conditioning is clear in this explanation: "The whole art of the master is to conceal restraints under the veil of pleasure or self-interest, so that they think they want everything they are being made to do." The phrase "so that they think they want everything they are being made to do" gives us a key to the interpretation of *The Social Contract*; we shall also find its analogue in *Emile*.

Rousseau's sociopolitical system is basically unvarying in all his writings. That is why it is not surprising to encounter other techniques employed in *La Nouvelle Héloïse*, such as public athletic competitions, in later works. "Imperceptibly, this custom has been turned into a kind of spectacle, in which the actors, animated by the looks of the audience, prefer the glory of applause to the prize itself." The words "looks" and "glory" again show how Rousseau urges the social (or directed) use of motives which he had condemned in the atomistic, antisocial individual of existing societies.

Thus manipulated, the servants will be stronger for their work and distracted from sexual temptations. A small cost in money is involved, Wolmar admits. "But," he says, "how many times that amount do you think I recover in my household . . . ?" Everything is planned, everything is calculated.

Parties or fêtes are also organized to provide harmless distraction on Sunday evenings, after the sermon. As far as possible, the women are kept apart from the men. The women are given treats of milk dishes, of which Rousseau supposed them to be naturally fond; his own relish for them may have a sexual significance, related to his fixation on women's breasts. The men are given wine, in order to keep them away from cabarets and women, and to prevent them from "losing their usefulness for their masters and for themselves." In the winter, the sexes are permitted to mingle at dances. Julie always makes her appearance at these events, to set a tone conducive to order. She even dances with her servants, this show of egalitarianism being obviously useful.

The most famous of the fêtes is that of the grape harvest. Then masters and servants all work and consort together on a footing of equality. But this is another sham. The illusion of equality is all that is

---

* In *The Social Contract*, Rousseau will urge the same technique upon the legislator (Book II, Ch. 12). In *The Social Contract*, to be sure, Rousseau is dealing with citizens, not subjects. What is usually forgotten is that not all the people are citizens. Furthermore, the next section of this chapter of *La Nouvelle Héloïse* (Part IV, Ch. X) makes clear that the difference is only one of degree, and that the strategy coincides with the sixth chapter of Book II of *The Social Contract*, where Rousseau says (among other interesting things) that the citizens need "guides," so that they may know their true will.

wanted, so that the work will be accomplished better. "Everyone is equal, and [i.e., but] no one forgets his place." In fact, the workers are even more respectful and grateful. Saint-Preux calls the fête "a means of instruction," a consolation, and a reestablishment of nature's order. This kind of "doublethink" is what we learn, in this book, to expect from Rousseau, the self-proclaimed enemy of masks, "veils," and seeming.

At night there is a real party. To prevent envy, nothing is displayed that the workers might not have in their own homes. Everyone serves everyone else. Old airs are sung, as solos or in chorus. Transparency, harmony, and peace are regained. Although Saint-Preux calls the fête spontaneous, it is carefully prepared and arranged; spontaneity is only the *effect*. All is illusion, and as Starobinski has remarked, the servants may not be the only dupes of this hypocrisy.[11] In a note Rousseau says that the spirit of the fête makes social differences *seem* unimportant. The means do not matter, apparently, as long as the *feeling* of equality and total participation is realized. What we have here, according to Starobinski, is the lyrical aspect of the general will: "To look at all your brothers, and to be looked at by all: it is not difficult to see in this, too, the postulate of a simultaneous alienation of all wills, in which each receives back all he has yielded to the collectivity."

Again and again Rousseau comes back to the separation of the sexes, a separation not only functional but physical. He rationalizes this sacrifice of freedom and nature to order, arguing that it heightens pleasure when contacts are allowed. Probably this intellectual fixation on the disorderliness of sex overlay some of his psychological quirks, in particular the need to reaffirm his masculinity by imposing a rigid distinction between the sexes.

The results of Wolmar's "system" leave nothing to be desired. Although servitude is admittedly *against nature*, here, in this realm of *false nature*, none of the domestics "can bear to have [Julie] compare her zeal with that of her comrades, and each wants to be the first in her favor." Harmony or order is achieved, by these and other hidden means. Thus, "they are united despite themselves, so to speak, by the services they are somehow forced to do each other." Self-interest and the oft-damned *amour-propre* are fully utilized to achieve unity in the common end.

They are all united only the better to serve . . . that is their greatest self-interest. But this word is scarcely appropriate here, for I have never seen any government in which self-interest was so wisely manipulated and in which it notwithstanding had less influence than here. Everything is done with eagerness.

The servants learn to think of themselves only in relation to "a household they consider as theirs."

The "household" is a concrete form of Rousseau's *moi commun*, or collective self, into which the natural self (the *moi humain*) is absorbed. Clarens is a microcosm of the greater society. Here, says Saint-Preux, "the state of war no longer exists." In Marxist terms, the class struggle has been abolished, by training the servants to identify themselves with their masters and to love them with servile devotion. "Moral" laws have been given the necessary quality of physical laws: "I know nothing less imperious than their orders, and nothing so promptly executed; they ask, and [the servants] fly; they excuse, and [the servants] feel their wrong." The devotion must be *absolute* and without reservation: "it is impossible to love the master sincerely without loving everything that belongs to him." Self-interest is utilized, but surpassed. "Whatever interest they have in loving themselves, they have a greater interest in pleasing him."*

Informing is another important mechanism in the prevention of privacy and keeping all acts in the light of day. It is essential, Rousseau declares, to destroy that "criminal morality" which makes it honorable not to "peach" on one's fellow-servants. "I cannot admire too much," he has Saint-Preux write, "how M. and Mme. de Wolmar have managed to transform the vile trade of accuser into a function of zeal, integrity, courage, as noble or at least as praiseworthy as it was among the Romans." The correct moral principle, according to Rousseau, is that failure to denounce a wrong makes one equally guilty; and this principle is true not only between master and servant, but "in general, from man to man." At Clarens, a wrongdoer may be forgiven, but failure to report another's wrong is unforgivable and is punished by expulsion. The informers and public accusers of the Reign of Terror and other totalitarian societies make their first appearance on Rousseau's stage.

The servants never understand what is being done to them, never realize how they are being used and "formed" not to be ends in themselves but means to other ends. Although Kant would have been shocked to know this about his beloved Jean-Jacques, there are men and women in Rousseau's world who are born to be the means to others' ends. In Julie's words: "Those who are destined to live in rustic simplicity do not

---

* R. J. Lefton has shown a primary part of forceful indoctrination is "the Great Togetherness," or the stage of group identification. "What we saw as a coercive set of manipulations, they put forth as morally uplifting, therapeutic experience." Emotional involvement is considered most important. A closed communication system is set up, in which all communication in the environment is controlled and manipulated. "Everything said or done can be observed and reported . . . and the information used to specify further manipulations within the group." Pressures for thought reform "strongly stimulate both guilt anxiety and shame anxiety," as well as fear of "the failure to live up to the standards of one's peers," with the "expectation of abandonment" and public humiliation ("Methods of forceful indoctrination," in M. R. Stein, A. J. Vidich, and D. M. White, *Identity and Anxiety: Survival of the Person in Mass Society*, pp. 480–92). Lefton might well have been describing Wolmar's domain specifically, instead of the People's Republic of China.

need to develop their faculties in order to be happy, and their buried talents are like the gold mines of Valais whose exploitation would be contrary to the public good. . . . Do not educate the villager's child, it is better for him not to be educated." Or in Wolmar's words: "Every man has an assigned place in the best order of things; the thing is to find that place and not to disrupt order." (In the eighteenth century, Leibnizian optimism was a frequent pretext for social conservatism.) Thus, there will always be an inferior species of men, and they will have no chance to rise.

Rousseau was no egalitarian, except in the sense of equal commitment to the common good and equality before the law. His concept of order involves hierarchic gradation. The important thing is not to abolish classes, but to put an end to class warfare (and to individual warfare). It is important, for example, to prevent the situation Samuel Johnson describes in *Rasselas*, where the shepherds' hearts "were cankered with discontent" because "they considered themselves as condemned to labour for the luxury of the rich, and looked with stupid malevolence towards those that were placed above them."

The most curious part of the plan, in *La Nouvelle Héloïse*, is the self-deception that accompanies deception. "Man," proclaims Julie even as she explains "the system," "is too noble a being to be used only as an instrument for others. It is never permissible to degrade a human soul for the advantage of others. . . ." Another example of doublethink. We have only to consider the words in which Rousseau describes his ideal model: "His servant was a stranger to him; he makes him his property, his child, he takes ownership of him. He had had authority only over his actions; now he gives himself authority over his will."

This is precisely what in "Political Economy" Rousseau says the ruler of the State must do; and in *Emile*, what the preceptor must do. There is a basic unity among all of Rousseau's ideological works. Critics who have denounced him as contradictory have only failed to discriminate among perspectives.

Rousseau's theory of manipulation and deception (the "hidden hand") is best formulated by him in the symbol of Julie's garden. She has arranged a favorite and private retreat. It is a closed garden, sheltered from the corrupting world. It *seems* natural, but nature could never have created it. Saint-Preux is completely deceived: "You did nothing but let nature alone. . . . I see no sign of human work." This deception is the mark of her success. Since on this occasion Julie's purpose is not to deceive Saint-Preux but to instruct him, she reveals her technique. "It is true," she says, "that nature has done everything, but done it under my direction, and there is nothing there that I have not planned." Her lengthy explanation uncovers a remarkable series of adroit manipulations that have produced the desired effect. The words "seem," "artificial," "art," "appearance" are recurrent. Again we realize that in this supposed realm of *being*, it is *appearance* that reigns. "The hand of the gardener is not to be seen." How incredible, and how profoundly significant, that Rousseau should condemn the *open* artificiality of the French formal gardens as unnatural!

In the garden is an aviary in which Julie has induced many sorts of birds to live together voluntarily; by utilizing the motives of action along with the time and patience required for conditioning, one can control the behavior of living beings. As usual, in this domain of the "natural," everything is the result of a scheme. But why take so much trouble, asks Saint-Preux, to hide your work? Nature by herself, explains Julie, doesn't do things right. Men are consequently "reduced to doing her violence, to forcing her in a way to come and live with them; and all this cannot be done without a little illusion." Nature, in short, must be made to bend herself to our ends, else she is not "natural." We must force, trick, and disfigure her if we are to make her correspond to our rational idea of the natural. Thus, Rousseau wants to replace existing societies, which he calls "artificial" and unnatural—although they are societies that in a real sense have developed "naturally," without rational plan—by models of artificial societies, which he calls "natural"! What he would like is to recover in a social state the peace and harmony of the natural or presocial state, by means of the artifices and pressures of culture. He has already shown how disastrous nature is in the cultural state. At Clarens one lives in the realm of culture (work, property, morals, and proprieties) while escaping culture's penalties (the endlessness of new pleasures and needs, the competition for their satisfaction and for prestige). At the same time, an attempt is made to recover nature's transparency and to substitute an iron-willed virtue for innocence.

In accordance with his view of the disparity between the sexes and their complementary roles, Rousseau has Wolmar and Julie control their little society in different ways. Wolmar is the "penetrating eye," the omniscient eye, the prototype of Big Brother. "If I could change the nature of my being and become a living eye," he says, "I should gladly make the exchange." The model of Rousseau's "guide" and Lawgiver, he is perfectly reasonable, above egoistic passion, almost godlike. The master plan and all its details are his. He believes (as Karl Marx was to believe) that if men are evil, it is because society has not shaped them properly. "There is no scoundrel whose natural inclinations, had they been better directed, could not have produced great virtues." His one all-absorbing motive is "love of order."

If Wolmar is the brain, the father-image, the God-figure, Julie is the heart of Clarens. She is at least as severe as Wolmar, but inspires love and radiates a warm benevolence. As Claire writes, she is one of those souls who have a natural ascendency over all around them. "You are made to rule. Your empire is the most absolute one I know; it extends even over the will . . . your heart vivifies all who surround it and gives them, so to speak, a new being. . . ." In the poetic scene of the grape harvest, she becomes, in Guyon's words, "the evocation of a rite . . . of a true cult paid to Julie, the goddess-woman, goddess-mother, the eternal feminine."[12]

The system of artifice and deception is consistently carried out in all aspects of life at Clarens. It is applied to the upbringing of the children, for as Wolmar puts it, to mold men it is necessary to "form"them when they are small children. The analogy with Julie's garden is best expressed in a phrase in the first book of *Emile*: "We shape plants by cultivation, and men by education." As in the much earlier *Projet pour l'éducation de M. de Sainte-Marie*, the method relies largely on the "hidden hand." Saint-Preux summarizes Julie's educational philosophy: "Explaining her maxims to me at length, she showed me under the appearance of negligence the most vigilant attention."

Education at Clarens converges on the same target as the training of the servants and workers. It is to make the children "docile," that is, to make them conform spontaneously to a desired pattern of social behavior. This is Rousseau's concept of "freedom." In theory, the children are not subjected to discipline. What, asks Saint-Preux, the perfect foil in all these discussions, has Julie put in its place? "A far more inflexible yoke," replies Wolmar, "that of necessity." It works by making the child constantly feel his "dependency" and "the heavy yoke" of what has to be. He has found a way of controlling behavior, more powerful than discipline which, being overt and personal, leads to resentment or revolt. The yoke of "necessity" has several advantages: it is inflexible, impersonal, and hidden; and most important, it is *freely* consented to. The analogy with *The Social Contract* (which obtains in almost all phases of the ideology of *La Nouvelle Héloïse*) is clearly seen when Wolmar explains that his purpose is to make the child at once "free" and "docile"—a remarkable paradox that can be explained only as a more subtle and complete process of control which reaches (as he states) the will itself. Like the citizen, the child will do freely what the "guides" think he should do for his own good. To transpose Rousseau's vocabulary in *The Social Contract*, he will be "forced to be free." Rousseau never hesitates to deform vocabulary to his own purpose. Thus "direction" and "constraint" turn into "freedom," and "artifice" into "nature."

The child is "bent to refusals," and each refusal is irrevocable. So is every consent. This system produces the effect of mechanical necessity that Rousseau demands. Reflection is bypassed, and reflexive behavior takes over. Children are never to be reasoned with, but made to think that reason is beyond their years, "for then they suppose it to be on the side where it is supposed to be." The result is that the child "is no more bothered by having the box of chocolates closed to him than by seeing a bird he'd like to hold fly away, for he feels the same impossibility in both. . . . In everything that vexes him, he feels the empire of necessity." After hearing all this, Saint-Preux finally asks the crucial and unavoidable question: "But . . . how do you reconcile so much happiness with so much constraint, and what becomes of all the freedom you pretend to give them, in all these restrictions?" Julie's answer to this question is a masterpiece of sophistical obfuscation.

Rousseau is wholly consistent when he tells us that Julie's *art* eventuates in *nature*'s own simplicity. Forthwith we are given an example of this strange but characteristic confusion of nature and artifice. The elder child has taken the younger one's drum. So Fanchon, the governess, does the same to the elder child a bit later. His tears produce no more effect on her than the younger one's had on him. When she later wants to return the drum to its proper owner, Julie stops her, "for that was no longer the lesson of nature. . . . In losing his drum, the younger boy suffered the harsh law of necessity; the elder one felt his injustice." Now what we really see here are the results of the doctrinaire rigidity that characterizes Rousseau's thought, a kind of thinking typical of the totalitarian shape of mind. Justice is not taught, in this lesson, but perverted. Nature and justice are confused, and the only lesson taught is the law of the strong. How ironic, when one recalls Rousseau's criticism of La Fontaine in *Emile!*

Since the children are never scolded or overtly punished, they feel free and speak and act without reserve. As a result, explains Julie, "we can study the impulses of nature even in their most secret springs. . . . They reveal without restraint whatever is at the bottom of their hearts. . . . I listen to them with the greatest attention without their suspecting it, and keep a detailed account book of all that they do and say." Thus the system of spying used among the servants is ingeniously applied in this modified fashion, and the "eye" of the master sees all through a technique of unsuspected surveillance. Even Claire's daughter, Henriette, is utilized as far as possible, without her knowing it, to shape the boys' behavior, "and with all the more success because her lessons are less suspect."

What Saint-Preux terms "transparence"—the absence of secrets—is a means of control, and we shall see how Wolmar utilizes it with the former lovers. Its function is to destroy the substance of autonomy and freedom, while keeping the names. *The only freedom is the freedom to conform.* "Openness" is a way of living under the constant "look" of the "other," the key for effectuating the absorption of private worlds into the collective consciousness, for creating a state of dependency, among equals or unequals. We are also about to see how difficult it is to make it work, to make it open all the locked doors and secret chambers.

It is evident that Rousseau's "freedom" is not a value in itself or for self-realization, but only one of the means used to "form" the children. How fitting that near the end of this exposé on education Julie should return to the image of the garden: "I weed the garden," she says laughing, "I root out the weeds." Such, then, is the application of Rousseau's method of the "hidden hand" to the raising of children.

Of course, Rousseau's theory should not be taken as a sinister plot against the human race. On the contrary, he is seeking the salvation of the individual and of mankind and is proposing a theoretical solution to the problem. Social man is inevitably more wicked than virtuous; the goal is to contain and direct his egoistic vitalities by putting an end to his inner contradiction. Other writers in the eighteenth century, anarchists or nihilists, made the same proposal, but with opposite implications.

### 4. THE WORLD WITHIN

Reconciliation of inner contradictions is precisely the problem besetting Rousseau's protagonists, whose private drama is worked out in the third and final division of the novel. Saint-Preux's reappearance has brought about a crisis in Julie's life which Wolmar thinks he will solve by initiating a remarkable project of psychological conditioning designed to "remake" the luckless lover. Wolmar will fail even as he succeeds, because despite his all-seeing eye, he cannot (as indeed he knows) penetrate his wife's inmost being. He wants Saint-Preux to remain with them—partly, he says, to bring up the children in accordance with his "method," but more importantly because he knows Julie will never be happy if, by depriving her of one she loves, he reanimates the nostalgia of memories and frustrated hopes. He decides, then, to reunite them, but to "regulate" their feelings and to remake them. To do this, he must reshape Saint-Preux's inner world and bring into harmony the conflicts between natural impulses and social law. In fact, the first must be submitted to the second. Saint-Preux must be "socialized" before he is given the right of citizenship.

Wolmar's ostensible method, which critics have mistakenly accepted at face value as his real method, is openness and "transparency." "I have always recognized," he tells Saint-Preux, "that there is nothing good one cannot obtain from fine souls with confidence and frankness." His true method and the real role of "confidence" and "frankness" are quite another matter.

First, let us turn to the famous scenes of "transparency." They take place in closed off rooms, into which strangers or servants are never admitted, where the chosen few of the realm (Wolmar, Julie, Claire, Saint-Preux, and the children) come together for the occasion. These gatherings are "an invitation to intimacy," a "society of hearts." Either they talk at supper with complete abandon ("what a delightful mélange of familiarity, of pleasure, of union, of ease . . ."), or at a *matinée à l'anglaise* they sit together in a harmony of silence, sensing each other's presence, "in an immobility of ecstasy"—exactly as Jean-Jacques had once done with Mme. Basile and with Maman—each enjoying the expansion of his own being, and their interpenetration, in a gentle tide of emotion that is not hindered or corrupted by the falsifying mediation of language. "How much was said without anyone speaking! What ardent feelings were communicated without the cold mediation of words!"

Rousseau's aversion to language is a basic part of his psychological make-up, and is theorized in the second *Discourse* and the *Essay on the Origin of Languages*. Doubtless it was a form of infantile regression, even of phylogenetic regression, to a stage when the extrinsic expression of our intrinsic experience is not through the symbolic distortion of speech. These scenes, on which Rousseau lingered with especial fondness, were a realization of his desire to retreat from the full implications of life, especially from the "factitious social life" that had made him so unhappy. Their ideal tone, in contrast to *Candide*'s, for example, is contemplative, not active. They embody in a peculiar way the fear of passion that is a leitmotif of the story. In them Rousseau is trying to spiritualize the abnormal and perverted passions associated with his fixation on the *ménage à trois*. Within the small dining room, as in the larger estate of Clarens, the drive toward self-expression is immobilized into a static perfection that, because it frustrates deep human needs, cannot bring emotional peace.

These scenes crystalize another leitmotif of *La Nouvelle Héloïse*, the yearning to restore broken unity with the world. Language, appearance, "opinion," *amour-propre*—these had all broken the unity of his childhood (in the incident of the comb, among others),* the unity of Les Charmettes, the unity men had known among simple peoples. All these enemies are banished from the "little group's" isolated communing. In the impenetrable shelter of the secret room, a momentary, fragile state of innocence, without conflict or rivalry, can be recaptured, and paradoxically, Jean-Jacques' being can expand to encompass the infinite. Surrounded by imaginary "creatures according to my heart," he can feel independent of the world, but not alone.

These are, I repeat, among Rousseau's most enduring fixations, earlier patterns that had been successful adjustments and that reasserted themselves in difficult and threatening situations. As in dreams and fantasy (and what else was *La Nouvelle Héloïse* for him?), there is a regression along the path of least resistance and in obedience to the pleasure principle.

If we examine the physical and psychological structure of Clarens, we discover that its architecture, so to speak, contains an infinite regression of security. The estate itself is a closed world, sheltered from the dangers of intrusion and contamination. But it surrounds other closed shelters within it. Julie's garden is cut off from the rest of the estate, and within

* See L. G. Crocker, *Jean-Jacques Rousseau: The Quest (1712–1758)*, p. 26.

the larger garden is a smaller enclosure, the Elyseum, to which no one
but herself is usually admitted. This is her own little corner in the secret
garden within the walled domain. The manor house is also a shelter,
and within it are rooms, like the Apollo, that are sacred and prohibited
territory. This peculiar phenomenon springs directly but unconsciously
from Rousseau's own psychic experience, from the security he had found
in a succession of closed worlds.

The moments of spontaneous transparent intimacy, like all else at
Clarens, are carefully prearranged and planned. They can take place
only in specific rooms and at set times. It is as if the happy few say to
themselves, "Now we are going to have a session of transparency and
harmony." They are all prepared. Actually there are only three brief
scenes of this kind throughout the length of this long novel. They stand
out, in a sea of misunderstanding, self-delusion, and artifice, as didactic
examples artificially set up by Rousseau to show how the characters of
his El Dorado live, according to the "method" of Wolmar. But it is
obvious everywhere else that they do not always, or usually, live this
way.

Wolmar's real method is not frankness or transparency, but a subtle
process of operant conditioning, which relies in good measure on duplicity and the "hidden hand." Part of it aims to make Saint-Preux believe
that his invincible love for Julie is not for *this* Julie, but for a different
Julie, Julie d'Etange, who no longer exists. "Take away his memory,
and you will take away his love." The very act of living together in the
existing circumstances will gradually condition his outlook. Wolmar explicitly avoids the psychoanalytic method of bringing truth to light in
order to make Saint-Preux understand his hidden self. "We shall do
better by making use of his error [delusions] than with knowledge."
The secret of making him forget lies "in adroitly substituting other
ideas for those that are dear to him." New associations will efface the
old, a method Wolmar calls "putting his imagination on the wrong
scent." Thus, "instead of his mistress, I force him always to see the wife
of a gentleman and the mother of my children; I efface one tableau with
another and cover the past with the present." For this reason he makes
them kiss when they meet, and later reinforces his lesson by taking them
to the grove where the fatal kiss had once been exchanged, and making
them kiss again.

In such fashion, then, the process of conditioning begins. Wolmar
proposes to Claire that she collaborate with him in this little conspiracy,
warning her not to judge his actions "by ordinary rules," but by the
ends that inspire them. The subject, Saint-Preux, is of course unaware of
all this. How well it works we see by his thoughts when he takes a
solitary stroll in the Elyseum. He thinks that the Julie of old has been
replaced by a new Julie, whereas they really coexist. "I said to myself:
peace reigns in her heart." He, too, is deceived by this world of appear-

ance. Julie was at peace only as long as her dreams of love were confined to the past, to impossible memories with no relation to present reality.

Needless to say, Wolmar intends the same process to be working simultaneously on her. Julie will be encouraged to delude herself into thinking that she no longer fears Saint-Preux, that her passion has been transmuted into a true affection. Wolmar also profits from the "confession" she has finally made, and from his act of forgiveness, to strengthen her resolution to be redeemed. Gradually he will accustom the former lovers "to the familiarity in which they will have to live if my purposes are accomplished." It will not turn out the way he expects.

The constant insistence on openness, or the free and undisguised expression of feelings, is a part of the method. Private worlds must, as far as possible, be abolished. Just as with the children, the less they can hide (or conversely, the more that is seen by the "eye"), the more effective the control and the more complete the individual's integration. Obviously, this process involves a show of confidence on Wolmar's part, but the confidence is itself a mechanism for conditioning rather than a real fact. In Julie's words we see how effective it is: "He raises me above myself, and I feel that by his confidence he teaches me to merit it." To Saint-Preux he says, "The more familiar you are with her, the better I shall think of you. But live in your tête-à-tête as if I were present, in my presence as if I were not there; that is all I ask of you." Saint-Preux, who is a weak character ("easy to subjugate," Wolmar later says), resolves always to keep his heart "in such a state that it could be seen by him." This is precisely what Wolmar, the "living eye," wishes.

A third mechanism, utilized both by Wolmar and Julie, is Saint-Preux's need for approbation. Saint-Preux, the image of his creator, has remained, despite Julie's erroneous initial judgment, an insecure and alienated individual in search of identity and belief in his own worth. He affects to be independent of "opinion," but in fact he would be most eager to follow it, if only "opinion" would accept him. The autarchy of self-approbation is no more sufficient for him than for Rousseau. Security, for both, depends on the approval of certain individuals with whom they identify themselves. Saint-Preux requires Julie's approbation and will increasingly need Wolmar's to satisfy these deep emotional needs. He requires it in order to become *what they make him think he wants to be*. He tends constantly to see himself in other people's eyes—in their "look," to be more exact. From this time forth, he tells Julie, "I really believe I am a person of worth, *for I am esteemed by you*." Both she and Wolmar use his longing for their approbation and esteem—a motive they had already found effective with the servants—to reshape his affective life. From the very first day, Wolmar's show of esteem for Saint-Preux made it impossible, the latter admits, to belie him. The outcome is that Saint-Preux, who had earlier conceived his identity as Julie's lover and husband, now conceives it as Julie's and Wolmar's satellite, thus enabling them to exploit his fear of being expelled from their Garden of Eden. The transposal of Rousseau's own experience is obvious.

Despite Wolmar's declarations and displays of confidence, he does not really trust Saint-Preux, and perhaps does not entirely trust his wife. We cannot blame him for this, but the duplicity involved is not to be overlooked. A good part of the remaining action of the novel consists of a series of tests to which the hapless Saint-Preux is rather cruelly submitted.

The first and simplest of these is to observe whether Saint-Preux pretends to like him. When the test is passed, Wolmar is sure that he will eventually bring the man of whom he says, "I stole what belonged to him," to love him dearly. In other words, a simple and honest man is the kind that can be most easily controlled and manipulated—to bad ends or to good.

The second test is to leave the former lovers alone for five or six days. Saint-Preux passes the first part by expressing his pleasure at the prospect. But Julie is just as much involved in this plan. Wolmar's X-ray eye detects her uneasiness. He reproaches her for a virtue "that needs to choose its time and place." Like the fanatical husband in Cervantes' *Celoso extremeño*, he will be satisfied with nothing less than an absolute. As Julie puts it, "Wolmar seemed to want to push me to the wall." He not only wants her loyalty, but says that her having the slightest doubt of it would be an offense to him. He then humiliates her by bringing out some of the old love letters and solemnly proclaiming: "I entrust my wife and my honor to the woman who, when she was a seduced girl, preferred an act of kindness to a sure assignation." Julie can react in only one way: "I fear to lose part of his esteem, if he thinks I need more reserve than he allows me." Thus, the esteem-approbation motive remains Wolmar's most powerful weapon. But his action is, in fact, even more subtle. While he is constantly telling Julie to forget the past (for it is dead and he has confidence in her), he does not allow her to. And so her letter concludes with this final emphasis: "Despite such long repentance, I feel with sorrow that the weight of an old fault is a burden that one must carry throughout life."

Wolmar leaves. Claire, who also assures Julie that she has nothing to fear, has so little real confidence that she urges her to take the most careful precautions. This duplicity is reflected in the proposed precautions themselves. "Above all, take these measures in such a natural way that they seem like the effect of chance." And yet Claire has just condemned polite society, "where everything is only vain appearance." It is the same story: artifice and *seeming* rule this world of supposed frankness and *being*.

We see this again in Wolmar's explanation of his conduct to his ally, Claire. "I would be insane to establish this lover in my house before making sure that he has forever ceased to be one." Thus, he has been less than frank in assuring Saint-Preux that he was "cured."

Then an incident occurs that brings out dramatically the power of the repressed emotions. Saint-Preux and Julie take a boat excursion, in the company of several oarsmen. A sudden storm puts them within an inch of foundering. They reach shore, savor an outdoor luncheon, then walk in the woods together, enjoying the beauties of wild nature. They reach the spot where he had once waited in loneliness, meditating suicide on the high rocks, engraving her initials on the trees. "Seeing them again after so long a time, I felt how the presence of objects can powerfully reanimate the violent emotion which agitated you near them." The whole past wells up and breaks through the dikes of conditioning. He pours out all that is in his heart. "Too constantly loved girl, oh, you, for whom I was born!" Julie is profoundly moved and grips his hand. He keeps her hand in his on the ride back, as they both remain plunged in silent, melancholy reverie. He thinks of upsetting the boat and drowning with her, Rousseau's original ending to the novel. They both weep quietly. At last he speaks in a low voice: "I see that our hearts have never stopped understanding each other."

There has been no "cure," no real transmutation, only a victory of discipline obtained by Wolmar's success in displacing the force of will, or value, from one set of motivations to another. The nature of this victory is defined by Bomston when he urges Saint-Preux to delight in the spectacle of his own soul, "a pure and sublime soul, conquering its passions and ruling over itself." The revolt is only a fleeting moment of rebellion against overwhelming psychological pressures, against the desperation born of time's work. But struggle and temptation will never be eliminated. Time has changed everything, except the changelessness of memories, in which love still lives, impervious to time's corrosion. Not even Wolmar can "take away this memory." It can be repressed, and behavior transformed, even made reflexive. How impossible it is to eradicate the "weeds," after childhood is past, becomes clear once more when Saint-Preux, at a later point, returns to a room that again awakens tender association with *other* days. Instantly, he is plunged into desperate melancholy.

O time, happy time, you are no more. I loved, I was loved. . . . I savored in long draughts the delightful emotion that made me live. . . . You don't even have the right to weep any more. . . .

"Why is she not dead!" I dared to cry in a transport of rage. . . . But she lives, and she is happy. . . . She lives, and her life is my death, and her happiness is my torture. . . . She lives, but not for me. . . . I am a thousand times further from her than if she were no more.

In these two episodes we see the flaw in Wolmar's process of conditioning, or brainwashing. The deeper layer of repressions is ever at the mercy of circumstance. Circumstance, by arousing its own associations, can summon forth the buried dead. Memory is not within the control of the will. In one sense, we may say that *La Nouvelle Héloïse* is a drama of time, of the past and the present coexisting and struggling for supremacy in the psyche.*

Within these limits, then, Wolmar succeeds in making what he wants of Saint-Preux. He succeeds with Julie, too, in the same way and in the same measure. Her inner struggle, like Saint-Preux's, is unending, and so they can properly speak, according to Rousseau's definition, of their virtue. "My sweet friend," writes Saint-Preux, "do you not know that virtue is a state of war, and that to live in it, one always has to be fighting with oneself?"

The last act of the drama, the anagnorisis, or recognition, shows that Julie has deceived not only Wolmar, but herself. Their relations, as we have seen, are governed by something less than the desired absolute of openness.

Wolmar is an atheist. Following his consistent policy of duplicity (which in this instance can only be termed hypocrisy), he goes regularly to church in order to set a good example for the servants and the children. "Appearances are so well saved," in this realm of *seeming*, that Saint-Preux has been completely taken in. But his sham provides little satisfaction to Julie, who perhaps needs Wolmar's faith to confirm her faith, without which she would be lost. She hides from him the sadness she feels because of his atheism. He, too, has been tempted to deceive Julie, but (according to Saint-Preux) he is incapable of dissimulation! We may assume he esteems such a sham too difficult to carry off and too risky for the atmosphere of frankness he needs to maintain.

Another test to which Saint-Preux is submitted is a reunion with Julie's father, who has ruined his life and deeply offended him into the bargain. This test is passed when he evinces great affection for the old curmudgeon. Such progress should evoke increased trust. But a much more difficult test awaits him, originated this time by Bomston. Saint-Preux will be sent to Rome to extricate Bomston from the imbroglio in which his affairs with two women have involved him.†

How brilliantly Wolmar has succeeded in modeling his human clay can be seen in Saint-Preux's first letter to him:

---

* It has also been pointed out that "Rousseau is the first novelist to isolate nostalgia as a distinct psychological malady. That is what makes *La Nouvelle Héloïse* such a modern novel. Everything is seen nostalgically, filtered with regret" (Judith Shklar, "Rousseau's Images of Authority," p. 926). However, it is not quite accurate to say that the lovers do not "long for a lost happiness: they did not enjoy their love affair." First, because memory makes the past seem more beautiful, especially by comparison with the present. (As Dante's Francesca says, "*Nessun maggior dolore che ricordarse del tempo felice ne la miseria.*") Second, because the longing is for the promise of *unfulfilled* happiness, for what they have missed.

† Actually, Bomston has possessed neither of the two women who are desperately in love with him. As in Rousseau's *ménage à trois*, his erotic life ends in narcissism, flight from commitment, and the avoidance of responsibility.

Accept the homage of a purified heart, which you have made worthy, by your great efforts, to be offered to you. . . . To you I owe the moral life to which I feel myself being reborn. Oh, my benefactor! Oh, my father! in giving myself to you without reservation, I can only offer you, as to God himself, the gifts I have received from you. . . . Dear friend, shall I then belong to you? Shall I bring up your children?

Saint-Preux has signed the social compact. He accepts complete dependency, complete docility, complete absorption of the egoistic self into the collective body formed by the Lawgiver-guide. Such total ego-shrinkage is the inevitable regressive result of total identification with a leader. "The more painful this departure was to me, the more I felt honored by such a sacrifice." This letter reminds us, too, of still another technique that has been used, a combination of criticism and self-criticism, followed by contrition. Saint-Preux refers to a scene of this kind with Bomston, and this letter (like others) is in itself such an act.

What then is the truth in regard to Saint-Preux's state, and Julie's? Is the true Saint-Preux the one who identifies himself with the collective will, formulated by the "guide"? The one who, reduced to the security of an avowed (and revolting) childish dependency, basks in the sunshine of his master's favor and worships those who, having undone him, now control him? Rousseau's masochism has found its perfect sublimated expression here. Or is it the Saint-Preux who fleetingly rebels in helpless frustration, cursing his ill fate and those who have caused it, knowing his unhappiness as he does know it? How far can we believe him when he repeats his indoctrinated catechism at the end of this letter: "All my transports are extinguished." The "veil" or obstacle—passion—has been lifted. "I see all my duties, and I love them."

While such questions cannot be answered, so complete is the dissociation of Saint-Preux's personality, we can be sure that his dependency is now fixed and that his overt behavior will remain under Wolmar's control. Some may feel repulsion on reading Wolmar's lines to him: "Lucky youth! Everything conspires to make you happy; all the rewards of virtue seek you out to force you to deserve them." This is not only part of the system of indoctrination. As Wolmar well knows, Saint-Preux needs to be reassured that he is happy, that he is esteemed, that he is *worth* something as a person, that he has only to keep on trying to make the grade. And the reply is: "What would I become without you?"

The Nazi concentration camps and Negro slavery both testify to the fact that when survival depends on meeting the expectations of a single man, the result is infantilism, or childlike modes of behavior. Rarely is there rebellion; instead, the personality of the victim changes. Destruction of autonomous initiative and forcing an individual to act against his own values are ways of breaking down his self-respect and reducing him to the state of a submissive child. This is the process Saint-Preux has undergone. Wolmar has become a father and a god, Julie a semi-incestuous mother, like Mme. de Warens. Applied to a group, such a process transforms it into a depersonalized mass capable of acting only according to the designs of those who guide it.

The test to which Saint-Preux is being put is a cruel temptation for him to favor his own self-interest at the expense of Bomston's. If he favors Bomston's marriage to the noble-minded harlot he loves, then Bomston promises him they will all live together at Clarens; but if he does not marry her, he will return to England, and Saint-Preux, his loyal friend, will be expected to follow his benefactor. This cruel plot is artfully and deceptively arranged by Wolmar and Bomston. "I pretended to give this trip more importance than it really had," the latter writes to Wolmar; "it is desirable that the plan of this test should never be known except by you and me." The test must *seem* to be "natural," authentic, to its subject. Again we see that expressed confidence in Saint-Preux has been a mask for lack of confidence, even as Rousseau's belief in man's goodness masked his deeper conviction (which his friend Conzié once noted) that men are wicked. Without a recognition of this psychological transposal we cannot understand Rousseau's work. Julie and Claire will also be deceived, then. Either they, too, cannot be completely trusted, or else the conspirators are secretly ashamed of what they are doing. The former is the more likely reason. We are made to feel, at this point, that all are treated, in varying degrees, like children, that nobody can be completely counted on or can count on himself—except Wolmar.

This is to be the final test. Again Saint-Preux passes it, proving by his sacrifice to virtue that he has been sufficiently socialized to fit into the organic body of the "collective self" that is Clarens. So completely has he been "socialized" that he refuses Laura (Bomston's unfortunate but *virtuous* mistress) the chance of redemption that had been granted Julie. Still more interesting, the unwilling prostitute is, in her alienation from society and her relationship to Bomston, in a position analogous to what Julie's had been. But Saint-Preux now belongs to the "other" side and has become the defender of the social order, Wolmar's man. "Respect opinion!" he warns Bomston.

At the outset, virtue had been confused with nature, in the minds of Saint-Preux and Julie. Now it loses its normal meaning altogether. No longer does it apply to the concrete individual, but only to the abstract society. Laura's own virtue and merits, as well as Bomston's duty to her and the very fact that her fall (unlike Julie's) is society's fault and not her own—all these factors might imply a different course of action. Saint-Preux recognizes this, only to reject it. "I tremble at the thought that his intrepid love of virtue, which makes him despise the public opinion, may lead him to the other extreme." How can we help experiencing a certain malaise at this point, a feeling that Saint-Preux is behaving like the dog who licks the hand of the master who is beating him?

We may feel a mixture of repulsion and pity for Saint-Preux, but only repulsion for his tormentors. In these cleverly disguised tests, they have used him like a laboratory animal. He has been treated like an object, to be shaped into a useful instrument. Their mode of dealing with the unfortunate Laura is no different; she is to be used as the touchstone of Saint-Preux's virtue before she is discarded. We had thought such treatment was reserved for the helots. But Saint-Preux, in Wolmar's system, cannot be treated otherwise until he has been *dénaturé*, transformed from the atomistic individual still living partly in the state of nature into a socialized unit of the corporate whole, *freely* and lovingly devoted to the collective self.

As for Laura, her happy marriage would not only outrage the social order, but would mock the fate of the virtuous Julie. Even in this paradise, redemption is not within the reach of all—just as only a chosen few are admitted to citizenship. Perhaps Rousseau is defending himself here, for his refusal to marry Thérèse. Marriage is a socially sacred institution, not to be thought of between a hierarchically superior man and an inferior woman. Nature and the individual must be sacrificed to order.

And now, at the very moment when Saint-Preux has passed all the tests and is ready for citizenship in the circle of the elect, a new and unexpected obstacle arises. Julie is overcome by fear that her unsated love will prove stronger than her will to virtue. This sudden turn is a dramatic revelation of the true facts of her life. In her panic she hits on the plan of marrying Claire to her former lover. She informs Claire that she now understands what her most intimate soul-companion had all this time kept hidden from her; she had also loved Saint-Preux and would have let herself be seduced if Julie had not anticipated her. Her analysis is devastating, and it is designed to force Claire to accede to her design.

At this point we may allow ourselves a few speculations. First, Julie doubtless intuited Claire's love even earlier, but now desperation, overriding discretion, impels her to use this weapon. Second, if we think back to Claire's manipulation of Julie and Saint-Preux—which had effectively separated them, prevented them from coming together again, and induced Julie to marry Wolmar—is it not tempting to believe that her actions had been prompted by female rivalry, by jealousy, by the instinctive impulse, conscious or unconscious, to keep them apart? and that all her reasoning about virtue had been self-deceptive rationalization, if not worse? And that Julie now suspects this strategem of her dearest friend, a friend from whom supposedly she had no secrets and who had none from her, a friend who had collaborated in "saving" her by means of a lifelong frustration? And may it not be a conscious or unconscious feeling of guilt that explains why Claire cannot bring herself to marry Saint-Preux? To profit from her friend's misfortune (in which she has had a hand) would be to make her earlier actions treasonable, even if they were not originally so.

No wonder Julie exults at her discovery. "You are caught, my poor cousin . . . you're in the same net you went to so much trouble to free me from. . . . So my turn to laugh has come, has it?" In vain she tries to cover the tone of triumph. Now it is she who is planning to treat Claire as an instrument, though she rationalizes her proposal into a design for her friend's happiness. If that were so, why has she not thought of marrying Claire to Saint-Preux before? What she is seeking is her own security, which is threatened by her inner turbulence. If Claire does not agree to the marriage, she says, "My advice is that we get rid of this dangerous man, at any cost." To Saint-Preux she will write that there is no implied threat of her sending him away if he does not consent to the marriage.

But Claire is clairvoyant. With a Wolmarian eye she penetrates Julie's secret motive, which in itself confirms the two women's intuitive grasp of all that has been unavowed and carefully dissimulated. The masks are off. She accuses Julie of really wanting to save herself. "I understand your tricks, my cute one; it is in order to give yourself the right of reprisal that you accuse me of having once saved my heart at the expense of yours. I am not duped by that trick." And this situation uncovers still another little duplicity and manipulation. It was out of fear for herself that Claire had encouraged and favored Julie's and Saint-Preux's love, even as it was out of love and jealousy that she had later worked to separate them.

Julie's motives are more complex than even Claire perceives. She wants to keep Saint-Preux, but to keep him without danger. Doubtless, too, giving him to Claire as a substitute would allay her feelings of guilt for her vows forsworn and his ruined life. I shall also speculate shortly on possible sexual motives.

Claire, too, has unresolved problems of sexual frustration. Her appetites are keen, she admits. (We must remember that Rousseau made her a brunette, in his concept more passionate than a blonde.) "How can I remain a widow at my age, and not feel sometimes that days are only half of life?" Virtue can win the battle with tricks and self-deception, during the daytime, but night brings with solitude and darkness a confrontation with the naked self. "How many times, in the silence of the night, when one cannot escape oneself, have I driven away importunate ideas by thinking of stratagems for the morrow!" While one cannot escape from oneself during the night, this is something one must do during the day, if life is to be bearable in this world of virtue and transparency. Perhaps Claire's suffering and self-denial explain her harshness, her smugness and pride of caste in her attitude toward Laura—an attitude far from the Christian charity and humility so calculatingly displayed by the inhabitants of this realm. There are numerous traces of sadistic cruelty in Claire's earlier letters.

Blocked, at least momentarily, by Claire's resistance, Julie now tackles Saint-Preux. She congratulates him and herself on the triumph of virtue, but reminds him that they must adore the guide who has made it possible. Then she goes on to express a complete lack of confidence in his virtue, and to affirm that he will probably seduce one of the women in the household, if he does not marry Claire. She admits that only this marriage can restore her peace of mind. "With what delight then would I give myself without constraint to all my affection for you!" This exclamation reveals everything. It evokes another passionate outburst of Saint-Preux's pent-up love. Then he reassures her that there is no need for her to worry (as if such an outburst would not confirm her fears), now that "the penetrating Wolmar has enlightened me about my real feelings."*

No, the marriage will not do for him, either. He prefers the masochism of the *ménage à trois*, its eroticism without virile responsibility, to the satisfactions of possessing Claire, although she is physically desirable. "When the redoubtable Julie pursues me, I find refuge with Mme. de Wolmar, and I am tranquil. . . . But this passing tranquillity is only a truce; and it does not avail to raise myself to you in your presence, I fall back into myself as soon as I leave you. Julie, in truth, I think I have two souls."

He is frightened by the threat of being sent away. His security—like Rousseau's at Les Charmettes—depends on his being allowed to stay in this world in which he has found his identity as Wolmar's and Julie's satellite.[13] Most telling are his reproaches. "Oh, Julie! Oh, Claire! I have lived in a storm, and it has always been you who brought it on. . . Julie, have you forgotten my oaths as well as yours? . . . I have lost everything; my faithfulness alone has remained to me." And now the bitter truth comes out. "Do not try to draw me out of the annihilation into which I have fallen, lest with the feeling of my existence I recover that of my suffering, and a violent turmoil reopen all my wounds." Claire, in their present relationship, has been a harmless outlet. "I congratulated myself on an emotion that helped me delude myself [Claire had used the same phrase, *"donner le change"*] and enabled me to bear your image with less suffering. . . . If some vain transport agitates me for a moment, everything represses it and stills it." Yes, this is the truth about Wolmar's realm of sincerity and transparency. But Saint-Preux is no longer man enough to have any will: "The decision belongs to you alone . . . tell me what I should do." *Le pauvre!*

Julie's threat of sending Saint-Preux away, her tormenting him as she does, is not the first time we note a touch of sadism in her, too. Her letter announcing her marriage had many cruel barbs, and none more cruel than when she told him that even if she had a free choice, she would choose Wolmar over him. That was really kicking him when he was down. Now she says that she will be open with him and tell him "with each feeling that stirs me: 'This is what I have preferred to you.' "

---

* Again there is an analogy with the "guide," in *The Social Contract*, who reveals to the citizens their real will.

This reaction is part of a paroxysm of virtue into which she sublimates her frustrations, forming a shield against self-confrontations, "this elevation of soul and this inner strength that we feel near each other." She comes to cherish her renunciation and her guilt, her hurt and her suffering; they give focus and value to her being after love is lost.

Contrary to the generally held view, I take Julie to be a highly egocentric personality. This characteristic, intensified by the neuroticism induced by what she calls her "great sacrifice," is obvious throughout. She has given up Saint-Preux, but she constantly shows that she would not like him to give her up. It is to keep him safely that she exhorts him to virtue, and then to marriage to Claire. Giving him nothing except sermons and scoldings, she wants to retain all her rights over him and prescribe his way of life. She does not hesitate to deceive him. She wants him to live in her house, where his passion will be fed, and chooses a wife for him who will keep him near her, knowing full well he will continue to love her. In this way her repressed sexuality seeks compensations. Both Julie and Saint-Preux would experience vicarious sexual enjoyment through Claire. She knows (and Saint-Preux practically says as much) that she would be present in their love-making, and in a way she would share him with Claire. Doubtless she, too, thinks of Saint-Preux when she responds to Wolmar's chill embraces. "*Comme il savait aimer!*" The marriage would equalize and balance the situation, with vicarious love substituted for the real in double transfer. This is a new and more subtle, more complex variation of the *ménage à trois*. *La Nouvelle Héloïse* is in this respect the result of a sick imagination. Here as elsewhere, Rousseau cannot go outside of himself, and we realize that sexuality in this novel only reflects his own experiences, fantasies, and attitudes.

At this point, Julie thinks of her happiness when they were all together:

I said to myself: That little room holds all that is dear to my heart, and perhaps all that is best on earth; I am surrounded by everything I care for; for me, the whole universe is here; I enjoy at once my affection for my friends, the affection they return to me, and that which they have for each other; their reciprocal good will either comes from me or is related to me; I see nothing that does not expand my being, and nothing that divides it; it is in everything that surrounds me, no part of it is far from me; my imagination has nothing else to do; I have nothing left to desire; feeling and enjoying are one and the same thing for me; I live at once in all I love; I satiate myself with happiness and life. O death! Come when you will, I no longer fear you, I have lived."

These lines reveal both her egocentricity (first person pronouns occur twenty-six times!) and the hollowness under the outer shell. Julie's confession, like Saint-Preux's, is one of defeat and unhappiness beneath the rationalizations of victory and happiness. It leads gradually into a justification of her other escape mechanism: a pietistic absorption with God, to which she has had increasing recourse ever since Saint-Preux's return. The strength of her religious emotion and of her love of virtue is a reciprocal of the strength of her passion. With her as with him, passion provides the stimulus to its own sublimation, which is the condition for their being together. Like Wolmar, God is described by Julie as the "guide." A person cannot count on himself, she insists. In the grip of passion one can be happy, for there are always hope and the charms of illusion. "Woe to him who has nothing left to desire!" she cries, thinking of herself; "we are happy only before we are happy."

Is it not clear that to have nothing to desire is really to have everything to desire? Voltaire, in *Candide*, had already laid bare the flaw in Wolmar's plan for an El Dorado where there is no desiring and no discontent. This "happiness"—what is it worth? That is why she says that happiness lies in dreaming, "such is the nothingness of human things." Only God can do without the pleasure of desiring; "any other deprivation would be more bearable." But what she desires is a forbidden desire; she cannot even admit its existence to herself. And so she concludes:

That is what I feel in part since my marriage and since your return. Everywhere I see only reasons for contentment, and I am discontent; a secret languor creeps into the bottom of my heart; I feel it empty and swollen, as you once said about yours; my attachment to all that is dear to me is not sufficient to fill it; a useless force remains in it with which it does not know what to do. This suffering is strange, I know it; but it is none the less real. My dear friend, I am too happy; happiness bores me.

Such is the duplicity and self-deception of this realm, that her happiness is an unhappiness, the greatest of illusions, a rationalization partly self-induced, partly induced by Wolmar.

Only God, Julie declares, can fill this emptiness that is destroying her, an emptiness in the supposed world of happiness and fulfillment. Only God can teach her to overcome her "vile yearnings." The mystical emotions she experiences as she tries to fuse her soul with God are both a protection against the danger of her subsisting love and a surrogate for the fulfillment that love alone can give her. It is the supreme evasion ("my faculties are alienated") whose consummation is the death for which she now longs. But in this mysticism, too, life offers more frustration than fulfillment. God is a hidden God, who "veils his face." One can touch him only by the mediation of his works and his providence. Although he is immanent in us, we cannot experience the *immediacy* of his presence. (Even Moses could see only the burning bush.) And so Julie must admit defeat here, too. "When I try to raise myself to him, I know not where I am; perceiving no relation between him and me, I do not know how to reach him. I see and feel nothing finally. I find myself in a state of annihilation." In her haunted mind, life has become a maze from which there is only one issue.

Death will come when it is most needed. Claire and Saint-Preux have refused the marriage. Enter *deus ex machina*. When Saint-Preux had left for Rome, he experienced a horrible dream in which Julie was separated from him by a veil, and he was told he would never see her again. Believing, like Rousseau, in oneiric predictions and other superstitious signs (a common trait of neurotics, especially obsessionals), he had rushed back to Clarens to defeat the dream. Unfortunately, he had contented himself with hearing her voice behind the garden hedge, and Claire had scolded him for this inefficiency. Now the prediction will come true. Julie jumps into the water to rescue her drowning son. A fatal illness (possibly pneumonia, but Rousseau is vague) follows, and there is no will to live, only to die.

The death scene is long, long enough for many speeches and confessions. After she expires (from talking too much, one might almost say), a rumor that she was resuscitated runs through the household. Wolmar, understanding "that it [is] impossible to make the common people listen to reason" (Rousseau's true opinion), postpones the burial until the flesh starts to corrupt. Claire then puts a golden, pearl-embroidered veil, which Saint-Preux had brought from the Indies, over Julie's face and cries: "Cursed be the unworthy hand that ever lifts that veil! Cursed be the impious eye that looks upon that disfigured face!" The dream has come true. The veil is Claire's final gesture of possessiveness and perhaps the symbol of the lovers' separation until death do them unite. The final "unveiling," the removal of all obstacles to unity and transparency, belongs to death, not to life; to God, not man.

As Julie lies dying, the penetrating "eye" will know the truth. Yes, says Wolmar, "I have penetrated you. You are glad to die; you are happy to leave me." Chagrined by his defeat, he complains that he has not deserved this. Julie, who had described their group as "each feeling himself to be such as he should be, shows himself to all such as he is," has hidden her deepest and truest self from him, and from herself. The flaw lay in the phrase, "feeling himself to be such as he should be." This "should" is determined from without, not from within; one must be *made* to feel as one ought to feel. This has been the whole aim of Wolmar's "system," and it has failed. Precisely at this point, Julie admits that her heart was born for love, that she was indifferent to the social standards ("opinion") to which she had bowed. Yet she still insists she was happy in her marriage, and doubtless this is true in Rousseau's sense, because her conscience was at ease.

My earlier criticism of the famous scenes of immediate transparency is, I think, amply confirmed at this point. Spontaneity and transparency would have involved sincere and total communication of Julie's and Saint-Preux's feelings toward each other, as well as Julie's toward Wolmar. This is not possible, of course, and all the less possible because they are not allowed to be sincere with themselves. The description of a society where "each shows himself to all such as he is" is patently untrue. The spontaneous and the sincere are rejected, in Wolmar's domain, in favor of illusions and psychological pressures in the name of social imperatives. All of life at Clarens is planned and calculated with an exquisite logic, according to the "system." Saint-Preux may write, "The sweet equality reigning here brings back the order of nature, and everything breathes an air of ancient simplicity." But Clarens is not the realm of equality, and there is nothing less natural than this return to a more natural life, nothing more intricate than this life of simplicity. Transparency is never won back except in fleeting, contrived situations. This is precisely the realm where the spontaneous, the "immediate," the transparent do not exist, cannot exist. How utterly incredible is the statement that Clarens is the model of a "society of hearts without mystery," or that the characters have "complete confidence" in each other!

Here as elsewhere, we may well extend the sphere of self-deception to Rousseau himself. The name "Clarens" is supposed to imply the realm of clarity or openness. The most "transparent" of the characters is Saint-Preux, and he is manipulated by all the others. If we compare Candide's garden with Julie's, we see the difference between a truly voluntary but limited cooperative society and a totally controlled collective in which every pressure, direct and concealed, is applied to obtain total participation. In the one, there is a compromise with life's ills and no illusion of perfection; in the other, no compromise with the utopian goal.

Final confirmation comes in the dying Julie's last letter to Saint-Preux. Wolmar's plan was wrong, she now knows: "This reunion was not good." She was never really cured of passion's disease. "You thought I was cured, and I thought I was." It was all an illusion, and "that illusion was salutary." Love had only been repressed ("it became concentrated in my heart"), and she is weary of the unending struggle. Wolmar has really created the realm of illusions and deceptions. "One more day, perhaps, and I was guilty. . . . All the tests have been passed; but they might have come back too often. Haven't I lived long enough for happiness and virtue?" This last question contains a charge of irony that blows Wolmar's world to bits. And she takes leave of her lover with these final words of farewell:

When you see this letter the worms will be gnawing your mistress' face, and her heart, where you will no longer be. But will my soul exist without you? Without you, what happiness would I enjoy? No, I am not leaving you. I am going where I shall wait for you. The virtue that separated us on earth will unite us in the eternal dwelling place. I die in that sweet expectation, only too happy to purchase, at the cost of my life, the right to love you forever without transgression, and to say it to you now, once more!

Here, in death, Julie at last achieves the transparency, the immediate presence of truth that has been the supreme *illusion* fostered in this society in which illusion is praised as more salutary than truth. One can only wonder what poor Wolmar will do when he dies, all alone in paradise.

Wolmar's plan had been to create an organic, unanimous social body. Love, the focus of egocentricity, was to be "socialized," sublimated into a reflexive devotion to virtue or the group. Saint-Preux's desires were not only to be abandoned, but transformed into a willing, ardent enthusiasm for the collectivity, into admiration and gratitude for those who are dispossessing, depriving, shaping him. Mauzi has made this astute comment:

In *La Nouvelle Héloïse*, the inhabitants of Clarens are the prisoners, without knowing it, of a trumped-up universe. The virtuous happiness they enjoy [?] has devoured their freedom. . . . Not only would there be no conflict between the *individual* and the *collective*, but the distinction between the two would lose all meaning, since the citizen is precisely that man who cannot conceive of the individual and the collective separately.[14]

In his writings on political theory, Rousseau is little interested in the individual, save as part of a collective group. These speculative works, in sharp contrast with his personal writings, are striking by their inhuman quality of absoluteness, by their sacrifice of concrete men to an abstract notion. Never does he count on love, on good will, or on self-discipline to create harmony and order; they can be brought about only by coercive pressures that mold motive, emotion, and will. This is sufficient evidence of what he really thought about man's goodness.

To create Wolmar's truly social state, to "make man one," involves a remaking of the personality, which turns out to be a disastrous warping of the personality. In Julie's case, the combination of repression, frustration, and fear which make up the atmosphere of Clarens, and which the rule of transparency is powerless to touch, has led to a flight from reality. She enters a neurotic state in which she seeks from mystical ecstasy the security she cannot find in life. Her self-justification, that her mystical practices are only a "recreation" and do not interfere with her active duties, is another form of self-deception. It masks the fact that it is only at the price of these compulsive, convulsive, cathartic exercises that she *can* carry on her duties. This retreat leads to progressive deterioration of her autonomous ego-defenses until, no longer able to face the reality of Saint-Preux's permanent presence, she attempts the last, desperate tactic of manipulating Claire and Saint-Preux into marriage, and then, when that fails, resigns herself with profound relief to the victory of the death wish over the life force. The pressures on her personality have disturbed its structure and brought about a flight into the refuge of psychic illness. Such has been the result of the frustration, pressures, and lies of this *terre inhumaine*.

As for Saint-Preux, we have seen how his personality is dissociated ("In truth, Julie, I think I have two souls"), how he is made into the willing instrument of the society that has crushed him. Especially in the Laura episode, we have the impression of a betrayal or renunciation of his self. In this society, where the individual is indoctrinated, "denatured," refashioned in his personality and conscience until he is made to realize "what he really wants," Saint-Preux is eviscerated. He uses the word "annihilation" to describe his state, just as Julie uses "annihilated" to describe hers. His dignity as an autonomous and responsible being has been demolished.

One of the remarkable aspects of this book is the suffusion of sophistical thinking applied to problems of the conscience. Julie in particular becomes a constant and truly remarkable casuist. She uses casuistry against others, to make them do as she wishes, and against herself, to rationalize her feelings and actions. This is another evidence of the principal lack at Clarens—honesty and sincerity.

There is an essential unity not only in Rousseau's works, but also between his work and personality, a unity of dynamic tensions and polarities. Political life and personal life, at Clarens, are governed by the same principles and the same tactics. The system of behavioral control operates on three levels—the plebes, the children, the chosen few. The basic method—deception and self-deception under a heroic profession of sincerity—suffuses the *Confessions*. Rousseau could not help transposing into his artificial world the way of confronting reality and of protecting his ego that he used in real life. In the strategies and subtleties that govern the personal relations at Clarens, such as those between Julie and Claire, do we not recognize the intricate mentality that conducted the intrigues over the wider checkerboard at the Hermitage? The richest and most subtle of Rousseau's works, *La Nouvelle Héloïse* combines his subjective world of personal experience and longings with the abstract world of his rationalistic writings.

Saint-Preux's and Julie's failure to find happiness shows that Rousseau is unable to resolve the human problem in a totalitarian society, which Clarens is. Here we have already the paradox and problem of Rousseau's democracy, the ideal of freedom and the monistic discipline of a single right way. The crushing of the personality and its dynamism warps all the characters into robots of virtue concealing unconscious hypocrisy and latent revolt. None of the three who are in love, despite their professions of confidence, can really count on himself. Julie does not even think that Wolmar (a man-god according to Saint-Preux, like Rousseau's Lawgiver) can: "What spectator prompts his secret good acts?" In Wolmar's realm of order, everything is in repressed disorder.

Nobody is *really* happy in this realm of happiness—not Julie, not Saint-Preux, not Claire. The impoverishment and denial of the self are so punishing that Julie gives up happiness as something that can exist only as a dynamic and ever-unfulfilled quest; its apparent realization according to preconceived definitions is only its inevitable frustration. The conflicts between nature and cultural repression, the cause of neuroses and unhappiness, have not been eliminated or pacified; on the contrary, they have been exacerbated. The erotic drives and the need for order have been harmonized only tenuously, on a shallow surface. Wolmar has not realized Rousseau's aim, to reconcile passion and virtue, "to make man one."

*La Nouvelle Héloïse* abounds in ambiguities, which explains why it has been interpreted in different ways by different generations. Rousseau surely believes that love and natural desires are good of themselves. The trouble is that in society they are not *by* themselves. If we insist on considering them as self-justifying ends, they disrupt all else. Disorder and unhappiness ensue. And yet, if such a love is frustrated, the ego is warped and crushed, and disorder results again. Saint-Preux was right when he said that the impulse of the heart is invincible; "to put yourself in a position where you must resist it is to court disaster."[15] This is the moral dilemma of the book, and Rousseau cannot work his way out of it. Julie falls from goodness or innocence only to rise to virtue, and then only to verge on falling again. Love and passion are praised and damned, associated with virtue and divorced from it. Nature and cultural norms seem to be now right, now wrong. "Opinion" is condemned time and again as false prejudice, and the independence of the conscience is proclaimed; but often enough, the reverse is upheld. Happiness is made the criterion of acts, only to have duty replace it when they are found incompatible; but sometimes they are incompatible and sometimes they are not. In the end all choose virtue, duty, and culture over the egoism of passion (a choice which is not "natural," but is natural in a "true" society)—and all are unhappy.

Rousseau's obsession with order, unity, and harmony towers above the ambiguities. Order stands out as an absolute. But in the human world there are few absolutes, except in the mind. The dialectic of contradiction is the human condition and the condition of growth and evolution. Rousseau cannot live with this human truth. To live in uncertainty is anguish for him. He wants neither contradiction nor the process of change. He would like to be outside of time, and would like society to escape from history, into which it "fell" when it began. This would be a release and a triumph. Feeling his own inner disorder and uncertainties, he attempts a flight from psychic anguish in his work. The constant recurrence of words like "order," "control," "direct," and "form" is more than an answer to the social problem; it is a response to his own inner conflicts and disorder. "My passions have made me live, and my passions have killed me," he writes in the *Confessions*, adding that the passions were trivial and puerile, yet all-powerful. They were powerful enough to impel him to satisfy them or to exorcise them in his writings. The conflicts he could not resolve for himself are the very ones he tried to resolve for the world. Will against temperament, independence against dependence, masculine against feminine elements, nature against culture, emotion against reason—all these were his conflicts, and they are the conflicts that beset his hapless characters in *La Nouvelle Héloïse*. This is why his life and work together pose the problem of existence, and why he could give no clear answer, for he could not solve in his fictitious or sublimated world what baffled and rent him in his real life.

Rousseau's problems are entwined with his basic personality disturbances. Passion animated him, but he feared and condemned passion. His acute sensuality was erotic, and regressively erotic, strongest in the oral and olfactory areas. He reacted to his shame by an evasion into a fictitious realm of nonphysical sensuality, a sensuality that sublimated itself into a passion for virtue. Some of his favorite phrases, "calm sensuality," "voluptuousness of angels," "intoxication of virtue," describe such a self-induced state. It was the hoped-for terminus of his love affairs, for it would annul all taint of guilt. It was also the evasion that justified his failure to take the active role with women. In relating the incident with Mme. Basile, for instance, he writes: "The possession of women has never made me feel anything that equaled the two minutes I spent at her feet without daring even to touch her dress."

Both physical and nonphysical sensuality represent an expansion of the self, unity with the other and with the world. Although Rousseau limited these results by a separation of the two forms of sensuality (and he did so specifically in the later *Dialogues*), he conceived of their union as the highest satisfaction. Unfortunately, he could not attain a nonsensual voluptuousness without cheating his "ardent sexuality." There seemed to be no woman with whom both needs could be fulfilled through reciprocal experience, no woman to whom he could give both his soul and his body. With Mme. de Warens and Mme. d'Houdetot the play-element was missing; with Thérèse and Mme. de Larnage, the moral dimension was impossible. Perhaps Mlle. Galley would have been perfect! At least he dreamed it, in dreaming Julie d'Etange. Total love requires a total confrontation between man and woman, and Rousseau was the seeker of absolutes. But frustration was inevitable. The total woman was a threat to his security and his ego-defenses; he became figuratively impotent before her. Her demands for satisfaction filled him with fear or even aversion, and he tended to seek a "spiritual" escape or to identify with the feminine role. It is only when he divided her into parts and symbolized her as physical or moral that he could cope with her, for then he no longer felt the threat of a too-demanding, total confrontation.

In Rousseau's own day, his reputation was based largely on *La Nouvelle Héloïse* and *Emile*. The popularity of *La Nouvelle Héloïse* among eighteenth-century readers was probably due more than anything else to the novelty of its lyrical *amour-passion* in an age of cynicism about love; to its wild and grandiose landscapes, its unashamed eloquence, and perhaps also to curiosity about its author's personal life. There may be still another explanation. Rousseau led his readers into a dark and complex world where the conscious and the unconscious intermingle, even as they truly do in the psyche, a world of troubled consciences, inner conflicts, and psychological ambiguities. Nowhere had eighteenth-century readers encountered such an experience, and they may not have been aware of all the reasons for its fascination. Whether or not this be so, it is doubtless the major reason for the novel's renewed life among twentieth-century readers. We must emphasize its astonishingly modern quality, not in its form, to be sure, but in its psychology, which is far in advance of other novels of its period, even in advance of Stendhal. From the aesthetic viewpoint, *La Nouvelle Héloïse* is a bad novel, but it is a great book. When we recall that Rousseau wrote to Mme. de la Tour (May 29, 1762), "If I imagine aright the hearts of Julie and Claire, they were transparent to each other," we realize how a writer may be unaware of important dimensions of his own work. He may not know how much the sway of its autonomous dynamism and his unconscious self-projection and catharsis has left to the discovery of future generations. As it so often happens with great books, Rousseau put far more into his creation—more of himself, more of his truth—than he knew, plunging into deep and unexplored regions of the soul, into the "misty mid-region of Weir."

# III. Strange Vicissitudes

J E A N - J A C Q U E S completes the tenth book of his *Confessions* on a somber note of recollected foreboding. He will continue to tell his story, but without access to his file of letters which (quite selectively, as we know) had guided his steps along the uncertain path of time gone by. The keenness of his memories, he assures us, will in great measure compensate for the loss. "They are such, in this cruel period, and I have kept so strong an impression of them, that I cannot forget the details of my first shipwreck, although what happened is confused in my recollection."[1]

That shipwreck—not the first, but the most calamitous—was not to come about for another year and a half. The first half of 1761 was a time of relative euphoria, marred only by Rousseau's self-torment and physical illness. Disaster came later.

Although reaction from some quarters was unfavorable, even bitterly hostile, *La Nouvelle Héloïse* was an immediate, unmatched popular success. On January 24, the Genevan government forbade its distribution by lending libraries. But only four days later the French publisher Robin put his unauthorized edition on sale, and Rey's second printing was out within a week. Evenhandedly, the Genevans ordered Voltaire's surreptitious blast, *Lettres à M. de Voltaire sur "La Nouvelle Héloïse,"* destroyed.

In France, town and Court, the Academy and the booksellers—all were thrown into a state of excitement by the sensational novel. By and large, Rousseau's generation, like the one that followed, was entranced by the passion and the problems of Julie and Saint-Preux. Most recognized his moralizing intent. Literary men, however, were more critical than the public, and *philosophes*, as well as theologians, resented his attacks on their own interests. Some critics ridiculed the novel's lack of verisimilitude, calling it ridiculous.

[ 99 ]

In general, the intellectual elite found the novel offensive to good taste and morality.² An anonymous letter published in Geneva in 1762 accused Rousseau of trying to subvert the nation's morals "by confusing every idea of decency and propriety; by offering us as models characters who are false, vicious in their maxims, extravagant in their behavior."³

Grimm, as may be expected, attacked the novel savagely in his secret *Correspondance littéraire*. After calling Jean-Jacques "a clever and eloquent sophist" who sweeps you away by "the charm of his eloquence," he goes on to describe *La Nouvelle Héloïse* as a book filled with the love of paradox and "the bitterness and peevishness with which its author is obsessed." Everyone, he affirms, can see "the absurdity of the story, the lack of plan, the poverty of execution which make this novel, despite the bombast of its style, a very flat work." Its characters act in exact opposition to reasonable people. Who can be interested in his pedantic Julie and her pitiful preceptor? "This bluestocking is a cruel prude who goes to bed with her teacher hoping he will give her a child and, when this fails, marries a certain Russian, an atheist and a gentleman, as a result of reflection and to please her father." She has the effrontery to spend the night with her lover in her own father's house, "a cheek which the most dissolute creature would not dare to have." The characters are all "almost crazy and out of their minds." Lack of genius, bad taste, the stamp of falsity, platitudes and coarseness, consistent misanthropy, a monotonous, heavy, bombastic style, obviously that of a sophist and misanthrope—every possible defect is to be found in this work, "one of the worst novels in a long time."⁴

This hatchet job was surpassed only by Voltaire. Protecting himself, as he so often did, by writing under another's name (this time, the "Marquis de Ximenez"), in February 1761 he published four *Lettres à M. de Voltaire sur "La Nouvelle Héloïse."* He even wrote to friends asking them to let him know who was the author of the pamphlet! Pitilessly Voltaire makes fun first of Rousseau's bad taste, bad style, and emphatic rhetoric, and then of the action and the characters. His biting irony is at its best, but sometimes gives way to ill-concealed venom. The second letter ends:

Never has a whore [Julie] preached more, and never has a valet-seducer of virgins been more of a philosopher. Jean-Jacques has found the happy secret of putting into this beautiful six-volume novel three or four pages of facts and about one thousand moral discourses. It is neither *Télémaque* nor the *Princesse de Clèves*, nor *Zaïde*: it is pure JEAN-JACQUES.⁵

Rousseau, begins the third letter, had no intention of writing a novel. "That kind of work, however frivolous, requires genius, and especially the art of preparing events, of linking them to each other, of knotting and unknotting a plot." But no one reads this boring book. In the last letter, Voltaire uses his own inimitable narrative skill to imagine an incident in which Rousseau was roughed up by some musicians, offended by what he had written about French music. Escaping to one of those garrets "where he says you can best learn the manners of the city," he finds the same prostitute from whom he had learned the secrets of what he calls *"la petite vérole."** The letter ends with a recital of Jean-Jacques' contradictions. This is the best of Voltaire's barbs: "He went to Geneva to abjure the Catholic religion in order to live in France." But "we must forgive a poor man with a deranged mind . . . it is better to ignore him than to beat him."

Voltaire's private letters were no less biting. "One of the infamies of this century was to have applauded the success of this monstrous work for a time. . . . Jean-Jacques' novel? In my opinion it is stupid, impudent, boring; but it has a fine piece on suicide which gives you an urge to die."[6] "The hero of Jean-Jacques," he quipped, "is a tutor who takes his pupil's virginity for his wages."[6] Not all the *philosophes* approved of Voltaire's slashing strokes. D'Alembert protested, and Grimm said that such gross insults only helped the enemy.

Mme. Necker, the unromantic wife of Louis XVI's minister of finance, later condemned the work as immoral. "Nothing is less moral than an edifice of virtue built on the debris of vice." Richardson was far more moral, she argues, in having Clarissa's disobedience to her father lead not just to remorse, but to disaster, while Rousseau shows a guilty woman enjoying "all the good things that belong to an innocent life." The trouble, it seems to Mme. Necker, is that in *La Nouvelle Héloïse* the charm of passion comes out in stronger colors than the sweetness of innocence; Saint-Preux is a seducer, nothing less. "Rousseau put morality in his book, but it is not a moral work." Mme. Necker also blames Jean-Jacques' love for women of a higher rank than his, and his tendency to see vice only in violent and premeditated acts, never in weakness. She was perceptive on all counts.

None of these strictures, however merited, affected the vast reading public. They were as touched and enraptured by the long sermons as by the sentimentality; both appealed to the aspect of the times that delighted in Richardson's novels and the *comédie larmoyante*. Rousseau took up the great problems which concerned them: love, marriage, family, education, household economy, government in a larger sense, relations between men, death. In brief, the reaction to the book was deeply emotional. For most readers Rousseau touched the heart and preached the morality of the heart. He was deluged with letters. A few were hostile (he was a corruptor of morals), most were favorable, many were worshiping. One wrote from Geneva: "I have devoured the six volumes, I am rereading them with rapture. This book should never come to an end. I have shed delicious tears."[7]

---

* Smallpox; ironically intended for *"la vérole,"* syphilis.

It was a book for women, and they loved it. Through Saint-Preux, they fell in love with Jean-Jacques. The Dauphine demanded to have it instantly. Few believed, or wanted to believe, that these were imaginary beings. The Duchesse de Polignac wrote to Mme. de Verdelin begging for a portrait of the heroine. "What a book, my dearest! and what a soul one must have to write it! . . . Everyone tells me that it is so with the *Citoyen*, and I wish to believe it. So sensitive, virtuous, and delicate a soul honors mankind. . . . Julie, dying, was no longer a stranger to me: I thought myself her sister, her friend, her Claire . . . if I hadn't left off reading, I should have felt as ill as all those who surrounded that virtuous woman in her last moments."[8] The Maréchale de Luxembourg was of the same opinion. "Your *Julie* is the most beautiful book in the world. Only a soul like yours could have written it."[9] The booksellers could not supply enough copies. Rousseau himself tells how the Princesse de Talmont missed the great ball at the Opéra because she began the new book and stayed up all night reading it.[10] This has always made him wish to meet her, he comments, because one could not be so entranced by his novel "without having that sixth sense, that moral sense with which so few hearts are endowed, and without which none can understand mine." But Mme. du Deffand, who was Voltaire's close friend and who disliked Jean-Jacques, condemned it as "an ocean of turgid eloquence" and as "contrary to good morals."[11]

One amusing tidbit was Jean-Jacques' answer to a gushing admirer who invited him to have coffee with her, using as a lure the promise to let him drink out of a gold-encrusted cup given to her by Voltaire. "I shall gladly visit you and take coffee with you," he replied; "but not, if you please, in the gilded cup of M. de Voltaire, for I do not drink out of that man's cup."[12]

The very pleased author had praise from men, too. D'Alembert was as ever courteous, if not entirely sincere. "That eloquence of the heart, that fire, that life which characterize your works shine especially in this one, which, I think, is bound to put the seal on your reputation. . . . The critics will fall silent and the work will remain."[13] Elsewhere he expressed a more moderate opinion.[14] Jacques Necker apparently did not share his wife's view. He wrote to Jean-Jacques, exclaiming about the sublimity of his novel.[15] Moultou, in Geneva, was ecstatic. "O Julie! O Saint-Preux! O Edouard! In what globe dwell your souls, and how may I be united to you!"[16]

On March 7 another work of Rousseau's, his condensation of the Abbé de Saint-Pierre's *Projet de paix perpétuelle*, came out. Deleyre, enthusiastic as usual, was sure that the English would take the lead in putting the peace scheme into effect, but foresaw some difficulties arising from religious and colonial rivalries. What Rousseau should do next, he urged, was devise a plan to reconcile the Protestant and Catholic churches.[17] Rousseau was not interested in squaring that circle. Vernes was more skeptical. "I fear, my dear friend, that French music will continue despite your letter [*Lettre sur la musique française*], sciences will spoil men despite your discourse, and war ravage the world despite your project; but at least you are teaching men and it is not your fault if they shut their ears to your lessons."[18] When Vernes complained that Wolmar, being an atheist, could not be a good man, Rousseau replied that one of his purposes in *La Nouvelle Héloïse* was to reconcile the two parties, *philosophes* and *dévots*, "by teaching the *philosophes* that one can believe in God without being a hypocrite, and the believers that one can be a freethinker without being a scoundrel."[19]

The *philosophes* were less than enthusiastic about this latest production, too. Grimm's thrust was clean and hard.[20] "This project has become under his pen more absurd than in the work of its author. No profound insights, no notions of politics, no idea that would at least make you dream about the idle fancy in a pleasant and touching way." But how could an "austere misanthrope," who has made it his task "to make men's lives hateful to them," serve as interpreter for the gentle and worldly Abbé de Saint-Pierre? Both men belong in the insane asylum, but at different ends, and the abbé's kind of madness is a good deal more pleasant. More soberly, Grimm argues that the project, if "carried out according to Jean-Jacques Rousseau's gospel, would put peoples under the sword of the most unlimited despotism and plunge them into an unheard of slavery."

Voltaire told his friends that he would say nothing in public. This time it was he who warned d'Alembert that such tactics would only divide "the little flock."[21] Private letters were something else. "So there is Jean-Jacques become a politician," he writes mockingly to a friend; "we shall see whether he will govern Europe the way he governed the house of Mme. de Wolmar. He is a strange madman."[22] Indeed; but no less strange is Voltaire's obsessional preoccupation with this madman. On every possible occasion he breaks out against him. "Jean-Jacques is a *jean-f...*,"* he exclaims again to d'Alembert, "who writes every two weeks to those priests to agitate them against the theater. Deserters who fight against their country should be hanged."[23] More elegantly, to Mme. d'Epinay: "As for Jean-Jacques, he is only a despicable wretch who has abandoned his friends and who deserves to be abandoned by everyone. In his heart he has only the vanity of displaying himself in the remains of Diogenes' barrel and of stirring up passers-by to make them stare at his pride and his rage. 'Tis a pity, for he was born with some *demi-talents*, and he might have had real talent if he had been docile and honest."[24]

Jean-Jacques knew nothing of these hostile reactions. He was more concerned about the feeling that he was losing favor with Mme. de

---

* *Jean-foutre*, a somewhat vulgar expression, signifying a person who cannot be counted on.

Luxembourg since he had nothing more to read to her. He thought that
a telling sign of her disaffection was her failure to insist that he sit next
to her at table. He noticed a decline in their conversation. In later
recollection, the fact that she asked him about Grimm but never told
him whether or not she knew him seemed a sure sign of double-dealing.
More and more he gravitated toward the duke's end of the table, joined
him in long afternoon walks through the forest of Montmorency, and
grew closer to him, consoling him for the grievous family losses he had
suffered—sister, daughter, son, and grandson. Rousseau was particularly
angered by the grandson's unnecessary death, which he ascribed (and it
was not unlikely) to the starvation diet imposed by the doctor. He
protested and pleaded, on occasion even fed the child, and reflected on
the misery of the great as he watched this scion of the highest nobility
"devour a little piece of bread with the greediness of a beggar."[25] He
was saddened to watch the aging maréchal's health broken by these
bereavements and his own increasing infirmities.

Everywhere he saw signs of hostility in the Luxembourgs' entourage.
He blamed the young Abbé de Boufflers (later the Chevalier de
Boufflers), whose clever wit discountenanced him and who, he was sure,
was trying secretly to turn the maréchale against him. Rousseau attempted unsuccessfully to please Boufflers and win him over. Then he
committed the blunder of saying that a portrait Boufflers had done of
the maréchale, which she detested, was an excellent likeness. The recollection led him to reflect that he was born not to praise men, which he
always did maladroitly, but to tell them useful and harsh truths. Later
in the year came another blunder. Playing the role of Alceste, he told
Mme. de Boufflers that a play she had written was not too good, and that
it bore an extraordinary resemblance to an English work. Infuriated, she
protested vigorously. Jean-Jacques also tried unsuccessfully to become
friendly with the great *salonnière* Mme. du Deffand, one of the century's
most brilliant women. He could not stand her despotic ways, her admiration for scintillating conversation, and her friendship for Voltaire.
She disliked him even more, especially when she recognized his dislike
for her, and never missed an opportunity to vent her feelings in her
letters. "Jean-Jacques is repulsive to me," she was to write in 1764; "he'd
put everything into chaos. I have seen nothing more contrary to good
sense than his *Emile*, nothing more contrary to good morals than his
*Héloïse*, and nothing more boring and obscure than his *Social Contract*." And two years later: "Is there a sadder madman than that Jean-
Jacques?"[26]

Even Lorenzy was not to be trusted. Was he not d'Alembert's friend
and the constant companion of the Comtesse de Boufflers, who was also
d'Alembert's friend? Everyone was working against him, but still the
maréchale, though increasingly bored with him, maintained their
friendship. He made her his confidante, he relates, told her all about

Thérèse and what he had done with their children. Far from shocked, she pampered Thérèse with little gifts. Then, he relates, she offered to search for one of his lost children.

Once again Jean-Jacques has rearranged the facts slightly. The *Confessions* would lead us to think that this offer preceded his imminent illness and that it was voluntary. Neither inference is true. Rousseau's chronic suffering returned in aggravated form in June, not in the autumn, as he apparently remembers it. On June 12, believing himself near death, he wrote to Mme. de Luxembourg, confessing his wrongs and asking her to search for his first child, the only one whom he had left with a mark of identification, at the orphanage. "For several years now, remorse for my negligence has troubled my tranquillity and I am dying without being able to make amends. . . . The ideas with which my fault has filled my mind have contributed in large part to making me plan the *Treatise on Education*." He closes his letter with sentimental solemnity: "Adieu, my dear and affectionate friends. Love my memory a little. As for me, I hope to love you still in the next life; but however that dark and dreadful mystery may turn out, wherever death overtakes me, I am sure it will find me thinking of you."

The search was unsuccessful, and Rousseau was forced to give up making amends. It has been speculated that the investigation may have uncovered the child's identity, a certain Joseph Catherine Rousseau, deceased, and that the Luxembourgs decided to keep this information from the supposedly dying Rousseau. There is no sound factual basis for this supposition. Rousseau was more relieved than disappointed. His conscience was to some extent assuaged, and he had never been sure about his desire. If the child had been found, he admits, he would always have doubted whether they had not given him another in place of his own.[27]

Meanwhile his malady grew more severe. The maréchal persuaded him to let Frère Côme, renowned for his method of extracting kidney stones, treat him. He considered it a mark of true friendship that the duke stood by while Côme probed him three times, a torture that lasted several hours. Côme's diagnosis was doubtless accurate. There was no stone, but the prostate was enlarged and had a fibroid tumor.

Rousseau managed to continue his work. Word of the forthcoming publication of *Emile* was spreading. Geneva knew about it. "There is no object worthier of your superior talents," an acquaintance assured him, "nor one which better expresses the great views you have in mind for mankind."[28] He must have been pleased to learn that the people of Geneva had acclaimed him noisily during a festival, on June 5, to the undoubted displeasure of the oligarchy. On June 23, d'Alembert wrote that he had heard about *Emile* and was impatiently waiting to see it. By December 30, Mme. de la Tour was able to write that *"tout Paris"* was saying that *Emile* was about to appear. The report was premature, and the whole process of publication was to be a great torment to Jean-Jacques, a torment intertwined with his physical and psychological suffering.

Turk, Jean-Jacques' dog, had been put down in July, and he was deeply depressed by this event. The duke and duchess, Prince de Conti, Comtesse de Boufflers, all sent their condolences, with real sympathy combined with a great effort at seriousness. "What news have I learned! I share your grief, I myself am in despair. Poor Turk! What a pity!"

Rousseau's drive to finish his projects was not to be deterred by illness or bereavement. The pride he placed in his work and the personal importance it had for him were incitements not to be denied. *Emile*, like *La Nouvelle Héloïse*, was truly an extension of himself. Pride was adulterated by incessant regrets, to be sure. "I've tried the path of glory; all my writings have been successful; no living man of letters, not even Voltaire, has had more brilliant moments than I. And yet I assure you that from the moments I began to publish, my life has been only grief, anguish, and pain of all kinds."[29] He had a second motive for finishing: he was counting on *Emile* and *The Social Contract* (much less on the uncompleted *Dictionnaire de musique*) to buy a life annuity and to retire with Thérèse to some distant province where he would forget the public and write his memoirs (for some future public).

With this in mind, he informed Rey in August that his treatise on political theory was ready for publication. Rey could have it for one thousand francs and the promise to print this, "the last work that will come from my hand," on beautiful paper. On August 29 he received a contract for *Emile*. Duchesne was to publish it in Paris, Néaulme in Holland. That had been arranged by the maréchale, with Malesherbes' agreement. Despite the unorthodox section on religion, the *Profession de foi*, Rousseau was not worried about an untoward reaction from the civil or ecclesiastical authorities. He laughed at the concern of Guérin, Duchesne's associate, and was unruffled when Duclos, to whom he read the *Profession*, asked him never to mention to anyone that he had. After all, Malesherbes was director of publications, and had he not extended his approval and protection?

Rey comes in for a word of praise at this point in Rousseau's story. Minimizing the distrustful and harsh letters he had sent Rey during the printing of the *Lettre à d'Alembert*, he says that of all his publishers, Rey is the only one about whom he has never had to complain in regard to his scrupulous honesty. Anticipating a bit, he tells how Rey, quietly and on his own initiative, gave Thérèse a life annuity of three hundred francs, in gratitude for what Rousseau's writings had done for him. Jean-Jacques was more touched by this gesture than by the noisy but empty zeal of many highborn self-proclaimed benefactors. "Was it their fault or was it mine?" He calls on us, the readers, to judge. "Are they only vain, or am I only an ingrate? Wise reader, weigh, decide; as for me, I shall say nothing."[30] The rhetorical appeal, with its concealed prejudgment, is one of Rousseau's devices as he places himself before the bar of justice, the Areopagus composed of all mankind, and pleads his cause.

Rey's gift was especially welcome because Jean-Jacques was worried about Thérèse's inability to keep track of money or to control her expenditures. This is one of her faults, he asserts—she has no vices. Truthfully, he complains about his enemies' malicious allegations that he took money given to her. Just as with Maman, all his efforts to build a sum against the future were always frustrated by Thérèse's simpleminded lack of care.

Thérèse, who was often left alone during the long hours when Jean-Jacques was working in his "donjon," had made friends with a mason's daughter. Often he lunched with the nobility and supped with the mason and his family.[31] It is tempting to try to imagine how he felt in each milieu.

As Rousseau's malady became more acute, his general unhappiness and suspiciousness intensified. On August 12, as we have seen, he told Dom Deschamps that he was "ensnared in the traps of perfidy." On October 17 he informed the Benedictine that he was working and walking around with a probe in him, without which micturition was impossible. He refers in letters to his pain and languishing state. He tells Dom Deschamps that he owes his life to his "housekeeper," as he calls Thérèse. She was indeed assiduous in her care for him, despite the unpleasantness of the tasks his condition involved.

Rousseau's state of mind is revealed when he asks Rey to begin Thérèse's pension, on a reduced basis, on January 1, 1763, instead of after his death. He added a note to *La Nouvelle Héloïse*, to the effect that the expectation of an inheritance could lead a person to make a horrible wish. Was he thinking that Thérèse, by her own instinct or advised by her family, might hasten his death?[32] No, he assures Rey on January 23, 1762, "the poor girl's heart is too good to long for the time when she would enjoy her annuity." Still, he prefers the other arrangement. When Rey asks for more information about Thérèse, he immediately suspects that Rey thought he planned to take some of the money for himself. "If that's what you are thinking, you can keep your gifts," he warns. He will accept no gifts, no charity.

In October he had started to worry about *Emile*. He asks Duchesne why he was beginning with the second volume. Had he lent the first manuscript volume to some one?[33] Duchesne is not to be trusted. An incident on November 6 disturbed him. Duvoisin, the chaplain of the Dutch embassy in Paris, was taking Rousseau's manuscript of *The Social Contract* to Rey, together with a corrected and annotated copy of *La Nouvelle Héloïse*. The gates to Paris were guarded by inspectors. Duvoisin dropped the manuscript, the inspector leafed through it, and returned it only when Duvoisin demanded it in the name of the ambassador. Duvoisin then read it. That work was no longer a secret, then.

Soon after, Jean-Jacques became possessed by a genuine obsession. He was aware of it but unable to control it. "For some time dark and sad forebodings were upsetting me without my knowing what they were about. I received strange anonymous letters and even signed letters which were no less strange."[34] One fact stood out: half a year had gone by since he had given his manuscript to Duchesne, and there was no sign of a book. And he had lost possession of his manuscript. All his efforts to get a clear explanation seemed to fail. Never, declares Rousseau, did misfortune upset him if he understood it; "but my natural tendency is to fear the darkness, I fear and hate its *air noir*; mysteriousness always disturbs me."[35] Several times, in *Emile*, the *Rêveries*, and his letters, Jean-Jacques expresses his fear of darkness or of a face hidden under a white sheet. "All the images of plotting and persecution which abound in the *Dialogues* will be images of mystery and darkness."[36] As he put it in a famous letter to Saint-Germain (February 26, 1770), "they built around me an impenetrable edifice of darkness." Light, clarity, and transparency are the images of happiness.

He knew that the Jesuits did not like him. Guérin was devoted to them, as was Malesherbes' father, the Chancellor Lamoignon de Malesherbes, Choiseul, and Mme. de Pompadour. "Everywhere I saw only Jesuits." He became certain that Guérin had betrayed him and given them the manuscript of *Emile*. He appealed to Malesherbes for help on November 18: Duchesne was only pretending to print *Emile*—that was why he had sent so few proof pages. Either the Jesuits wanted to suppress the work, Rousseau explained, or else they were waiting for him to die in order to put out a completely falsified edition.

Rousseau sent an accusatory letter to Duchesne, but when some printed proofs arrived, he wrote back on November 20 offering a half-apology. "My preceding letter is unintelligible if you have done no wrong, in which case I am in the wrong, although your negligence is not undeserving of blame. Time will clarify everything and will destroy or confirm the suspicions which your procedure has given me." If he turns out to be wrong, Rousseau promises to forfeit one hundred écus on his contract. On the same day he apologized, in a quite different tone, to Malesherbes, and begged him to keep his letter a secret if it was not already too late.

Ah! Monsieur! I have done an abominable thing! I fear it, or rather I hope it; for it is a hundred times better that I should be a madman, a fool worthy of your disfavor, and that there should be one more honest man on earth. Nothing is changed since the day before yesterday, but everything looks different to me and I no longer see anything but uncertain signs where I thought I saw the clearest proofs. Oh, how cruel it is for an ill and depressed hermit to have a disordered imagination and not to be able to find out what he wants to know!

On the twenty-fourth a probe broke off, leaving part of it in the neck of his bladder. The cruelty of his suffering was accompanied by a rebound of his paranoid obsession. He writes again to Malesherbes on the thirtieth, suggesting that Duchesne either return his manuscript, fix a date for its publication, or allow him to make a contract with a new publisher. Failing this, he will have to take other measures.

Both Malesherbes and the maréchale tried to reassure him. Malesherbes' letter of December 7 was not entirely honest. He "doubts" that Duchesne has a secret agreement with Néaulme (although he knew there was such an agreement); he "has reason to believe" that *Emile* is not being printed in Paris (but he knew it was). At all events, the letter failed to accomplish its purpose. On December 10 off went another letter to Malesherbes, reiterating Rousseau's conviction that there was a plot to substitute another book for his. On the twelfth he dispatched a long letter to Moultou, in Geneva. He tells his friend that the manuscript of *Emile*, "the most useful, best and last of my writings," is forever lost, suppressed by a plot; his publisher has tried to delude him into thinking that the book was being printed, while the Jesuits were reworking it in anticipation of his death. Try to imagine, he asks Moultou, the effect on a poor, lonely, dying man "who has perhaps sought fame too avidly, but who has at least sought it only in writings useful to his fellow men." He has only justice and right on his side, and they are of scant use in a world run by the powerful. He now proposes, in the brief time left, to rewrite the entire work from his sketch and confide it to Moultou, whom he also charges with making a public protest when the false *Emile* comes out. How he would like to go back to Geneva, to die in "that beloved land where I have not been able to live."

Nonetheless, he rejected Roguin's suggestion that he travel incognito to Switzerland. "Rousseau I am and Rousseau I shall remain, no matter what the risk." The next day he informs Malesherbes that he is withdrawing his request for secrecy; there can no longer be any doubt about the plot. An ambiguous statement in a letter from Duchesne to Rey, which the latter had transmitted to him, makes it clear that Duchesne is controlled. "My book is lost," he writes to the maréchale, "the Jesuits have seized it."

Malesherbes made a thorough investigation and tried to calm him with a rational explanation for the delays. Expressing his regret for Rousseau's "*violentes agitations*," which he attributes to an author's concern intensified by solitude and illness, he speaks to Jean-Jacques quite frankly: "Allow me to tell you that I think I have seen your soul quite completely in the several letters you have written me on this matter. I have seen the succession of anxiety, suspicion, and then remorse for unjust suspicions . . . I have concluded from half of your letters that you are the most honest of men, and from the other half that you are the most unhappy."[37]

It was difficult to keep secrets in a scandal-hungry society. "They are saying that . . . you are on bad terms with your publisher," wrote Mme.

de Verdelin. "Your book is awaited with an impatience and interest such as I have never seen."[38] Soothed, Jean-Jacques again apologized to Duchesne: "My wrongs towards you are great, and not only towards you."[39] One day later, he wrote a letter to Moultou that he would never send. He no longer knows what to believe and so is finishing the new copy of the *Profession de foi* just in case. He does know that death is at hand, if not from his illness, then by his own hand.

It's all over, dear Moultou; we shall never see each other again except in the dwelling place of the just. . . . You will understand that the profession of faith of the Savoyard vicar is my own. I desire too strongly that there be a God not to believe in him, and I die firmly confident that I shall find in his bosom the happiness and peace that I have not been able to enjoy down here. I have always loved my country and my fellow-citizens dearly; I dare to expect from them some sign of kindness toward my memory.[40]

The sign he asks for is protection for Thérèse, so that she should not spend the rest of her days in lonely poverty. One thing makes it hard for him to die. "These last six weeks I have done nothing but villainies, imagining only calumnies against two honest publishers. I do not know what blindness, what somber melancholy, inspired by a frightful malady in the midst of solitude, has made me invent this tissue of horrors to blacken my life and the honor of others."

Frantic in his remorse, as in his terror-filled accusations, he touches depths of self-abasement such as he had not indulged in since the slow and bitter parting from Maman. I am no longer worthy of your friendship, he writes to Malesherbes on December 23.

I shudder as I open my eyes to myself and see myself as despicable as I have become. Become? No. The man who for fifty years has lived with the heart I now feel reborn in me is not the same man who was able to forget himself to the point that I have done. One does not beg for pardon at my age because one no longer deserves it. Sir, I take no interest in the man who has usurped and dishonored my name; but he is dead and will not be reborn.

These lines reveal the same unhappy Jean-Jacques we have known from the early years, the man who dissociates his "true self" from his acts, which are impulsive and uncontrollable, but never ill-intentioned, and so never wicked. Yet this is the man who affirms that "the first impulse of nature is always right," and who considers himself the unique exemplar of nature freed from the corruptions of social degeneracy. What we really see, as so often before, is the catharsis of guilt.*

Malesherbes' reaction to Rousseau's self-humiliation was characteristic

---

* Grimsley comments that Rousseau believed his fame and personal reputation to rest on *Emile*, the "objective embodiment of his ideal self." In his mind, this, not the public figure seen by his contemporaries, was his real self. "Rousseau also acknowledges that the other's hostile gaze has the power to disturb his peace of mind by arousing in him an awkwardness and embarrassment which add still further to the misrepresentation of his true personality" (R. Grimsley, *Jean-Jacques Rousseau: A Study in Self-awareness*, p. 168).

of him. Jean-Jacques is not wicked, he assures him, but "hypersensitive, melancholic, and inclined to see things in the blackest light." Consumed by bile, he sees horrors where Democritus would have laughed at human follies. His celebrity and strange way of life make him the subject of public talk, and he is not really displeased by that. His virtue is that he yields to truth and justice when he recognizes them.[41] After this candid assessment, Malesherbes promises to try to recover the wild letters written to Duchesne. His sincerity is attested by a simultaneous note to the Duchesse de Luxembourg. Enclosing Rousseau's letter to him, he comments: "You will see in it as in the rest of this affair the depths of his soul and that mixture of honesty, nobility, and at the same time of melancholy, sometimes of despair, which makes his life so tormented, but which has produced his works." And the maréchale's own sincerity is corroborated by her reply. "You are full of kindness and humaneness, Monsieur. Poor Rousseau needs them. . . . He deserves whatever you do for him."

On the same day (December 26), Rousseau received the first proofs of *The Social Contract*. On the thirty-first, he heard from Rey that *Emile* was being printed. Rey also asked him to do something he had long hoped for, something, he assured Jean-Jacques, that the public would relish—write his autobiography, to be placed at the head of an edition of his complete works. The idea appealed to Rousseau, but he gave no positive reply.

Doubtless because of the tensions of the moment—because of his illness, he claims—Rousseau returned a rude answer to de Brosses, a distinguished jurist, scholar, and belle-lettrist, who had invited him to write remonstrances for the Dijon Parlement. De Brosses had promised secrecy. We do not have Rousseau's reply, but he adds it to the list of actions about which he feels guilty, explaining that such a project was against his "principles" and may well have been a plot of his enemies to destroy him. De Brosses, after all, was on good terms with the Encyclopedists.[42] But Jean-Jacques, as usual, was to bring about his own debacle, without any connivance on the part of his enemies.

## 2. THE FIRST APOLOGIA

In Rousseau's psyche self-justification and justification in the eyes of the world were inseparable. Almost from the beginning of his story, they were a compulsion in his mind. Not only did the public (and Malesherbes) not know his real self, and consequently misjudge it; worse, they were being deliberately led astray by the malevolent connivings of his enemies. Of this he was to grow ever more convinced. He could not bear to leave "such an unjust opinion" of himself "in the minds of honest people."[43] Self-examination was imposed on him. His professed scorn for "opinion," and all the actions that expressed that scorn, were a futile effort to shake off the tyranny of his obsession. He now felt that he

had to justify himself in Malesherbes' eyes. His hysteria in regard to
Duchesne required it. Malesherbes' phrase, in his last letter (December
25) about his "singular way of life" was worrisome. His protector might
have been affected by the gossip circulated by the Encyclopedists.

For these reasons, as well as to catheterize his inner conflicts, Rousseau
composed a series of four letters which he sent to Malesherbes between
the fourth and the twenty-eighth of January. They form a self-portrait,
Jean-Jacques looking into a subjectively satisfying mirror.

The letters were part of a long process that was to occupy a major part
of Rousseau's remaining years, the effort to organize a coherent picture
of his personality. We must note that the basic mistrust in his self-
delineation, the basic doubt of the possibility of any relationship of
mutuality, unquestionably embody an element of infantile regression.
Doubtless he had the idea of an autobiography in the back of his mind.
While he expressed reluctance to Rey about it, on the ground that his
secrets were also the secrets of others, the idea appealed to him.[44] Rousseau promises Malesherbes that as he tries to explain why he has followed Alceste's example and withdrawn from human society, he will be
completely open. "I shall paint myself without make-up and without
modesty. I shall show myself to you as I see myself and as I am. . . .
Nobody knows me but myself alone." The opportunity for exhibitionism, as always, pleases him.

Why, then, had he withdrawn from the world? (Actually he had done
so only in a certain measure.) He has never wanted to be a misanthrope,
he declares in his first letter, nor is he trying (as was often said) to play
the role imposed by his fulminations against society. Such a course
would imply that public opinion was important to him. No, he affirms,
"I love my pleasure and my independence too dearly to be as much the
slave of vanity as they suppose." What more proof is needed than that
he waited forty years before making his talents known to the public?* It
was not hatred of men's injustice and wickedness that drove him away
from Paris—he is not that noble, either. His motive was his love of
solitude, "which has only increased as I have gotten to know men better," his preference for living in his fantasy world of "imaginary beings
with which I surround myself." But "others" could not understand him,
because they judged him as if he were one of them, instead of realizing
his uniqueness.

Rousseau, having blithely overlooked his own shortcomings and mal-
adjustments, broaches an important point, and in so doing reveals the
depth, if not necessarily the accuracy, of his introspection and self-
awareness. He had long attributed his unhappiness among men to his
discomposure and clumsy conversation (though he had no awareness of
their underlying causes), and also to the feeling that he did not occupy

---

* It had not been "forty years," nor a matter of "waiting."

in the world the place to which his merit entitled him. This was the correct explanation, but now he repudiates it. When he won fame he found that he was unhappier among men than before. And so it is necessary to search for another cause. Now he claims to have discovered the real reason for his unhappiness. He does not fit in, cannot fit in with other men because of an invincible need for freedom and independence, which comes in turn from an incredible laziness that makes writing a letter or paying a visit unbearable burdens. Freedom means not having to do whatever he has an aversion to doing, especially fulfilling the obligations of gratitude.

Rousseau, in coming to this conclusion, has protected himself by self-delusion from tearing away the "veil" (one of his word-fixations). "Laziness" was a symptom, not a cause; he was a prolific letter-writer and paid countless visits. The drive for independence was, we have seen, a compensation for dependency and feminine passivity. "An active life," he admits to Malesherbes, "has no temptations for me." Indolence, aversion to "duties," are excuses for withdrawal and narcissism.

He still has to explain how this "indolence" tallies with the search for fame that had impelled him to publish his writings over the last ten years. Here is an inner contradiction, not one between himself and the world. Rousseau begins his second letter (January 12) by going back to his childhood in order to explain his peculiar disposition, a contradictory combination of ardor, timidity, moroseness, and hypersensitivity. From his early years, he explains, he had lived in books and in fantasy, in a heroic and romantic world. That formation spoiled the real world for him, forever. People and things were never what he expected them to be. Everywhere he saw or felt the injustice of other men, and they led him to "disorders" of his own. Thus he learned that he could never fit into this world which he despised and that he could find happiness in his private, imaginary world. Then came the Crisis of Vincennes. He describes the mental and physical effects of that semimystical seizure or revelation in graphic lines that have become famous. No longer would his heart be in contradiction with his mind. Now he knew what he had to think, and do: free himself from the false opinions of men which had created their misery and wickedness. "Ah, monsieur, if I had been able to set down a quarter part of what I saw and felt under that tree, with what clarity would I have revealed all the contradictions of the social system, with what force would I have exposed all the abuses of our institutions, with what simplicity would I have shown that man is naturally good and that men become wicked by their institutions alone."*

---

* We must remember that in Rousseau's vocabulary, "naturally" refers to men (or prehumans) before they became social beings; and that social living develops their inherent evil potentialities which express themselves in their "institutions." If the latter become forces of corruption, then, it is only because of the evil which is already in men, but which the institutions develop.

Of all this wealth of ideas, he retained only those he developed in the two *Discourses* and *Emile,* "which three works are inseparable and together form a single whole."

And that is how he became a writer *malgré lui.* After his first success he was ensnared by fame and the barbs of critics. Yet he immediately knew one truth: "If I wanted to be consistent and once and for all shake the heavy yoke of opinion from my shoulders, I had not a moment to lose." Now that all the great trials have been passed, "it is forevermore proven to me by experience that my way of life is the only one in which man can live good and happy, since it is the most independent, and the only one in which one never finds himself having to hurt others for his own advantage."* At last he is free from those false friends who had wanted to reign over his life and make him happy in their way, instead of understanding his. Now he knows that nobody is better than he— indeed, he seems ready to confer moral superiority on himself, after all, inasmuch as his way of finding happiness is the best way.

Jean-Jacques would like next to tell about his happiness. This is the subject of the third letter, on January 26. He is proud of his wisdom, for he has sought the only happiness he could have, found it within the limits of the possible and to the greatest degree possible. How wrong then are Malesherbes and the public in judging him "the unhappiest of men"! If everyone knew the truth, they would rush to imitate him, men would no longer hurt each other, peace would reign. Utopia, Rousseau implies, need no longer be a dream. But what can a solitary enjoy?

Myself, the entire universe, all that is, all that can be, all that is beautiful in the world of perception, all that is imaginable in the world of intellect. I gathered around me all that could delight my heart; my desires were the limit of my pleasures. No, never have the greatest voluptuaries known such delights and I have enjoyed my fantasies a thousand times more than they their realities.

When he tosses in pain during long sleepless nights, the past comes back with its sweet recollections and its stinging regrets. Then he knows that in his life happiness lay not in an unrecoverable past, with its rare intervals of light in the somber texture of his memories, not in an illusory future, but in the immediacy of the present, in his solitary walks, in "days spent alone, with my good and simple-minded housekeeper, my beloved dog, my old cat, the birds of the field and the does of the forest, with all of nature and her inconceivable author." Only in this way lies release from anxiety. In all of this picture, Rousseau, it would appear, is endeavoring to shunt aside, for Malesherbes and probably for himself as well, the erotic obsessions which had haunted him throughout the composition of *La Nouvelle Héloïse* and *Emile,* and which had

---

* Isolation, at one extreme, fulfills this condition. At the other extreme, total control by the organic society will offer an alternative.

played so important a part in his life during these last years. Now he would like to exclude them from his innocent idyll.

There are no men, no women, in this picture. He dreads their approach. They would rupture the states of his own awareness. Happiness lies within himself alone. Within this tightly bound circle, his inner being, untrammeled and uninhibited, experiences infinite expansion. What joy when he reaches a certain spot in the forest of Montmorency beyond which he is sure no one will find him, and he is master of himself! Quickly he rushes to some wild sanctuary where nothing "revealing the hand of man announced servitude and domination." In this favorable environment, he can climb his own ladder of exaltation. First there is the rhapsody of nature's beauty all around him. From there he mounts to the rapture of close fellowship with people. None that he knew or had ever known intrudes into the exquisite harmony of his solitude. "I soon peopled it with beings according to my heart . . . with men worthy of inhabiting it." They had no care for "opinion," prejudices, or artificial passions.

I formed a charming society with them, of which I did not feel myself unworthy. I created a golden age according to my fantasy, and filling those beautiful days with all the scenes of my life that have left me sweet memories and with all others that my heart could desire, I melted into tears in the presence of mankind's true pleasures, pure, delicious pleasures, forevermore so far from men.

Exaltation is not yet concluded, for unity is not *completeness*, or the perfect realization of the self, external reality, and their relationship. It leads to the final height, a mystical paroxysm of union with the divine. He leaves the earth and reaches out to "the incomprehensible Being who includes everything." Now he will attain the spiritual orgasm, the achievement of completeness through the loss of self in an ecstatic union, as the female partner, with the universe.

Then, my mind lost in that immensity, I did not think, I did not reason, I did not philosophize. I felt myself crushed, with a kind of voluptuousness, by the weight of the universe. I surrendered myself with ravishment to the turmoil of these vast ideas, I exulted in losing myself, in my imagination, in space. My heart, confined within the limits of beings, was boxed up inside. I was stifling within the universe, I longed to soar away into infinity. I believe that if I had uncovered all of nature's mysteries I should have felt myself in a less rapturous state than in the vertigo of this ecstasy, to which my mind abandoned itself without restraints and which, in the commotion of my paroxysm, made me cry out at intervals: "O great Being! O great Being!" helpless to say or think ought else.

The paroxysm at an end, gentle fatigue and a contented calm accompany Jean-Jacques as he returns home to sup outdoors, feeling the communion of his little ménage and freedom from servitude and dependency. How different on days when people came to visit him! Then, as Thérèse remarked, he was sullen and ill-tempered.

One letter remained, dated January 28. You can see, he tells Malesherbes, that noble sentiments did not motivate my solitude—only the courage to do what I had to do to put my life in order. How many men can say as much? Now invective enters. As we have so often witnessed, he cannot dismiss other people, cannot cease to see himself through their eyes, cannot have a secure image of himself without their confirmation. Contrary to what his enemies charge, he now declares, he is more useful, even the peasants of Montmorency are more useful, to society, "than that heap of idlers who live off the fat of the people so that they can spend the week jabbering in an academy." His role is "to give men the example of life they should all lead." It is to sound the voice of truth from out of the depths of his retreat and to show them the error of their ways. Because he has freed himself from artificialities, he has retained or recovered man's natural goodness, and his estrangement has enabled him to draw lessons from it.

Rousseau descends from the sublime to petty recrimination and self-apology, then returns to self-analysis. "I have a loving heart, but one which can be self-sufficient." (Here indeed is a paradox.*) If he hates injustice, it is because he loves all men, "men in general." "It is because I love them that I fly from them; I suffer less from their hurts when I do not see them. This interest in the species is sufficient to nourish my heart. I do not need particular friends; but when I have them I have a great need not to lose them." Nor does he require to see his friends, but only to know that they love him; his friends of yesteryear had only put on a show of loving him. Only the Duc and Duchesse de Luxembourg have been true friends. There is a paradox in this. "I hate the great," he dares to tell Malesherbes, one of France's greatest nobles. "I hate their class, their hardness, their prejudices, their pettiness, and all their vices; and I should hate them still more if I despised them less." But for the Luxembourgs there is no sacrifice, however painful, he would not make, even "the only glory that ever meant anything to me, the honor I expect from posterity and which it will give me, because it is due to me and posterity is always just."

In this account Rousseau, as he will do in the *Confessions* in his relation of the years at Les Charmettes, telescopes an uneven, emotion-filled period into a simplified, rosy picture. We know that Rousseau was deeply disturbed and often depressed in his solitude. Not only were there lingering memories of shame, strife, and humiliation; he was troubled by the cooling-off of the "burning enthusiasm" for truth, liberty, and virtue that had stirred him when he lived in Paris—perhaps because the irritant was gone. The serenity and inner harmony he described to

---

* Grimsley comments: "his overwhelming 'need for love' made him quite unfitted to live in a state of self-sufficient detachment" (*op. cit.*, p. 180).

Malesherbes were elusive and fragile. His inner revolution, as he admits in the *Confessions*,[45] had been too swift and severe. "From that moment, my oscillating soul could never rest at its center of gravity, and its ever-recurring fluctuations have never allowed it to stay there."

The four letters to Malesherbes were a continuing effort in Jean-Jacques' lifelong quest to form a clear image of his identity. Neither his "reform," nor yet the entangled confusion of *La Nouvelle Héloïse*'s fictional world—the perfusion of reality with fantasy—had been adequate to an acceptable harmony of inner contradictions. He did not realize that the heart of the problem was the impossibility of conquering his own sincerity, a necessary conquest if he were to accept himself in the role of moral superiority that was the safe-conduct through the thicket of his inner world to the haven of self-esteem. He could convince himself intellectually that he was the apostle of virtue, but how to quell the deeper doubts and resistances? It was much easier to be sure that he was the prophetic voice of truth chastising society for its false values; but it was his self that he had to redeem, and that, as he knew, could not be achieved by intellect. When he said that he could not give himself to men because his task was to serve mankind, did the second statement really explain the first? When he condemned the exclusiveness of close friendships, was he not deceiving himself, inasmuch as all his life he had longed for the happiness of close, exclusive friendships with "beings after his own heart"? Knowing as he did that he could not reconcile himself to the world, he had to idealize his inadequacy and transmute self-deprecation into self-esteem. His problem, in brief, was that he had to try not only to live his role, but to *be* the man of his role—and that he could not.

Grimsley has shown that the "Lettres morales" which Rousseau had written for Mme. d'Houdetot in 1757–58 were the prelude to the letters to Malesherbes.[46] The reform of 1756 had been an action, but not a sufficient act of self-comprehension. It did not justify him as a "certain kind of person," with a legitimate claim to self-esteem. In the "Lettres morales" we see him struggling toward integration and self-awareness in the face of his betrayal of his own moral standards, toward catharsis of the feelings of guilt and unworthiness. He was unique and no heart could respond to his. Others lived in the world of "appearance" and "opinion." He alone did not. Therefore he could not be judged as we judge other men. Despite his grave lapses, he was the being of authenticity. His intrinsic worth was not damaged by his lapses, because they belonged to "a kind of peripheral self still dominated by the false values of the world." We can see how Rousseau is preparing to rescue himself. But he goes beyond absolution to positive value. His example will show mankind how natural goodness may be salvaged from the havoc of the artificial self created by participation in social life. The prophetic mantle, and the quest for identity and self-esteem through literary fame, had been essential steps; but they had involved his own life in such a way that self-ordering and self-justification were impossible by those means alone. To acquire absolute confidence in the worth and quality of his own being, he would have to delve into his own self, and by absorbing himself in his own past, determine the meaning of his life and justify his essential moral nature. What Rousseau calls his "cruel imagination" will constantly create acute anxieties and forebodings in relation to present events; but it will be more beneficent in helping memory in its work of idealization and self-justification, as well as in the unrelated activity of fantasy-building. Idealization relieves the stress of feeling the world's hostility. Both forms of imagination will hamper his ability to relate himself to people and the real world, will increasingly distort that world and isolate him in his own realm of fantasy.

It was to devote himself to the "happiness of living"[47] that Rousseau decided to abandon writing and the quest for fame. Such a course, if it led to deeper intimate enjoyment, had the danger of "throwing him back on his own conflicting inner resources."[48]

Rousseau, in these letters, has admitted contradictions in his life, but they are in a way explained, in his mind, as a progressive search for his authentic being, which he has now at last recovered. His life and his image come out quite simplified. "He consciously chooses those aspects of his being with which he wishes to be specifically identified," and suppresses, for example, "the feelings of guilt and anxiety by which he is so frequently tormented, as well as the heroic moral ideal which no longer has the same importance now that he has chosen a life of solitude in which the expansive needs of his 'free' self will play a determining role."[49] Is this to be attributed to age and illness, or to the crushing *échec* of his only true love, his love for Mme. d'Houdetot?

### 3. DEBACLE

About this time, Rousseau decided to break off a desultory correspondence he had been carrying on with a Mme. de la Tour, or more accurately, the correspondence she had been carrying on with him. Marianne Alissan de la Tour, *née* Marie-Anne Merlet de Fousomme, sprang from a family of the upper bourgeoisie and the lesser *noblesse de robe*. Her marriage to Alexandre Alissan de la Tour in 1750 turned into a disaster. A disorganized personality, he was unable to perform the duties of his job on the staff of the Hôtel de Ville and soon dissipated his money. His parents had a steward named to take care of his affairs. Mme. de la Tour's unhappy marriage was a common experience under a system of arranged unions. Unlike many others, she did not console herself with a lover, even though at the time of her first letter to Rousseau (August 5, 1761), she had been separated from her husband for several years. In 1774 she stopped using his name and called herself

Mme. de Franqueville. She never remarried and died childless on September 7, 1789.

It was after reading *La Nouvelle Héloïse* that she decided to engage in correspondence with Rousseau. Signing her letters "Julie," and sometimes enclosing shorter notes from a friend, "Claire," she combined the clever wit that characterized so many eighteenth-century French noblewomen with deep admiration for this strange man and his writings. Patiently she withstood his gruffness, which covered a coyness she doubtless detected. Reluctant to write at first, he was gradually caught in her net. When her letters annoyed him, he became insulting. She begged forgiveness and cleverly turned the tables on him. He grew tired. Now, when he felt she had not fully understood or sympathized with his foibles, he declared their letter-writing at an end. "You have seen nothing in my letters," he wrote peevishly on January 31; "it is, Madame, because your heart has less wit than your mind [*votre coeur n'a pas autant d'esprit que votre esprit*]. . . . You can forbear setting a price on the return of your esteem; for I swear to you, Madame, that it is a restitution about which I do not care a fig."

Insults were not enough. It was not possible to break off with this tenacious admirer. On March 8 she returned his fire in her own way. "Although you have wronged me, you are still the most eloquent of men, and the one who for me has carried the knowledge of the human heart to its furthest reach; I still owe to you the infinite pleasures I have enjoyed in reading your writings and the voluptuous tears they have a thousand times drawn from me; finally, your ideas, sometimes bizarre but always noble and just, seem nonetheless to me the completion of my own."

Jean-Jacques not only resumed the correspondence, but in May sent her two copies of *Emile*, one for her and one for "Claire," even though the latter had dropped out of the game because of his rudeness. He is almost ready to allow Mme. de la Tour to visit him. "Your trip is something to think about; for I confess that, despite my condition, I am very much afraid of you."[50] He went further. He told the maréchale about his epistolary friend and aroused her curiosity. Does he have her permission, he asks his admirer, to reveal her name to Mme. de Luxembourg? But he is worried about the projected visit. "No, I have never feared a woman as much as you."[51] Yet he really is tempted. He will have to plan a day to be with her alone.

Two letters from Mme. de la Tour followed in rapid succession, on June 5 and June 7. The first reveals a very alarmed woman. She urgently begs Jean-Jacques not to give her name to the maréchale, for "the strongest reasons" which involve her husband, her family, and herself. The second is a cry of alarm about Rousseau. "Please, Monsieur, a word to calm me about your fate. The most disquieting rumors are being spread about you."

They were more than rumors. Rapidly, events had built up to disaster.

Already on February 3, Rousseau's friend Moultou, a liberal pastor, had warned him not to publish the *Profession de foi*. "Have you taken into reckoning all the harm that may result for you?" In France he would be crushed between the opposing "parties." Jean-Jacques was not impressed by these forebodings. He had always obeyed the law and could not be attacked justly. "That is enough for my tranquillity." Besides, he is honored and esteemed by the French, and that hospitable people would not persecute *"un pauvre malade"* who is in no one's way and who preaches only peace and virtue.[52] No thought of the "plot" seems to cross his mind now. Yet only a few days before, he had written Rey about certain "bold" ideas that were bound to antagonize the censors.[53] And again, on February 18, he urged Mme. de Luxembourg to have his book printed outside of France, "for the publisher's safety and my own tranquillity." Under no circumstances would he allow a word of his text to be changed.

Moultou replied on March 15. He had taken time to reread the *Profession* carefully. Rousseau's natural religion, he admits, is really *"le christianisme bien entendu."* "He who thinks like Jesus Christ is his disciple." But the people believe only because of miracles, which they need. Therefore he must renew his warning. Rousseau will be considered an *"incrédule,"* and the field will be open to his enemies.

The printing of both *The Social Contract* and *Emile* was now proceeding smoothly. Little occurred to distract Rousseau. The Luxembourgs paid him their usual visits, and even Malesherbes came to see him. He was a bit aroused by a letter from Tscharner, in Berne, to which we have only his reply, in which he restates some of his basic ideas.

You wish to begin by teaching men the truth to make them well-behaved, and it is necessary, quite to the contrary, to make them well-behaved first in order to make them love the truth. Truth has accomplished almost nothing in the world because men always act upon their passions more than their lights and, while approving the good, they do evil. The century in which we are living is among the most enlightened. Is it among the best? What good is knowledge, then, for the advantage of society? Books are good for nothing. . . . Has a single abuse been corrected by the maxims [of great writers]? . . . You may teach the people, but you will never make them better or happier [that way].[54]

In these significant lines, we can clearly see Rousseau's consistent opposition to the main drift of Enlightenment thought. To be sure, the Enlightenment, a complex and dynamic movement, contained a strong current of pessimism, and Rousseau's ideas immediately recall the message of another great Protestant, Bayle. But the underlying difference is striking. Rousseau's pessimism is limited, never radical. Many things cannot be done or hoped for; the *philosophes* especially were on the wrong track. But men *could* be made "better and happier." However, that goal required an entirely different path, a brave—indeed a shocking—new concept of political organization, social relations, and behavioral control. Of all this Rousseau of course says nothing in his letter; but the letter reflects the substance of his thinking.

On April 13, Rey sent out bound copies of *The Social Contract*. On the twenty-ninth Rousseau returned final errata sheets for *Emile* to Duchesne. He had already heard of a pirated edition being put out in Lyons. Malesherbes, through intermediaries, urged Rey to persuade Rousseau to eliminate his name from the title page of *The Social Contract*: "The principles contained in this work are capable of bringing disaster upon him in France."[55] Rey knew Rousseau too well to think of removing his name, and he did not believe that Malesherbes would carry out his threat. Rousseau understood better. "M. de Malesherbes," he warned Rey on May 9, "is good and helpful, but unfortunately he cannot always do what he would like to do." On the twelfth Rey was informed that Malesherbes, having read *The Social Contract*, had forbidden its distribution in France. Rey was shocked, but not Rousseau—if a monarchy had censorship, it was to protect itself. Nevertheless, Rey advised Rousseau that copies had been sent to London, Paris, Dunkirk, and Switzerland.

Meanwhile, Rousseau had again responded to Moultou's warnings, on April 25, this time with a touch of bitterness. Discounting the influence his *Profession de foi* could possibly have on the religion of the common people, he affirms that the publication could harm no one but himself. "For a long time now *j'ai mis les hommes au pis*." Yes, the hatred smouldering against him will be unmasked, and so much the better. "Can you believe that I do not see that my fellow-citizens resent my reputation, and that if Jean-Jacques were not from Geneva, Voltaire would have been less fêted there?" From all over Europe visitors journey to Montmorency to pay homage, but never any from Geneva, except Voltaire's spies. That is why he can never go back. "I love my country too much to bear to see myself hated there."

Moultou denied the allegations (May 19). True, Jean-Jacques has some enemies. "Come back to your country, and they will not dare to raise their heads. . . . How impatiently I am awaiting your *Social Contract! Mon Dieu!* why am I not a king, why do I not have a Pennsylvania to give you! Then at last we should see men happy and yet living in a society." But Rousseau was not in good spirits. "I have only one journey left to take," he wrote to Dom Deschamps on May 22, one that "will take me into an unknown land." His two works are not, he says, worth very much. He had been suffering from his usual physical and psychological torments. The Jansenists (not the Jesuits, now), perhaps in collusion with d'Alembert, had, he suspected, been rifling his papers.

A minor work on the raising of young children, published on May 22, was nothing, he was convinced, but a pirated plagiarism of the first part of *Emile*.[56]

The explosion was drawing closer and tension was growing in informed circles. On May 22, Néaulme complained to Rousseau that the *Profession de foi* was an attack against religion, too dangerous a book to publish, even in Amsterdam. Jean-Jacques was more worried about his other book. He imagined that Rey's shipment of *The Social Contract* had been captured by the English. Writing to Duchesne on May 23, he remarks significantly that *The Social Contract* "should be considered as a kind of appendix" to *Emile*, and that "the two together constitute a single whole." Together with this statement we must put another in a letter to Moultou (May 30). Complaining as usual that only the Genevans do not seek his books, he adds that *The Social Contract*, banned in France, should be acceptable in Geneva, "for in it I loudly proclaim my preference for aristocracy over all other forms of government." Never, he informed Rey (May 29) would he consent to removing his name from the title page of a book he is proud to have written and which he stands ready to defend before any tribunal. But he is in no personal danger, he reassures Rey. France would not violate *le droit des gens*, not persecute "a poor sick man whose peaceful residence in France is perhaps not less honorable to the government than to him." What Jean-Jacques did not admit was that he was banking on the support of Choiseul, the prime minister, against the ill will of Mme. de Pompadour.

Despite the ban, a few copies of *The Social Contract* had been surreptitiously circulated in Paris. There was nothing to impede *Emile*, which was published there. On May 22 copies were sent to the Luxembourgs, for themselves and for complimentary distribution to persons on a list Rousseau had drawn up. Three of them at least, Duclos and the scientists La Condamine and Clairaut, responded at once, the latter two with extravagant praise, the prudent Duclos vaguely, without mentioning the title. Rousseau's apprehensions were only slightly aroused. Mme. de Boufflers' enthusiastic response ended with the request that her letter be returned to her forthwith. D'Alembert, for the first time, did not sign his letter of commendation. All this praise was enough to confirm Rousseau's conviction that "this was the best and most important of all my writings."[57] At a private reading at the home of de Blair, an attorney of the Parlement, the official remarked to Mathas, a friend of Rousseau's, "That is a very fine book but it will soon be talked about, more than it would be desirable for the author's sake."[58] Still Jean-Jacques had no foreboding of catastrophe, and laughed when the remark was repeated to him. Choiseul, Malesherbes, Conti, the maréchal—all were in back of him. And there was nothing reprehensible about the book. On the contrary, it was a manual of virtue. This was the work that would crush his envious enemies.

On May 24, Duchesne, having received tacit permission, put *Emile* on public sale. By the twenty-sixth, all Paris was buzzing about Jean-Jacques' daring new work and eager to lay hands on it. On that day Bachaumont noted in his *Mémoires secrets* that the book "is causing a great stir" and that it contains "very bold ideas against religion and the government."[59] By the end of the month a pirated edition was being widely peddled, and the scandal had become a storm. Rousseau wrote retrospectively, "The muffled roar that precedes the storm began to sound, and all who were perceptive saw that a plot was brewing, around my book and myself, which would soon break out. As for me, my sense of security, my stupidity were such that, far from foreseeing my misfortune, I did not even suspect its cause after having felt its effect."[60] It is indeed surprising that Jean-Jacques, who had been so wildly suspicious during the printing of *Emile*, should have felt so secure now. There is no doubt that he felt himself to be an exemplar of *le juste*, the defender of truth and virtue.[61] He did not understand that the authorities would consider his ideas to be a direct challenge to established doctrines and institutions. But Bachaumont noted on May 31, "The Sword and the Censer are uniting against the author, and his friends have told him that he is in danger."

At this point Rousseau for the first time did begin to feel endangered, but reluctantly. The judges of the Parlement were saying that it was time to stop burning books and to start burning their authors. He laughed and put it down to a plot of the d'Holbach clan: if they could frighten him enough, he might run away. Only when the Luxembourgs reached Montmorency did he suspect that the affair might be serious. The maréchal asked him whether he had spoken ill of Choiseul in *The Social Contract* or *Emile*. It was a strange question, certainly disquieting. Rousseau replied that he had praised Choiseul in the former work. "Ah," replied the maréchal mysteriously, "you should have done the same in the other work." But the maréchal, says Rousseau, was too much the courtier to reveal more, friend though he was.

On the morning of June 1, Malesherbes, acting on the instance of Sartine, the lieutenant of police, ordered the sale of *Emile* stopped and all copies seized. The police carried out the order on the third. Bachaumont noted: "Rousseau's *Emile* is confiscated by the police. This affair will not stop there." On June 5, Duchesne informed Rousseau of the seizure and Rousseau replied to Néaulme (whose letters have disappeared), regretting the trouble he had caused him, but maintaining that "no power on earth" could make him remove "one syllable" of *Emile*. He expressed confidence that so wise a body as the Parlement would not be foolish enough to prosecute him. "By praising God and speaking out for the true good of man, I have done my duty." Let men praise or blame as they would.

When Rousseau wrote again to Moultou on June 7, he had not received his friend's letter dispatched two days previously. Moultou had congratulated him on the great success of *The Social Contract* in Geneva —few of the two hundred copies were left. *Emile* had just arrived, in the pirated Lyons edition. Rousseau's message, which crossed Moultou's, was one of alarm. Justice, he cries, is always subordinated to the self-interest of institutional bodies. Such are men; such is the society of which men are so proud. The time may be at hand for him to show that his life is worthy of his motto. Also on June 7 came Mme. de la Tour's note of alarm and warning.

Still he could not quite believe all the warnings. He was counting on his protectors. Malesherbes, after all, had not only given tacit approval to *Emile*; he had actively patronized it and exercised a general surveillance over its publication. What Rousseau forgot was that Malesherbes was an extremely prudent man, who twice before had narrowly avoided being seriously compromised; in 1752, when the *Encyclopédie* was condemned, and in 1758, when his friend Helvétius and the *Encyclopédie* (which he also protected) provoked the authorities into a wave of persecution. Malesherbes had not heeded Rousseau's own warning against publishing an edition of *Emile* in Paris simultaneously with the Dutch edition. But his antennae were evidently finely tuned to possible trouble. Shortly before publication he had asked Rousseau, through the maréchal, to return all his letters referring to *Emile*. It was an elementary precaution in case of search, but this never occurred to Jean-Jacques until much later. He could think only with gratitude of Malesherbes' constant solicitude ever since he had come to Montmorency.

Mme. de Luxembourg seemed so calm and unconcerned! Indeed she never talked about the situation. Rousseau did not understand that she was trying not to alarm him. Mme. de Boufflers, *au contraire*, was obviously agitated. While assuring him that Conti was using his powerful influence, she urged him to fly to England, where he would be well received by her friend David Hume. When he declined, she asked him not to bring in the maréchale's name if he were interrogated. Rousseau admits he might not have kept the promise he gave her, for he had to tell the truth cost what it may. Mme. de Boufflers then suggested the possibility of a royal *lettre de cachet* which would confine him in the Bastille for a time but protect him from the Parlement. Rousseau made no objection, but the idea was not followed up.

The rumors were about to become fact. June 7 was the day on which Gervaise, the syndic of the Faculty of Theology, denounced *Emile* to the Sorbonne. Official sanctions followed so swiftly that there is no doubt every move had been planned. At six in the evening the Abbé Marin, a friend of Grimm and Mme. d'Epinay, informed the Duc de Luxembourg that Rousseau was to be charged before Parlement that day, and his arrest ordered. Another trick of the Holbachians, thought Rousseau. Normally an inquiry had to precede an arrest.

The same day he received an urgent warning from the Marquise de

Créqui. He replied at once that he would not heed her advice: "Jean-Jacques Rousseau does not know how to hide." A warrant for his arrest had been issued. "*Au nom de Dieu! allez-vous-en,*" she pleaded again on June 8, in a note he did not receive in time. "Your book, burnt, will do you no harm. Your body cannot stand imprisonment." She was a good friend. Four days later, after Rousseau had fled, she wrote to Abbé Trublet: "Inform me of what you know about Rousseau. His madness does not detach me from him."

June 8 was just an ordinary day for Rousseau. He spent a gay afternoon picnicking with two Oratorian professors. Improvising straws from reeds, they competed to see who could drink the most from the same wine bottle. Following his custom, he read the Bible in bed late into the night, until he felt sleepy enough to snuff his candle. That night he read the Book of Judges and was greatly moved by the story of the Levite (Judges, XIX–XX). "I was musing about it when I was startled from my reveries by noise and light." It was Thérèse lighting the way for the maréchal's steward, La Roche. "Do not be alarmed," he said to Rousseau, who had sat up. "It is Mme. la Maréchale who is sending you a letter from M. le Prince de Conti." Conti's letter informed her that despite all his efforts the harshest measures were to be taken against Rousseau. "Nothing can prevent the blow from falling; the Court demands it, Parlement desires it. At seven in the morning his arrest will be ordered and men will be sent to seize him. I have obtained this much: if he leaves, he will not be pursued."

It was two o'clock. The maréchale's own note to Jean-Jacques read: "It seems that you do not have a moment to lose before bringing over all your papers and seeking safety from all the persecutions that can be directed against you when one wields power and justice does not always accompany it. In God's name, come." He dressed and left for the château with La Roche.

Jean-Jacques observed that the maréchale was discomposed. Never had he seen her like that. His own agitation vanished as he thought of the troubles she would suffer if he allowed himself to be taken. There could be no vacillation: he would do for her what he would never have done to save himself. He did not await her persuasion, but said at once that he would leave. Ever the romantic, Jean-Jacques was ready to display the gallant heroism of his devotion to his lady. She expressed no gratitude and seemed indifferent. Shocked, he was at the point of changing his mind. Then the maréchal came in, followed by Mme. de Boufflers. They flattered and thanked him. The maréchal proposed hiding him in the house for several days while they deliberated on the best measures. Rousseau refused. He would not hide. He would leave at once.

Quickly scanning the possibilities for a refuge, Jean-Jacques eliminated Geneva, which would have been his preference. To begin with, the French ambassador was too powerful there. More important, the

Council had never forgiven him his *Discourse on Inequality*, and had been at the point of condemning *La Nouvelle Héloïse* on the urgent solicitation of Dr. Tronchin. He rejected Mme. de Boufflers' renewed exhortations to seek exile in England. "I have never liked England or the English," he declared. The more she argued in favor of England, the greater repugnance he felt for that country. No, he would go to Switzerland, but not to Geneva.

La Roche, making several quick trips, brought over the papers Rousseau had been accumulating for his memoirs. Thérèse was kept in ignorance of his resolve. He spent the morning going through the papers, burning what he decided not to take with him. Even with the maréchal's help, the morning was not long enough for the task, and he accepted his noble friend's offer to complete it. Only then did La Roche bring Thérèse over to the château, without even telling her that Jean-Jacques was still there. She had been consumed with worry and kept looking for the bailiffs to arrive. When she saw him, she screamed and threw herself into his arms. At this recollection, Rousseau allows himself some retrospective exclamations. "O friendship, understanding of two hearts, habit, intimacy! In this sweet and cruel moment so many days of happiness, tenderness, and peace spent together were assembled in order to make me feel more keenly the laceration of a first separation." The maréchal wept and left them alone. Thérèse did not want Jean-Jacques to go without her, but he told her she had to take care of his possessions and his finances. Knowing she might be questioned, he would not tell her where he was going but promised she would rejoin him before too long. Filled with an uncontainable emotion, he embraced her and bade her goodbye with an eloquent parting speech. *"Mon enfant*, you must summon up your courage. You have shared the prosperity of my good days. Now, since it is your wish, you will have to share my ordeals. Expect nothing to follow me but affronts and calamities. The fate of which this day marks the beginning will pursue me until my last hour."

He had not been too good to her these last three years. Despite the happy hours he writes about, he had been absorbed, with the neurotic's self-absorption, in his writings, his visits, his moral and physical problems. Thérèse attended him when he needed her, suffered his moods of dark melancholy and the long periods during which, according to his own admission, he would not say a word to her.

It was four in the afternoon of June 9 when he set out. The bailiffs should have arrived by ten o'clock, he thought. Doubtless they had counted on his taking the post stage and apprehending him en route. But the maréchal gave him a cabriolet and a postilion to take him to a relay where he had fresh horses waiting. Jean-Jacques noted that the maréchale's final embraces seemed cold, those of Mme. de Boufflers more affectionate. The maréchal accompanied him to his carriage without uttering a word, pale with emotion. He took Rousseau's key with a vivacity that in retrospect seemed disturbing. In the back of Jean-Jacques' mind lay a growing, gnawing doubt: were these people really his friends, in the total sense that he could alone accept, or were they eager to be done with him? But at the moment it was no more than a flash. Then a long and silent embrace which both men knew was a last adieu. "I have never had a more bitter moment in my life."

It was none too soon. A carriage containing four bailiffs passed him on the road. Rousseau was mistaken in expecting them to have arrived at ten in the morning. The judgment had been pronounced at that hour. In view of the necessary legal and police procedures, their arrival at Montmorency toward four in the afternoon shows that the utmost urgency had been used in expediting the warrant. The authorities were indeed determined to take Rousseau prisoner and to inflict the harshest punishment on him. *Emile* was to be torn up and burnt, an event that took place on June 11 in front of the Palais de Justice. He himself was to be "physically apprehended and incarcerated in the Conciergerie," the prison where Marie Antoinette was to spend her last days.

Jean-Jacques had had the misfortune to choose a bad moment. The established institutions were on the *qui vive*. Jean Calas had been broken on the wheel in March in Toulouse. The Jesuits had been condemned and their schools closed. This drastic action made it all the more necessary for the authorities to deal severely with the enemies of the Church. The Parlement, in Rousseau's case, had met with a minimum quorum composed of elderly magistrates hostile to new ideas. All those who might have taken his side, such as Malesherbes and Hénault, were excluded. The judgment was made in haste, in an hour and a half. Rousseau's courage in putting his name to *Emile* was taken as an impudent gesture of defiance, not, as he hoped, as one of honesty and courage.* This act in itself, ran the edict, required an exemplary and severe punishment. Rousseau understood nothing of the mentality or the procedures, writes Lanson, "which paralyzed Malesherbes and Luxembourg, and even the Prince de Conti, and did not allow them to resist the religious party openly."[62] Once the Parlement had docketed the case, all overt protection came to an end, and Rousseau could only be warned to leave at once. He would not have been spared.

When Rousseau, as he became increasingly disturbed, suspected a plot, he was not off the mark. Where he erred was in the direction he gave to his suspicions. In his mind Grimm, Voltaire, and the Encyclopedists were the center around which all other enemies gradually accreted. This group did write against him on all occasions, but they never sought his persecution. What Jean-Jacques never suspected, until much

* If Rousseau had followed the usual practice of anonymous publication followed by denial of authorship, he would probably not have been personally molested. Such denials usually fooled no one, but allowed the government to save face by condemning the book.

later, was that the only real plot was that of his *friends*. In frequenting
the highborn aristocracy—with overt reluctance but inner eagerness—in
accepting their protection, he had ventured into treacherous waters that
he could not possibly fathom and in which he lost control. He had
become the naïve victim of their designs.

The highest born of his lofty friends was the Prince de Conti. He was
the commanding figure in what had happened and in much more yet to
come.[63] It is worthy of note that Conti had in earlier years protected
other writers rebellious to authority. The Abbé Prévost had been his
almoner. As Grand Prior of the Order of Malta in France, Conti had
offered a refuge to Diderot in the sanctuary of the Temple, one of his
homes. There was a reason for his preferences. He was both a disappointed man and a crafty intriguer. Louis XV, his cousin, had prevented
him from reaching the highest rank in the army, in the diplomatic
service, and the government. The monarch, and even more Mme. de
Pompadour, resented his pretentions and sensed an enemy in him. The
throne has a long memory. In the seventeenth century, Conti's ancestor,
"le grand Condé," had been involved in the Fronde, the last rebellion of
the aristocracy against royal absolutism. His family had maintained that
tradition, one still feared by the monarchy and still carried on, in another way, by the Parlements and the *philosophes*, who wanted the
ancient "constitution," with its "intermediary powers," restored. A considerable sector of the nobility and the magistracy were thus allied, and
it was Conti who, from 1756 on, was "the advocate, the artisan, and the
great hope of this union."[64] He was, in short, the leader of the unde-
clared opposition, and on one occasion led the peers into a session of
Parlement in defiance of the King's order. In 1771, when the Parlement
was exiled and then suppressed, Conti was banished from the Court for
his opposition.

There are few letters from Conti to Rousseau, for he prudently wrote
few letters, preferring to act through agents or friends. It was in this
manner that he had made his initial overtures to Rousseau, who was
subsequently overwhelmed by his two personal visits. The *Confessions* treat him with enthusiastic praise, and only at the end did Rousseau add this footnote: "Note the perseverance of this blind and stupid
confidence in the midst of so many maneuvers which should have most
turned me away from it. It has ended only since my return to Paris in
1770."

Conti was not shocked by either *The Social Contract* or *Emile*. The
former condemned absolute authority, and the latter was if anything too
devout for the unbeliever that he was. Conti was to be the first prince of
the blood to die refusing confession and the last sacrament. For him this
writer, the most fashionable and scandalous of the day, the most sought-
after since he had turned his back to society, could be a valuable recruit;
he had already seen that. Not only was Rousseau a shock-trooper in the

fight against "legal despotism"; he had publicly broken with the radical wing of the *philosophes*, whose ideas and politics were disliked by Conti and his group. He was indeed "unique" and uniquely valuable. Rousseau's new friends—and two of them, the maréchal and Malesherbes, were really his friends—were not entirely disinterested when they patronized and adulated him. Conti, working through his mistress and confidante, Mme. de Boufflers (who Rousseau unjustly felt harbored a secret hatred for him), had convinced them that he could be useful to their political schemes.

In conniving for the publication of *Emile*, however, their overconfidence had led them into a serious miscalculation. The Sorbonne, they foresaw, would raise its voice against the *Profession de foi*; but the Sorbonne, wracked by quarrels between Jesuits and Jansenists, was no longer powerful. Sartine, the lieutenant of police, could be influenced. But the blow came from where it was least expected, since Malesherbes and Conti were Rousseau's protectors—from the Parlement, where they had the strongest connections. Rousseau, with his abnormally suspicious but sometimes uncanny intuition, had guessed right after all. The Jansenist Parlement, reaching the victorious climax of its long campaign against the Jesuits, had, as we have seen, a powerful motive to appear as defender of both throne and altar. This was emphasized in its decree, which condemned *Emile* as destructive to royal authority. Ironically, Malesherbes' own father, Chancellor Lamoignon de Malesherbes, a staunch royalist and reactionary, had led the counteroffensive against the new Fronde. The play of forces was such that the Parlement's harsh legal judgment not only made Rousseau a criminal—since he was to be arrested without a hearing—but threatened his abettors and supporters.

Rousseau's patrons were now in an acutely embarrassing, even dangerous, position. Malesherbes especially was in the line of fire. The year before he had been warned after the publication of a "republican" book, and now he was deeply involved in *Emile*. He admits that he, not Rousseau, was the real target.[65] It was evident, to him and to Conti, that above all else *Rousseau must be prevented from appearing in court*. They knew—and Jean-Jacques himself affirms it—that this strange fanatic would tell the whole truth. Nor were they surprised when, on June 9, the threats of imminent danger with which they faced him did not shake his intention of appearing before the French judges and convincing them of the illegality and injustice of their decree. Malesherbes admits as much. "The more we spoke about the danger, the more he stiffened and insisted on taking the witness stand."[66] He confirms the essence if not the letter of Rousseau's own account: only by holding up to him the danger of the Duchesse de Luxembourg's being compromised did they persuade him to become a fugitive. (Rousseau, of course, takes the credit for himself and mentions no effort of persuasion.) Malesherbes adds this significant statement: "It was not true; Mme. de

Luxembourg had no fear of that, but she agreed to using [the pretext] to urge him to seek safety." The statement is not entirely accurate. The maréchale was undoubtedly worried for her husband, and she would not herself have escaped unpleasantness. Jean-Jacques' "safety" was of such great concern to his friends because it was the only way of assuring their own. Malesherbes' worry is evidenced by his letter of June 10 to his father, the chancellor, denying that he had given tacit permission for the publication of *Emile* and mentioning nothing about his role in it.

Conti, especially, did his best to frighten Rousseau; and that was also to be his later tactic in controlling the man he was affecting to save.* Conti was of course in no personal danger. It was his political role that was menaced, his stance as leader of the group associated with and supporting the Parlement. How curious that we have Mme. de Luxembourg's note that La Roche brought to Rousseau late that night, while Conti's has disappeared! How strange the maréchal's eagerness to work so tirelessly with Jean-Jacques in going through his papers, and his zealousness in promising to complete the task by himself! We can credit Rousseau's affirmation to Moultou (June 15): "I swear to you, my dear Moultou, . . . that not only was I completely within the law, but I had the most authentic proofs to protect the security of others."

As the unwitting victim fled, helpless, into an unknown future, he could fathom almost nothing of what had gone on behind the scenes. Perplexed, he had only the uneasy feeling that his friends were relieved to be rid of him, and perhaps that, despite his thirst for independence, he was not the master of his fate.

One can only sympathize with Rousseau's conviction that all his life was ruled by a special destiny which had selected him to be a unique witness. His childhood home, Bossey, Les Charmettes, the Hermitage, and now Montmorency—each refuge from a hostile, uncomprehending world had been violated. From each he had been traumatically, cruelly ejected, in circumstances that seemed to him unjust and incomprehensible. Once more he was the wanderer, banished from those he loved, proscribed, deprived of the secure insularity in which he could live in peace with his dreams and the chosen few.

The troubles that lay ahead were to surpass Jean-Jacques' most dire

---

* The account which was circulated in the gossip sheets may have been "leaked": "They say that he absolutely refused to leave; that he insisted on testifying; that M. le Prince de Conti having urged him to in the most pressing and affectionate way, the author asked His Highness what they could do to him, adding that he'd just as soon live in the Bastille or Vincennes as anywhere else, that he had to uphold the truth, etc.; that the Prince having explained that it was a matter not only of prison, but of the stake, Rousseau's stoicism was shaken, whereupon the Prince added: 'You are not yet enough of a philosopher, my friend, to stand such a test,' following which they packed his things and sent him on his way" (Jean Fabre, "Rousseau et le prince de Conti," *AJJR*, XXXVI, 1963–65, p. 28).

forebodings. Before we follow him on his flight, we must inquire carefully into *Emile* and *The Social Contract*. They were not only the immediate causes of his persecution; they are the greatest products of his intellect, the pillars of his social and political thought, the books through which he has exercised his most enduring influence.

# IV. The Hypothetical Emile, or the Reconstructed Individual

*Combien d'art pour rentrer dans la nature!*
LA BRUYÈRE

## 1. THE DISGUISE OF FREEDOM

NOWHERE in *La Nouvelle Héloïse* is there a viable individual. None of the main characters is able to cope with the conflicting demands of nature and society, of egoistic needs and moral order, of independence and dependence. Even Wolmar, who is really the hypostasization of the suprahuman Lawgiver or "guide," rather than a personality, is frustrated. If Rousseau reflected on his finished work, he must have realized that he had not really solved any problems. At least he had gained insight into their complexity. Saint-Preux had been saved from the contamination of corrupt societies, but the effort to integrate this "natural" man into a small socialized unit had ended in the disintegration of both the individual "citizens" and the collectivity.

It was plain where the trouble lay. When Wolmar set to work, it was already too late. To "denature" man, to "form" him, one must begin with the child—indeed, with the newborn infant. After that, it is too late. Rousseau had long been thinking along these lines; his *Projet pour l'éducation de M. de Sainte-Marie*, the *Discourses*, the article "Political Economy," the pages on education in *La Nouvelle Héloïse*, all hint broadly at such "behavioral engineering" and move more and more strongly in that direction.

*Emile*, we must remember, is not an isolated work (although, like *The Social Contract*, it has too often been considered as such). Both are steps toward Rousseau's grand plan for the good society. *Emile* contains a section on politics in which the ideas are identical with those of *The Social Contract*. *La Nouvelle Héloïse*, which precedes *Emile*, has an important chapter on the education of children, containing ideas that are again identical with those of *Emile*. All these works are political, in the large sense of that word. Their subject is how to govern men. In Rousseau's ideal society, control and valuation are located in the state or community. Yet, in a quite different sense, his thinking is individual-oriented. Whatever Rousseau may have written about man not being naturally evil, as a good Calvinist he knew that evil is radical in the species. If society has corrupted man, as he so often says, it is really because man corrupts society.

In view of Rousseau's critique of present so-called societies, what can be done to make an individual fit for the ideal "true" society, and yet able to live, uncorrupted, amidst the corruption of the present regime? He will search for a solution to this problem in *Emile*, an experimental construction in behavioral control.

As Rousseau undertakes the perilous journey of bringing a human being from infancy to manhood, two questions come to mind at once. What is the goal or end that imposes a directive pattern on the individual's formation? What is the process itself? A precise reply to the first question will not be easy or satisfactory, for *Emile* must be viewed in all its complexities. The difficulty is made crystal clear by Rousseau at the outset. It is the dominating problem of his work, and of eighteenth-century philosophy: how to reconcile nature and culture. On the one hand, *nature* must be preserved, for as he states in the first lines of the book, "everything is good when it leaves the hands of the creator, everything degenerates in the hands of man." (Yet, as I have already noted, if man spoils all good things, then his nature contains a principle of evil.) On the other hand, the goal of the whole process is the formation of a man fit to live in *society*. Can we unite the apparent irreconcilables? We can, if we remember that in *Emile* Rousseau's "nature" is no longer that of the state of nature, but as he declares, what is natural to a social, *human* man. Natural man, in this sense, is an as yet unrealized entelechy, something belonging to a hypothetical future, not to a prehistorical past.

Rousseau's uniqueness, in the context of the French Enlightenment, lies to no small degree in his full understanding of the concept that culture is a rupture with nature, that it in effect takes man out of nature, or separates him from it. For him it could not be, as for the other *philosophes*, a rather simplistic matter of "reconciling" nature and culture, of finding a middle term. The only two possibilities for a solution to the problem of "making man one" were either to regress to the chaos of the natural state (an impossibility, he declared), or else to move forward to the true dominion of culture.

Jean-Jacques, in the sheltered seclusion of his sylvan retreat, once

more gives wings to his imagination, his sovereign remedy for the inadequacies of reality and the stings of human misunderstanding and wickedness. Once again he builds an ideal world, a second reality to which
he will become more attached than to the other. Rising above his rejection by the world, he persists in playing his role of moral guide to men,
of showing them the right path. "Readers," he warns in Book II of
*Emile*, "remember always that he who is speaking to you is neither a
scholar nor a philosopher, but a simple man, a lover of truth, without a
party or a system; a solitary man who, living little with others, has fewer
opportunities to imbibe their prejudices and more time to reflect on
what strikes him when he has relations with them." The result was a
treatise on education that turned into a kind of educational novel, in its
last part, and was followed by a sequel, *Emile et Sophie, ou les soli-
taires*, which is entirely a novel, though unfinished.

Rousseau lays down some of his basic principles at the very outset.
They include many valid ideas and insights. "To live is the trade I want
to teach him [Emile]." To live, he declares, is to act. One aspect of his
method is to avoid verbal teaching, to make the child learn by himself,
learn by doing. Another of his insights is that the child's faculties do not
develop all at once. He progresses in a series of stages in which mental
and physical development are interlocked. New needs and new powers
dominate each stage. The educator must utilize these periods of functional maturation by appropriate exercises. In other words, each thing
should come at its proper time. "We must consider the man in the man,
and the child in the child." This sound concept was destined to have a
lasting influence on educational theory. Unfortunately, Rousseau's customary spirit of absolutism leads him to exaggerate his idea to the point
of absurdity, by making each stage a sudden emergence instead of a
gradual unfolding. While it is true that learning must wait upon certain
stages of development, attainment of these stages can be accelerated by
education, and proper preparation can make learning at each stage
more effective.

Rousseau's keen interest in the natural course of development of the
child's faculties and interests has two motives. One is to avoid harmful
acts and attitudes; the other is to manage him better. *Emile* is a book
about child management and behavioral control.

How can we bring up a moral man in an immoral society? There is no
Clarens, where education and life are conducted in a harmonic style. In
the absence of a true society, the education of the citizen must be theorized outside the social context. Emile will be raised in isolation. There
is, then, an implicit assumption of a fundamental harmony between the
man-citizen created in *Emile* and the reconstructed society of *The Social
Contract*.

The first stage, infancy, extends to the age of two. In a famous plea,
Rousseau urges doing away with swaddling clothes and giving the baby

freedom of movement. Constraint is not only physically bad, but hurts his disposition and character. It is followed by another plea that was equally famous and influential: mothers should nurse their own children. This they must do not only for the child's sake. The touching spectacle of dutiful mothers will keep husbands faithful and create the atmosphere of a true home. (It is said that the fashion became so widespread, as a result of *Emile*, that women were seen nursing their babies in the theater and other public places.)

The tutor or master (Rousseau himself!) will have sole and absolute control over Emile's upbringing. He will *make* that child and the man into whom he grows. Rousseau, losing himself in the world of his fantasies, gradually becomes exalted by the power he has given himself. At one point, he specifically emphasized the importance of close relations between mother and child: "No mother, no child." But Emile, to all intents, has no mother. Rousseau also writes, "A father who will not fulfill his duties has no right to be one." We shall not, like Jean-Jacques' enemies, point a mocking finger at him for writing that phrase, but only remark that in effect Emile has no father, either. Because a child needs a father and mother desperately in society, does he need them less when isolated with an ideal tutor?

The child should be put to the test of a Spartan regime, hardened to all rigors. One out of two children will die before the age of eight. This is nature's law, says Rousseau, and it is wrong to work against it. Cold
• baths, exposure to harsh weather, hunger and thirst—all must be borne. Most of all, one must avoid pampering the baby. His cries quickly become commands, and he knows when he is master.

It is man's natural inclination to consider everything that is within his power as belonging to him. In this sense Hobbes' principle is true up to a certain point: multiply our desires and the means of satisfying them, and each will make himself the master of everything. Therefore, the child who has only to want in order to get thinks himself the owner of the universe; he looks on all men as his slaves. And when you are finally forced to refuse him something . . . he takes this refusal for an act of rebellion. . . . Without ever being grateful for complaisance, he becomes indignant at any opposition.

This brings us at once to a key problem in interpreting *Emile*. Rousseau claims throughout that he is bringing up his ward to be free. He urges preparing the child, even in his early years, for "the reign of his freedom" by teaching him always to be "master of himself and to do his will in everything." One might conclude that Rousseau was either self-contradictory or preparing the reign of anarchy; but freedom and liberty have special meanings in his terminology. Emile is "free" because he is (supposedly) dependent only on *things*; but things are under the control of the "guide," who manipulates them secretly. His purpose is clear: it is to teach the child to limit his desires to his powers, so that he will grow up to be independent (a word Rousseau constantly stresses) and, at the same time, to submit *willingly* to *necessary* limits. Consequently, if we make the limits we desire to impose on the child *seem* like necessary limits, he will still feel independent and free. This is the theory in a nutshell. Thus, it is permissible to distract a crying child with a toy; but it must never be forgotten that "it is of the greatest importance that the child should not perceive the intention to distract him, and that he should be amused without realizing that anyone is thinking of him." Here we have Rousseau's favorite technique of *la main cachée*, or the "hidden hand," which in all his writings underlies his programs for behavioral control.

The second stage begins at the age of two. We are now dealing with the *puer*, not the *infans*. Before long we come upon Rousseau's eloquent plea that we allow the child to be a child, and to be happy. "We must consider the man in the man, and the child in the child." Rousseau means what he says, but we should not rush to conclude that he intends really to give up anything. "I say it again, the child's education begins at his birth. . . . If you want him to keep his original form . . . grab hold of him as soon as he is born, and do not let him out of sight until he is a man." *Emile* is a program for doing exactly that.

What we must do to make our subject happy is to order his passions according to man's natural constitution. Once it is clear that the so-called natural man does not exist naturally, and never has existed, it follows that we must make the natural man. Rousseau's great parable of Julie's garden, in *La Nouvelle Héloïse*, teaches us that nature, in its ideal or proper form, never makes itself. A natural education becomes then, almost by definition, an education controlled by artifice. Here indeed is a deep paradox. The very touch of man corrupts nature, according to Rousseau, and yet he calls on men really to create the natural.

Of course it is not a "natural" man that Rousseau is aiming at. In the third *Dialogue* (*Rousseau juge de Jean-Jacques*), he speaks of *Emile* as "this book which is so widely read, so little understood."[1] And he goes on to say: "Nature made man happy and good, but society depraves him and makes him wretched." This was a sincere belief, not a slogan. But in *Emile* we are told that man alone has "superfluous faculties," more than are needed for self-preservation.[2] Doubtless this explains his unique "perfectibility," so important a point in the *Discourse on Inequality*. And it results in the intellectual powers of a child developing more rapidly than his physical powers, except during the storm of puberty, when the reverse occurs. Education must repress these *natural* excesses, since happiness depends on an equilibrium between desires and powers. The idea of limit thus governs each stage in Emile's development, and the end product as well. It is therefore necessary constantly to guide nature, constantly to repress it.

At the same time, freedom is a necessary condition for happiness. In Rousseau's mind there is no contradiction. "The truly free man wants only what he *can* do and does what he wants." The problem is obviously the same one of limiting the will. One cannot be free if he is dependent on other individuals. Rousseau had himself learned the bitter lessons of personal dependency. Necessity, however, especially impersonal necessity, does not frustrate a sensible person in the way the will of other persons does. The idea has an immediate political reverberation, and Rousseau repeats one of the central themes of *The Social Contract*. If we substitute for personal dependency an impersonal, inflexible dependency on the laws of the general will, "Men's dependency would then become once more a dependency on things; we would unite in the Republic all the advantages of the natural state, and those of the civil state; we would join to the freedom that keeps man free of vices, the morality that raises him to virtue."

We see then that the two antagonists, independence and dependence, are united by Rousseau in this very special way, without either being sacrificed. Absolute submission to impersonal necessity is considered to be consonant with liberty; when it is willing submission, it *is* liberty. All of this is based on a fundamental idea in Emile: we must find a way to give to moral laws the compulsive force of necessity.*

The essential thing, then, is to control desire, or the will. This philosophy is the basis of the child's education. Today we should say that the normal acquisition of behavior depends on the repression of impulses as the result of disapproval by adults or the resistance of impersonal, unchangeable conditions in the environment. Rousseau would in theory eliminate the former in favor of the latter. In reality he means something quite different—to conceal or disguise the tutor's direction, as he manipulates conditions and works through them. Since the child does not resist "things" (which are inevitable and unchangeable) in the same way he resists people, the result will be total control by the tutor, together with complete docility on the part of the child, who will nonetheless have the feeling that he is free. Rousseau tells us, "Use force with children and reason with men." But the force must never be overt; it must never seem to come from a person's will.

Never never command him to do anything . . . never let him even imagine that you think you have any authority over him. Let him only know that he is necessarily at your mercy . . . let him soon feel on his proud head a heavy yoke of necessity . . . let him see that necessity in things, never in caprice. . . . There

---

* This idea Kant was to incorporate in his categorical imperative, stating that "the unconditional command leaves the will no liberty to choose the opposite; consequently, it alone carries with it that necessity which we require in a law" (*Fundamental Principles of the Metaphysic of Morals*, in Kant's *Critique of Practical Reason*, trans. T. K. Abbott; London, 1909, p. 37). But Kant passed by Rousseau's fundamental utilitarianism. He would have reversed Rousseau's sentence: "I have made lying less odious than useless."

is no middle term. Either you must require nothing at all or you must from the start bend him to the most absolute obedience.

This, then, is what Rousseau calls "controlled freedom," or "guided freedom" (*"la liberté bien réglée"*). It enables the tutor to "govern the child as he wills," by tightening or loosening the sphere of the possible and the impossible. Since the child remains ignorant of their real limits, "you will make him supple and docile by the force of things alone." Obviously then, the program will have to be carried out by tricks, by the "hidden hand."

Another famous principle, associated with Rousseau's belief that a child's faculties develop in sharp and discrete stages, is "negative education." The important thing is to lose time, not to gain it. Until the age of twelve the chief emphasis should be on prevention; after that age it is too late to uproot the weeds. This process requires much planning and close supervision. Forgetting—as he so often does—his slogan "The first impulse of nature is always right," Rousseau now says, "Beware of all his feelings until he has judgment to evaluate them."

Negative education is another justification for raising Emile in relative isolation. Nothing is to be dreaded so much as the contagion of human beings. Isolation also helps the tutor to control the environment, for Emile must be allowed to see and to know only what his master decides he should. "You will not be the master of the child, if you are not master of all that surrounds him." In this way he will be kept in a state of innocence, unaware of good and evil.

One exception is the idea of property, which is the source of our experience of justice and injustice. Our first feeling, Rousseau correctly remarks, is not of what we owe to others, but of what they owe to us. This is the occasion for the tutor's first programmed lesson: the planting of beans, which Emile finds, one fine day, plowed under. His anguished complaints are answered by the reproaches of the gardener, who claims to have had his prior planting of melons ruined. None of this is true; the gardener has been coached and the lesson arranged. Thus, we see Rousseau again following his oldest and most persistent technique, the "hidden hand," which he had urged in his very first writing on education. The means do not matter. The end is what counts.

The child has learned, in action, the right of the first occupant. A little trickery also provides Emile with the necessary motivation to learn how to read. He will receive invitations to dinners and parties, but by the time they are read to him, he will have already missed them. Soon he will want to read them himself. He will get a little help, but not enough to quite make them out. (What child would not get furious at this sadistic treatment?)

Emile will learn to read, but there will be no studying before the age of twelve, and no books. "Reading is the curse of childhood, the child's greatest torture," says Jean-Jacques, who had found solace in books.

Shall we teach him facts without a grasp of causes and the moral springs of action, and call it history? Shall we let him hear such things as La Fontaine's fables? Taking "The Fox and the Crow" as an example, Rousseau in a famous analysis shows that the child can learn from it only how useful it is to be a flatterer, rather than to beware of flattery— another revealing commentary on what Jean-Jacques thought of human nature. To the child the fox will be the hero. He will also prefer the ant to the grasshopper and learn to be miserly, harsh, and cruel. From the lion he will learn to grab as much as he can at the expense of the weak. (But isn't that nature's law, and are we not to give Emile a natural education—as in the episode of the drum in *La Nouvelle Héloïse?* Or are we forgetting that Rousseau is redefining nature as man's social nature, but free of all vices which originate in society—if that combination of ideas really means anything?)

Before long Rousseau reemphasizes his objectives. Emile will be "nature's pupil," self-reliant and self-sufficient. He will be the master of his own will, and do only what he wants to do.

Is this freedom, then? The question returns. No, not if we read the rest of the page. Emile will do only what he wants to do, but the master's job is to see that he wants to do only what he *should* do.

Let him *think* that he is always the master, but be sure that you are always the master. There is no subjection so complete as that which keeps the *appearance of freedom*; that is the way to *capture the will* itself. Isn't the poor child at your mercy? His work, his games, his pleasures, his pains—isn't all that in your hands without his knowing it? Of course he should only do what he wants; but he should want to do only what *you* want him to do. [Italics added.]

Could there be a clearer affirmation of the doctrine of the "hidden hand," of complete control by deception? It was the same in *La Nouvelle Héloïse*, where Rousseau also speaks of freedom and immediacy, in the face of planned intervention and management that make of them a subjective illusion. Rousseau again relies on the apparent lack of constraint to induce the child to be completely open, for a purpose which he states unequivocally, in order that the child may be manipulated more surely without his ever realizing it. The triumph of the master's art is to make the child do as the master wills, without orders or refusals, without lectures or exhortations, but leaving him thinking that he is acting freely. The child is a shapeless dough to be kneaded. "I can't imagine anything for which we could not inspire a taste, even a rage, in children, with a little skill." Social scientists of our time affirm that, through motivation research, a world of unseen dictatorship is conceivable, still using the forms of democratic government. This, I believe, was Rousseau's plan. In *Emile* and *La Nouvelle Héloïse*, he originated motivation research and behavioral engineering. "Freedom" has the sense of automatic response of the desired kind, a specific output to a specific input.

As Rousseau's stratagems and stage settings grow more complex, they give us a deep insight into the intricacies of his own mind. To teach Emile the judgment of distances, the master manipulates a foot race with shameless dishonesty, secretly making the distances unequal. When after a time he allows Emile to discover the trickery, and is covered with reproaches, he tells the boy that all he has to do is to take the shortest route and win all the races. Emile soon learns to judge distances very accurately—and to win dishonestly. What complexities to teach a simple lesson! What a pathological confusion of values! And Rousseau dared to criticize La Fontaine!

By the time Emile reaches the age of reason, at twelve, he will have known only pleasure and play. He will—somehow—know how to behave in company and not be egocentric. But how can we believe this, when he has lived for himself alone, except for his tutor, without need for human intimacy, without social relations or obligations? "Whence," remarks one critic, "that strange construction of a child without emotions, without affection, without pity, even without love, of a child completely closed up within himself, in sum, a child without a soul . . . and who—let us admit it frankly—if we met him in life, would make us shudder?"[3] If you deny Emile something, he will immediately accept the refusal, not as a denial, but as an impersonal necessity. "Opinion," or what others think, has no effect on him. He is happy and "free." Some would say he is a monster of Rousseau's imagination.

At twelve, the veil of darkness that covers Emile's mind, "nature's sacred curtain," must be carefully disturbed. Knowledge may lead to fatal error; "ignorance has never done any harm."* To discover what it is natural to learn, we should suppose a philosopher abandoned on a desert island—apparently the natural situation.

"I hate books; they teach only how to talk about what we do not know." How often was this sentence turned against Rousseau by his enemies! Was it not proof of their accusation that he was a lover of paradoxes whose life belied his theories? But Emile will be allowed one book, *Robinson Crusoe*, which corresponds to the philosopher cast on a desert island. Believing erroneously that Robinson Crusoe was deprived of all the instruments of culture, Rousseau draws the equally fallacious conclusion that "the surest way to rise above prejudices and to make one's judgments according to the true relationships of things is to put yourself in the place of an isolated man, and to judge everything as that man would, in reference to what is useful to him."

The tutor's motto in teaching is "Never substitute the sign for the thing, except when you cannot show it." This wise precept leads to one of Rousseau's most complex deceptions. In order to teach Emile the

* "Rousseau," writes Jouvenel, "is the antiprogressive philosopher *par excellence.* His stance is that of the contradictor of all the tendencies that will be increasingly the characteristic of our modern civilization ("Rousseau évolutionniste et pessimiste," p. 12.)

phenomenon of magnetism, the tutor takes him to a fair, where he enlists the services of a performer who has entranced the boy by making a waxed duck move in response to a piece of bread that conceals a magnet. With what pride Emile imitates his performance with a piece of bread the tutor has prepared! Even the mountebank congratulates him. But the next day Emile, expecting another triumph, is thrown into confusion when the bread has been switched and he can get no results. When the performer easily carries out the tricks, the boos of the crowd cover Emile with humiliation. The next day the tutor's accomplice calls on them. After complaining that they have tried to discredit him and deprive him of his living, he reveals the secret of his act. Then, well coached, he turns to Emile's tutor and tells him that it is his duty to guide his pupil in all things. Such is the lesson of magnetism.

Even Emile may stray. The master is never to let him out of sight, but "to spy on him without cease and without his being aware of it, to intuit his feelings in advance and to forestall those he is not to have. . . ." The tutor must "pry out carefully the secret conclusions Emile draws in his heart from his observations." There is to be no secret chamber, like Julie's, which the tutor is unable to penetrate, else control would not be complete.

Soon we come upon another example of Emile's freedom. The tutor will say:

Where shall we dine today? Around that mountain of silver that covers three-quarters of the table and those beds of paper flowers that are served on mirrors at dessert, among those hoop-skirted women who treat you like a toy mario-nette and want you to have said what you do not know, or in that village two leagues from here, among those simple people who welcome us so gaily and give us such good cream? We can be sure what Emile's choice will be.

Indeed we can. Here is an excellent example of how the guide leaves him the illusion of freely choosing, while manipulating him by suggestion, a process to which he has been conditioned since earliest childhood.

Emile will learn to appreciate the dependency inherent in social relations through a knowledge of the useful trades and arts. Despising "opinion," he will, like Robinson, esteem a locksmith above a jeweler and tools above trinkets—as if the true value of things is their worth for a castaway and not for a man living in a civilized society. He will be taught a trade, one that will be manual, useful, and make him relatively independent of fortune and of other men. He will learn carpentry.

Emile's mind has been rigidly directed and limited. Any questions on matters such as history, morals, or metaphysics have been skillfully turned aside. Morally, he is still a child, without a conscience. "He considers himself without regard to others, and is satisfied if others do not consider him. He demands nothing of anyone, and feels no duty to anyone. He is alone in human society. . . . He loves his sister as he loves his watch, his friend as he loves his dog." From this egocentric monster, whose development has been tailored to the Procrustean bed of rigid divisions and categories, Rousseau will now proceed to make the social being, the citizen. But first there is another problem. Puberty is at hand. "As the roar of the sea precedes the tempest from afar, the stormy revolution is heralded by the murmur of nascent passions." But we shall manage, never fear.

Since sexuality leads to depravity, Emile must be virginal when he marries. No modesty is to be taught him, since the very notion of shameful things arouses curiosity about them. The proper method is to prevent curiosity from arising. This requires strategy in replying to the boy's questions. Above all, the master must never be *caught* in a lie, for that would ruin the absolute confidence that is necessary to Rousseau's system of manipulation by deception. To the inevitable question, "Where do babies come from?" the most judicious reply is "My son, women urinate them with pains that sometimes cost them their lives." The unpleasant associations provoked by such an answer are sure to turn aside the child's curiosity. By delaying sexuality, Rousseau reiterates, we shall be *following nature* and keep the passions in order.

Ignorance, artfully preserved, will thus postpone the eruption of sexuality. But this is not enough. Emile must be allowed spectacles or entertainments of a rustic nature that will "throw his imagination off the scent. . . . By carefully providing examples, lessons, images, you will blunt the spur of his senses for a long time, and *deceive nature* by following her own directives. . . . As the desires become enkindled, find the right kind of *tableaux* to repress them." Rousseau is not trying to follow nature. The whole point is to elude and deceive nature.

Rousseau's preoccupation with sexuality, in so many of his writings, reveals that for him it is a great enemy of order and control. It must be delayed, limited, governed by whatever means. Like several other eighteenth-century writers, he realized, even before Sade, the essentially aggressive quality of sexuality.

I have always observed that young men who are corrupted early and given up to women and debauchery were inhuman and cruel; the fire of sexuality made them impatient, vindictive, furious; their imagination, filled with a single object, could see no other; they knew neither pity nor compassion; they would have sacrificed father, mother, and the whole universe to the least of their pleasures.

An essential ingredient of sexuality is *amour-propre*, which Rousseau, in the *Discourse on Inequality*, had distinguished from the beneficent *amour de soi* ("self-love"). *Amour-propre* is the enemy of the good society. It is comparative and can never be satisfied, because it would require that others prefer us to themselves. "It feeds itself unendingly at the next man's expense." Therefore, the fewer men's needs, and the less their competitive rivalry, the better they will be. "On this principle, it is easy to see how the passions of children and men can be directed to good or to evil." This, too, is part of what Rousseau considers a "natural" education. In his reasoning, the passions engendered by *amour-propre* (including sexual aggressiveness) are unnecessary to life and harmful to others, and so are "unnatural." Rousseau, in his puritanism, is trying to accomplish what the Christian religion had tried to achieve in different ways: control of the egoistic instincts and above all the sexual. At the same time, he always believed that true love is noble. By the singularity of its choice, it is a brake to nature's unruliness.

Rousseau wants Emile to be generous and compassionate, but again we cannot count on nature to assure these qualities. We need the skill of a clever tutor "who knows the art of penetrating hearts while working to shape them." The tutor takes advantage of the youth's not having learned to dissimulate (which *he*, of course, has constantly done!) "to read in his face all the movements of his soul; by spying them out, he succeeds in foreseeing them and finally in controlling them. . . . Do you see what new empire you are going to acquire over him? How many chains have you tied around his heart without his realizing it!"

Few would agree with the bizarre notion, which Rousseau next sets forth, that we should postpone the development of sensibility and sociability until the age of sixteen. Behind his reasoning lies his desire to build a strong and independent ego. The child who becomes a social being too soon will be alienated from his own self by his dependency on the approval and disapproval of others, on what Rousseau terms "opinion." "The man of the world is all in his mask. Scarcely ever within himself, he is always a stranger to himself, and uncomfortable when he has to go back within himself. What he is is nothing to him, what he seems to be is everything." There is a deep well of truth in Rousseau's continued criticism of social life. But we scarcely refrain from asking, what is this strong and independent ego, which is strong and independent in its relations with men, but weak and helpless in its master's hands?

Emile is now a moral being. No longer does he live within the circle of his own self. To learn about the unpleasant reality of the social order, he will become a spectator, studying how society has depraved man's natural goodness, how laws inevitably favor the strong, sacrifice the multitude to the few, the general interest to the private. Rousseau's powerful indictment lacks only the words "exploitation" and "class struggle" to make it Marxian. But the sense is the same, and it helps us to understand the revolutionary implications of his political writings. The spirit is also the same: "Those who try to treat politics and morals separately will never understand anything about either of them."

Emile will also learn to estimate the worth of individuals and to despise the masses, *la multitude*. History—more exactly, biography—provides the safest way of doing this. "Directed readings" will have a powerful effect on the blank slate of his mind. A curious but detached spectator, like Wolmar, unspoiled by passions and "opinion," he will understand the springs of action in others. But will Emile really understand anything, we may well wonder, in his vacuum of personal experience? In this regard, Rousseau deludes himself about his Emile, who is the secure child and youth he would have liked to be. He is sure that Emile, "free," "self-sufficient," "dependent on no one," will scorn both the ambitious, struggling for power, wealth, or knowledge, and the wastrel, flying hopelessly from boredom. His only danger, Rousseau says, will be pride, failure to recognize (and here we see the truth peeping out again) that he is his master's creation.

Perhaps we get a more accurate view of what Emile really is, in his independence from "opinion," when we learn that he will not accept an insult or a slap, with its stain of dishonor; but neither will he, in such a situation, endanger his life to remedy what the civil law is unable to avenge. Law being insufficient, he recovers his natural independence. He will simply murder the offender in some way, perhaps by shooting him in the back.

The mental distortions of the authoritarian shape of mind are again evident when we read that the more abstract our love of mankind is, the more virtuous it becomes. If we are not careful to "generalize" pity and "extend it over all mankind," it will degenerate into the weakness of pitying unworthy individuals. We should sacrifice pity to justice or to what best serves the general welfare. "What does it matter who is made happier, as long as it is for the greater happiness of all? That is the first interest of the sage, after his own; for each is part of his species and not of another individual. Reason and self-interest tell us to pity our species even more than our neighbor." This is the attitude and the spirit that, with a little twist in the right circumstances, will give us Robespierre, and the Committees of Public Safety. All we need is more Emiles, who are certain that they possess "the true principles of justice, the true models of beauty, all the moral relations between beings . . . the right place of everything."

Rousseau goes even further in his fantasy. He says of Emile: "Without having experienced human passions, he knows their deceits and their operations." Emile is sixteen years old. But he is different from all others. "He is not man's man, he is nature's man." Perhaps. If true, it took a man and all his devious artifices to make him so—as with Julie's garden—and I do not know that he is the better for it.

Rousseau, then, is almost satisfied that his Emile is sufficiently protected against passion and "opinion" to play his role in society. But first it is necessary for him to have a personal religion and a sound moral conscience. Emile has not yet met God—not even heard his name. Before the age of sixteen, one can have only an idolatrous, animistic, and anthropomorphic idea of God. If a child tried to explain the catechism he recites, he would lose his sanity. Is it enough to repeat words to be saved? Will he be rewarded for having been born in Rome rather than in Mecca? No. Emile will not be the slave of opinion in religion more than in anything else; he will choose for himself. More exactly, Rousseau will write a disquisition on his own metaphysical and religious beliefs, which we are to assume Emile will somehow have chosen for himself.

These and other arguments ring with the tone of the "philosophic" group with which Rousseau had been associated. He knew they were dangerous. Boldly he proclaims his defiance of persecution. "Readers, do not fear that I shall take precautions unworthy of a friend of the truth. I shall never forget my motto ['To risk one's life for the truth']." But he was no longer of the "philosophic" group, and his former friends were to pillory him almost as cruelly as the Church. Rousseau's disquisition, entitled *Profession de foi du vicaire savoyard* (*Profession of Faith of the Savoyard Vicar*) grew, in fact, out of a long, soul-searching confrontation between the reason of the *philosophes* and his own religion, which he had learned, not from the Protestant or Catholic churches, but from Maman, the Abbé Gaime, and the Abbé Gâtier. Near the end of his life, Rousseau relates in the third "Promenade" how his skeptical friends had shaken the security of his beliefs, how he had, after his "reform" in 1751, submitted them to the unrelenting challenge of his reason, and how they had come out of the test unscathed. From then on he was never again to have doubts, never even to pay heed to the arguments that were hurled at him. His own conscience was sufficient.

Now Rousseau departs from his usual techniques and pretends that he will not count on himself. There is no direct instruction of Emile. After recounting a romanticized version of his friendship with the Abbé Gaime during the Turin period, he combines the personalities of Gaime and the Abbé Gâtier, fuses their doctrines with his own, and gives us the most celebrated part of *Emile*. The scene is the high hill overlooking the Po and the distant snow-covered Alps; the rising sun sends its myriad colors and long shadows over the hills, fields, and houses. This is the proper setting in which to speak of God and the eternal verities.

## 2. THE *Profession de foi*

The abbé speaks. He tells Jean-Jacques about his spiritual pilgrimage, more like Descartes' than Dante's, except that his, like the poet's, began with sin. Unlike other priests, he had respected marriage and so had a child by an unmarried girl. Having fled from persecution, he began the search for truth in the seclusion of a safe retreat. His first conclusion was that the Church's authority is tyrannical and vain; his second, that the philosophers in their pride lead us only into the kingdom of confusion. One way is left: "Let us consult the inner light." Whatever "the heart" (substituted for Descartes' "reason") admits as clear and evident, will be true.

So much for the method. Only it is not really his method. In reality, Rousseau is a reasoner and a rationalist. He will reason as hard and as far as he can. He is also a dogmatist. Knowing in advance what he wants to prove, he will abandon reason, mock and vilify it when it abandons him, and turn in triumph to the "inner light." The "inner light" is infallible because it is an immediate intuition, preverbal in form, unfiltered by reason. He sees no contradiction in his attitude: reason, "properly" used, within its "proper" sphere, is man's attribute. But he also decries reason, because he is hostile to its effects as men have used it in civilization. That had been enough to turn him against Voltaire, Diderot, and the Encyclopedists, and to turn them against him.

In writing the *Profession de foi*, Rousseau hoped to settle once and for all his religious position, in his own mind and especially in that of the public. He wanted to establish his opposition to atheism, materialism, and determinism, but without becoming an ally of the Church. Thinking through his positions, he made the unhappy discovery that Condillac's sensationism, which he, like all the *philosophes*, had followed, was one basis of the doctrines he was assailing. Now at the "pitch of his antiphilosophic fervor," he was forced to double back.[4] In order to refute a theory that eventuated in such detestable ideas as those he had condemned in Helvétius' *De l'Esprit* (1758), he now had recourse to the old Cartesian mind-body dualism, defended free will, and postulated conscience as a motive of behavior alongside self-interest. Like Descartes, again, he insists that the mind is "an active force." Free will becomes possible, and Helvétius' paradox, that to feel and to judge are one thing, becomes untenable. "According to me, the distinctive faculty of the active or intelligent being is to be able to give meaning to the word *is*." The idea foreshadows existentialism. The point Rousseau wishes to establish is that in man the response to external stimuli is mediated (if we may use modern terminology) by a set of internal mental states. Man has unique powers of judgment which make freedom possible. But from this fact Rousseau draws this paradoxical conclusion: the less we judge, the closer we shall be to the truth. "Thus my rule, to be led by feeling rather than reason, is confirmed by reason itself. . . ." We may be astonished by this *non sequitur*.

God exists. The materialists' idea that matter is self-moving, and the universe self-regulating, is nonsense. Intuition cannot accept it. Scientific laws explain nothing, he adds, failing to understand that scientific laws do not explain at all. He goes on. If motion proves a will that moves the universe, "matter moved according to certain laws shows me an intelligence." If only we listen to inner feeling, we shall see God.

"Not only in the skies that turn, in the star that shines on us; not only in myself, but in the sheep that grazes, in the bird that flies, in the stone that falls, in the leaf that the wind sweeps away." Chance cannot produce life. So much, then, for the arguments of the *philosophes!*

Man, because of his reason and moral conscience, is king of the earth. But he is a dual being in another sense, too, in the Christian sense. One part of him is animal passion and egoism; the other is spiritual. He is both slave and free. "I see the good, I love it, and I do evil." That is why the human world is the realm of disorder.

Rousseau's psychology goes beyond the pleasure-pain mechanism of Condillac and the materialists. To follow your passions is not to do what you want to do, he affirms. Freedom is the overcoming of instinctual desires, and virtue exists only where there is struggle. Respect for order is the sign of freedom and virtue. In his exaltation of moral responsibility, Rousseau seems to be replying to materialists who had argued that man is not free and therefore not responsible morally, but answerable only to society's laws and power.

Part of man's uniqueness is that there is no limit to his will for expansion and power. Rousseau, before Sade, realizes that man, longing to escape his contingency, strives for godhood. "Something in you seeks to break the links that confine your mind; space is not your measure, the entire universe is not big enough for you. Your feelings, your desires, your disquiet, your very pride have a different principle from that of the narrow body in which you feel yourself chained."

I have a soul, then. "No material being is self-actuating and I am. You will argue in vain; I feel it, and that feeling which speaks to me is stronger than reason which combats it." Thus, we have the third principle: man is free and animated by an immaterial substance. This being so, God is exonerated. "Take away man's work, and all is right." Here Rousseau uses the Christian argument: God made us free so that we could choose the good, have merit, and be virtuous. All of Bayle's arguments, about God being either not good or not omnipotent, and responsible for evil in his own creation, are swept by in this theodicy. "No, God of my soul, I shall never reproach you for having made me in your image, so that I could be free, good, and happy like you." Rousseau might have seen that we are not free like God, or inversely, that God is not as free as we are. We can choose between good and evil, but God cannot; we are not omnipotent, while he is. And if we are happy, it is not like God, either. Rousseau has forgotten what he had written earlier in the book: God is happy because he desires nothing (being all-powerful), whereas man is happy only in desiring and striving. Doubtless Rousseau here betrays his secret wish to be happy in the same way as God.

Thus, Pope and Leibniz, routed by Voltaire's *Candide,* make their bold return, to triumph again in the works of Rousseau's sentimental disciple, Bernardin de Saint-Pierre. But Jean-Jacques, unlike the earlier optimists, has a bitter grudge against mankind, whom he affects to love. Man is the culprit, for having spoiled God's world. "All is good when it leaves God's hands, and all is spoiled in the hands of man." Man has put an end to innocence and the neutrality of the *is*. He has created a new world of freedom, of good and evil, and much as Rousseau admires it, much as he approves of it, he simultaneously condemns it as the principle of disorder. Man, finally, has brought God's goodness into question and dared to hail the Creator before the creature's bar of justice.

The vicar's inner voice speaks again. Although he has said God is unknowable, he now finds this promise inscribed in his heart: "Be just, and you will be happy." But Rousseau, who was convinced of his own goodness and his misfortune, was pricked by the thorn that stung the conscience of many eighteenth-century writers: "The wicked prosper and the just man is oppressed." Was he not the living proof? In Rousseau there was to be no metaphysical revolt against this disorder, nothing of the attitude of the nihilists (such as Sade) toward a wicked God and a blind universe in which man is an alien. For him this betrayal is the very proof of the soul's survival: "So shocking a dissonance in the universal harmony" can only indicate that "order is restored after death." If it were not so, God would be dishonored (Psalm 115), and he would only be a principle of disorder.* To Jacob Vernes he wrote (February 18, 1758), "God would not be just if my soul were not immortal." This is one of the finest examples of rationalized wishful thinking in Rousseau, and there are many. If he had not been able to cling to God, and the future "restoration of order," he would (like Julie) have been lost. Perhaps he would have been a rebel and a nihilist, like Sade; for he admits that "if God does not exist, only the wicked man is reasonable, the good man is insane." But that would have been another Rousseau.

He knows what paradise will be like. Paradise is the narcissistic enjoyment of private worlds. "I aspire to the moment when, released from the fetters of the body, I will be *myself* without contradiction, without sharing, and I shall need only myself to be happy." The aspiration to godlike autarchy that runs throughout Rousseau's life and writings will at last be fulfilled. The inner contradiction between self-esteem and self-abasement, between longing and guilt, will disappear in the harmony of unity. No longer will the "other" be the insuperable obstacle to his self-acceptance.

The vicar now takes us into the realm of morals. Natural Law is

---

* In a twentieth-century version of the same argument, one of Anouilh's characters says: "All the same God must keep his promises, otherwise the just who, like you, have bet everything on it, will be robbed just as by a highwayman" (Jean Anouilh, *L'Invitation au château*, act III, scene 1). There are those who are not satisfied with Pascal's wager, who want to be sure to win.

inscribed in his heart in ineffaceable letters. "I have only to consult myself on what I want to do; whatever I feel is right is right, whatever I feel is bad is bad." Although Rousseau assumes the silence of the passions in this consultation, such a statement has been justly criticized as foreshadowing the anarchism of Romantic morality. But he himself will not stay with it. With his distrust of the common man's egoism, or *amour-propre*, he raises the impersonal conscience of the general will, in his political writings, above that of the individual.

His passages about the conscience are studded with famous phrases. "God has given us conscience to love the good, reason to know it, freedom to choose it." But they are confusing statements, too, since he cannot decide whether conscience is a feeling or a judgment. He also says that while reason may err, conscience will not. It is likely that he takes reason to be the mediator between instinct and conscience, which are both immediate. In its mediating function, reason destroys the unity of consciousness and our unity with the world.

Growing lyrical, Rousseau pens the famous hymn to the conscience which inspired Kant, who saw in Rousseau the Newton of the moral world:

Conscience! conscience! divine instinct, immortal and celestial guide of an ignorant and limited, but intelligent and free being; infallible judge of good and evil, that makes man like unto God: It is you who make the excellence of his nature and the morality of his actions; without you I feel nothing in me that lifts me above the beasts except the sad privilege of straying from error to error with the help of an understanding without rule and a reason without principle.

Each of us, he had written in *La Nouvelle Héloïse,* has a divine model of order and perfection inscribed in our hearts, and fortunately we do not have to be philosophers to distinguish right from wrong.

Like Kant, Rousseau holds that the morality of acts lies in intent or good will. "The entire morality of human life," he wrote to Mme. d'Houdetot, "is in man's intention." His frequent defense of his own or of others' reprehensible acts as coming from a good heart that was too weak to be virtuous is related to this position, which is subjective, romantic, and even capricious. For Rousseau, subjective truth, his own truth, was all that mattered in his own life; he resented the contradictoriness of objective intrusions. In a fragment of a letter written in 1767 to the economist, the Marquis de Mirabeau, he says: "I let myself go to the impression of the moment without resistance and without scruples; for I am absolutely sure that my heart loves only what is good. All the wrong I have done in my life was done from reflection, and the little good I may have done was done from impulse." The statement is not accurate, as the incident of the ribbon suffices to show. But Rousseau was always divided between the man he was and could not accept and the man he would have liked to be or dreamt that he was.

No act is moral unless it is experienced as such. We must do the good, then, for its own sake, for the love of it (as a maxim, Kant will say), if we are to be virtuous. All men, the vicar assures us, love virtue when they cast aside their own interest. Obviously, the conditional phrase changes the nature of the question, since men are evil principally out of self-interest. Rousseau does not consider the possibility, upheld by some eighteenth-century writers, that men may do evil for the love of evil.

Virtue speaks for the general interest, and against self-interest. But reason, he argues (to the same effect as Hume but in a different way), cannot establish virtue, moral laws, or any proof of the proposition that men should be virtuous. It is a natural need of the heart, or it is nothing. But why, asks the vicar, echoing the argument of all the moral nihilists, should I prefer virtue to my own well-being? After all, vice, like virtue, is the love of order, but an order of a different kind. "The difference is that the good man orders himself in relation to the whole, and the wicked man orders the whole in relation to himself." Thus, Rousseau remains consistent with his political thinking, even if he does not supply a good answer to the question.

Further considerations on conscience lead Rousseau into a paradox that holds a profound truth: society is the very condition of the moral life, but it is destructive to morality. To some extent, our moral experience originates in pity which, although it is self-centered, becomes other-directed. (Another source is in the offenses we experience as wrongs.) Self-love, however, having degenerated into *amour-propre*, often stifles pity. Conscience may also be stifled, but never extinguished. Not present in "natural man," it flourishes as soon as he becomes a social being. Opposed to it are the pride and envy that result from the human comparative process in which we see and judge ourselves through the eyes of the spectator, of the "other."*

Now the vicar launches into a long and forceful critique of so-called revealed religions, their dogmas, churches, and priests, their intolerance and cruelty. This section was damned by the devout and applauded by Voltaire and all the *philosophes*, any one of whom might have written it. How odd that this disparager of reason should exclaim: "It is useless for them to cry to me, 'Submit your reason'; a deceiver would tell me as much. You must supply the reasons why I should submit my reason. . . . The God of darkness has not given me an understanding only to forbid my using it."

Not that a public cult is unnecessary to the welfare of the State, but this is a political matter, to be established by the government as one of its instrumentalities. In God's eyes the only cult that counts is that of the heart, and for it no churches or priests are needed. "How many men between God and me!"

---

* In Rousseau's political tracts, the accent is quite different. Conscience and Natural Law play no part, because he sees them overwhelmed by egoism and aggressiveness, which it is his whole intent to control.

Rousseau had been both Catholic and Protestant, but he was not really a Christian, though he may have been the most religious man in the eighteenth century. Revelation and grace are excluded from his natural religion. In a way he is a disciple of the Stoics and Plato, but his essential originality is the personal emotion he put into his worship of God and the effusion of his self into a religious communion with nature and the universe. It was this that influenced the Romantic generation in their unorthodox Christian religiosity.*

In an interesting parenthesis, Rousseau excoriates Christians for their persecution of Jews and demands that they be allowed schools, universities, freedom of speech, and self-government. He was the only major *philosophe* in the Enlightenment to take such an enlightened attitude, although he does speak of the ancient Hebrews as "the vilest of all peoples." Voltaire hated and reviled the Chosen People, who had given the world the *infâme* of Christianity. None of the other *philosophes* included the Jews in their plans for a modern state and an open society.[5] They looked on that mysterious group with a natural aversion for the alien tinged with the scorn of popular folklore.

The most astonishing ambivalence in the *Profession de foi* is Rousseau's attitude toward the Scriptures. He ridicules the so-called miracles and the other proofs of Christ's mission, and scorns the religion they preach which, if followed scrupulously, would put an end to all civil life. The Gospels cannot be accepted because (of all things!) they are repugnant to the reason. But then he admits their emotional power. "I confess to you that the majesty of the Scriptures astonishes me, and the holiness of the Gospels speaks to my heart." The death of Jesus was that of a God. Yet it is most curious that Julie, in all her religious effusions, never mentions Christ. She, too, needs no revelation, no church or mediator. Her relationship is directly with God, who will judge her according to the purity of her intentions. Rousseau himself read the Bible often, and he prayed; but his prayers did not include Christ, the Virgin, nor any Christian dogma. Nor is his concept of virtue a Christian one. Essentially social, it values the negative rule, to do no harm, above the doing of good. The golden rule is dangerous; the negative virtues are the most sublime and also the most difficult, since they remain unknown and reap no reward.

Thus the *Profession de foi* ends. But we cannot take leave of it without referring to an interesting footnote near its close. Rousseau was a defender of religious tolerance. Here, however, he defends fanaticism, even when it is cruel and sanguinary, as a noble passion "that lifts up man's heart, makes him despise death, gives him a tremendous source of

---

* Guéhenno puts the matter cleverly: "He certainly had a profoundly religious soul, but he was the only priest of his religion and he alone wrote its Gospel. He admitted neither books nor men between God and him" (Jean Guéhenno, *Jean-Jacques: En marge des "Confessions," 1712–1750*, Vol. II, pp. 39–40). Yet the religion of *Emile* is systematic in contrast with the spontaneity and spiritual aspiration of Rousseau's personal religious experiences. He seems to be looking for a religion acceptable to his time.

energy which only has to be better directed to draw from it the most sublime virtues." This thought is another link with political theory. Religious skepticism, he argues, concentrates the passions "in the vileness of private interest, in the abjection of the human self, and so quietly undermines the true foundations of all society; for what private interests have in common is so slight that it will never balance their antagonisms." These lines express Rousseau's basic political outlook. Self-interest, the *human self*, must be superseded; another type of relation between men, and between men and society, must be found. The liberal idea of consensus, of a compromise or equilibrium of interests, is implicitly rejected for the ideal of unanimity. Rousseau's words breathe the authoritarian spirit.

As a philosophical treatise, the *Profession de foi* is feeble. It represents Rousseau's need for subjective certainty, his tendency to perceive reality in accordance with his wishes, interests, and fantasies. An individual of this psychic complexion always fights against any disturbance of his cherished certainty and resents it bitterly.[6] This typology explains, better than anything else perhaps, Rousseau's underlying aversion to scientism and to the *philosophes*, the group that most disturbed the security of his beliefs. At the same time, the presence of God provides, seemingly at least, an objective ground for security and certainty.

Rousseau's idea of God, and his ethics, are close to the Platonic tradition. To know God—a vision of beauty and order—man must turn his mind away from the inferior things of sense toward the inner reality of his own soul which, as part of the World-Soul, reflects the divine Ideas. Passion and *amour-propre* are evil regions of matter which can be overcome by looking upward to the sphere of spirit—virtue. As in Plato and Plotinus, this outlook leads easily into the ideal of community or collectivity.

Such a doctrine is related in spirit to modern anti-intellectual and mystical currents. That is why the aspect of the *Profession de foi* that has most perplexed critics and commentators is the duality of Rousseau's rationalism and antirationalism. At times he seems Socratic in advancing an ethic of acting on principle, with a courageous acceptance of all its risks; but more often he places obedience to a mysterious inner conscience above an intelligent estimation of the values involved in a situation of choice. For him (as for Kierkegaard) existential truth, as opposed to the abstract reasoning of his former friends, is a total commitment to something objectively and rationally uncertain, a commitment equivalent to faith.

Yet nothing could be more erroneous than the popular view that Rousseau urged complete license to follow our feelings. The charge is contrary to the entire tenor of his writings. The *Profession de foi* has been justly called an attempt to reconstruct man's psychological unity, to harmonize reason and sentiment, man and the world, exactly as in his sociopolitical writings he seeks the way to social unity. That is why the vicar defines virtue as the love of order rather than of justice or right, an emphasis we earlier found in *La Nouvelle Héloïse*. With his "sense of the disintegration of the human personality in modern society," of "internal strife and loss of the self . . . he evolves an almost utopian vision of an end to *mauvaise foi* and self-alienation and the creation of a unified moral consciousness 'when all the powers of the soul are alive to the beauty of order.' "[7]

Rousseau is both a rationalist and an antirationalist. Reason is properly human; but it is dangerous, because it is also human to abuse it. Throughout Emile's education, as well as in the other writings, distrust of the intellect is a dominating factor; paradoxically, the structure of that education is as much a work of the pure intellect as is *The Social Contract*. In his personal relations, Rousseau valued sentimental communion above intellectual attainments or activities. He distrusted reason as the instrument of "progress," which had alienated men from nature. He abominated reason when it was not amenable to the subjective truth he needed. At times he seemed possessed by a childish rage against reason because he could not make it yield that truth, or again when his adversaries used it to deduce conflicting truths. In such instances he was ready to appeal to the deeper forces of feeling and conscience that could make the certainties he needed, *his* truths, immune to rational criticism. Reason has its place, and in its place is good and noble; but for Rousseau it was not enough to say that the dignity of man demands a life presided over by reason.

While it is deceptive to say, as Cassirer does, that Rousseau set "the pure ethos of law" over the utilitarian theories of the Encyclopedists[8]— for Rousseau's concept of law was utilitarian, and he held justice to be established by law—it is true, more exactly, that he set moral law apart from and above individual *self*-interest. While his idea of virtue, like that of the *philosophes*, was beneficent social behavior, he denied this was enough without the dedication to the moral purity and perfection, the moral beauty in the inner life, that makes man the image of God. This heritage of Calvinism sets his moral philosophy apart from the others and accounts for its influence. There is no doubt that he considered himself dedicated to it. To prove it to himself, to witness it to the world of corrupt men who would not recognize or could not understand his moral superiority, he, the prophet, the leader to the right way, was willing to incur their wrath, bear their contumely, and suffer their persecution.

Impregnated with the glow of Rousseau's conviction and eloquence, the *Profession de foi* has had a deep impact. He was to say quite truthfully, in the third "Promenade," that his purpose had not been to convince, but to display his personal religious outlook at the end of a long itinerary. It is the imprint of Rousseau's *expérience vécue* that makes the

*Profession de foi* a human document of lasting interest and significance.

This man, whose inner being was filled with shame, guilt, and self-abasement, took fright and withdrew when approached or put in the center of the stage. In the shelter of his loneliness, he became strong, courageous, outspoken, and in so doing, sought his identity and his redemption.

### 3. THE DISCOVERY OF SOPHIE

At this point Rousseau summarizes the progress he has made with his creature. "To make man one" he has "deceived Emile's nascent sensibility," or sensuality, until the heart could catch up with the body. Now that Emile's moral and intellectual development are well advanced, these faculties serve to increase the tutor's power over him. "What new means of control we have given ourselves over our pupil," he exults.

An astonishing reversal follows, one of many points in *Emile* that critics have passed over. The tutor will teach Emile to love the good not only for its own sake or for the sake of order. Men, we are assured, will never love the good for any reason except self-love, and "every man always prefers his self-love" to the love of order. To pretend otherwise is only to cultivate hypocrisy, for in this competitive world self-interest always wins out. This reversal underscores Rousseau's opinion about men and their social relationships.* It is the basis of his reliance on deception and coercion (in education, in political and social life) and of his dream of the transformation of the self in the ideal society. He does not, after all, rely on conscience or on voluntary good will. On the contrary, he makes no effort to hide his dependence on deception and coercion.

Up till now you obtained nothing from him except by force or by rule; authority, the law of duty, were unknown to him; you had to coerce him or deceive him to be obeyed. But now you see with how many new chains you have bound his heart. . . . The first of all passions, self-love, puts him in your power; habit does as much. . . . Keep him from being corrupted, and he will always be docile.

Emile must never be aware that there even is such a thing as deceit. How much better this way than to attempt Wolmar's work with an already corrupted Saint-Preux!

After this long detour, we are brought back to the problem of Emile's

---

* Rousseau, like the materialists, like Sade, declares that we pity others out of enjoyment of the fact that we are not suffering, like them, ills from which we feel ourselves not to be immune. Happiness in others inspires envy. Green remarks: "It never occurred to him that the primitive man who resides within each of us might be just as ready to laugh with his fellows or to weep with them" (F. C. Green, *Jean-Jacques Rousseau*, p. 238).

sexuality. Following "nature," then, Emile's master will keep him unaware of sexual desires until he is twenty. This athletic youth has had no voluptuous dreams or nocturnal emissions. Hard work and hunting have exhausted his energies. The youth must not be let out of sight, day or night, not allowed to go to bed unless dead with exhaustion, and then the tutor should preferably share his bed. Sexual desire does not represent a genuine physical need, but is only the work of the imagination, which can be controlled. "I am convinced that a man brought up in complete solitude, in the wilderness, without books, without learning and without women, would die a virgin there regardless of his age."

But now, at the age of twenty, appropriate lectures will uncover to Emile the "inconceivable mystery of reproduction." He will not be allowed to forget that chastity and fidelity are the basis of order in society, their violation the source of disorder. Emile's mind "will be docile." His master once more counts especially on his not having learned to deceive or to dissimulate—unlike himself! The problem is to "guide" Emile's unleashed imagination, rather than to stifle it. "Spare no effort to become his confidant; it is only with this title that you will really be his master." And the "independent" Emile, just like Saint-Preux, will respond; "I want to obey your laws, I shall always want to. . . . Make me free by protecting me against my passions—force me to be my own master by obedience to my reason, not to my senses."

This astonishing reply combines the submissive masochism of the pupil with the master's fantasy of domination.* Both are projections of Rousseau's psyche and unconscious wish-fulfillment. Emile's reply is the fanciful culmination and triumph of the whole "method." Despite the lack of *overt* interference with free or spontaneous expression, his behavior has on every occasion been foreseen, regulated, or corrected, with the end result that it must lose spontaneity and become—like physical laws —automatic and predictable. The appearance or illusion of freedom is a necessary element in the process of control. Emile's whole life has been carefully mapped out for him, controlled at every step. He will have the freedom and the spontaneity of a computer, to act and react as he has been programmed. He cannot even choose his own wife, do his own courting, or make love to his wife without supervision. The link with *The Social Contract* is evident. There, too, the "guide" will force the citizen to be free by obedience to public reason, the will of the collective self.

From now on the tutor will no longer fight against Emile's inclinations.

I shall consult them, so as to be their master; I shall enter into his view, in order to direct them. . . . How dull one must be to see in a young man's

---

* "I control comparisons, and I easily impede the illusion of real objects." This is only one of the expressions of the fantasy of power.

nascent desires only an obstacle to reason's lessons! I see in them the real means for making him docile to those same lessons. One can control passions only through passions. . . . You cannot imagine how at the age of twenty, Emile can be docile. . . . It took me fifteen years of careful work to win that hold on him. I was not bringing him up then, I was preparing him to be brought up. He is now sufficiently brought up to be docile. . . . I leave him, it is true, *the appearance of independence*, but *never has he been more completely subjugated* to me, for he is in my subjection *because he wants to be*. As long as I was not able to *make myself the master of his will*, I remained the master of his person; I never left him. Now I sometimes leave him by himself, because I still control him. [Italics added.]

What a lesson about the real meaning and purpose of Rousseau's system of education and politics! Education is a form of control, just as the State is a mechanism for control, of wills, of acts, of thought.

The remaining pages of Book IV and all of Book V are devoted to Emile's courtship, and to the education of his future wife, Sophie. This section becomes more and more novelistic in character, which may explain why contemporaries preferred it, along with the *Profession de foi*. Rousseau's biographers and critics usually pass it over rapidly. It is the sorriest part of the work and, together with Book IV, his favorite part. Into it he unconsciously projects his perversions, for we are dealing with sex, ever guilt and shame laden for him. It is curious indeed that this is also the part of *Emile* in which the tutor's stratagems and trickery become most intricate and devious. He has already selected the future wife and goes to all lengths to build up in Emile's mind an ideal image that corresponds to her. This he does so thoroughly that in the sequel to *Emile* the hero says, "I loved Sophie even before I knew her."

First, however, Emile will be further readied for Sophie, whose image he already cherishes, by a stay in Paris. There he will come to know worldly and artificial women, and to feel repugnance toward them. Of course, with the upbringing he has had, he will fit smoothly into the world of the salons (even without knowing anything of its manners), while remaining superbly cool and aloof, the impervious spectator of the foibles and weaknesses of the "slaves of opinion." How Jean-Jacques triumphs now, in his imaginary world! What sweet revenge! Yet—strange contradiction!—Emile will esteem "opinion" just enough to develop a keen *competitive spirit* and excel in everything, except such things as ready wit and clever speech—which are of course to be despised! Knowing himself to be good, he will want the approbation of others—not because he needs it, but because it will prove them to be worthy of him. We can feel only pity for the unhappy Jean-Jacques who projected his troubled inner world into these fantasies.

Rousseau's ideas about women reflect his authoritarian shape of mind and his need to compensate for his feelings of inadequacy by belief in male superiority. (He never forgave Parisian women for making sport of him, scorning him, or laughing in his face outrageously.) Sophie does not imitate men and knows that women have a different natural and social role. A woman's role is to please a man; it is less important that he please her. His role is to be strong, while hers is to be passive and weak. She must know how to provoke him to use his strength, and how to enslave him by her charms. Modesty, according to Rousseau's theory, is a male protective device against woman's insatiable sexual desires. (Had Mme. de Warens taught him that?) The double standard is nature's law. Rousseau pinpoints the danger (which religion is powerless to meet) that women represent to the social order. A beautiful woman will never despise her body or feel sorry for the sins her beauty makes her or men commit. She will never regret being an object of lustful desire. The goal, then, must be to make her submissive, as well as content with her intellectual inferiority. Her destiny is to bear children, and her horizon limited to the home.

Here, as in *La Nouvelle Héloïse*, Rousseau supports the Spanish honor code, according to which it is not enough that a woman be faithful; she must "be judged so by her husband, those around her, by everybody." For a woman, but not for a man, appearance and "opinion"—what others think of her—are everything. "Opinion is the tomb of virtue among men, and its throne among women." With girls, the magic question is not, as with Emile, "What is it good for?" but "What will people think?"

Women must be healthy and strong so that they can bear strong sons. In a word, women are made for men's pleasure, and men are made to fight. Such is nature's law. After she is married (Rousseau says it twice), a woman should rarely be seen outside her home; both nature and reason (or at least Rousseau's nature and reason) demand that she be like a nun in her cloister. Moreover, since "that sex" is wheedling and tricky by nature, we shall not trust their words—a lesson doubtless learned from Thérèse.

It follows that a girl's education should be entirely different from a boy's and entirely relative to what her husband will expect of her. She must be able to think, to be sure, but learn only what is proper for her to know. Women have only a practical kind of reason, designed to get what they want. It follows that girls can conceive of religion even less than boys and should be submitted to authority in this as in all things. Rousseau takes advantage of the opening to deride the Catholic dogma and catechism, and to insist on the social necessity of a belief in a God who rewards and punishes in the next life. "Whoever combats [these principles] deserves without question to be punished; he is the disturber of order and the enemy of society."

There is another reason for us to beware of cultivating women's minds. They are superior to us in the qualities of their sex; "if we make them our equals in the rest, what will this be except to give the wife the superiority that nature has given to the husband?" In these words Rousseau's deep-seated fear of women and his acute sense of sexual rivalry come out sharply. Emphasizing man's limited sexual powers and women's unlimited appetites, he judges monogamy natural to the male. Women's naturally libidinous instincts are whetted by our social institutions, and their fidelity can never be counted on.

Rousseau's ideas about women may seem antiquated, tyrannical, intolerable. They certainly go in a direction òpposite to that taken by modern civilization. Yet it may be argued in his favor that he felt woman's complexity, compared to man, her ability to function behind the scenes, as mover and manipulator, and as supporter of man's ego. He not only feared women's competing with men, he deplored its consequences: the masculinization of women, the feminization of men. He wanted no homogenizing of the sexes. In Rousseau's world, the male has the lead, the authority and primacy; but he recognizes woman's peculiar qualities and powers, her ascendancy over hearts—one may almost speak of a respect, even a fear, of her magic powers. He does not attempt to suppress their play, but only to direct and utilize them.

We shall skip the details of the long courtship, which is controlled by the tutor, aided by Sophie's father, with incredible trickery and deceptive maneuvers. The complexities and subtleties of the tutor's stratagems for manipulating Emile often give the impression that they could spring only from an abnormal mind.

There are, to be sure, pages suffused with tender, idyllic sentimentality, highlighted by occasional erotic touches; pages in which Jean-Jacques, in his vicarious imaginative experience, lives out his dream wishes; pages that even include his desire to be imperiously commanded and mistreated by his mistress. Other perverted tendencies make their way into the idyll. The tutor prepares Emile, with sadistic cruelty, for a long test separation from Sophie, during which he will travel and study political institutions. As Starobinski writes,* "The preceptor seems to take secret pleasure in those tears he causes to flow; but we have not had to wait until the fifth book of *Emile* to discover his sadism."[9] On the emotional level this episode is a transposition from Rousseau's own life, echoing his recurrent theme of separation and return, the renewal of lost beginnings.

Emile's political observations reinforce Rousseau's view of existing societies as essentially nihilistic in character. They are so because of human nature itself. "Needing civil life," men are "unable to get along any more without devouring men." This brutal, barely disguised warfare, which Rousseau had portrayed in the *Discourse on Inequality*, is another way of phrasing the basic motive for his system of regimentation.

---

* Jean Starobinski, *Jean-Jacques Rousseau, la transparence et l'obstacle*; Genève, 1957, p. 157.

After Emile's return the wedding will take place, but not before Rousseau has served as marriage counselor. When the marriage is consummated, he seems actually to become sexually excited as he plays the role of *voyeur*. After their sexual initiation, he looks at the couple carefully and with erotic pleasure. Closely, he observes their reactions, their sexual provocations. When Emile tells him that Sophie has refused him one night, the tutor gives her a long lecture about her sexual relations with her husband, and urges her not to worry about over-indulgence affecting his health.

Rousseau's role in the imaginary love affair he has created has been astutely analyzed by Jean Starobinski.* He overcomes his dependency and inferiority as an intruder by acting as the sole possessor of the science of happiness. His own sexuality is vicariously satisfied by participating in the young couple's erotic games; he mediates them, and they confide intimately in him. He is the author of their joy: "How often, contemplating my work in them, do I feel overcome by an ecstasy that makes my heart proud! How many times do I join their hands in mine, blessing providence and sighing ardently! How many kisses I give to those two clenched hands!" He is in a sense above their emotional dependency and detached from it, free of all ties. Yet, from this outside position, he contrives to be in the center of their eroticism and to partake of it. An accomplice in their sexual intoxication, "he turns aside the erotic joy or pain that he has aroused in others and on which he does not want to be dependent." Rousseau, in his imaginary world, has fulfilled his secret longings for sexual satisfaction without emotional obligations or other responsibility, without risking the adequacy of his manhood, without commitment.

This, then, is what Rousseau calls a "natural education." But the "natural," as it is expounded in *Emile*, does not exist naturally, and has never existed. It is "natural" that men should be corrupted by society; but this is precisely what must be avoided. As we saw with Julie's garden, nature, in Rousseau's sense, never makes itself. A natural education becomes, almost by definition, an education controlled by artifice. The very touch of men corrupts nature (in his sense of the word), and this makes it necessary for men to create the natural according to an ideal model. As one scholar has pointed out, this "is not the condition that man would reach if he were left to develop it naturally."[10]

From quite another viewpoint, what is "natural" in Emile's education is his acceptance of what is done to him on an induced conviction that it has a natural necessity. This necessity is also his freedom. "It is you, O my master, who have made me free by teaching me to yield to necessity." This "freedom" means following a predetermined pattern of thought, feeling, and behavior *freely*, a result that can follow only from a devi-

---

* *Ibid.*, pp. 219-21.

ous, concealed, and powerful conditioning process. Quite self-conscious about his manipulations and his arbitrary use of the words "nature" and "natural," Rousseau tries to forestall the obvious objection. "You will say that the dreamer is still pursuing his fantasy; in giving us a pupil of his fashioning, he does not only shape him, he creates him, he plucks him out of his brain; and always thinking he is following nature, he abandons her at every step." His reply to the objection (which he knows to be true) reveals with complete sincerity the drift of his philosophy: "There are so many contradictions between the rights of nature and our social laws that to harmonize them we must use dodges and evasions; it takes much art to prevent social man from being completely artificial."

If *Emile* was only a theory or a dream, it was one in which Rousseau believed. In his letter to M. de Beaumont, he says that *Emile* was written to show how men can be prevented from becoming evil. "I have not affirmed that in the present order the thing was absolutely impossible; but I have affirmed and I still affirm that to reach that end there are no other means than those I have proposed."

But for what has Emile been educated? This is the first question we posed. Rousseau himself sees the dilemma in relation to present societies: "Forced to combat nature or social institutions, we must choose between making a man or a citizen, for we cannot do both." He obviously believes he can do both. Emile is "nature's man," yet Rousseau also declares that he is educated to be a citizen. Indeed, just as he says that morals and politics are inseparable, so he believes that education and politics are inseparable. Political action is considered to be educational, and educational activity to be political. What happens in such a fusion is that pedagogy, like morals, becomes political, rather than the contrary. Nevertheless, the relation between Emile and his life as a citizen remains vague and undefined. A child normally goes through a stage of narcissism which gradually fuses with attitudes toward others as he becomes a part of social groups. Emile, in the image of his maker, has been made to cultivate a prolonged narcissism. In fact, Rousseau does not intend that he ever be really integrated into society. "Emile will be, if he will, a likable stranger." Can we form someone for society by keeping him out of society?

Emile is educated for independence from other men; but beneath this inculcated belief in his independence lies the deepest, most permanent dependence on his guide. Rousseau's own dualism is replicated in his creation. It is the underlying dependency that will make him a *citizen*— which men in our societies are not. "Natural man is everything for himself. He is an absolute whole, having no relations except to himself or his fellow. Civil man is only a fraction depending on the denominator, whose value is in his relation to the whole that is the social body." The individual is fast swallowed up. Rousseau continues:

Good social institutions are those that know how best to denature man, to take away his absolute existence and give him a relative one, and to transport the *self* into the common unity; so that each individual will no longer believe himself to be one, but part of the unity, and will no longer be recognizable except in the whole. . . . He who wants to keep the primacy of nature's feelings in civil order knows not what he wants. Always floating between his inclinations and his duties, he will never be either a man or a citizen; he will be good neither for himself nor for others.

Emile will be a citizen because he has been indoctrinated to prefer duty to pleasure reflexively, to want all the things he should want and not to want those he should not want. He will submit with docility to necessity, including the necessity of the law. But he will never yield to the opinions of other individual men. Thus, he will be both a citizen *and* himself.

Dependency, conditioning, and indoctrination, hidden and deceptive, are the mechanisms that accomplish this complicated maneuver. They are implicit in the key idea of "denaturing" man. Rousseau places his hero, Lycurgus, above Plato. "Plato only purified man's heart; Lycurgus denatured it. . . . It is not enough to mold our species half-way. . . . Plants are shaped by cultivation, men by education. . . . Happy is he who is led to wisdom despite himself! What matters the guide, as long as he leads him to the goal?" To understand this goal, we must bear in mind Rousseau's implicit distinction between "original human nature" (which he described in the *Discourse on Inequality*) and "true human nature." The latter, that of men who are sociable, rational, and moral, living in a state of harmony and order, is something to be achieved. Contemporary civilized man represents *neither* nature, but a perversion of both.

In view of this process, it is difficult to accept Rousseau's statement about the role Emile will play in society. "He is made to guide, to govern his equals. . . . Everywhere he will become the leader of others. . . . Without realizing that they are obeying, they will obey." Emile, then, is supposed as a leader to use the same deception to guide others that has been used on him. That is why he has been taught to despise "opinion" and to "raise himself above the common herd," for "you cannot lead the people if you resemble them." But has Emile really been brought up for such leadership? The constant victim of manipulation and deception, he never is aware of the process to which he has been submitted; awareness, Rousseau warns us, would automatically have nullified it. How then is he prepared to use this "guidance" on others? "It is necessary to know the instruments that give you control over men."

The word most frequently used to describe Emile is "docile." Is he not perfectly conditioned to be the helpless victim of another guide like his tutor, a civil guide who does understand the process? In a word, is he not conditioned to be a model citizen? If *La Nouvelle Héloïse* portrays the regenerated family and small community, and *The Social Contract* the regenerated society, then Emile is the citizen who will fit into those collectivities. The three works, written at about the same time, are variations of a single doctrine.

The strong expression of obscurantism in *Emile* is a common facet of the authoritarian mind. The search for truth is condemned because of the errors that accompany its discovery. Rousseau, whom we may define as a rationalistic anti-intellectual, asserts that all the ideas men need were discovered long ago; the rest are "pernicious and deadly to the human race." Enlightenment is a progress we have paid for by our vices. This opposition to progress has, to be sure, its laudable side. Rousseau feared the advancement of science toward what Husserl has called "exact essences." There are also "inexact essences." These are valuable, because they qualify the perceived world, the world we live in. They are the true world of men, a world, Rousseau would have maintained, in which we live by intuition and feeling, not by intellect. But social man, with his life of artificiality and inauthenticity, was losing contact with that world, the world of *intériorité.*

In the fixed society Rousseau would like, "all the places are assigned, and each must be brought up for his own." To leave one's place is destructive to order. Education is therefore harmful except for the chosen few. "The poor man has no need of education." This view echoes *La Nouvelle Héloïse* and, as in that work, Rousseau asserts that "the widening of the worker's mental horizons and the increase in his education do not improve but rather worsen his attitude to work."

As we have already noted, Rousseau really despised the common people, although—with typical ambivalence—he also praised them for being their authentic selves and liked them because he could be at ease with them and feel superior. This attitude of superiority recurs throughout *Emile*. To rise above the herd and its prejudices is a lesson Emile must be taught. The people can have no true idea of God. "A spirit is only a body for the people and for children." Such problems as eternity and creation have no obscurity to them, "for they understand nothing at all about them." The *Profession de foi* is not for them, for simple minds must not be alarmed or disturbed in their faith. In government, it is useful to have pomp, thrones, scepters, crowns, and so on, for they overawe the people.

That Rousseau was one of the first to exalt patriotism and nationalism is well known. A man owes everything to his country, he affirms; he should not be, as the other *philosophes* urged, a citizen of the world. A good mother thanks God if all her sons are killed in battle. Rousseau might also be placed among the first racists, not in the sense that he held one race superior to another, but inasmuch as he thought it important to maintain the purity of natural groups and to prevent the mongrelization that has come about because nations, unfortunately, are no longer "locked up within themselves." As a result of invasions and immigrations, "the Frenchmen of today are no longer those tall, blond-and-white bodies of yore. . . . The Europeans are no longer Gauls, Germans, Iberians, Allobrogians; they are only Scythians diversely degenerate in shape and even more in their mores."

French society, in Rousseau's eyes, was not only artificial and corrupt; it had lost its stability. European monarchies, he predicts, cannot last much longer. "We are approaching the state of crisis and the century of revolutions." His Cassandra-like prophecy was to be fulfilled.

In the eighteenth century there was a prolonged controversy over the relative value of truth versus falsehood and prejudice.[11] Those inclined to liberal views generally maintained the ultimate utility of truth. Rousseau, however, believed in illusion and beneficial falsehoods. Reversing the liberals' formula, he says that the useful is always true. Thus, to destroy the Persians' false superstition about a bridge to the afterworld would only relieve the conscience of the wicked. "It is therefore false that the skeptic's doctrine was not harmful; it could not therefore be true." It is at times difficult not to sympathize with those who call Rousseau a sophist.

The political implications of *Emile* and its intimate relationship to *La Nouvelle Héloïse* and *The Social Contract* have often been overlooked. Leaving aside the vast impact of the *Profession de foi* on the history of religious sentiment in France, we may say that *Emile*'s deep influence has always been as a treatise on child psychology and education. Though its absurdities and repulsive ideas were passed by, its many shrewd insights often took root in other minds. This is as it should be. Here, however, I have insisted on looking at the whole.

Those who look selectively at Rousseau's innovations find much of enduring value. He was the first to expound a pedagogy that described the psychic evolution of a child, a methodology that is at the heart of the reform movement from Pestalozzi to Froebel. He recognized that reason does not function in isolation but "develops in conjunction with the realization of other human potentialities."[12] Really independent reasoning takes years to develop; the first twelve years are mostly passive ingestion of prejudices and attitudes. The "education of the senses" anticipates the Montessori method. Learning by doing, the stimulus of pleasure, the awakening of curiosity before teaching, emphasis on things rather than words, treating the child as a child and not expecting him to understand adults' reasoning, physical development and manual training—all these have entered, with modifications, into the mainstream of modern pedagogical thought. Although Rousseau often misunderstood the child's psychology and development, his essential idea, that education should be adapted to the pupil's potentialities, is sound.

The reform of the schools under the Revolution took little from him, but the idea of public or civic celebrations, borrowed from *Emile* and the other writings, was accepted enthusiastically. Under the Third Republic, the influence of the first three books was more considerable, at least that of the theoretical principles outlined above. John Dewey called Rousseau the prophet of the new education.[13]

Of course, Rousseau's thought was fed by his readings. It is possible to trace most of his ideas to Montaigne, Locke, Fleury, Rollin, the Abbé de Saint-Pierre, Pluche, Nollet, Mme. de Lambert, Vandermonde, and others.[14] It matters little. With the exception of the first two, none of these writers aroused significant intellectual reverberations, and none stirred men's hearts and emotions. Whatever Rousseau took he infused with a new life, and it became uniquely his. "Works take their power," writes Picon, "not from the past from which they come, but from a future toward which they did not know they were going."[15] There never has been another *Emile*.

There is no doubt, then, that *Emile* is truly great, an incredibly rich work. But I believe that the sense and direction of Rousseau's theory of education and its intimate connection with his political theory have not been correctly gauged. One critic, for instance, calls Rousseau "the guide of the permissive concept of education." But as we have seen, the education of Emile, a puppet whose strings are pulled by his tutor-guide, is exactly the antithesis of permissiveness. What are we to think of this statement in a widely read book: "Educationally, Helvétius' theories were dramatically opposed to Rousseau's, for he stressed the deliberate conditioning of group education against the spontaneous natural growth of the privately tutored Emile."? (The group conditioning, too, will come in Rousseau's later political writings; but he reserves public education, even the raising of children in common by the State, to his ideal societies, where the citizen has been completely assimilated by the group. Emile has been educated for this society, where there is no *patrie* and there are no citizens.) Still another outstanding critic, caught in the snares of the Rousseauian vocabulary, thinks he sees how his education proceeds through successive stages of freedom, culminating in the achievement of moral freedom in the State; while in fact, instead of liberating Emile gradually, the tutor gradually assumes greater and more absolute control over him, teaching him at each step to accept new necessities and disciplines by conditioning him to want to accept them. Rousseau invents a ladder of "necessities." The duplicity of the "hidden hand," trickery, manipulation, and conditioning are the mechanisms of the tightest control over thoughts and emotions. Their avowed purpose —and why should we deny it when Rousseau clearly proclaims it?—is to capture the will and to mold the human clay.

In *Emile* there are strong elements of individualism in thought and feeling. Happiness is intensely individualistic, to the point of autarchy. It requires golden mediocrity and the nourishment of the inner self.

Let us measure the radius of our sphere, and remain in the center like the insect in his web; we shall always be sufficient to ourselves. . . . Looking ahead, which constantly carries us outside of ourselves and often places us at a point we shall never reach, is the true source of all our wretchedness. What mania in a being as fleeting as man to be always looking far ahead to a future that comes so rarely and to neglect the present of which he is sure! . . . Thus we cling to everything. . . . Our own self is at least part of ourselves. . . . Close up your existence within yourself, and you will no longer be unhappy.

It may be said that "looking ahead" is a specifically human quality. But doesn't Jean-Jacques really resent the human condition? "The happiest man is the one who suffers least. . . . Always more suffering than enjoyment. . . . Man's felicity here below is therefore only a negative state."

In Rousseau's political nationalism, the circle is enlarged to the community, and the self (the "human self") replaced by the "collective self." But the principle of self-sufficiency and the tight enclosure are identical.

The strong elements of individualism in *Emile* are undeniable. At the same time, however, the individual is deprived of value, while seemingly exalted. He is treated as an object to be manipulated for ends determined from without, even if they are for his benefit, and he is allowed no autonomy.

It may certainly be argued that Rousseau wishes to form the best and happiest person possible. But is it truly a "person" who is to be happy? Is not Rousseau's "education," in important respects, a process of dehumanization? Means surely count; and we must not forget that the most significant word in *Emile*, repeated again and again, is "docile." What is human is not specific, predictable responses, but flexibility, creativity, the imagining of new possibilities, judgment according to our values. According to Martin Rang, Rousseau's notion of extending the law of necessity to the moral domain implies taking men as things. I am afraid that this is basically a correct analysis. Rousseau considered education, as he conceived it and illustrated it in *Emile*, to be all-powerful. In other writings he will tell us that education is the most powerful instrument at the disposal of the State. Human dignity can scarcely be secured by means that violate human dignity.

It is usually said that *The Social Contract* is Rousseau's most abstract and rationalistic work. In a sense, *Emile* is even more so. True, it deals with an individual. But no one like that individual has ever existed or could exist. Like his tutor, he is an abstraction, or a series of abstractions, modeled to fit certain theories.

There is a final irony. We are about to see, in the sequel to *Emile*, that the tutor has no more succeeded with his subject than Wolmar with Saint-Preux. Both protagonists, the subjects of his demiurgic experiment, are himself, and are equally unviable. The process itself defeats the end, and Emile's dependence on his Pygmalion replaces dependence on opinion. In *La Nouvelle Héloïse, restructuring* of the personality led to its breakdown, as a result of the resistance of intractable elements in it. In *Emile, structuring* of the personality through concealed dependence creates a permanent infantilism. How can we account for Rousseau's becoming trapped into these ironic reversals? Only, I think, if we regard these works as representative of the contradictory aspects and needs of his own personality, as the outpouring of his narcissism. On the one hand, they express his longing for dependency, the deep-seated masochism that permeates his life. On the other hand, they express the obverse, the reaching out for compensation through the fantasy of being godlike and having others in his absolute control. The need for power that in the figures of Wolmar and the tutor attains the point of omnipotence fulfills neurotic needs. From the feeling of powerlessness derives the need to win approval and love, to force one's will on others. By doing so Rousseau proves his masculinity and avenges himself for his hurt and his failures. It is this kind of a drive, in its sublimated forms, that leads to the creation of a work as original and compelling as *Emile.*

It is a strange book, *Emile,* one in which Rousseau expressed his inner self, a great book, but a monstrous book. Rousseau's cosmos is constellated with fragmented images of himself. *Emile* has his wisdom and his absurdity, his decency and courage, and his perversity. It expresses the polar tensions of his ideal of life: action and withdrawal. As in his own life, withdrawal finally wins the upper hand. Emile turns aside, or is turned aside, from the struggle for rank, power, and wealth, from "artificial needs," from comparison with others, from the competitiveness and integration with "opinion" that social life demands. He settles for a middle-class, bourgeois happiness in the country, with an ideal Sophie. Rousseau gave to Emile and his tutor all the qualities and virtues he lacked, the fulfillment of all the dreams he never realized. They are his mirror image, the anti-Rousseau.

### 4. *Emile et Sophie*

When Rousseau finished *Emile,* the problems of education were less in his mind than the erotic fantasies that had excited his imagination. He set to work on a sequel, with the ostensible purpose of showing how well Emile's education had prepared him for the trials life held in store; but this was only an unconscious pretext or disguise to enable him to find substitute gratifications for his aroused eroticism. His need was largely discharged in masochistic form in the long first letter of *Emile et Sophie.* This may be the reason he abandoned the project when he was not far into the second letter, even though he thought enough of what he had done to read it to a visitor at Môtiers, on November 17, 1762. Years later he asked Du Peyrou (July 6, 1768) to return the manuscript:

"I still have for this project a weakness that I cannot resist." What we have was published in 1780, two years after Rousseau's death.

The story begins in the form of a dramatic exclamation. "I was free, I was happy, O my master!" "Freedom," we remember, means having no dependency on other individuals, and no obligations imposed by them. Now, we are informed, all that is gone like a dream. Emile has lost everything. He is writing to his old tutor to give a faithful account of what has happened to him since those happy days. "Cherished days of my first loves, exquisite days, why can you not begin over and over again and fill my whole being forever? I could want no other eternity. Vain regrets! Empty wishes! Everything is gone, gone never to return!" The Romantic poets had little to add to this theme.

Now that the tone has been set, the events of the interval will be narrated in a long flashback. With a loving wife, a son and a daughter, and faithful tutor ever at his side, Emile was indeed happy. But as the tutor had emphasized, in one of his lectures, love puts us in a vulnerable position. And it is the tutor's departure (for reasons unknown) that was to precipitate disaster. Everything went to pieces after that. Emile blames the tutor squarely for his misery, thus confirming that despite his wonder-working education, he has never acquired the maturity to accept responsibility for his own life. In a short space, Sophie loses her parents and then their little girl. To dispel her depression, Emile decides on a sojourn in Paris. For Rousseau all cities are evil, capitals the worst of all cities, and Paris the worst of all capitals. As Emile enters the city, he is filled with premonitions of misfortune. They will come true. In the two years that follow, he forgets all the lessons of his master, becomes well adjusted (one might say!) to the frivolous life around him, and loses interest in his wife. Each follows his own way, while remaining "good friends," according to custom. The search for pleasure turns into an endless flight from boredom.

Suddenly Sophie puts an end to her social life and shuts herself morosely in her room. Since they no longer confide in each other, Emile cannot discover the cause of her brooding. He decides to merit her confidence again, devotes himself to her, only to discover that she adamantly refuses to let him make love to her. He persists, until a day comes when she is about to surrender to his caresses. Then she breaks down in dramatic revelation. Pushing him away, looking at him with wild and desperate eyes, she cries out: "Stop, Emile, I am nothing to you any more. Another man has soiled your bed. I am pregnant. You will never touch me again." Whereupon she runs into her boudoir and locks the door, leaving Emile utterly demolished—as well he might be.

Judging from Rousseau's preoccupation with adultery in *La Nouvelle Héloïse* and *Emile*, his repeated insistence on its most vicious consequence, deception of the husband by introducing another man's children into his home to share his love and his property, and the central

place of this type of situation in *Emile et Sophie*, we may conclude that
he had a masochistic obsession in this regard. It is possible to speculate
that one cause of this obsession was his suspicion—perhaps even his
knowledge—of having been deceived by Thérèse, and his uncertainty
about the paternity of his children.*

The remainder of the "letter" is taken up mainly by an analysis of
Emile's thoughts, emotions, and rationalizations, an analysis of such
acuity and subtlety that the least one can speak of is its remarkable
empathy into the psychology of a man suffering from the blow Emile has
been dealt. Among his curious reflections is one admitting that he had
been a weak character (despite all his tutor had done!), while Sophie
was strong (despite hers!), and wilful, and another about her refusal to resume marital relations: "Why could I not have spent centuries in that
happy state, esteeming, respecting, cherishing her, sighing at her tyranny, trying to make her relent without ever succeeding, asking, im-
ploring, begging, desiring endlessly and never obtaining?" These
reflections of Rousseau's own preferred sexual posture are clear indica-
tions of his self-projection and intimate involvement in this situation.

Emile summons the courage to leave Sophie forever. He indulges in
fury, scorn, thoughts of vengeance—and looks for pretexts to forgive her.
He blames himself for neglecting Sophie while fully aware of her ardent
temperament and his own tepid inclinations. He thinks of how she must
have struggled with herself, of her refusal to deceive him, and concludes
that she is virtuous even in crime and that, hating her crime, she is more
unfortunate than guilty.

By the time Emile reaches this conclusion, he has taken a job in a
carpenter's shop in a small village—how well his tutor had foreseen
everything!—in order to continue his reflections in greater calm. Should
he go back to her? After all, according to his principles, he is "above
public opinion." But it is no use; to go back and forgive would be
cowardice and infamy. They could never be the same to each other.
"What! Will nature herself authorize crime and force my wife, by dividing her affection between her two children, to divide it between two
fathers?" This idea reawakens his rage, and he decides to take their son
away from Sophie, a decision he changes when his employer tells him
that a strange woman and child had stopped outside the shop; that she
had watched him through the glass door, knelt down sobbing, and cried
out, "No, he would never take you from your mother!" and then had
reluctantly torn herself away.

Emile now faces the future "rationally." He will leave the country
and wander in search of some unknown destiny, unconcerned with the

---

* Green attributes Rousseau's interest to the affair with Mme. d'Houdetot, claiming
that he had never accepted the prior rights of Saint-Lambert (Green, *op. cit.*). This is
not only dubious, but overlooks the fact that no adulterine children, and no confession,
were involved.

past or the future, freed from the restlessness born of hope. "I said to myself that all we do in life is to begin, and that there is no link in our existence but a succession of present moments, the first of which is always the one at hand. We die and we are born at each moment of our lives." In his new life he will be sufficient to himself and stoical before the world. From this rhapsody emerge the three correlated themes that, according to Green, "composed the inner melody of Rousseau's own existence: self-renewal, escape, solitude."[16] In Paris, Emile had fled his true self to discover the world; now he will do the reverse.

If the first chapter seems outrageously romantic, the fragment of the second that we have is even more so. As if to reinforce our impression that this whole episode constitutes a psychological regression, Rousseau returns to adventure tales he had devoured in his childhood and relates Emile's capture by pirates and his incredible but stereotyped adventures as a slave. Let us note just one or two of Emile's reflections. First, his attitude toward leaving his country reproduces Rousseau's own feelings toward Geneva and the Swiss. He speaks of his "fatherland, for which I had to blush, and to which I owed only scorn and hatred, since, happy and worthy of honor in myself, all I got from it and its vile inhabitants were the ills to which I was prey, and the opprobrium into which I was plunged." Second, Emile does not mind being a slave, for his tutor had taught him to accept necessity, and what is freedom? "If freedom consisted in doing what you want, no man would be free; all are weak, dependent on things, on harsh necessity; he who can best desire all it orders is the freest, since he is never forced to do what he does not want to do." In these words, Rousseau again confirms the definition of "freedom" that I have attributed to him.

Scholars have been embarrassed by *Emile et Sophie*, because of the apparent failure of Emile's and Sophie's education. To judge this problem, we must reconstruct the unwritten part of the story. First there is the evidence within the remaining fragment. From this we know that the son, sent to Emile's family, dies; that Sophie has been the victim of a false friendship and human weakness, and that she has been redeemed. "It is about your regenerated children that I have to speak to you," he writes to his tutor. "What a character hers must have been to come back from so far to all that she had been first!" Sophie, too, is dead at the time of writing. But first she and Emile had been reunited, as a result of their child's death, and having expiated their faults by suffering, had experienced the happiest days of their lives.

Beyond these foreshadowings, we have two variant accounts of Rousseau's outline for the rest of the story, as reported by two of his friends, Pierre Prévost, a Genevan professor, and Bernardin de Saint-Pierre. It would be difficult to say which is wilder. Both end with Emile on a desert island. According to Prévost's version, which he heard from Rousseau in his old age, Emile pays daily visits to a temple on this island, a temple served by a mysterious priestess, who later turns out to be Sophie. She explains how she had been the victim of fraud and violence on the part of her friends. Knowing herself to be unworthy of him, she attends his wedding to a young girl with the announced intention of being their slave. (Rousseau's fascination with slavery is another curious phenomenon in this novel.) After Sophie has been punished for several days, Emile tells her that the marriage is only a show, that her "rival" is a married woman. (He has learned some of his tutor's trickery, after all!) Her involuntary fault, expiated by cruel punishments, is forgiven, and she is reunited with Emile, who only now begins to realize the extent of her virtue.

In Bernardin de Saint-Pierre's version, Emile finds a shipwrecked Spaniard living on the island with his fifteen-year-old daughter. Emile has been attracted to the island by the tale of a "perpetual miracle," centered on a statue of the Virgin in a grotto, at whose feet food and refreshments were always to be found. This "miracle" is the work of the Spaniard, who is always on the watch for passing ships. The sailors, in turn, always leave valuable gifts for the hermit, an exchange of services accomplished without the mediation of language (and so, for Rousseau, more valuable). The Spaniard persuades Emile that Sophie's infidelity has annulled their marriage and marries him to his daughter. Shortly after, Emile begins to see a phantom woman appearing and disappearing among the rocks. This turns out to be his wife, who likes to play tricks on him. Then Sophie comes on the scene. Repenting her crime, she joins the newlyweds as a concubine. On the day of her death, she relates her systematic seduction by a young man, assisted by an old friend, a pair of rogues who foreshadow Valmont and the Marquise de Merteuil in Laclos' *Les Liaisons dangereuses*. (One of the most popular themes of the eighteenth-century French novel, the misfortunes of virtue, thus finds an echo in this version.)

The second account is probably the more authentic, since it was set down before the publication of *Emile et Sophie* and contains an accurate summary of the extant chapters. In both, we have two of Rousseau's obsessive themes, that of woman's sin, expiation, and redemption, and that of separation followed by reunion with the beloved.[17] These themes had been the substance of the plot of *La Nouvelle Héloïse*, although there the ultimate reunion takes place in the next life. In both stories, death is the final expiation and liberation from guilt. There is perhaps some confusion of values in Sophie's case, since the element of moral guilt is dubious. In accordance with Rousseau's view of the importance of "opinion" in the management of women, the adulteress must be punished and die. Simultaneously, there is a contrary element of masochism in the desire to forgive the straying wife and to renew their love. Emile's torments, which Rousseau experiences vicariously, reveal the conflict in his emotions. The novel eventuates in a new *ménage à trois*, one that reverses the usual pattern of two men and one woman.

Although there are reminiscences of the Abbé Prévost's romantic novels, of Anson's *Voyages* and *Robinson Crusoe* in Rousseau's sequel to *Emile*, his principal source is the sixteenth-century legend of Lampedusa, an island between Malta and Tunisia.[18] The legend tells of a grotto, in which a dual chapel, Muslim and Christian, was a refuge for fugitive prisoners on both sides, a sanctuary of tolerance and mutual assistance. Other elements of the legend were a helpful hermit and specter. It has been convincingly suggested that the episode of the grotto was a belated reply to Diderot, whose reference to the isle of Lampedusa had so irritated him.[19]

Rousseau may have been drawn to this theme for another reason. In a story like *Emile et Sophie*, in which he has lost contact with reality and has surrendered to fantasy gratifications, the isle of Lampedusa took him back to a state akin to that of nature, outside of a changing and corrupt history, one in which self-love, not having degenerated into *amour-propre*, walks hand in hand with compassion. In this state, men live untroubled by the inner or outer war. With a minimum of rules and conventions, they enjoy a harmony conducive to the immediate pleasure of the "existence-feeling," rather than the "happiness" that depends on artificial and mediate factors. This is the "golden age" of the *Discourse on Inequality*, "the true springtime of the world," he called it, a harmony of interests that does not need the coercive force of the State and the general will.[20] It approaches Emile's way of life and that of Rousseau at the time he wrote his *Rêveries*—not solitude and isolation from others, nor yet integration into their way of life.

Returning to our original question, whether *Emile et Sophie* represents a failure of Rousseau's educational system, it is now apparent that we can argue it both ways. Emile is successful, because he has surmounted life's most bitter trials and found a better way of life. On the other hand, his education did fail the moment he tried to integrate himself into society, and he freely admits it.[21] He never achieved the independence about which his tutor constantly prated. The tutor's departure was a psychological disaster to him. If the tutor had remained, he complains, none of his misfortunes would have occurred. His later "success" results only from his withdrawal from society, and from a romantic miracle that belongs entirely to Rousseau's fantasy-world. Referring to *Emile et Sophie* in his *Confessions*, Rousseau says that its theme was the necessity of avoiding temptation if we are to remain virtuous.[22] And in the second *Dialogue*, he wrote that the only way to escape situations in which we can benefit ourselves by hurting others is to withdraw from society. There is no doubt that if Emile ever returns to society, he will be at best an alien, possessing only himself, behind the parapets of a psychological wall. This was precisely Rousseau's condition. And the interest of his sequel to *Emile* is less in any ideas it may symbolically enfold than in its revelation of Jean-Jacques' inner world of frustration, perversion, self-torment, and escape into fantasy.

# V. The Reconstructed Society

T H E *Social Contract* is the capstone of Rousseau's rationalistic pyramid. It is one segment of a single sociopolitical system, carefully worked out in his mind and reflecting the needs of his personality, a system designed to make men virtuous and happy. The theoretical mode of political institutions it contains corresponds to the architectonics of his broader plan, his grand plan, to fashion a man and a society "according to his heart."

Over the base of a broad critique of society, he had conceived a monumental work, *Institutions politiques*, based on his theory of a *morale sensitive*. The abandonment of that project provided the ideological skeleton for the three great works of reconstruction. *La Nouvelle Héloïse*, an experiment with the ideal social microcosm, treats the problem of the refractory or corrupted individual, of romanticism versus order. *Emile* explores what can be done with an individual *ab ovo*. *The Social Contract* gives us the political structures. To be sure, we may reverse the picture and consider *Emile* as logically (as it was chronologically, by some months) subsequent to *The Social Contract*. This is so because Rousseau finds himself at an impasse. The reconstructed society cannot be realized without postulating the reconstructed individual, and the latter cannot be realized without the former. The case of Emile, a hypothetical individual raised in virtual isolation, only confirms the dilemma. Rousseau cannot escape from this circle, which is one reason why he says that his principles can be applied only to new and uncorrupted societies. He will not be entirely faithful to this restriction, for in later years he will grasp eagerly at the invitation to write constitutions for Poland and Corsica. These practical exercises, with their realistic adaptations to national situations, will shed invaluable light on the true character of his thought.

Geneva is constantly in the background of Rousseau's political the-

[ 173 ]

orizing. His idealization of its constitution, the partisan tracts of 1718–38, and the upheavals that took place during his own lifetime were always hovering in his mind.[1] His speculations ranged far beyond Geneva, however, to encompass his admired Spartan *polis* (but not the Athenian), the semimythical beginnings of the Roman republic, and above all, his own view of man and of a true society.

The character and originality of his thought hinges on this last element. And it is this, the character of his thought, that has provoked the most bitter and enduring controversy of all the controversies waged over Rousseau. The most seminal of eighteenth-century writers, he is also the most debated. It has been said that he was "the revolutionary thinker who first inscribed on the political banners of modern times the opposing slogans both of democratic and totalitarian government."[2] "Liberal" would be a better word than "democratic." Although the two words are used today as loosely equivalent, the twentieth-century authoritarians also call themselves "democratic," and that word, denoting popular sovereignty, may be applied to either type of society. A liberal society is a pluralistic and open one that does not demand total conformity as the price of being a good citizen. Such a society fosters variety and individualism. It emphasizes the limits to the power of the State or collectivity, for it admits of no will that has the right to constrain all wills, though it may constrain acts. A totalitarian society, on the other hand, imposes a unique mold on ideas, feelings, and acts. Since no private will may oppose the general will, which alone is right, the rights of individuals and minorities are severely limited or suppressed, and violators become enemies of the nation or people.

It is obvious that both words, "liberal" and "totalitarian," are partly anachronistic when applied to Rousseau. He did, however, have a clear idea or model, in his beloved Sparta, of a totalitarian collectivity. In any event, the appropriateness of words cannot affect the appropriateness of recognizing clear tendencies. Eighteenth-century thinkers, living in an archaic social and political structure that was out of tune with the economics and ideologies of a new stage in Western culture, were groping for ways to reorganize society on a rational basis and to solve the unending problem of the relation of the individual to the group. The basic philosophies of liberalism and of totalitarianism were both developed in the Enlightenment, the former by men such as Montesquieu, Voltaire, and Diderot, the latter by Mably, Morelly, Helvétius, Mercier, Restif, Rousseau, and other utopians.

In the *Discourse on Inequality*, Rousseau had painted a vivid picture of a competitive society as one whose values are perverted by a false notion of "progress" and "good," one in which men have every interest in hating each other and in hurting each other. He saw that Western civilization espouses a Christian ethic of brotherhood, but practices a cutthroat, exploitative way of life.

Rousseau's apparent "primitivism" had a powerful appeal to his contemporaries, as well as to men of later times. Some followed the logic of his *Discourse* to its obvious end, dreaming of an egalitarian, communistic society, or even of an anarchistic social state. But Rousseau himself, as he turned to the constructive part of his work and sought a way out of man's dilemma, rejected primitivism. While he urged a simple way of living and abjured none of his criticisms of society, he realized that the simplistic solutions of "abolition" were pure fantasy. There can be no return to innocence. Evolution is an irreversible process.

For Rousseau, society is the original sin, but it is also the testing place, as earthly life is in the Christian tradition. The direction man must take is not a "return to nature"—neither to the hypothetical, metaphysical nature of "natural man," nor to the empirical laws of nature. We must leave all this behind and forge a new destiny, unknown to nature, one that is truly man's own.*

To be sure, Rousseau still speaks of "natural" ways of living; but in *Emile* he clearly says, "We must not confuse what is natural to the savage state and what is natural to the civil state." It is the latter he is concerned with now. Montesquieu, he thought, had made this error, overlooking the opposition between the natural order of things and the civil order. Natural instincts are good in the state of nature only. Society brings out other, latent instincts of aggression and selfishness. These always become dominant in any unguided society, that is, in a sense, in any "natural" society. In physical nature, man depends on things, which have necessity and stability. In society, man depends on men, on the caprices of power. Rousseau's hope, clearly expressed and exemplified in *La Nouvelle Héloïse* and in *Emile,* is to give to human laws the necessity and inflexibility of physical laws; then men would depend only on an impersonal necessity. In this way (and in this way alone), they would be equal. By so doing, "we would unite in the Republic all the advantages of the natural state to those of the civil state." But in order to accomplish this, we must overcome what is "natural" in man: impulses and self-centered passions. We must also prevent the conflict of values imposed by social living ("Political Economy"). Internal unity, however, even if it were still attainable, is no longer enough. Collective unity must now replace the natural unity of the self. Independence must become dependence. The remedy, "art perfected," will give man entirely to the State, Rousseau declares, thus creating a cooperative, organic unity. By "denaturing" man, we shall socialize him. In this way, and only in this way, will he be able to satisfy his natural needs in an artificial social existence.

However complex and intricate Rousseau's theorizing may become in

* The first sentence of the first *Discourse* reads: "It is a great and beautiful spectacle to see man rising, in a sense, out of nothingness by his own efforts." Rousseau calls on man to create himself, that is, to give primacy to culture, not to nature.

*The Social Contract,* it rests on this set of simple assumptions. To him they have all the self-evidence and certitude of Descartes' "clear ideas."

Ever since Pascal, the search for happiness and emotional security has been an increasingly important problem in Western civilization. Rousseau was not concerned with men's basic irrationality or the lack of purpose in human existence. He had no feeling of the absurd, of cosmic alienation. Like some other millenarian theorists, he believed that the human problem could be solved in human terms, by the true society.

*The Social Contract* opens with a famous first sentence: "Man was born free, and everywhere he is in chains." It would be wrong to take these words as a protest. They are only the statement of a fact, that man in society no longer enjoys the freedom of "natural man." The prime purpose of Rousseau's inquiry, as he says immediately afterwards, will be to determine what conditions justify this civil status; in other words, what are the foundations of a legitimate political society. Here he breaks with most other thinkers of his time, who, like Montesquieu, were seeking to found the body politic on natural laws, or else on a rational "Natural Law." Following his view that society is not natural to man, he looks elsewhere, to artificial and deliberate conventions. In this, Hobbes' influence was doubtless great. In nature, argues Rousseau, there is only force. In society, men create right, which, though using force, supersedes it. Force under law is quite different from force without law. Right comes into being by the convention of the social compact.

Rousseau's version of the social contract theory is brilliantly original.[3] For him, as for Hobbes, it terminates the state of nature, with its natural freedom and equality. But a legitimate political society gives men, in their stead, something new and far more precious: political liberty (as Rousseau understands it) and civil equality. The compact is the one unanimous act that obviates the need for further unanimity in voting. It creates the obligation to submit to the will of the majority: legally, since the individual has agreed to its rule; morally, since he is still obeying his true will, which is that the general will shall rule. Rousseau shows in detail what is lost forever on accepting the compact, and the gains which, point by point, are substituted for the losses. Possession, for instance, a usurpation which is limited only by strength, becomes property, a right which is both secured and limited by the community. Further, society is assumed, in Rousseau's theory, to be prior to government. The consequence is revolutionary. The so-called rulers of men have no part in the contract; they are only the instruments and servants of the people, in whom all sovereignty inalienably resides, and they may be dispossessed by the simple will of sovereign citizens.

This summary points to the two great problems of *The Social Contract* that have exercised the minds of countless commentators. The first is the expression of the will of the community, which is to be the determinant of justice and social control. This involves Rousseau's famous notion of the "general will." The general will is to be ascertained or formulated by the process of majority vote, that is, a process of cancellation, in accordance with what Rousseau considered to be the workings of the mathematical laws of probability. But we must not err, as many commentators do, by confusing the nature of the general will with this positivistic process of its expression. The "general will" is essentially a rationalistic notion and involves the same type of hypothesis as "natural man" or the "state of nature." Rousseau does not deny what we might call "empirical man," man as he is, fighting primarily for his own interest. But beyond this he assumes a rational unity among all men, consisting of what their reason would desire if all individual passions and desires could be stilled. This is the "general will." It is questionable whether in majority rule Rousseau has found a procedure that would realize it, or whether he was really convinced that he had. It is on the general will, and on the participation of each citizen in the voting process, that he bases his theory that political and civil liberty consist not in doing what we as individuals want, but in doing what this hypothetical or metaphysical "general will" wants. Thus, when we suppress the individual's protest, even the protest of his conscience, we merely "force him to be free," force him to do what he *really* wants to do. The peculiarity of Rousseau's idea, and its basic fallaciousness, lies in its attempt to mingle in one concept a real, empirical situation (the will one experiences as his own) and a purely metaphysical postulate (the will which, the citizen is told, is really his own).

Eighteenth-century French political thought is characterized, in varying degrees, by a duality between what might be called a certain mythical substructure (the "myths" of what was called "nature" and those of reason), on the one hand, and the reality of human nature and of political institutions, on the other. The utopians especially, in their effort to translate myth into reality, were confronted with the difficult problem of imagining a "real" that would embody the ideal. This problem is nowhere more evident than in Rousseau. Thus, in the matter of voting, Rousseau excludes what he calls "the will of all," which is something real (a count of votes expressing the actual will of the components of the community), in favor of the intangible "general will," which has to be "discovered," because it preexists the vote, which only actualizes it.

Rousseau conceives, then, of an organic State, one in which (as he put it in "Political Economy") a unanimous corporate or collective self has absolute control over all its parts, on the analogy of the body of an animal. By the terms of the social contract, the individual has surrendered, without reservation, all his natural rights to the collectivity, which may give him such rights as it wishes. The collective will creates right and justice and supersedes the individual conscience in matters of public concern. But only the State, through the general will, determines what is of public concern. As it works out, almost everything is in the realm of public concern. We should expect this, given the dynamics of power. Rousseau's concept is obviously dangerous and disturbing to those who favor pluralistic or "open" societies.

Scholars have puzzled over the seeming contradiction between the individualism and spirit of rebellion in the *Discourse on Inequality* and the ideal of submissiveness and docility to the univocal will of an organic society in *The Social Contract*. Rousseau himself denied any real contradiction in his writings, and in this regard, at least, there is none. Rousseau's individualism, like his exaltation of the individual conscience, applies only to existing societies, which are corrupt, unjust, and exploitative. It is in the true society of which he dreams, where men are socialized, that the new, emergent conscience of the community, the "general will," supersedes individual conscience and individual will.

The second difficult problem, the new relationship of the individual citizen to the State, is the inevitable sequel. Is Rousseau's thought totalitarian or liberal? A remarkable quantity of ink has flowed in the attempt to prove it one or the other. Rousseau of course was not thinking in such terms. He wanted only to secure men's happiness, through a just, legitimate, political society. This could not be done without sacrifice and control. If we are to make a successful transition from a natural state of force to a civil state of right, we must think of men as citizens who have become part of a greater whole, and not as independent, self-centered individuals. The mutuality of the sacrifice, the application of laws to all,* the respecting of others as we wish them to respect us, the limitation of the sacrifice by the sovereign people itself—this is the theoretical justification.

In the working out of Rousseau's plan, however, both individual dissent and political groupings are excluded. Not only are there no minority rights; there cannot even be minorities. Rousseau constantly uses the word "liberty," but for him it does not have the same meaning as for us. Liberty, for him, is first of all the independence or sovereignty of the State. Second, it is the independence of any individual from all others, or from group pressures. It is the prevention of exploitation, either by individuals or by groups. This goal is achieved by the complete dependence of all on the collective self—an impersonal, inflexible force like that of nature in the original state of nature.† Third, liberty is law self-given, or consented to—in other words, the sovereignty of the people as expressed in the general will. But this stipulation, as we shall see, cannot be taken at face value.

---

* These are the two conditions of equality. Rousseau does not demand economic equality, but only a narrowing of the gap, and he supports hierarchical inequality. Aristocracy, he tells us here and in his correspondence, is the best government, as long as the people retain sovereignty.

† In Rousseau's political vocabulary, the idea of liberty is frequently associated with words and phrases such as "docile," "docility," and "submissive to the yoke"; they constitute a leitmotif and an implicit definition. In *Emile*, too, "docile," "the appearance of independence," "subjected," "master of his will" are key words and phrases.

A liberal society, as Locke declared, assumes that we sacrifice *part* of our freedom in order that the remainder of it may be protected. Freedom is limited, in order to be secured. Rousseau demands a complete alienation of all rights to the State. The sovereign may not be limited by a bill of rights, a constitution, custom, or precedent. Yet he claims that the individual in his society is as *totally* free as in the state of nature. What is changed is the nature of liberty and of the self. Liberty is now the freedom to do the "ought"; and the will the citizen "freely" obeys is no longer that of his subjective or egoistic self (in several writings, Rousseau calls it, deprecatingly, the "human self"), but that of a new social self (*le moi commun,* or "collective self"). However, liberty, at least as we view it, though it certainly means obedience to majority rule as expressed in the law, must mean more than this. The liberal view, as developed in the eighteenth century and thereafter, fears and rejects Rousseau's concept of a "total alienation" of the individual to the collectivity, with the latter returning only what it wishes—even if he does keep an equal voice in the expression of its will. Liberty is not merely the right to participate, but the protection of individual rights against encroachment. Liberalism fears the tyranny of the majority, even the tyranny of the "whole" which it supposedly expresses. Can a people be called "free" if it freely decides to be enslaved? Rousseau, it seems, fails to discriminate between the promotion of individual good through collective action and the sacrifice of the individual to the collective whole.

Still more important, we must not forget the lesson of the *Discourse on Inequality.* Historical or social man, because of the very conditions of social living, is inevitably evil; he is impelled to selfish actions that will hurt others. The more civilized the society, the more evil he will be. The development of virtue (as contrasted with natural man's merely instinctive "goodness" or sympathy) is therefore Rousseau's principal consideration, and virtue takes on a strictly political meaning. He has no confidence in good will, reason, or Natural Law. Virtue is placing the general good above one's own. This is *against* nature, and can be achieved only through social discipline. We must "form" citizens. Social man is an artificial man. When men are exposed to all sorts of artificial needs and urges, the liberty of individualism, a vestigial hangover from the state of nature, leads to luxury, acquisitiveness, power drives, and all the other evils of a competitive society which it is precisely Rousseau's intention to eliminate as destructive to the true happiness of the individual. In order to create a society of harmony and cooperation, an organic society, we must create a new man, a social man, overcome the natural in him, and govern behavior by "the impersonal necessity and inflexibility" that characterize physical events.

When we realize what kind of society Rousseau is dreaming of, we can better understand the function of the political processes outlined in *The Social Contract.* Sovereignty belongs to all the citizens and cannot be alienated or limited. This "democratic" doctrine turns out to be an absolutist doctrine. The sovereign power is in effect unlimited, even if it is (supposedly) held by an all-powerful general will rather than a despot. In fact, the potential tyranny is greater, because it is to take on a different coloration, that of impersonal necessity. Oppression by the State becomes, by definition, impossible; no self can want to hurt itself, Rousseau argues. It thereby tends to become unlimited. Rousseau's expressed intention is to reach beyond overt conformity and to "capture wills."

The illusion of self-government is founded in the doctrine that the legislative power, being the fundamental expression of sovereignty, cannot be represented and resides in the whole citizenry. Rousseau's rejection of representative or parliamentary government divorces him from nineteenth-century democracies, of which some writers mistakenly call him a source. It is the vote of the assembled citizens that is to discover the general will. They are not called on, as in Western democracies, to "create" a will by debate and compromise. The will exists. In fact, it has been tentatively formulated by the Lawgiver, and the people must confirm or deny the validity of that formulation. The assembled citizens, however, cannot find it by themselves; they "need an organ" to express the general will. Fortunately, there are Lawgivers and "guides" to accomplish this end.

The voting process, then, has no resemblance to that of Western, liberal democracies. Its purpose is not to find a consensus among opposing group interests, each of which freely expresses its will, but to abolish all group interests, or "particular wills," by "discovering" the general will. There is no debate or discussion, and each citizen must deliberate in isolation. The proposition cannot be amended, and the citizen is called on only to say "Yes" or "No"—and to say it (if we may interpolate a statement from the *Proposal for a Constitution for Corsica*) openly, in front of all. Even more significant, the citizens may not vote until they are sufficiently "informed" by a "guide," who, as the proponent of the law, apparently knows the general will *before* the vote.\* After the vote, no dissent or contrary will is allowed. The citizen who has voted the wrong way was "mistaken," and he must surrender his own will, his own ideas, his own conscience.

In regard to the work of the "guide," it is of some significance that Rousseau warns of the futility and danger of trying to reason with the people, who are too stupid to see beyond their immediate self-interest. Lamenting the lost art of demagoguery, he calls on the Lawgiver "to persuade without convincing." The relationship between this methodology and the conditioning designed to produce automatic reactions

---

\* We may perhaps find a modern analogue in Fidel Castro's telling a million assembled citizens that there will be no rationing of sugar unless they approve, and, after stirring up their zeal (an ability Rousseau says his leaders must have), calling for a voice vote. Castro, incidentally, admits to having been inspired by *The Social Contract*.

in his "educational" theory is evident. In both cases, the intent is to avoid enlightenment, or the preparation for rational, deliberate choice (which is the aim of what we call education). This ever-present suspicion of the people implies a separation of rulers and ruled into "we" and "they."

Rousseau's condition that the people be the sole judge of whether the will of the Lawgiver or "guide" is the general will simply cannot be fulfilled. As one scholar has put it, "It is precisely because the people does not in fact judge according to the general good that the Legislator is necessary in the first place; how then can it judge whether or not the Legislator's will is really the general will?"[4]

We must look beyond the voting process itself for its ultimate function. In the main, its purpose is to obtain, through total participation, the total commitment of all individuals to the general will, and thus to achieve a unanimous, cooperative society in which they will think of themselves as part of the whole, rather than as self-centered units. The vote is an important factor in creating the *moi commun*. It also serves to make the law seem an impersonal necessity, and in Rousseau's political vocabulary "seem" always plays an important role. For these reasons, he wants the act of voting to have the tonalities of a national consecration or a semireligious ritual. His concept of the function of the vote is an underlying reason for his opposition to representative government, in which the citizens' participation and commitment are only partial, never total.

The vote, then, is one factor in the complex process of remaking the individual, the Lawgiver's principal task. At the heart of the concept of an organic collectivity is Rousseau's idea that it can have only one will. Once formulated, there can be no legitimate opposition to it. To oppose the general will is to be an enemy of the people, and such a person must be "forced to be free"—or expunged. It is therefore necessary both to control the ever-lurking enemy, the *moi humain*, and to prevent all groupings that, as lesser general wills, would become the foci of conflicting interests—whereas the whole purpose is to eliminate conflicting interests and conflict.

There is an important element of duplicity in this operation. *La Nouvelle Héloïse* and *Emile* have shown that duplicity and the "hidden hand" are constant and conscious mechanisms in Rousseau's methodology for conditioning and indoctrinating the individual. How often has he said that the best way to control men is to capture their will, and that control is most complete when they think they are doing freely what their guide wants them to do, and makes them do?

The method of duplicity seems to be involved in a vital function of the vote; it gives the citizenry the illusion of self-government. (Rousseau not infrequently speaks of the beneficent utility of illusion.) Indeed, he seems to give the game away when, reiterating one of his most constant beliefs, he writes that law is inadequate: at best, it can control actions, but it cannot control wills, opinions, or passions. It cannot change men. And it is this control, he adds, without which laws are futile, that must be the constant preoccupation of the Lawgiver, the work he must unremittingly carry on *in secret* (Book II, Chs. 7, 12). Rousseau has assured us that his citizens are free because they obey only the law. But in view of these later statements in *The Social Contract*, is it not obvious that they will be obeying something other than the law—the whole secret process of control, which is the *really* important thing?

In view of his theory of human nature and society, Rousseau was bound to fear individual liberty. The remaking of the individualistic, ego-centered personality involves the harnessing of natural competitive instincts to collective purposes, and a process of coercive conditioning through education and law. All the forces of the collectivity are brought to bear to assure the socialization of the egoistic self. The most important force—though Rousseau strangely neglects it in *The Social Contract*—is education. Popular sovereignty is tenable because the citizens have been "educated," "formed," "guided." Another technique developed in other writings is the institution of popular festivals and demonstrations; these create patriotism, pride of citizenship, emotional involvement, and a feeling of belonging to one unanimous body.

Two other mechanisms are carefully described in *The Social Contract*. One is censorship, Rousseau's word for what we now call thought control, a force he complains statesmen have always overlooked, and one he deems essential: to control people's opinions is to control their behavior. Here, too, we have duplicity and the fostering of an illusion of freedom. The people, he says, must believe that the censorial tribunal is not the arbiter of their opinions, but only the means of expressing them. But again no dissent is permitted, and the censors' judgments are not subject to debate or revision. Nor are we told how they are to determine public opinion. It is not unjust to infer that from censorship would flow the State control of publications and the regimentation of art, the theater, and all means of communication.

Here and elsewhere, Rousseau insists on public inspection of private actions or a severe restriction of privacy. "The better the State is constituted, the more do public affairs supersede private ones in the minds of the Citizens. There are even many fewer private matters . . ." (Book II, Ch. 15). Nothing must be allowed to rupture the unity of the collectivity, or to impede the State in its work of socializing or "denaturing" refractory individuals. In the *Confessions*, Rousseau declares that morals and politics are inseparable. In his system, both become politics, and every phenomenon has a political significance. Nothing is neutral or indifferent. This is one prime characteristic of a totalitarian state. In Rousseau's theory, in sum, the State is coextensive with society.

As we conceive a free society, power, like freedom, is limited. To that end, we spell out the powers that government may exercise and the rights and protections enjoyed by individuals which put effective limits on governmental authority. All this Rousseau opposes. He emphasizes the openendedness of the power of the State, the community, the majority. Its limit is what the State itself determines, with the vague protection that nobody can wish to do himself harm. A second protective limitation, that the general will cannot pass laws affecting individuals, is partly nullified by the reservation that it can legislate on groups or classes of citizens, and determine who is and is not a citizen. In fact, the sovereign power has no limit other than the general will. "There is no right to put anyone to death, even for the sake of an example, except him who cannot be kept without danger" (Book II, Ch. 5). But where does danger to the social body begin?*

Religion is another force that must be harnessed to the total effort. In the fourth book of *The Social Contract*, Rousseau, writing from a strictly political point of view, directs a withering criticism against institutional religions, and especially against Christianity, which he considers a source of dissension and resistance to social control. Religion must be one of the mechanisms of the State. Better still, religious fervor must preferably be transferred in great measure *to* the State. In the *polis*, the cult of certain official deities was recognized as a necessary function of organized society.[5] Rousseau proposes a "civil religion," a "purely civil profession of faith whose articles it is the Sovereign's task to determine, not exactly as religious dogma, but as feelings of sociability without which it is impossible to be a good citizen or a faithful subject" (Book IV, Ch. 8). Among these dogmas (he does use the word) are belief in a providential and all-powerful God, immortality, the reward of the good and the punishment of the wicked, and the sanctity of the social contract and of the laws.

What gives us pause here is the intolerance and persecution implied. Rousseau does indeed demand toleration of all faiths, for intolerance would only promote the dissensions and disharmonies he is eager to suppress. After all, what matters to him is not the truth of religion, but its coercive and emotional power. However, two categories are excluded from toleration. One consists of religions that are themselves intolerant,

---

* Referring to the nascent belief in the eighteenth century in a science of human behavior, Sir Isaiah Berlin speaks of the "simplifiers whose . . . moral purity seemed to make them all the readier to sacrifice mankind again and again in the name of vast abstractions upon altars served by imaginary sciences of human behavior." Montesquieu (in contrast to Rousseau) "distrusts all central authority, all the great managers of society, all those who confidently and tidily arrange the destinies of others. . . . Societies organized by such persons, however well ordered and enlightened, are necessarily tyrannous. . . . He distrusts zeal, however benevolent, because it threatens to suffocate individuals ('virtue itself needs limits'), and values personal liberty above all. . . . Only those societies are free which are in a state of 'agitation,' unstable equilibrium; whose members are free to pursue—choose between—a variety of ends or goals. A state might itself be free, that is, independent of other states, but if it becomes frozen and suppresses opinion in the name of no matter how sacred a principle, its citizens are not free but enslaved. . . . It is more important that people should be free to err than be coerced into holding correct opinions. . . . Willing slaves are still slaves" (Sir Isaiah Berlin, "Montesquieu").

particularly Roman Catholicism. The other comprises those who either refuse to take an oath that they believe in the civil religion or, having taken the oath, violate it. The former are banished, the latter put to death.

This imposition of a religious test will recall to Americans the loyalty oaths of the 1950's. It is obvious that Rousseau's intention is to control consciences, beliefs, and opinions. The citizen can no more escape this religion than he can the censorship. Beliefs become a matter for punishment. Implied are the rights of inspection and inquisition. Still worse, Rousseau speaks of executing those who *act* as if they do not believe. Whether or not he realized it, the potentialities of this statement are immeasurable. It would allow the State to interpret actions, or nonactions, as indicative of belief or opinion. This is tantamount to the doctrine of arrest on suspicion of wrong thinking. We need take only one further step to punish people for lack of enthusiasm. The effect of such a state of affairs on people's conduct can only be imagined from the worst excesses of the Terror, or Stalinism, or of Chinese communism.

We are reminded that Rousseau, in *La Nouvelle Héloïse*, establishes a system of spying and informing, and that in a personal letter to M. de Beaumont, which we have not yet come to, he sets forth the theoretical justification for personal and governmental surveillance of ideas, with the inseparable implication of denunciation. It is found earlier, in the *Lettre à d'Alembert*. As we know, this is a strangulating, terror-inspiring system to which it is difficult to set a limit. But how can we expect otherwise? When rulers fear dissent and free thought, terror results. Yet how many have failed to see these perils in Rousseau's political writings?*

An essential aspect of Rousseau's system is the separation of sovereignty and government. The government executes laws and manages the society. Only the citizenry can consent to laws (but not formulate or propose them). Rousseau tells us that this is what sovereignty really means. It is also the power to choose and to remove at will those who govern. This arrangement has almost always been seen as one designed to protect freedom against the power of government. Rousseau, I believe, had no such intention. His purpose was rather to protect the system from abuses or revolution from within, to prevent those who govern from seizing or perverting their powers for their own interests. It was not the *extent* of

---

* We cannot help wondering about statements such as the one we find in Bretonneau's turgid and misguided book, in which he cites "the respect for the personality" as one of Rousseau's highest values (G. Bretonneau, *Valeurs humaines de J.-J. Rousseau*, p. 281 ff.). Saint-Preux, Emile, and the citizen—all are violated in the depths of their personality to serve a supposedly beneficent end, conceived and imposed by a superior intelligence or "guide."

It is tempting to quote Justice Louis Brandeis on the right of privacy. "The makers of our Constitution . . . conferred, as against the government, the right to be left alone—the most comprehensive of rights and the right most valued by civilized men."

their power that worried him, but its *use*. "Le peuple, convaincu que ses chefs *ne travaillent qu'àfaire leur bonheur*, les dispense par sa déférence de travailler à affermir leur pouvoir" ("Economie politique," p. 350, italics added). "C'est l'ordre le meilleur et le plus naturel que les sages gouvernent la multitude" (Book III, Ch. 5).

When used for the purposes set out by Rousseau, the power of those who govern is immense. It is checked only by the periodical assemblies of the people, who act under the "guidance" of the same leaders who govern them, and who are called on to say "yes" or "no" to their regime and to their proposals for laws. Furthermore, the very notion that sovereignty can express itself only in laws means that acts of the government do not inhere in the sovereign (that is, the citizens), and are in themselves beyond their competency and reach. The formulation and execution of laws, control of morals and opinions, of patriotism, "education" and "zeal" by the various on-stage and backstage methods Rousseau has specifically proposed—all are within the unchecked hands of the leaders. We are told very firmly that the people cannot even exercise their sovereignty wisely, cannot be trusted without this direction and manipulation.

There are solid reasons, then, to conclude that to take the separation of government and sovereignty as a libertarian or liberal provision is to reverse the reality of it. The whole system of "forming citizens" obviously depends on managers having such unchecked power; once they have it, their accountability for it—at least, as long as they do not violate the system itself—is illusory.

The foregoing discussion points to two further conclusions. One is the falsity of the accusation leveled against Rousseau by his enemies, that he was a romantic who wanted the anarchy of popular sovereignty. On the contrary, the individual and the mass are controlled, in his system, to the very depths of their beings. The second is the importance of reading all of Rousseau's sociopolitical writings in order to understand the true meaning of *The Social Contract*. His article "Political Economy" lays the basis for the monistic State and control of the individual. In *La Nouvelle Héloïse* and *Emile* we see this control carried out by various means of indoctrination, operant conditioning, and duplicity (hidden control, or the "hidden hand"), which make of these works the first manuals of behavioral engineering. His political theory of education is developed in *Considerations on the Government of Poland*; while in the *Proposal for a Constitution for Corsica* we shall see how the total control of private lives reveals the meaninglessness of his contradictory assurance, in *The Social Contract*, that the individual surrenders only those rights the State judges of social importance.

Democracy and totalitarianism are not exclusive terms. Democracy is rule by the people. Totalitarianism is the attempt to impose a single pattern upon the thought, feelings, and actions of a community. The opposite of totalitarianism is not democracy, but the pluralistic society, in which people are free to differ and to judge the law itself, one in which complete conformity is not the test of good citizenship. Obedience to law is one thing; Submergence into a "higher unity", surrender of one's judgment and will are quite different. We are inclined to cry out with the other Rousseau, the *romantic* Rousseau, "I am I, a sacred I. Thus far do I surrender myself, thus far do I *belong*, but no further." The libertarian will not accept Rousseau's "people's democracy." The general will belongs to the realm of myth; in the realm of reality, it can be expressed only by an individual or a group that speaks in its name and exercises the real power. It is difficult not to conclude that this is what Rousseau really intended, with his "Lawmakers" and his "guides," and all the mechanisms of control of thought and behavior.

In the ideal society Rousseau so ardently longed for, men are made to be happy, because in each man a harmony is created between wish and possibility, and a harmony among all men by the elimination of exploitation and aggressive, self-centered competition. It will also be a just society. Justice will never come from individual conscience or Natural Law, which are simply useless. They could never form the kind of *social* man of whom he was thinking. In their place he put the general will, a juridical, not a moral phenomenon, one that concerns the general welfare. We may wish to assume (as Rousseau probably does) that to act immorally would involve the collectivity's hurting itself, and consequently that the general will cannot will to do so. But if it cannot, it is not for a moral reason, but from motives of self-preservation and self-interest. Rousseau refuses, in the political context, to consider justice as part of the category of moral intuitions of right and wrong which he includes in Natural Law and in his exaltation of conscience. Justice is the child of the general will, of the political will, a matter not of pure ethics in individual relations, but the very essence of the functioning of the State as a political, not a moral entity—or, more exactly, as a moral entity *sui generis* (a notion Hegel and Fichte were to develop). Justice, then, is the decree of the general will as expressed in law. This scission from ethics, or absorption of ethics, is pregnant with possible consequences.

It would be hard to imagine a more dramatic contrast than that between the *Discourse on Inequality* and *The Social Contract*. Little wonder that many critics, in Rousseau's lifetime and in later years, have accused him of inconsistency. Yet, as I have already pointed out, there is no basic contradiction between the two works, for their frames of reference are different. The basic value, happiness, remains unchanged. Freedom, however defined, is in both an instrumental value. The independence of natural man assured freedom and an existence without unhappiness. The imposition of society on this natural man created a situation of conflict, inequality, distorted values, and misery. Social interdependence makes dependence on the collective whole the necessary condition for independence from oppressive individuals or groups.

Happiness can come only from the good society, one in which men would be made to live according to virtue. Its realization depends on the factors that make up Rousseau's disputable concept of political liberty, on equality and control; these in turn must inhere in the organization of a legitimate polity.

The starting point of Rousseau's politics is the assumption that man is naturally (presocially) nonaggressive ("good"). If he is aggressive now, then society has made him so. But the essential fact is that he *is* so. Unlike the modern utopian socialist, Rousseau denies that man is not intrinsically self-centered and can be persuaded to work for the good of the community. He must be denatured and remade. As long as a society is individual-centered or motivated by gain, with little or no check on rivalry for prestige, position, and power, no significant improvement can be effected. Cruelty and exploitation reign, and a real society is impossible. Aggressiveness results from the frustration of unlimited desires. In the state of nature, the desires of the brute man were strictly limited by natural factors and an undeveloped psyche. Once men are beyond this stage, only the strictest control can institute the civilized analogue of the primitive condition, by the creation of a group mentality, by a "negative education" which confines the consciousness to what is healthy, by the systematic control and channeling of behavior into automatic social patterns.

Rousseau's use of the word "natural" can be justified by Pascal's definition of the natural as a habit. Realizing that aggressive impulses are "natural" to men in society, Rousseau found a solution in their diversion to socially controlled activity. Realizing, from the torments of his own self, the deep need for self-esteem, he recognized that other ways can be found to satisfy those needs and the equally deep need for identity by an emotional association with the impersonal group—in other words, by a fictitious identification of the ego with something that is not itself. Thus, one of Rousseau's highest values is order. A communitarian culture is an orderly culture, but that is only because it is not a subjective or permissive culture.*

Utopianism leads to rigorism, for all other ways are wrong. History shows utopianism to be conducive to cruelty and fanaticism, since its theories ignore the persistent refractory elements of human nature. Rousseau expressly favors fanaticism.† Ultimately, then, unlimited con-

---

* Rousseau knew Pascal's aphorism: "We are born unjust, for each of us inclines toward himself. That is against all order. We must incline toward the generality. And the tendency toward self is the beginning of all disorder."

†In *Emile* (p. 386), he writes: "Fanaticism, though sanguinary and cruel, is nonetheless a great and strong passion which exalts the heart of man, makes him despise death, gives him a prodigious spring, and which only has to be better directed to produce the sublimest virtues." Skepticism, on the other hand, makes men effeminate and attached to their lives. It "concentrates all the passions in the vileness of personal interest, in the abjection of the *moi humain*, and quietly saps the true foundations of any society; for what personal interests have in common is so very little, that it will never outweigh what sets them against each other."

trol of individuals is implied, because that is what is required to make them act in a fashion consonant with utopianism. Most often, as in Rousseau, a utopian myth serves to rationalize coercion. To be sure, his political theory in *The Social Contract* is an attempt to transcend experience and is unrelated to action. However, when theory is ruthlessly applied to human affairs, freedom is its victim.

There are, we know, the primitivists and naïve utopians, who claim that social institutions have corrupted men (instead of the reverse), and assure us that if only we leave men alone, their natural goodness will operate unhindered. We have seen that Rousseau was never one of these, and that when he says that society has corrupted men, it has a special meaning, that of unleashing their latent, inherent aggressiveness. Most of the *philosophes* believed that it was enough to change or reform institutions in order to modify men's behavior adequately. Rousseau, Helvétius, and a few others realized that it was not enough. Rousseau rejected reform as a trap to perpetuate what we should call exploitation by the "establishment." The only hope would be to wipe the slate clean and make a new beginning; but he did not really have that hope, for corrupt societies cannot be redeemed, he thought, except, very rarely, by revolution.

At some future point in time, historical perspective will doubtless perceive the social evolution of man as bifurcating into two great streams arising out of the dying feudal order. They emerge as abstract ideas in the eighteenth century, become coherent systems in the nineteenth, and finally enter the realm of actuality in the twentieth. Marxists might call them the bourgeois and the proletarian societies, although in one sense the antithesis is false, since it masks the real locus of power. We call them democratic and authoritarian, but those are slippery, fuzzy-edged words. It is in Rousseau's thought that we can discern the most exact labels, the individual-centered society and the organic society. All the rest flows from this distinction: who sets goals and values; truth and law; the relations between individuals (either moderated or controlled by the State); the very atmosphere breathed. When Mao Tse-tung declares, "Freedom is the recognition of necessity," how can we help being struck by the identity with Rousseau's repeated declarations in *La Nouvelle Héloïse* and *Emile?*[*]

When we criticize Rousseau's theories, candor requires us to admit that we do so from within the framework of our own definitions, traditions, and predilections. It would be possible to argue that his citizens, like the men of the fourteenth century, enjoy a freedom more basic than ours, one which derives from an adjustment between their lives and

---

[*] It is likely that Rousseau would have added Mao, who has said, "It is necessary to remake men, as well as society," to his triumvirate of heroes, Moses, Lycurgus, and Numa Pompilius. Who can say whether Mao, who has applied and perfected Rousseau's technique, was not inspired by him?

their institutions, and from the absence of alienation. We can conceive of their feeling at home within their world. To such a definition of freedom the political regime is irrelevant. I think there can be no doubt that for Rousseau feeling at home in one's world was the real freedom, far more precious than civil liberties.

Whether or not we like Rousseau's "new society," we feel his incomparable candor and the courage he drew from absolute conviction. In one sense, his message is one of hope. Neither society nor human nature is beyond the reach of man's will and rational powers; under certain conditions, both can be turned in new directions. Rousseau thought he had pointed out the paths toward a more human existence.

The *Discourse on Inequality* tells us what men may have been, in their remote origins, or what they still are in their fundamental substructure, and what has happened to them because of social experience. *The Social Contract*, a purely theoretical work, indicates a new direction. It tells us how to overcome and transform this "natural man" within us. It tells us what men may become—or rather, what Rousseau thought they must become, if the unique *human* experiment in a *natural* universe is to succeed and to survive.

Was he "a false prophet," as Irving Babbitt once called him? We cannot, at this point in history, say that he was wrong. His criticisms of our kind of society have surely lost none of their validity. And in such matters, only history can pronounce the verdict.

## 2. THE AUTHORITARIAN PERSONALITY

Rousseau's work is rooted in his personality and his intimate problems. To separate them is to risk losing a whole dimension in our understanding of either one. It would not, for instance, be inconsistent with his remarkable power of self-delusion if in *The Social Contract* he really believed that he was protecting the individual and his rights in alienating them to the all-powerful collectivity (even as he thought he had proved that men are naturally good), despite the oppression it would take to remove the causes of an exploitative society.

This is not to say that Rousseau's political philosophy is reducible to a mere expression of his personality. It had its own intellectual credibility to him and the allegiance of his acute intelligence. To later generations, it has stood by itself. But his politics are not only an intellectual construct. The complexities, problems, and needs of his inner being are involved quite inextricably, as they are in all he wrote. We cannot separate this man from his work, because he writes constantly about himself. Where he is not talking about himself, he projects himself into everything else. He is his own subject. The biographer, wishing to see the man *whole*—his person and his writings which are one—will find in the relationship an illumination of both aspects.

The unity of Rousseau's thought lies in the pervasive antithesis of the independence-dependence polarity. Through it, his personality conflicts are projected onto the written page, an extension of his inner self. It was because he was so dependent, and longed for infantile dependency, that guilt and shame made him yearn for independence. Independence was a "reaction formation" to dependence, comparable to the antitheses of inferiority and boastfulness, exhibitionism and puritanism, which he also displays. The middle road, the normal path of interdependence or integration, had failed him time and again. He alternated between two abnormal extremes.

Independence, as Rousseau sought to live it, is also an escape from other-directedness, a defense—or rather the avoidance of having to make a defense—against implicit or projected criticism from the "other," an escape from the "opinion," and the "look," of others. The goal is to live according to the "pure self." Release from masochism and sadism, from inferiority and superiority, is the valued reward. In modern terminology, the outsider seeks escape from superego and from social limitation.

Such independence from "opinion" is the impossible objective of an abnormal mind, impossible because it involves undoing the work of the parents and the whole process of socialization that makes a human being out of the infant. Its pursuit contributes to a further disorganization of the personality. Inability to cope with society and its demands is evident, and the guilt is projected on society. Revolt seems justified. Jean-Jacques' search for independence was, then, a way both of compensating for his dependency and of avenging his failure to integrate into a normal state of interdependence. It signifies a radical *regression*.* It calls forth his sociopolitical theory, which is the counter-movement: complete dependency in a perfect process of socialization. It is a radical progression into a wished-for state that has never existed. Was it his subconscious wish to achieve the security he found in a dependent relation? Or to create an imaginary world of interdependence, the higher synthesis that would dissolve the inner tension of his polarities? Doubtless it was both of these. In the world he imagines, he finds his true and proper place, denied to him in life by the corruption of men and society. These were compulsive goals, no doubt.

We must not forget Rousseau's fear and distrust of other individuals. How comforting to build something superior to them and above them, an impersonal force like nature's forces, to which they would have to bow! In this imaginary world of socialized men, alienation is overcome.

---

* The emotional potency of the millenarian dream is rooted in deep psychic experiences, in "a hope for rebirth, for another chance." These are childish fantasies. Messiahs, when they get the chance, "turn out to be as horrible in the flesh as the monsters they have slain" (F. E. and F. P. Manuel, "Sketch for a Natural History of Paradise," pp. 122–3).

Rousseau illustrates to perfection the modern psychological theory that neurotic characters have not been able to sublimate nonsocial demands in the normal adjustment process. Yet they cannot follow through their original tendencies because "they have also developed a rigid code of behavior. They are both oversocial and nonsocial at the same time."[6]

The road of independence was the path of the primitive, leading back toward the innocence and immediacy of the state of nature. The road of dependence led into the moral and political realm, where virtue and the work of culture replaced or remade nature. In the *Discourse on Inequality* and in many emotional outbursts—sometimes, towards the end, seemingly psychotic outbursts—Jean-Jacques expressed a preference for nature, a hatred of man's rational powers, a love of the spontaneous, a distrust of language itself, in sum, an aversion to the entire human work of culture, to all that men had superimposed on nature. But in works such as *The Social Contract*, culture had its revenge, and he was its defender. It was too late, he knew. Immediacy was forever gone. Men would be good if they followed their first impulses (as he did!), if they acted without calculation, reflexively, not reflectively. That, too, was forever gone, lost to the corruption of *amour-propre*. Virtue, the "guide," a remaking of men—was there any other way? We can understand why Rousseau was the first man in history to place politics above all else, to extend it to a universal scope, absorbing morals, education and all else.[7]

Albert Schinz was unable to understand how Rousseau could be accused both of individual extremism and collectivist extremism.[8] Gustave Lanson thought he saw a flat contradiction between the individualism of the man and the statism of his thought. Our own study explains the disconcerting antithesis as two poles of a single phenomenon. Rousseau's condition has been well described by Talmon:

A motherless vagabond starved of warmth and affection, having his dream of intimacy constantly frustrated by human callousness, real or imaginary, Rousseau could never decide what he wanted, to release human nature or to moralize it by breaking it; to be alone or a part of human company. He could never make up his mind whether man was made better or worse, happier or more miserable, by people. He was . . . a recluse and anarchist, yearning to return to nature, given to reverie, in revolt against all social conventions . . . abjectly self-conscious and at odds with his environment, on the one hand; and the admirer of Sparta and Rome, the preacher of discipline and the submergence of the individual in the collective entity, on the other. The secret of this dual personality was that the disciplinarian was the envious dream of the tormented paranoid.[9]

This explanation becomes clearer still when Rousseau's attitudes are held up to the light of modern psychology. Recent studies have developed an empirically grounded theory of the "authoritarian personality," and Rousseau qualifies as a classic case of this syndrome. His need for subjective truth and certainty turns out to be a central factor in the authoritarian mind. An outstanding student of this psychological complex, Walter B. Simon, has put it this way: "A basic problem in human action is presented by the gap between the multi-dimensional reality to which man has to react and the necessity that such reaction be unidimensional."[10]

In confronting the problem of adjustment to reality, Rousseau reacted in ways typical of the authoritarian personality. He maintained an infantile tendency to perceive reality in accord with his wishes, interests, and fantasies. His insecurity face to face with a chaotic, unpredictable, hostile world, a pluralistic world of complex and transient relationships, created in him a longing for certainty, a need to perceive and interpret reality in certain and unambiguous ways that fitted his inner reactions and needs. Uncertainty, he admits in the *Profession de foi*, was an intolerable psychic burden. "As the need for certainty," writes Simon, "is only based upon a desire for psychic comfort that comes from subjective certainty, it impedes the quest for objectively testable knowledge." This torment explains Rousseau's resentment of his friends' efforts to modify his opinions and behavior ("response patterns") as threats to his psychic security. It is a mental aberration that habitually "induces eagerness to consider inconclusive moments of suspicion as conclusive evidence." The world, to such a person, is a frightening place, a jungle, and his hatred is projected upon the outside world. How true this was of Jean-Jacques the rest of his story will make only too clear. It is typical of the Messianic complex that its victim flees his inner anxiety by separating himself from the society that disturbs him.

The authoritarian personality finds neat packages and solutions for every situation and is intolerant of ambiguities. His need is to perceive everything in black and white dichotomies. He rejects what disturbs his intellectual and emotional defenses. He admires military virtues and idealizes the soldier because of his envy of superior strength, his need for order, certainty, and security. He is ready to surrender his independence to a stronger protector.

Those in quest of subjective certainty will seek authority that is unlimited in scope and unrestrained in the exercise of its power. In their . . . contempt for authority that operates under limitations and restraints, members of this group occasionally seem to be indomitable anarchists and rebels. That they are in fact pseudorebels only shows when they have occasion to submit to the total authority they crave, or exercise it themselves. *Ibid.*

A person lacking ego security "is apt to feel threatened not only by the comparative permissiveness of democratic [liberal] norms, but also by the complexity of pluralism itself." Authority is what matters, whether they submit to it or exercise it; in this we recognize the sadomasochistic complex.

The dialectic by which Rousseau seeks in the voluntary submissiveness of the citizen the supreme flowering of his freedom has deep connections with his own masochism. The all-powerful, godlike masters of men he creates in the three works we have studied, and in whom he finds wish fulfillment by creative self-projection, is the other side of the coin. He is the demiurge, giving himself godlike power to create better men and better society according to his dreams. Men become simple material for the building of dreamworlds. We may also think of Rousseau's treatment of sexuality, where we see the contrast between the anarchic in his own life and the authoritarian in all his writings. It is not unreasonable, then, to speak of his three epiphanies—Wolmar, the tutor, the Lawgiver —through whom he avenges his ego after having been kicked around through life—and of his three exorcisms—Saint-Preux, Emile, the docile citizen—in whom he discharges or propitiates the real Jean-Jacques.

If *The Social Contract* has any indisputable feature, it is the creation of a totality. It has been shown that the human personality needs to achieve a sense of wholeness, a sense of inner identity. When this process fails, the self responds by restructuring itself. This is an alternate, more primitive way of dealing with experience, one which has adjustment and survival value where a higher tolerance of tension and diversity is lacking; for in this case the lower level "needs totalities and conformities to preserve a sense of security." Such deviations are related to the problem of identity which every individual experiences. Identity is the feeling in an individual of "a continuity between what he has come to be and what he promises to become," between "that which he conceives himself to be and that which he perceives others to see in him and to expect of him." Its achievement depends on "protection in a well-integrated childhood and collective assurances from social institutions in regard to accrued anxieties." Obviously, Rousseau never achieved a normal stage of identity, and he sought help in the manner Erikson has described: he invented an imaginary role for himself as a prophetic voice, superior, but spurned and persecuted. For some years, he was able to maintain that fiction.

Many other traits and tendencies in Rousseau are typical of the authoritarian. Some of these are ethnocentrism and nationalism; exclusiveness of the in-group; the perception of an abyss separating men and women; homosexual tendencies; antagonism to providing education for the "inferior"; pronounced tendencies to avoid or not to admit responsibility for one's own fate; achievement of pseudosecurity through routine and compulsive-obsessive mechanisms; obsession with secrecy and duplicity, with unity and harmony. We recognize them all. Another common element is the secret snobbery of the proletarian who envies the class he attacks. Jean-Jacques' need for stability and thirst for permanence are equally typical. In the authoritarian personality, the obsessive pursuit of justice can become savagely unjust—in Robespierre, for instance. It leads to a revolutionary mentality, characterized by an abstract love of humanity allied with contempt of individual men. (Jean-Jacques wrote that when away from men he loved them again.) Obsessionality, not uncommon to this personality type, tempts its victim to recourse to magic. Rousseau's ideal *polis* is a magical way of escaping from the entrapment of history. It is the dream of the man who fashioned an Emile, a Saint-Preux, a Pygmalion, and breathed his breath into them to give them life.

Rousseau, like all authoritarians, was a man of absolutes. What could be more conclusive than the first lines of the *Confessions?* His undertaking is unparalleled and will never be imitated; he is unique. Other men are either for him or against him; since the "for" is an absolute, almost all are "against." The authoritarian personality sees plots everywhere and inclines to a conspiratorial theory of history. Rousseau did both. In the *Discourse on Inequality*, he attributed the very origin of society to a vast plot of wicked exploiters. If we interpret Rousseau's voting procedure as a ruse, and see deception in his censorial tribunal and secret technique of behavioral control, we are in effect, it may be charged, accusing him of a conspiracy. Precisely. A conspiracy is necessary to cheat nature (as in *Emile*) and make men happy in society. It would be folly to think that a man who was the pathetic victim of a conspiratorial paranoia could escape this pathological trait in his own thinking.

A person of the type we are describing assumes unquestioningly (and Rousseau said it many times) that his conscience is always right. He takes on the mantle of God's "scourge and minister," of prophet and accuser. To a compatriot, Perdriau, Jean-Jacques wrote:

Isolated by men, clinging to nothing in others, I at least believe myself to be exempt from political prejudices. . . . If the detachment of a heart which values neither glory nor fortune, nor even life, can make it worthy of proclaiming the truth, I dare to believe that I have been called to this sublime vocation. It is in order to do good to men according to my capacity that I abstain from receiving any good from them, and that I cherish my poverty and my independence.[11]

He writes constantly in the tone of absolute certainties, of a prophet proclaiming the truth. His judgments are unquestionably the only correct ones. "He would not halt until he had sorted out the good and the wicked, and found again the order of creation."[12] *The Social Contract* is marked by rigidity of thought and structure: there is only one right way, with no modifications. The rules for happiness he lays down in *Emile* are absolute rules.[13] He begins the *Lettre à d'Alembert* by proclaiming that he is speaking in the name of justice and truth. He condemns Alceste, Molière's misanthrope, whom he otherwise idealizes, for being insufficiently cruel in the scene of the sonnet, "for, if one allows himself the slightest compromise, the least alteration of truth, what will be the sufficient reason for stopping until one has become as false as a courtier?"[14] But the examples are too numerous, the phenomenon too constant, to continue.

Finally, like other authoritarians, Rousseau was possessed by the mirage of a better, simpler time, of a simple, disciplined, uncorrupt world, to which he looked back from the confusion of present realities. Unlike many others, he not only looked back, but projected a renewed Golden Age into a revolutionary future which his love of order and stability prevented him from applying to his own corrupted society.

The importance of all this is best summarized in Simon's words:

It did not take long to establish the fact that a person's attitudes are not isolated from one another, but combine to form consistent patterns and configurations of attitudes that emerge as political or social ideologies or as systems of value. As such they provide consistent forms of reference that play crucial roles in cognition and perception.

Rousseau's life was a search for identity. Identity and ideology are two aspects of the same process. Ideological choices correspond to an inescapable inner need and are "vitally related to the the existing range of alternatives for identity formation."[15] But Rousseau, it will properly be said, was also a creator. There are, from one viewpoint, two categories of creator: the devotee of the perfect, and the devotee of the imperfect, who is a lover of spontaneity.

The devotee of the truly perfect upholds the [cultural] conserve as the ultimate value and is skeptical of spontaneity. He is a devotee of theory and a master of words. That is why he is compulsive, authoritarian. . . . He loves to develop magnificent theoretical systems, physical, social, and cultural projects. He sponsors theories of religion, of altruism, of love, and preferably on the theoretical reflective level. He shrinks from experimenting existentially.[16]

Once again, we recognize Jean-Jacques.

From all the preceding we derive a rather obvious answer to a persistent question: how does one reconcile Rousseau's longing for innocence and spontaneity with the regimentation that is the substance of his six sociopolitical writings?

The ambivalence of Rousseau's attitude toward "opinion" and authority is an expression of fundamental character traits. Guilt and inferiority feelings led to social inadequacy. Because he was weak and sickly, he compensated by a form of self-rejection, exalting strength, power, and the military spirit. Because his life was undisciplined and disorderly, he created authoritarian societies in which order is the highest value, and discipline an "inflexible yoke." Unable to cope with the problems of interpersonal relationships, he fantasized himself as a master in governing others, as an all-powerful person who bends them to his will, for their good. The weak finds compensation in associating himself with the strong; the humiliated, rejected individual fancies himself with the power to control others and exercise his will over them. Thus, Rousseau's massive inferiority feelings and his sadomasochism, which are indissociable, led to his characteristic ambivalence: fantasies of godlike power in imaginary worlds and assertions of an unreal independence in life, on the one hand; and the satisfactions of submissive docility, on the other. A deeper psychological analysis leads back to his basic obsessionality, a character disorder whose etiology and symptoms center on ambivalence. The play of two conflicting impulses and needs—dependence and independence—suffuses his life. His security required him to sublimate them into his writings, from *Pygmalion* to *La Nouvelle Héloïse, Emile,* and the others.

Rousseau's life is a history of increasing estrangement and self-doubt. From the time he confronted an awesome, ambivalent father to his confrontation with an alien, ambivalent society, his striving to adapt to reality generated overcompensations for his inadequacies, in the shape of goals of perfect adaptation. While inventing techniques to compel the desires of the will to coincide with a cleverly devised "objective necessity," Rousseau, unable to adjust his own dreams and desires to an objective reality incompatible with them, was pursuing the fantasy of fulfilling them by changing reality.

The first and climactic consequence of the inevitable failure of his fantasy-adaptation, or achievement of identity, had been the Crisis of Vincennes, the Olympian perception of the world as a crazy nonsociety, a world of injustice, war, and disorder. From it sprang the vision of a true society in which his perfect adaptation—the reconciliation of dependence and independence, of submission and power—takes place. His true value as the bearer of a truth that will bring happiness and reconciliation to men would be recognized. His psyche would be healed in the process of perfect socialization. His crippling self-absorption would be overcome in a community of other-directed citizens. The unrecognized hope for a magical therapy directs this adventure, necessarily self-defeating because it takes place outside the context of real life. In real life, he was summoned to another role: to be humiliated, lonely, and unhappy; to be proud and rebellious; and above all, to be what he wanted to be—a prophetic voice.

Whatever viewpoint we choose, whatever evidence and authorities we consult, we are brought back to the same conclusion. The man and the work are one and illumine each other with an unfailing light. The contradictions in both are the same, and when their relationship is understood, they are embraced in the complex unity of his self. They are seen not simply as a basic contradiction or split, but rather as a dynamic tension of polarities which constitutes the organic unity of his personality. No biographer can "explain Rousseau's genius," or anyone's. What can be explained is the peculiar forms it takes to express itself.

# VI. The Fugitive

## 1. A TROUBLED REFUGE

O N E might have expected that Rousseau, as his carriage rolled un-
comfortably along the hot, dusty road toward Switzerland, would
be gloomy and bitter. For a few hours he did sink into rancorous despon-
dency, to which he alludes briefly in a later piece. What is the worth of
a society that never rewards the good and punishes only the show of evil,
he asked himself.[1] No question was more common in the novels of the
time and in the discussions of the *philosophes*, but for Jean-Jacques it
had the caustic sting of reality. The action taken against him had immeasurable consequences. It had stunned him. He had never imagined
that his message of truth, justice, and virtue could be considered dangerous and seditious; and he mistakenly believed, all his life, that the threat
of arrest had been a ploy of the "conspirators" to make him leave France,
so that they would be free to weave their plot unhampered. He might also
have reflected—as he later did—that the social institution had acted to
confirm his role as prophet, truth-bearer, outsider. It was no longer
his choice; it was his lot. Ironically, his firm desire, as his letters to
Malesherbes and others testify, was now to give up the role of seer and
moral guide, although he twice succumbed, in later years, to an invitation
to prescribe a political organization for another country.

The sensations of movement drove the dark thoughts from his mind.
He entered a phase of euphoria not uncharacteristic of paranoid cy-
clothymia. A sense of release swept over him. He was free, alone, wandering across the open country. It was easy for him to turn his mind
away from the past and set his fancy loose. "The Parlement and Mme.
de Pompadour, and M. de Choiseul, and Grimm, and d'Alembert, and
their plots, and their accomplices" were forgotten. Between June 10 and
12 he spent most of his time composing a prose poem, *Le Lévite d'Ephraïm*, based on the biblical episode that had so fascinated him on the
fatal night. It was his favorite work; he eulogizes it in the *Confessions*.[2]

Another reason for Rousseau's high spirits lay buried in his mind. His masochism fed willingly on a diet of martyrdom. "Persecution seems to respond to a secret desire of Rousseau. It delivers him from acts and their consequences. . . . It is no longer *his* failure, it is *their* misdeed. He is no longer responsible. . . . He would have liked . . . to be condemned to an island or a prison for the rest of his life."[3] There he could have lived entirely within himself, dreaming and existing, instead of being compelled to act and to be answerable to reality. The wish comes out clearly in the fifth *Promenade*: "I should have liked them to make this refuge [the island of Saint-Pierre] a lifelong prison."[4] The image of the island solitude interwove in his psyche contrasting notions of exile and refuge, suffering and happiness. Saint-Preux, an alter ego, says it for him: "I was perhaps the only man who was not frightened by such a sweet exile; am I not evermore and everywhere in exile?"[5]

The roads and carriage made for a rough journey. Too shy to command, he was treated contemptuously by the postilions, and his excessive tips evoked their scorn. He reached Switzerland on the fourteenth. Stopping the carriage, he got out and kissed the ground. "Heaven, protector of virtue!" he cried out, while the amazed postilion stared. "I praise you, I am touching a land of freedom." Reality was soon to shatter that illusion. A few hours later he was at Yverdon, in the Vaud canton. There he fell into the welcoming arms of his old friend Daniel Roguin.

As he opens the twelfth and final book of the *Confessions*, Rousseau reveals the disturbed mental state from which he is reviewing this period of his life:

Here commences the work of darkness, in which for eight years past, I have been entombed, without ever having been able, in spite of all my efforts, to penetrate its frightful obscurity. In the abyss of misfortune in which I am submerged, I feel the strokes of the blows which are directed against me. I perceive their immediate instrument, but I cannot see either the hand which guides them or the means which it employs. Shame and misfortune fall upon me as if of themselves, and unawares. When my heart, torn with grief, gives vent to lamentation, I seem like a man who complains without reason, and the authors of my ruin have discovered the incomprehensible art of making the public the accomplice of their plot, without their suspecting it or perceiving its effect. Therefore, while narrating the events which concern me, the treatment which I have suffered, and all that has happened to me, I am not in a position to trace them back to the moving spirit, or to assign the causes, while stating the facts.[6]

Jean-Jacques, who thought he had found another refuge in a land of freedom, soon learned better. Yverdon lasted barely a month. At first he experienced relief and pleasure, the joy of renewing an old friendship with Roguin and establishing a new one with Mme. Boy de la Tour. Roguin's niece, and the widow of a Lyonnaise merchant, she had come to visit her family. Rousseau was to maintain a correspondence with her for over a dozen years. She gladly performed the innumerable services he asked of her.

Bad news was not long in coming. In Geneva—where several over-imaginative persons spread the rumor that they had seen Rousseau—sale of his two books was banned on June 11. On the nineteenth the Petit Conseil condemned them to be torn up and burnt "as bold, scandalous, impious, tending to destroy the Christian religion and all governments." Should the author enter the city, he was to be arrested. The justifications were set forth plainly. With a show of objectivity, Rousseau's two books were declared to "sparkle with audacity and genius." Unfortunately, they combine "sublime truths and pernicious errors," confuse liberty with anarchy. Christianity is exalted and insulted. The political theory is dangerous because it allows the basic, constitutional laws to be revoked by the passing whim of a majority and puts those who govern at the mercy of the governed. Rousseau's periodic assemblies, charges the edict, "would make liberty more oppressive than servitude." (This was precisely his intention; more than once he speaks of "the harsh yoke of liberty.") Moultou foamed with indignation when he read such opinions. Why, *The Social Contract* was the greatest product of Rousseau's genius, superior even to Montesquieu; *Emile* provides the model according to which all men should be formed.[7] The Genevan aristocrats were not wrong, however. *The Social Contract* became the philosophical basis of the political claims of the restive *Citoyens*.

Rousseau's resentment of this action by his fellow-citizens was deep and unending. He had written, he was to declare many times, to defend the cause of God and morals against the materialists, against Helvétius in particular. Besides, the action was strictly illegal: his book had not been printed in Geneva; he was not residing there; he had never been given a hearing in court. Many Genevans felt as he did. It is not too much to say that the action against Rousseau was a spark that renewed the long-smoldering civil strife in that republic.

Dr. Tronchin, in a speech against unbelievers, approved the edicts. He had written to Pastor Vernes: "It is true that he had broken all the windows. . . . He can boast of having done a lot of harm and of having stabbed mankind while embracing it. I should like that wretched man to die. Yes, I say I wish he were dead, for his last two works will do a lot of harm."[8] Two days later he wrote to Albrecht von Haller, urging that Berne follow Geneva's example. In Geneva it was now rumored that Rousseau was a prisoner at Vincennes or a refugee in Holland.

This blow was dealt him by his beloved native city! It was hard to believe, and to bear. He feared, he says, meaning "hoped," that the people would rise up against the decrees, but the wave of anger and scorn, there and elsewhere, was directed against him.

These two decrees gave the signal for the cry of execration which went up against me throughout Europe with unexampled fury. All the newspapers, journals, and pamphlets sounded a most terrible note of alarm. The French especially—that gentle, polite, and generous people, who so pride themselves on their good breeding and respect for the unfortunate—suddenly forgetting their favorite virtues, distinguished themselves by the number and violence of the insults with which they vied with one another in overwhelming me. I was called an infidel, an atheist, a lunatic, a madman, a wild beast, a wolf.[9]

Jean-Jacques, unable to find a rational motive for this wave of execration and insults, thought the world had gone mad. It was enough to make his disturbed mind reel. "I had secret enemies," he writes. The danger was everywhere.*

There were also loyal friends. Various letters of support had reached Montmorency after his departure. Coindet, in Paris, offered to follow him wherever he went: "O Rousseau! how sweet it would be if you tested whether this heart which loves you is worthy of you."[10] Moultou was so distraught that he had a fit of vomiting and had to break off his letter, which was finished by Roustan. Belatedly, he urges Rousseau to flee: "In the name of God! Preserve the supporter of honest men, the consoler of the unhappy, the model of the poor, the teacher of free men."[11] D'Alembert, whom Rousseau numbered among his secret enemies, expressed his outrage that a herd of fanatics should persecute him "for having been right and for having given men the outline of a reasonable religion." He urged Rousseau to seek the protection of Frederick the Great, in Neuchâtel, which he ruled, and offered to intercede with that monarch. Like Roustan, he compares Rousseau to Socrates, and assures him that men of letters place him at their head. "You will find everywhere a thousand tongues to defend you and a thousand arms open to welcome you. . . . Posterity will pronounce your name with respect and will not even know the names of your despicable enemies."[12]† D'Alembert was right, not only in the longer view but more specifically in the next generation. On December 23, 1790, the French National Assembly voted to erect a statue to the author of *Emile* and *The Social Contract* with the inscription: "The free French nation to Jean-Jacques Rousseau." About two months later, on March 2, 1791, the Council of Geneva publicly declared the decrees of June 19, 1762 to be "null and void, because he was never given a hearing."

Rousseau knew only the present. He expressed his bitterness and discouragement in a letter to Moultou (June 15, 1762) informing him of his place of exile. He is an "unhappy outlaw." His only wish is to be forgotten. "Give my address to nobody; speak no more of me; never mention my name. Let my name be effaced from the earth! Ah, Moul-

---

* Moultou wrote to Rousseau on June 22: "The passion with which you have been judged is strange and astounding; with the exception of three or four wise men who have resisted the torrent, all the rest were unanimous in favoring the warrant."

† Rousseau's own admiration and self identification had earlier abandoned Socrates (the martyred philosopher), their first image, for Cato the Younger (the selfless citizen), . and for his trio of god-like Lawgivers.

tou! providence has erred. Why did she make me to be born among men while making me of a different kind from them?"*

What about the little clan of his aristocratic friends? A letter from Mme. de Verdelin hints, in its ambiguity, at the relief they felt. "I paid court at the château [of the Maréchal de Luxembourg]. Since they know you've reached a safe haven, they seem to me to look much better."[13] Mme. de Chenonceaux urged him to go to England. Rousseau kept in touch with his protectors, not without a note of recrimination. "You have wanted it this way," he begins his letter of June 17 to the duchess. "Here I am far away from all that attached me to life. Is it worth having at that price? At least, while losing the happiness to which you accustomed me, it will be some consolation in my unhappiness to think of the motives which decided me." He was reminding her he had left only for her sake. With this letter went one to the Prince de Conti and another to the Maréchal de Luxembourg. To Conti he writes briefly: "I owe Your Highness my life, my liberty, my very honor, which is more enhanced by the interest you have deigned to take in me than diminished by the inquiry of the Parlement of Paris." He reaffirms his allegiance to the prince, his wish to put his life at his service, and signs, "your very humble and very obedient servant." He had never written to Conti before, precisely because he was loath to use that conventional formula. In these words he puts his fate in Conti's hands and signifies his willingness to follow the prince's decisions.

He informs the maréchal that he will not choose a final refuge until he knows whether Thérèse plans to join him; but he urges his friend not to try to persuade her. In this letter he encloses one to her, very affectionate. "I shall be consoled for everything when I have you at my side." There follow many detailed instructions about the things she has to do. No less touching is Thérèse's reply, written at four in the morning on June 23, in an almost undecipherable spelling. "My heart has always been yours, and it will never change as long as God gives us life. . . . I have always told you that wherever you were I would go to join you, even if I had to cross seas and precipices to find you." The maréchal reassured him, in veiled terms, that Conti was still working for him. "We are on the watch, and you cannot imagine all that the man for whom you sent a letter yesterday is doing, and the marks of friendship he has shown for you on this occasion."

The little clan was indeed "on the watch." They suspected that Rousseau would not be able to stay where he was. On June 24, Mme. de Boufflers put further pressure on him to go to England and told him she had written to Hume and other friends in that country. She exalts Conti's friendship for him and for Thérèse and urges him to put a halt to

---

* Pastor Künzli, an admirer, exclaimed that Rousseau was unique: "Does he eat, does he drink like other men?" (*Corr.*, XI, 62.)

his recriminations against the Parlement, which was only doing its duty in condemning a book destructive to the established religion. "Rousseau is forewarned," Fabre points out; "his 'protectors' were dissociating themselves from him on the question of substance."[14] Rousseau's reply to Mme. de Boufflers (July 4) was biting and rancorous. He slashed at the illegalities and calumnies of the Parlement, and even more harshly at Geneva. He pointed his finger at Voltaire, whom he considered the true villain. "It is at M. de Voltaire's instigation that the cause of God has been avenged, against me." The same thing, he predicted, would happen at Berne, when his book reached that city, and he would be expelled from Yverdon. It would happen everywhere. He would be hounded from frontier to frontier, until even air and water were denied him. He would never go to England.

In view of Rousseau's later conviction that the Comtesse de Boufflers had been his secret enemy and had plotted with Hume from the start, her letter of June 14 to Hume is a significant document.

M. Rousseau is held by most people in this country to be a singular man. Taking that epithet literally, it is properly given, for he differs from men as they are in many ways of acting and thinking. He has an upright heart, a noble and unselfish soul. He hates any kind of dependency, and for this reason he has preferred, while in France, to earn a livelihood by copying music rather than to accept benefactions from his best friends. . . . He shuns social life, enjoys only solitude. . . . But, despite his apparent misanthropy, I do not think there lives a gentler man, more humane, more sympathetic to the sufferings of others and more patient in his own. In a word, his virtue seems so pure, so constant, so even, that those who hate him have been unable up to now to find reasons to cast doubt on it, except in their own hearts.

Equally significant is Hume's letter of July 5 to a friend, Gilbert Elliot, expressing sincere sympathy for Rousseau, and broaching for the first time, but not the last, the idea of securing a royal pension for him. He could not suspect that his suggestion was to have disastrous consequences a few years later.

Hume, on July 2, addressed a most cordial letter to Rousseau from Edinburgh, expressing his esteem and admiration. He was under the impression that Rousseau was already in London, and offered his help and friendship. Rousseau received this letter months later, and did not reply until February 19, 1763.

As for Voltaire, Rousseau's accusation was to some degree an exaggeration born of his anguish and resentment. In numerous letters he blames "the buffoon Voltaire and his pal [Dr.] Tronchin," or "the poet Voltaire and the jongleur Tronchin," for maintaining the public excitement and animosity. While the Patriarch of Ferney did maliciously foment gossip and hostility toward Jean-Jacques, it is not certain that he desired Rousseau to be persecuted or harmed. At least not yet. On the other hand, one must adopt a strongly Voltairean perspective to write that "after many years of patience and restraint, he blazed forth against Rousseau, who seemed to be jeopardizing, both by his conduct and his attacks, the sacred cause of philosophy."[15] Voltaire not only despised Rousseau, as a person and as a philosopher; he had never forgiven him his "Lettre sur la Providence" (1756) or his *Lettre à d'Alembert*. It was widely suspected that he had been the moving force behind Geneva's condemnation of *Emile*. On June 18, the day before it was issued, he wrote snidely to Tronchin, "Let me know how they are taking, in Geneva, the little accident that has befallen Jean-Jacques." The oligarchs, however, did not need a nudge from Voltaire, in their eagerness to toady to France and slap down this pestiferous plebeian.

While Voltaire's claim that he offered his persecuted adversary a refuge is without foundation, at this stage of their relationship it may still have been possible for him to feel compassion. "Since this bastard of Diogenes' dog is unhappy," he wrote to Gabriel Cramer on June 12, "we must forgive him. He is a man who belongs neither in a republic, nor in a kingdom, nor in a society." On September 8, d'Alembert informed him of the rumors being spread by Rousseau's friends to the effect that he was persecuting Jean-Jacques and working to have him expelled. He advised the Patriarch not to crush his foe. "Remember, moreover, that if Rousseau is persecuted, it is for having thrown stones, and pretty good stones, against that *infâme* which you wish to see crushed." It would not be good for the "party" to be involved in this persecution.[16] Many of Voltaire's friends, and also Diderot's, disapproved of his endless volleys of jeers. Replying to d'Alembert on September 15, Voltaire denied persecution:

I have made fun of his Emile, who is surely a sorry character. His book bored me, but there are fifty pages in it which I'd like to bind in morocco. Really, am I the kind who persecutes? Do they think I have influence with the priests at Berne? . . . You can see that the poor fellow is mad. If only he had a shred of sense left, he would have come to the Château de Tournay, which I offered him. It is a free land. He could have thumbed his nose at the Aryan priests, the imbecile Omer [Joly de Fleury], and all the fanatics; but his pride did not allow him to accept the generosity of a man he has offended.

D'Alembert accepted this apparently clear statement at face value. Unfortunately it is not clear at all, and its sincerity is subject to the strongest doubt. In July 1762, Voltaire had written to Charles Pictet: "I am so far from being his enemy that I offered him, several years ago, one of my houses so that he could regain his health." Was Voltaire referring, as some have thought, to his letter about Rousseau's *Discourse on Inequality* (August 30, 1755), in which he suggested that he come back to his native land and lead a healthy life there? But in that letter there is no such offer. It may not be irrelevant to note that Voltaire, in his letter to Pictet, also says: "It is false that I have ever written anything against the Christian religion." Later references confuse the issue further. On January 15, 1765, Voltaire wrote to Damilaville: "I had offered him, despite his stupidities, a fate as happy as that of Mlle. Corneille* and if, instead of a bushel of pride, he had had a grain of common sense, he would have accepted my offer. He took offense at the offer of help. He is not Diogenes, but Diogenes' dog, who bites the hand of one who offers him bread." And to Hume, on October 24, 1766, he asserts that he had offered Rousseau a country house, called the Hermitage, in 1759. In 1755, however, Voltaire did not own the Hermitage, and in 1759 he had exhibited only fury and spite toward Rousseau.

Rousseau said on one occasion that he remembered no such invitation. Twice, in 1764 and 1767, he denied it categorically.[17] Some third-party testimonials from Voltaire's friends, which support such a claim are highly dubious and at times outright mendacious.[18] How little the pragmatic Voltaire understood the idealist Rousseau is clear in an incident reported by Moultou. At a social gathering Voltaire volunteered the prediction that Jean-Jacques would return to Geneva, promise to respect religion, and declare that the printer had added a few pages to his book. "No, Monsieur," Moultou responded impetuously, "Jean-Jacques does not put his name to his works in order to disavow them." Voltaire, *touché*, remained silent.[19] Nonetheless, Rousseau was prescient. Before too long, Voltaire became one of his most implacable persecutors.

Rousseau would have liked to stay on at Yverdon, and asked Moiry, the city's bailiff, for his protection. Moiry's opinion was that he would not be molested; he would, if worse came to worst, give Rousseau warning. On July 3, with tears in his eyes, Moiry told the fugitive that the government at Berne had ordered him expelled, giving him two weeks' grace. A man of character, Moiry wrote to the Senate of Berne, asking them to respect the exile's person and virtue, even though his book was unorthodox. But Berne was an even more closed oligarchy than Geneva, and its rulers felt as threatened as their neighbors by Rousseau's doctrines. Despite an appeal for delay by Moiry, the expulsion order was confirmed on July 9. He later related to Boswell how he broke the news:

A second order came. Then I communicated it to him, but tactfully. "Are you contented here?" "Yes, but I see too many people." "I think you would be better off at Môtiers." He fixed me with his piercing gaze. "I believe I understand you." "Yes, you understand me." I had already engaged the house where he now is. He left that same day. He came to take leave of us. There were tears in his eyes. He said. "They are tears of joy for having known you."[20]

Moiry tried to console Jean-Jacques. "Great reverses make a great name illustrious," he wrote on July 27.

---

* The grandniece of the great tragedian, whom Voltaire protected.

On the ninth, then, Jean-Jacques left for Môtiers in the lovely Val-de-Travers, a village in the province of Neuchâtel. Two factors made the move favorable. Mme. Boy de la Tour offered him a furnished, unoccupied house belonging to her son. It was a rambling, rustic house with a gallery, or porch, on the second floor, and Rousseau found it to his taste. Moreover, Neuchâtel was ruled by Frederick the Great, who—although Rousseau had on more than one occasion expressed his aversion toward that unprincipled monarch—was known to protect dissident *philosophes*.

On that same day, Thérèse left Paris to join him. Jean-Jacques, as we have seen, had been ambivalent about this. Twice he assured the Luxembourgs that she should not be urged to come, not realizing that they could scarcely wait to see her out of the way. In the *Confessions* he explains his hesitancy with candor. Their relations, he was convinced, could no longer be the same. Either she would suffer because of his sufferings (and thus add to them), or else make a merit of her sacrifice. For some time, he adds, her feelings toward him had cooled. "I felt that she was no longer for me what she had been in our *belles années*." He does not indicate the probable cause: the cessation of sexual relations between them in 1755, for the sake of his health and in order not to make her pregnant again. Thérèse, at forty-one, had lost none of her natural appetites and had gained nothing in the way of intelligence or understanding. (Nevertheless, she resisted the insolent advances of two men in the coach that took her through France.)[21] Rousseau assures the reader that his feelings toward Thérèse had not changed, but a year later speaks of his boredom with her.[22] Deep down in his heart, he declares, he felt he could not get along without her and wanted her with him. She reached Môtiers on July 20. The joy of their reunion released fountains of tears.

On July 11, the day after his arrival at Môtiers, Rousseau sent a note to Lord Keith, hereditary earl marischal of Scotland and governor of Neuchâtel. He was depressed and had written to Roguin, "I am so unhappy that everything good that happens to me makes me fear something bad."[23] George Keith, a partisan of the dethroned Stuarts, had followed them into exile after the Jacobite rising of 1715. In 1719 he led the Spanish expedition to Scotland in behalf of the Old Pretender, and escaped after its defeat. Disillusioned by the Stuarts' tyrannical ways, he fought for Spain, then became a diplomat in the service of Prussia. Keith was a man of wit and wisdom, tolerance and understanding. Like Jean-Jacques, he had been in tight straits, suffered humiliation, and had come to prize independence. At seventy-six, he was emaciated and tired. In a few months he was to leave the principality, wearied by the strife-ridden people he was supposed to govern, and by their petty religious controversies.

Rousseau asked him, in a tone of desperation, to grant him refuge. He penned a proud note to Frederick. "I have said unfavorable things about you, and I may say more. . . . Sire, I have deserved no consideration from you, and I ask for none. But I thought I should inform Your Majesty that I was in your power, and that I wanted to be. You can dispose of me as you wish." A most unusual way to ask for protection. He decided not to send the note. It was unnecessary. Keith, a man of noble character, though eccentric and unpredictable, assured Rousseau that he could stay, and that he was writing to the monarch. Jean-Jacques was worried that Voltaire and Tronchin would pull the strings of other puppets in Berlin, but permission was granted on the condition that he abstain from controversial writing and cause no trouble among the pastors. The exile replied proudly that he would accept no conditions, that as a free man and a republican his thought was his own, but that anyhow he had no intention of writing anything more.[24] On November 1 he sent a letter to Frederick, urging his "benefactor and protector" to stop making wars and see that his people had enough to eat.

Rousseau accepted an invitation to visit Keith.

The venerable appearance of that illustrious and virtuous Scotsman touched my heart strongly. At once there began between him and me that strong attachment which on my part has always remained unchanged and which would have, on his part, if the traitors who have taken away all the consolations of my life had not taken advantage of my absence to deceive his old age and disfigure me in his eyes.[25]

Keith returned his visit and spent two days at Môtiers. After that Rousseau went to see him every two weeks, walking the nine miles, but breaking the journey by staying overnight at an inn. "How many tears of tenderness I often shed on the way, thinking of the fatherly kindness, the lovable virtues, the gentle philosophy of that respectable old man. I called him my father, he called me his child." It was ever thus with him. He rejected protectors, including kings, unless he could feel that the protector was a supervising father, an understanding father, such as he had never had. Jean-Jacques would not accept class arrogance, but he craved emotional subservience, just as Saint-Preux had willingly placed himself under the firm hand of Wolmar. Nonetheless, jealous of his independence, he turned down Keith's repeated invitations to live with him.

Rousseau is so filled with emotion as he writes about Keith that he cannot help adding another exclamation: "O my good lord! O my worthy father! how my heart still throbs when I think of you! O the barbarians! what a blow they struck me when they turned you away from me! But no, my great man, you are and will always be the same for me, as I am always the same. They have deceived you, but they have not changed you."[26]

Rousseau was as happy as could be expected. He was ready to stay in his new refuge. Lenieps, in Paris, urged him to go to Prussia, a land where men were free and enlightened. Mme. de Boufflers tirelessly pressed him to go to England. She translated part of Hume's letter to her, in which he expressed his admiration and warm welcome, but worried about the problem of his not knowing English. She offered two alternatives: Mme. de La Marck's château near Aix-la-Chapelle, a free and tolerant principality; or else "the château of a man" (referring, in covert language, to Conti) "to whom you are already obliged and whom you mention in your letter."[27] Hume, replied Jean-Jacques, was the truest philosopher he knew and the only objective historian, but how could he, loving the country, live in the murky streets of London? He puts her off about the other suggestions, and even prevaricates by saying he had not yet heard from Frederick.[28] Mme. de Boufflers had an answer to all his objections: the country around London was charming; Conti would assure a safe-conduct through France; he could even supervise a new edition of his works.[29] Mme. de Luxembourg seconded her exhortation in a letter of her own.[30] One cannot help noting this eagerness to see Rousseau on the other side of the Channel. At a later time he was to interpret it, rightly or wrongly, in a sinister way.

He must have told Keith about these offers. The prospect of Rousseau's going to Britain delighted the old earl marischal. He dreamed of going home to Scotland and of living with Hume and Jean-Jacques, each of whom would have "a couple of rooms" and contribute to the household expenses. The pressures were so strong that Rousseau wrote to Mme. de Boufflers on October 7 that he might go to England in the spring. Meanwhile, Frederick the Great had offered to build him a hermitage in Prussia. This was not appealing. Jean-Jacques, the enemy of kings, could never live in a house built by a king.

To solidify his position in Môtiers, Rousseau on August 24 wrote to its pastor, Frédéric-Guillaume de Montmollin. Asking permission to take communion, Rousseau assured him of his constant attachment to the reformed religion, and stated his motive to be the edification of the faithful. The letter, actually intended as a public manifesto, was widely circulated. Permission was granted, after an interview. (Rousseau reverses the facts by claiming that Montmollin came to see him.) He attended Holy Supper on August 29 and thereafter became a regular communicant. Many were shocked by this action, by the letter to Montmollin, and by his calling a religion he had condemned "holy." The *philosophes* and the clergy could not believe he was sincere. Security had of course been his primary motive. He answered one imputation of hypocrisy by an angry correspondent: "Truth for us is covered with a veil, but peace and union are a sure good."[31] In this he was not insincere. Communion was a great consolation. He suffered from his isolation, from the verbal vilification that was coursing like a fever throughout Switzerland, from anonymous letters, from the ceaseless drumfire in the journal of Neuchâtel. "To live always isolated on the earth seemed to me a very sad fate, especially in adversity." Môtiers was a prison more than a refuge. In church, taking communion, he felt as one, for a moment, with his brothers.

Montmollin, an ambitious man who had given himself the title of professor, was doubtless flattered to have the eminent Rousseau under his protection. On November 27 he assured Jean Sarrasin, the powerful Genevan pastor who was Rousseau's enemy, that his protégé was docile to his lessons on religion and that he hoped to win him over to the true faith. Montmollin's feelings towards Rousseau were most friendly, even though he had not counted on all the *tracasseries* his visitor was to bring him—countless letters, many of them hostile, the suspicions, and finally the disapproval of his colleagues.

Reassured about his safety, Rousseau settled down to as pleasant an existence as he could devise. This was the time, he decided, to satisfy a long-standing whim, to give up normal clothing and don the Armenian garb. The robe would be more convenient than breeches for his infirmities. The rationalization covered the deeper motive, the satisfaction of a psychological need: his strange dress made him "stand out from his fellow-men as a bizarre and unique figure who could not fail to arouse considerable public interest."[32] Caftan, belt, and the rest (such as we see it in Allan Ramsay's famous portrait) were acquired on August 30. The townspeople, at first aroused to anger by the feminine garb, got used to it. Montmollin allowed him to wear it to church. Keith, seeing it for the first time, said only "*Salamaleki!*"

This step was the first in a willed feminization. On August 21, a young bluestocking, Julie von Bondeli, reports Rousseau to have said: "I have thought like a man; people have disapproved of it, I am going to make myself a woman." He took to lacemaking as his favorite occupation, and to embroidery. He wanted his lace to be pretty and multi-colored. "I would go to work on my doorstep like a woman and gossip with the passers-by."[33] It made him feel good. "I'm wearing a long robe and making lace," he tells Mme. de Verdelin. "That makes me more than half a woman. Why have I not always been one!"[34] Soon he took to baking his own bread.

At the same time he was still easily aroused by young women. He mentions one, Isabelle d'Ivernois. She was twenty-six, and Jean-Jacques called her "*ma fille.*" When she was married, that September, he gave her a large lace cloth on the condition that she would nurse her children, as he had urged in *Emile*.

He makes no mention of a second young woman. While we cannot speak with certainty, it is possible to deduce from his *Lettres à Sara*, which he probably wrote during his stay at Môtiers (though at a later date than these first months), that "Sara" was Salomé-Charlotte Montmollin, the younger daughter of the pastor. She was just eighteen. Rousseau tells us in a Preface that he wrote these four letters to prove that a man of fifty can write love letters "to a girl of twenty" without losing the respect of decent people. More likely, it was a last temptation of his undying romanticism, of his longing for the perfect love, or perhaps, it has been speculated, "a rebellion against his aging body."[35] His imagination was always at the service of his sensuality. But experience had at least made him lucid, and he admits he is too old to be loved by a young girl. That admission does not inhibit his own passion. "For six months my eyes and my heart have been devouring your charms; for six months you have been the only thing on my mind and I have lived only for you."[36] Sara did not love him, but she knew how to tease and torment. With his customary masochism, he takes pleasure in his servitude and his humiliation, yet exults in his passion: "I was young with your youth, wise with your reason, virtuous with your virtue. . . . I was humiliated, I was mad, I was ridiculous, but I was happy. . . . I have lost all repentance, all shame. . . . For you I have a young man's heart."[37] The paroxysm passed, and he regained a "stoical" calm.

We have other evidence that Rousseau continued to have erotic longings accompanied by an unwillingness to accept the realities of growing old. He admitted as much to a friend, Henri Coignet, in 1770.[38] A visitor, Chassaignon, reports a conversation during which Rousseau said, "I suffer to see all beings renewing themselves around me . . . while my body, changed by the years, becomes decomposed and wrinkles of decrepitude furrow my brow. . . . No, I have never been more attracted by women than I have been since I have become an object of aversion for them."[39]

There were many visitors at Môtiers, and some new friends. Most important was a close friendship with Alexandre Du Peyrou, who lived in Neuchâtel. They met in September 1762. His junior by fourteen years, Du Peyrou was wealthy, generous, and entirely devoted to Rousseau. The portrait in the *Confessions* is not wholly favorable; Rousseau pictures him as taciturn, secretive, cold, and giving the appearance of a sage. In fact Du Peyrou was ever at his service, ever tolerant of his moods and whims. But the *Confessions* were written after Rousseau had quarreled with him—as he did with almost all his friends. Although Du Peyrou did not always agree with Rousseau, he respected his ideas and admired his genius.

Right now Jean-Jacques wanted only to be forgotten. There would be no more writings, that was definite. "I have accomplished my mission, I have said what I had to say, I consider my career as ended. All that is left is to suffer and to die."[40] Why bother to tell men useful truths, when they only stop up their ears and persecute? Well, at least the persecution would prove to the future that he had not exaggerated.

Even the peace of oblivion was denied him. He was sick of unwanted well-wishers and turned them away. "You are a lieutenant-colonel,

Monsieur, I am very glad to know it. But even if you were a prince, or a farm worker (which is worth more), I have only one tone with everyone, and I shall take no other with you."[41] The Prince de Conti? Well, that was something else.

It was the Rousseau-haters, not the Rousseau-lovers, who were the worrisome torment. Fomented by Voltaire, who was to write that "the city of Calvin has become the city of *philosophes*,"[42] and by his acolytes, controversy would not die down. Rousseau was sure the two "parties," *dévots* and *philosophes*, had joined forces against him, and was fearful of being driven from Môtiers.[43] Moultou was always offering to defend him, but was careful not to compromise himself by taking an open stand.

The real trouble came from the Church. Montmollin allowed copies of Rousseau's letter to him to be spread throughout Geneva. The acrimonious controversy it caused would not die down. A requisitory issued in Paris by Joly de Fleury, the attorney-general, further stirred up the Genevan ministers. Rousseau received a mocking letter, "reeking of Voltaire," from an imaginary baron asking him to take him in as a boarder for two years, without charge, so that he could be taught how to be happy.[44] Pamphlets and newspaper articles against him came out regularly, and the flood of anonymous letters was endless. A Colonel Pictet who issued a letter defending him and blaming Voltaire and Tronchin for influencing the Council was imprisoned, suspended from the Grand Council and from citizenship, and forced to make public apology. This was another unpopular move on the part of Geneva's government, as was its refusal to answer the request of Rousseau's relatives to make their judgment public. Pastor Vernes, a friend of Rousseau's, scolded him for promoting incredulity by stripping the religion of Jesus of what men have added to it.[45] Vernet followed suit, but more harshly, demanding a retraction.[46] Rousseau broke off with both. Enraged when a M. Comparet sent him an abusive letter, he retorted in kind, but did not send his reply: "Monsieur, I have never heard your name. What have I done to you? Is your heart so strangely depraved that you deliberately provoke an unhappy man, browbeat him for no reason, when he wasn't even thinking of you?" Why is Helvétius, who wrote a much more dangerous book, unmolested, while *his* only crime is to have wanted to make men better? The innocent Jean Calas would not have been broken on the wheel if his judges had been disciples of the *Profession de foi*.[47]

Protestations were futile. Had the Genevans gone mad? Every day he had visitors whom he took to be spies from his native city. It was enough to make him decide to renounce his Genevan citizenship, his proudest title—an act he was to carry out on May 13, 1763.

Ustéri, in Zurich, reassured him that he had many partisans. He did indeed; martyrdom has that effect. Hirzel, author of the popular *Le Socrate rustique*, dedicated a copy to him: "To the first among men." A

friend in Dijon, Legouz de Gerland, urged his "dear orang-outang" to
return to society, arguing that men are no worse than they have always
been.[48] His ever-faithful admirer, Mme. de la Tour, sent her encouragement: "You are indifferent to no one. The privileged creatures whom
your works have formed or reassured adore you; the others detest
you."[49]

Detest him they did. The letter to Montmollin and Rousseau's admission to communion outraged the *bien-pensants*. One Genevan, Jean-
Louis Dupan, expressed his sentiments to a friend: "Fortunately there
are not many heads like his, or the world would soon be a chaos. That
man has wanted to make a name for himself, and he has succeeded very
well."[50] Rousseau was deluged by letters, some idolizing him, many
reviling him, all emotional. One woman declared flatly: "You are a
plague to mankind."[51] Anyone daring to speak in favor of *Emile* was
immediately suspect of heresy. One thing is certain: in the inexhaustible
letter-writing of the Swiss, Rousseau was the dominant topic. "Very well,
my dear friend," writes Julie von Bondeli, "*parlons Rousseau, et parlons-
en souvent.*"[52] When Montmollin's Genevan colleague Jean Sarrasin
scolded him roundly for admitting Rousseau without a public retraction, he defended himself vigorously. Rousseau had assured him he was
a sincere Christian and Protestant, a defender of the faith; the *Profession de foi* was directed against Helvétius and the *philosophes*; and the
people were impressed by his obvious piety.[53] Suspicious and hostile,
Sarrasin kept up a drumfire of monitory letters to Montmollin. Among
the things that shocked him was that the Vicar, in the *Profession de foi*,
professed the Catholic religion without believing in it, and that he
advised Emile to do the same. Isn't Rousseau's behavior, he asked on
December 3, to be interpreted in the same light? Rousseau, in fact, had
given out various exculpations for the *Profession*: it was an attack
against Catholicism only; it was a defense of Christianity; the Vicar's
faith was not to be taken as Rousseau's; Christianity is only the Vicar's
natural religion clarified and perfected. Few were convinced by these
protestations.

On September 9, *Emile* was put on the Index. On November 14 the
Sorbonne published its *Censure* of that work, written by the Abbé
Gervaise.

### 2. REACTIONS TO *Emile* AND *The Social Contract*

Copies of *Emile* and *The Social Contract* were infiltrating Paris. The
political tract aroused little interest, but even Gervaise admitted that
*Emile* was eagerly sought after. People in high places used influence to
get a copy from the authorities. The book smugglers did good business.
"Everybody wants to have it with him day and night, when he's out
walking and in his study, in the country and in the city. . . . Not to

declare yourself one of his disciples is practically to be put to shame."[54] The influence of the work was incalculable. The *Profession de foi*, however, left little permanent impression on Catholic thought; Rousseau defended personal faith, and his "insistence on re-examining the entire basis of religious belief and observances was an implicit rejection of the church's authority . . . and of its claims to present the truth as revealed by the creator."[55] Outside the clergy, his work had a moral influence and undoubtedly brought a general spiritual renewal to many individuals.

Voltaire covered the margins of his copy with derisive comments. But he could not help feeling grudging admiration for it, despite his animosity and many satirical comments of detail.

It is true that in this book, which is a program of education, there are many ridiculous, absurd things. He has to bring up a young gentleman of quality, and he makes a carpenter of him. That is the substance of the book. But in the third volume he introduces a Savoyard vicar who attacks the Christian religion with much eloquence and wisdom.[56]

Jean-Jacques, who has written both against the priests and the *philosophes*, has been burned in Geneva in the person of his dull Emile, and banished from the canton of Berne, where he had taken refuge. Presently he is between two rocks, in the Neuchâtel country, still thinking he is right and looking pitifully at human beings.[57]

And in a different tone: "Oh! how we would have loved that madman, if he had not been a false brother!"[58] Jean-Jacques would have been a Paul, if he hadn't preferred to be a Judas. "How horrible that such a scoundrel should have written the *Savoyard Vicar* [*Profession de foi*]. That wretch has done too much harm to philosophy; but he resembles the *philosophes* only as monkeys resemble men."[59] Voltaire, clearly enough, hated Jean-Jacques for party reasons as much as he detested him personally. He predicted that *Emile* would be forgotten in a month.*

D'Alembert, Voltaire's close friend, was as usual circumspect, but fair. He found *Emile* "full of flashes and smoke, of warmth and puerile details, of light and contradiction, of logic and irrelevancies; in a thousand places the work of a writer of first rank and in some others that of a child."[60] Diderot rarely made comments on his former friend's writings.

---

* Theodore Besterman, the outstanding Voltairean, inclines to Voltaire's side: "Needless to say Rousseau was well able to keep his end up. When he received a mad letter from a crank he at once attributed it to Voltaire; and soon after he composed an amusing little dialogue between Voltaire and a workman, in which the former is made to appear a calumniator and a hypocrite. And henceforth he lost no opportunity to exercise his bile at Voltaire's expense. Worse was to come. In the meanwhile he implacably vetoed an attempt at a reconciliation initiated by Moultou." Besterman properly speaks of Rousseau's "obsessive hatred of Voltaire," but of course the feeling was reciprocated (T. Besterman, *Voltaire*, pp. 429, 450–51).

But he could not miss the opportunity, in one of his gossipy letters to his mistress, Sophie Volland, of telling her about the Genevan people's demonstration against the Consistory. "It is precisely because that *Profession de foi* is confused balderdash that their heads were turned. . . . I see Jean-Jacques flirting with a friary in which he'll get caught one of these days. His ideas have no stability. He is a man of excesses who is tossed from atheism to piety. Who knows what his stopping point will be?"[61]

Grimm was teutonically thorough. On June 1 he had predicted Rousseau's expulsion from France to the readers of his *Correspondance littéraire*. "Intolerance and bigotry will not miss such a good opportunity to torment a famous writer."[62] A fortnight later, he gave a summary, full of venom and distortions, of Rousseau's career. On July 1, July 15, and again on September 1 he devoted many pages to a critical analysis of *Emile*, mingled with his own ideas on education. Grimm is severe, but objective. Like d'Alembert, he sees in *Emile* a combination of fine truths and beautiful passages and of extravagant, absurd, and false ideas. As a system of education, he judges it impractical and worthless. With his keen, critical mind, he hits on many of the book's weaknesses. "What is not less strange is to see this writer preaching the love of truth everywhere, and constantly using artifice and lies in order to succeed with his pupil. It is not so easy to fool children as M. Rousseau thinks."[63] The source of all of Rousseau's extravagances, Grimm finds, lies in the "ideal and chimerical man which he has created and substituted throughout for man as nature made him," and as he has always been as far back as we know.[64] Emile, he comments, "is a rather stupid child, and his mistress [Sophie] a little prude, shrewish and unbearable."[65] Grimm also has the rare perspicacity to see the relationship between *Emile* and the *Discourse on Inequality*.*

"They say," adds Grimm at the end of his first piece on *Emile*, "that *The Social Contract* is of the same quality: obscure and involved in its principles, often futile and dull, often bold, lofty and admirable." Unfortunately, he continues, it is not possible to get hold of the book in Paris. One must go to Holland and smuggle it in.

Probably few of those who bought *The Social Contract* as a *succès de scandale* ever read it through. The French, unlike the Genevans, had not bothered to condemn the book, but only interdicted its sale. It had relatively little impact in France until the 1780's. Outside of Geneva it provoked little fuss except for its political attack on Christianity. By the

---

* Julie von Bondeli, like Grimm, is struck by Rousseau's confusion of artifice and nature. She wonders how it is that "Emile is the work of nature and not that of men," when as a small boy he says to some angry men, 'You are such unfortunate people, I pity you' " (*Corr.*, XI, 234). Bachaumont remarks: "This pupil, adorned with all virtues . . . ends up by being a misanthrope with an aversion to any place in society, fills none, and goes to the country to plant cabbages and give his wife children."

public at large, Rousseau was not considered a political thinker, although the summary of his ideas in *Emile* doubtless gave them wider diffusion. As an abstract, speculative work, it had, of course, some serious readers. Bachaumont's comment (September 3) is to the point: "*The Social Contract* is gradually being distributed. It is very important that such a work not ferment in excitable minds; great disorders would result. Fortunately the author has enveloped.himself in a technical obscurity that makes him impenetrable to the average reader." Bachaumont's next sentence reveals how true was the last remark: "He only develops maxims that everyone has engraved in his heart; he says commonplaces in such an abstract way that they seem marvelous." But if that were true, why did Bachaumont fear "great disorder"?

La Popelinière, a tax farmer and "establishment" figure, acknowledged the theoretical validity of Rousseau's theories, but took comfort in the admission that they were useless and inapplicable in the present state of society. "It will be necessary, I think, for the natural revolution of things to return us to our original state of barbarism."[66] Such an eventuality left plenty of time.

Voltaire quipped: "*The Social Contract*, or unsocial contract, is noteworthy only for some coarse insults he hurls against kings . . . and for four insipid pages on the Christian religion."[67] But he was angered by the burning; books, he declared, should be refuted, not burnt. He read his copy carefully, covered the margins with comments, and missed its import completely. Rousseau had said correctly that he could not be understood in his own time.

Despite Voltaire's dictum, there were only two published and two unpublished refutations of *The Social Contract* during Rousseau's lifetime. Several more commentaries appeared during the Revolution, when both sides tried to put him to use. Luzac's expert examination (published in 1789) pointed out clearly the revolutionary character of Rousseau's doctrine: not that sovereignty might inhere in the people—which is the character of democracies—but that it could inhere only in the people, who could never alienate it to a king or an aristocracy—thus making the other two forms of government, as they were understood, illegitimate.[68] One of the published refutations appearing in a little-known periodical, *La Religion vengée*, made this criticism: "Will the agreement of a crowd of vile commoners form more just decisions than wise and enlightened men, although in a smaller number? It is for M. Rousseau to prove this; that is to say, it is up to him to show that to make good laws, intelligence is useless, and it is enough to count votes."[69] The writer pays no heed to Rousseau's expressed preference for aristocracy or to his plans to control popular opinion.

Often overlooked among these few early refutations is Voltaire's *Idées républicaines* (1762), a good part of which is devoted to a severe criticism of Rousseau. He derides as conducive to anarchy the notion that the people can dismiss any of the officers of government "when it pleases them." To Rousseau's ideas he opposes his own belief in representative government and inalienable civil liberties.

It was in Geneva, where the oligarchy had already on several occasions put down abortive revolts, that *The Social Contract* was most feared. There is little doubt that it did stir up anew the demands of the Bur-ghers and created an unrest which was heightened by events we are about to examine. Only in Geneva were both of Rousseau's works burnt by the public executioner. The crisis was to grow until the Burghers and the Natives were granted a few token concessions in 1768, and then begin again in 1780. A revolt occurred in 1781–82, in which an impor-tant role was played by political clubs, although the basic factors were political and economic.[70]

In a more general way, Rousseauism triumphed where Rousseau did not. Even in 1765 one Genevan decried the acceptance of a new emo-tional philosophy. "Our youth especially are intoxicated with the prin-ciples of Rousseau, and believe we can refuse nothing asked from us in the name of liberty. . . . Rousseau is their God."[71] The essence of the new mood was equality and opposition to discriminations of honor and status. Constitutional objectives became insufficient. When the Revolu-tion finally arrived in Geneva, Rousseau was "worshipped as its prophet and moral authority." He had created "a new and universal criterion of value with irresistible appeal"—not blood or wealth, but "virtue" and noble sentiment.

Of course there was a large disparity between intent and influence. Rousseau was an aristocrat in most of his aspirations and theorizing, though pulled at times to the plebeian class of his origins, largely be-cause he had not been able to enter the aristocratic world on a footing of equality. The lower classes, however, felt ennobled by him. He did teach his followers that an inner conviction of rectitude was more valuable than the social and literary standards that governed accepted judgments. Few looked or saw beyond, to the immobile, hierarchical society he envisioned, in which equality meant that the State exacted equal sacri-fice from all as the only way to eliminate exploitation by individuals or groups. It is interesting—though by no means conclusive—that a Genevan terrorist, Jean-Robert Argaud, who had been reared literally on the pattern of Emile, would draw sketches of his victims before the tribunal and vote monotonously for their conviction, often on trumped-up charges, while maintaining his moral superiority.[72] Revenge and sadism may find their justifications in the name of virtue (as Rousseau understood that word).

The 1780's witnessed a surge of interest in Rousseau's political theo-ries. Adam Smith, who had sided against Rousseau in his quarrel with Hume, declared that *The Social Contract* would avenge him for all his persecutions.[73] Revolutionaries in France, in the 1780's, men like

Mirabeau, Brissot, and Mercier, had spent some time in Switzerland and undergone the influence of Rousseau's ideas. "Already in 1766 Choiseul feared Geneva as a hotbed of subversive ideas, and this was one of the motives for French pressure and eventual military intervention."[74] Of course Rousseau's influence was augmented during the French Revolution and has continued to exercise a profound impact on later ideologies.[75]

### 3. CONTROVERSY, CALUMNY, AND CONFUSION

On October 4, Rousseau learned from Conzié that Mme. de Warens, his dear Maman, had died. She had closed her eyes on an unhappy life on July 29, at Chambéry, administered to by the same Philibert Gaime who is portrayed in Rousseau's unlucky *Profession de foi*. The last years had been very hard. Her aged protector had died. Assailed by creditors, she had slipped lower and lower, unable to see the limits of her own abilities even after an incredible series of failures, unable to recognize her own faults and follies. Forgotten by all except Conzié, she may well have died of malnutrition, after spending much of her last two years in bed.

Rousseau had been uninterested in her last undertakings, and would not have known of her death if Conzié had not sent him a letter expressing his regrets at the condemnation of *Emile*, in answer to which Rousseau inquired about Mme. de Warens. Long after, in 1787, Conzié sent Count d'Escherny a brief relation of her life, in which he pronounces this judgment:

I have always condemned Jean-Jacques, to whom she had given the name of adopted son, first of all for having preferred the interest of LeVasseur to those of a maman as worthy of his respect, in every way, as his washerwoman LeVasseur was unworthy. He should have suspended his pride from time to time and worked only to earn his sustenance in order to return at least a part of what he had cost his generous benefactress.[76]

There is some truth in this harsh judgment. Of course, from Jean-Jacques' viewpoint, it was he who had been wronged—replaced and then thrown out. But Conzié knew only that Maman had felt bitterness toward him. She remembered all his protestations and vows. "It was she who, young and shining, had appeared to him one unforgettable day."[77] She had taken him in, guided him. Each time he came back— from Turin, Lyons, Besançon, Paris—penniless and abandoned, it was in her house he had found his supper and his shelter. She had helped him to become a musician and to study, taught him about society, men—and, regrettably, women. She was the most important person in all his life. His debt to her was infinite. He had not forgotten; but neither had he forgotten the hurts and the humiliation, the unforgivable rejection. Mme. de Warens was incapable of deep attachments, and Jean-Jacques had never meant to her anything like what she had to him. It was the tardy realization of this lack of reciprocity that stung.

As time went by, and nostalgia spread its golden glow over the lost years, the image of Maman regained all its radiance. In the depths of Rousseau's misery, Les Charmettes shone like an island of light in the midst of darkness. He says his adieu in the *Confessions*, confusing the time of her death, placing it after that of the Maréchal de Luxembourg. "The best of women and mothers" had left "this vale of tears and gone to the dwelling-place of the good. . . . Go, sweet and charitable soul . . . go taste the fruit of your charitableness and prepare for your pupil the place he hopes to take next to you some day. Happy in your misfortunes because Heaven, by ending them, has spared you the cruel spectacle of his!"[78]

Jean-Jacques was too busy with his controversies, his huge correspondence, and his own writing to keep Maman's death long on his mind. He was working in a desultory fashion on his *Dictionnaire de musique*, which he was to offer to his French publisher, Duchesne, the following February. Several other pieces excited him more than that tedious labor, and he told Rey, who pressed him, that he would like to write his autobiography, but had no time. In actuality, he had made a positive decision before the end of 1761, and was soon to begin transcribing documents.[79]

On November 22, the young Anton Kirchberger, a Bernese patrician and one of Rousseau's worshipers, described to Julie von Bondeli how he had succeeded in seeing the great man. Rousseau liked him, read to him part of *Emile et Sophie*, which Kirchberger found "very strong": "I was frightened, transported, shaken. I felt my eyes filling with tears, and Rousseau, the great Rousseau, wept too." Pleased with his listener's reaction, Rousseau proceeded to read his dramatic monologue, *Pygmalion*. He was fond of this work. Years later, in April 1770, he sent it to a composer, Coignet, to set it to music. Despite what seems to us exaggerated, rhetorical posturing, *Pygmalion* was well considered at the time. One scholar interprets it as an expression of Rousseau's narcissism, of his desire to find himself in the mirror of his own creation, to grasp the permanence of his self, while seeking a complete fusion of the sexes.[80] However, one may also view this ecstatic dithyramb as the sublimation of his frustrated sexual longings. Jean-Jacques was still aspiring to his ideal woman. The disappointment with "Sophie" d'Houdetot left no alternative but to create her. He had already done so, in words. Galatea is an imaginary reification of Julie, in whom he had infused his soul. "I have given you my entire being," Pygmalion says to the statue. Jean-Jacques could not bring his creations to life. There remained only ineffectual longing and the last futile sparring with young women.

Most of all, his intellectual and emotional energies were absorbed by a new polemical piece. On August 28 the Archbishop of Paris, Christophe de Beaumont, had published his *Mandement*, or *Pastoral Letter*, a combined fulmination against *Emile* and a critical analysis from the viewpoint of Catholic orthodoxy. D'Alembert thought it would turn out to Rousseau's advantage. "The archbishop," he wrote to Voltaire on September 8, "has just issued against him the very devil of a pastoral letter, one which will make everyone who doesn't know his *Profession de foi* want to read it. An archbishop's pastoral letter is an added title of fame; that is called to leave the field with the honors of war."

Rousseau did not feel that way. When he later read the Sorbonne's condemnation of *Emile* (he wrote to Mme. de Verdelin, March 27, 1763), "I threw it on the floor and spat on it for all reply. But I could not read the pastoral letter of the Archbishop of Paris with the same disdain." This public flagellation was more than he could swallow. To be singled out in this way, misrepresented and attacked by so powerful a figure at a time when he was seeking refuge, what was this but to hold him up for vilification to all Europe? Already deeply disturbed by Geneva's hostile reaction to *Emile* and *The Social Contract*—he had been wrong in discounting Moultou's warning that they would unite Genevans against him in defense of their religion and country—Jean-Jacques saw in this latest philippic an opportunity to justify himself and strike down all his enemies. He set to work with that intense energy of which a lazy man is often capable when he is thoroughly aroused. After two months he dated his reply on November 23, though he was not to send it to Rey in Amsterdam until early in January.

The *Lettre de Jean-Jacques Rousseau, citoyen de Genéve, à Christophe de Beaumont, archevêque de Paris* is a polemical masterpiece. It opens on a tone of challenging indignation: "Why is it necessary, Monseigneur, that I should have anything to say to you? What common language can we speak, how can we understand each other, and what is there in common between you and me?"[81] It closes on a note of justified indignation:

Monseigneur, you have publicly insulted me. I have just proven that you have calumniated me. If you were a private individual like me, and I could hail you before an equitable tribunal, and if we appeared before it, I with my book and you with your pastoral letter, you would certainly be declared guilty, and condemned to a reparation as public as your offense. But you have a rank which makes it unnecessary for you to be just; and I am nothing. Nevertheless, you who preach the Gospel; you, a prelate devoted to teaching others their duty, you know what yours is in this case. As for me, I have done mine. I have nothing to say to you.[82]

In between the exordium and the conclusion is a serried refutation of the pastoral letter, passage by passage, hard-thrusting and at times almost insulting, but always dignified. Nor is Rousseau sparing of the agile parrying of the skillful debater, of the side-stepping his enemies called "sophistry." The style "reflects a strange confusion of emotional states: vituperation, bitter irony, megalomania, evangelical mansuetude, righteous indignation and prophetic solemnity."[83]

The essence of Rousseau's argument is that his natural religion of the *Profession de foi* is the true Christianity of the Gospels and is best suited to men since it expresses their true nature. The morality and doctrine of the Catholic church is built on a lie—the doctrine of original sin. So-called "believers" must bow to law and custom, but they do not really believe the absurd dogmas of Catholicism. He defends the civil religion of *The Social Contract* as the only universal and social religion. True faith rests not on miracles, but on intuition. No man needs the Church to interpose itself between him and God.

Ernst Cassirer justly remarks that Rousseau has placed himself in an untenable position.

On the one hand he upheld—against the Church—the original goodness of human nature and the right and independence of human reason—art, science, and all spiritual cultivation. Could he still legitimately complain of his complete isolation, an isolation which he himself had created by estranging himself from the dominant forms of faith as well as by quarreling with the philosophical Enlightenment?[84]

Some of his boldest lines he excluded from the final text, as when he speaks of "that rage to decide everything, to explain everything, to make pronouncements on the matters we understand least, that audacity to be constantly making God speak."[85] Or again: "Of all religions in the world yours is the most tormenting, precisely because it is the least reasonable. You always have to intimidate, frighten men. As soon as you allow them to reason, you are lost."[86]

Not unexpectedly, some of Rousseau's basic tenets make their way into the document. Men have vices because their interests clash in society, and because their ambition increases with their knowledge. They have a natural self-love, which is not vicious in the state of nature. Their conscience or love of order, equally natural, develops only in society, but the results are not happy.

When finally aroused personal interests vie with each other, when excited self-love becomes *amour-propre*, when opinion, making each man feel he needs the entire universe, makes them all born enemies of each other and makes each find his own good only in the hurt of others, then conscience, weaker than aroused passions, is stifled by them, and remains in men's mouths only as a word used for mutual deception. Then each pretends to want to sacrifice his own interests to the public interest, and all lie. No one wants the public good except when it suits his own. Consequently this agreement is the object of the true politician who seeks to make people happy and good. But at this point I begin to speak a foreign language, as unknown to my readers as to you.[87]

The "foreign language" was indeed not understood in Rousseau's time, and it is, as we have seen, the key to his political system. Another significant passage refers to the techniques of thought control to be used in his "true society," the organic society.

Why does one man have the right of surveillance over the belief of another, and why does the State have the right of surveillance over that of its citizens? It is because one supposes that men's belief determines their morals. . . . In society, each has the right to inform himself whether another believes himself obliged to be just, and the Sovereign has the right to examine the reasons on which each person bases that obligation.[88]

This condition of cause–effect does not obtain in our corrupt pseudo-societies. One would infer that the attempt to exercise this right .in present conditions would be called, in Rousseau's terms, persecution.

The "clan" in Paris seemed far away now. He had a sharp exchange with Mme. de Boufflers, who disapproved of his letter to Montmollin, and their correspondence fell off. The Maréchal de Luxembourg continued to send brief notes in desultory fashion. Keith was an effective surrogate. Possessed of a rare sympathy and understanding, he readily forgave his protégé's idiosyncrasies. He was not bothered by Jean-Jacques' churlish letter to Frederick or by his declaration that as long as that monarch ruled as he did, he would rather "graze on grass and gnaw roots" than accept a crust of his bread.[89] They wrote back and forth about their dream of living together in Scotland. Keith wavered in placing the accent on its possibility or its illusoriness. Jean-Jacques relished the idea of being completely isolated, of being unable even to speak to the people around him.

Mme. de Verdelin had lost none of her warm friendliness and served him in various ways. When she sent greetings from Saint-Lambert, Mme. d'Houdetot, and the Encyclopedists, he replied with affected indifference.

I have always esteemed them and wished them well, even when they mistreated me; for my self-esteem is well enough nourished by my self-approbation so that I can get along without that of others. . . . As for the Clique, first of all they lie, because they are all false and liars, and because they have done me too much harm to be able to like me; and then I don't care if they are not lying, because the affection of people I despise can bring neither pleasure nor good.[90]

Rousseau's long-drawn-out and half-unwilling correspondence with his persistent admirer Mme. de la Tour took an unexpected turn, as the new year, 1763, arrived. Only a few months before, on October 15, he had sent her a nasty little note saying that he was fed up with letters and asking her to put an end to her harassment. She parried the blow so adroitly that on December 18 we find him asking her what she looks like. "I think that your face torments me even more than if I had seen it. If you do not wish to tell me what you look like, tell me at least how you dress, so that my imagination can attach itself to something I am sure belongs to you." The devoted lady took full advantage of the unexpected opening. The description she supplied was intended to be alluring. Her face was a perfect oval, with a pleasing profile; her eyes, large, dark blue, were enhanced by dark eyelids. "My arms, hands, fingers, even my nails are modeled like a painter's dream." Her height was scarcely over four foot nine—an average height in the eighteenth century.[91]

Rousseau, enchanted that his dream was not at odds with reality, was fired up. He replied with a gallantry that is both audacious and insipid. He even dared ask the question one never puts to a woman, how old she was. Openly flirtatious now, she admits to being thirty-two. The response was eminently satisfactory. "I thought you were going to say at least forty, you were so shy about telling me. I remember that my last passion—and it was certainly the most violent—was for a woman over thirty.* . . . She loved another man, and never had more than an interest in me."[92]

Mme. de la Tour then proposed that Rousseau help her find a property not too far from Môtiers, so that she could see him from time to time. Rousseau made some investigations, but nothing came of that. Soon she was baiting him. She had much to tell him, but first he would have to allow her to call him *"ami"* instead of *"monsieur."* When nearly two months passed without Rousseau's hearing from her, the roles were suddenly reversed; now he pleads with her to reassure him. The explanation was not long in coming. It aroused sympathy: "Overwhelmed by all kinds of troubles, victim of the bad faith of all those whom I have served well, and especially of the ingratitude of a husband who owes me his welfare, his honor and his freedom, all my thoughts are filled with despair."[93] Nevertheless, she is going to have a miniature portrait painted. If he would like to see it, she will lend it to him. Rousseau, properly sympathetic and philosophical, assured her that he added her troubles to the burden of his own. Unfortunately, he continues, he has forgotten her first name. Would she forgive him? As for the portrait: "Would I like to see your portrait! Oh, not alone see it, but keep if it were possible." But does she still feel warmly enough toward him?

That last question made Mme. de la Tour feel authorized to graduate from *"monsieur"* to *"ami."* "Have my warm feelings toward you cooled down? What a cruel doubt! . . . Believe your sincere Marianne. . . ." But he cannot keep the portrait. "I hope only that after you have seen it, you will find it easier than you imagine to give it up."[94]

---

* The statement is not true. Mme. d'Houdetot, like Mme. de la Tour, was born in 1730, but Rousseau had fallen in love with her in May 1758.

Rousseau makes no mention of this correspondence, which continued, in his *Confessions*. Was he afraid of appearing too foolish?

The "troubles" to which he refers were no more serious than vexations and worries, for the time. A part of them revolved around the *Lettre à Christophe de Beaumont*. Rey gladly accepted the manuscript, but infuriated Rousseau by wanting to print the archbishop's *Mandement* and the decree of the Parlement along with his refutation—a very sensible idea. Then he became apprehensive and wished he could cancel the whole project. Du Peyrou regretted that he had allowed himself to become excited and to risk new troubles. On March 6 he informed Malesherbes that he was sorry to have done something so foolish. Keith, on reading the manuscript, called him a hothead, but Moultou went into his usual raptures: "Let the fanatics and the courts howl, let them burn your books; you burn your readers' souls."[95]

The *Lettre* came out in March. The archbishop was crushed as if by a massive blow, and avoided talking about Rousseau. Grimm praised its eloquence and powerful reasoning, its touches of humor, rare in this somber man. Then he adds: "What is no less singular, but more in conformity with the author's character, is that in a piece in which he develops the strongest arguments against Christianity and revelation, he declares before heaven and earth that he is a Christian at the bottom of his heart." As usual, he sins by sophistry and love of paradox. If he had spoken the language of humanity he would have said that "every citizen who fulfills his social duties has a right to the protection of the laws, and cannot be legitimately harassed because of his religion and his personal opinions. . . . Whoever [like Rousseau] speaks otherwise deserves to be persecuted."[96]

Grimm provides his avid readers with another bit of information. "The few copies there are in Paris are being snatched from hand to hand. I do not doubt that we shall soon be able to get this letter as easily as *The Social Contract*, which they were so careful to suppress last year and which anyone can get for an écu today."[97]

Voltaire, too, made fun of Rousseau's protestations about being a Christian while condemning and ridiculing that faith. "There are a dozen sublime pages against that holy religion. Perhaps he goes too far; after all, Christianity has wiped out only about fifty million people of all ages and types in fourteen hundred years, because of theological disputes."[98] His vitriol was stronger when he wrote to d'Alembert a week later:

He claims that it is quite credible that Christ, when he instituted the Holy Eucharist, ate of his consecrated bread, and that it is clear, then, that he put his head in his mouth. But to that we shall reply that the bread was not larger than a pinhead. Besides, Jean-Jacques talks too much about himself in his letter. He asserts that all civilized States owe him a statue [Rousseau had written precisely that]; he swears he is a Christian and covers our holy religion with every imaginable mockery. . . . [De] Luc gives him one suit a year, some wood, some wheat, and he lives quite arrogantly in his barrel at Môtiers-Travers between two mountains.

The *Lettre* was at first well received in Protestant Geneva, although its sale was soon forbidden as a result of pressure from the French résident. Rousseau's friends advised him that now he would be well received in his native city. Nothing was further from his thoughts. In February he had been enraged by suggestions that he, the injured party, ask to be forgiven. "I am a Christian. I tolerate everything except intolerance. . . . I look on inquisitors as the devil's satellites."[99] He did not know about a secret decision of the Petit Conseil to the effect that he would have to stand judgment before it if ever he returned to Geneva, a decision which betrays the authorities' fear of his influence over the citizenry. In fact, they did not want him to face charges; they preferred to be rid of him. He snapped to one of his innumerable impudent and unknown correspondents: "I do not know why you speak of bringing me back to Christianity. I have never left it. I wish someone would undertake to bring most of our clergy back to it."[100]

He was still nursing the idea of renouncing his citizenship. Bitterly, he wrote to Moultou, "The Genevans have done me too much harm not to hate me, and I know them too well not to despise them. . . . My only crime is to have loved them too much."[101] He had not forgotten that four hundred citizens had been excluded from voting because of their taking a stand on his side.[102] He would, by this gesture, bring the world's attention to the wrongs inflicted on him by an ungrateful country and win its admiration for the courageous defiance of a man alone. Keith, experienced in the ways of the world, urged him not to take a step that could only alienate his supporters in Geneva. Jean-Jacques would not be deterred from his heroic gesture. He had finally received and answered Hume's letter, saying that in his own country he had gotten only "insults and injuries" when he had expected "if not gratitude, at least consolation."[103] Now he knows he would like to spend the remainder of his time in England, with the good and wise Hume, enjoying his philosophical hospitality. "In such sweet company I should bless the misfortunes that had led me to it and I should believe I had begun to live only on the day it began. May I see that happy day, more longed for than hoped for." Rarely have more unprophetic words been written! He thought of changing his name, so that no one would recognize him in England. Useless! Keith scolded; unable to change his ways or his mind, Jean-Jacques would soon be recognized.[104]

The earl marischal left for Berlin on April 30. Jean-Jacques felt suddenly shorn of his protection. For some time he had been suspicious that a recent visitor, a Hungarian pseudobaron named Sauttern (his real name being Ignatius Sauttersheim) was a spy set on him by the French. At his request, both Keith and Ustéri made inquiries and found the suspicion to be purely imaginary. He saw himself surrounded by enemies, ready to pounce on an unhappy, defenseless man.[105] Keith had done what he could. Before leaving, he had succeeded in making Rousseau a naturalized subject of Neuchâtel, thus putting him under the protection of its laws.

Sauttersheim, an adventurer, captivated Rousseau much as Venture de Villeneuve had done years earlier. Jean-Jacques, from whom he adroitly extracted money and confidences, was shocked to discover that his protégé lied to him constantly, that he was having an affair with a married woman, and that the reason for his sudden departure was not "business," but to escape the consequences of leaving a serving girl pregnant. He urged Sauttersheim to return and defend his innocence, and was taken aback by his lack of eagerness to embrace the suggestion. It was not Sauttersheim's fault, Rousseau remarked regretfully, after the scamp had died in poverty in 1767, but that of circumstances.[106]

On May 12, outraged by hostile sarcasms directed against his *Lettre à Beaumont*, Rousseau sent a letter to Jacob Favre, the First Syndic of Geneva: "I abdicate in perpetuity my rights as Burgher and as Citizen. . . . I have neglected nothing in order to make myself loved by my compatriots. . . . I want to please them even in their hatred." His friends were thunderstruck. On the twenty-sixth he defended his action in a letter to Marc Chappuis, a letter that became known as *"le Tocsin de la sédition."*[107] A man as enlightened as Chappuis, he declared, must know that "any public act made by the magistrate is held to be made by the entire State when none of those who have the right to disavow it does so. When the government speaks and all the citizens are silent, know that the nation has spoken." Rousseau "was standing up against a whole city, his native land, just as in writing his letter to the archbishop, he had stood up against the Church. But the same gesture, dictated by the same pride, was more singular this time. He who was proclaiming that he was neither Swiss nor French, was telling both peoples what they should be."[108]

Grimm, an assiduous collector of news and gossip, was obviously very resourceful. Rousseau would have been amazed to learn that in the May 15 number of the *Correspondance littéraire* he had provided his aristocratic readers with this tidbit:

He [Rousseau] has just written to the Council of Geneva to be struck from the list of citizens. It is hard to see the purpose of this solemn madness; but it proves the uneasiness and agitation of his mind. They say that he will follow the earl marischal to Scotland . . . and that [he] exclaims: "At last I shall have the happiness of living with men whose language I shall not understand."[109]

The blow in the face of Geneva had all the dramatic effect Rousseau had anticipated, and more. "Your affair is still stirring everyone up here," Moultou informed him on June 7. "The bourgeoisie [citizenry] is in despair at your abdication; in order not to have to reproach themselves, they are taking it out on you." That is the way men are, replied Rousseau; "they won't allow you to be better than they with impunity."[110] This judgment reflects his distortion of realities, the lack of empathy that so often characterizes neurotics. There is, writes one psychiatrist, "an implicit mutual contract between the individual and society"—a fact Rousseau certainly recognized in his political theory, but not in his own life. The community feels "recognized" by the individual "who cares to ask for recognition; it can, by the same token, feel deeply—and vengefully—rejected by an individual who does not."[111] Rousseau felt rejected by Geneva, and so he rejected it. Geneva reacted precisely in this way. And Geneva was more powerful. The sensation was no less great in France, where Rousseau's letter was published in the *Gazette de Paris* on May 20. It was rumored, wrote Lenieps on June 9, that he had left for Scotland.

On June 18 a group of citizens headed by De Luc handed a written remonstrance to the syndic protesting against the illegality of the procedures against Rousseau and the condemnation of his books. They asked for revocation. "By this patriotic act," they told him, "our laws will be restored, and the resignation of a citizen who brings as much honor to his country as M. Jean-Jacques Rousseau does, by his virtues and superior talents, will be null and void."[112] Rousseau thanked De Luc, approving the text, but warned of reprisals. De Luc, wrote Moultou, was a hero.

De Luc's action marks the beginning of the long struggle between the oligarchic Petit Conseil and the Bourgeoisie, or rather, the renewal of the old struggle. More than two hundred citizens had signed the remonstrance. The Council felt it necessary to issue a reply, which the syndic handed to De Luc and four of his associates, arguing, *inter alia*, that Rousseau had really only been summoned to defend himself. Between June 18 and September 29 the citizens presented three remonstrances, protesting against violations of the laws of the Republic and the liberties of its citizens. All were summarily rejected by the Petit Conseil.

Grimm, a wily politician and diplomat, had foreseen the event a year before (though not quite as it happened), as soon as *Emile* and *The Social Contract* were condemned to the fire and Rousseau's arrest ordered. "The rash and improper procedure," he told his subscribers in the July 1, 1762, number of the *Correspondance littéraire*, "could easily make Rousseau go back to his country, for he does not lack supporters. . . . Then he would become head of the people's party and, as a result of these contrivances, M. de Voltaire might be harassed even in his refuge at Les Délices. These are conjectures."[113] A year later, on July 19, 1763, Grimm reported to the Duchess of Saxe-Gotha that Rousseau was admired by many Genevans. He sets down the remonstrance, however, less to love of Jean-Jacques than to hatred of the oligarchy. The action, he goes on, has been a failure, and Rousseau-Diogenes is about to set out in his barrel for Scotland. "This poor devil drags out his wretched life, and the Pope is a sovereign with an income of fifteen million. That's the way of the world."[114]

Voltaire was not worried, if we may believe what he wrote to Damila-ville on August 31. Six hundred people, he reports, had made a third protest to the Council, demanding freedom of the press and respect for the rights of man. "They say it could end up in armed insurrection. I should not be sorry to see a civil war over the *Vicaire savoyard.*" In the agitation that ensued, however, between 1763 and 1770, the Rousseau affair was to assume a very minor role. As Grimm had surmised, the citizens, including the faithful De Luc, were interested in the larger issues. Rousseau's renunciation of citizenship and his letter to Chappuis had brought them together and set things off.

Rousseau must have realized that, after his actions, vexations could only increase. In the summer, Voltaire published an anonymous *Caté-chisme de l'honnête homme, par D. J. J. R. C. D. C. D. G.* (Dom Jean-Jacques Rousseau, former citizen of Geneva). The ideas of the *Profession de foi* are transformed and mutilated, making of Rousseau a Voltairean, an enemy of religious faith. So much the better if some simple-tons thought it had really been written by Rousseau! "How can I recog-nize God," writes D. J. J. R. C. D. C. D. G., "in this Jew from the rabble . . . sweating blood in his fear of death?" Voltaire even insinuated that Rousseau might have written the *Sermon des cinquante,* which he had penned![115] Perhaps it was a satisfaction for Jean-Jacques—even while he was proclaiming his desire to be forgotten by the world—to know that he was being talked and written about all over Europe.

Bachaumont assured his readers, on July 13, that Rousseau would not go to Scotland. At about the same time, Mme. de Chenonceaux, writing to him about her quarrels with her mother-in-law, Jean-Jacques' old protectress Mme. Dupin, informed him that a letter was being circulated in Paris, attributed to him, in which "you break out in fury against the human race."[116] The letter was amusingly entitled "Letter from Jean-Jacques Rousseau, of Geneva, containing his renunciation of society and his last goodbyes to men, addressed to the only friend he has left in the world." It was probably written by a lawyer in Toulouse, Pierre-Firmin de Lacroix. Bachaumont records:

Freed by his having been proscribed, he considers himself to be without master or country. He declares that he prefers the forests to cities infected by cruel, barbarous men, wicked by principle, inhuman by education, unjust because of laws dictated by tyranny. One is tempted to believe that the letter is not really Rousseau's, so extraordinary is it . . . but the style . . . leaves almost no doubt that it is the work of this modern Diogenes.[117]

Later that month Rousseau's former friend Vernes published his *Lettres sur le christianisme de Jean-Jacques Rousseau*, which Moultou called an insolent, malicious, and wretched book.[118] Rousseau gave no answer, although Tronchin had feared that he might embarrass Vernes by divulging a letter the latter had once written to him defending Helvétius' condemned *De l'Esprit*.

Rousseau, having no desire to become involved in Genevan politics, rejected De Luc's persistent efforts in that direction.[119] "The letters of appeal or praise to the new Socrates, to the new Lycurgus, even to the new Christ, are even more numerous. We know that they correspond to the deep choice of Jean-Jacques, which is to become a great man halfway between the sage and the prophet."[120] So it was; but above all it was not to compromise himself in the arena of a political power struggle. His role was above that of party leader, above that of the righter of wrongs. Or at least so he rationalized his refusal of responsibility and social action. These were both foreign to his nature, which combined the outwardness and courage of the prophet's role with the neurotic's emotional self-centeredness. The prophet is the truth-teller, and this is what Rousseau felt he was doing. "For Zion's sake I will not be silent." But his Zion was not the Republic of Geneva.

Even his theoretical position was compromised by one of those antitheses that were so typical of him—his profound belief that truth is not always useful, and that in the governance of men, illusion and deceit are beneficent and necessary. That, too, was a truth. Moreover, it was "man" he loved, "not men." Consequently, he shrank from becoming a prophet-activist in Geneva, where it was hoped he would be head of the populist party, Les Représentants.

Appalled by what he had started, he urged De Luc to desist from further remonstrances and political activity, which in his opinion could never succeed but only hurt the republic. True, he had written to Chappuis that if only a few citizens had used their right of petition, he would not have given up his citizenship. But the subsequent action he had "neither desired nor approved." To emphasize his appeal, Jean-Jacques vows: "I shall never in my life set foot again in your walls . . . never take again the title of Citizen of Geneva."[121]

Life was only too busy, with innumerable and mostly unwanted visitors, and an endless correspondence. Keith left for Scotland at the end of July. He urged Jean-Jacques to join him, avoiding France by traveling to Basel, up the Rhine and through Holland. Lenieps warned against the idea. Rousseau would never thrive in a cold, damp, sunless climate, amid a narrow-minded, unfriendly people. And, limiting himself to Keith's company, what would happen to his independence?[122]

Are the rumors true? asked the ever-serviceable Mme. de Verdelin. Have we lost you forever? inquired the unhappy and most likable Mme. de Chenonceaux. Even the Maréchal de Luxembourg was moved to send him a brief note. "Let me know, at least , since I have the misfortune of not seeing you, where you are living. . . . I supped with the Prince de Conti yesterday; we spoke about you. . . ."[123] The maréchal sent an even briefer note five months later (December 12). One gathers that the clan was hoping the news was true.

In the midst of these vexations, exchanges with the mysterious Mme. de la Tour provided a diversion. On July 17, Jean-Jacques penned a most gallant missive. "O that charming Marianne! What will she think, what will she say now of him whom she has honored with the precious name of *ami?*" Marianne replied that she was no longer insisting on his returning her portrait. Her admiration was boundless. "You should de-pénd on no one except the Being who has allowed you to share his perfections, as far as any creature may."[124] But Rousseau was tardy in answering. His pains had returned with renewed force early in August. Certain that he was near death, he gave the will he had made out in February, making Thérèse his sole heir, to Martinet, the *châtelain* of Val-de-Travers. More solicitous than usual, he had in January asked Mont-mollin's permission to take her to mass in a Catholic village. Now he wrote to the curate of Ambérieu, asking him to protect Thérèse after his imminent death. "She has faults, of course . . . but she has rare virtues, an excellent heart, pure morals, an unbreakable fidelity and disinterest-edness."[125]

Meanwhile, the Burghers had made a second remonstrance on August 8. In Paris, Bordes' *Profession de foi philosophique*, directed against Rousseau, had appeared. Marianne complained of his neglect: "My heart is ulcerated."[126] But on that day (September 27), the Genevan attorney general, Jean-Robert Tronchin, published the first four of his five *Lettres écrites de la campagne*, the last of which, appearing on October 23, was called "The Torch of Truth." This work was a defense, based on the Genevan constitution, of the actions of the Council. Coolly and persuasively argued, it made a profound impression. Tronchin was called a new Cicero who had saved his country from a new Catiline–Rousseau. Another remonstrance, on September 29, brought into use the terms "Négatifs" and "Représentants" as respective designations for the oligarchs and the popular upstarts.

Oblivious to all this, Mme. de la Tour kept protesting Rousseau's neglect, and finally sent the precious portrait. He acknowledged its re-ceipt on October 23, in a few hurried lines, saying that the portrait did not resemble her self-description, but assuring her that it would be "like having two mistresses at the same time . . . without being unfaithful."

Rousseau was absorbed by the new Tronchin business. On October 25 he reluctantly agreed to write a refutation of the lawyer's all-too-success-ful work. He had learned from earlier experience that the defender is always at a disadvantage, since the refutation leads only to further expo-sure. In 1753 he had resolved to make no more replies to critics. But now the circumstances were different. What was at stake was not only his ideas, but his character and image. The task was to be a long and arduous one. He was about to challenge a lawyer who was an authority on the Genevan constitution. It was necessary to be on sure ground. Responding to his appeals, De Luc and another friend, Vieusseux, supplied the necessary research in the archives. (In fact, they were preparing a refutation of their own. Published shortly after Rousseau's, their *Réponse aux Lettres de M. Tronchin*, though forgotten today, was regarded as even more dangerous.)

In this situation, Mme. de la Tour's complaints were exasperating. He was not even mollified by her relating how the Chevalier de Méhégan, on visiting Montmorency, had been overwhelmed by the peasants' questions about Rousseau and their loving admiration for him. "He was a father to all of us. . . . He was our protector with Monseigneur le Maréchal; we lost everything when we lost him"—and so on, all to the accompaniment of tears. Untouched by the lachrymose homage, Rousseau suddenly turns on his admirer and vents his spleen. "Marianne" disappears and is replaced by "Madame." He will not answer her imputations. "Since I can have with you only a stormy correspondence, I prefer to have none at all. . . . I warn you that it will be enough for you to ask once more for a prompt reply to be sure that you will have none at all."[127]

The decision about rejoining Keith was put off till spring. Besides, the Scottish *château en Espagne* was no longer so alluring. Hume, harassed for his opinions by his compatriots, had gone off to spend a couple of years in France. Keith reported that he was depressed by the "bigotry" of the Scots and their hostility toward Hume. Not all was bad. He was getting acquainted with his manor and found it warm and comfortable. "There are hidden stairways, trees, a stream, and a well-stocked vegetable garden." He promises to find out more about the neighbors.[128]

Mme. de Verdelin now urged Rousseau to return to France, to some place outside the jurisdiction of the Paris Parlement; he would only have to change his name to be quite safe. Never, he replied, would he change his name or hide in any way whatsoever.[129]

The winter of 1763–64 was a rude one. Rousseau stayed close to home, working on his reply to Tronchin and the *Dictionnaire de musique*. His frequent book orders show that despite his statements to the contrary, he devoured books of many kinds: novels, history, philosophy, travel, utopias, and treatises on botany, his newest passion. He was vexed and persistent when the volumes of Buffon's *Histoire naturelle* did not arrive on time.

With his fame ever spreading, he was detested by some and worshiped —the word is not too strong—by others. Rumors of all kinds were current. It was said that he had composed a poem, a sequel to *La Nouvelle Héloïse*. Writings were falsely attributed to him. He expected Duchesne and his friend Lenieps, in Paris, to keep him informed. From men and women he received a stream of letters expressing adoration and asking for advice about their lives or how to bring up their children. He had succeeded in creating the image of moral mentor and guide which he had tried, too late, to assume with Mme. d'Houdetot. As one young woman, "Henriette," put it, "After reading your works, I have seen in you a character, a heart, a tone, an air which have inspired in me confidence and the desire to consult you. . . . Pity [my sick soul], Monsieur, and show me the road that can lead, if not to happiness, at least to peace of heart."[130]

For some time he had been exchanging letters with the Prince of Wurtemberg, who, in his passionate admiration for Jean-Jacques, wanted to raise his little daughter on the model of Sophie. This correspondence was nearly brought to an end when the prince informed Rousseau that his wife was unable to nurse his newly born second daughter. "It is indeed odd," he wrote, "that such a respectable and tender mother can have breasts that are so pretty and so ungenerous. I am sorry for the babe, for I am certain that she would have the same pleasure in suckling them as I have in covering them with a thousand amorous kisses."[131] Rousseau's severe reply blamed the prince. "You speak to me of that pretty breast like a husband who is jealous of keeping all its freshness and who, if harm must come to it, prefers it to come from his own doing than from the child's. But marital pleasures are fleeting, and the lover's sensuousness does not make the happiness of the father or the husband."[132] The prince denied the charge of such "criminal voluptuousness," and the correspondence continued.

The correspondence with Mme. de la Tour also went on fitfully, despite Rousseau's brusque bursts of temper. He did not succeed in making her, distant and unseen, into the ideal woman of his heart. She was lacerated by his harsh letter of December 25 and replied: "I had not expected to be so humiliated. Nevertheless, the disdain with which you try to overwhelm me does not numb my modest feeling of my own worth." After his "offensive" letter, he will, she expects, write no more.[133] A clumsy apology brought the reply that she had been too cruelly disappointed, too often. But then it was "chère Marianne" again, and a humble tone.[134] This evoked further confidences from the devoted lady, who pointed out that sexually they were of equivalent ages: "Since women live only in their charms, a man of fifty and a woman of thirty must be considered to be of the same age."[135] Jean-Jacques, with equal coyness, warned her that the only thing in her letters he would not answer was her praises of him. In Marianne's next letter, Rousseau becomes "*mon cher Jean-Jacques*—why should I hesitate to call you that?"[136] Further bickering and further explanations ensued. Even though Marianne was moved to write: "*Mon cher J.-J., mon adorable ami*, never will anyone love you as I do," their correspondence becomes more desultory as he is taken up by other matters.

A letter of March 4 to the Abbé de Carondelet shows Rousseau still struggling to clarify his ideas and perplexities on moral questions. Love of order (an idea that includes the general welfare) is, he explains, an abstract idea which can never equal the force of self-interest. A man makes himself the center of the order of which he is a part, and considers everything according to its relation to his own good. Love of order cannot therefore lead to virtue, which is defined as a victory over ourselves. Can conscience serve? Powerful as it is, it cannot, for passions and pride change or stifle it in society. Since self-love is the only motive of actions, the problem of founding virtue, "taken absolutely and as a metaphysical entity," on it is insoluble. The current ethics of enlightened self-interest is dismissed as it had been in the *Discourse on Inequality*. Here, as in that work, Rousseau borders on moral nihilism. The motives of crime, to avoid a hurt or to secure a good, are quite natural (and so not subject to disapprobation). Pragmatic considerations confirm that crime often pays, and pays well. "Justice and scruples make only dupes in this world. Were it not for the afterlife and eternal justice, I should see in virtue only an insanity to which we give a fine name." (Excepting the last sentence, Rousseau's thinking would have a perfect place in the subcurrent of eighteenth-century moral nihilism which leads to Sade.) Finally, Rousseau declares, if we accept moral determinism, as the abbé does, there can be no morality in actions, and so no virtue or vice.

What Rousseau is saying—and Hume had shown it to be so—is that morality cannot be justified rationally. That is why his solution, as we see it in his great works and in his refutation of Diderot's "Droit naturel," is a political one. If the individual is socialized, "so that he thinks of himself only in relation to the whole of which he is a part," it will never occur to him that it is to his self-interest to will something that is contrary to the general interest; or if it does instinctively occur to him, he will have been so conditioned and controlled that he will respond reflexively, not reflectively, in the way society terms "virtue." "You wish to begin by teaching men the truth in order to make them well-behaved," Rousseau had replied to a correspondent; "and quite to the contrary, it is necessary to make them well-behaved in order to make them love the truth."[137]

Rousseau had lost, or was about to lose, his two dearest friends. He missed the absent Keith. "Come back to Colombier, Milord, cultivate your garden."[138] (The echo of *Candide* surprises.) The *château en Espagne* was no longer even a dream. Keith, discouraged by the Scottish climate and environment, soon left for the Court of Frederick the Great, where he found life more to his liking.

The other friend lost was the Duc de Luxembourg. In April, La Roche, who frequently served as intermediary between the Luxembourgs and Rousseau, informed him of the maréchal's serious illness. Rousseau penned a modest note designed to accompany a gift of the new Duchesne edition of his works: "Receive the homage of my heart, and may my writings, conquerors of time, transmit to future ages this monument of my respect and attachment." The maréchal died on May 18. Rousseau, with supreme egotism, wrote to La Roche: "I feel Madame la Maréchale's grief by my own. But she does not lack consolations; and I, abandoned by the whole world, remain alone on earth, crushed by troubles, without friends, without resources, without consolation."[139] On June 5 he expressed his grief to the widow:

How can those he loved remain divided? Shouldn't their hearts unite to mourn? If yours no longer has any feeling for me, at least take some interest in my misfortunes because he did. . . . But I am doubtless flattering myself. He had ceased to be interested in them; following your example, he had forgotten me. . . . What is my crime, except to have loved you too well? . . . I lost you both while both were living, I am more to be pitied than you.

To De Luc he confided, "The loss of M. de Luxembourg leaves me only one desperate consolation. I am at the bottom of the wheel and nothing worse can happen to me any more."[140] The duchesse, in her reply, reproached him for his injustice and assured him of her unbroken friendship; her letter, he wrote back, brought him great consolation.[141]

The *Confessions* contains a eulogy of the maréchal, but expresses the belief that Mme. de Luxembourg had turned her husband away from him, and that she hid her changed feelings. The brevity and infrequency of their letters had convinced Jean-Jacques that they were really glad to be rid of him.

Rousseau wanted to leave Môtiers because he thought the air unhealthy. Yet his life was not unpleasant there. In one of his rare letters to Mme. de Boufflers, he speaks of "delightful days, wandering without cares or affairs, from wood to wood and from rock to rock, always dreaming and never thinking. I should give anything in the world to know botany."[142] He asked Duchesne to send him books on the subject. "I have a rage to learn botany without having a single book to guide me."[143]

Count d'Escherny, who was to establish a close friendship with Jean-Jacques despite the latter's coolness toward his first advances, devotes many pages to Rousseau in his *Mélanges*, or memoirs, published in 1811. D'Escherny had rented a house near Môtiers, and Rousseau was attracted by his lively conversation and his acquaintance with all the literary figures in Paris. D'Escherny reports favorably on Thérèse's cooking.[144] Meals were simple and well prepared: succulent vegetables, leg of lamb steeped in herbs, salmon, trout, quail, and woodcocks that were served like "balls of fat." The wines, of which Rousseau was extremely fond, were excellent. Conversation flowed as freely as the wine and touched on every kind of subject.

Rousseau, when he had guests, did not allow Thérèse to eat with them. She came in from time to time, breaking into the conversation. Unfailingly gay, reports d'Escherny, Jean-Jacques would make jokes at her expense or at his own. After dinner he might go to the spinet and accompany himself or d'Escherny. They took long walks, one excursion lasting three days, and relished the wild landscapes. D'Escherny, incidentally, blamed Thérèse for Rousseau's desire to leave Môtiers. She would constantly bring him tales, "true or fabricated," about the nasty things the townspeople were saying about them. She had a fishwife's tongue and got into frequent brawls with the local women.

With d'Escherny, Rousseau undertook several unsuccessful trips looking for another residence. His friendship with Du Peyrou was growing closer. Rousseau made frequent visits to his house in Neuchâtel, and Du Peyrou sometimes went along on excursions. It was with him that, at d'Escherny's urging, he was to leave his papers when circumstances necessitated his departure from Môtiers. Together the three friends plunged into the study of botany, d'Escherny with boredom, the other two with a zeal that soon became a passion. Describing these excursions, d'Escherny relates that Rousseau enjoyed excellent health, a lusty appetite, and good sleep. One night they piled into a haystack in a barn. When asked, the next morning, whether he had slept well, Rousseau replied, "I never sleep well." Colonel Pury, one of the companions, stopped him short. *"Par Dieu*, Monsieur Rousseau, you astonish me. I heard you snoring all night. It is I who could not close my eyes; that damned hay was damp!" After breakfasting on rich cream, which always sent Rousseau into sensuous ecstasies, at five in the morning, they went into the fields and woods to collect specimens.

D'Escherny has left us an interesting personal evaluation:

He wanted it to be thought that he was above the needs of common men, that he could live without sleeping and that his immortal pages sprang from the midst of suffering and pain. Surrounded by admirers, he called himself persecuted, receiving only ingratitude from men as a reward for the good he had done or tried to do them; in any other country, statues and altars would have been raised to him. And so that no one could doubt that he was persecuted, he, the bard of liberty . . . asked to lose it, to escape persecution, and implored to be put in prison as an act of mercy. By despising riches, he put himself above the rich. There remained only to put himself above himself as writer and philosopher, and that is what he did, in a way, by abjuring letters and philosophy, by heaping anathema and scorn on them. . . . By hiding, he redoubled people's desire to see him . . . and his brusque way of treating visitors enhanced the worth of those times when he was gentle and affectionate.*

Clearly, for d'Escherny, who is not entirely fair, Rousseau was enacting a role.

Who would believe it? This man, this Jean-Jacques so known for his misanthropy, his brusque fits of humor, his paradoxes, his sophistry, his explosions

---

* H. Buffenoir, *Le Prestige de Jean-Jacques Rousseau*, pp. 302–03.

of vanity (when he thought he was hurt), when he spoke only of statues and altars which he raised to himself, was with us . . . the simplest, gentlest and most modest of men.

Both sides were, of course, true. The role was the man, but the man overflowed the role.

After Rousseau was forced to leave the Val-de-Travers region, d'Escherny did not see him again for five years. When they met in Paris, in 1770, he found his great friend sadly changed, the helpless prey of an obsession of a universal conspiracy against him. "He was suspicious of all who approached him. The beautiful days at Môtiers were never to be born again."[145]

Early in June, Rousseau received reports from Mme. Verdelin that Hume was in Paris, lionized by the Holbachian circle, pursued by the ladies. He was not pleased by the news. It made little difference, for he was resigned to spending the rest of his days in Switzerland, but preferably near a lake.[146] One thing was certain; he would never go back to Paris, where, he quipped sarcastically, his friends might give him fresh evidence of their friendship.[147] Duclos, whom he no longer trusted, still wrote occasionally, professing his friendship and urging him to write his memoirs. Rey had done as much, several times. While he did not admit it, he was fitfully assembling documents. "Wasn't there in him," asks R. A. Leigh, "something like a 'confessional fibre,' and had he not continually 'unburdened his heart' since the age of eighteen?"[148] His four "Letters to Malesherbes" had been an important rehearsal of self-display. Another was a series of comments and epigrams, entitled "Mon Portrait," written between 1758 and 1763. It begins this way: "Readers, I enjoy thinking about myself and I speak as I think. Do not bother to read this preface if you do not like people to talk about themselves." This sketch is still very far from the *Confessions*, however; the time was not yet ripe.

How much more appealing, how much more satisfactory to his vanity and his intellectual interests, was a proposal he received in September. In *The Social Contract* he had declared that the only nation young, unformed, and uncorrupted enough to be made into a true society was Corsica, which in 1755 had revolted and won its independence from Genoa under the leadership of Pascal Paoli. On August 31 a young Corsican officer, Matteo Buttafoco, invited Rousseau, in the name of the provisional government—actually in the name of Paoli, the effective dictator—to be his country's *Législateur*, or Lawgiver. Buttafoco was in France, negotiating unsuccessfully to get the French to withdraw their troops from the island and to confirm its independence; however, he was no match for the wily Choiseul. He thought that Rousseau's name would help the cause of Corsica, or perhaps his own.

Rousseau, having already projected himself into this role, the loftiest he could imagine, was now offered the incredible opportunity of enacting the role in real life. Buttafoco's description was most attractive. The people had never "borne the yoke of laws"; the women were subservient and rarely left their hearths; the country had no arts, sciences, or luxury.

Rousseau responded on September 22 with a mixture of enthusiasm and caution. "The very idea exalts my soul and excites me." But he cannot perform without a vast amount of information about the people and the country; he is concerned also about his own health and by the danger of the French swallowing up the island. Buttafoco (October 3) reassured him on the last score, promised full cooperation, and urged Rousseau to visit the island, where he would enjoy the climate and the style of life. On October 15, Rousseau in effect accepted the proposal. "The object is so great that my temerity makes me tremble." With this letter went an addendum listing the subjects on which he required detailed memoirs. He hoped to complete the work by 1769, but the project was doomed to disaster, first by calamitous events in his own life which were unsuspectedly close at hand and then by the French annexation in 1768.

What we do have of Rousseau's Proposal for a Constitution for Corsica is an important fragment, which we shall examine in due course. Meanwhile, word of the invitation spread rapidly. "The request of the Corsicans," writes Lenieps on November 30, "has covered you with honor and created a sensation. I am not surprised that your enemies, clever and wicked as they are, have tried to belittle its importance." Bachaumont's *Mémoires secrets* notes, on November 21, "a fact too extraordinary not to be related." The Corsican rebels have asked "Rousseau and Diderot" to draw up a constitution and a code of laws; the former has accepted, the latter has refused. Rousseau is worthy of the task, concludes the gossip sheet; Diderot has done nothing to deserve it. Malesherbes asks Rousseau for confirmation of the rumor. "I am passionately desirous of knowing whether the fact is true and whether you have decided to work on this important project." He is sure—and right he is—that French jurists will be astonished "by the roads they will see you take."[149] And Duclos in turn: "Tell me what is this Code for the Corsicans that you have been asked to do."[150]

Although Rousseau declared that he had reached a stage where he desired no new friendships, he continued to make new friends. A young Scotsman thrust himself on Rousseau and captured his fancy. At the age of twenty-four, James Boswell was making the conventional grand tour. He had letters of introduction, but disdained to use them. "My romantic genius, which will never be extinguished, made me eager to put my own merit to the severest trial."[151] His initial letter to Rousseau, written in quaint French on December 3, reveals his characteristic ingenuity and his determination in getting to meet celebrities he wanted to know.

Boswell himself says: "It can neither be abridged nor transposed, for it is really a masterpiece. I shall ever preserve it as proof that my soul can be sublime." After first describing his background to Rousseau, Boswell goes on:

I have heard, Monsieur, that you are very difficult, and that you have turned away visitors of the highest distinction. I respect you all the more for it. If you gave entrance to all whose vanity wishes to be able to say, "I have seen him," your house would no longer be the refuge of exquisite genius and lofty piety; and I should not be so enthusiastically eager to be received there.

I present myself, Monsieur, as a man of incomparable merit. As a man with a sensitive heart, a keen and melancholy mind. Ah! if all my sufferings do not earn me a unique merit in Monsieur Rousseau's mind, why was I created thus? Why has he written thus?

Mingling effusive panegyric with casual personal confidences and in-credible vanity, Boswell concludes with an appeal. He is presently in a delicate predicament and desperately needs the advice of the author of *La Nouvelle Héloïse.* "Then open your door, Monsieur, to a man who dares to assure you that he deserves admittance. Have confidence in an exceptional foreigner." Rousseau succumbed and received the romantic Scotsman, who had been preparing himself by strolling in a wild valley, gazing at high mountains and "frowning rocks" and thinking "great thoughts." He felt prepared to see "the wild philosopher."

They chatted easily, talking mostly about Rousseau. "My books have saved my life," he said, as Boswell reports the conversation. "When Monsieur Rousseau said what touched me more than ordinary, I seized his hand, I thumped him on the shoulder. I was without restraint." He found that he really pleased the wild philosopher. "I live here in a world of fantasies," Jean-Jacques told him; "I cannot tolerate the world as it is. . . . Mankind disgusts me."

The next day, Jean-Jacques being in a gay humor, they joked about Thérèse's keeping him under lock and key. It is indeed apparent that she protected him and regulated the flow of visitors. After a while Rousseau said to Boswell, "You are irksome to me. It's my nature. I cannot help it." Boswell replied, "Do not stand on ceremony with me." "Go away," answered his host. Thérèse showed him out, saying: "I have been twenty-two years with M. Rousseau; I would not give up my place to become Queen of France." "She is a very good girl," comments Boswell, "and deserves to be esteemed for her constancy to a man so valuable."[152]

The next day there was a third interview. Fearing that Rousseau was not going to allow him to talk about himself and his personal problems, Boswell spent that afternoon writing a sketch of his life and a letter in which he once more set forth his estimate of himself. "I consider myself an excellent man in the world as it is. But I have an idea that it is possible for me to put myself above the world as it is; and until I do, I shall not be content."[153] The sketch of his life dwells on the episode about which he desired Rousseau's advice: his affair with a married woman in Scotland. Of course he did manage to bring the conversation around to himself, speaking of his earlier conversion to Roman Catholicism, his melancholia, and his moral weaknesses. Rousseau's advice aroused his enthusiasm to such a pitch that he asked his idol to become his guide and mentor. "Monsieur, will you take care of me?" Rousseau replied impatiently, "I cannot. I am good only for myself." Boswell turned to religion. He had the temerity to look Rousseau in the eyes and ask him whether he was really a Christian. "His countenance was no less animated. Each stood steady, and watched the other's look. He struck his breast and replied, 'Yes—I pride myself on being one.' "

Before setting out in the dark, alone on horseback, Boswell wrote to a friend: "These three days I have visited that sublime sage. He has enlightened my mind. He has kindled my soul. . . . My present sentiments give me a force and a vigour like the lion in the desert."[154]

Considering it prudent to leave his prey for a while, Boswell spent ten days in Neuchâtel. On December 14 he returned to Môtiers, and to talking about himself. Rousseau was ailing, and Boswell had to force his way in. Rousseau reassured him that he could yet become a man, advised him never to see a priest, and pleased with himself, gave his unwanted acolyte permission to return in the afternoon—if he kept his watch on the table. The afternoon conversation covered a wide ground, including education and sex. "I should like to have thirty women," Boswell admitted. "Could I not satisfy that desire?"

Rousseau: "No!"

Boswell: "Why?"

Rousseau: "Ha! Ha! If Mademoiselle [LeVasseur] were not here, I would give you a most ample reason why."

Boswell: "But consider: if I am rich, I can take a number of girls; I get them with child, propagation is thus increased. I give them dowries, and I marry them off to good peasants who are very happy to have them. Thus they become wives at the same age as would have been the case if they had remained virgins, and I, on my side, have had the benefit of enjoying a great variety of women."[155] Rousseau did not approve the plan.

Their discussions continued on the fifteenth. Boswell was enraptured by Rousseau's invitation to have "a simple meal" (six dishes and dessert) with him. "Gods! am I now then really the friend of Rousseau? . . . 'Come, Boswell, will you dine with us today?' 'No, Gentlemen, excuse me; I'm engaged. I dine today with Rousseau. . . .' My tone, my air, my mature pride when I pronounced this!"

He dared to criticize *Emile*. "You say nothing in regard to a child's duties towards his parents. You tell us nothing of your Emile's father." To which Rousseau answered, "Oh, he hadn't any." Hearing Samuel

Johnson described, Rousseau commented—correctly—"He would detest me. He would say, 'Here is a corrupter.' "[156] He told Boswell that he admired the Abbé de Saint-Pierre because he was an individualist who did what he wanted in complete indifference to men's opinions, "saying that they were overgrown children." At dinner, when Boswell asked, "May I help you to some of this dish?" Rousseau replied: "No sir. I can help myself to it." When Boswell asked: "May I help myself to some more of that?" the answer was: "Is your arm long enough?"

Boswell reluctantly said adieu, having several times refused to be thrown out. Rousseau embraced and kissed him several times. "Goodbye. You are a fine fellow," he said. "You have shown me great goodness," replied Boswell, "but I deserved it."[157] As Thérèse showed him out, she let him know that she thought well of him—how well, we shall see later. He asked her what he could send her, and she requested a garnet necklace, which he did send. Meanwhile, he gave her a handsome tip.[158]

The following day Rousseau's friend, the bailiff Moiry, related many anecdotes about him to Boswell. "Women are his ruling passion. You see what fire he has in his eyes when he speaks of them. He considers it no crime to have a mistress. He advocates laws for the citizens of a state, but he regards himself as a being apart."[159]

From there Boswell went on to Geneva, where he captivated Rousseau's archenemy, Voltaire. The two men had a raging dispute over the Bible, in which Boswell admitted that he was defeated by "the daring bursts of his [Voltaire's] ridicule." To Rousseau, Boswell wrote, on December 31, "His conversation is the most brilliant I have ever heard."[160]*

If Rousseau was able to accept the Corsican project, it was because he had completed his *Lettres écrites de la montagne,* a work to which he attached the greatest importance. His relationship to Geneva was now ambivalent. On March 1 he had affirmed to Colonel Pictet that his former country was indifferent to him. In July he was resisting attempts to suck him into the populist conspiracy.[161] But in August and September we find him making several trips to clandestine meetings with De

---

* A rather remarkable description of Voltaire's conversation is found in Boswell's *Private Papers:* "The magician appeared a very little before dinner. . . . I placed myself by him. I touched the keys in union with his imagination. I wish you had heard the Music. He was all brilliance. He gave me continual flashes of Wit. . . . When he talked our language, he was animated with the soul of a Briton. He had bold flights. He had humour. He had an extravagance; he had a forcible oddity of style that the most comical of our *dramatis Personae* could not have exceeded. He swore bloodily as was the fashion when he was in England. He hum'd a Ballade. He repeated nonsense. Then he talked of our Constitution with noble enthusiasm. I was proud to hear this from the mouth of an illustrious Frenchman. At last we came upon Religion. Then did he rage" (James Boswell, "Private Papers of James Boswell from Malahide Castle," Vol. IV, pp. 17–18).

Luc, d'Ivernois, and other rebellious citizens. Some of his correspondence with them uses code for their names. Passing through Nyon, he could see in the distance the forbidding towers of the walls of Geneva, a sight that must have evoked distant memories and also made him reflect that those walls were now forever shut to him.

When Rousseau wrote to Rey on June 9, offering him the *Lettres,* he explained quite candidly that it would not be to the Genevan government's liking, "since it is my apology and that of the bourgeoisie of Geneva." He insists on the most careful avoidance of printing errors: "My honor, my tranquillity, my very safety depend on it." Moreover, the work must be done in the strictest secrecy. Not even his fellow republicans in Geneva knew he was writing it. Jean-Jacques, then, was aware of danger, but not of the extent of the danger into which he was putting himself. On August 27 he warns Rey that when he announces the work to his correspondents, he should make no reference to its political aspect but present it as Rousseau's defense of his religious beliefs: the interests of "justice, of your country and your friends," he warns, are at stake. On September 9 we find him worried that their correspondence may have been intercepted by the Swiss. When Rey explained that he had been painfully ill, Rousseau graciously replied, "While you were suffering your pains, I was suffering from your silence."

Rey, expecting a large sale, sent a thousand copies to Geneva on October 27 and three thousand to Paris on November 5. But the word was already out. On the sixth Mme. de Verdelin sent the news on to Rousseau. "There's a great deal of talk here about the *Lettres écrites de la montagne,* which they say is an answer to those from the *Desert* [sic] of Tronchin. They insist you are the author. Nobody here can get it. One of my friends made a tour of all the bookstores yesterday." A few days later Sartine denied the book an entry permit, a step Rousseau protested to Malesherbes (who, however, had resigned from his post as director of publication),[162] and, more bitterly, to Mme. de Verdelin.

It is cruel not to have the right to defend oneself without attacking anyone when one is so barbarously attacked himself. . . . I foresee that the publication of these letters is going to turn into a very stormy time for me. . . . I'll be blackened, vilified, harassed; I believe I can assure you they will not go beyond that; but what I can certainly assure you is that they will never get me to do anything cowardly.[163]

Keith, to whom Rousseau sent a prepublication copy, warned that the Genevans would be furious at his continued denial of miracles; he makes no note of the political side of the polemic.

Obsession with secrecy led Rousseau to distort the truth by word-quibbling. He assures Philibert Cramer (the Cramer brothers, Philibert and Gabriel, were Voltaire's publishers and influential Genevans in the "establishment") that no new work of his was being sold in Paris, and that he was not the author of a work entitled *Lettres de l'homme de la montagne.*[164] He was more open with Montmollin. "Since they like war so much, they shall have it, and, after a thousand aggressions on their part, this is my first act of hostility."[165] It was a brave defiance, but the forces were not equal.

Rousseau's newest bomb had reached Geneva on December 18. Some copies were put into circulation. The furor was immediate, but did not prevent Rousseau from writing a preface to his *Dictionnaire de musique* two days later. Voltaire's comment to d'Argental, on December 23, was typical: "It breathes the flames of discord, it excites all the little factions of this little State against each other; on a first reading, I thought there would be a civil war." To the aristocrats Rousseau was a false patriot ready to sacrifice his country on the altar of his pride and personal rancors. His old friend Moultou, with whom he had broken after a quarrel in the summer of 1763, pleaded with him to restore their friendship. "I have read your book: they are the sighs of a hero; they have broken my heart. . . . It is for Europe to pronounce judgment now; if it absolves you, what can they reply?"[166] But the Prince of Wurtemberg asked whether it was true that he had written a book, *Lettre de l'homme de la montagne* [*sic*], which, it was said, "undermines the foundations of religion, tears apart the social bonds and tends to upset the form of government in Geneva."[167] Reading this note, Rousseau was filled with a towering rage he could not control. "So then, as long as there are wicked and vile men on earth I shall have to justify myself to you against their imputations! No, prince, I do not wish to maintain a correspondence in the role of an accused man who justifies himself. Therefore I beg you to allow ours to end today."[168]

Cramer's reply to Rousseau's evasive letter was even more disturbing. Cramer had read and reread the copy of the *Lettres* that Rousseau did, after all, send him. One sentence of Cramer's, brief and clear, amounted indeed to a declaration of war. "Forced to look on you today as the enemy of my country, I have wished to say it to you frankly, so that you would no longer count on the feelings I expressed to you before your last work."[169] On December 29 the Council submitted the *Lettres écrites de la montagne* to Jean-Robert Tronchin for judgment. He had the honesty and dignity to disqualify himself as a principal party. Agitation among the ruling clique was mounting steadily. As Boswell reported from Geneva on December 31:

Your letters from the Mountain are causing an immense furor here. For the most part I have found myself among the partisans of the Magistracy, consequently with your implacable enemies. I should be ashamed to repeat to you what I have heard some frenzied men say against the scoundrel Rousseau. You are the cause of a terrible ferment in this seat of the sciences. I consider Geneva as Athens; but it is Athens during the persecution of Socrates.

In his *Confessions*, Rousseau compares the *Lettres écrites de la montagne* with his earlier *Lettre sur la musique française*, for the hatred it aroused against him. "Nobody in Geneva or Versailles could believe that a monster such as I was allowed to remain alive."[170] Nevertheless, the Council took no official action, partly because De Luc and his friends, on January 1, had published their own *Réponse aux Lettres de la campagne*.

On December 27 an anonymous satirical pamphlet, eight pages in length, entitled *Le Sentiment des citoyens*, rolled off the Genevan press. "Vernes has just published against me," Rousseau notified Rey on the thirty-first, "a satire which makes me shudder and which will bring harm and dishonor to my adversaries. As for me, I can swear to you that I am not upset." He was, in fact, very upset. That same day he wrote to Du Peyrou: "Such, Monsieur, are my enemies and the arms they use against me. . . . Oh, some day, when the veil is drawn aside, how posterity will love me! How it will bless my memory! As for you, love me now, and believe that I am not unworthy of it." The attribution to Vernes, his former friend turned enemy, was erroneous. The unrecognized poison pen, the *main cachée*, was that of Voltaire. His diatribe, however, was not unmotivated.

Unlike Rousseau, the Patriarch of Ferney never signed what he wrote if it was at all dangerous, always denied authorship, and frequently attributed his objectionable writings to a dead man or a living enemy. These, he felt, were tactics justified by persecution and authorized by sane common sense. Thus, on July 16 he had written to d'Alembert about his own *Dictionnaire philosophique*: "I have heard about that abominable little *Dictionnaire;* it is a work of Satan." Of course d'Alembert, like everyone else, knew who the author was. Even Rousseau knew and was honest in his opinion: "It is enjoyable reading. It contains a sound morality; one would like to see it in its author's heart and in that of all men." But what Voltaire writes about the Bible is another matter; there his use of mockery is "an outrage against society and punishable before men's courts."[171] Voltaire was soon to say the same about him!

Voltaire's authorship was not always so easily discernible. He cried to heaven and earth that the scandalous *Sermon des cinquante* was not his. One of his most trenchant broadsides, it assailed the Old and the New Testaments. It summarized the horrors and absurdities of the one, the contradictions, frauds, and absurdities of the other, and proposed in their stead the universal, natural religion of deism. Even Voltaire might find himself in hot water for this no-quarters fusillade and his standing with the aristocratic, liberal pastors of Geneva compromised.* With

* Although the *Sermon* was generally ascribed to Voltaire, an open accusation in print was another matter. The police of the *ancien régime* rarely prosecuted authors who remained anonymous. "By printing what he did Rousseau blew the gaff on this pretense and exposed Voltaire to the greatest dangers" (Besterman, *op. cit.*, p. 451).

what furious resentment he was filled, then, when Rousseau not only made him an unmentioned, hidden butt of his polemic, in the first four of the *Lettres écrites de la montagne*, but, in the fifth letter, openly mocked him and pinned on him the authorship of the *Sermon!* The strokes were telling:

These gentlemen see M. de Voltaire so often; how is it that he has not inspired in them that spirit of tolerance which he never tires of preaching, and which he sometimes lacks? If they had consulted him a bit in this affair, it seems to me that he might have spoken to them in this fashion: "Messieurs, it is not the reasoners who do harm, it is the bigots. Philosophy can go merrily along without risk; the common people do not understand it or pay no heed, paying back all the scorn it has for them. . . . I, of course, do not myself reason; but others do, and what harm comes of it? . . . And even if I do not reason, I do better, I make my readers reason. Look at my chapter on the Jews, look at the same chapter more amply developed in the *Sermon des cinquante*; there is reasoning there, or at least the equivalent, I think!"[172]

Voltaire would never forgive this thrust. An anecdote in Grimm's *Correspondance littéraire* in January 1766 relates that when he came across Rousseau's denunciation, he exclaimed in fury, his whole body trembling: "Ah, the scoundrel! ah! the monster! I shall have to have him beaten to death. Yes, I'll have him beaten to death between his housekeeper's knees." He wrote numerous plaintive or indignant letters to his friends.[173] "There is no excuse for such a criminal and cowardly act," he declares to Rousseau's patroness, Mme. de Luxembourg.[174] Rousseau is an informer and a calumniator; such is the man she honored with her protection. The letter goes on to summarize Rousseau's aggressive acts toward him, and his own generous defense of *Emile*. At the same time, he drew up a brief for François Tronchin, a member of the Council, summarizing all the counts on which Rousseau's work might be prosecuted. In these notes, dictated but not signed, he declares that it is not enough "to burn a book which is not hurt by burning," but that its author must receive the severest punishment. And if the Council does not take action, "he will be exposed to public derision and dragged in the mud by the populace."[175] Voltaire kept whipping up Tronchin, reassuring him, "on my head," that the Duchesse de Luxembourg would make no move to protect Rousseau.

But this was not enough. Voltaire's real counterblow against Rousseau was to be swift and of a different kind. It took him barely a week to write, publish, and distribute *Le Sentiment des citoyens*. In a horrified tone that clearly pointed to a priest as its author, he defended Christian miracles with the holy wrath of a man fighting for his faith. The writer was obviously a native Genevan, defending his country as well. How, he asked in the final line of his summation, like an attorney at the bar, how should we treat such a man as the author of the *Lettres écrites de la montagne*, the enemy of religion and of laws? "We must teach him that if we chastise an impious novelist lightly, a base revolutionary receives capital punishment."[176]

In Voltaire's mind, one foul blow deserved another harder one in return. Jean-Jacques, in a fight of this kind, had taken on more than his match. Voltaire's ferocious rhetoric has to be read to be believed. He stops at no hypocrisy. But the really low blow was personal, mendacious, and revolting. Asking who is this man who dares to cast reproaches at the good pastors of Geneva, he supplies an answer in a way that cleverly entangles truth with falsehood:

We admit with grief and blush to say that it is a man who still bears the deadly marks of his debauchery; one who, disguised as a mountebank, drags with him, from village to village, from mountain to mountain, the wretched woman whose mother he killed* and whose children he exposed at the gates of an asylum, rejecting a charitable person who wanted to take care of them, abjuring all natural feelings even as he casts off those of honor and religion.[177]

One could scarcely paint a blacker villain. That in itself was not what made the blow almost unbearable to Rousseau. His deepest secret, the abandonment of his children, which Voltaire had learned from Dr. Tronchin or from Grimm, was now the pabulum of all the gossips in Europe. His shame, his guilt, his violation of the principles he professed so loudly, on which his image and self-esteem depended, were proclaimed for all to know. The enterprise of self-justification would henceforth be more difficult, and more pressing.

Helpless, beside himself, he covered his copy of *Le Sentiment des citoyens* with denials. "I should rather have done what I am accused of in this passage than to have written it."[178] The broadside was so vicious that the Genevan government ordered it to be burnt. Losing his head, Rousseau sent his own copy to Duchesne and asked him to print it, with his own notes and a letter to Duchesne, holding the author up to condemnation. (The notes, incidently, do not tell the truth about his children.) In a private letter to Duchesne, not to be published, Rousseau asked for secrecy and a limited edition of twelve copies, to be strategically distributed. To confront an enemy, a man of the Church (we remember that he believed Vernes to be his tormentor) who used such base tactics, this was his first impulse.

Voltaire, meanwhile, continued to send up smoke screens and to kick his beaten rival. "Jean-Jacques," he writes to Bordes on January 4, 1765, "is putting the torch to his little republic. . . . I still haven't read his book,† which the magistrates find to be very seditious, and the people very good. Diogenes was run out of Sinope, but he did not agitate in it."

* Mme. LeVasseur, Thérèse's mother, was still alive, but Voltaire was no slave to truth when attacking his enemies.

† The *Lettres écrites de la montagne*, against which he had fulminated in *Le Sentiment des citoyens*.

To Damilaville, on the same day, he was a bit more brutal. "According to all appearances they are going to make him feel sorry for trying to set fire to the toy country he has left. You saw, in my last letter, how vicious he is. I cannot get over my astonishment that a man who calls himself a philosopher should publicly play the role of stool pigeon and calumniator. . . . I see that Jean Jacques' great fault is to be mad at the human race; that is a very ugly passion." To d'Alembert he quipped, "Jean-Jacques would be delighted to be hanged, provided his name was mentioned."[179] Not long after, writing again to Bordes, he refused to believe (or so pretended) that Rousseau had been asked to draw up a constitution for Corsica. "How can people have imagined that the Corsicans had written to him? I assure you there is no truth in it. All he needed was this new *ridicule*. Let's abandon the wretch to his infamy."[180] But letters were not enough. In February, and again in March, he fired off two new anonymous pamphlets.[181]

Condemnation of the *Lettres écrites de la montagne* was as widespread among the *philosophe*s as among the devout. Grimm devotes most of his January 15 issue to a long list of charges against it. "His reply [to Tronchin] is a masterpiece of eloquence, of sarcasm, of bitterness, of madness and atrocity; never has one seen such an abuse of talents. . . . He says he believes in Jesus Christ, despite His miracles. . . . He says the Gospels are a divine book, and draws up an indictment against it. . . . Another hypocritical act must not have been difficult for him." The political part is even more atrocious: "He wants no less than to arm citizen against citizen." And so on.

Little wonder, indeed, that Jean-Jacques, a neurotic with the most fragile equilibrium, should see himself surrounded by plotters! Voltaire and Grimm, the Genevan oligarchs and pastors were determined to silence if not to destroy him, resolved to drive him out of Switzerland. He was not overstating his position when he said, in the sixth of the *Lettres écrites de la montagne*: "the great ploy of my enemies consists in accusing me of being admitted nowhere, while they work to have me expelled everywhere."

The modern reader finds the *Lettres écrites de la montagne*, which caused Rousseau all his grief, among the least interesting of his works. Having read Rousseau's defense of his faith elsewhere, knowing little and caring even less about Genevan politics and constitutional law in the eighteenth century, he finds the interminable argument tedious. Grimm expressed exactly the same opinion in his attack. Yet a closer look shows why its passion and logic generated such commotion.

From the religious viewpoint, it was a shocker because Montmollin's defense for admitting Rousseau to communion had been based on the belief (of which Rousseau had persuaded him) that *Emile* was directed solely against the Catholic church. Indeed, Rousseau had used this argument time and again. He had also promised Montmollin never again to write about religion. What a surprise, then, to open this new book and to find the Genevan clerical establishment indicted for wilfully distorting what he had written, for inflicting injustices upon him and for failure to understand the true spirit of the Gospels. Once again Rousseau argues against the evidence of miracles to support the Christian faith. The disciples of the Savoyard Vicar, not the persecuting Genevan church, are the true Christians, the true Protestants, since they are tolerant. They practice Christ's teachings, instead of arguing about them. Rousseau's attempt "to clear himself from the charge of having written two 'rash, scandalous and impious works' "[182] only compounded the scandal.

In the political sphere, Rousseau has been made to recognize, once and for all, that the Geneva of actuality was a mockery of the "real" (in the sense of ideal) Geneva that he had carried around with him as a model, a composite of readings, memories of childhood, and wishful thinking. It had inspired a strange combination: his peculiar concept of "liberty" and his rigid, Calvinist moral and political absolutism. But to him the strange combination was a republic dominated by clergy and enamored of Voltaire. Taking up Tronchin's challenge, he has no difficulty in showing that the condemnation of both *Emile* and *The Social Contract* violated the fundamental laws and procedural practices of the State, and that a condemnation without a hearing was against all equity. He shows that more radical works were frequently published in Geneva—those of Montesquieu and especially of Voltaire. (The Council, of course, recognized who was the real danger, the real revolutionary.) And, most unjust of all, he had written to vindicate religion against atheism and to "exalt the constitution of Geneva above that of all other States!"[183]

On constitutional grounds, Rousseau challenges the claim of the Council to a right of veto on representations by the citizens. What was at stake here was the fundamental question of sovereignty, which, in Geneva, inhered precisely in that right, a right granted by the mediating powers during the troubles of 1738 and approved by the General Council of the citizens. Sovereignty, he maintains, belongs to the body of citizens, legally assembled as a General Council. Faithful to the doctrine of *The Social Contract*, he claims for this assembly the sole power to pass new laws and also the right to decide whether the government, the Petit Conseil, has acted properly or improperly. It must be this or tyranny. And the possible reactions to tyranny, he declares, are submission to enslavement, foreign intervention, or civil war. There is no other choice. Rousseau goes on to say that of the three courses, civil war is the worst. Despite this appeal, the government of Geneva considered the *Lettres écrites de la montagne* to be revolutionary and a danger to the oligarchy's control of the State. Their judgment was accurate. "The effect of the *Lettres écrites de la montagne* was to give fresh courage to the Représentants and to increase their numbers."[184]

In this polemical work, Rousseau largely eschews the difficult—and most original—aspects of his political theory, such as the notions of the communal self and the general will. For polemical reasons, he follows Locke, whereas his real mission, as Vaughan points out, was to confute Locke and "to strike out on a new path of his own."[185] Nevertheless, a number of statements would have enabled an astute reader of *The Social Contract* to recognize Rousseau's consistent doctrine. Thus, the individual's alienation of himself to the organic social union "is absolute, without conditions, without reserve"; for which reason the action of the body can never be unjust or tyrannical, by definition. The will of all is "the supreme rule."[186] As long as men live under laws, "they are always free, no matter how one is governed."[187] "It is the essence of sovereign power not to be limited; it can do everything, or it is nothing. . . . It can recognize no rights other than its own and those it grants."[188] In a good society, the citizens are wholly devoted to the public weal. The Genevans, Rousseau charges, concerned only with commerce and money-making, "never think of the public interest except when their personal interest is attacked."[189] As one Marxist disciple of Rousseau puts it, he "denounces the snare of bourgeois freedom."[190]

Irving Babbitt, who in so many ways misunderstood Rousseau, struck the mark when he wrote: "The Rousseau who has moved the world . . . is Rousseau the extremist and foe of compromise."[191] And Babbitt quotes Gustave Lanson's perceptive comment:

The writer is a poor dreamy creature who approaches action only with alarm and with every manner of precaution, and who understands the applications of his boldest doctrines in a way to reassure conservatives and satisfy opportunists. But the work for its part detaches itself from the author, lives its independent life; and, heavily charged with revolutionary explosives which neutralize the moderate and conciliatory elements Rousseau has put into it for his own satisfaction, it exasperates and inspires revolt and fires enthusiasms and irritates hatreds; it is the mother of violence, the source of all that is uncompromising, it launches the simple souls who give themselves up to its strange virtue upon the desperate quest of the absolute, an absolute to be realized now by anarchy and now by social despotism.[192]

# VII. Where Can I Go?

IN November, Rousseau had written to Henriette Maugin, one of his many female admirers, about her personal values:

I cannot tell it to you too often, I know of no happiness or peace when one is alienated from himself; on the contrary, each day I feel more keenly that happiness on earth is possible only in proportion as one becomes detached from things and grows closer to himself. If there is any sweeter feeling than self-esteem, if there is any occupation more enjoyable than increasing that feeling, then I may be wrong; but that is how I think.

Solitude meant the exclusion of the world and free narcissistic self-indulgence—a comfortable wall to protect his self-esteem, to shut out "opinion." As Jean-Jacques knew and admitted, he had failed to achieve independence *in* the world. He yearned, or so he believed, to leave it behind. Both literally and figuratively, there was—it was now a settled fact —no home for him.

The first four months of 1765 did bring isolation. Illness, pain, and the severe winter confined him indoors. "The sensitive soul, which dreams and suffers more than it acts, finds in its illness an excellent excuse for its isolation and introvertedness."[1] This was in general true for Rousseau. But now correspondence was heavier than ever, and the political situation allowed no tranquillity. He warned d'Ivernois (January 17) not to answer a gazetteer who had written against him: "Why am I not forgotten by mankind! Why can I not, by sacrificing that petty glory which has never appealed to me, enjoy the repose I worship, the peace so dear to my heart, which one can taste only in obscurity?" "They"—Voltaire and his group in Geneva, and now the clergy all around him—were out to get him. "They are making a big straw mop out of religion, covering it with mud and shoving it down my throat so that they can cut me up at their convenience, without my being able to cry out."² Rumors were spread that Voltaire had set a trap for him by writing to him in Paoli's name, and that Helvétius and Diderot had also been asked to devise a constitution. Had Voltaire made up the letter to them, too? he asked sardonically. It was another *canard*. Rousseau alone had received such an invitation; but the *philosophes* were spiteful about the signal honor. Jean-Jacques, as might be expected, for a while grew suspicious that Buttafoco was in league with his enemies and only trying to make him an object of public ridicule.

He was still able to jest about the persecution. "When the inquisitor Voltaire," he wrote to Du Peyrou on January 31, "succeeds in having me burnt at the stake, it will not be funny for me, I admit; but admit, too, that the thing in itself couldn't be funnier." On January 17 the *Lettres écrites de la montagne* was confiscated in Holland, and condemned to the flames. "Considering how cold it is," he punned badly, "there are many burning people. How many bonfires glow in Europe in my honor!"³

The ever-widening conspiracy and the libelous *Sentiment des citoyens* now made the project of writing his memoirs inescapable, he confided to Duclos on January 13. Doubtless Mme. d'Epinay had provided Vernes with information or misinformation about his past. How much could he "spill" about her! But no, he will not reveal her secrets. He has enough material, even without them, to paint her portrait; and even that, he assures Duclos, will be known only after his death. "I have a lot to say, and I shall say everything. I shall not omit a single one of my faults, not even one of my evil thoughts. I shall paint myself as I am: the bad will almost always cloud over the good. And, despite that, I find it difficult to believe that any of my readers will dare to say, 'I am better than that man was.'" The famous exordium of the *Confessions* was already sketched out.

Du Peyrou asked him to draw up a list of manuscripts to be published in a posthumous edition of his works. He will settle on Rousseau an annuity revertible to Thérèse after his death. Rousseau agreed and gave Du Peyrou power of attorney over all his literary property. In Paris, he learned from Lenieps, contraband copies of the *Lettres* were being snatched from the hands of their lucky possessors. Rousseau waited in vain for Geneva, in turn, to order it burnt.

When Vernes denied authorship of the *Sentiment des citoyens*, Rousseau wrote to Duchesne asking him to halt reprinting it. Some copies, however, had already gotten out. An insulting correspondence followed. Despite Rousseau's resolve to break off, Vernes forced him to admit that he still thought him guilty of the infamous pamphlet. So certain was Jean-Jacques that Vernes was the culprit that he was ready to submit his case to the Genevan Council which had condemned him. It is astonishing that he never recognized Voltaire's mordant style or his allusions to Jean-Jacques' life in Paris, or paid heed to whispers in Geneva.

Simultaneously, he quarreled with Mably, whose letter to a Genevan friend was being widely publicized. "I thought him a decent man," wrote Mably. Now he recognized him as a conspirator and trouble-maker.[4] Rousseau protested, but Mably was firm. "I pitied you in your misfortunes, as I pitied Socrates; but allow me to tell you that Socrates, to revenge himself on his judges, did not try to incite sedition in Athens."[5] Jean-Jacques at first would not believe that Mably, whom he admired, could have written such a letter; and in the *Confessions* he claims that Mably never answered his protest. Now he knew one thing: Mably had gone over to his enemies. Such a public denunciation, un-called for, against a man who was in distress, could be interpreted in no other way. Mably's reason, Rousseau was persuaded, was jealousy of his superior political writings.

On February 12 the government of Geneva finally issued a manifesto against the *Lettres écrites de la montagne*. It was proclaimed in the streets by the town crier. The following day the pastors of Neuchâtel denounced the *Lettres* to their government and magistrates. The Coun-cil of State of Neuchâtel forbade the reprinting of Rousseau's works. On the twenty-fourth, Rousseau ordered the De Luc brothers never to write to him again about Genevan affairs—or anything else. Since, "with so much love for justice and truth, I have done only wrong on earth, I wish to do no more, and I retire within myself." More than by anything else, perhaps, he was annoyed by the fact that the bourgeois party, or Les Représentants, who had sought his aid and leadership, completely avoided mentioning his *Lettres écrites de la montagne* in their petitions and polemics. His petulance comes out strongly in the *Confessions*.[6]

The Neuchâtel Council, on March 4, transmitted the pastors' protest to Frederick the Great. Four days later Montmollin asked Rousseau to desist from communion. On March 10, hoping to appease the aroused clergy, he gave his written promise never to write again about religion, but rejected a word substitution demanded by Montmollin. The pastors, however, declared that he could no longer be considered a Christian or worthy of partaking in the communion of the faithful unless he satisfied them with a formal retraction and a profession of faith in the risen Christ and Revelation. Following this, he was summoned before the Consistory of Môtiers on March 29. "The ministers and their satellites are roused* and furious," he wrote to Mme. de Verdelin on March 24; "it is known that Geneva and Voltaire are whipping up revolt against the prince [Frederick] and persecution against me." Instead of appearing in person, Rousseau pleaded illness and sent a letter, insisting that the procedure against him was illegal and that a Protestant church had no right of inquisition into the faith of a private citizen. "Once received into the church, I owe no one an accounting for my faith except God

* Rousseau uses the word *ameutés*, which refers to dogs in a hunting pack.

Himself." He had, in fact, wished to appear in person, and had stayed up all night rehearsing his vindication. "In the morning I no longer remembered it. I hesitated at each word, I thought myself already before the illustrious assembly, I became confused, I stammered, I lost my calm; finally, when it was almost time to go, my courage failed completely."[7]

Meanwhile, the first of fifty so-called *Lettres populaires*, directed against him, had appeared. Du Peyrou was about to publish his "Lettre de Goa," the first of a series defending his friend. This time it was Rousseau's turn to warn him to be careful. In Paris the *Lettres écrites de la montagne* was publicly burned on March 19. Fréron, in his journal *L'Année littéraire*, adroitly made public Rousseau's attestation of a miracle performed by Bishop de Bernex. The attestation, something Rousseau had written in a private letter to Father Boudet in April 1742, was acutely embarrassing in the light of his present denial of miracles, all the more so because Fréron perfidiously suppressed the date of Rousseau's letter, thus allowing the reader to think it was something recent.

Most annoying to Jean-Jacques was the change in attitude of the people of the Val-de-Travers. Montmollin, not content with arousing the pastors, was stirring up the people.

I dare to say that I should have been loved by the common people of that country, as I have been in all those where I have lived, distributing charity at every step, . . . putting myself, perhaps more than I should have, on terms of familiarity with them, carefully avoiding any distinction that might excite jealousy.[8]

None of that, complains Jean-Jacques, prevented the populace "from being aroused against me in increasing degrees until they became a fury, insulting me publicly in broad daylight, not only in the countryside and on the roads, but in the streets."

Doggedly, Rousseau set to work on his memoirs. Proposing to Rey a new edition of his works in exchange for an annuity of one thousand francs, he informs him about "the great enterprise of my life. . . . Never will any man have attempted such an undertaking and accomplished it as I propose to do."[9]

As week followed week of tension, he realized that the time had come to seek another refuge. But where? His faithful friends who wrote letters of encouragement pressed various suggestions on him. He kept vacillating, finding advantages and disadvantages everywhere. England? It was far away, the climate vile and the cost of living high, but the people were free from clerical oppression. Italy? He loved Venice, the Inquisition was not too vigorous there—but they would never forgive what he had written about them. Savoy would be delightful, but would they allow him to go back? Berlin and Breslau were proposed, and the Duchess of Saxe-Gotha invited him to her capital; but Germany had no appeal. Best of all would be some remote corner of France; but France, he was sure, would never forgive. "Wherever I turn, I see only claws to tear me and open jaws to devour me."[10] Keith urged him not to delay too long. "The bad thing is that time is short. You'll see what the Neuchâtelois will do. They catch fire like straw."[11] But on April 6, Jean-Jacques was still writing to d'Escherny, "I do not yet know where my fate will take me."

A sudden turn put a brighter light on the situation. After debating Rousseau's letter, the Consistory voted not to excommunicate him. Joyfully he assured Mme. de Verdelin, on March 30, that "the paltry clergy (la ministraille) could founder in this affair, and M. de Voltaire, who is boasting loudly that he will chase me out of here despite the King of Prussia, will probably not succeed." Yes, he will leave, but only when it is clear to all that he can stay. On the same day, a royal order placed him under the protection of the Council of State and removed him from the Consistory's jurisdiction. Assured of royal protection, Rousseau promised the Council to write nothing subversive. His friends rejoiced. Relieved, Rousseau withdrew his frantic request to Mme. de Verdelin to secure him a passport allowing him to cross France on the way to England.

Still there was no cessation of harassment. A passage in the Lettre à M. de Beaumont, praising Montmollin as a model of Christian charity, was exploited. Rousseau, it was charged, had written that women did not have souls, and the ladies of Môtiers cursed him. The pastors, incited by Montmollin, preached sermons against him in the churches. "I was pursued," Rousseau relates, "throughout the countryside, like a bogey-man . . . by the booing of the rabble and sometimes by their stones."[12] Some threatened to shoot him. But he walked quietly among them, never hastening his pace. Keith wrote to a friend that "the very worthy Sacragorgon [Montmollin] has assured people that Jean-Jacques was really the antichrist in person, and that he has told the women they have no souls."[13] When Vernes published his correspondence with him, Jean-Jacques must have winced, and Voltaire rubbed his hands with glee.

Safety was assured, Rousseau thought, but it was not enough. "They will never let me alone here," he declared to Keith on April 6; "Geneva is no further away than before." His anguish did not prevent him from exchanging flirtatious letters with Marianne Guyenet, the daughter of a friend.

Jean-Jacques' friendship with Mme. de la Tour, on the other hand, took a sudden turn toward disaster. Misjudging her idol, she had the imprudence (to him impudence) to tell him, on February 25, quite frankly, that a man with his philosophy, who teaches virtue to others, should have greater calm and firmness in the face of misfortunes. After all, he has been rash in his challenge of accepted opinions. To Rousseau this reprimand was unforgivable. In a cold and brutal letter ("You flattered me in my prosperity, you become frank in my misfortune"), he told her to write no more.[14] Again and again she sent him letters of explanation, humble apology, adulation, accusations of vindictiveness.

Am I to believe that your virtues are only in your mind . . . that your writings are a mask you have used to usurp public esteem and the almost religious adoration I have given you? . . . Give me back a happiness so dearly bought. . . . Remember how much I have loved you, since you do not wish to know how much I love you still, how often I have forgiven your harshness![15]

And the distressed lady quotes his own phrases back at him, some from letters that are lost. Had he not written, "You are too much *ma dame* for me to call *Madame* any longer"? Jean-Jacques could ape the French gallantry on which he so often heaped scorn. Not until August 11 did the wounded god relent. "Dear Marianne, you are unhappy and I am disarmed. I am softened when I picture your beautiful eyes wet with tears. . . . Let us try to forget our childishness. . . . Forgive me and let us love each other."

With a former friend, however, Rousseau was unrelenting. It was at this time that Diderot (though he later denied it) asked d'Escherny to try to effectuate a reconciliation. D'Escherny pleaded in vain:

I would not have the temerity to speak to you about the natural disposition in noble and generous souls to forgiveness. I do not know your motives. But, whatever they may be, whatever atrocity, whatever villainy I can suppose in M. Diderot's actions, and putting things in the worst light, can you refuse to forget the past, reject his disavowal of that fateful note,[16] after twenty years of friendship with a man you have mortally wounded, and who begs you to forgive?

Rousseau's reply, on April 6, was decisive:

I do not understand, Monsieur, what M. Diderot can suddenly want of me after seven years of silence. I ask nothing of him, I have no disavowal to make. I am far from wishing him any harm, further still from doing or saying any. I know how to respect the rights of friendship, even when it is dead. But I do not enkindle it again. That is my most inviolable maxim.

Harsh and unforgiving though he was, Rousseau was right. They could not have been reconciled. Each had too much guilt of his own to be able to confess. Each had too much resentment for the other's guilt to regain the confidence necessary to friendship.

Even the long friendship with Lenieps came within a hair of sudden death. A paragraph of Rousseau's letter to him of February 10, in which he derided the citizens of Geneva as stupid dupes of the Council, was made known in that city, in a corrupted text, and widely circulated. Bitterly, Jean-Jacques accused Lenieps of having lost him all his friends in that city. Several of them indeed asked him whether it was true that he had written the insulting lines. It was true, he admitted to De Luc, but they were written in a desperate moment. Forgiveness was granted

Lenieps following a humble and pleading letter (April 20, 1765) and an explanation that he had given no one a copy of the letter, but had only read it to trusted friends.

Better news came from Paris with the approval for publication of the *Dictionnaire de musique*, on April 15. Duchesne was offering him an annuity of three hundred livres for it, and Rousseau was most satisfied. The fine weather returned in May and he could not wait to leave Môtiers. Together with Du Peyrou and the latter's architect, Ritter, he journeyed to the village of Bienne, on the lake of that name. From there he went to Neuchâtel, looking at several houses, before returning to Môtiers. He told Du Peyrou he wanted to be called "Citizen" in their correspondence, not "Monsieur"—although he was no longer really a citizen. The word had republican connotations and was to be adopted during the French Revolution.

On May 31, Rousseau sent a final letter to his archenemy. Voltaire had been telling people that Rousseau had never been the ambassador's secretary in Venice, but only his valet. The letter is blunt enough:

If M. de Voltaire has said that instead of having been secretary to the French ambassador in Venice I was his valet, M. de Voltaire has been lying impudently.

If in the years 1743 and 1744 I was not first secretary to the French ambassador, if I did not perform the functions of secretary of the embassy, if I did not receive the appropriate honors at the Senate of Venice, then I am the liar.

Voltaire made no reply, but one can assume that Rousseau's challenge did not shut his mouth. When he quoted Rousseau's letter, he changed the words significantly, omitting the reference to having been a valet.

The Montmollin affair seemed to have been settled, as far as Rousseau was concerned, although pamphlets and letters continued to come out. Du Peyrou became more and more involved and even endangered in his attack against the fanatical clergy. To assist him in replying to Montmollin, Rousseau sent him, on August 8, a long philippic in which he pointed out, among other things, that the minister had approved his writing about religion when he replied to Beaumont. In this way Rousseau voluntarily continued the quarrel, and again when he wrote a labored diatribe, *Vision de Pierre de la Montagne*. Published in September, it served only to redouble the wrath and resentment of his enemies. The most curious fact about this rag is that Jean-Jacques conveniently forgot his *Vitam impendere vero*, and warned Du Peyrou that "it is essential that nobody know I am its author," although he didn't care if people suspected it, *à la manière de* Voltaire.[17]

It has been said that if Rousseau had stuck to his earlier resolve never again to take up his pen, he could have lived out his life quietly at Môtiers, but that this was impossible for him. "Paranoiacs generally conduct themselves in a way to draw attention to what they consider their martyrdom and endangered position, while infantilists delight in making themselves conspicuous."[18] This explanation is valid, but not adequate. Rousseau had been thrice attacked in print, his ideas, motives, and character impugned. And his enemies had no intention of letting him live in peace. Of course, he made matters far worse for himself.

He continued to take happy excursions around the region, and in July spent ten days with d'Ivernois on the Isle of Saint-Pierre in Lake Bienne. He was thinking of taking an apartment in the house Du Peyrou was building in Neuchâtel, or of going to Paris and spending the winter there supervising the publication of his *Dictionnaire de musique*. No longer does the Parlement worry him, he writes to Guy, the director of the Duchesne publishing house since Duchesne's death. "I am so used to the persecutions of men, that they have become in a way my element."[19] Guy sent his welcome and offered him a small apartment. The Paris Opéra had just put on *Le Devin du village* again, and its success would not hurt him.

Mme. de Verdelin, Jean-Jacques' ever-faithful and devoted friend, informed him in July that she would journey to visit him at the end of the summer. He agreed, setting the conditions that would suit him. She reached Môtiers, after an arduous journey, on September 1. Jean-Jacques, though he had at times doubted the sincerity of her friendship, could not remain insensitive to this clear evidence. He was grateful for her offer to use powerful influences to secure a passport for him to traverse France, a matter that had to go as high as the King, none of the ministers having the courage to take that responsibility. But he was puzzled by her apparent lack of interest in the insults and attacks on him which she was about to witness. Like so many others, she had urged him many times to exile himself to England. Later, he included her among the plotters. Could so many people have misdirected him at once (or directed him to his doom), if they had thought and acted separately?*

On the very day of Mme. de Verdelin's arrival, the first of a sudden rush of events that were to change Rousseau's life took place. It was a Sunday, and Montmollin delivered a sermon that aroused the populace against him. That night, pebbles were thrown against his windows. The next day, three emissaries came from the town of Couvet to offer him shelter there. During the night, two harrows with rocks on them were set up in front of his door in such a way that the rocks could easily fall on him. When Mme. de Verdelin left on the third, a group of mowers hurled insults at him, and one shouted that it was time to get a gun and shoot him down. The Council of Neuchâtel, the next day, ordered the

---

* Writing about one of his friends in the Roguin family who had secretly turned against him and worked for his expulsion from Yverdon, while covering him with affection, Rousseau comments: "He was following faithfully *le plan chéri de mes persécuteurs*" (*Confessions*, Pléiade, p. 631).

*châtelain* of Môtiers to warn the community against such behavior. But two nights later, a window of Rousseau's house was smashed by a volley of stones. "The rioting is so great here among the rabble," he wrote to Guy on September 7, "that last night my doors were broken down, my windows shattered and a rock almost as big as my head just missed my bed." Thérèse and he pressed themselves against the wall out of range of the window. The servant of a lodger downstairs ran to the *châtelain's* nearby house. He came at once with the guard, which was out because of the village fair. He was amazed to see the number of stones on the gallery and concluded that the mob had tried to get to Rousseau through the broken door.

Grimm reported, on November 15, that a few drunkards had gathered in front of Rousseau's house, "without any plan," and tossed a few pebbles into his windows. If "poor Jean-Jacques" had gone through hell, it was in having to listen to Montmollin's sermons each week. Montmollin was displeased with him, true enough, but it was because Rousseau had given signs of his boredom. Then the *Lettres écrites de la montagne* had provoked the stupid pastor's wrath.

Inquiry failed to uncover the malefactors. Two guards were stationed on the gallery of Rousseau's house. He received and courteously refused a renewed offer from the town of Couvet. It was too close. "I must live far from them as from poisonous snakes who spread their venom in their breath where their teeth cannot reach." On the nineteenth the Council offered a reward of fifty écus and immunity to informers.

But Rousseau had left Môtiers the day before, vowing never to go back. After stopping at Neuchâtel, he reached the Isle of Saint-Pierre on September 10 or 11. He had received two assurances that the government of Berne would let him alone, and had been offered rooms in the house of the tax collector, who lived there. At a hasty conference, it had been decided that once he was gone, Thérèse would probably not be molested; she could stay to take care of their possessions, as usual, and join him two weeks later. The excitement did continue even after his departure, with a public lampoon. A straw man was set up by the rabble near the town fountain. On a bandolier he had a sack, which contained a paper covered with insults. Thérèse was threatened for "the scandal she has caused." The *châtelain*, also menaced, prudently posted guards around his own house. A rescript of Frederick the Great ordering the Council to protect Rousseau and condemning Montmollin reached Neuchâtel too late on September 28.

Although the shoreline and landscape of the Isle of Saint-Pierre have changed somewhat, and the house of its one family has become a noisy inn reached by an excursion boat from the mainland, we can still recapture the serenity of this retreat and understand the peace of mind it brought to Rousseau. The little island was flat on the edges, allowing some farming and fruit orchards, especially in the southern part, where the house stood. Farther back a thickly wooded hump extended along its breadth. The mainland, beyond the circumscribing blue waters, revealed only an occasional house on tree-covered slopes and, at a further remove, high hazy hills with towering mountains in the distance. In the house, Jean-Jacques had two rooms, pleasantly rustic. A bedroom, with a couch and straw mattress, had two windows overlooking lake and shore. Adjoining it was the kitchen-dining-sitting room. At the Hermitage or Montmorency there had been no real solitude. Here he left the world behind. Escaping from the storm he had aroused, he withdrew into the island fastness for which he longed. Here there was no conflict, but innocence and harmony, within himself and with nature, enabling him almost to feel that he was realizing his quest for an earthly paradise and redemption. Communion between his spirit and nature had a religious quality, even as it had a quality of sensuality. Underneath was a half-conscious feeling of exultation, "at being, in this state, out of reach of the villains. . . . I cried out at times, with emotion: 'O nature, O my mother, here I am under your protection alone; here there is no clever or knavish man who can interpose himself between you and me.' "[20] On Saint-Pierre he could conceive of a world of his own, a hermetic existence, a total unity: independence, self-sufficiency, pure solitude.

I acquired the habit of going to sit on the bank in the evening, especially when the lake was rough. I felt a singular pleasure in seeing the waves break at my feet. They became in my mind the image of the world's tumult and the peace of my dwelling, and this sweet idea sometimes moved me to tears.[21]

He longed to be sentenced to life imprisonment on this isle; that fate he would have embraced with joy.

The isle was "a half-league" in circumference. Five hundred feet to the south was a smaller, uninhabited islet. On these two islands Jean-Jacques wandered, studied botany, dreamed in that state of idleness and self-absorption that was so delightful to him. He divided the island into sections and planned to make a collection of every plant on it. He would row on the lake, accompanied by his dog, Sultan, let the boat drift, and float away into a nirvana of reveries, which he was to describe in the unforgettable fifth "Promenade" as a pure feeling of existence. He was approaching the happiness he had once known at Les Charmettes; unfortunately, instead of Maman, there was only Thérèse, and his mental outlook was considerably changed.

In 1765, when he arrived at the Isle of Saint-Pierre, the universe which surrounds him has reached such a degree of opacity, his "co-efficient of aggressivity" is so high, that to secure his protection he needed a new kind of rampart: water will serve him as an isolator, and the consciousness of a solitary, of a fanatical admirer of Robinson [Crusoe] will soon become an insular consciousness. Soon he will perceive that prison alone, true incarceration, could afford him adequate help.[22]

It was harvest time. Jean-Jacques, thinking back to Les Charmettes, pitched in with his host's family. His Bernese friend, Kirchberger, found him one day perched on the branch of an apple tree, filling a large sack tied around his waist. It would be good, Rousseau thought, if the Bernese know how innocently he was spending his time. He had decided to stay permanently on this enchanted isle, where bliss was spoiled only by the uneasy premonition that he might once again be driven out from his Eden. Keith and Du Peyrou had both settled pensions on him, the former out of love, the latter in anticipation of an edition of his works; he also had a small income from Duchesne in payment for the *Dictionnaire de musique*. What if his enemies mocked and defamed him from now on without fear of reply or reprisal?

In the noble enthusiasm which dictated my writings and in the constant uniformity of my principles, I was leaving a testimony of my soul that matched the testimony which my entire conduct gave about my character. I needed no other defense against my calumniators. They might paint another man under my name, but they could deceive only those who wanted to be deceived. I could give them my whole life to comment on from one end to the other; I was sure that beyond my faults and my weaknesses, beyond my inability to bear any yoke, one would always find a just man, good, without bitterness, without hatred, without jealousy, quick to recognize his own faults, quicker yet to forget others'; seeking all his happiness in loving and gentle passion, and carrying sincerity in all things to the point of imprudence and the most incredible disinterestedness.[23]

Such was the portrait Rousseau wished others, in his own time and in all time to come, to have of him. It was what he thought to be his *real* self, the other self of the innumerable lamentable episodes of his life being only an ephemeral, fortuitous, inexplicable simulacrum, or else the malicious invention of his host of enemies.

Rousseau's affirmation—more than once repeated—that he was unable to bear any yoke, is of peculiar interest. His political utopianism rested precisely, as we have seen, on the imposition of an unbreakable yoke on the individuals in an organic society, although he calls it "the harsh yoke of *liberty*." I have attempted to explain this paradox in discussing Rousseau as a model of the "authoritarian personality." And it was precisely at this time, when he was free of any yoke, that he was writing his outline of the proposed constitution for Corsica, one which imposes the severest restrictions and control on individual thoughts and actions.

Written in two small notebooks, the *Projet de constitution pour la Corse* was abandoned, in the form of a rough draft, when Rousseau's stay on the island came to an abrupt end. It remained entirely unknown until published by Streckeisen-Moultou, the great-grandson of Rousseau's friend, in 1861. As Vaughan remarks, only in the work on Corsica (in contrast to Geneva and Poland), did Rousseau have a free hand as *Législateur* or Lawgiver.[24] Only in this instance is he able to inaugurate a nation-state with the formalities of a contract. The oath he imposes on each citizen reads: "I join myself—body, goods, will, and all my powers—to the Corsican nation, granting her full ownership of me—of myself and all that depends on me."[25] The contract is irrevocable; no individual may renounce it (as Rousseau had himself done in Geneva), nor may it be dissolved by general consent. Total surrender of the individual and the religous basis of the State are proclaimed as clearly as in his earlier writings.

The Lawgiver, Rousseau warns, must use much "art" to keep the Corsicans in their present state of a people uncorrupted by the arts and by luxury. Employing the techniques of control and deception we have already examined, he leads them where he wants while convincing them that they are free. In the *Projet* Rousseau comes closest to state social-ism. There will be a minimum of private property and strict control of every aspect of economic life, which will be kept on a Spartan level. This is essential if the people are to remain "virtuous" (in Rousseau's politi-cal sense). Control is used to maintain living at a primitive level, and this simple living, or lack of sophistication and intellectual develop-ment, enables control to be effective. To a large extent Rousseau outlines the idea of what present-day Chinese communists call "com-munes."[26] Authoritarian methods prevent the natural movement to-ward cities, luxury, commerce. They must extend over the "passions," then, as well as economic activity. The people must not be able even to *imagine* a better condition. Complete devotion and self-sacrifice to the collective good ("virtue") will ensue. Morals having been absorbed into politics, the one virtue that matters is thinking of oneself only as part of the whole. That is why Rousseau says that we must form "the nation for the government," not adapt the government to the nation, thus reversing Montesquieu.

It follows that arts and letters will be prohibited. Egalitarianism and military service are emphasized. Instead of taxes, an easy and meaning-less sign of devotion and sacrifice, forced manual labor is exacted of all. But the main point remains the psychological captivity of the individ-ual, his subjugation and docility. "The people must be made to practice this system, to love the occupation we decide to give them, to find in it their pleasures, their desires, their tastes, their happiness in general, and to limit their ambitions and projects to it." The State or community will "possess men and all their powers."[27]

In the second part of this treatise, Rousseau draws up a truly astound-ing program of regimentation. Every aspect of life, including sexual life, marriage, and procreation, is controlled. "I will not preach morality to them; I will not order them to have virtues. But I will put them in such a position that they will have those virtues, without knowing the word, and that they will be good and just, without knowing what goodness and justice are."[28] Thought, feelings, and action must be absolutely certain and automatic. The people are always to be treated as children, watched over and guided, because they easily go astray and succumb to nature. Never does Rousseau place any confidence in men's rationality or reasonableness or good will. They will be reflexive. "Those who control a people's opinions control its actions."[29] The voting process, as in *The Social Contract*, fits into the pattern. The leader speaks: "Corsicans, be silent. Let those who do not agree leave, and let those who do agree raise their hands."[30] This is what Rousseau calls "a system of liberty," but which is rather a system of the death of choice and the withering of the individual before an impregnable State.[31]

While Rousseau has not altered the basic tenets and aims of his theory, he has tried to learn what he could about the realities of the Corsican people and life. He had hoped to live on that island, in order to make theory conform more closely to actual conditions. He does try to use such information as he was able to assemble and to keep in mind what he thought to be the temper of the nation. In the last analysis, however, political realism is considered only as a necessary limitation or guide in the service of political idealism.

Alas, Rousseau's dream of a haven for himself and of happiness for the Corsicans was suddenly destroyed by a single blow. "It is time," he tells us, "to relate the fatal story which crowned my disasters and swept away, in my ruin, an unfortunate people whose nascent virtues promised to equal someday those of Sparta and Rome."[32] On October 16, Emmanuel Graffenried, bailiff of Nidau, reluctantly informed Rousseau that the Council of Berne had ordered his expulsion. It was a bewildering blow. He had just written to Mme. Boy de la Tour (October 13), as to other friends, "Now I am thanks be to Heaven in peace and security on this isle." He had given no cause for such action. How true the words of the great Buffon, he must have thought, who wrote to him: "You have been the victim of your love of truth and even of your patriotism. . . . I know that your [virtue] is sustained by a great courage and that your soul is as strong as it is noble."[33] But Graffenried's consolation was too flattering: "I am certain that a virtuous man, a philosopher, a friend of truth and mankind like you, Monsieur, will easily bear this trifling misfortune. . . . The entire world is the homeland of a good man. . . ."

Jean-Jacques' state of mind comes out in a hastily dispatched note to Du Peyrou on October 17.

I am being run out of here, my dear host. The climate of Berlin is too harsh for me. I have decided to go to England, where I should have gone right off. I urgently need to take counsel with you, but cannot go to Neuchâtel; see whether you can for pity's sake escape from your business and come out here. I embrace you.

"Where should I go?" asks Rousseau in the *Confessions*. "What would become of me at the beginning of winter, without a destination, without preparation, without a carriage or driver?"[34] He pleaded for a few weeks' delay, or else to be sent to prison for life without paper or ink and without any direct communication with the outside world.[35] A paranoid reaction? Perhaps, but certainly that of a frightened, desperate man. Where else could he shelter himself from the hounding of his enemies and end his life in quiet oblivion? Both requests were refused. He was given five days, until the twenty-sixth. He had already written to Mme. de Verdelin, asking her to send the French passport with utmost speed.

Thursday, October 24, was Jean-Jacques' last night on his happy isle. He and Thérèse had dinner with the collector's family. Then he accompanied himself on a lute as he sang the songs he had composed that day to bid his hosts farewell. The next day, accompanied only by Kirchberger, he went to Bienne, thinking he could spend the winter there. It was at Bienne that he received Hume's letter of October 22, expressing his commiseration, his friendship, and recommending him to his friend in London, Elliott; obliged by his diplomatic duties to go to Ireland, he would not be able to accompany Rousseau, as he would have liked.

Du Peyrou felt obliged to send Rousseau a word of warning about Thérèse. "Let her avoid as much as possible getting friendly with other women. Its consequence is always gossip, which upsets peace of mind more than all persecutions." The warning continues, repeated, and concludes: "Just between us, I am very sorry to hear it said that when she was at Brot she spoke quite improperly about the conduct of the *châtelain* Martinet. Often a careless word is enough to gain the hatred of people whom we do not think we have offended."[36] These lines are enough to help us imagine what turbulence she must have caused Rousseau with her gossip, exciting his suspicions and animosity; doubtless, too, starting quarrels and arousing resentment among the townspeople. Thérèse's champions, however, assert that she was only defending Rousseau, to whom she was loyal and protective. The two assertions are not necessarily exclusive.

Rousseau was mistaken in thinking Bienne a free town. It, too, depended on Berne. On October 28 he learned that he was about to be asked to leave. "I have been deceived," he writes to Du Peyrou. "I am leaving tomorrow before I am kicked out." Already, the whole town had been stirred up against him. An acquaintance in Basel offered to take him in, "hoping, he said, that I might avoid being stoned there. The advantage did not seem flattering enough for me to tarry amidst such hospitable folk."[37] Graffenried had the courage to visit Rousseau in Bienne, dressed in full regalia, to give him a passport through Bernese territory. "Finally, after having with great difficulty obtained a chaise, I left that homicidal land the next morning."

The next stop was Basel, after all, on the way to Berlin. He stayed a day, and on November 2 reached Strasbourg, where he was to remain six weeks because of the cold and the bad condition of the roads. It was on the whole a most pleasant time, but ended with physical exhaustion. At first he was delighted to be honored as he deserved to be. Two of his plays were performed, and he was given a private, grilled loge in the theater. The opera put on *Le Devin du village* for him. He went to the rehearsals and performances. He attended concerts and dinners given in his honor, and enjoyed strolling about the city. It mattered little now that the Swiss gazettes described him to the people as a man pursued by the wrath of heaven, one whose presence spread sterility over the land he inhabited.[38] He was interested in learning that Voltaire, angered by the burning of his *Dictionnaire philosophique* in Geneva, had welcomed an approach from the dissident Burghers. Turmoil in that republic had increased. The Burghers (Représentants or Citizens), frightened by the demands of their allies, the Natives (who were not Citizens), were drawing closer to their enemies, the oligarchic Patriciate. On the pretext of a plot, the leaders of the Natives were imprisoned and many fled into exile. Voltaire, going over to the other side, took in some of the émigrés and helped them to find homes, even though they were admirers of Rousseau. As for Rousseau, he was delighted; he would forget Voltaire's wrongs, devote himself to admiring him and making wishes for his happiness and glory.[39] Later Voltaire made fun of both sides in his burlesque epic poem "La Guerre de Genève."

Rousseau now decided definitely to go to England, provided he could stay in Paris for two months of rest.[40] Rey wanted him to travel through Amsterdam and to stay with him. Without consulting Rousseau, he sent his clerk, Potinius, to Strasbourg, to accompany the infirm traveler. Rousseau, in a high dudgeon, sent him back. But Mme. de Verdelin kept pressing him to go to the land of freedom. Hume had found a quiet farm twelve miles outside of London. He was willing to meet him on the way and go to London with him.

The final decision was made on November 30. Now he expected to stay in Paris only a week or ten days, to rest from the rigors of an exhausting journey in a freezing carriage. He charged Guy, with whom he was to stay, with secrecy. He was to see no one except a few close friends, and de Luze, a friend from the Môtiers region, with whom he would push on to England. Leaving on December 9, he reached Paris, after traveling in easy stages, on the sixteenth. He was ill, exhausted, and in a bad temper. Four days later, he succumbed to strong pressure from the Prince de Conti and Mme. de Verdelin and moved to one of Conti's houses in the Temple.

Conti was an excellent host. He lodged and fed his guest with splendor and even staged a performance of *Les Muses galantes* in his private theater. For two days he put intense pressure on Rousseau, to persuade him to settle on one of his estates near Paris, the Château de Trye. The fugitive was tempted, but declined, "because of a necessary condition he made which I could not accept."[41] The condition was probably a promise to publish—perhaps even to write—nothing without Conti's approval; word of the projected memoirs had leaked out. He had no choice but to go with Hume, if he was to keep any freedom.[42]

Jean-Jacques, who had wanted privacy, was busier than ever. Far from hiding his guest, Conti displayed him. He would show that the Temple had not lost its ancient privilege of shelter from royal authority and also, perhaps, intimate to Jean-Jacques that he was an outlaw. Between nine and noon, and again between six and nine in the evening, Rousseau received visitors. It was said that Diderot solicited a meeting, but was turned down. The famous sculptor Lemoyne did a bust of him. At the same time, he was pressing Du Peyrou to send him the documents he needed to continue his work on the *Confessions*; the third Book was being written.

Malesherbes was one of Rousseau's visitors. The storm that had struck *Emile* had narrowly missed him, since he had been responsible for its publication, and he was grateful to Rousseau for having taken his advice to leave the country. At a later time, toward 1780, Malesherbes scrupulously set down the facts as he remembered them. He relates that when he visited Rousseau at the Temple, he admitted that he was the indirect cause of Jean-Jacques' troubles, and that anything he could do for him would be only the payment of a debt. This admission moved Rousseau deeply. He felt his esteem and friendship for this man soar.[43] He asked for one thing: a note attesting to the fact that if *Emile* had been printed in Paris instead of Holland, it was without the consent, and at first without the knowledge, of its author. This was the key to the defense he hoped to make someday before the tribunal that had condemned him without a hearing. On January 2, 1766, Malesherbes gave him the requested certificate. Though the language in which it was couched was not as clear as Rousseau would have liked, he kept it as a precious piece of evidence.

Malesherbes was to have afterthoughts. Before long he wrote to Hume asking him to persuade Rousseau to return the certificate in exchange for a more exact one, and to promise to make no public use of it.[44] The tone of Malesherbes' letter is joking, but it is evident that he wanted Rousseau's defense to be posthumous. The idea of a public trial frightened Malesherbes and the Conti group. Their determination not to allow it explains many of the tribulations Rousseau was to suffer following his return to France.

Malesherbes continued to be worried that Rousseau might be planning to publish all his letters. We learn from a letter sent to Moultou in 1780 or 1781, after Rousseau's death, that he had confided personal and family secrets to him, and that he feared that Thérèse would sell his correspondence.[45] The apprehension was groundless. Rousseau, a loyal friend, had destroyed the letters that were personal or potentially embarrassing.

On December 28, Mme. de la Tour finally got to meet her great man, but not without difficulty. To her letter of December 21, written in Italian, complaining that though everyone knew he was in Paris, he had not gotten in touch with her, he made no reply. Two days later she expressed her deep chagrin and gentle reproaches: "My dear Jean-Jacques, you have forgotten the keen, tender, and constant interest I have always taken in you, despite the unevenness of your conduct towards me." Even if he does not consent to see her, she will always love him. The second letter brought a churlish reply. "Always reproaches!" He cannot visit anyone, he explains, but he does not invite her to visit him. Besides, hadn't she always wanted to keep their correspondence a secret?[46] She was not to be fooled. "Your stay here is not a secret, Monsieur, and you do not give me your address. [She had sent her letters via Mme. de Luxembourg.] I feel what that means. . . . I can assure you that you will never hear about me until after my death. . . . I hope you keep all your friends, and acquire more, that they will be happier than I, and above all, that your misfortunes, ills, and humor do not cost them as many tears."[47]

Then, on December 28, she presented herself at his house, sending up a note explaining that she had heard he would welcome her visit. "I am at your door." It was not during his visiting hours, but she hoped he would understand. "I am naturally so shy, your presence will so overawe me, I shall be so discountenanced, so stupid, so ill at ease, that I should be most unhappy to find anyone with you." Jean-Jacques' reply was sent downstairs at once. "I am not alone, Madame, which will not prevent me from receiving you with the greatest pleasure if you care to come in." The lady did care. What was said between them, when they looked upon each other after years of correspondence, remains their secret. But two notes followed. "At last I have seen you, my interesting friend," she wrote on January 1. "But that was four days ago, which seem as long as the four years that preceded them. . . . My dear Jean-Jacques, let us not lose hope. Heaven owes reparations to a feeling as keen, as pure, as star-crossed as the one it has given me for you." He replied the next day. "I am leaving, dear Marianne, regretting that I cannot see you again. . . . Pity me without condemning me. Since I have seen you, I have a new interest in not being forgotten by you. I should much like for you to love me, to stop making reproaches, and for me to stop deserving them. But it is too late to mend my ways. I shall remain such as I am, and it is no more in my power to be more lovable, than to stop loving you."

On New Year's Day, 1766, Rousseau informed Du Peyrou that he was leaving with Hume and de Luze on the fourth. He adds somewhat mysteriously that his stay in Paris has not been fruitless. "I have acquired new information about the source of my misfortunes which should be given to the future public." All this in view of his all-consuming project, the *Confessions*. Mme. de Verdelin added her love to that of

Mme. de la Tour. "I do not say, 'Love me, remember me'; but I do say, 'Keep well for my sake, I could not bear the loss of my friend.'"

Rousseau and Hume, whose lives were soon to become so strangely entangled, met for the first time a day or two before their appointed departure. Their earlier exchanges of letters, Keith's praise, their common feud with the "Llamas" (as Keith called the pastors), all predisposed him in favor of "le bon David." Hume also took an immediate liking to the eccentric exile, despite all the unfavorable remarks he had heard in Paris. Secretary to the British ambassador for two years, "le bon David" had been idolized in the salons, especially by women. He frequented d'Holbach's coterie, where he had been warned that he would never get Rousseau to England without a quarrel. It took a bit longer than that.

Hume, de Luze, and Rousseau left Paris together on the morning of January 4. They stayed the second night at Roye, where, according to Rousseau, the three slept in the same room. We are about to see that this detail, which would seem to be of no importance, was to play a disproportionate role in convincing him that Hume and de Luze were plotting against him.

That day, too, Thérèse left Saint-Pierre and went to stay with Du Peyrou at Neuchâtel on her way to join Jean-Jacques in England. "The poor girl is languishing until she can leave to join you," writes Du Peyrou on December 24.

The journey continued without incident, and on January 10, at 11:00 P.M., the three men embarked at Calais for Dover, and what was to be the strangest and most nightmarish of Rousseau's experiences.

# VIII. "Cette affaire infernale"

## 1. THE TRIUMPH OF DELUSION

WET and frozen after a rough Channel crossing with all three travelers seasick, Rousseau rejoiced at having at last reached "this land of liberty" which was to be, he thought, his final place of exile. He threw his arms about Hume's neck, covered his face with kisses and tears. In London, he was delighted by Hume's zeal in serving him and even more by visits from distinguished Englishmen, including the Duke of York, who came to pay homage to the illustrious refugee. He was deluged by letters from admirers. Truly, he had made a wise decision. England was a civilized country which knew how to treat great men. "English manners are much to my taste," he informed Du Peyrou. "They know how to show esteem without flattery. . . . My stay here is making a greater sensation than I should have believed." Following hard upon the attention and admiration lavished on him in Paris, the acclaim of the English did much—for a brief moment—to restore his equilibrium and his feeling of worth after the discomposing persecution in Switzerland. Ever the faithful friend, Du Peyrou had made arrangements for Rousseau to draw on his London bank. "My dear Citizen, may you like that country and find peace, tranquillity, and health there."

The wish was not to be granted. Already, in Paris, the seed-cloud of a great storm had been sown. Horace Walpole, a notoriously malicious character and a friend of the Encyclopedist group, had written a mocking letter, supposedly from Frederick the Great to Rousseau, whom that monarch had in fact protected. The letter invited Jean-Jacques to the Prussian Court.

Your reveries, which (I may say in passing) absorb you too much and too long, amuse me. . . . Show your enemies that you can sometimes have common sense. . . . If you persist in racking your brains to find new misfortunes, choose

[ 265 ]

the ones you prefer. I am a king, and I can arrange to suit your tastes; and, unlike your enemies, I shall stop persecuting you when you stop seeking your glory in persecution.

This spurious letter was probably inspired by a joking remark by Hume, though he never admitted it. Its style suitably polished by Mme. du Deffand and Helvétius, it made the rounds of the Paris salons in January, to the great merriment of the sophisticates. Jean-Jacques heard of it, but it was still only a vague rumor, and he attributed it to a Genevan source. Unruffled, he savored the articles about his life and his persecutions appearing in the *London Chronicle* and other newspapers. The great Garrick took him to a command performance at the Royal Theater in Drury Lane. In his Armenian costume, Rousseau attracted more attention from the King and Queen than the players. "It is incredible," Hume commented, "the enthusiasm for him in Paris and the curiosity in London."[1] He tried hard to learn English, but never achieved more than a fair reading knowledge. In June he admitted defeat to Du Peyrou: "[Thérèse] has not learned a single word of English; I had learned about thirty in London, all of which I have forgotten here [at Wooton], so undecipherable to my ears is their terrible gibbering." Nonetheless, he read all of Hume's letters, written in English.

Despite the severe weather—the winter of 1766 was one of the worst in memory—he made a number of excursions with Hume, who was doing everything to find him a suitable residence in the country. London was not possible. He wanted only to be left alone and to be forgotten by all men—so he affirmed in letters to several friends. A temporary retreat was located in Chiswick, at the home of a grocer, and he settled there on January 28 for the duration of the winter.

None too soon, for Thérèse was on her way, and she would have furnished great sport to the London *haut monde*. She could scarcely restrain her impatience to rejoin him, Jean-Jacques was informed by his friends in Switzerland. Making her way by stages through the bitter winter, she reached Paris on January 23. But how would she journey to the land of the Britons? Rousseau was worried. Then a stroke of luck: his charming Scots friend Boswell, having completed his tour of Corsica, was passing through Paris on his way home from the grand tour. He had hoped to see Rousseau there and talk to him about the island that had invited the Citizen of Geneva to write its constitution. He found, not the philosopher whom he had besieged at Môtiers, but his housekeeper, whom he had at the time thought rather attractive. At the townhouse of the Duchesse de Luxembourg he still found her attractive, even though she was forty and he twenty-four. She looked at him appealingly. "Mon Dieu, Monsieur, if we could make the journey together!" "That," replied the gallant Scot, "is what I came to suggest."

No time was lost. The next day a carriage was hired, and off they went, the "housekeeper" and her "chaperone." The journey was to last two weeks, and it was not to be an idle one. Hume, when he heard they were to travel together, foretold what was to happen. "He [Boswell] has such a rage for literature," he wrote to Mme. de Boufflers, "that I dread some event fatal to our friend's honour."

A discreet descendent of Boswell's has destroyed the twelve pages on which he carefully set down the intimate details of the amorous feats with which Thérèse and he occupied the time of their leisurely journey. Fortunately, Colonel Isham, who collected Boswell's private papers, was allowed to read the naughty sheets before their deletion, and he has summarized what he read.

No intention of laying siege to Thérèse seems to have occurred to Boswell before he started for London in her company. But the intimacy of travel and the proximity in which they found themselves at the inns each night soon precipitated an intrigue. The complications which ensued were so comic that it would have been a pity if they had been utterly lost to the world. In the simplicity of his conceit Boswell had thought to win the gratitude of Thérèse by allowing her to experience the superiority of his own vigorous youth over the senile fondness of Rousseau. But Thérèse stunned and humiliated him by flatly denying any superiority; she granted him youth and vigor, but maintained that he lacked art, and of the two she preferred art. Then, seeing him crestfallen, she begged him not to be hurt; there was still time, and she would take it upon herself to give him a thorough course of instruction *in arte amoris*. Boswell approached the first lesson not with eagerness, but with trepidation. The apartment in which they were lodged that night was a private dining room with the bed in an alcove at the end. Thérèse retired early, urging him to follow. Boswell, overcome with terror, devised a pretext for going back to the main room, where he seized a full bottle of wine which, by his direction, had been left in a corner, and drained it on the spot to bolster his flagging spirits.[2]

Boswell felt that Thérèse was treating him like a child, not a lover, and her lectures bored him. He brought up the subject of Rousseau, "hoping at least to gather a few *dicta philosophi* for his Journal." But Thérèse found that subject dull and wanted to turn back to the matter of her lessons. It was a mistake, Boswell finally reflected, to run away with an old man's mistress.

Only a few lines of Boswell's original account remain. They refer to the last day of the crossing. "Yesterday morning had gone to bed early, and had done it once—thirteen in all. Was really affectionate to her." That evening they rolled into London. Boswell was too excited sexually in the carriage to observe the city, despite his long absence.

This episode adds weight to our earlier surmise that Thérèse, before she went to live with Rousseau, had been a trollop ready to give herself for hire. As with Mme. de Warens, he had been credulous enough to believe her story of having been seduced, and by only one lover. Perhaps he was convinced that she, like Maman, had a frigid temperament. More likely, he suspected infidelities and doubted his paternity of at least some of her illegitimate children.

When they reached Chiswick on February 13, Boswell was glad to be relieved of his charge. In the grocer's parlor he watched the tender effusions of the reunited couple. "*Quanta oscula,* etc.!" he remarked cynically. "He seemed so oldish and weak you [Boswell] had no longer your old enthusiasm for him." Indeed his attitude toward the man he had once idolized was in the process of change. In Paris he had observed that almost all the people who counted spoke of Jean-Jacques in mocking or scornful terms. By nature "a born weathercock," Boswell was turning with the prevailing winds.

It was Rousseau who was to break with him, the following summer, when the quarrel with Hume had exploded and he was withdrawing into a despairing spiritual isolation. In reply to Boswell's complaint of neglect, he wrote sarcastically, on August 4, "Allow me to recommend to you in my turn to take care of your health, and especially to have yourself bled from time to time; I think it might do you some good." Had Thérèse confessed, as some biographers conclude? It would be strange for a woman to do so, especially one as wily as she. More likely, she pictured Boswell as having annoyed her with persistent solicitations, even as she had done once before, in the Gauffecourt episode.

Happy to have his "*gouvernante*" back, Rousseau turned his mind to other annoyances, such as a lost trunk, the delay in receiving the papers Du Peyrou was to send to him, papers he needed to continue work on his *Confessions.* The volumes of the *Encyclopédie* had not arrived, and he seems remarkably eager to have them. Dr. Tronchin was in Paris adding fuel to the flames of animosity against him. (Patients were flocking to the famous doctor's door—he would make no house calls. Pullets and sirloin were his prescription for diarrhea.) Nasty rumors about the concocted letter from Frederick continued to arrive in England. Why do you attribute it to Walpole? Rousseau asked Du Peyrou; that was incredible. Hume, at least, was constant and true. He could only agree with Keith's warm recommendation: "He is a real man of honour, a *preux chevalier.*"

Hume was still trying assiduously to find him a permanent residence. Rousseau leaned toward the isolation of Wales, where he had located "a lonely house amid forests, and rivulets, and rocks and mountains." Hume urged him strongly not to go that far, even enlisting Mme. de Boufflers' help. Keith proposed an inviting spot near Plymouth, where he would be the guest of a retired Frenchman and thus avoid the language problem. Hume made other suggestions. But Rousseau was characteristically indecisive. "Everyone pulls me in his own direction, and when I make a resolve they all conspire to make me change it." Thérèse made it all the more difficult. Once, when he had come to a decision, he stipulated that she take her meals at the *table d'hôte.* Unthinkable!

exclaimed his would-be host, a wealthy squire. How could an illiterate servant girl, without table manners, share a gentleman's table?

Thérèse was almost as notorious throughout Europe as Rousseau himself. Her reputation had preceded her to England. As Hume informed Mme. de Boufflers (not that she needed to be told), de Luze had warned him about her.

She passes for wicked and quarrelsome and tattling, and is thought to be the chief cause of his quitting Neuchâtel. He himself owns her to be so dull, that she never knows in what year of the Lord she is, nor in what month of the year, nor in what day of the month or week; and that she can never learn the different values of the pieces of money in any country. Yet she governs him as absolutely as a nurse does a child. In her absence his dog has acquired that ascendant. His affection for that creature is beyond all expression or conception.[3]

Jean-Jacques, as always, was ambivalent and unpredictable in regard to his Thérèse. He refused a dinner invitation from Lady Aylesbury and General Conway, the King's minister, on the ground that "Mlle. LeVasseur, a very good and estimable person, is not made to appear *dans les grandes compagnies.*"

The evidence of Hume's letters indicates great esteem for his protégé; at the same time he was fascinated by his eccentricities. In view of the approaching fracas, we must recall that from 1762 on, he had tried to befriend Rousseau in various ways, sometimes unknown to him. Now that Hume knew him in person, he found him amiable, polite, sociable, often gay. He so informed the Comtesse de Boufflers on January 19, 1766. But Jean-Jacques' hypochondria puzzled him:

He is one of the most robust men I have ever known. He passed ten hours in the night time above deck during the most severe weather, when all the seamen were almost frozen to death, and he caught no harm. . . . His wearing the Armenian dress is a pure whim, which, however, he has resolved never to abandon. He has an excellent warm heart, and, in conversation, kindles often a degree of heat which looks like inspiration. I love him much, and hope that I have a share in his affections.*

* *The Letters of David Hume*, ed. J. Y. T. Greig, Vol. II, p. 2. In the same letter, he informs the comtesse that Rousseau is writing his memoirs, and that he intends to portray himself "in such plain colours, that every one may boast that he knows himself and Jean-Jacques Rousseau." This news spread alarm among Rousseau's enemies. On February 11, Hume described Rousseau to Hugh Blair as "a very agreeable, amiable man; but a great humourist" (Greig, *op. cit.*, Vol. II, p. 13). Before he had left Paris, d'Holbach had warned him about Rousseau: "I tell you frankly that you are about to warm a serpent in your bosom." Hume mocks the warning: "I think I could live with him all my life, in mutual friendship and esteem. I am very sorry, that the matter is not likely to be put to a trial. I believe one great source of our concord is that neither he nor I are disputatious, which is not the case with any of them."

All quotations from Hume's letters will be found, in chronological order, in *The Letters of David Hume*, ed. J. Y. T. Greig, Vol. II; Oxford, 1932, except for letters appearing in later publications.

To his brother, Hume wrote: "He is a very modest, mild, well-bred, gentle-spirited and warm-hearted man, as ever I knew in my life," but he is also "the most singular man surely in the world."* He is surprised that this very sociable man should want to live in solitude, and that he is so independent as to have refused pensions from Frederick and other benefactors. At the same time Hume, with Rousseau's consent, was working with Conway to obtain a royal pension for him.

In still another letter to the Marquise de Barbentane (February 16), he defends Rousseau against the current charges of insincerity. "I declare to you, that I have never known a man more amiable and more virtuous than he appears to me."† He is gentle, modest, affectionate, disinterested, and above all sensitive. But he is also impatient and can be insulting.

He is apt to entertain groundless suspicions of his best friends; and his lively imagination, working upon them, feigns chimeras, and pushes him to great extremes. I have seen no instance of this disposition; but I cannot otherwise account for the violent animosities which have arisen between him and several men of merit, with whom he was once intimately connected; and some who love him much [doubtless the Luxembourg-Boufflers set] have told me that it is difficult to live much with him and preserve his friendship; but for my part I think I could pass all my life in his company, without any danger of our quarrelling.

Hume was right on all scores except the last. He did not suspect that Rousseau's suspiciousness was soon to be focused on him. In these lines we see, too, that Hume, an intimate of Diderot and the Holbachian circle, was not about to take sides against them.

He was so struck by Thérèse's power over Rousseau that he comes back to it more than once in his letters. "His maid," he tells the marquise, "has an uncontrolled authority over him." Rousseau had revealed to him that it was Thérèse's unwillingness that had made him cancel the project of a stay in Corsica. "His dog also has great influence with him." Because Sultan howled when they were leaving for the theater, Jean-Jacques turned back, and only Hume's insistence that the King and Queen would be disappointed not to see him induced him to relent.

Early in March, Rousseau posed in his Armenian dress for Allan Ramsay. The La Tour portrait ("the only one which resembled me") had shown him in a gallant costume and powdered wig, more the smiling *homme du monde* than the fierce satirist or the severe Cato. Because this appearance did not suit the plot, *ces messieurs* arranged (he was later to charge) to have Ramsay execute his somber chiaroscuro in which he was made to look like "a dark Cyclops."[4] It was part of the plot to

* Greig, *op. cit.*, Vol. II, pp. 7–8.
† *Ibid.*, Vol. II, p. 14.

destroy his image, his identity, his self. His certitude is not surprising; a mentally disturbed person has a distorted view of how he looks. The Ramsay portrait was to haunt him, as if it had captured and imprisoned for all time the nightmare of his soul, the distorted lineaments by which his enemies wished future generations to recognize him.

While posing at Ramsay's, Rousseau met Richard Davenport, a wealthy Cheshire merchant and a man of fine character. He was capable of understanding the eccentric genius, though not so completely as Keith or with his warmth of affection. He invited Rousseau to settle at Wooton Hall, near Dovedale, Derbyshire, where he resided only occasionally. Having strained everyone's patience by his indecisiveness, Jean-Jacques finally consented to be Davenport's guest, on the condition that he accept thirty pounds a year.*

In the last days preceding his departure for Wooton, Rousseau began to conceive some doubts about Hume. When he asked Hume whether it was true that Walpole had disseminated "Frederick's" letter, the answer was evasive, and Rousseau could not pry a yes or a no from him. Doubtless Hume did not want to compromise Walpole, but Rousseau immediately became suspicious. Later Hume's evasiveness on this occasion became one sign of the plot. Then he asked Hume to recommend a reliable person to bring his papers over from Paris. To his surprise, Hume proposed Walpole. It occurred to him that the translation of Du Peyrou's letters against his Swiss persecutors, which Hume had agreed to take in hand, had made no progress. His protector was evasive about this, too. At about the same time, he learned from his London cousin, Jean Rousseau, that the son of one of his bitterest enemies, Dr. Tronchin, was living with Hume. Then Hume had the imprudence to defend d'Alembert. Walpole, Tronchin, d'Alembert—the conjunction was scarcely fortuitous.

An innocent deception made matters worse. Hume agreed to Davenport's proposal that they should spare Rousseau the expenses of transportation by pretending that a chaise was to leave for Ashburn (near Wooton) on Friday, March 19, on its return journey, so that a special

* Some French or Swiss scholars, in their endeavour to prove Hume a villain and to justify Rousseau, have been guilty of mistranslating passages in Hume's letters. One instance concerns the move to Wooton. Musset-Pathay makes a big point of his writing to Mme. de Boufflers that he is pleased with the move (April 3), and at his having earlier written to the Marquise de Barbentane (February 16) that he did everything possible to prevent it. "Let us try to understand why the same man says to one of these ladies that he has tried in vain to foil the project, and to the other that he is glad to see it realized" (C. G., XV, 144, n. 2). It happens that what Hume had written on February 16 was something quite different: "In a few weeks he will certainly remove *to Wales*. . . . I have endeavoured to throw a hundred obstacles in the way, but nothing can divert him; his obstinacy here is an invincible proof of his sincerity" (Greig, *op. cit.*, Vol. II, p. 16, italics added). Even more curious, the more common accusation leveled against Hume is that he wanted to "bury" Rousseau at Wooton. Yet the evidence is absolutely clear on this point: it was Rousseau who wanted to "bury" himself from the public view and concern, and it is he who chose Wooton.

arrangement would not be required. Hume so informed Rousseau, in a note, on the thirteenth or fourteenth. Rousseau was extraordinarily alert to deceptions, even benevolent ones. He was abnormally suspicious about the most trivial gift, taking it either as a form of obligation that threatened his independence, or (as he once admitted to d'Ivernois) as the sign of some secret purpose. On the eve of the departure, an extraordinary scene took place in Hume's lodgings. Rousseau, as Hume recounts it,[5] laid bare his suspicions, and cried that he would rather live like a beggar than be treated like a child. Hume denied complicity, whereupon Rousseau started to pace the room. Suddenly he sat on Hume's knee, put his arms around his neck, kissed him and wept, and asked for forgiveness. "I love you, I esteem you; and not an instance of your kindness is thrown away upon me." Hume responded by embracing him "twenty times, with a plentiful effusion of tears. I think no scene of my life was ever more affecting." On March 30, Hume wrote a note of apology assuring Rousseau that his only part in the deception was to have concealed it.

Hume was unable to understand the absoluteness of his protégé's principles, and there was no way to overcome this psychological barrier. Rousseau's emotional outbreak was a desperate attempt to maintain the confidence and the rapport he so greatly needed, feeling, as he did, disoriented and isolated in a strange land.

Rousseau's own narration of these events is in several important respects different from Hume's.[6] His imagination is feverishly at work, bringing all his recollections together and interpreting them with obsessional single-mindedness. He had been worried and suspicious. Expected letters had not arrived. Others, which came through Hume, seemed to have been opened.* Then, one evening, Hume could scarcely forebear looking over Rousseau's shoulder as he was writing a letter. When it was finished, he insisted on posting it. Jean-Jacques declined, and gave it to a visitor, Lord Newnham, who promptly asked Hume's lackey to give it to his own. Rousseau's intuition told him that Hume would follow hard upon the heels of the servant—and he did. He did not doubt that the letter was read before it was sent. After supper, the two sat silently before the fire. Hume was staring at him. The look was relentless, at once burning and mocking. He tried to stare back. But such was the malevolent intensity of that look, he was seized with a trembling and had to lower his eyes. Where did "le bon David" get those eyes? It was at this point that Rousseau, filled with a sudden wave of remorse, embraced him and sobbed, "No, no, David Hume is not a traitor; if he were not the best of men, he would have to be the basest." To this tender effusiveness Hume responded with "cold caresses," a few taps on

---

* In fact, one or two letters were delayed, Hume having removed his lodgings. One letter (from d'Ivernois) was unsealed, doubtless a routine police measure, if not an accident.

the back, and some embarrassed words: *"Mon cher Monsieur, quoi donc, mon cher Monsieur!"*

Hume later protested that Rousseau's account was cleverly concocted for effect, and indeed it was, for Hume had promptly written a detailed account of the amazing episode to Blair and Mme. de Boufflers, before Rousseau had leveled any accusations against him. Nonetheless Hume, although *au fond* an emotional person, was accustomed to the reserve characteristic of his compatriots. He was undoubtedly embarrassed by Jean-Jacques' unabashed emotionalism and perhaps was unable to share openly in it. Even if he did say *"mon cher Monsieur,"* his *gêne* was not *prima facie* evidence of bad conscience, as Rousseau took it to be, but only of a temperamental and cultural inability to respond in kind.

When Rousseau reached Wooton on March 22, the unpleasantness momentarily seemed less important, but he was still deeply troubled underneath. Immediately he sent a letter back to Hume with the carriage driver. He was delighted with his new home. "One of the happy things in my life will be to think that I owe this to you." He begged Hume to love him and to keep his friendship for him, and never again to indulge in ruses.

Wooton Hall struck him at once as charming and congenial. A neat house built on a slope, with a large terrace and the thickest lawn he had ever seen, looked out over a pleasant landscape punctuated by occasional farmhouses or more pretentious homes. A winding stream with the murmur of its cascades came down from the high hills. The valley, with its enchanting nooks, would supply his main need, long walks and opportunities to "herborize," as soon as its mantle of snow melted. The bedroom of his apartment, on the second floor, was in the forepart, and so had a magnificent view on three sides. The only problem was inability to communicate with the servants, except through Thérèse's sign language. There was the compensation of not being annoyed by intruders. "I am not only the master, but my own master, which is more important." He wrote Coindet on March 29 that he was regenerated and rebaptized. Nothing that went on back on the Continent could bother him any more. It was goodbye now to the acrid smoke of glory. Jealousy, intrigue, persecutions—none of those could touch him again. What did it matter if a new document was put out against him in Geneva, or if Frederick had unleashed a crushing thunderbolt against the rebellious pastors of Neuchâtel? Or if Geneva was about to legalize a theater, despite the *Lettre à d'Alembert* and all that had ensued?

As usual the euphoria passed. On the day he wrote to Coindet, he told Du Peyrou that he had only two friends he could trust, Keith and him. The muted apprehensions were stirred up, the suspicions fanned into hot flames. Only two days after his letter to Coindet, he informed d'Ivernois, in Geneva, that he no longer trusted Hume. His friendship with the Encyclopedists, Tronchin's son, the opened letters—to these grievances a new one was added. Whereas he had always had a good press in England, now the papers either ignored him or spoke ill of him. "I thought I was at the end of my misfortunes, and they are only beginning. . . . I cannot yet fathom his intent, but I cannot help believing it to be sinister." From now on, all letters must be carefully sealed, and the seal submitted to vigilant scrutiny on their receipt.

It was on the third of April that the St. James's Chronicle published the purported letter from Frederick, by then notorious, in French and in English. Two days later the English text was reprinted in two other newspapers. On the seventh Rousseau wrote a letter of protest to the Chronicle. "I inform you, Monsieur, that this letter was fabricated in Paris and—a fact that upsets and rends my heart—the impostor has accomplices in England." He was absolutely certain that the "letter" was the work of d'Alembert, that arch-hypocrite who posed as his friend only to stab him the better. He scoffed at the idea that Walpole could have written it and assured everyone that he recognized d'Alembert's style. He asked Lord Strafford to use his influence to have his letter printed. His enemies would try to prevent it, he assured him. "The public should know that there are secret traitors who, under the mask of a perfidious friendship, are working relentlessly to dishonor me." There is, then, no longer any doubt in his mind. The specter of Môtiers rose up in his imagination. Were his enemies preparing to stir up riots against him? Were they trying to force him to leave England?*

---

* Musset-Pathay, one of Rousseau's nineteenth-century editors, in order to make Hume an accomplice, mistranslates a passage in his letter to the Marquise de Barbentane (Histoire de la vie et des ouvrages de J. J. Rousseau, Vol. I, pp. 113–14, reproduced in C. G., XV, 63). These are Hume's words: "Assure her [Mme. de Boufflers] that Horace Walpole's letter was not founded on any pleasantry of mine: the only pleasantry in that letter came from his own mouth, in my company, at Lord Ossory's table; which my Lord remembers very well" (Greig, op. cit., Vol. II, p. 16). The French "translation" reads: "The only pleasantry I allowed myself relative to the supposed letter from the king of Prussia was made by me at Lord Ossory's table." Traduttore, traditore! French scholars who have relied on the translation have been misled.

The matter, however, is rather more complicated. Hume, in his later reply to Rousseau and summation of the whole affair (Exposé succint de la contestation qui s'est élevée entre M. Hume et M. Rousseau; Paris, 1766) affirms that he did not know the contents of the false letter before it was published. However, it is difficult to believe that he had not heard it talked about while in Paris and it is still more unlikely that General Conway (to whom Walpole wrote about it gleefully, including a copy, on January 16 or 17) did not show it to him or at least tell him about it. Yet Hume did not inform Rousseau who the author of the letter was. On the nineteenth, he wrote to Mme. de Boufflers, "M. Rousseau says that the king of Prussia's letter is a forgery and he suspects M. de Voltaire." (The statement was factual. Later Rousseau's suspicions fastened on d'Alembert.) A French scholar, Henri Roddier ("A Propos de la querelle Rousseau-Hume. Précisions chronologiques"), among many other vague and tenuous suppositions, points out that when Hume received Rousseau's grande accusation of July 10, he wrote to his friend Hugh Blair, "I own, that I was very anxious about this affair but this letter has totally relieved me." However, there is no reason to suppose that Hume was referring specifically to this incident. I take it from the context that he is referring to Rousseau's accusations as a whole, which he summarizes in such fashion as to bring out the abnormal suspiciousness on which they were based (Greig,

On April 9, Rousseau sent out three letters. In one he accused the tardy English publishers of Du Peyrou's letters of connivance with the plotters. The others informed Mme. de Verdelin and Mme. Boy de la Tour that he had been betrayed. He makes his first open accusation of Hume and gives the details of all he believes Hume has done. Now, for the first time, he refers to an incident that occurred at Roye, where the three travelers had spent the first night after their departure from Paris. We shall refer to the version in Rousseau's *grande lettre d'accusation* of July 10, where it is related in greater detail as the rhetorical crescendo to all the other charges, and is associated in particular with the famous "stare."

We were sleeping in the same room, and several times during the night I heard him cry out in French, with extreme vehemence: *"Je tiens Jean-Jacques Rousseau!"* ["I've got Jean-Jacques Rousseau!"] I do not know whether he was awake or whether he was sleeping. The expression is remarkable on the tongue of a man who knows French too well to mistake the strength and the choice of his words. Nevertheless I took and at that time could not help taking those words in a favorable sense, although the tone indicated it even less than the phrase. It was a tone which it is impossible to convey to you, and which corresponds quite well with the look of which I have spoken. Each time he said those words I felt a shudder of fright of which I was not the master. . . . And there is not a night when those words, *"Je tiens Jean-Jacques Rousseau,"* do not ring in my ears as if I were hearing them anew.

Hume, in his reply to Rousseau's accusations, could not very well deny the allegation; but he pointed out that it would be rather odd for him to dream in French. The reply is of course not conclusive. Hume had been speaking French all day, and always spoke to Rousseau in that language, so that the association in the dream may well have produced the expression. Yet one must also note that on April 3, Hume once again summarized his opinion of Jean-Jacques in a way that seems objective, but not hostile.

I must however confess, that I have not the consolation to think he will long be happy there [at Wooton]. Never was a man, who so well deserves happiness, so little calculated by nature to attain it. The extreme sensibility of his character is one great cause; but still more, the frequent and violent fits of spleen and discontent and impatience, to which, either from the constitution of his mind or body, he is so subject. These disqualify him for society, and are the chief reason why he so much affects solitude. When his health and good-humour return, his lively imagination gives him so much entertainment, that company,

---

*op. cit.*, Vol. II, pp. 63–4). Of what can we be certain? Only that Hume did not wish to betray Walpole, and that he tried to isolate himself from whatever had been done in Paris. Beyond this, there are only suspicions and hypotheses—for instance, that the "pleasantry" at the end of the spurious letter was Hume's own witticism, which Walpole used in his fabrication, and that Hume was concerned lest any imputation fall on him. But there is nothing to indicate a plot.

by disturbing his musing and meditation, is rather troublesome to him; so that, in either case, he is not framed for society. He is commonly however the best company in the world, when he will submit to live with men. Every one who saw him here, admires the simplicity of his manners, his natural unaffected politeness, the gaiety and finesse of his conversation. For my part, I never saw a man, and very few women, of a more agreeable commerce.[7]

As at the Hermitage and at Môtiers, Thérèse was to be a major contributing cause of Rousseau's growing dissatisfaction, suspiciousness, and emotional turbulence. In London she had aroused him about the "hostility" of the domestic staff at Hume's lodgings. At Wooton, it did not take her long to start filling his ears with complaints about Davenport's servants and to quarrel with them, even without any English. Mme. de Verdelin warned her bluntly, in her letter to Rousseau of April 27, to hold her "female tongue" and to stop pestering him with complaints. When Jean-Jacques spoke of his suspicions, Thérèse doubtless encouraged them, for she did not want to stay at Wooton, or even in England, where she was deprived of her greatest pleasure, gossiping.

Like many people of low intelligence and extreme ignorance she had a highly developed animal cunning which she knew how to use with good effect. It is one of the curious paradoxes of Rousseau's life that this "stupid female," as Mme. de Verdelin called her, should have gained such an extraordinary ascendancy over a man who was in so many ways her superior.[8]

Later Davenport was to write to Hume about her quarreling with his ninety-year-old housekeeper, adding, "His Gouvernante has absolute power over him and without doubt more or less influences all his actions" (July 6). By all accounts an expert cook, she doubtless disliked the English cuisine and insisted on supervising Rousseau's meals. Rousseau's own comment about Thérèse, in the *Confessions*, is revealing: "But this very limited, if you will very stupid person, is often of excellent counsel in difficult situations. Often, in Switzerland, in England, in France, in the catastrophes in which I found myself, she saw what I myself did not see, and gave me the best advice to follow."

The quarrel gradually came to a head over the affair of the King's pension, which Hume had sought through the intervention of Conway. On May 2, Conway informed him that the King had consented to give Rousseau a pension of one hundred pounds, "desiring only that it might be a private one." On the same day, Hume informed a French friend (possibly Malesherbes) of the news. Some have pounced upon this as a sign of his enmity. This is an absurd exaggeration. There was no monstrous wrong in his telling another friend and protector of Rousseau about the latter's good fortune. He states, quite accurately, that the secrecy was pleasing to Jean-Jacques, and there is no sign of "Tartufferie" in his letters.[9] Nor can we call him a false friend on the grounds that he has come to understand his protégé's character as lucidly as he does understand it, without blindness, and that he conveys his judgment with forthrightness:

One of his little weaknesses is to want to make himself interesting by complaining of his poverty and ill health; but I have discovered by chance that he has some financial resources, slight in truth, but which he concealed from us when he gave us an account of his financial state. As for his health, to me it seems robust rather than weak, unless you count the fits of melancholy and spleen to which he is subject. It is a pity. He is very likable in his manners; he has an honest and sensitive heart; but these moods estrange him from society, make him ill-tempered, and sometimes give his behavior an appearance of strangeness and brusqueness, traits which are not natural to him.*

Hume, however, is guilty of one interesting deception in this letter. It is not true that his discoveries were made "by chance." He had made enquiries of Mme. de Boufflers and Mme. de Barbentane concerning Rousseau's financial resources and asked them in turn to make discreet enquiries. Later Rousseau reproached him for having tried to pump Thérèse on the same score. On the other hand, Jean-Jacques had not been honest with him about the matter. The canny Scot obviously suspected as much, with good reason, but did not want Malesherbes to know that he had been prying into Rousseau's private affairs.†

Other incidents aggravated Rousseau's susceptibilities. He may not have known about Walpole's anonymous reply to his protest in the *Chronicle*, "Lettre d'Emile à Jean-Jacques Rousseau," which Mme. du Deffand circulated in manuscript. Letters against him were appearing in the London papers, some doubtless by Walpole. There were cartoons, too, and this public ridicule was a torture to him. Other letters defended him, but these counted not at all against the "evidence" of a plot, and he refers only to the hostile ones. In April he heard of the "Lettre de M. de Voltaire au docteur Jean-Jacques Pansophe," a slashing vilification, which was soon to appear in English. A "tale" in the *St. James's Chronicle* depicted him as a quack who forces everyone to take his pills and then is chased from place to place because of the ill effects of his last prescription (the *Lettres de la montagne*). He must have smiled bitterly on reading Deleyre's letter from Parma: "At last you will have found a haven in that island which has always been called *hospitibus ferum*."

His own letters are increasingly unhappy. He knows there is a plot, or he would not have lost the great esteem in which he was once held by the English. There is a secret cause, a hidden villain, a group of traitors taking advantage of his helplessness. He is alone and friendless. The scoundrels, by their furtive slanders, have destroyed a lifetime of moral

* Greig, *op. cit.*, Vol. II, p. 319.

† In the *Concise Account*, Hume would reply that he had only one tête-à-tête with Thérèse. "I admit that it did not occur to me to talk to her about anything except M. Rousseau." This reply is obviously evasive.

uprightness and untarnished honor. His letter of April 9 to Mme. de
Verdelin had already directly accused Hume, citing sly remarks made in
his presence, the hostile attitude of his circle, the night at Roye, and the
spying on his correspondence. That honorable lady, protector of one
and friend of the other, found the charges hard to swallow. Why, she
asked Rousseau on April 27, should Hume want to dishonor you in
England, when he has tried in every way to help you? Before her and
before other people she knows, he has always spoken of Rousseau in the
highest terms. Keith replied to a similar letter in similar terms. Either
Rousseau's suspicions were paranoid, or Hume's devious game had succeeded in taking in all the honorable people who were not "allied" with
him.

When Hume reassured Jean-Jacques on May 2 that there were no
calumnies against his morals in the London papers, only a satirical letter
of Voltaire's, the reassurance produced a countereffect. Carefully, he
composed a long letter to Malesherbes (May 10), but for some reason
decided not to send it. It was a dress rehearsal for the forthcoming
indictment of Hume, and drips pathos and self-pity. The famous Rousseauian rhetoric is not missing. Just to think that the man who "holds
his arms out to me in my distress, crushes me when I have thrown myself
into them. . . . If I live a thousand years, I feel that never until my last
hour will David Hume cease to haunt me."

At this point Rousseau threw his first counterblow. He had decided to
strike in a different direction. He informed Conway on May 12 that he
could not at the present time accept the King's pension, feeling too
depressed by new misfortunes which no one could have foreseen. Hume,
to say the least, was put out. To Davenport he expressed his indignation.
Rousseau had let the matter come to a conclusion, with great trouble to
a number of people. Now he slights the King, with not even a word to
inform Hume, much less an apology. On the same day, May 17, he
protested to Rousseau. He assures Jean-Jacques that Walpole regrets
having given him offense; there can be no other cause for this "affliction" of his, which gives Hume great uneasiness. To Mme. de Boufflers
he wrote more openly.

I am afraid, my dear Madam, that notwithstanding our friendship and our
enthusiasm for this philosopher, he has been guilty of an extravagance the
most unaccountable and most blameable that is possible to be imagined. . . .
You see that our friend objects to the pension's being a secret; whereas, in his
letter to Lord Marischal, he said that he liked it better on that account.

He cannot imagine what causes Rousseau's distress and will endeavor
to find out from Davenport whether it is something other than Walpole's letter.

He did so at once. His May 17 letter to Davenport expresses his
bewilderment. Davenport, who was spending three weeks at Wooton,

informed him that his guest was in excellent humor. Hume was more perplexed—some say worried—than ever. Rousseau had told Conway that he was desperately unhappy. He decided to press the matter of the pension further.

Rousseau did not reply to Hume's letter. Nor did he heed Keith's reassurance about Tronchin's son: he too is obliged to receive him, out of friendship for those who have recommended the young man. Rousseau had written again to Mme. de Verdelin (May 25), denouncing both d'Alembert and Hume as traitors. He will give up all correspondence, die to the world, live in himself and for himself, write his memoirs and tell everything—as no man before has ever done. Her reply ridiculed Rousseau's suspicions and spoke of the innumerable occasions on which Hume had gone out of his way to help him. No rational argument, no evidence could counter his obsession.

Rousseau was so convinced that his correspondence was being tampered with that he began to write to d'Ivernois using a code for names. He longs only to go back to Neuchâtel, to live with his dear Du Peyrou and die near him. It is the only castle in Spain he has left.

The publication in the *St. James's Chronicle* on June 5 of an anonymous letter sent his temper to a new high. It was to become a chief piece of evidence in Rousseau's indictment; two of its three charges, he concluded, were facts known only to Hume: that he had treated his cousin Jean coldly in Hume's presence, and that he changed friends frequently, opening his door to the great and closing it to the humble. In his *Concise Account* Hume claimed that he had never seen the piece, "neither before nor after its publication; nor has it come to the knowledge of anybody to whom I have spoken of it."[10] While some may consider the reply scarcely credible, the letter was almost certainly written by a Swiss, Deyverdun, and Jean-Jacques' statement that only Hume could have known of some of the facts stated in it is patently absurd, as they could easily have been public gossip at the time.

Hume now brought the matter of the pension to a head. He made a new application through Conway, requesting that the condition of secrecy, which Rousseau had at first welcomed but which now struck him as conspiratorial, be dropped. On June 19 he so informed Rousseau and entreated him not to expose His Majesty to a second refusal. Two days later he again begged Rousseau for a reply and asked Davenport to use his influence on his guest. At the same time he made an enquiry of Davenport which may be interpreted as the expression of genuine bewilderment, or else, as various biographers have preferred, as a cunning device to find out how much Rousseau suspected or knew:

Were he not the most unaccountable man in the World, I should be very much scandalized and very much offended at this long silence. After his arrival at Wooton, I received a Letter from him full of the highest expression of esteem and affection; and as there has been since no intercourse between us, except in this affair, where he sees the strongest proof of my friendship, it is impossible for me to imagine that he can in any way be disgusted with me: yet perhaps something has struck his Fancy, which I shall never be able to guess or imagine. Did you ever hear from him any surmises of that kind? Or have you ever discovered what that deep affliction was, which he said overwhelmed him about the time of your arrival at Wooton? Could your people ever discover it from Mademoiselle? Or was there really any affliction at all?[11]

Included in Hume's letter to Rousseau was one from Mme. de Boufflers, expressing her surprise about his melancholy, as Hume had described it to her. Surely, she ventures, there can be no cause for this depression; the spurious letter, a silly thing, cannot be that important. On the twenty-first, Du Peyrou warned Rousseau not to break with Hume. A public quarrel with a man who had done so much for him would only furnish fresh ammunition for his enemies. It was too late. On the twenty-third, Rousseau sent Hume his first letter of accusation. "I thought that my silence," he began, "interpreted by your conscience, said enough; but, since it enters into your plans not to hear it, I shall speak." Hume knows, he continues, what his own secret conduct has been. He wants no more favors from his "patron" and will never write to him again. "I give free rein to your friends' maneuvers and your own, and with little regret, I abandon to you my reputation during my lifetime, convinced that some day justice will be done both of us."

Did Hume read in these words a covert threat referring to the *Confessions*? Surely, he might have let the altercation drop there. What little fallout would have ensued would have been favorable to him. Whether he was sincerely distressed or fearful of the future, according to the interpretation one prefers, he did not choose that course. Instead, he appealed to Davenport, on June 26, sending him a copy of Rousseau's letter. "You and you alone can aid me in the most critical affair which, during the course of my whole life, I have been engaged in. . . . You will be astonished, as I was, at the monstrous ingratitude, ferocity and frenzy of the man."* So upset was he, that he dispatched a similar letter to another residence of Davenport's. "I shall not have peace of mind," he adds, "till you have met with this man, and have given me an account of your conference with him." If we are to believe that Hume was the mastermind of a vast plot, then he had indeed succeeded, or was about to. He insisted that Rousseau detail and justify his accusations, or "pass for a liar and calumniator." Simultaneously, he made the same demand in a letter to Rousseau which begins: "As I am conscious of having ever acted towards you the most friendly part, of having ever given you the

---

* Roddier (*op. cit.*, p. 465) furnishes another example of reading into Hume's letters what is not there. He asserts that Hume charged Rousseau with refusing the pension in order to free himself from the burden of gratitude, and with the intention of "obtaining it later by his own means." The latter phrase is a purely gratuitous addendum. Roddier, it must be added, does not believe in "the plot."

most tender, the most active proofs of sincere affection, you may judge of my extreme surprise on perusing your epistle." He adds a warning: Rousseau should know that he had kept his earlier effusive letter of gratitude.

It would seem that Hume, confident of his innocence, was demanding that everything be brought into the open. This is the obvious interpretation. Those who believe in the plot claim that he was so certain of having covered his tracks that Rousseau would only make a fool of himself, even degrade himself, in the public view. But why should Hume have wanted to do this?

It is nonetheless evident that Hume was growing ever more disturbed, especially when no reply from Rousseau was forthcoming. He requested a friend, the Reverend Hugh Blair, never to show anyone the letters he had written in favor of his protégé, and to recover any copies from any correspondent to whom he might have sent them. Already (July 1) he is thinking of making a public affair of the squabble:

He is surely the blackest and most atrocious villain, beyond comparison, that now exists in the world; and I am heartily ashamed of anything I ever wrote in his favour. I know you will pity me, when I tell you, that I am afraid I must publish this to the world in a pamphlet, which must contain an account of the whole transaction between us. My only comfort is, that the matter will be so clear as not to leave to any mortal the smallest possibility of a doubt. You know how dangerous any controversy on a disputable point would be with a man of his talents. I know not where the miscreant will now retire to, in order to hide his head from this infamy.

A week later, with still no word from Rousseau, Hume tells Davenport that he no longer expects a reply. "I see that this whole affair is a complication of wickedness and madness; and you may believe I repent heartily, that I ever had any connections with so pernicious and dangerous a man." With a shrewd understanding of the workings of Rousseau's unconscious mind, he adds that Jean-Jacques was doubtless seeking an opportunity "of picking a quarrel with me, in order to cancel at once all his past obligations to me." And he asks Davenport to prod Rousseau into a reply.

Three days later he requested Davenport to send him copies of his letters to Rousseau, the latter having sent some to his host. "It would be of no consequence for me to have copies of them, were he not the most dangerous man in the world, on account of his malice and his talents." How had Rousseau reacted, he enquires again, to his recent letter?

Rousseau had read Hume's letter of June 26 to Davenport. The accusation of black ingratitude demanded a reply. Whether or not Rousseau, left to himself, would have made one is uncertain. On July 6, Davenport informed Hume that he had gone to Wooton on the first and had had a long conference with him. He insisted that Rousseau make "an open answer." Rousseau, he reports, quite upset by this, gave him a long history which, with his faulty French, he could not follow. Davenport concludes: "In short, I perceive his disorder is jealousy; he thinks you are fond of some *savant hommes* whom he unfortunately thinks his enemies."

The answer was finally sent on July 10. Rousseau had taken days to prepare it, working up the unsent letter to Malesherbes. A huge document, it comprises eighteen folio pages of manuscript, some twenty-five pages of printed text. But not length alone, it may well be imagined, had required so much time. The letter again shows Rousseau as a master rhetorician, and in this sense, at least, justifies Hume's fears.

Of hard evidence of a plot he really has nothing at all to offer. But all the charges are brought together, marshaled in a crescendo that follows not chronology but forensic effectiveness, narrated in a style that combines eloquence with subtle changes in tone. Following an old tactic of his, he admits some good things in order to make the others seem more believable. Jean-Jacques could have been one of the great barristers of all time. He begins plaintively: "I am ill, Monsieur, and scarcely in a condition to write; but you insist on an explanation, and I shall have to give it to you." He does not live in the world, and is ignorant of its ways. He only knows what he feels to be true. The first care of villainous plotters is to make sure there are no juridical proofs against them; Rousseau thus turns the very fact that he has no proofs into an accusation. "Inner certainty allows another kind of proofs," the only proofs needed by an *honnête homme*. He will speak with his usual openness, for he is "the enemy of all artifice." "You ask, with great confidence, that I name your accuser. That accuser, Monsieur, is the only man in the world who, testifying against you, could have been listened to by me: it is yourself."

In this fashion Rousseau brings together all his suspicions, persuasively tries to turn them into facts, interprets them in his own way, and by their very mass and number succeeds in writing a condemnatory document, one which would require another clever lawyer to take apart—or at least someone who knew Rousseau and his compulsion to judge the actions of others in the light of what his might have been in the same circumstances. Thus, he cannot conceive that Hume did not recognize his intimations of no-confidence, even his insults; and the wilful nonrecognition is the sign of guilt. Insinuations abound: Hume was jealous of the way he was treated by the Prince de Conti; his generosity toward Rousseau was motivated by the desire to enhance his own reputation. His insistence on having Ramsay do his portrait was too ostentatious. (Hume pointed out that the idea was Ramsay's own.) If Voltaire's letter against him appeared in English translation, Hume must have had a hand in it. Yes, Hume took much trouble and time to help him, but we must evaluate benefactions by their results. Guilt by association is introduced at the appropriate point. Why are his enemies Hume's friends?*

We see another example of Rousseau's procedures in the accusation, already made to Mme. de Verdelin and others, that when Thérèse arrived in London, Hume's staff treated her, and him, with hatred and disdain. From this, he says, one can readily conclude how Hume must have spoken about his two guests. Am I guilty, Hume was to reply, because my servants, who do not know a word of French, looked at him coldly? As for the pension, Hume deliberately put him in the position of having to refuse it, "for assuredly I had to, or else make myself the vilest of men by voluntarily incurring an obligation to the man who had betrayed me." Even deliberate insolence enters Rousseau's plea, when three times he says that he (figuratively) "slapped my patron in the face," and that each time it was ignored—obviously the reaction of a guilty man. And yet . . . and yet this emotional inculpation ends with an emotional plea to Hume, asking him to exculpate himself, if he can. Highly significant, this unexpected plea shows Rousseau to be aware of his own thought processes, suspicious of his own accumulations of suspicions even as he convinces himself that he is absolutely convinced of them, unable to control the tide that has swept him on into his denunciation of the villainous plot.†

Mossner's summation is excellent:

Granted his extreme sensibility, his persecution mania, his candid admission that "I know only what I feel," the malignant whisperings of Thérèse LeVasseur, the course of publications in the English journals, Hume's inarticulateness in expressing affection, the basic inability of the two philosophers to understand one another in social intercourse—granted all these facts, Rousseau's letter is consistent with the complete logical consistency of dementia. It remains one of the most brilliant and fascinating documents ever produced by a disordered mentality.[12]

The receipt of Rousseau's indictment on July 15 prompted Hume to write six letters. Rousseau's letter, he informs Blair, "is a perfect frenzy. . . . He there tells me that d'Alembert, Horace Walpole and I had from the first entered into a combination to ruin him; and had ruined him."

* Hume protested that he had never met either Voltaire or Tronchin, and had only once received a letter from the former. "As for M. d'Alembert, I am proud that he is my friend."

† We should note Grimsley's explanation of Rousseau's behavioral pattern. "If the other upon whom he was emotionally dependent did not behave in the appropriate way, then Rousseau was compelled to have recourse to a different, more desperate kind of strategy: the appeal for sympathy and affection having failed, he had to provoke him by more aggressive means. The other is attacked and reviled, but in a way that is intended to elicit the contrary reaction: he is repelled in order to be brought closer. Painful, heart-rending estrangement will be followed (Jean-Jacques hopes) by rapturous reunion" (R. Grimsley, *Jean-Jacques Rousseau: A Study in Self-awareness*, pp. 208-9).

To Mme. de Boufflers he reviews his relationship with Jean-Jacques, and explains that he had really thought some calumniator had poisoned his protégé's mind. Rousseau's "counterfeit distress," at a time when Davenport wrote that he was in excellent spirits, proves that he was deliberately trying "to stab" him. Actually, Hume hesitates between this interpretation and a feeling of relief—the man was mad, not wicked. What should he do now? "Should I give the whole account to the public, as I am advised by several of my friends. . . . I utterly ruin this unhappy man. . . . I cannot resolve to commit such a piece of cruelty. . . . But on the other hand, it is extremely dangerous for me to be entirely silent. He is at present composing a book, in which it is very likely he may fall on me with some atrocious lie." If Rousseau publishes his memoirs posthumously, his own justification will lose much of its credibility—assuming he is still alive to make one. Clearly worried about what Rousseau might do to his posthumous reputation, he asks Mme. de Boufflers to consult Conti and Mme. de Luxembourg, and to forward their advice. Another letter, to d'Alembert, somewhat more detailed, is not dissimilar, but he is less restrained in his anger:

His plan was to have a pension offered to him to have the glory of refusing it, and at the same time to efface at a stroke, by picking a quarrel, all the obligations he may have to me, and which weigh too heavily on his pride. He was also looking for a quarrel which would make himself talked about, although much to his disadvantage.[13]

The last statement is unfair to Rousseau and clearly reveals the animosity Jean-Jacques had succeeded in evoking in his former protector. As for his projected history of the quarrel, Hume informs d'Alembert that he intends only to circulate it among mutual acquaintances, and to send a copy to Rousseau, with a list of recipients, so that he might have an opportunity to justify himself.

Rousseau felt constrained to inform Keith of what he had done. Again he asks only to be forgotten. He is busy writing his life, "not my external life, as others have done, but my real life, the story of my most secret feelings. I shall do what no man has done before me, and what probably no other will do in the future. I shall tell everything, the good, the bad, everything in short. I feel that I have a soul that can show itself." If Keith replied, his letter has disappeared; but early in the month he had assured Rousseau that Hume was innocent and a true friend.

On July 22, Hume did reply to Rousseau, on one count only. He condemns him for having altered the true account of the scene during which Jean-Jacques had thrown his arms about his neck and wept. "It necessarily follows that either you or I are liar [sic]." Doubtless Rousseau has thought that Hume could not disprove his version of something that occurred in private. But he reminds Rousseau that he possesses his letter of March 22, which confirms the truth of his own account, and warns him that he had related the story, hard upon the event, to Davenport, Mme. de Boufflers, and other friends. No one will believe that at that time he was preparing an apology. And who will believe that because he was plunged in reverie, he was staring at Rousseau with the eyes of a traitor?

Meanwhile Hume had been marshaling his friends in Paris, and they rallied to his support. The signal was his letters to d'Holbach on June 27 and July 1, recounting what had occurred. D'Alembert and his mistress, Mlle. de Lespinasse, replied with a joint letter of support (July 6);* but d'Alembert, on his part, urged Hume not to publish an account which could only splash mud on both antagonists. Adam Smith, then in Paris, called Rousseau a base rascal, but urged Hume not to risk disturbing the tranquillity of his whole life by unmasking the hypocrite in public—precisely what his foe would like. "Your whole friends here wish you not to write, the Baron, d'Alembert, Madame Riccoboni, Mademoiselle Riancourt, Mr. Turgot, etc." "It is a fine thing," wrote d'Holbach, "to make ingrates and to despise ingratitude." All your friends, he insisted, are unanimous in urging you not to engage in polemics. Mme. de Meinières scolded Hume for the violence of his letter to d'Holbach. In Paris, she related, they are talking about nothing but the quarrel, and the air is thick with conjectures. Why should the most enlightened people in Europe tear each other to pieces? Mme. de Boufflers, on July 22, urged Hume to show his superiority to the unhappy, ungrateful wretch. "Rousseau's letter is atrocious; it is the furthermost excess of the most complete insanity. There can be no excuse for it. . . . Do not think, however, that he is guilty of artifice or lies, that he is an impostor or a scoundrel. His anger has no basis, but it is real, I do not doubt it."† Mme. de Boufflers knew her Jean-Jacques well. And she had been a true friend to Rousseau, in her way. Hume must then dismiss the idea of a premeditated attack by Rousseau. He is guilty of pride, of madness. Shouldn't Hume, then, have responded with compassion, avoided a scandal that could only hurt both parties and, with them, all the *philosophes*? In a postscript added several days later, after her return to Paris, Mme. de Boufflers condemned Hume for urging his friends to circulate his letter to d'Alembert and for seeking additional information about Rousseau. "I cannot suppose you will write anything against that unfortunate man which is not pertinent to your defense. You will not be an informer after having been his protector." Keith expressed similar sentiments: "le bon David" would not answer.

In a subsequent letter (July 21), d'Alembert, still regretting that Hume had ever bothered to complain openly about Rousseau, now thought that things had gone too far for him to avoid a complete publication of his side of the affair. As chance had it, Hume's letter reached

* Greig, *op. cit.*, Vol. II, p. 408.
† Greig, *op. cit.*, Vol. II, p. 416.

him when he was in the company of Turgot, Morellet, Roux, Saurin, Marmontel, Duclos. They were now unanimous in urging him to take this course, and to justify it by the threat of a posthumous publication of Rousseau's memoirs. Above all, he must limit himself to the facts, narrated "without bitterness, without the slightest insult." Moderation, clarity, precise detail—these are the only arms against Rousseau's compelling eloquence. And speed is essential. One more thing: Hume must prove that he had no part in Walpole's nasty joke, a trick of which d'Alembert thoroughly disapproves, "because it is cruel to torment an unfortunate person who has done you no harm." At that time d'Alembert did not know that Rousseau had denounced him for being its author. In his letter of July 15, Hume had written only that he assumed that d'Alembert was one of the *"savants"* for whom he supposedly felt greater friendship than for Rousseau himself. On July 15, Hume informed d'Alembert about the *grande lettre* of July 10, and detailed Rousseau's indictment of d'Alembert, including the Walpole letter and the charge of a conspiracy entered into before the departure from Paris. Turgot, meanwhile, in a letter of his own (July 27), urged Hume not only to adhere to the strict truth, but to admit his own errors or wrongs, particularly his having revealed Rousseau's accusatory letters to others. Publication of Hume's defense became inevitable in August, when London newspapers printed part of Rousseau's letter to Guy (August 2), replying to Hume's notorious letter to d'Holbach of June 27. Nevertheless, d'Holbach, as late as August 18, urged him to keep silent and publish nothing against Rousseau.

An examination of the preceding events and maneuvers lends no support to the still widely held theory of a conspiracy against Rousseau organized before he and Hume left Paris. Not only is positive evidence lacking, but as we have seen, Hume first tried to avoid a break. Then his supposed co-conspirators urged him, at least at first, not to accuse Rousseau or defend himself. Only when Rousseau's accusation became a public scandal, and when the menace of unanswerable memoirs published after the death of one or both men took shape, did Rousseau's adversaries—and such they were, without doubt—rally in sincere support of Hume. Surely, he had a right, seeing his character besmirched, to do all he could honestly do to defend himself. Grimm's lines in the *Correspondance littéraire* for October 15 (Hume's *Exposé succinct* appeared at about that time) are particularly significant: "M. Hume, who up till now had always resisted the mania for squabbling, has finally joined the club, for fear of catching a legacy in Jean-Jacques' testament. There is reason to believe that so many decent people will be calumniated in that testament that the Scottish philosopher may have resolved to take his risks with them."

We must now take into account Hume's letter of July 26 to Walpole. It is a surprise to read there that if d'Alembert and his friends urged

Hume to publish an account, it was because he had decided not to; and that he still is disinclined to do it. His earlier correspondence and the disapproval of his French friends indicate precisely the contrary. On close view, however, it seems possible that he had changed his mind.

D'Alembert had also urged him to refute the allegation that he was party to the spurious letter from the king of Prussia. Hume writes to Walpole:

I am told by Crawford [a mutual friend] that you had wrote it a fortnight before I left Paris, but did not show it to a mortal, for fear of hurting me; a delicacy of which I am very sensible. Pray recollect, if it was so. Though I do not intend to publish, I am collecting all the original pieces, and shall connect them by a concise narrative.[14]

In his reply, Walpole urged Hume not to print, unless Rousseau did so first. As for the letter, he had written it "several days before you left Paris, and before Rousseau's arrival there."* For the rest, he confirms Hume's presumptions, and adds: "I have a hearty contempt of Rousseau. . . . If there is any fault, let it lie on me." Rousseau is a mountebank and an ingrate.

Was Walpole's letter a *"lettre de complaisance,"* as some think, concocted, like Hume's, as part of the campaign?[15] There is, at least, a distortion of time, for Rousseau had arrived in Paris on December 16, which was more than "several days" before Hume and Rousseau left that city, on January 4. Walpole, however, was not famous for strict accuracy.

Although some of Rousseau's friends stuck with him, others who were acquainted with both sides did not. Du Peyrou, distressed by the widespread condemnation of Rousseau, asked him to publish irrefutable proofs. Mme. de Verdelin wrote to Coindet on July 20: "Nothing will convince the public that Mr. Hume has been capable of a villainy, not that simple and virtuous man who carefully conceals the good he does." To Rousseau she expressed her complete disbelief. Duclos, whom Rousseau had never trusted, told d'Alembert that he had been a friend of Rousseau's, but now finds his conduct so villainous that it must be revealed to the world. Mme. de Boufflers (July 27) did not hesitate to tell Rousseau what she thought. "M. Hume has sent me, Monsieur, the scurrilous letter you wrote to him. I have never seen anything like it. All your friends are filled with consternation and reduced to silence." His irrational and odious suspicions, his insults, directed against a man whose life is without a stain, and who has no interest in hurting him, his black ingratitude, finally, are beyond comprehension. As we have seen, Mme. de Boufflers also told Hume that she condemned his lack of self-control and moderation in his handling of the quarrel. The hardest blow for Rousseau was to come later, when Keith turned against him.

* That is, in Paris, not, as in the French translation, "in London." (*C. G.*, XV, 349).

Rousseau was not to be moved. "The league against me," he writes to Guy on August 2, "is too powerful, too clever, too determined, too accredited, for me, in my position, with no support except the truth, to face it in public." Hume, he is certain, will never dare to publish the documents. Twisting the facts to his convenience, he compares himself, the helpless man in a foreign land, to Hume, the intriguer surrounded by influential friends, able to control the newspapers, and asks which of the two set traps for the other. Can anyone believe that he had allowed himself, alone, sick and abandoned, to be taken to Hume's country in order to conspire against him? (Of course Hume had never made such an accusation.)

Hume saw matters quite differently. As he wrote to Mme. du Deffand (August 5): "Above all, the method I used to ruin him is rather extraordinary. It consists in having lodged him at the home of a gentleman . . . to whom he pays only thirty pounds sterling for his board and his housekeeper's and in having gotten him a pension from the King." The famous *salonnière* assured him that there was no shame in his being the dupe of his good heart and that Jean-Jacques' carryings-on did not surprise her. In her letters to Walpole, however, she blamed both men. Jean-Jacques is a rascal and a madman whom she has always despised. "But neither do I have much esteem for the Peasant," her nickname for Hume. She was maliciously amused at the disturbance the quarrel caused among the Temple group: Conti, Mme. de Boufflers, and Mme. de Luxembourg.[16]

The correspondence between Hume and his French friends continued throughout the summer and autumn months. In August he sent his *Concise Account* to d'Alembert for his opinion, but he assures Adam Smith that he will not publish it unless forced to. He urges Mme. de Boufflers and Mme. de Barbentane to read the documents, convinced they would show Rousseau to be a dangerous madman. Nothing is more reprehensible, he affirms to Turgot in September, than implicating d'Alembert in an affair in which he had no part. Rousseau's conduct toward himself reveals "extreme depravity of heart," "perversity of mind," fury worse than a tiger's or hyena's, a malign suspiciousness seeking to put a malicious interpretation on every word, look, or gesture, a proclivity to cunning lies and invective. "I really believe him to be one of the worst and most depraved men."

These impassioned invectives reveal Hume's real state of mind and his fury against Rousseau. They are equaled by those of d'Alembert in a letter to Hume of August 4, in which he expresses his outrage at the accusations Rousseau had directed against him, whereas he, far from ever harming Rousseau, had done all he could to cool Voltaire's justified rage. This, indeed, he had done, as we can see in their correspondence. D'Alembert could have said much more, for he had many times gone out of his way to show friendship to Rousseau, who twisted many of these gestures to fit his paranoid views. Thus, an unsigned letter was clear evidence of treachery, although d'Alembert not infrequently, out of caution, sent his letters unsigned.[17] It is notable that on September 1, after reading Hume's complete account, he still condemns Walpole and, even more, Mme. du Deffand, who had urged Walpole to write the letter and had corrected its style. His views were repeated in an addendum to the *Exposé succinct*. Turgot (September 7) also condemns Walpole and declares Rousseau to be more mad than wicked. Hume, he insists, must publish his account, because Rousseau has written to his friends all kinds of accusations against him and has challenged him to publish the documents without bringing dishonor upon himself.

Before considering the impact of Hume's *Concise Account*, we should pause to reflect on the deeper causes and the explanations of this second imbroglio which shattered Rousseau's emotional equilibrium. Few if any writers have inspired as much passionate partisanship as he. However, while no one any longer accuses him of having been a scoundrel in this affair, a number of prejudiced apologists have struggled hard to make "the great plot" credible and turn Hume into a monstrous and subtle knave.

There is no doubt that Rousseau had many enemies. Some, like Voltaire, had a vicious hatred of him. The Holbachian clique, and others, like Mme. du Deffand and Samuel Johnson, either sincerely despised him, feared him, or resented his "apostasy" and his influence. They were malicious, sometimes outrageous in their correspondence, their conversation, and in some of their published writings.* Their lack of pity for a sick and hounded man is unquestionably reprehensible. The anger evoked in Rousseau's admirers by such cruel and paltry behavior has sometimes misled them into accepting his own delusional interpretations. In particular, the influential book of Henri Guillemin seems as paranoid as Rousseau's letter of July 10.[18] In Guillemin's rhapsody, as lyrical a document as that famous letter, everything is twisted or interpreted to support the foreordained conclusion. Rousseau's enemies become the ogres in a fairy tale. But plots must have motives. Guillemin has no trouble in finding them: the *philosophes* wanted to punish Jean-Jacques for having abandoned the side of irreligion; Hume wanted to win the plaudits and gratitude of the *philosophes* by delivering them from their most dangerous enemy.[19] From the beginning the servile agent of the clique, he had been working in secret to betray Jean-Jacques. Of course one cannot ignore Rousseau's own psychic unbalance and obvious distortions. Guillemin, again taking a leaf from Rousseau's

---

* One of the most telling testimonials on this score was given by Deleyre, who remained Rousseau's steadfast friend even after Rousseau had added him to his list of traitors. In a letter written after Jean-Jacques' death, he speaks of the end of his own friendship for Diderot. "My heart had long been alienated by the insidious and malicious innuendoes which he used to detach me from my admiration for Rousseau." (*Corr.*, V; Appendix, 292–3)

own tactics, affects to demonstrate his objectivity by acknowledging them. But why was Jean-Jacques unhinged? That, we are asked to believe, was precisely the technique of the conspirators—so to confuse him as to drive him into insanity, a result that was finally attained rather abruptly, after Hume published his *Exposé succinct*. Accounts such as Guillemin's are not history, but a combination of fantasy and uncontrolled hatred.

A sound explanation must take into account the long and increasing accumulation of Rousseau's neurotic afflictions, his disastrous experiences just before the journey to England, and above all, his conspiratorial mentality, as we have seen it in many episodes of his life, from the Venetian affair to the intricate involvements at the Hermitage and the "plot" of the Jesuits against *Emile*. It also suffuses his writings and must be taken into account if we are properly to understand them— something the critics have not done.

At Wooton, as at the Hermitage, two conditions were united: solitude and the influence of Thérèse LeVasseur. The former was of course more important, but possibly both were necessary. The refuge in solitude sprang from his maladjustment to society and from the urgent impulse to proclaim his independence, and to believe in it. However, his independence, as we have seen, was a reaction against, and an intolerable betrayal of, his deeper need, which was for a loving dependence. This need was not acceptable to him, since it confirmed inferiority and violated the self-image he wished to believe in and so to project to the world. Thus, he proclaims his relief on escaping from the social obligations of London, while he had profoundly enjoyed being the object of attention. Solitude led to brooding, enhanced by his absorption in the writing of the *Confessions*. The admiration in the London newspapers was followed by a series of satirical letters, with devastating effects on him.

What ensued has been lucidly explained by Grimsley.[20] Hume had not been able to understand that for Rousseau he was a father-figure. Jean-Jacques had attached himself to him, looking to him to satisfy his profound needs for dependence and emotional outpouring. But while he had a tormenting need to be taken care of, he also had to reassure himself about his independence by remaining free from all sense of obligation.*

With Rousseau, as he himself said, it had to be all or nothing. When he succumbed to his delusion, his anxiety and resentment inevitably

---

* W. H. Blanchard (*Rousseau and the Spirit of Revolt*, pp. 213–14) has analyzed this phenomenon. Rejecting his own dependency, Rousseau imagined that an enemy from outside was attempting to seduce him. His own gifts were free gifts from the heart; those of others were traps, and his tension turned outward into an angry attack on the giver. Blanchard also points out that Rousseau was in fear of becoming dependent on a man who, not responding totally, could not be trusted not to withdraw his affections.

fixed themselves on the very man toward whom he felt dependence, who had done everything he could to help him. As Freud has pointed out, the delusions of persecution are first directed upon loved persons who have exerted an important influence on the subject's emotional life, in this case the very men—Diderot, Grimm, d'Alembert, and now Hume— for whom he had once experienced gratitude, affection, and admiration. And so, with remorseless logic, he interprets every trivial incident as the sign of a sinister plot to defame him in the eyes of the world. The enthusiastic initial welcome was only a feint to put him off his guard. One man only could be responsible—the very man who had made such a show of befriending him in the first place. Like Diderot, but in a much more evil and demonic way, Hume had plotted to lure him into his power in order to degrade and humiliate him as the recipient of ignoble charity and the sophist who was false to his professed principles. The conviction of universal hostility, it should be noted, derives "from an initial assumption that degradation takes the form of dependence on others."[21] Hume's very benefactions were the means of "transforming him into a 'monster of ingratitude.'" For the weak man, ever wounded by his inferiority feelings, "to be in another's power is to be exposed to universal opprobrium." In Rousseau's mind, Hume's intention could not be doubted. The words *"Je tiens Jean-Jacques Rousseau"* are con- clusive to him. The lack of hard evidence for his interpretations only makes the hostility seem more terrifying and malevolent. Since it is hidden and subterranean, he must beware of every look, of every expres- sion. The paranoid imagination "interprets a shrug, a glance, a chance word, into corroborative material."[22] Increasingly, he lived in a world of "signs."

The skein of motives which dictated Rousseau's response pattern in the Hume affair probably includes still another thread. It is difficult not to see his response as, in part but perhaps an important part, a defense mechanism against a homoerotic attraction to Hume, aroused by the intimacy of the shared bedroom at Senlis and Roye. "I still see him taking [putting on?] his short-sleeved, pleated nightgown," he will write to Du Peyrou on October 4, 1766. It is not impossible that the repressed wish took the form of the hallucination of an exclamation from the sleeping Hume. In London, Rousseau, emotionally upset, had sat on the astounded Scot's knee, embraced and kissed him. The pattern of infatu- ation is a repeated one in his life.*

Psychological analysis has shown that anxiety, guilt feelings, and the need for self-punishment are responses to internal threats to basic in-

* Like Grimsley, Blanchard sees Rousseau's relationships with men as tinged by un- conscious homosexual desire toward which he reacted with revulsion, desires rooted in the feminine identification which had been his defense mechanism vis-à-vis his father (*loc cit.*). He also remarks pertinently that the danger Rousseau felt from women "was not that of being sexually attracted to them, but the dread of being turned into a woman—of releasing the female within himself" (*op. cit.*, p. 286).

stinctual demands, so that anxiety exists as a permanent condition. When external threats meet the inner anxiety, they are experienced as more dangerous than they really are, and intensify the anxiety, which takes the form either of depression or of persecution. Thus, the residue of inner shame and guilt from childhood and adolescence leads to compulsive doubting and eventually to paranoiac fears concerning hidden persecutors.*

### 2. FLIGHT

In the autumn of 1766 the social and literary circles in Paris were buzzing with news of the quarrel. As Hume wrote to Mme. de Boufflers (August 12), "If the King of England had declared war against the King of France, it could not have been more suddenly the subject of conversation." Suard was translating Hume's *Concise Account*; it appeared in the middle of October. Copies of Rousseau's letters to Hume and to Guy were passed from hand to hand. Fresh rumors sprang up daily. Jean-Jacques had had a meeting with his enemy and there had been a tearful, tender reconciliation. Jean-Jacques was leaving or had left England. Jean-Jacques was going back to Geneva, to write a new constitution for that republic.

Rousseau found himself in an extremely vulnerable position. There was no longer any need for a plot, such as he imagined, to have existed. He had himself created the effects that he accused his enemies of having conspired to create. Throughout Europe he was regarded as a madman, an ingrate, a scoundrel, or all of these together. His enemies had a field day. He was condemned in countless conversations and letters. Tronchin rejoiced. "The open expression of this madness and wickedness of Rousseau can only be useful to us," he wrote to Charles Bonnet on August 21. "Scorn for his person will rebound on his principles, and many of his enthusiasts will abandon him."

Voltaire exultantly joined the fray, in letters to Hume and others. He seemed tireless in his denunciations, combining indignation, sarcasm, and irony as only he could do.

In his fifth *Lettre* [*de la montagne*] he becomes an informer against me. That is not very nice. A man who has taken communion in both rites, a sage to whom statues should be erected, seems to degrade his character a bit by such a

---

* At the heart of paranoid behavior are two processes, denial and projection. "Denial" is the refusal to consider that certain standards of evaluation might apply to oneself. "Projection" is the practice of attributing one's own thoughts, motives, and reactions to others. Both processes are constantly at work in the paranoid, producing a personality which is incapable of admitting its own errors, and which can see no point of view save its own. The victim subconsciously projects his own faults and mistakes into others, and refuses to admit any but the most noble motives and qualities in himself. Someone else is always to blame. (Summarized from *Encyclopaedia Britannica*, 1969 ed., s.v. "Paranoid Behavior."

maneuver; he risks his safety and his reputation. . . . You see, Monsieur, that this poor fellow has never been able to live under any master, nor keep any friend, inasmuch as it is against the dignity of his being to have a master, and as friendship is a weakness whose touch a sage must repel. You say he is writing his life story. It has been too useful to the world, and too filled with great events, for him not to serve posterity by publishing it. His taste for truth will not allow him to disguise the least of those anecdotes which can be used to educate princes who would like to be carpenters like Emile.[23]

Nothing riled Voltaire more than Rousseau's statement in his "Lettre à M. de Beaumont" (1763), that if there were enlightened governments in Europe, they would raise statues to him instead of persecuting him. A tone of savagery and unscrupulous distortions marks these attacks, of which Rousseau's whole life, rather than the quarrel with Hume, is the substance. Bringing out only Jean-Jacques' extravagant accusations against him, Voltaire conveniently overlooks his well-founded grievances.

Voltaire's letter to Hume was widely circulated, but not widely enough to suit him. About this letter Grimm wrote to his correspondents, in November, that it had done more harm to Rousseau than Hume's *Exposé*. "He has, so to speak, given this poor Jean-Jacques the *coup de grâce*." All the arrows were shot off at once, for the public edification, in Voltaire's *Lettre au Docteur Pansophe*, which appeared in November. No doubt it is a masterpiece of its kind. No doubt Voltaire was not proud of it, for in his usual way he tried his best to attribute it to others, first to the Abbé Coyer and then to Bordes. Nobody was fooled, least of all Rousseau.

Diderot was an honorable exception. His correspondence avoids all mention of the scandal of the day. Grimm, on the other hand, gave his readers a gleeful account of the excitement in Paris ("What food for the idle!"), and of the discomfiture of Rousseau's supporters. He does not approve of writers making the public the judge of their quarrels, and strongly condemns Hume's action. Grimm then takes off on a general attack against Rousseau's character, referring in particular to his own quarrel with him. "I have no objection to someone's being mad; but I do require him to be an honest man." He does, however, add: "I think that nobody can read this strange contention without feeling deep pity for this unhappy Jean-Jacques; for, if he manages to offend his friends, we must admit that he punishes himself cruelly for it." He reveals that he possesses letters of Rousseau's that are far more damaging than those published by Hume, but promises not to make a public spectacle of himself. And in fact, Grimm did not; but we have recounted his underhanded work, and Diderot's, in falsifying Mme. d'Epinay's *Histoire de Madame de Montbrillant* in the hope of tarnishing Rousseau before the bar of history.

Rousseau's efforts were now focused on retaining the few friends he had left. His relations with Du Peyrou are most revealing. At first he counts on his "host," as he calls Du Peyrou, unquestioningly. Hume will never publish his accounts, he assures him (August 16), or if he does, he will falsify the letters. He has no worry on that score. His repetition of this opinion in several letters would indicate that he really is worried and trying to reassure himself.[24] He does not doubt his friend will agree when he asserts: "Hume's plan was to serve me in public with great ostentation and to defame me skillfully in private." It was a shock to read Du Peyrou's warning that the public was against him and that he had better supplement his suppositions with hard proofs or else hold his pen. Rousseau saw only too clearly that Du Peyrou was also skeptical, most particularly about the Walpole letter. Hume's reputation, he was reminded, was too solidly founded, he had done too much for him, and he had nothing to gain. Worse still, Rousseau had a well-earned reputation for quarreling with friends.

Rousseau's cousin Jean also pleaded for evidence with which to defend him. But Jean-Jacques despised and distrusted his kin, and did not become emotional. To Du Peyrou, on the other hand, he replied with wrath and outrage. "*Tu quoque!*"[25] He declares that it is for Du Peyrou to justify *himself*, but pages of self-justification follow. He was on the point of breaking off. The ensuing correspondence was stormy. Du Peyrou finally managed to disengage himself, but not without warning Rousseau again, like a true friend, that everywhere the voices of men were raised against him. Can he prove his charge that Hume tried to turn Davenport against him? Does he know it from Davenport himself? If so, the traitor is unmasked. But where is the proof? Rousseau crossed out a passage in one of his heated letters: "As long as I exist I shall be a too disquieting object for *ces Messieurs*, and everything that is going to happen to me now will be only the beginning of their project; for *ces Messieurs* are not stupid enough to stop there; as long as I live I shall be in their way."[26]

To Mme. de Verdelin he concedes that Hume doubtless has hated *only him*, an argument he was to repeat again and again.[27] With Mme. de Boufflers, as with Du Peyrou, he leans heavily on still another argument: *he* had kept the whole matter secret. It was Hume who had made it public, in his letters to d'Holbach and other French friends, and then by publishing his *Exposé*. The argument struck others, rightly or wrongly, as disingenuous. As Voltaire wrote to Damilaville on November 3, "It is obvious that this charlatan, in writing his letter [of July 10, to Hume], is thinking of making it public. Art is plain in every line. It is clearly a carefully meditated piece, destined for the public. . . . He has not hesitated to calumniate his benefactor in the hope that his false eloquence will excuse his infamous acts." It is not possible to know whether Rousseau anticipated that his letter of August 2 to Guy would be circulated. As it happened, that letter in effect challenged Hume to publish all the documents, by its assertion that he would not dare to do so. Even Du Peyrou (February 5, 1767) told Rousseau that it left Hume no choice but to go ahead.

It is probable that Rousseau had wished to avoid a public éclat. To make a public outcry would be precisely to fall into the trap that had been set for him. After the scandal broke, he kept silent for the obvious reason that he could offer no convincing proofs. If Hume, on the other hand, wrote to all and sundry, it was first of all because of his incomprehension, bewilderment, and indignation; and later, because of his apprehensions concerning the *Confessions*. The different courses of action furnish no evidence relevant to the theory of a plot.

During all these months the Rousseau-Hume affair was the great scandal in England, as well as in France. Unlike the French, the English national habit was, then as now, to write letters to the newspapers. Partisans and enemies of Rousseau filled the columns with prose and verse. Two examples are interesting enough to recall. In the *St. James's Chronicle* for December 11, a defender of Rousseau expressed himself with poetic fervor:

> Rousseau be firm! tho' Malice like Voltaire,
> And supercilious Pride, like d'Alembert
> Tho mad Presumption W—le's form assume,
> And baseborn Treachery appear like H—e,
> Yet droop not thou, these Spectres gathering round,
> These night-drawn Phantoms want the power to wound:
> Fair Truth shall chase th' unreal Forms away;
> And Reason's piercing Beam restore the Day;
> Britain shall snatch the Exile to her Breast.
> And conscious Virtue soothe his Soul to rest.

A reply, "Parody on Poem of December 11," followed in the next issue:

> Rousseau, be firm! Though Satire like Voltaire,
> And Genius, in the shape of d'Alembert
> Though Walpole's Form sly Ridicule assume,
> And honest Friendship wear the Guise of Hume,
> Yet feel not thou! nor hear the Silver Sound
> Of annual Pension of One Hundred Pound.
> Rank Arrogance shall chase all Help away,
> And pedant Sophistry turn Night to Day.
> From Land to Land a wretched Exile fly,
> Then, mad with Pride, curse all Mankind and die.

Rousseau's most anguishing experience was his failure to keep the friendship of his beloved Keith. Their correspondence continued fitfully for seven months. At first (August 9) he expresses his "confidence" that his friend and protector will not believe what is being said against him. Not knowing the facts, he will not judge.

The earl marischal was indeed trying to remain impartial and act the conciliator. Just as he had earlier defended Hume to Rousseau, and was to do so again on August 24, so he urged Hume, on August 15, not to publish his charges and to be charitable toward a man who was not an ingrate but the victim of his unbalanced imagination. Again on September 5, he wrote to Rousseau, defending the sincerity of Hume's friendship. Jean-Jacques did not dare reply to Keith as he had to other friends, such as Du Peyrou. Instead he pleaded for understanding, and when no answer came, responded with cries of alarm. Can Keith have fallen prey to Hume's schemes? Has he lost the only consolation remaining to him on earth? Nobody has really known Hume. *"Il n'a jamais haï que moi seul."* *"Moi seul,"* the very words that give dramatic accent to the exordium of the *Confessions!* How well they epitomize the pathology and the pathos of his alienation and isolation! But if Keith has not answered, it may be that he has not received Rousseau's letters. "Have they been lucky enough to escape the nets that are stretched out all around me, through which very little passes?" There is no doubt now that "they" are trying to cut him off from the Continent.[28]

Keith's reply (September 25), a strong defense of Hume, brought Rousseau no consolation. He begged his old protector not to speak of Hume any more, at the same time reopening the whole argument about the pension. He apparently destroyed his copy of his letter of November to Keith, a letter that so exasperated the patient and faithful friend that he informed Rousseau on the twenty-second that he was putting an end to their correspondence. This decision evoked an outpouring of anguish, pathetic and lyrical (December 11). "If you keep your cruel resolve, I shall die. This is not the worst thing; but I shall die in sorrow, and I predict that you will regret it." By February 8 he could bear it no more and sent another plea. "My protector, my benefactor, my friend, my father—will none of these names move you? I kneel down at your feet to beg you for a single word."

Keith was not moved from his resolve. Instead of replying, he explained to Du Peyrou, on December 24, that since he could not persuade Rousseau that he was wrong, or be persuaded that Rousseau was right, further correspondence would be fruitless. Hume was an honest, decent man, and the whole world, even his enemies, admitted it. It was only left for Rousseau to write the epitaph, on March 19:

It is all over, then, Milord. I have lost forever your favor and your friendship, without my being able even to know or imagine why, not having a single feeling in my heart, not an action in my conduct which, I dare affirm, should not have confirmed that precious favor of which, according to your so frequently repeated promises, nothing could ever deprive me. . . . Some phantom must have been shown you under my name. I abandon it to you, and I shall wait until your illusion dissipates, convinced that as soon as you see me as I am, you will love me as you once did.

It was a typical dramatic flourish, of the kind that brought upon Jean-Jacques the cry of "sophist," the charge of guileful use of his gift of eloquence. But the rhetoric overlay a deep feeling and a significant defense mechanism. Repeating a response pattern which went back to the critical childhood incident of the broken comb,* he was convinced that an opaque veil (this time the work of his enemies) was preventing his real self from appearing to others, who were judging a "phantom." The cry from his heart was genuine when, describing his friendship with the marischal in the *Confessions*, he exclaimed: "O good Milord! O my worthy father! how my heart is still torn when I think of you! Oh, the inhuman wretches! what a blow they struck me when they alienated you from me!"

There was one unshakable friend and admirer toward whom Rousseau felt some fleeting gratitude. Mme. de la Tour had published a letter in a rejoinder to Hume's *Exposé succinct* put out by Rousseau's supporters. In a five-line note, he tells her how his heart beat fast when he recognized his "dear Marianne."[29] The note called forth her usual tender complaints about his neglect, which was hastening her death. Although Jean-Jacques had appealed to Keith on the same grounds, he filed away the lady's plea without an answer.

On the other side, Hume was not entirely comfortable with his role. On September 2 he defended himself vigorously to Davenport. He will not publish Rousseau's *grande lettre* until Rousseau attacks him, "which I expect every day." We do not know whether word of Rousseau's letter to Guy had reached him or what his real intentions at the moment were, but of course he did not keep this pledge. On the other hand, contrary to what Rousseau was to claim, he strongly urged Davenport to continue to protect his guest, "a very dangerous man," but not possibly dangerous to Davenport, because he was not a writer. After the *Exposé succinct* came out, Hume wrote (November 8) as follows to Davenport:

You would see by the newspapers that my friends at Paris have found it necessary to publish an account of this strange and ridiculous affair between Rousseau and me, together with the original letters. He had wrote defiances against me to the different parts of Europe; his friends had been very industrious in showing these letters; some of them had even got into the public papers, and on the whole, things had come to that extremity that my silence would universally have been interpreted as a sign of guilt.

He is also concerned that Rousseau will still claim that he has falsified the correspondence and asks Davenport to warn him that he is depositing all the originals in the British Museum. (The Museum refused them, and they are now among Hume's papers at the Royal Society of Edinburgh.)

It is evident that Hume felt apprehensions, if not compunctions, about what he had done, and was afraid of tarnishing his reputation as "le bon David."

---

* L. G. Crocker, *Jean-Jacques Rousseau: The Quest (1712–1758)*, pp. 26–7.

The remaining months of Rousseau's stay in England were to envelop him in an ever-darkening nightmare, relieved, in his typical pattern, by intervals of calm, during which his botanizing soothed him. Toward the end of December, his suspicions turned against Davenport. He had not come to visit Rousseau, had not given him the explanations requested as to "what footing I am on in your house." Should he leave? How can he, helpless, friendless, unable to speak English? A few days later he informs Davenport that he can no longer stay on, and asks him to find him some peasant's cottage in which he can live in peace. Davenport wisely took no offense. Feeling abandoned by his friends in France, Rousseau asked Guy, on January 20, to find out why he had not heard from the Duchesse de Luxembourg.

A little earlier he had news of another lost friend, Sauttersheim, the scamp who had so attracted him. On learning that Laliaud occasionally saw him, Rousseau wrote a paragraph expressing his affection for Sauttersheim: "He committed some youthful mistakes which make him only the more estimable now by the way in which I believe he has reformed. I have lived with him in a great intimacy which I found delightful and do not regret. . . . Love him for himself and for love of me."[30]

In February, Rousseau received from the Marquis de Mirabeau* a letter sent to him on October 27, the first of an exchange that was to continue over the next months. Interminably long, written in a colorful, colloquial idiom, the first letter spoke bluntly to Rousseau of his faults and his philosophy, and of Mirabeau's own philosophical prescriptions for the right way to live. Considering that he did not know Jean-Jacques, his understanding of his character is remarkable. "You have lived too much in the opinion of others," he notes shrewdly. The ultimate purpose of the letter was to offer Rousseau a choice from among some half-dozen domains he possessed in various regions of France. Jean-Jacques would have bridled at such a letter from most men, but Mirabeau was too important and highborn, or perhaps he felt an affinity for this eccentric character who was so interested in him. He, too, wrote a long letter, talking about his own character and his tastes, regretting that he saw no way of taking advantage of the generous offer. Another offer of hospitality also came from Count Orlov, lover and favorite of Catherine the Great, but the idea of St. Petersburg and the frozen north sent chills down Rousseau's spine.

In March, after some further negotiations through Davenport, he finally agreed to accept a royal pension of one hundred pounds per annum. Now that Hume was no longer the intermediary, so large a sum was not to be refused. The good news did nothing to dispel his phobias. He was more than ever convinced that "they" were trying to isolate him

---

* Victor Riquetti, Marquis de Mirabeau, economist and physiocrat, is not to be confused with his son, Honoré-Gabriel, Comte de Mirabeau, the Revolutionary leader.

by cutting off his correspondence with the Continent. He was desperately worried that his papers and the manuscript of his *Confessions* might fall into his enemies' hands. He planned to burn them if he found himself *in extremis*. "As far as I can discern the project, it is to make me die of grief, as soon as possible, in this island, the surest way they have thought of for stifling my complaints."[31]

Tormented by his doubts and certainties, obsessed by the fear of being poisoned, harassed by Thérèse, who was desperate to quit the isolation of Wooton, Jean-Jacques advised Davenport that he was leaving for London. He had the paranoiac's perpetual illusion that a change of residence would bring relief from persecution. Actually, he had no intention of going to London, if he could help it, and was afraid to. He had decided to look about on his own in the provinces. He was now convinced that his cousin Jean was a spy, "*l'âme damnée du bon David,*" alerted to intercept and open his mail. He advised Du Peyrou that his situation was becoming desperate (April 2). "I am surrounded by snares." Only Cerjeat, a Swiss friend of Du Peyrou's who was married to an Englishwoman, might be able to save him, above all save his papers, the prime objective of the conspirators. But did Cerjeat get his letters? "The men who bring and take my letters, those at the post office—everything is equally suspicious to me. I am in the hands of everybody, and there is no movement I can make to free myself." The net is stretched between London and Wooton, "nothing can escape it." To assure secrecy, he has arranged a two-step cipher for their messages. "I have the letter and the cipher ready, but will anyone come for them? Will anyone come for me? O fate! O my friend! pray for me. I think I have not deserved the misfortunes which overwhelm me."

Two days later, Rousseau sent Du Peyrou a modified duplicate of the preceding letter, hoping that one of the two would get through. "I am trying to get to London, but I doubt I shall succeed." It would be very dangerous, because of his papers. "The desire to get hold of them on my death, and perhaps during my lifetime, is one of the main reasons I am kept under such close surveillance." It is obvious that the *Confessions*, which were indeed the focus of worry for Rousseau's enemies, had become the most oppressive incubus in his nightmare-world.

Rousseau succeeded in getting to Cerjeat the manuscript, bound in calfskin, of a revised version of the *Confessions*. Cerjeat was to transmit it to Du Peyrou. On May 1 Rousseau and Thérèse slipped out of Wooton, after sending Davenport a letter which must be described as insolent, even though it closed with an expression of gratitude and eternal friendship. He wrote, in part:

The master of a house, Monsieur, has the obligation of knowing what is going on within it, especially in regard to foreigners who are his guests. If you are not aware of what has been going on in yours, in regard to me, since Christmas, you are at fault. If you know it and allowed it, your blame is the greater.

protector, to feel the prestige of this highborn aristocrat as a kind of magical power.

On June 3 he departed, and two days later was installed at Fleury. Conti was annoyed. Rousseau had kept him in ignorance of his moves, and now he had put himself into the keeping of another protector.

Jean-Jacques was to have only two weeks at Fleury. Mirabeau wanted to take him to a more remote and safer domain, but was forced to yield to the pressure of a prince of the blood. "The oak is putting you in his shade." At least Jean-Jacques had been able to see his dear friend, Du Peyrou. Unable to make the promised journey to England, Du Peyrou arrived in Paris on June 11. On the nineteenth, Conti's henchman, Coindet, came for Rousseau, and whisked him away to Trye-le-Château, in the province of Oise, north of Paris. On Conti's urging, he now took the name "M. Renou" and solemnly promised never again to write for the public, "on any subject whatsoever," and to allow no work of his to be printed before his death. Thérèse was to pass as his sister.

Within the large, walled park of Trye, so heavily wooded that the sun could scarcely pierce the foliage, Rousseau was to dwell for a year. The isolation of a walled domain appealed to him at first. "I hope to spend tranquil days here," he wrote cheerfully to Du Peyrou. But tranquillity had been banished from his life. There was to be no peace, especially while he depended on any other man. Soon the strong autumn winds and the snows of a bitter winter became oppressive. The peasants, who hated their harsh and distant master, turned on him. The servants were sly, mocking, or surly. "Scandals brooded; pregnant girls, poachers taking revenge, dogs found poisoned. Anyone could be a spy or an informer."[2] To the peasants, a botanist bent over flowers could only be a sorcerer looking for poisons. So, at least, Jean-Jacques saw and felt his new surroundings, and there was much truth in his mental picture. Deschamps, the new *concierge*, arrived on June 23. He was obviously an enemy to be feared. The large round tower quickly became an oppressive domain of dark shadows, spying on him, conspiring against him, the agents, not of Conti, but of Rousseau's relentless, impalpable pursuers.

Jean-Jacques was a frightened man, struggling to shore up his inner security and equilibrium against the mounting tides of helplessness and loneliness. Much of his behavior, throughout his life, was that of a neurotic beset by crippling, obsessive inferiority feelings. Not daring to admit them to others or to himself, he was ever on guard lest some chance shaft pierce his defenses. The more vulnerable he was, the more self-centered he became. By now, however, Rousseau had gone beyond this stage. He had entered the terrifying realm of paranoia. The world (that is to say, other men), which had always been to him a hostile, menacing, impenetrable presence, was now subject to a systematic interpretation according to a fixed idea, an obsession, one that compulsively exaggerated or distorted phenomena. In England, this lifelong tendency had finally overcome his psychic defenses, following the series of persecutions to which he had been subjected since 1762. Don Quixote is the classical paradigm in literature of paranoid distortion. Rousseau's reaction was different: bewilderment and helpless terror, leading to a series of withdrawals, until he finally reached the ideal of autarchic self-enclosure that is a recurrent theme in his writings.

From July on, his letters are filled with increasing complaints about the hostility, vexations, and insults he has had to suffer from the domestic staff of the château. He does not know whether they are there to serve him or to guard him. "I see clearly that there is a secret motive in all this; but as of now I am unable to penetrate it."[3] No doubt there is a hidden hand, "*la main cachée*," he writes to Mme. de Verdelin. The *concierge* has several times locked him in or locked him out of the grounds. No one would believe what he is going through, he tells Mirabeau; "may it remain unknown to the world!" Deschamps and the vicar, he reports, are stirring up the peasants and villagers into open hostility. Mme. de Verdelin is convinced that Thérèse's gossiping and nagging are at the bottom of it. She is, Rousseau admits, unbearably bored.

He did not know whether to stay or to leave. The *concierge*, he thought, was trying to get rid of him, and that made him determined to stay. But in almost every letter to the prince, in every meeting with him, he asked: "Give me permission to follow my destiny and to dispose of myself."[4] What he meant to do was to give himself up to the authorities and face the charges. Then he would either be a free man or would find in the Bastille another prison, more secure and tranquil than this one. Once before he had begged the rulers of Neuchâtel to imprison him for life. Conti warned him not to take such a step and exerted every possible pressure on him. He forbade Jean-Jacques to write to Mme. de Luxembourg. He nevertheless did, on August 16, pleading with her to obtain Conti's permission for him to leave Trye. If she replied, we do not have her letter.

Mme. de Verdelin reassured him repeatedly. The prince did not intend to keep him in the château forever, just long enough for the public to forget about him. People were saying, she added, that he was about to go to Prussia.[5] To Jean-Jacques it seemed that his enemies were trying to hound him, drive him out of this refuge, then wait for him again at the next. There would be no stopping place. Thérèse now urged him not to leave: "Do you want to give your enemies the advantage they are looking for, of shouting that you can't live anywhere?"

Conti had to keep this dangerous man under wraps, if he could not get rid of him. His tactics were to calm him down and temporize, and finally, when he had to, negotiate a compromise. Directly and through Coindet, he kept insisting that there was no safety in any other part of France, no possible incognito. Jean-Jacques, in direct pleas or through Coindet, implored Mme. de Verdelin to sound out Choiseul, the King's minister, about the government's attitude. "You are still my refuge," the agitated, hapless man wrote to her: "I turn to you today again. Where can I live? Must I leave the realm?" She did want to be Rousseau's friend and had always tried to be, in her way; but she belonged to her set and could not betray it. She informed Conti, not Choiseul. To ask and to be refused, she replied through Coindet, would be highly dangerous; but if he were still interested in going back to Italy, it would be possible to find protection there.[6] Be patient, she urged again and again: "I begin to see a glimmer of light in your future."[7]

Rousseau began to suspect Coindet, associating him not with Conti's maneuvers, but with Mme. de Verdelin and through her with the arch-enemy, Hume, and the Encyclopedists. After all, it was she, along with Mme. de Boufflers, who had urged him to undertake the fatal journey to England. "I return caress for caress. They dissimulate in order to destroy me, and I dissimulate in order to save myself." Conti and the maréchale had sincerely done their best for him. "But sooner or later the storm must break."[8] How incredible, he thought, that the French had become the Scot's satellites, tools of his implacable rage!

Desperate, Rousseau finally disregarded his protector's admonitions, and sent a pleading letter to Choiseul on March 27, 1768. This rash move was prompted by relentless pressures from his environment, which had been worsened by an unexpected, dramatic episode.

On November 4, Du Peyrou came to visit Rousseau at Trye. Rousseau was overjoyed. He had feared that his enemies, eager to get at the papers he had entrusted to his friend's keeping, would prevent the reunion. Du Peyrou, when he came to Rousseau, was ill with gout. In the eighteenth century both diagnoses and treatment often belonged to the realm of fantasy. Du Peyrou was treated with spirits of urine poured into his ear and mustard applied to his feet. He was Rousseau's only remaining friend, the one he trusted. He dreamed of spending his last years in close and tender friendship with Du Peyrou, the most recent of a number of men with whom he would have liked to fulfill such a dream. Together they would botanize and discuss the wide range of subjects with which Du Peyrou, an intellectual and a bibliophile, was familiar. (Rousseau never suspected that his friend was the head of the Neuchâtel lodge of Freemasons, and one of the European leaders of that freethinking, occultist secret society.) To Mme. de la Tour he wrote about Du Peyrou: "It is from him that I have my subsistence and my independence."* To Du Peyrou himself he wrote: "The day you leave me will be the last I'll wish to live."[9] Only these feelings can enable us to understand the crisis of November 9.

Suddenly Du Peyrou became seriously ill, to the point of delirium. Rousseau and the doctor assured him that it was the gout, but the

---

* The date of this letter is uncertain—Sept.–Oct. 1767. See *C. G.*, XVII, 291.

patient, feverish and scarcely able to walk or even stay awake, was convinced that he had been poisoned. His stomach was upset and he could not eat. He became agitated, and his looks and words finally brought Rousseau to the "realization" that his friend suspected him of having administered the poison. Rousseau, in turn, became convinced that Du Peyrou's servant, Grisel, had been bought by his enemies, in an effort to get rid of the guardian of his papers. On the sick man's insistence, the doctor prescribed an antispasmodic. As Rousseau handed him the blackish liquid, Du Peyrou said, "I take it with complete confidence." He drank the potion, then became frightened again when he saw grains of powder at the bottom of the cup. When Rousseau shed tears, Du Peyrou accused him of trying to upset him. "At that moment," Rousseau writes in the detailed account he sent to Conti, "I felt all my esteem, all my attachment, all my tenderness, extinguished to the last spark." Du Peyrou again grew drowsy. Rousseau, frightened at the thought of being accused as a poisoner, sealed the two vials of medicine, put them in his pocket, and wrote out a declaration renouncing any share in his friend's estate. That was the night of November 9, "the most anguishing in my life."

The next day he wrote a note to Du Peyrou, annulling all their agreements. Du Peyrou recovered and sent Rousseau a letter of apology, claiming he had been delirious, if indeed he had said the offensive words. Jean-Jacques grudgingly forgave him, but his feelings were never the same.

Just what Du Peyrou said, and to what degree Rousseau may have distorted his words and acts, we cannot know. Yet the similarity with the memorable scenes with Hume is striking. In both instances he releases his emotions in tender, almost erotic embraces. There is, it seems to him, a lack of adequate response. Suspicions, distortion—perhaps hallucinations—follow. Then comes another transport of emotions and tears, the expression of regret. Finally, suspicions harden into certainty. One suspects that, in both cases, the presence of the longed-for friend alerts repressed homosexual tendencies. A quarrel ensues in which a projection of suspicions and hatred serves as protection from the internal threat.

On November 26, Rousseau's *Dictionnaire de musique*, on which he had labored for many years, was finally put on sale in Paris. He was worried that any book bearing his name might be a pretext for trouble and wished that he could have suppressed the work. There was no trouble, but the publication gave him no joy. His mind was filled with other, darker thoughts. On December 13 he wrote to Colonel Abraham de Pury, a state counsellor of Neuchâtel and Du Peyrou's future father-in-law, asking him to come and take the unwanted guest home; he did not trust Grisel. Pury made the journey, and Du Peyrou finally departed on the third of January.

The dreary days went on as before. He was looking forward to the release of death, he wrote to Mme. de la Tour. For years he had been saying that. "Whatever my contemporaries may do, my memory will not always remain unhonored."[10] This, indeed, was prophecy.

Conti finally gave Rousseau tentative consent to go to Dombes, in Burgundy, provided he kept the name Renou and stayed outside the jurisdiction of the Parlement of Paris. Nothing came of this idea. Two weeks later (February 16), Rousseau had a violent quarrel with Coindet, their go-between, about the Hume affair. Feeling himself more and more a prisoner of the château, he was moved to throw himself figuratively at the feet of Mme. de Boufflers, whom he distrusted and disliked, beseeching her in the name of her past favors to rescue him from "the abyss of indignities," warning her that her conscience would be haunted by the memory of a good man "choked to death in the mud." The countess reassured him of her constant friendship and inquired what she could do. The salons in Paris were buzzing with talk of impending publication of Rousseau's "memoirs." This gossip did not make the *philosophes'* or Conti's circle less uneasy.

From these events came the desperation that led to Rousseau's violating Conti's injunctions by sending his plea to Choiseul. The plea is written with his typically eloquent combination of humility and pride. It is in part the letter of an advocate, denying the charges that had led to the warrant issued against him in 1762, asking to be allowed to live in peace and freedom under the duke's protection. It concludes: "If you honor me with a reply under the name of Renou, three words suffice: '*I believe you;*' and I shall be content." He was offering Choiseul an easy way. Choiseul did reply, without delay, on March 29, but his letter is either lost or was destroyed by Rousseau.

Only one more incident was needed. Deschamps, the hated *concierge*, died on April 17. Jean-Jacques, believing himself suspected of having poisoned him, requested an autopsy at his own expense. He informed Conti on April 8 that he would stay no longer, *coûte que coûte*; if the servants prevented him from leaving, as he expected they would, and if he had no news from Conti, he would ask to be put in the dungeon until the prince consented to bring him before his judges. The prince replied immediately, telling him he would come on the tenth. He must do nothing until then. Apparently the interview produced no satisfactory results, for on April 18, Conti again sent Rousseau a stern warning against his plan to give himself up to the authorities. "If your project is to come here, I can only sigh, as I told you. But if it is a new resolve to hasten that misguided and extravagant *démarche*, against all your pledges and my promises, I owe it to my very friendship for you to tell you that it is to be unfaithful to everything at once."

He was struggling for survival, helpless in the hands of the powerful. Little wonder he paid no attention to Voltaire's burlesque, scurrilous poem, "La Guerre de Genève," copies of which reached Paris in April.

Relentless in his hatred of his beaten-down foe, the Patriarch of Ferney described him in choice words:

This enemy of human nature, devoured with pride and rancor, flies from the world and fears to see the sky. And yet his dismal, ugly heart has felt the flame of the god of love. He has found, to charm his boredom, a beauty most worthy of him, like Charon enamored of Megaera. That hellish, hideous witch follows the peripatetic monkey everywhere, as the she-owl stays with the owl. . . . Ingratitude is his highest virtue. Out of greatness of soul, he hates his benefactors. . . . His nature is of the canine species: he yelps and snaps at whoever caresses him.

Early in May, Conti yielded in part. Rousseau could leave Trye, provided he remained outside the jurisdiction of the Paris Parlement, renounced the wild idea of confronting the law, and agreed to keep the name Renou. In other words, he held firm on the main point. Until another refuge was found, Jean-Jacques would once again be hidden in Paris, at the Temple, Conti's secure domain.

Rousseau did not leave Trye and reach the Temple until June 12. In the interval he had broken with Coindet and branded him a false friend. Conti meanwhile arranged for him to stay in Grenoble, under the protection of the Comte de Tonnerre, commander of the city.

Now two years of wandering begin. Rousseau was an exile from Paris, from Switzerland, from everywhere. First there were brief stays at Lyons and Grenoble. At Lyons he stayed with his friends, the Boy de la Tour family, but Conti had limited the time he could remain there. He reached Grenoble on July 11, in a cheerful frame of mind. The name of that city evoked memories of his youth. Conti had assured him of the favor of the authorities and a proper reception from his host, Bovier. When he reached Bovier's house, he found no room and no host. When Bovier returned, Rousseau had decided to seek a room elsewhere. He did not know that Bovier was a barrister and a fervent admirer of Voltaire. Perhaps he smelled out an enemy. Why did Bovier urge him to give up the name Renou and tell him that everyone would welcome him under his real name?[11]

The next day everything brightened. Bovier had all of Rousseau's works in his library, and following his precepts, he gave his baby a cold-water bath outdoors. Better still, Mme. Bovier nursed the baby herself. He must have been wrong. The next two days he was greeted triumphantly by the people, wherever he went. Again Bovier tempted Jean-Jacques. "Well, M. Renou, it is you who are stirring up this crowd; you see the power of a great man. . . . Believe me, give up the surname of Renou, resume that of Jean-Jacques." The incognito was ineffective, a sham for official purposes.

Bovier was sincere, but he was striking at Rousseau's weakest point, the temptation to resume his nerve and his role and, with them, the circle of fear and the delusions from which he was trying to escape. Conti had warned him repeatedly about this, warned him to avoid the popular acclamation he so loved. Conti thought he was sheltering Rousseau from the warrant for his arrest; he was really protecting him "against a more redoubtable risk: the danger of becoming Rousseau again, with his glory and his obsessions."[12] To be sure, "M. Renou" had obsessions enough.

Jean-Jacques abandoned all caution. A serenade beneath his window filled him with delight. He appeared at the window and the applause would not end. Then he tried to retreat, spent some days botanizing with Bovier and a magistrate, Servan. He had read a pamphlet by Servan, defending marriages between Protestants and Catholics. It had pleased him. But Servan had also anathematized concubines as corrupters of public morals. Rousseau did not dare to pretend to Servan, who knew his past too well, that Thérèse was his sister. He said that she was his wife. That lie was to have unexpected and drastic consequences. It was to bring about his flight from Grenoble and precipitate his marriage to Thérèse.

Rousseau became uneasy. Were there not spies in those crowds? We know from a letter of Conti's that there were police spies, but Jean Jacques was thinking of his enemies'. He caught Bovier reading one of Voltaire's pamphlets, and Servan may have mentioned his visit to Voltaire at Ferney. In a desperate tone, he wrote to Conti, asking for permission to live in Lyons. Permission denied.

On July 25, Rousseau went on a short journey. He revisited one of the magic landmarks of that long-ago which lingered nostalgically in his memory, Chambéry. There he made a pilgrimage to the grave of Mme. de Warens, "that tender mother" whom he had the misfortune to survive, and visited his friend of yesteryear, Conzié. Alas, Conzié had changed. He was cold and unfriendly. Rousseau, already upset by his situation in Grenoble, feeling uneasily that his life was in danger, was certain that Conzié, too, had been "reached" by the conspiracy.

He returned to Grenoble, convinced that there was no escape. To Thérèse, still at Trye, he wrote that he wanted to give his enemies every opportunity, so tired was he of living in a nightmarish world in which he was surrounded by their satellites. For a while, he seemed to calm down and went on several excursions with the Bovier family. Then, on August 12, after having invited them to visit a hermitage, he fled the city, leaving Bovier in the lurch, Servan and the other people he knew astounded.

What had happened? Bovier had kept prodding Rousseau to show himself, to make official visits. One day Bérulle, chief magistrate of the Parlement, had received him cordially—until the leave-taking, when he remarked, "Of course, Monsieur, I do not know any of your works. I have never read a single one." According to Bovier—and Rousseau was satisfied to let everyone think so—this offense to a writer's vanity was the motive of his sudden departure. "M. Renou turned pale," wrote Bovier, "and without a gesture of adieu, went out the door and ran without stopping to the stagecoach office."[13] The story was good enough to mask the real reason.

A more likely reason was the excitement caused by a young professor, Abbé Gattel (later the teacher of Stendahl) who announced that his public lecture that year would be a refutation of Rousseau's philosophy, especially of the *Discourse on Inequality*. The efforts of Bovier and Servan to avoid distressing their hypersensitive guest by keeping the excitement from his ears could only have produced the contrary effect, for Rousseau was afraid of nothing more than of mystery and "darkness."

The real motive of Rousseau's agitation was to remain his secret. He had just learned that Thérèse had left Trye on August 4. At any moment she might arrive. Keep her in Lyons until I send further instructions, he wrote to Mme. Boy de la Tour on August 11. "I do not want Mlle. Renou to come here; she would be inevitably mocked and insulted by the *belle jeunesse du pays*." He was referring to Gattel's students, no doubt. But what he feared, far more, was Thérèse's wagging tongue. He had told everyone that she was his wife. That fiction would not last a day. The prospect of the scandal and shame that would follow, as soon as she called him *mon frère*, was one he could not face. Two decisions were rapidly taken. He would slip away and go to the not-distant town of Bourgoin. And he would put an end to this whole situation. He would marry Thérèse, and that would be that. Such were the consequences of Bovier's pushing Rousseau out of his planned obscurity into the limelight he so loved. One more disastrous result soon followed, the Thévenin affair.

On August 13 we find him in Bourgoin, ill, alone, and depressed. The warm and ceremonious greeting of the mayor and councillors of Bourgoin he accepted as his due, but it did not relieve his anxieties. He penciled a notice on his door, entitled, "Sentiments du public sur mon compte," a brief summary of the attitude toward him of the various classes and groups in France. A few choice sentences are worth quoting:

The priests, having sold out to the *philosophes*, bark at me in order to court them.

The wits insult me to get revenge for my superiority, which they feel.

The people, who were my idol, see in me only a badly combed wig and a proscribed man.

The women, dupes of two morose men who despise them,* betray the man who is the most deserving of them.

The Swiss will never forgive me for the harm they have done me.

Voltaire, whom I prevent from sleeping, will write a parody on these lines. His coarse insults are the homage he is forced to pay me despite himself.[14]

---

* Probably Grimm and Hume. The phrase in French is *deux pisse-froid*.

Rousseau's unhappiness, his wounded ego cry out in these lines. He was so pleased with them that he sent copies to several friends.

At this point what was to be known as the "affaire Thévenin" came as a culminating blow. On August 22, Bovier sent Rousseau a demand by a certain Thévenin, a chamois-worker, for reimbursement of nine francs he claimed to have lent him years before. Rousseau, with his remarkable memory, knew that he had never met this person, never made such a loan. Clearly, this was a fabrication of his enemies.

Long experience told him that some trouble was in the offing. All the phobias crystallized. He was afraid that when Thérèse rejoined him she would be publicly insulted. He did not want to submit her to his harsh fate, he told her. "I know that they will follow me all over the earth, or rather that they will wait for me." Everywhere, he wrote her on August 23, "I have found only the effect of the machinations which preceded me. Everywhere, the object of hatred and the laughing stock of public derision, I have seen those who were seemingly most eager to serve me, the most zealous to hurt me." He urged her to remain in Lyons or turn back to Paris. He was sure that a new Trye was being prepared for him. "You will not be able to protect either me or yourself, and your sufferings will redouble mine." He was being urged to settle in the remote Château de Lavagnac. It would be, he tells Thérèse, a prison for the rest of his life, a prison where he would be cut off from all human faces. How safely they could defame him, then!

He will not return to Grenoble to face Thévenin. "Note that those who control me, knowing my plan to go to Grenoble, have drawn up all their batteries there against me; when they have us there, they will do what they want with us." Bovier, he is now sure, is another Hume, and in Grenoble the horrors of England are to be replayed for him. In Rousseau's mind Conzié, conniving with Choiseul, has closed off the possibility of Savoy. He has only one hope: Conti's benevolent protection. They have deceived the prince, but his good will is beyond doubt. Perhaps, he suggests to Thérèse, they should go to Turin, where he can earn a living as a copyist, for his enemies plan to make him die of hunger or beg his bread from them. That is why they have hounded him from place to place. He tells her to provide herself with a passport.

He was really hoping that Thérèse would rejoin him. He needed her, in his loneliness and his fear. Otherwise he would not have sent her these revealing instructions: "It does not seem advisable to me that you should give me the name of brother here. . . . In the prince's house we had to comply. . . . Let us be friends and relatives in the expectation of something better. I'll say no more now."

This letter never reached Thérèse. On August 26 she arrived, without a passport and still playing the role of Mlle. Renou, his sister. He kept up the fiction for four days. On the thirtieth, without any notice or word of warning to Thérèse, while they were at the Fontaine d'Or inn, he asked the mayor of Bourgoin and an artillery captain to witness their marriage, by mutual consent. Legal marriage between a Protestant and a Catholic was forbidden. Rousseau solemnly declared that he took Mlle. Renou for his wife, and asked her whether she shared his feelings. The question brought a tender "*oui*," following which he made so eloquent a speech about the duties of marriage, and his own life, that his listeners shed torrents of tears, until his discourse became so sublime that they could no longer follow.[15] After the wedding repast, Rousseau was gay and sang a song he had composed for the occasion. He announced his decision to spend the rest of his life in Bourgoin. Where else could he go? He had been married under the name "Renou." Renou he would stay, in the happy obscurity which he so often claimed he longed for. As for marrying Thérèse, he made that seem a gesture of *noblesse oblige*. He gave it out that it had been an impulse of gratitude toward the companion of his illnesses and misfortunes. "I have never carried out any duty more cheerfully or freely, since I had never given her any hope of it and she had no idea of what I wanted to do two minutes before. . . . Since she will not leave me, at least I want her to follow me with honor."[16] Rousseau's responses followed certain patterns. There is a close analogy between this masking of his real motives and his explanation of his first conversion. Shame requires him to hide the deeper motives: fear and, in this case, shame itself.

The Thévenin affair grew like an incubus in Rousseau's mind. The Comte de Tonnerre, his protector in Grenoble, was not helpful. Rousseau refused to believe that the accusation against him was the result of innocent error. He was determined to clear his name. Though at first he had balked at returning to Grenoble until the mystery was cleared up, when there were no gestures in that direction, he demanded a confrontation. It took place on September 14. He cross-questioned Thévenin with the skill of an examining magistrate, trapping him into contradictions and absurdities. Although Thévenin had supposedly accompanied him for three days, he had seen Rousseau only from the back, and could not describe what he looked like or what he wore, except that he had on a gray suit with a blue or green lining. There was more of the same. Rousseau pointed out to Tonnerre that at the time of the alleged occurrence, he was living at Montmorency, not in Switzerland, and that in Switzerland he wore his Armenian garb, which dould not help being noticed. At first Tonnerre did not reply to this irrefutable invalidation of the charge. Finally he offered to impose silence on Thévenin. Rousseau, outraged, demanded that the scoundrel be obliged to make a public avowal of his imposture.

Rousseau sent letters to Roguin and other friends in Switzerland, asking them to search for further proof. Roguin discovered that Thévenin had once been condemned for forgery, whipped, branded, and sent to the galleys.* Then the innkeeper at Verrières, where the loan

* A year later, Du Peyrou sent Rousseau a copy of the edict sentencing Thévenin to the galleys for three years, for imposture and calumny.

supposedly took place, signed an affidavit denying the whole incident. Tonnerre offered to put Thévenin in prison for a few days. Again Rousseau was infuriated. Tonnerre's duty was to uncover the instigators for whom Thévenin was working. "You cannot imagine the anguish this stupid affair has given me." The populace had taken sides against him, and he feared violence.

Where could he go? The question became a constant torment again. "They" were trying to reduce him to begging for his bread by keeping him at Bourgoin, where his purse was becoming exhausted. He had to leave France. On November 2, in answer to his request, Choiseul sent him a passport. He toyed with the idea of going to Minorca, or to Cyprus, where, under Turkish rule, he would be safe from Christian charity. He even entertained the notion of going to America. Finally he decided to go back to Wooton. On the same day the passport came, he wrote to Davenport, asking him to take him back.

Repeatedly, Rousseau expresses to his correspondents his complete confidence in Conti's unreserved devotion to him, and declares him to be ignorant of the maneuvering carried on behind his back. If Conti did not reply to his letters, it was because they had been intercepted. He was really afraid of losing his only remaining powerful protector. "There is nothing I will not endure rather than deserve the disfavor of the prince. . . . Among all the torments with which they have determined to overwhelm me to my last hour, there is one at least from which I shall be able to protect myself, whatever they do: losing his protection and favor through my own fault."[17]

In November, Rousseau took a rare initiative. He wrote to the Comte de Saint-Germain, whom he did not know, asking him whether he would be willing to receive his confidences and whether he could visit him. The request was accepted graciously. The meeting took place and was followed by correspondence.

Seven years earlier, in preparing his papers for the writing of his *Confessions*, he had been puzzled to discover that a number of letters concerning the Encyclopedists were missing. At that time he could think of no explanation. Later he concluded that d'Alembert, who had slipped into the Maréchale de Luxembourg's graces, had stolen them. But why? Now an explanation dawned upon him. On November 8, 1768, he heard that a man implicated in an "execrable assassination" had been apprehended on the frontier. The individual, it was said, had passed through Bourgoin. Something clicked in his mind, and the two facts meshed. The period of the missing letters was precisely that of Damiens' attempt to assassinate Louis XV, on January 5, 1757. In a flash he "understood." The conspirators were trying to implicate him in that plot! On November 9 he wrote a hysterical letter (now lost) to Conti, to which the latter replied, reassuring him that he was not being accused of any crime.

Fearing that Walpole was plotting with the English ambassador,

Rousseau decided to remain in France, *coûte que coûte*, despite Davenport's warm invitation to return to Wooton. He was suffering from a
painful intestinal inflammation, which he attributed to the water and
swampy air of Bourgoin. On January 30, 1769, he moved to Monquin, a
town situated on high ground in the same region. There he would stay,
he resolved, until he died. He was trying to regain serenity through faith
in the afterlife. God exists, he exclaims to Moultou (February 14), or
else the justification of moral values is destroyed.

Can we believe that the just man who is a prey to all the ills of this life,
including infamy and dishonor, has no indemnification to expect when it is
over, and that he will die like an animal after having lived according to God?
No, no, Moultou. Jesus, whom this century has misjudged, because it was
unworthy to know him, Jesus, who died because he wanted to make his vile
compatriots into an illustrious and virtuous people, sublime Jesus, did not
entirely die on the cross. That is enough for me, who am only a miserable man
full of weaknesses, but with a heart which I feel never to have been touched by
guilt, to feel, as I sense the dissolution of my body drawing near, the certainty
that I shall live.

Serenity was not to be attained. A complaining letter to Conti
brought a reply, on April 5, in which the prince denied that a secret plot
against him existed, and declared his suspicions about Mme. de Luxembourg to be reprehensible. He warns Jean-Jacques to control his misin-
terpretations of other people's acts. If he is unhappy, it is the doing of
his own imagination.

Rousseau continued to harass Conti, asking him to set him free from
his promises, and to allow him to do what he wished with his life. Conti
refused even to grant his protégé an audience. Rousseau threatened
(May 31) to defy his orders: "Since nothing can release me from my
duty to myself, I shall, in the extremity in which I find myself, dispose of
myself as my heart dictates." Dismayed by this threat, Conti, on June 16,
warned him again about keeping his promises and about the danger of
coming to Paris. He relented to the extent of inviting Jean-Jacques to
visit him at his summer residence at Pougues, near the Loire. But he
cannot, must not, move about in France. If he wishes to leave the
country, however, that can be arranged. A month later, Rousseau
traveled to Pougues. The results, apparently, were unsatisfactory, for on
September 2, Conti writes again to his recalcitrant protégé, saying that
the steps Rousseau forced him to take (in order to allow him to return
to Paris, one must suppose) have, as he had forewarned, failed. If Rousseau moves, he will lose his protection. And he must continue to use the
name Renou.

A domestic crisis added to Jean-Jacques' misery. During the summer
of 1769, bitterness and rancor brought him and Thérèse to the point of
separation. He wrote her a long, emotional letter on August 12. It is

only too obvious, he says, that any feelings exist only on his side, that she can scarcely bear to stay a few minutes with him, such is her aversion. Despite all he has done for her, despite all his present efforts, he can no longer make her happy. He does not ever want to leave her; he wants to have her beside him in the ground. But she has suggested, time and again in the heat of their raging disputes, that they separate. What will he do when he has no heart in which to confide? She is his only resource. Without her, he will be absolutely alone, he will die. Yet to go on in this state of war is impossible. He urges her to think of going to live in a convent, at least until they both realize that they cannot live without each other. Meanwhile, he is leaving on a fortnight's journey, one from which he may never return. (The projected trip, possibly to Chambéry, was not undertaken.) If he dies, she is to do nothing about the plot which will pursue his memory. "Let providence and time do their work; it will be done sooner or later." While he is away, she should be thinking.

Think of what you owe to yourself, of what you owe to me, of all we have been to each other for so long, of what we should be to each other until the end. . . . We both have faults to regret and to expiate, but, thank heaven, no villainies or crimes to reproach ourselves for. Let us not destroy, by the imprudence of our last days, the sweetness and purity of those we have spent together.

Rousseau was rocked by the crisis. It is obvious that Thérèse's wrath came from his persistence in not cohabiting with her. At forty-eight, she had not lost her lascivious temperament. The incident may have been provoked, however, by Rousseau's discovery that she was amusing herself with a monk. In 1770 Grimm reported a choice bit of gossip: Jean-Jacques, having caught Thérèse *in flagrante* with the monk, discarded his Armenian garb, seeing that he was now no different from ordinary men. Some corroboration is supplied by Rousseau himself. In his letter to Thérèse, he gives her a warning. In case they are separated, "let no monk have anything to do with you or your affairs in any way whatsoever." Not without significance, while at Monquin he wrote the ninth book of the *Confessions*, in which he promises to reveal some day "the wounds, the lacerations with which she rended my heart in the depth of my misery."[18] Rousseau never wrote the final book of the *Confessions*. But in the second of the *Dialogues* he does allude to the "*monastiques oeuvres*" (the anterior position of the adjective could well indicate irony) of a Jacobin monk who was serving in Monquin, and says that he finally conveyed to the monk "that which he was stupid enough not to have suspected until then."[19]

We hear no more of this quarrel. The incident, however, did not contribute to his well-being. His defense mechanisms were breaking down, and he was entering a period of acute emotional disturbance. Most

of his letters, in the early part of 1770, and some even later, are headed
by a quatrain:

> Pauvres aveugles que nous sommes!
> Ciel, démasque les imposteurs,
> Et force leurs barbares coeurs
> A s'ouvrir au regard des hommes.*

He felt the darkness closing in on him and, like Don Quixote with the
wineskins, flailed about wildly at the giants who were relentlessly persecuting him, whose spies and informers, he told his correspondents,
dogged his every step. Come what may, he would use his own name, and
he would leave this accursed place, go to Lyons, near Mme. Boy de la
Tour. They concerted on the arrangements. Only the snows and bitter
cold forced a delay.

In April of 1769, Rousseau had turned down Rey's urging that he
finish his memoirs. It came during one of the intervals of relative tranquillity, when he was trying to follow his oft-announced policy of withdrawal. Distinguished visitors were turned away. His life would be spent
quietly, with Thérèse and his dog, with botany, music, and Tasso. Then,
in November 1769, he could no longer resist a new fear. He was going to
die without justifying himself for having abandoned his children. There
would be no defense against the vilification his enemies would heap
upon him as soon as he was gone. He made up his mind. He would give
up botany and work again on the *Confessions*. Courage and determination returned, in the midst of his terrors. He felt himself capable of
crushing his enemies' clever phrases with the power of his eloquence, as
he would crush an insect. As he mulled over the fatal events of 1762 at
Montmorency, he began to understand the pressures, the blackmail
which had been brought to bear on him, and for the first time, he began
to suspect Conti, but not for the right reasons. His own prudence had
been cowardice.[20] In February 1770, despite a final admonition from
Conti, he decided finally to use his own name, which he "should never
have quit." He was determined to clear his name, to go back to Paris. He
was thinking of provoking his arrest and trial or, possibly, of reading his
*Confessions* to influential people. In some way or other, he would force
his enemies to show their hand. He knew he could not publish the
*Confessions*. Even to read them would at least foil the secret agents who
were trying to get hold of his manuscript and take away the weapon of
truth on which he counted to win his great victory.

His turbulence became uncontainable. On February 22, 1770, he
poured his distress into a long letter to Saint-Germain, a remarkable
psychological document which reveals how far his psychic disturbance

---

* "Poor blind men that we are! Heaven, unmask the impostors, and make their
barbarous hearts disclose themselves to the eyes of men."

has progressed beyond the comparable letter of accusation written to Hume on July 10, 1766.

The letter is suffused with two cries: "I am innocent!" and "I accuse!" It is the paroxysm of an agonized paranoid who feels himself enmeshed in the web of a net, in which he is thrashing about helplessly.

Rousseau is now certain that Choiseul, France's foreign minister, has taken complete charge of the plot. Much of Choiseul's time, it would appear, is devoted to organizing schemes and a vast network of personnel, in order to make his life a torment worse than death by dragging him through the mud, vilifying his character, and making him "the fable of the people and the sport of the *canaille.*" Even the French takeover of Corsica was motivated only by Choiseul's desire to spite Jean-Jacques, who had declared its people the only ones capable of living according to his ideas. By seduction or pressure, he has turned all of Rousseau's friends against him, even Du Peyrou, in order to get at his papers, even his childhood friend Conzié, even his publisher, Rey. All his correspondence is intercepted and read. People are sent regularly to ask him for favors, in order to find out whether he has any protectors remaining to him, so that they can be alienated in their turn. They lure him into making promises to Conti in order to bind him hand and foot. Word has been spread that he is a rapist, arsonist, poisoner, and murderer. Every step, every movement of his finger, is spied on and noted down. If he remains immobile, it must be that he is contemplating the worst of all crimes, telling the truth.

The plot, Rousseau tells Saint-Germain, began long before Choiseul, in his unmotivated hatred, assumed control of it. He now goes back over his whole life. The trouble started when he told men the truth and expressed his devotion to virtue in his early writings. The first villains, the originators of the plot, were Diderot and Grimm, especially the stealthy implacable Grimm, who hated Jean-Jacques because he had wronged him. The next to join was Mme. de Boufflers, who never forgave his having written (before he knew her) that a charcoal-seller's wife was more respectable than the mistress of a prince. When she asked him what he thought of a play she had written, he told her it reminded him of one he had read. But most of all, she could not forgive him for not making love to her.

Many others hate him, relentlessly. The Maréchale de Luxembourg, Tronchin, d'Holbach—and we wonder why Voltaire is omitted from the list.

Rousseau proceeds to a defense of his character. He is not avaricious, only a pinchpenny, out of fear of having to obtain money for his simple needs. He was never debauched, never frequented bordellos, never had venereal diseases, as they were saying. "The love I conceive of, that I have been able to feel, is inflamed by the unreal image of the perfection of the beloved; and that very image exalts it into an enthusiasm for

virtue, for that is part of the idea of a perfect woman." Yes, he loves
solitude; but Diderot's charge, "only the wicked man is alone," reverses
the truth. Yes, he has loved fame. But how does a man win glory if not
through virtuous, noble works?

Of what, then, am I guilty? he cries out, again and again. In these
pages we witness the agony of Kafka's hero in *The Trial*. What is the
accusation? Why am I not charged? Let me go before the bar and defend
myself! This is what he had been requesting of Conti for years, always to
be denied. And this is what they will never allow him to do—because he
is innocent! The nub of the whole plot is to spin a web of mysterious
innuendo.

To make me drink the bitter cup of ignominy, they will take care to circulate it ceaselessly around me in the darkness, to make it drip and trickle down
my head, make it soak me, inundate me, choke me, but without any shaft of
light ever reaching my eyes or letting me see what it contains. They will isolate
me from all men, even while I live with them; for me everything will be a
secret, a mystery, or a lie. They will make me a stranger in society, without
seeming to expel me. They will build around me an impenetrable edifice of
darkness; they will bury me alive in a coffin. . . .

Groups of people will fall silent when I arrive; women will lose their
tongues; barbers will be discreet and untalkative; I shall live among the most
loquacious nation as among a people of mutes. If I travel, everything will be
prearranged to control me wherever I go; the word will be given to passengers,
coachmen, innkeepers. . . . Such horror of me will be spread on my road that
at each step I take, at each object I see, my heart will be lacerated. That will
not prevent my receiving everywhere, like Sancho, a hundred mocking obei-
sances, accompanied by compliments, respect, and admiration.

It is a curious phenomenon that Rousseau so precisely defines the
"hatreds" that have united against him, while declaring that this "black
mystery is still enveloped, for me, in an impenetrable veil." Where he
does not see clearly, he is convinced that his intuitions guide him with
their almost unerring light. Have Grimm and Diderot, the initiators of
the grand plot, withdrawn? This is not to be believed. Doubtless they
are busy forging "abominable writings" which are being attributed to
him. Not books—it would be too difficult to forge his handwriting over
such a span—but letters. That would not be hard. Diderot knows many
artists, and Choiseul commands everything. Who else but Choiseul
could have set Thévenin upon him? But surely it was Grimm who devised the most clever schemes, with Choiseul behind, or rather in front
of him. *Emile* had given them their great chance. They had seized it,
used the maréchale's honor to get him to flee, while Mme. de Boufflers
and Hume plotted to reduce him to helplessness in England. When he
refused and went to Switzerland, they worked until he had to leave that
refuge. Then, desperate that he might escape them altogether by joining
Keith in Berlin, they set so many snares for him that at last they caught

him, never again to let him go. So relentless and thorough are these
fiends that they have destroyed all the portraits which look like him,
spreading everywhere the Ramsay portrait, commissioned and plotted
by Hume, in which he looks like a Cyclops. "In a word, the details
involved in the execution of the plan are for me immense, inconceivable."

Death will not end their work. They will try to cover his memory with
obloquy. On that score, he is not worried. His enemies, too, must die.
Time will sift the gold from the dross. The plots will be uncovered.
Future generations will weep over his misfortunes and bless his memory.
But for him only one thing remains: death, which will surely bring him
the happiness "for which I was born and which I have sought in vain on
earth." It will not be denied him, though he is not without sins. "I feel
myself to be just, good, virtuous, as much as any man on earth. . . . If I
were offered the choice on earth of what I want to be, I should reply
*dead.*"

Rousseau has entered his nightmare world. He was a prisoner, not of a
vast plot such as he imagined it, but of his own delusions and, it must be
added, of the contrivings of the Conti set to keep him from returning to
Paris. In his tormented mind, all his disparate misfortunes since 1757 co-
alesced into a single, indivisible phenomenon, the "plot." It is a common-
place of psychiatry that unjustifiable hostility toward others is a projection
of guilt that can no longer be repressed.* Rousseau's continual self-defense
in his letters and other writings was an effort to exorcise that guilt. In
his case, however, there was enough reality in the persecutions he had
suffered and the hostility of his enemies among the *philosophes* and the
Church to make his delusional world absolutely convincing.

The outstanding element in the letter to Saint-Germain, according to
Grimsley, is the theme of an unbridgeable chasm between "the most
loving of men" and the "horror of his fellowmen" for him. The notion
of a "false" and "evil" Jean-Jacques, whom his enemies were trying to
pass off as the authentic Rousseau, was an obsession, and his personality
was split between these two images. His enemies, determined to hound
him to his doom, have contrived to put him in a situation in which he is
powerless to justify himself. "The tone of Rousseau's references," comments Grimsley, "suggests that his attitude involves at times a regression
to more primitive and infantile modes of emotional response."[21] Thus,
his persecutors are identified with animals and birds, or with devilish
creatures, who take a sadistic pleasure in tormenting their helpless
victim. They are always "unseen," moles burrowing under earth. He is
beset with genuine terror in the face of this secrecy and silence.

---

* Mauzi remarks that Rousseau carried his hell within himself, "vibrating with a
good conscience when attacked, gnawed by remorse as soon as nothing is opposed to
him" (*L'Idée du bonheur au XVIII<sup>e</sup> siècle*; Paris, 1960, p. 633). "Myself am Hell," says
Milton's Satan.

All psychosis is an attempt to find a viable psychic state when reality is unbearable. Grimsley's analysis is most acute:

The whole gigantic edifice of Rousseau's delusional system emerges finally as a desperate attempt to regain a stability and equilibrium that had been so seriously undermined by the events of the previous years. The obsessive preoccupation with others' hostility was not intended to serve as a mere screen to conceal his own feelings of inadequacy and guilt, but as a positive basis for a new affirmation of his own "goodness." If he was persecuted by all, was it not *because* of his own goodness? Was it not because others knew him to be innocent and good that they took such fiendish pleasure in pursuing him with their hatred? Persecution, therefore, was not a mere aberration, but an essential condition for the renewal of his efforts at self-realization. It created as it were the stable background against which the striving for personal fulfillment could be carried on.[22]

Saint-Germain, in a soothing reply (February 28), assured Rousseau that his hypersensitivity to self-evidently false accusations was his enemies' greatest weapon against him. He urged Rousseau not to go to Paris to start again "a useless, dangerous, untimely war" in which he could only be hurt. But Rousseau thought that "nothing is so great or so beautiful as to suffer for the truth. . . . I envy the glory of the martyrs."[23]

To the numerous unwanted correspondents who thrust themselves upon him, Rousseau usually replied courteously, sometimes obsequiously, when they were aristocrats, especially aristocratic ladies. One of these was Mme. Rose de Berthier, with whom he had a mildly flirtatious correspondence, reaching the point of calling her by her first name. The longing for the lovely lady of his dreams never quit him, but his anguish penetrates even these letters.

You have esteemed me for my writings. You would esteem me even more for my life if it were known to you; and even more for my heart, if it were open to your eyes. Never was there a heart more tender, better, or more just. Neither wickedness nor hatred has ever touched it. Certainly I have great vices, but they have never hurt anyone except me. . . . Remember three words with which I finish my adieux: I AM INNOCENT.[24]

Unless he touched Rousseau's heart in a special way, a stranger of no distinction was likely to get short shrift. When a doctor and would-be poet, one Gagnière, asked Rousseau to give an opinion on his long poem, *Les Principes de la physique*, Jean-Jacques refused abruptly, disclaiming any knowledge of what was suitable for the public. "Thus, not having the honor of knowing you, and unable to serve you, I do not wish to see your poem." Gagnière, unlike most of the rejected admirers, replied with pique. If you do not know what the public likes or dislikes, he asks, "why did you take it on yourself to be its reformer, in education,

legislation and the priesthood, even to the point of trying to persuade us
to walk on all fours?" The angry doctor was obviously acquainted with
Voltaire's famous letter to Rousseau about his *Discourse on Inequality*.
He thrusts a sample of his poetry on his former idol:

> Quittez cet esprit pointilleux!
> Ne vantez plus votre sagesse!
> Et devenant moins orgueilleux
> Vous connaîtrez la politesse.*[25]

When a certain Henriette, with whom he had exchanged some letters
years before, requested him to see her, he abruptly asked her to explain
in detail who she was, what she wanted, why she had not written for so
long, and why she suddenly had decided to come on the scene again.
Then he would consider her request. "I have a greater need of friends
than you, but I don't want them to choose me. It is I who wish to choose
them." If she calls without his consent, then she is "judged" and will be
turned away.[26]

Pierre de Belloy, the famous dramatist, author of *Le Siège de Calais*,
was worth several letters, in one of which Rousseau writes:

I consider my misfortunes to be linked to my status as a man and a lover of
the truth. I see the wicked man who persecutes and defames me as I should see
a rock tumbling down a mountain to crush me. I should push it away, if I were
strong enough, but without anger, and then I should disregard it and never
think of it again.[27]

How can Belloy write to him about his own troubles? "What can they
have in common with mine? My situation is unique, unheard of since the
beginning of the world, and I may presume that there will never be
another like it."

When Rey put out a new edition of his works, Rousseau was convinced that his old friend had mutilated one of his writings in a way
that would hurt him. Rey "had enlisted." Yet Jean-Jacques kept on
writing to him as if he had not suspected the treason.

The snows were heavy that year and lasted until early April. When
the roads became passable, Rousseau, throwing off Conti's yoke, left
Monquin. He would go where honor and duty summoned him, even if it
were toward imprisonment and death. Departing with his household
goods on April 10, he went to Lyons, where Mme. Boy de la Tour and
other friends entertained him. In his honor, *Pygmalion* and *Le Devin
du village* were performed at the Town Hall. Hearing that a subscrip-
tion was being taken to have Houdon do a statue of Voltaire, he sent in
his contribution, which was not accepted. The gesture, doubtless designed to show the nobility of his heart, irritated the Patriarch of Ferney
considerably. Perhaps Rousseau had intended that, too.

---

* "Put away this captious spirit! Stop boasting about your wisdom! And, becoming
less proud, you will discover politeness."

The two months in Lyons were relatively happy. He would have prolonged his stay, were it not for the failure of a motet he had composed; doubtless his enemies had formed a cabal against him. There could be no resting place. He must go on to Paris, to confront them in their lair.

# X. Return to Paris

But there is that within me which shall tire
Torture and Time, and breathe when I expire.

## 1. WHERE IS THE ENEMY?

ROUSSEAU may have taken soundings from Lyons and found that his return to Paris would be tolerated under certain conditions. It is evident that he was not concerned. Perhaps he really hoped for a confrontation. On the way, he stopped at Dijon, where he met the magistrate and *littérateur* Charles de Brosses, and at Montbard, where he discussed botany with two celebrated naturalists, Buffon and Daubenton. On June 24 he reached Paris, going at once to his old lodgings at the Hôtel du Saint-Esprit in the rue Plâtrière. He wrote Mme. Boy de la Tour of his joy at living in Paris again and finding friends of former days. Soon he was frequenting his old haunt, the Café de la Régence, matching his strength at chess with them. He went back to work copying music.

Contrary to Conti's dire warnings, the police did not bother him. What a fool he had been to allow himself to be Conti's dupe! He added a footnote to the tenth book of the *Confessions*: "Notice the perseverance of that blind and stupid confidence in the midst of all the vexations which should have certainly disillusioned me. It ended only after my return to Paris in 1770." A sure sign of his safety was the Comédie Italienne's giving him free admission. The Comédie Italienne put on musical plays, but we do not know whether he took advantage of the privilege.

According to the report in the *Correspondance littéraire*, permission to live in Paris had been granted (doubtless by Choiseul and the public prosecutor) on two conditions: that Rousseau give up his Armenian garb (which he had done) and that he refrain from any publication. Later he was asked to stay away from cafés and other public places, because curious crowds gathered to look at him. The bear, continues the report, has become a gallant and soft-spoken frequenter of fashionable *grandes dames.*

Voltaire was exasperated. "It is amusing," he wrote the Duc de Richelieu on July 11, 1770, "that a watchmaker's apprentice, with a warrant out for his arrest, should be in Paris, and that I am not."

Visitors came in an unending stream, some famous, like the Prince de Ligne. Rousseau could not accept all the invitations to dinner. A Swedish professor who succeeded in getting an interview set down his impressions at some length.

M. Rousseau has just married Mlle. LeVasseur, who was his housekeeper and had taken the most tender care of him during his illnesses; he wanted to reward her. She is already middle-aged, and it is easy to see that he did not marry her for her beauty. Yet she is not without charm; she is frank in her way and is obviously very attached to her husband.

M. Rousseau will soon be 59, for he was born in 1712. I should never have believed him to be so old, if he had not told me himself. He looks far younger. He is of average height, small and stocky rather than tall. His eyes are dark and fiery. He always carries his head bent to one side, and he generally averts his eyes from you. Sometimes, however, he darts a penetrating look at you, furtively. His face is full, with well-molded features, and prepossessing. His manners are pleasing and gracious, although he talks too loud and vehemently.[1]

Only one person was made unhappy by Rousseau's return, the ever-loving and all too frequently spurned Marianne de la Tour. Hurt and indignant, she learned early in August that her idol was almost her neighbor, that he had ignored her existence. When she offered to visit him, suggesting that she would be embarrassed if he came to see her, because their friendship was a secret, Rousseau, offended and proud, refused brusquely, almost savagely, closing his note with a cold and formal salutation.[2] Marianne immediately reversed herself, offered to receive him, and went on to ask his consent to her publishing their correspondence. He denied her request.

A young *littérateur*, Dusaulx, introduced by Duclos, appealed to Rousseau, and for about six months they were fast friends. He was the newest of a line of men for whom Jean-Jacques felt an infatuation that was at least partially homoerotic. Dusaulx was later to describe their friendship with some bitterness.[3] " 'At last I have found what I was looking for,' he told me, devouring me with his eyes; 'but I do not see you often enough, I want to see you every evening.' "[4] On January 4, 1771, Rousseau invited Dusaulx to a "little Epicurean supper," and asked for "a little 'yes' " in reply. Dusaulx replied: "Never has a bride, ready to surrender herself to her dear lover's arms, pronounced her 'yes' with greater joy than mine, as I hasten to send you 'that little yes' so graciously requested."[5] The inevitable quarrel came about in February.

Rousseau's suspicions were awakened when Dusaulx read him a composition, "Portrait of an Impostor." Rousseau, of course, took it for
himself. "The *je ne sais quoi*," he wrote Dusaulx, on February 16, "too
long to recount but striking to notice, has warned me that there was
some hidden mystery beneath your caresses." Sometime later, while he
was watching the roadworks at the Etoile, he ran into Dusaulx. Suddenly he was seized by fear. Dusaulx, he felt, was going to throw him
into a deep trench. Trembling, he raised his arms to heaven, as if to ask
his estranged friend's pity.[6]

Dusaulx was to have replaced Sauttersheim, who had replaced others
and was followed by Hume. It is worth recalling Rousseau's reaction to
the news of Sauttersheim's death, which had occurred at Strasbourg on
December 17, 1767, but reached him only a year later. He broke into an
emotional eulogy:

Poor boy, poor Sauttersheim! Too preoccupied with myself in my distress, I
had lost sight of him, but he did not leave my heart, and I nourished the secret
desire of drawing near to him again. . . . There remained only an illusory hope,
now I have none left at all. . . . I feel that the loss of this poor boy affects me
out of proportion to my other calamities. There must have been a very strong
affection between him and me, since, having already learned to beware of
gushing people, I received him with open arms as soon as he introduced
himself, and from the first days of our friendship, it was an intimate one.
[Rousseau mentions the letter he wrote, defending Sauttersheim, and the trip
to Pontarlier they took together.] On reaching Pontarlier, I embraced him with
rapture, then I showed him the letter. He read it with no emotion. We embraced again, and our tears flowed. . . . Heaven has taken him away from men,
among whom he was a stranger; but why has it left me here?[7]

The similarities and contrasts between this episode and Rousseau's
relationship with Hume are striking. Hume had not responded to his
caresses and his tears. Therefore, he was a false friend. Sauttersheim, an
adventurer, had not remained with him. Neither had Bâcle, Venture de
Villeneuve, Altuna, or Carrión. The homoerotic longings never developed to the point where they became a menace.

The end of 1770 again brought darker hues into Rousseau's mind,
and the opening quatrain cited earlier (p. 317) reappears in many of his
letters. His old friend d'Escherny writes of visiting him at this time. "I
perceived that the Rousseau I had found again was no longer the one I
had left five years before. I saw him weighed down by the despairing
idea of that muffled, frightening, universal conspiracy by which he
claimed to be surrounded." The conspirators wanted to persuade the
world that he was not the author of his books, deny his genius and
brand him a scoundrel. "Several days later, I found him better, for these
dark moods overcame him only at intervals and in sudden fits."[8]

Another lengthy justification went to Malesherbes on November 23.

Though less interesting than the letter to Saint-Germain, it illuminates several points and testifies to the deepening of his delusions. Mirabeau is now included among the conspirators. His letters inviting Rousseau to return from England were written in a strange style. Like other false friends at that time, he put a certain note of reservation and obscurity into his praises. We also have further evidence that Rousseau has finally suspected Conti of double-dealing. The prince was not aware of the mistreatment under which he suffered at Trye, "or at least, so I thought." The prince "seemed" to overwhelm him with his favors.

But the Maréchale de Luxembourg's image has darkened most. She is consumed with secret hatred for him. Its motive was not, as he had suspected, his clumsy remarks to her, but something else that had determined her to drive him to his doom. She, without doubt, allowed d'Alembert to steal the missing letters. She betrayed her hand by writing to him more and more infrequently, and less and less cordially. She had not helped him get the passport. It had come, after a delay—that is, after they had had time to prepare traps for him in the countries where they thought he might go. That is why he had decided to foil them by going back to England, until they drove him crazy with their harassment. That was when he understood why the letters had been taken: they had sworn to bring about his ruin. At that moment of understanding, he had decided to stand steadfast against all they could do.

During the autumn months Rousseau moved into a flat on the sixth story of a house on the same street where he had been living. The apartment had two rooms. Dusaulx and the Prince de Ligne called it a garret, infested with rats. Bernardin de Saint-Pierre, however, describes a neat little home, with Jean-Jacques copying music in his frock coat and white bonnet. Thérèse sat near him, sewing, while a canary sang in its cage and sparrows ate crumbs in the open windows. In the evening, he read aloud to Thérèse, from novels or from Tasso's *Jerusalem Delivered*.

By December 24 he had written the last pages of the *Confessions*. Seeing that he had not succeeded in forcing his enemies' hand by reappearing in Paris, he decided to challenge them again by reading his *Confessions* in influential salons. At the homes of selected friends, including the poet Dorat and the Marquis de Pezay, he gave readings which lasted from fifteen to seventeen hours at a stretch, his voice never tiring, with only an interruption for dinner. It was not merely a physical ordeal, but an emotional one, for a man so timid, to make a public display of his intimate secrets, secrets which few men would reveal to their friends. These readings continued into the following spring. In February the crown prince of Sweden was his listener. Now he was into the second part, which includes the quarrel with Mme. d'Epinay, Grimm, and Diderot. When he read from it at the home of the Comtesse d'Egmont (to whom he vowed devotion), Mme. d'Epinay asked Sartine, the head of the police, to forbid any more readings. They had become a public scandal and were brought to an end.

Rousseau was distressed by the results of his readings, as he interpreted them. At the climactic session, at the home of the Comtesse d'Egmont, he added a final postscript for his audience:

"I have said the truth. If anyone knows things contrary to what I have just related, even if they were proven a thousand times over, he knows lies and impostures. . . . As for me, I declare aloud and without fear: Whoever, even without having read my writings, examines with his own eyes my nature, my character, my morals, my inclinations, my pleasures, my habits, and can believe me to be a dishonest man, is himself a man worthy to be choked to death."

I concluded thus my reading, and everyone was silent. Alone Mme. d'Egmont seemed moved; she shuddered visibly; but she quickly regained her composure and remained as mute as the rest of the company. Such was the fruit I harvested from this reading and from my declaration.[9]

Rousseau realized that he had failed to achieve his purpose—opening a breach in the wall of silence by confronting his enemies. He had succeeded only in giving them a new hold on him, he was convinced, a new way of "disfiguring" his true image. He should have known that one can obtain nothing from "depraved hearts."[10] In fact, his listeners did not all react in the same way. The poet Dorat wept copiously and returned home intoxicated with pleasure and admiration. "What a work! How he paints himself in it! How one loves to recognize him in it!" Dusaulx, on the other hand, explains the listeners' patience and attention by the satisfactions of snobbery, of being among the chosen few: they "didn't want to miss a word, in order to have the pleasure of talking about it."[11] Dusaulx's cynicism was undoubtedly well founded. The elite of Paris had come to look at this notorious, mentally unbalanced genius, eager for stories to tell.

Rousseau did not intend his *Confessions* to be published during his lifetime. He had finished the first part at Trye, in the spring of 1768; the second, begun at Monquin in 1769, was completed in Paris in June 1770. The first half was given to the public early in 1782, the second in 1789. If Rousseau's foes sighed with relief on seeing that the first part ended before the quarrel of 1757, their uneasiness was not relieved by the eloquence and persuasiveness of the writing. Mme. de Boufflers' admiration for Rousseau had already turned into dislike during the Hume affair. When she read the *Confessions*, she expressed her indignation to the king of Sweden. "Infamous memoirs," she called them, "memoirs of a *valet de basse cour* [a poultry-farm boy], insane and vicious in the most disgusting way," boring, to boot.

The mad avowal of all his vileness strikes me as an act of providence which has forced this infamous man to snatch off his own hypocritical mask. . . . I regret the devotion I had for him (for it was that). I shall never forgive myself because it cost the illustrious David Hume, who to please me undertook to take that filthy animal to England, his life.[12]

The *Confessions* is a major work of world literature. Its influence on later generations has been vast. It brought into literature the entire subjective realm of the inner self, adding thereby many new dimensions: the isolation created by the consciousness of the protagonist, the immediacy of experience, the distortions of subjective time and the recapture of time through the subterranean storehouses of memory, the bending of reality through the unfathomable prism of sensitivity, the continuity of personality and its changes.* In the midst of writers whose main interest was to observe and illuminate the outer world, or man in general, here was Jean-Jacques, thrusting upon them the revelation of his *moi*. A style was set, and he has had many imitators, but no equals. No longer was a writer—sinning, perverted, agonized, or criminal—to feel shame at opening his mind and heart, with their soil and intimate pain, for all to see. Voltaire had once apologized for "falling into the ridiculousness of speaking about myself to myself." The eighteenth-century world had never seen the inside of a heart, until Jean-Jacques showed it his. "I should like in some way to make my soul transparent to the reader's eyes."[13] He showed his readers the difficulty of comprehending the incongruous individual, in his majesty and his misery, in any system of rational coherence; he can be understood, in Kierkegaard's phrase, only in "passionate subjectivity."

According to Jean-Paul Sartre, our death is the final triumph of the Other, since the Other can now decide how to think of us; once in the "public domain," we are defenseless against all judgments. We have seen that Rousseau was keenly aware of this human fate. His future name and reputation were the very bull's-eye at which the "conspirators" were aiming. Rousseau's enemies were equally worried about what he might do to theirs, and were indeed taking countermeasures.[14] Enough vicious gossip about him was going the rounds, in Paris, London, Geneva—all over Europe—for him to have reason to be concerned. A lot was known about some of the shameful pages of his past. But how much did they know? How much were they saving until after his death? There was no way of finding out, in this conspiracy of darkness. Rousseau, a clever strategist, must have realized that the best course was to tell everything himself, and in his own way. And above all, to put the stamp of complete sincerity—of the *confessional*—on every page.

He could not believe in the indifference of the world to him. The

---

* About memory, Rousseau makes the following remark: "Not only do I remember the times, the places, the persons, but all the surrounding objects, the temperature of the air, its smell, its color, a certain local impression which was felt only there, whose recollection carries me back to it again" (*Confessions*, Book III, p. 122; a similar statement occurs in Book IV, p. 174).

"look" of the Other had become the eyes of the world. He could not know that his distrust of the world was an inversion and projection of his distrust of himself. On the contrary, he "was indulgent toward himself and exacting toward others, a not very endearing characteristic; and he saw himself as a tiny flame of goodness and light in a world which was essentially dark and evil."[15] Yet he would ask all men to judge him. Not the men of his own time; their corrupted ears would not hear the truth. He would throw himself on the mercy of the unprejudiced tribunal of future generations, whom the plotters could not corrupt or ensnare, and, beyond mankind, on the mercy and judgment of God. When he defies his readers to dare to say, "I was better than that man!" Rousseau, like Clamence, the hero of Camus' *The Fall*, is adroitly trying to escape the noose of his own guilt by obliging others to share it. Confession, moreover, is a means of purging oneself, of restoring a sense of honesty. To make public confession was, he asserts, a heroic and unique act. But it was also an exorcism of what was evil in him: a fault, it has been said, "may appear as far less objectionable once it has been revealed to others and thus shared with them."[16]

The *Confessions* is not only the plea of a defendant at the bar. It is one of the two major pieces in Rousseau's lifelong search for himself. He was doing precisely what Voltaire, who could never begin to understand him, called ridiculous: speaking about himself to himself. He labored as hard on the creation of an identity for himself—both private and public—as he had worked on any masterpiece. The questions were the same as always. Why had he acted in a given way? Why had strange, unique things happened to him? The ends were the same: catharsis of guilt, self-justification, self-knowledge. Actually, it was perhaps less to find the truth that he wrote, than to correct it. Rousseau's need to create an acceptable image of himself, to cast himself in certain roles, to have a truth of his own which was a subjective certainty, had determined the events of his life. It was to determine also his recollection and narration of the events of his life. Only rarely did he purposely deform the truth, when the wounds of abjection and humiliation to his ego were too piercing to lay bare.

If Rousseau was often (though not always) aware of this warping, he was unaware of his monstrous egocentricity, which, according to one of his admirers, "bordered at times on megalomania."[17] He did not suspect that he was really engaged in the work of choosing his "authentic" self through memory, and at the same time, of alleviating his guilt, from the first pages on, by blaming others. The two themes of the *Confessions* are Rousseau's uniqueness, and the dialectic of guilt resolving itself into innocence or into pardonable weaknesses which never compromise the moral worth of his authentic self—the self which *is*, in contrast to its acts. By self-revelation, Rousseau strove to become the man he wanted to be and felt himself to be, to break through the "veils" and "obstacles" against which he had always been struggling. He is not recapturing the past for its own sake, but using it to explore and explain what he has become, what he is. The past, in the *Confessions*, is not a dead past, then. Its echoes resound in the present. We are always aware that Rousseau is living in both times at once. Not infrequently, three layers of time coalesce, as the old man bends over his past to recapture a younger Jean-Jacques, who is reliving an earlier moment of happiness. When he recounts events of long ago, he reexperiences the past in which they took place, which may include a more remote past, in all its amplitude. When he returns to the Hermitage, for instance, we know not only what happened, but the state of his physical and moral being. Following a passage quoted earlier,* he goes on:

I pursued these reflections in the most beautiful season of the year, in the month of June, in cool groves, amidst the song of the nightingale and the purling of brooks. Everything combined to plunge me again into that too-seductive indolence to which I was naturally inclined, but from which the hard and austere frame of mind, to which a long period of inner ferment had brought me, should have delivered me once and for all. Unhappily, I went on to recall the dinner at the Château de Toune, and my meeting with those two charming girls at the same season of the year, and in a spot almost like that where I was at the moment. This recollection, rendered still more charming by the breath of innocence which pervaded it, brought back others of the same kind. Presently, I saw gathered round me all the objects which had touched my heart with emotion during my youth—Mademoiselle Galley, Mademoiselle de Graffenried, Mademoiselle de Breil, Madame Basile, Madame de Larnage, my young pupils, even the piquant Zulietta, whom my heart can never forget. I saw myself surrounded by a seraglio of houris and by my old acquaintances, the liveliest desire for whom was no new sensation for me. My blood became heated and inflamed, my head swam, in spite of my hairs already growing gray: and the serious citizen of Geneva, the austere Jean-Jacques, close upon his forty-fifth year, suddenly became again the lovesick shepherd. The intoxication which seized me, although so sudden and extravagant, was, notwithstanding, so strong and lasting, that nothing less than the unforeseen and terrible crisis of the unhappiness into which it plunged me would have been able to cure me of it (*Confessions*, Book IX).

Rousseau's *Confessions*, despite its moments of degradation, self-deception, and self-pity, displays the great human virtue of inextinguishable courage in the face of acute maladjustment, intense suffering, endless loneliness, and anguish. To be sure, he experienced frequent periods of depression, some of despair, even a few of renunciation. But these pages shine with his commitment to life and to himself. Unlike many other self-revelations, such as those of Gide and Proust, which end in disintegration, morbidity, cynicism, or abnormality, Rousseau's con-

* See L. G. Crocker, *Jean-Jacques Rousseau: The Quest (1712–1758)*; New York, 1968, p. 293.

fession affirms the persistence of the spirit through the power of will and belief in oneself.

And yet confession, from another viewpoint, fails. It does not lead to penitence or the transformation that arises from penitence, a transformation that would effectuate a better contact with existence, as distinguished from life.

On every level, Rousseau's life is the failure of participation. He was not able to be Emile's tutor, nor Wolmar, nor Saint-Preux, nor Lycurgus. Pygmalion is only a dream. Existence has the risk of being only an exhaustion of life: it is necessary to stop acting and listen to the beating of one's heart.[18]

Rousseau ultimately reached that stage where the political solutions lose all interest, and only dreams act.

Lionel Trilling's judgment of Joyce is quite applicable to the *Confessions*: "James Joyce has taught us the word *epiphany*, showing forth—Joyce had the theory that suddenly, almost miraculously, by a phrase or a gesture, a life might thrust itself through the veil of things, and for an instant show itself forth, startling us by its existence."[19]

In 1771, Rousseau lost an old friend, Daniel Roguin, and gained a new one, Bernardin de Saint-Pierre, who was to become famous through his studies of nature and his idyllic novel, *Paul et Virginie*. A disciple and admirer of Rousseau, he has left interesting memoirs about their friendship.

Other relationships were stormy. In addition to the bitter quarrel with Dusaulx, he broke again with Mme. de la Tour, accusing his devoted defender of not telling him enough about herself, of harboring secret motives, of setting traps for him, and the like. Her unhappy letter of adieu brought a gruff concession: they might take up again sometime.

Once more he became involved in writing on political theory, despite his many vows to abandon both politics and writing. Poland was enjoying a brief period of respite from its aggressive predators, Russia, Austria, and Prussia. At a convention held in 1769, Polish leaders had resolved to consult preeminent French political theorists, to secure their advice about a new constitution. Count Wielhorski, one of the few members of the Diet who was trusted by the opposing factions, was charged with the task in the early part of 1770. Mably was approached first, and he complied with a treatise. When the matter was first broached to Rousseau is not certain, perhaps near the end of that summer of 1770. We know that he worked on the problem from October until April 1771. The resulting manuscript, *Considérations sur le gouvernement de Pologne*, remained unpublished until Du Peyrou's edition of the complete works in 1782. Unpublished, but not unknown. Wielhorski and Rousseau had agreed on secrecy, but the former had imprudently allowed a copy to get into the hands of a publisher. Copies began to circulate in April 1772. Grimm gave an account (and a mocking criticism) of the work in the issues of his *Correspondance littéraire* for January and February 1773. More than a year went by before Rousseau expressed his wrath in letters to Wielhorski on April 20 and July 1, 1774.

Why had Wielhorski approached Rousseau, and why had he accepted? These questions have been clarified by Jean Fabre.[20] Choiseul, the minister of foreign affairs, was an important man in Rousseau's mind, a man who controlled his destiny. When he had first known Choiseul, at Montmorency, Jean-Jacques had thought him capable of understanding him and of giving him another chance at a diplomatic career. Although he now considered Choiseul the leader of the plot, the man who pulled all the strings, he not only feared him but at the same time admired his political skill and policies. When Choiseul fell, during the last days of 1770, he judged the event a public misfortune.

It was doubtless on Choiseul's advice that another friend of Rousseau's, Ruhlière, approached him. Ruhlière, a soldier and diplomat *manqué*, had spent years in Russia. His scandalous *Anecdotes* on the career and the Court of Catherine the Great enraged the "Semiramis of the North" and delighted Choiseul, who was pointing French policy against her ambitions. Named to the post of researcher and writer at the Russian desk of the Foreign Office, Ruhlière composed his voluminous *Histoire de l'anarchie de Pologne*, a work directed against the role of Russia in Polish affairs. Poland was indeed in a state of semi-anarchy, with a virtual guerrilla war going on between its factions, one of which was backed by French money and advisers, another by Russian bayonets.

When Wielhorski reached Paris, Choiseul decided that Rousseau was to be the most brilliant recruit to their cause. After all the trouble he had stirred up, he could perhaps be useful. Ruhlière was one of the few who had *carte blanche* to visit Jean-Jacques whenever he wished. It was he who had taken him to the house of the crown prince of Sweden and the Comtesse d'Egmont. He brought Wielhorski to him. Rousseau took an immediate liking to the Pole, who was an accomplished musician and composer. He even overlooked Wielhorski's liaisons with the Encyclopedists. The cause of the defenseless and brave Poles appealed to his idealism. Poland's future, he thought, was important to the future of Europe. He could not resist this new opportunity to play the coveted role of Lawmaker, into which he had several times before projected himself. The temptation was whetted by the documentation put at his disposal, which included the first part of Mably's treatise for Poland. He was delighted to teach a lesson to a man who, he thought, had pillaged his own writings, and whose basic ideas he disliked.

During the winter of 1770–71, Rousseau worked with the relentless fervor that this "lazy" man bestowed on all his major writings. He was convinced of the importance of his task and encouraged by the victories of the "Confederates," whom Wielhorski represented. But the last pages of the *Considérations sur le gouvernement de Pologne* are filled with somber forebodings. The events of May, when the Russians overwhelmed the opposing faction with brute force, were to confirm them. The manuscript was finished in April, but revisions took until June, when he handed the final version to Wielhorski.

The first partition of Poland was to be carried out in the summer of 1772. The fate of Poland plunged Rousseau back into a dark misanthropy. Ruhlière had been dismissed in May 1771 by d'Aiguillon, Choiseul's successor. Ruhlière's protection became illusory, his company compromising. Before long the whole incident of the *Considérations* had become, in Rousseau's mind, another episode in the great conspiracy.

This last political writing of Rousseau is worthy of consideration. As with his treatise on Corsica, he was faced with a concrete situation, and he endeavored to be practical and realistic, learning all he could about the traditions and circumstances of the country. The task was quite different this time. Whereas Corsica was a primitive country with no defined fabric, Poland had a corrupt, archaic political and social system, disunified and apparently impossible to reform. Not surprisingly, Rousseau proposes relatively few institutional changes. He never believed in the utility of reform. His theory was revolutionary, but his attitudes were always conservative in regard to existing institutions. Stability and order, two of the aims of his speculative utopianism, were for him very high values in the present order, too.[21] He would not, for instance, touch the power and wealth of the aristocracy and the Church, or ameliorate the miserable condition of the serfs. (His utopianism, contrary to the usual opinion, never contemplated the abolition of hierarchies, and he had used and abused the plebes in *La Nouvelle Héloïse.**)

And yet, the essence of Rousseau's thinking is entirely in accord with his earlier writings. He frequently refers back to *The Social Contract*. The only hope for the Poles lies not in changing laws and institutions—he had never believed them to be the crucial element. Rousseau's utopianism was not that of the primitivist or of the naïve idealist, but that of a man who knows he is working with the most perverse and recalcitrant of all materials, human nature. The only hope, then, lies in another *kind* of revolution, one that would rekindle the national spirit of independence ("liberty"), and do so by creating a fanatical ardor of patriotism, the complete devotion of the individual to the *res publica*. In essence, then, Rousseau does not deviate from any of his basic positions, although he realizes that one cannot impose an abstract plan, *tel quel*, on an existing, historically conditioned situation without a violent *political* revolution, which is abhorrent to him.

---

* Vaughan mistakenly attributes this conservatism to the influence of Montesquieu. He is correct, however, in qualifying "the popular image of Rousseau as the fanatical champion of abstract rights" as a pure delusion.

Working, then, within the framework of Polish traditions and institutions, modified in some ways but not radically changed, Rousseau outlines the method of effectuating *his* kind of revolution—the molding and remaking of men, so as to control them with their own "free" consent. The State must mobilize every possible means to "form citizens." Anyone can write better laws. But how do we make them supreme over the passions of self-centered individuals? "There will never be a good and solid constitution except one in which the law rules over the hearts of citizens. As long as the legislative power does not go that far, laws will always be evaded. But how do you reach hearts? That is a matter about which our pedagogues scarcely think."[22]

Passions must be captured, turned into "enthusiasm" or "zeal" for the nation.* "How then shall we stir hearts, and create love for the fatherland and its laws? Shall I dare to tell you? By children's games; by practices which seem frivolous in the eyes of superficial men, but which form cherished habits and invincible attachment."[23] Condemning the institutions of existing societies for fostering individual "egoism," he once again holds aloft his models, Moses, Lycurgus, and Numa Pompilius. Moses knew how to form a people. By weighing them down with rites, by confining them in a thousand ways, he gave them institutions that have not changed in fifty centuries; he created a permanent autarchy. As for Lycurgus, he imposed on his people

an iron yoke, such as no other people has ever borne; but he attached them [i.e., emotionally] to this yoke, identifying them with it, so to speak, by keeping it constantly in their minds. He showed them their country unceasingly, in their laws, their games, their homes, their loves, their feasts. He did not allow them a moment to be with themselves alone. And from this continual constraint, ennobled by its object, was born that ardent love of country. . . .[24]

Destruction of privacy, living under constant surveillance: these remain his primary techniques. Public games, athletic exercises and competitions; nationalistic ceremonies of a semireligious character; historical spectacles designed to arouse patriotic emotion and to stimulate "a lively emulation"; poetry and literature harnessed to the same ends (he condemns unguided freedom of the arts and letters): these are means at the disposal of the nation's leaders. All citizens are infused with the spirit of competition. Competition, so destructive in individual-centered societies, when put at the service of the collectivity is an essential instrument of regimentation and unity. Every method must be used to keep the idea of "country" constantly in the minds of the people, "constantly under their eyes," and to make it *"leur plus grande affaire."* (Rousseau would have put billboards and television to good use.)

* The principle is expressed in *Emile*: "The passions of children and of men can be directed toward good or evil" (p. 249).

Many public amusements in which *la bonne mère patrie* enjoys seeing its children play. Let her constantly concern herself with them so they may always be concerned with her. . . . It is unbelievable to what extent the hearts of the common people follow their eyes, and how much they are impressed by ceremonial majesty. It gives to authority an appearance of order and regularity that inspires confidence and dissipates ideas of caprice and whim, which are associated with arbitrary power.[25]

In Rousseau's new Poland, those who have shown outstanding patriotic devotion will be honored in public ceremonies. The result of all these relentlessly applied techniques is a dependency that keeps the people, like Emile, in a state of childlike immaturity.[26] Ordinary amusements and spectacles (those which are not directed by the State toward its communal ends and so isolate them as individuals) will be banned, along with everything that leads to idleness, effeminate pleasure, and "luxury of the mind." Physical prowess and military virtues will be exalted. Illusions, stage-settings, pomp and ceremony, occasional mingling of the leaders with the masses—all must be used to impress the common people. A sheeplike mass, *des pauvres d'esprit*, the people are to be treated like children and to be led.

Above all else is the upbringing of the young. From his article "Political Economy" on, Rousseau had stressed this element (along with the element of deception) above all others.

This is the important article. It is for education to give souls the national form, and so direct their opinions and tastes, that they will be patriots out of inclination, out of passion, out of necessity. A child on opening his eyes should see *la patrie*, and until he dies see nothing else. . . . This love fills his whole existence; he sees only *la patrie*, lives only for it. As soon as he is alone, he is nothing.[27]

Rousseau adds many specifics, which include communal education, competition in public view to bring the children "under the eyes of their fellow-citizens and to desire public approval," and enforced participation.

To forbid things that are not to be done is an inept and vain expedient, unless you begin by making them hated and despised; the law's disapproval is never efficacious except when it supports that of judgment. Whoever puts his hand to forming a people must know how to control the opinions, and through them to control the passions of men. . . . Direct in this way the education, usages, customs, and mores of the Poles. . . . But without these precautions, expect nothing from your laws. . . . They will be eluded and vain."[28]

This, Rousseau tells us, is the price of what he calls "liberty": "Proud and holy liberty! If those poor people could know you . . . if they realized how your laws are more austere than the harshness of the tyrant's yoke . . . they would fly from you with fright as from a burden that would crush them."[29]

The original character of Rousseau's political thought, and his opposition to the liberal Encyclopedists, is again manifest. They relied on self-interest, enlightenment, and laws, aided by an uncoercive civic education. He sought the politicization of all activities. He believed that "forming" and "remaking" men were prior to all else.

You will give their souls . . . a vigor that will replace the delusive game of ideal precepts, that will make them do out of inclination and emotion what is never done well enough when it is done only out of duty or self-interest. It is on such souls that a well-thought-out legislation will be effective.[30]

As he had so often said, the task of a nation's leaders is to capture hearts, minds, and wills; only thus can they create the "docility" needed to form the *moi commun*. The only way to end the civil war that we call "society" is to subject men's minds and persons to a world of shadowy controls. His system is designed to reduce the development of the individual personality and rational thought, to weaken the boundary between the self and the nonself, to submit the horde to a new kind of "primal father."* The deep polarity that arises between his belief in the dignity of the moral person and his assignment of total moral responsibility and control to the organic collectivity, and to its guides or leaders, can be understood. The dignity is partly abstract, partly the attribute of the uncorrupted individual; but society (as we have known it) inevitably corrupts. In the great choice between collectivism and individualism, between the closed and the open society, there is no doubt which is Rousseau's way.

## 2. THE "REAL" JEAN-JACQUES?

From this time on Rousseau no longer visited other people's homes, making an exception only for Mme. de Créqui, a very old friend. His disappointment over the readings of the *Confessions* rankled. So many times before, ever since the picaresque years, he had "told his story" and conquered hearts. He had miscalculated, forgetting that men had closed their hearts to him. The plotters had done their dirty work too well.

The reprise of *Le Devin du village* in February 1772 gave him no joy, even though the popular enthusiasm should have made it a triumph. Rousseau was convinced that his authorship of the work was being denied, the applause intended to make fun of him. It is true that he had

* According to one psychiatrist, "Disintegration of social groups is due to this individualism. . . . The cohesion of a group . . . gradually increases by identification of group members with each other, their instinctive attachment to each other, and their dependence on their leader. With increasing interdependence, the tendency toward individual self-preservation becomes socialized." Rousseau has clearly anticipated this principle.

at various times been accused (and by no less a person than Rameau) of having stolen his airs from others, and these calumnies galled him. In 1772 no one was making such accusations, but he interpreted the addition of a ballet as a dagger thrust.

The following month, the Opéra put on his *Pygmalion* for the first time. Again the popular success brought him no joy. His permission had not been sought, and the intent, even if unsuccessful, was surely, he thought, to incite derision.

He was now working on his last apology, *Rousseau juge de Jean-Jacques, Dialogues.* The *Confessions,* he feared, might not be enough to assure him the vindication of future generations. The new defense was to turn into a deluge of a hundred and forty thousand words of accusations, apology, and intricate self-analysis. His phobias and delusions intensified as the writing progressed. Guy, because he came to visit him too often, without sufficient motive, and stayed too long, was now suspect. He dispatched a letter to Sartine. "There are clever little maneuvers in all this; a person in any position but mine, provided he made a little effort, could easily discover them."[31]

He was harsh to Mme. de la Tour, after he finally allowed her to visit him, on March 21. The devoted Marianne had seen him only once before. Six years had elapsed, and now he did not even recognize her. She was hurt by his openly admitting it, and by his brutal suspicion that her visit was prompted by hidden motives. A third and last visit, in June, resulted in a note requesting her not to disturb him again.

Much time was spent in botanizing in the parks and environs of Paris, and in writing letters on botany. These activities gave him a measure of calm and equilibrium without diminishing his obsessions. He has given up, he writes to the Marquise de Mesme on August 14, the useless task of trying to discover what is going on about him, of finding an explanation. His contemporaries are henceforth indifferent to him:

I neither esteem them, then, nor hate them, nor despise them. They are nothing in my eyes. For me they are inhabitants of the moon. I have no conception of their moral being. I know only that it has no relation to mine, and that we do not belong to the same species. I have therefore given up, along with them, the only society that could be sweet to me, which I have so vainly sought, that of hearts.

Another distressing, but typical episode occurred in the summer of 1773. Mme. de Créqui sent him a note, asking him not to come the following week, being too engaged to receive him properly. It was enough to put an end to that friendship. Mme. de Créqui was all too familiar with his hypersensitivity, and she may have intended the outcome. Whether or not this was so, Jean-Jacques, who so frequently rebuffed both friends and strangers with a rudeness which in himself he called frankness, could not take a little frankness directed at him.

"When I consent to call on someone," he replied, "it is to honor him, and to be honored by him. . . . If he has the misfortune to refuse me his esteem, he will soon be disillusioned or delivered from me."* Not long after, he was certain. "I understand you, Madame, the artisans of darkness have reached you." Mme. de Créqui offered this explanation to a friend:

I think his displeasure is feigned, that he was ashamed to have read me his confessions, of having seen me shed tears at the episode of the theft [of the ribbon], of the children left at the foundling home, at the horrors he writes about women I do not know but who are as good as others and whose weaknesses should be respected.[32]

The next year witnessed another quarrel, this time with Wielhorski. Several Russians had called on Jean-Jacques. That in itself was suspicious. More important, Grimm and Diderot had just returned from Russia and had stopped over in other countries on the way back. There could be no doubt that these stops had to do with the plot. On April 20, 1774, Rousseau sent Wielhorski an ultimatum. If Wielhorski can get to the bottom of it, then Rousseau will allow him to remain his friend. If not, their friendship is at an end. "I predict, M. le Comte, that if you survive me, as I hope, you will some day regret this letter scorned." He asks the count to note his decision at the bottom of the letter, so that "a less prejudiced generation may judge between you and me." In July, Rousseau discovered that d'Alembert had a copy of the treatise on Poland, and that it had been offered to Guy.[33] That, for him, was conclusive. "Adieu, Monsieur le Comte Wielhorski. I shall never think of you without feeling satisfied with myself. I wish with all my heart that you could say the same."

Wielhorski did not rescue the friendship, but he protested the theft of the manuscript to d'Alembert. It is curious that d'Alembert knew of Rousseau's letter to Wielhorski three days after it was written.

A happier event was acquaintance with Gluck. Rousseau, accompanied by Bernardin de Saint-Pierre, went to the general rehearsal of *Iphigénie*. His enthusiasm was so great that he sent Gluck a note of congratulation. Gluck's music, he said, reversed all his theories. It inspired him to start work on a new opera, *Daphnis et Chloë*. The composer gave him some music to copy and succeeded in getting the Opéra to restore his former privilege of free admission, which years before, in anger at his *Lettre sur la musique française*, they had withdrawn.

In April and May of 1775 bread riots swept Paris, Versailles, and other cities. Bakeries were sacked by mobs. These disturbances leave no

* In the autumn, Rousseau wrote to Rey that he welcomed his letters and might even occasionally answer them (October 15, 1773). He never failed to answer Malesherbes, with whom he corresponded about botany, and to do so promptly. He always knew who was important and how to be flattering and polite to such people.

mark in Rousseau's correspondence, which now becomes sparse. A letter to the Russian ambassador to the Court of Turin (May 27, 1775) reveals that the intensity and ambivalence of his feelings about Geneva are unchanged. "The cowards! I forgive their injustices; it is for posterity to avenge me." But he weeps when he thinks of his fatherland.

O lake, on whose shores I spent the sweet hours of my youth, charming landscapes where for the first time I saw the majestic and moving sunrise, where I felt the first emotions of the heart, the first flights of a genius which later became too imperious and too famous, alas! I shall never again see you.

Rousseau's delusions, though paranoid, left him intervals of calm. Botanizing, music-copying, and the writing of the *Dialogues* all served as safety valves. Between 1775 and 1777 he gave up botanizing, having reached a point of satiety. Two friendships remained. With Corancez, who had introduced him to Gluck, he composed, played, and sang. The other friend was Bernardin de Saint-Pierre ("almost as crazy as he," writes Guéhenno, "certainly as irritable and ill-tempered"), an adventurer in search of an Edenic desert isle where virtuous men could be happy. In general, the years between 1773 and 1776 were marked by lassitude and discouragement. Corancez notes that Rousseau was more suspicious than ever, but also more logical. "Not only did his suspicions multiply and derive fresh nourishment from every substance, trifling and remote; but like the reasons by which he attempted to justify them, sometimes assumed the character of real madness."[34] Corancez often found him

in a state of convulsive agitation which so distorted his features that I scarcely knew them and imprinted on the whole of his face a truly horrible expression. In this state his gaze seemed to embrace the immensity of space; his eyes seemed to see everything at the same moment, but in fact they saw nothing. He spun around on his chair and flung his arm behind it; thus suspended, it assumed the oscillatory motion of a pendulum. . . . When I saw him take this posture on my entering his chamber, my heart bled for him, and I was prepared to hear him utter the wildest extravagances. In this expectation I was never disappointed.*

The posture described by Corancez is characteristic of schizophrenia. Corancez was surprised by Rousseau's dejection on the death of Louis XV in 1774. Previously, Jean-Jacques explained, the hatred of mankind had been divided between Louis XV and himself; now he would have to bear the burden alone.

In February 1775 a provincial admirer, Mlle. Phlipon, the famous Mme. Roland of the Revolution, was turned away from his door by a

---

* I. W. Allen, "Therese LeVasseur."

hostile Thérèse. His flat had in effect been turned into a fortress in a state of siege, "of which the chief sentinel was Thérèse."[35]

The *Dialogues* had been on Rousseau's desk every day, for a quarter of an hour or so, starting in 1772. The manuscript was completed early in 1776. Then an incident brought on total loss of control over his delusional obsessions. As with *Emile* and the *Confessions*, he became convinced that the plotters were about to steal his precious testament to posterity and destroy it. On February 24, at two in the afternoon, he made his way into the Cathedral of Notre Dame, desperate and terrified. If he could leave the manuscript on the high altar, then he would be placing it in the protection of God. God would see to it that his justification would reach the King. To God he had already entrusted his redemption, his vindication, his eternal happiness. To his horror, he discovered that the choir gate, which was usually left open, was locked. The belief in signs is typical of the obsessional condition. (We recall the time when he had wagered his salvation on his hitting a tree with a stone.) What could this be, but a sign from God? God was shutting him out. God had taken the side of his enemies. He was damned, cursed, condemned, now and for all eternity. Ravaged and crushed by God's rejection, he wandered aimlessly through the streets, hour after hour, his whole being in a turmoil of emotion and despair, until night and exhaustion directed his steps home.

All at once he saw the shattering event in a new light. It was indeed a sign from God, but he had misinterpreted it. God had saved his precious work. God had saved him. What had made him think it would ever have reached the King? His enemies were everywhere. The walls had eyes, he had written at Trye; and the eyes were the eyes of his enemies. God had prevented him from foolishly putting the manuscript into their hands.

The next day, he gave one copy of it to his former friend, the philosopher Condillac. He did not trust Condillac completely, but to whom else could he turn? There was no one left. Condillac happened to be in Paris. This, too, was a sign from providence. Rousseau found out where he was staying, and gave him the manuscript "in a transport of joy." Now future generations would pierce the veil of darkness. The aging Condillac, always a cold and logical man, disappointed Jean-Jacques. "He spoke to me of that writing as if it were a work of literature." On April 6, when Brooke Boothby, whom he had known at Wooton, passed through Paris, Rousseau entrusted a second copy of the first book only to him. Boothby was the first to publish it, in 1780, at Litchfield. Still Rousseau was not sure. In all, he made six copies of this huge manuscript, hoping that one, at least, would survive.

Despite these moves, designed to provide reassurance and allay fears, Rousseau again lost control that month. In May he wrote out a circular letter, "A tout Français aimant encore la justice et la vérité." Going into the streets, he distributed the copies to passers-by. The pathetic cry of anguish was the same. Why have you abetted this satanic conspiracy of which I am the helpless victim? he asked the French people. Why can't I hear the accusations for which I have been condemned and wrecked? Why can't I face my accusers and be given a chance to prove my innocence?

Why is so public a scandal a mystery for me alone? Why so many machines, ruses, betrayals, lies, in order to hide from a guilty man his crimes, which he should know better than anyone, if it is true that he has committed them? If, for reasons which pass my understanding, persisting in depriving me of a right of which no criminal has ever been deprived, you have resolved to fill the rest of my days with anguish, derision, opprobrium, without letting me know why, without condescending to listen to my grievances, my reason, my complaints, without even allowing me to speak, I shall raise to Heaven, as my only defense, a heart without fraud and hands clean of all wrongdoing (*Oeuvres*, I, 990).

He went through the Tuileries, looking for honest faces. They would not take his letter. Some read the salutation and laughed, declining the implied honor. Other copies were sent to correspondents who had asked to call on him. He would allow them to, if they told him first what his crimes were. They seemed not to understand, but he knew they did. They were just pretending. Everyone in Europe knew the secret, except him.[36] Word had been spread: he was not to be allowed to know the charges against him. The distribution of letters went on for months. Anyone who praised him was a secret agent. "Whoever wants to see the rhinoceros should go to the fair and not to my house."[37]

Late in summer his frenzy calmed, and he wrote his "Histoire du précédent écrit," from which we have the foregoing account. It ends with an expression of confidence in God's justice, absolute resignation to his destiny, and nonresistance to his tormentors. He consents to being their prey and their plaything. "They will not prevent me from dying in peace."[38]

The primary motivation of the *Dialogues* is the attempt to counteract the "conspiracy" that has enshrouded him with darkness and an impenetrable wall. He is trying, all at once, to understand himself, to justify himself, and to appeal to others to recognize him as he really is. The central idea is that there are two Rousseaus, the true and the false. In the "look" of others, only the false Rousseau exists, the achievement of his enemies. The dialogue is between Rousseau "himself"—an allegedly impartial observer—and the "Frenchman." Hostile at the outset, because he is the dupe of the calumnies of *"nos messieurs"* (Rousseau's real target), the Frenchman is gradually converted. Rousseau's method is a splitting of the self. As he contemplates himself as object, he is both the judge and the judged. He imagines himself "looked at" by that Other, equitable and attentive, whom he would like to have as his judge.

It follows that the main interest lies in "the emergence of the real

Jean-Jacques as the writer wishes us to conceive him."[39] Rousseau is trying to understand himself by synthesizing his contradictory personality and by synthesizing his personality and his work, which he recognizes as a unity: the man and the author are one and the same. The schema of the apologia follows these purposes. The first dialogue is a complete history of the plot. The second presents the "real" Jean-Jacques. The third deals with his writings.

From this interminable work of a tortured mind, the reader carries away several dominant impressions. The first is of the hypertrophy of Rousseau's ego. The obsession with his uniqueness, a very old one, has reached a pathological dimension. The second is that "his efforts to bestow unity and stability upon his existence as man and thinker" do not succeed, despite a simplification and systematization of both.[40] He tries to present himself as the man of nature, the authentic man, and pictures the "new man" of scientific materialism and progress as the great threat. The Rousseau he portrays, however, is, as in the *Confessions*, the one he *chooses* to be. The choice is governed by the need to eliminate complex, disturbing elements, and to project "inadmissible feelings of guilt on to the figures of his persecutors."[41]

A Puritan or Calvinist conscience, such as Rousseau's, is a complex phenomenon. Even while it holds fast to its conviction of rightness, it is haunted by a need for the expiation of its sins. What it longs for is total innocence, and it torments its victim because its end cannot possibly be achieved. This lifelong need of Rousseau is a dominant theme of the *Dialogues*. That is why it is correct to say that his last apology is "the summa of his sentimental, moral and intellectual experience from boyhood to old age."[42] The remarkable lucidity of his unbalanced, paranoid intellect penetrates the shadows of his own psyche. Ultimately, to be sure, it gets lost, since he is unable to understand the fundamental causes of his problems except by relating them to a delusional system. But he realizes the limits of his own self-comprehension, and in so doing, he introduces the role of the unconscious in human behavior. The self cannot be completely known.

The third impression, which Grimsley has so well stated, is Rousseau's conviction that the distinction between self-love (*amour de soi*) and pride (*amour-propre*), which Rousseau had first made in the *Discourse on Inequality*, is the vital principle governing the interdependence of his ideas and personality, and also his relation to the world of men. Having lost his true self, man lives outside himself in a permanent state of conflict and contradiction. This condition is the result of *amour-propre*, a comparative, competitive drive, whereas *amour de soi* does not lead to envy or impair the stability and unity of the self.[43] Only Rousseau is governed by *amour de soi*, free from the corruption of *amour-propre*. His life and his political writings embody this principle, which society as it is cannot tolerate.

Turgid and repetitious, though often moving because of Rousseau's inner drama, the *Dialogues* do not have a wide appeal to modern readers. Bachaumont's *Mémoires secrets* (September 9, 1780) speaks of its "dark imagination, exalted to the point of delirium, combined with the best organized and coldest intellectual dialectics." La Harpe was to condemn its monstrous egocentricity. Today we can understand, and with understanding, sympathize.

In the autumn of 1776, Rousseau began his last and one of his most beautiful works, the *Rêveries du promeneur solitaire*. It opens with a dramatic sentence: "Here I am, then, alone on the earth, having no longer a brother, a neighbor, a friend, or any society except myself." A little further on we encounter an enigmatic passage:

Not two months ago complete calm was reestablished in my heart. I had lost my fears long before, but I still hoped. . . . An event, as sad as it was unforeseen, has finally effaced that feeble glimmer of hope from my heart and has made me realize that my destiny here below is fixed forever, with no reversal. From that time on I have resigned myself without reservation, and I have again found peace.[44]

What was this event, "as sad as it was unforeseen"? In all likelihood, it was the death of the Prince de Conti, on August 2. We must go back a few years in order to understand why Rousseau was affected in this way.

When Choiseul fell, at the end of 1770, he was succeeded by the Duc d'Aiguillon, whom the Parlement had exiled the year before. A month later, Parlement was disbanded by royal order. Malesherbes was exiled from the capital, and Rousseau lost contact with him. Resistance to these tyrannical acts was led by Conti. Little by little his allies, even his own son, deserted him. He stood alone and finally was exiled to one of his estates.

Rousseau, after becoming convinced that Conti had not always been a benevolent, disinterested protector, would not see any of his set in Paris. Still, he was filled with admiration for Conti's courage. And he knew that if anyone could have the Parlement's decree of 1762 revoked, it was Conti. Paradoxically, it was the prince who had always prevented this, as Rousseau finally came to realize, by preventing him from asking for a trial. "He used all the vehemence of his mind and all the ascendency he had over me to turn me away from a step which I shall never console myself for not having taken."[45]

After Louis XV's death, the tables were again turned. Malesherbes was recalled; but the new King refused to restore Conti to favor, saying that it would be an insult to his grandfather's memory to forgive that persistent oppositionist. Conti remained in Paris, shut up in the sanctuary of the Temple. Parlement was recalled, and once again Conti became the leader of the opposition, fighting now against all of Turgot's progressive reforms, which might have prevented the Revolution. Supposedly *"le patron de la liberté,"* he was in reality the dogged defender of feudal privileges. None of this seems to have struck Rousseau, who, in his solitude, once again thought of Conti in the image of his protector. Conti's death, then, put an end forever to his illusory hope that some day, somehow, before his own death, he might win public rehabilitation. "It would be to misjudge the man that was Jean-Jacques," writes Fabre, "his demand for dignity, truth, justice, if we were to fail to grasp what the sentiment of his 'infamy' and the mirage of this hope meant to him."[46]

Complete loss of hope for any redemption on earth was the inevitable aftermath. It brought him a larger measure of peace than he had known for years, a peace which he expresses lyrically in the *Rêveries*. Ironically, he finally won, to some degree, the independence from "opinion" which he had so often proclaimed. As Théodore Rousseau, a relative, said after Jean-Jacques' death, he was "always worried about what the public was thinking, and what he imagined it was writing or doing against him."[47] Now that he had been "branded as a moral leper,"[48] he was resigned, or tried to be. He was the solitary walker, *"le promeneur solitaire."* It was his fate, his uniqueness, that men, "whom he loved," should do this to him. He sometimes thought of himself in the role of Christ. "Whoever does not become passionate for me, or against me, is unworthy of me."[49]

He began writing the *Rêveries du promeneur solitaire* in the form of notes scrawled on odd slips of paper or playing cards. He was no longer thinking of appealing to future generations. "Everything is over for me on earth. . . . I am devoting my last days to studying myself and to preparing in advance the account I shall soon have to give of myself."[50] In the preceding decade, Rousseau had written the *Confessions*, the *Considérations sur le gouvernement de Pologne*, the *Dialogues*, and numerous minor pieces—a fairly full output for a man who had sworn so many times never again to take up his pen.

We can mark off the major stages in Rousseau's life. His disturbed childhood was traumatically ended by his father's flight and its sequels. After a time as a homeless wanderer, he sought to satisfy his need for security by dependency on a substitute mother. The guilt of Oedipal relations, and her rejection, sent him into the world resolved to find a place on its own terms, within the framework of its values and "artificial" ways. Out of failure to win identity and self-respect by pursuing this course came the revelation of Vincennes and self-projection into the role of truthbearer and prophetic voice. This new identity completed his alienation from the world and loosed the controls of reality over fantasy and narcissism. Then persecutions and the obsession of the "conspiracy" led to acute psychic disintegration. Only in the last stage, near the end, did he find a measure of peace in narcissistic withdrawal.

The *Rêveries du promeneur solitaire* was both an instrument and a

product of the final stage. It was Rousseau's last effort to render some
definitive account to himself of the value of his existence. Each *"Promenade"* is different from the others, and they do not speak with one voice.
Written over a period of almost two years, they are animated by a
diversity of moods and values, but there are basic significant elements.

The solitude of the *Rêveries* is a symbolic return to the state of
nature, with its independence and "goodness" (in contrast to the struggle Rousseau calls "virtue"). It is a search, even as his political and educational theories had been, for the innocence that is inevitably lost in
society. Simultaneously, this impossible quest for the grail of lost innocence is also a search for an end of self-alienation, which (as the
*Discourse on Inequality* shows) is society's penalty: it forces us to play
roles that cut us off from our own authentic selves. The central political
idea, of submitting the docile individual into an organic whole to which
he alienates his self (*le moi humain*), was intended to enable him to
recover it in another, higher form (*le moi commun*) thereby ending self-
alienation. The dream of a new life for a new kind of man, of which
Rousseau appointed himself the prophetic voice, arose from the frustration of the dream of his own happiness. It was an intellectual adventure,
both an exciting stimulant and a narcotic for his anguish. Now it was no
longer effective.

In order to recover the original autonomy and the primitive Eden,
Rousseau, in his solitary strolls, has two forces at his disposal: pure
sensation and imagination (considering memory as a form of imagination). The two coalesce into reverie. Unable to reconcile feeling and
being, world and self, he "abolishes" the world. No longer is the reso-
nant "I" throttled by the impervious "It." No longer is the richness and
spontaneity of the inner life imprisoned by the chains of abstract reasoning. In the famous fifth *Rêverie*, Rousseau reaches the apex of pure
existence, in a self-sufficiency, a self-enjoyment whose absoluteness is not
only a reunion with nature but an autodeification. "One is self-sufficient
like God."[51] Nature is drawn in, transmuted, and absorbed. This
shrinking into his self is, paradoxically, the condition for the self's infinite expansion and total experience of itself, as it enlarges its confines
to embrace nature and the macrocosm. Time as we know it is now
absent. It is only an intruder, putting an end to the perfect, ineffable
moment.

Escape from time is required for the ecstatic ascension, just as the
millennial utopia imposes the abolition of history. Time is not abolished,
however. Rousseau is one of the great poets of memory, of its consolation
and its bitterness.[52] But in his reverie the linear quality of time, with its
fragmentation of the self, is lost, to become pure duration, a kind of
eternity or eternal present that leaves no sense of emptiness. Past and
present are infused in each other, drawn together in a single point of
concentrated experience. The images and sensations of long ago, recap-

tured, are inseparable from present nostalgia. Rousseau's search for himself in time can be accomplished only by the conquest of time, because
only then can one speak of beginning to live again at each moment.

Although this attempt to overcome self-alienation is distinctively
human, in a deeper sense the desire to escape from time, and from
bipolarization to "oneliness," destroys the distinctive character of
human existence. It is a regression to a prehuman state. Rousseau's
condemnation of curiosity and its conquests, of "opinion" (the innate
desire for group approval), of *amour-propre*, even of language—all manifest his aversion to the human condition. To endure, without change, is
to aspire beyond it, both in the polity and the self. For Rousseau it is the
requisite of both kinds of happiness, public and private, antithetical as
the two ways are. While he was right to protest against the crushing of
the subjective, inner world by outside forces, self-absorption needs to be
controlled, and its healthy expansion is not through autistic intensifica-
tion, but in ways that were denied to him. Freedom cannot affirm itself
in passivity. The terminus of Rousseau's reverie is the ataraxia of
stoicism. Moreover, the quest for freedom and enjoyment, for authenticity and unity, can never be *absolutely* fulfilled. It must take place in a
dynamic dialectic with the Other, with what is outside oneself. In the
human condition one cannot possess one's self without also alienating
it—and who knew this better than the author of *The Social Contract*?*
Surely, he knew that his own attitude could be only the exception, valid
for the "unique" being he considered himself to be.

Only partly valid, however, even for him. The *Rêveries* are more
complex, more polyvalent, than this summary implies. The underlying
anguish of Rousseau's social isolation frequently breaks through the
idyllic calm. His serenity is ruffled by the slightest thing. The intermit-
tent composition of the work reflects the alternation between periods of
stability and instability. His preoccupation with other people is recurrent; he cannot stay within the circle of self within which he urges us to
circumscribe ourselves. He longs for companionship and love, and he
refers to his other dream, of collective happiness through fraternal concord. The fourth *"Promenade"* is another sophistical apology; here and
elsewhere he goes back to analytical reasoning in order to free himself
from the guilt that haunts his steps. The exercise in spiritual self-
preservation, then, the seeking for compensations for loneliness and
isolation, falls short of being successful. It is not a conquest of his psychotic persecution complex; the "plot" is as strong as ever, his enemies

---

* "The immediacy of the interior life is his alibi, his shelter; but it is also the
means of exempting himself from the means one must normally use to encounter
others. Jean-Jacques hopes to make himself loved without doing anything except being
himself; while remaining locked within himself, he wants to attract loving solicitude
and tender devotion. . . . Rousseau does not assume the risks and the effort of going
beyond himself that is required for authentic communication with others" (J. Starobinski, *Jean-Jacques Rousseau*, p. 216).

are still "moles." It is only a way of living with it, by concentrating on other aspects of his affective life. Jean-Jacques, who had so often, in overt actions, rejected himself, is trying to accept himself, by making the pure feeling of existence its own justification, trying to dissolve the dilemma of order and existence in a new "magical state of existence."[53] That is the real dynamic of the *Rêveries du promeneur solitaire*.

A poignant and beautiful work, it initiates the literature of contemplation and introspection, especially the experience and the psychology of reverie. Rousseau's sensuous apprehension of the world and of his self, the ecstasy resulting from a kind of self-hypnosis, the gamut of moods, affective states, and emotional nuances, all are conveyed in a delicate but exact notation. Nature is essential to his quest. In his loving descriptions, we feel their union and communion. Most of all, we feel that he is communing with himself and communicating with us. "His illusion, his dreams, are still at work."[54]

Through the *Confessions* and the *Rêveries*, Rousseau led the way to the hypertrophy of the self that characterizes Romanticism and all its anarchic varieties in the nineteenth and twentieth centuries. His rational doctrines and the expression of his personal anguish head in two opposing directions, precisely the two directions which stand in confrontation in our own time.

### 3. *Nunc Dimittis*

"The old couple was growing old."[55] His vitality ebbing, Jean-Jacques had to give up copying music in 1776. He got rid of his spinet and his herbarium, lost his magnifying glass and his cane. He went back to his dreaming. Thérèse was suffering from rheumatism. They engaged a servant, but none would stay with such irritable and fault-finding employers. In fourteen months eleven maids came and went.

An accident, on October 24, 1776, had a reverse effect. He had spent the day walking and dreaming on the heights of Ménilmontant, then a suburb of Paris. As he was making his way homeward, a carriage came hurtling past him, descending the slope at full speed. A large hound running alongside the carriage crashed into him. Rousseau was flung into the roadway with such force that he lost consciousness. It was nightfall when he came to. Blood was still coming from his lip. Yet, inexplicably, he felt good. It was *"un moment délicieux."* He made his way home. Only when Thérèse screamed on seeing his blood-encrusted face did he fully realize what had happened.

Word spread rapidly through Paris. It was rumored that Rousseau was dead. The *Courrier d'Avignon* even specified the cause of death: a gluttonous bout of overeating in the company of his old friend Romilly. The police made an inquiry. Enemies mocked him for having been run over by a dog. If only they had thought of Don Quixote trampled by pigs! Corancez and Bernardin came to see him. Mme. de la Tour wrote solicitously, hoping that her concern would end his "crushing indifference." It did not. Marianne nonetheless twice published defenses of her idol, after his death.

Excitement of a different kind marked the end of the year. A new friend, the young Comte Duprat, a lieutenant colonel in the Orleans regiment, stirred Jean-Jacques' fancy. It was "a most tender affection," according to one of his editors.[56] When he stayed away an entire week, Rousseau was alarmed. If we may believe one account, he discovered that Duprat had fallen ill. This put him in a dilemma, since his "principles" forbade him to call on anyone. Instead he directed his walks toward Duprat's residence, passing in front of its walls every day, until one afternoon he broke down and rushed into the count's apartment.

The triumphal reprise of *Le Devin du village* should have marked an auspicious beginning to the new year, 1777. It was not to be so. Jean-Jacques could no longer cope with aggravated domestic problems. The roles were reversed now. He was tending to Thérèse and the household chores. No longer able to work, he had to make ends meet on a tiny income of 1,440 francs a year (if not less) from the annuities he had from Duchesne, Keith, Rey, and Dutens. Expenses exceeded that amount. In his pride, he had, seven years before, refused the arrears of his pension from George III, amounting to 6,000 francs. Now he was gripped by the fear of helpless poverty. Thérèse carefully hid from him the gifts of food and clothing she had been accepting from Corancez and other friends. She remembered how angry he had been when Dusaulx sent him a dozen bottles of wine, and when Bernardin sent him a packet of coffee.

In February, desperation drove this proud man to distribute a public plea for assistance.[57] He offered to assign all he possessed in exchange for a place for Thérèse and for him in an old people's home or anywhere else, "locked up or in apparent freedom, with gentle or harsh people." He complained that the state of his health prevented him from giving Thérèse the care she needed. How curious that even in 1778, according to Bernardin, he was able to walk around the entire circumference of the Bois de Boulogne without appearing to be tired!

The *Rêveries* were gradually being written. In the spring he began to compose again, and to copy music. For diversion he went back to botany and to reading his beloved Tasso. The herbarium was reconstituted.

In December he read d'Alembert's eulogy of Mme. Geoffrin, the famous *salonnière*. Mme. Geoffrin was quoted as saying that every criminal about to be hanged should be asked this question: "Have you loved your children?" The reply, she was sure, would be negative. Jean-Jacques immediately concluded that these lines were intended for him. Filled with remorse again, he composed the ninth *"Promenade,"* with its plea for understanding: he had always loved children. He cites instance upon instance and, for the last time, defends the abandonment of his own children. But the remorse could not be dispelled. "Oh! If I could again have for a few moments pure caresses that come from the heart, were it only from a child still in his smock. If I could again see in some eyes the joy and contentment of being with me." He had been so lonely. As he felt death drawing near, his loneliness was a sharp pain, welling up across the years. He had wanted so much to love and be loved.

In December 1777 he was still looking for a last retreat. He asked Duprat to help him. Duprat suggested a refuge near Clermont, for eight hundred francs a year. He was tempted. But Thérèse did not wish to go back to the provinces, and he was loath to change his name again and attend mass, the two necessary conditions. Besides, he no longer had the energy to move and start all over. "It is a castle in Spain, and none of those I have built in my lifetime ever came true."[58]

In February his archenemy, Voltaire, returned to Paris for a triumphal visit after more than thirty years of exile. On March 30 he was crowned at the Comédie Française and acclaimed at the Académie. The crowds cheered him deliriously. When a flatterer tried to please Rousseau by deriding Voltaire's apotheosis, Jean-Jacques repulsed him. "How dare you censure Voltaire's being honored in the temple of which he is the god, by priests who have been living off his masterpieces for fifty years?"

April 12 was Palm Sunday. Rousseau began the tenth and last "Promenade," devoted to the sacred memory of Maman. It was not to be finished. Few pages in literature are as touching and nostalgic as these two in their simplicity and sincerity.

Today, Palm Sunday, it is just fifty years since I first met Mme. de Warens. She was twenty-eight years old then, having been born with the century. I was not yet seventeen [he was not yet sixteen] and my budding sexuality of which I was not yet aware put warmth into a naturally ardent heart. . . . She had sent me away. Everything called me back to her, and I had to go back. That return decided my whole life, and long before I possessed her I lived only in her and for her. Ah! If only I could have been enough for her heart, as she was enough for mine! . . . No day goes by without my recalling with joy and tender sadness that unique and brief time of my life when I was myself, fully, without alloy, and without any obstacle, when I can truly say that I have lived. . . . During that brief span of years, loved by a woman, gentle and caring, I did what I wanted to do, I was what I wanted to be. . . . My only pain was the fear that it would not last long.

How fitting that this page should have been his last! This unfinished reverie, about all that had been or might have been, distills the poetry, the longings, the anguish—and the self-deception—of all his life. How proper that his last lines should be in homage to the woman who, as he says, had made him what he was! The underlying pain is now a muted note. He has not forgotten his bitter suffering at her hands, but we feel that he has forgiven. In his idealized image she was, more than ever, the lost mother; if he could have returned to her, once again, all problems would have been dispelled or solved. Would he not have preferred the tender bliss, in the closed garden of Les Charmettes, to the storms and the torment of fame? Since those faraway days he had seen so much, done so much, written so much. Was it worthwhile for Jean-Jacques to have become Rousseau? A futile question, for he had not forgotten, either, that the other dream had been an impossible castle in Spain—the most cherished, the most regretted of all.

There is not much left to tell.

On May 2, Rousseau's old friend Paul Moultou, with whom he had not corresponded for eight years, visited him, with his son, Pierre. Rousseau gave him a copy of the *Dialogues* and one of the *Confessions*, together with some other writings. He was feeling ill. Lebègue de Presles, the doctor who was taking care of Thérèse, told him that the Marquis de Girardin, who had been giving him music to copy, was offering him lodgings in his beautiful estate near Paris, at Ermenonville. On May 20 he left suddenly, without informing Corancez or Bernardin, with whom he had an engagement the next day. According to Bachaumont, the police had gotten from him an avowal that he had written his *Confessions* and warned him to leave Paris to avoid a search. The story is apocryphal. The moment he spied Ermenonville, with its serene beauty, its groves, lake, and waterfall, he knew that this was where he wanted to die. He jumped out of his carriage and walked the three miles to the château. He was moved to tears when he found the marquis, with his wife and children, waiting to welcome him. He sent word to Thérèse, who was not eager to leave Paris or accept hospitality again, to pack up the household goods and join him. He had ever depended on her for such matters. As he had said to Duprat, as recently as March 15, "Any job to be done, any fatigue to be borne, frightens my indolence. . . . If, by myself, I could collect two nightcaps and five or six shirts, it would be a lot." Thérèse joined him on May 26.

During the night of May 30, Voltaire died, his fragile body exhausted by the emotional and physical excesses of his triumph. It had been an imprudence for an eighty-four-year-old hypochondriac, but the temptations of vanity had always been too great for him. Rousseau was shaken by this event. The marquis wondered why he was so moved. "It is because my existence was bound up with his," he replied. "He is dead, and I shall follow him before long." They were indeed bound up with each other, in more ways than one. "The air of the century vibrated with the ideas they had sown like an invisible dust."[59]

There was a last brave flicker. Ermenonville seemed to revive his strength and will to live. He took long walks with Girardin, even as far as Senlis, where the mayor honored him at a reception. There were no more letters or business affairs. He exulted in his freedom and his closeness to nature. As he had done long ago at Les Charmettes, he went out into the park each morning in time to greet the sunrise with a prayer.

Ermenonville offered new stimuli for botanizing, in the company of his host's twelve-year-old son. He would forget the hour, until Thérèse went after him for dinner. He enjoyed gossiping with the local curate and the villagers, dined at the château, sang old ballads while accompanying himself on the spinet. At night, enchanting concerts in the woods were arranged by his thoughtful host. As for Thérèse, she increasingly found solace in the wine bottle.

Alas, before June was over, if we may believe d'Escherny—and some of Thérèse's later statements agree with his report—Rousseau was quarreling with Girardin and brooding again.[60] He correctly suspected that Girardin was a money-grasper and intended to use him. He asked his host to find him a place in a public asylum; but Thérèse did not want to leave, perhaps because she had already taken up with her new lover, John Bally, Girardin's valet.

He died after brief but intense suffering on the morning of July 2. On June 27 he had reached his sixty-sixth birthday. The six accounts of his death, three by Thérèse, two by Girardin's son (who wrote what his father had told him), one by Lebègue de Presles, differ only in details.

On the preceding afternoon, Rousseau had felt intestinal cramps, after eating strawberries with milk and sugar. In the morning he was better and went on his usual early walk. At seven he was back and had *café au lait* for breakfast. While he was getting ready to leave for the marquis' daughter's music lesson, he suddenly became ill. He complained to Thérèse of a violent headache, chest pains, a tingling on his soles, and a strange feeling along his spine, as if an icy fluid were running down it. Thérèse, nevertheless, went out to pay a bill. When she returned, she heard him groaning. Perspiration was streaming down his face, and he was evidently in considerable pain. Alarmed, she sent for Mme. de Girardin, although Jean-Jacques forbade her to do so. When his hostess arrived, he gently brushed aside her pretexts for this unusual visit and asked to be left alone with his wife.

With great difficulty Thérèse helped him into bed.* He asked her to open the windows, so that he might see the trees. (Possibly he was having difficulty in breathing.) Thérèse wept. "Why do you weep?" he asked her. "Isn't it time for my life to end? Haven't men made me suffer enough?" He requested that an autopsy be performed and a precise description be made of the state of his organs. Upon that he was seized with unbearable pains. He struggled to get out of bed, crying, "Being of Beings! God! See how pure the sky is. There is not a single cloud. Don't you see that its gates are open and that God awaits me?" With that, he fell to the ground, striking his head against the tiles.

Lebègue's more prosaic account mentions no final words, and has Rousseau falling from the chair dead. Since Thérèse, an inveterate con-

---

* According to Lebègue, he was sitting on a chair—probably a *chaise percée*—when he died. He had drunk some bouillon and had been given an enema.

cocter of stories, was the sole witness, and since her versions of the last words were many and varying—indeed, she once said, "He died holding my hands tightly in his, without saying a single word"—we can only suspend disbelief. It is not usual for a man dying of apoplexy to break into poetic discourse. *Se non è vero, è ben trovato.*

It is more tempting to think that Rousseau died, not as Thérèse melodramatically recounted it, but peacefully, like his own Julie. He saw Maman smiling at him. She was waiting for him again, at the end of the long, dusty road, to welcome her tired wanderer to her warm and ample bosom for the last time. There would be no more separations, no more returns. Of this, too, we may surely say, *se non è vero, è ben trovato.*

Measures taken to revive the dead man—bleeding, vesicatories, alkali —were of no avail. Rousseau was *bel et bien* dead. The next day, Houdon made his death mask, which bears the mark of the bruise inflicted by his fall. The autopsy, disclosing "bloody, serous matter in the brain," led to the verdict of "serous apoplexy." Doubtless it had been brought on by uremia.* On July 4, near midnight, Jean-Jacques was buried on the Isle of Poplars in the lake at Ermenonville. Girardin had given it out that such was Rousseau's dying request, but he probably invented the idea for reasons of his own. However that may be, when "le culte de Rousseau" soon swept across France, the tomb at Ermenonville became a shrine, visited by countless pilgrims, and it so remains today.

Before long, stories were circulating. Rousseau had shot himself. Thérèse had murdered him with hammer blows. The Romantics—Mme. de Staël, Gérard de Nerval—preferred the suicide version, and Mme. de Staël even supplied the motive: he had discovered Thérèse's infidelity. (Surely it was rather late in the game for so drastic and untypical a reaction.) Both versions were pure fantasy. An exhumation carried out on December 18, 1897, showed that the skull was intact, and bore the mark of a superficial bruise.

Thérèse was to survive Rousseau some twenty-two years. She died in 1801, at the age of eighty. Not loath to gossip about her Jean-Jacques, she sometimes spoke about how good he was, more often told of his faults, retailing, according to one witness, "a thousand other nasty insults which should not be on her tongue, even if she were telling the truth. This woman combines every fault, for she is stupid, stupid enough to make you laugh."[61] She knew how to pretend, though, and spoke of "the great man whom fate has condemned me to weep over for the rest of my life."[62] She lived openly with John Bally, but decided not to marry him, realizing shrewdly that it was in her interest to remain "the widow of Jean-Jacques for all my life," as she sometimes signed her undecipherable letters. If one wonders why a comparatively young man

* The initial bladder infection would have led to the kidneys by ascending infection, resulting in pyelonephritis, which would inevitably produce hypertension and ultimately apoplexy.

like Bally attached himself to an ugly fifty-eight-year-old woman, the reasons are not hard to find. Thérèse was an expert in *arte amoris*. Even more, she had an income, and the possibility of obtaining more. Bally squandered what she had and endeavored to help her get more.

What happened, in brief, is that Girardin, upon his guest's death, seized all of his papers, including a precious manuscript of the *Confessions*.[63] He may have thought, or even told Thérèse, that he alone could protect them from Rousseau's enemies, who would surely find a way, by force, guile, or bribes, to take them from her. More likely, as his later actions show, he wanted to profit from the precious manuscript, which he excluded from a list of those he was holding. Over a period of years, Thérèse, directed by Bally, made every effort, including threats, to recover her property. Du Peyrou was working on his edition of the complete works. Girardin tried to ally himself with Du Peyrou, even journeying to Neuchâtel. Du Peyrou held Thérèse off, until he finally became convinced that Girardin had lied to him when he denied possessing any such manuscript. Girardin finally had to admit as much. He even had the insolence to pretend that he had concealed it only because Thérèse had begged him to, and to affirm that Rousseau had asked him on his deathbed to take back all his papers from Du Peyrou and Moultou, putting him in sole charge of them. A nasty quarrel ensued but still he refused to give up the manuscript, despite the threat of a lawsuit. Thérèse kept protesting that Girardin had cheated her of her inheritance, but the powerful marquis would, and Du Peyrou could, do nothing.

The Revolution treated Thérèse well. In 1790 the Assemblée Constituante voted to erect a statue to Rousseau, with the inscription, which he would have dearly loved, "The free French nation, to Jean-Jacques Rousseau," and also voted his widow a pension of twelve hundred livres. The bill was signed by Louis XVI. Girardin, however, waged a successful fight for two and a half years against the proposal to transfer Rousseau's remains to the Pantheon. The great man belonged to him. He had given him his last shelter, and Rousseau had expressly wished to lie there. In 1794, during the Reign of Terror, Girardin was under house arrest. The transfer was voted on April 14, but the fall of Robespierre and the Thermidorian reaction caused a delay of five months. On September 26, Thérèse appeared before the Convention. After a brief ceremonious speech, she presented to the Convention, and the French nation, the precious manuscript of the *Confessions!* She had recovered it, she later explained, by threatening to denounce the marquis. The menace of the guillotine had been more powerful than the pleas of the impoverished widow, the claims of justice, or the pressures of Du Peyrou.

Thérèse's dramatic gesture was undoubtedly designed by Bally as a maneuver to obtain a larger pension. It worked, but as time went on, she found her pensions and annuities harder to collect. When Rousseau's remains were transported to the Pantheon, with pomp and ceremony, over a three-day period (October 9–11), she created a small scandal by appearing for the occasion, accompanied by her lover. She stayed with Bally until her death, eking out a living by accepting gratuities from curious visitors who wanted to see her and hear her talk about Rousseau. They found her, more often than not, besotted with wine, garrulous, and childish.

Jean-Jacques' story, as he had known so well, was not ended. In a way, an important way, it was beginning anew. The reburial in the Pantheon symbolizes this life beyond life. Whether or not he had asked to be buried on the lovely little Isle of Poplars, I think that he would have preferred his last home to be there, rather than in the cold, august Pantheon, among the marble tombs of France's great men. But his destiny, as he himself had willed it, belonged to the future generations, to the world, not to himself. The history of his life beyond life, of his reputation and influence, of the altercations between those who have cursed him and those who have canonized him, is another story. An unfinished story.

# Notes*

### Chapter I: Fruits of Solitude

1. Paolo Casini, "Rousseau e Diderot," *Rivista Critica di Storia della Filosofia*, Vol. III, pp. 240–70.
2. J. Christopher Herold, "The Solitary Wanderer," p. 96.
3. Guy Besse, "Observations sur la réfutation d'Helvétius par Diderot," *Diderot Studies VI*, p. 43.
4. See Jean-Jacques Rousseau, *Lettre à M. D'Alembert sur les spectacles*, critical edition, edited by M. Fuchs, pp. xiv–xix.
5. F. C. Green, *Jean-Jacques Rousseau*, pp. 220–21; *Lettre à d'Alembert*, ed., Fuchs, p, xxi.
6. To Deleyre, October 5, 1758.
7. *Corr.*, V, xxiv.
8. P. H. Meyer, "Rousseau and the French Language," p. 188.
9. *Corr.*, V, 106.
10. A. Feugère, "Pourquoi Rousseau a remanié la Préface de la *Lettre à d'Alembert*," *AJJR*, XX, 1931, p. 144. See this article for the parallel texts of the two versions, and for useful explanations.
11. Plato, *The Republic*, sections 604–6.
12. R. L. Politzer, "Rousseau on the Theatre and the Actors," p. 251.
13. *Lettre à d'Alembert*, ed., Fuchs, p. 80.
14. *Ibid.*, p. 62.
15. *Ibid.*, p. 76.
16. *Ibid.*, pp. 106–7.
17. *Corr.*, V, 268–9.
18. *Lettre à d'Alembert*, ed., Fuchs, p. 80.
19. R. Grimsley, *Jean-Jacques Rousseau: A Study in Self-awareness*, p. 38.
20. *Lettre à d'Alembert*, ed. Fuchs, p. 135.
21. *Ibid.*, pp. 136, 138.
22. *Ibid.*, p. 148.
23. *Ibid.*, p. 74.
24. *Ibid.*, pp. 110–11.
25. *Ibid.*, p. 116.
26. *Ibid.*, pp. 61, 77, 155.
27. *Ibid.*, p. 78.
28. *Ibid.*, p. 89.
29. *Ibid.*, p. 90.
30. *Ibid.*, p. 147.
31. *Ibid.*, pp. 168–9. See pp. 89, 118, 154, 181.
32. *Ibid.*, p. 184.
33. *Ibid.*, p. 80–1.
34. B. de Jouvenel, "Rousseau évolutionniste pessimiste," in *Rousseau et la philosophie politique (Annales de philosophie politique)*, p. 12.
35. B. Waisbord, "Rousseau et le théâtre," p. 119.
36. Politzer, *op. cit.*, p. 257, n. 19.
37. *Lettre à d'Alembert*, ed. Fuchs, pp. 49–50.
38. *Ibid.*, p. 35.
39. *Ibid.*, p. 53.
40. J. Brody, "*Don Juan* and *Le Misanthrope*, or the esthetics of individualism in Molière," pp. 571–2.

* Abbreviations: *AJJR* = *Annales de la Société Jean-Jacques Rousseau*; *Corr.* = R. A. Leigh's edition of Rousseau's correspondence; *C.G.* = the Dufour–Plan edition of the correspondence; Pléiade = *Oeuvres complètes*, Pléiade edition. See Bibliography.

All letters of Voltaire quoted in this volume may be found in chronological order in his *Correspondance*, edited by Theodore Besterman, 107 vols.; Geneva, 1953–65.

41. *Ibid.*, pp. 573–4.
42. *Lettre à d'Alembert*, ed. Fuchs, p. 57.
43. *Ibid.*, pp. 176–7.
44. J.-J. Rousseau, *Oeuvres complètes*, 13 vols.; Hachette, Paris, 1884–87, Vol. I, p. 295.
45. D. Diderot, *Oeuvres*, ed. Assézat-Tourneux; Paris, 1875, Vol. II, p. 412, Vol. X, p. 417.
46. Feugère, *op. cit.*, pp. 158–60.
47. M. Grimm, *Correspondance littéraire, philosophique et critique*, Vol. IV, p. 54.
48. *Oeuvres*, Hachette, Vol. I, pp. 271–3.
49. *Corr.*, V, 208.
50. *Ibid.*, V, 217.
51. *Corr.*, V, xxiv.
52. *Ibid.*, V, 68.
53. *Ibid.*, V, 31.
54. *Ibid.*, IV, 19.
55. *Ibid.*, V, 155 (September 26, 1758).
56. *Confessions* (see Pléiade, I, 506).
57. *Corr.*, V, 66.
58. *Ibid.*, V, 296–7 (to Baron d'Allonzier, May 20, 1758).
59. *Corr.*, V, 74, 83.
60. J. Casanova de Seingalt, *Histoire de ma vie*, Vol. V, pp. 221–2.
61. *Confessions*, pp. 503–4.
62. *Ibid.*, p. 509.
63. *Ibid.*, p. 152.
64. *Ibid.*, p. 510.
65. *Corr.*, I, 197 (editor's note).
66. See L. G. Crocker, *Diderot, the Embattled Philosopher*, New York, 1966, for the further history of the publication of the *Encyclopédie*.
67. *C. G.*, VI, 146.
68. See J. S. Spink's introduction, Pléiade, IV, lxxvi–lxxvii.
69. *Ibid.*, p. 263. See L. G. Crocker, *Jean-Jacques Rousseau: The Quest (1712–1758)*, New York, 1968, pp. 182–3.
70. See Pléiade, IV, lxxvii–lxxxvii, and P. D. Jimack, "La Genèse et la rédaction de l'*Emile* de Jean-Jacques Rousseau," Parts I and II.
71. *Corr.*, VI, 37–8 (February 21, 1759).
72. *Ibid.*, p. 62.
73. *Corr.*, VI, 51.
74. *Ibid.*, p. 54.
75. *Ibid.*, pp. 78–9 (April 28, 1759).
76. *Ibid.*, pp. 94–6 (May 7, 1759).
77. *Ibid.*, p. 110–11 (May 30, 1759).
78. S. S. B. Taylor, "Rousseau's Contemporary Reputation in France," p. 1553.
79. *Corr.*, VI, 8.
80. *Ibid.*, p. 1 (January 4, 1759).
81. Taylor, *loc. cit.*
82. *Corr.*, VI, 7.
83. *Ibid.*, p. 9.
84. Grimm, *op. cit.*, Vol. V, pp. 92–106.
85. See Crocker, *Jean-Jacques Rousseau: The Quest (1712–1758)*, pp. 150–1, 263.
86. Quoted in H. Buffenoir, *La Maréchale de Luxembourg*, pp. 15–16.
87. H. Bonhomme, *La Société galante et littéraire au XVIIIᵉ siècle*, pp. 2–3.
88. *Confessions*, p. 517.
89. *Corr.*, VI, 84 (April 29, 1759).
90. *Confessions*, p. 521.
91. *Corr.*, VI, 102 (May 21, 1759).
92. *Ibid.*
93. See also Rousseau's letter to Dom Deschamps, October 17, 1761, *Corr.*, IX, 176–7.
94. *Corr.*, VI, 114 (June 4, 1759).
95. D. Diderot, *Correspondance*, Vol. II, pp. 154–5.
96. *Ibid.*, II, 145.

97. *Corr.*, VI, 116–7 (June 6, 1759).

98. *Ibid.*, pp. 128–9 (June 23, 1759).

99. *Ibid.*, pp. 122–3 (June 14, 1759).

100. See Crocker, *Jean-Jacques Rousseau: The Quest (1712–1758)*, p. 16. He repeats the statement on November 10, 1761, in a letter to Mme. de la Tour.

101. *Confessions*, p. 522.

102. *Corr.*, VI, 148–9 (August 13, 1759).

103. *Ibid.*, p. 152 (August 16, 1759).

104. *Ibid.*, p. 155 (August 18).

105. *Ibid.*, p. 156–7 (August 30, 31).

106. "But I shall see you here; you have told me that, and however much I might have desired it, I should never have dared to suggest it to you." (*Ibid.*, p. 152).

107. *Confessions*, p. 528.

108. *Ibid.*

109. C. A. Sainte-Beuve, "Mme. de Verdelin," Vol. IX, p. 435.

110. *Corr.*, VII, 32 (February 4, 1760).

111. *Ibid.* (no date).

112. *Ibid.* (December 28, 1760).

113. *Ibid.*, p. 239 (December 21, 1759).

114. *Corr.*, VI, 194–5 (November 15, 1759).

115. *Corr.*, VI, 225 (December 11, 1759).

116. *Ibid.*, p. 200 (November 18).

117. *Confessions*, p. 513.

118. *Corr.*, VI, 195–97. Margency's letter is dated ca. November 15, 1759.

119. *Ibid.*, p. 214.

120. *Confessions*, p. 514.

121. *Corr.*, VII, 98–9 (May 21, 1760).

122. *Confessions*, p. 537.

123. *Corr.*, VII, 106 (May 24, 1760).

124. *Ibid.*, pp. 205–6 (August 4).

125. *Ibid.*, p. 209 (August 12).

126. *Confessions*, p. 539.

127. Quoted in H. Buffenoir, *Jean-Jacques Rousseau dans la vallée de Montmorency*; Paris, 1904, p. 189.

128. *Confessions*, p. 546–7.

129. *Corr.*, VII, 139 (June 17, 1760).

130. *Ibid.*, 269–71 (October 29, 1760).

131. *Ibid.*, 210–11 (August 13).

132. *Ibid.*, 374–5 (December 26).

133. *C. G.*, V, 37 (January or February 1760).

134. *Corr.*, VII, 142–3 (June 19).

135. W. H. Blanchard, *Rousseau and the Spirit of Revolt*, p. 118.

136. *Confessions*, p. 523.

137. Blanchard, *op. cit.*, p. 120.

138. *Ibid.*, pp. 120–21.

139. *Confessions*, p. 535.

140. Sainte-Beuve, *op. cit.*, Vol. IX, p. 173.

141. *Confessions*, pp. 542–3.

142. I. Grünberg, "Rousseau joueur d'échecs," p. 164.

143. *Confessions*, p. 543.

144. W. H. Blanchard, *op. cit.*, p. 122.

145. *Ibid.*

146. J. McManners, "The *Social Contract* and Rousseau's Revolt Against Society," p. 7.

147. *Confessions*, pp. 524–5.

*Chapter II: "La Nouvelle Héloïse": The Problem of Reconstruction*

1. *Confessions*, p. 427.

2. *Ibid.*, p. 548.

3. *La Nouvelle Héloïse*, ed. R. Pomeau; Paris, 1951.
4. R. V. Sampson, *Progress in the Age of Reason*, pp. 126–7.
5. I am here following Pomeau's excellent outline.
6. *La Nouvelle Héloïse*, ed., R. Pomeau, p. vii.
7. For a detailed analysis see L. G. Crocker, "Julie ou la nouvelle duplicité," pp. 105–152.
8. "The firmest virtue avoids taking chances; he who exposes himself to danger is looking for his downfall." (Corneille, *Polyeucte*, Act II, Scene iv).
9. This has been suggested by a woman, Renée LeLièvre, in her article, "Julie d'Etange, ou la maternité frustrée," p. 367.
10. R. Mauzi, "La Conversion de Julie dans *La Nouvelle Héloïse*," pp. 29–38.
11. J. Starobinski, *Jean-Jacques Rousseau, la transparence et l'obstacle*; Paris, 1957, p. 121.
12. B. Guyon, "Un Chef-d'oeuvre méconnu: *Julie*," p. 343.
13. "When an individual cannot gratify his emotional needs on an adult level, he regresses to a more infantile and dependent attitude. . . . There is a protest against adult independence and an insistence upon being loved and cared for, if necessary at the sacrifice of others. This regression creates new emotional problems. Shame may develop and express the tension between the regressive behavior and adult standards, which are not wholly relinquished" (F. Alexander, *Fundamentals of Psychoanalysis*; New York, 1963, p. 69).
14. R. Mauzi, *L'Idée du bonheur en France au XVIII^e siècle*, p. 622.
15. A similar warning occurs in *Emile*, ed. F. and P. Richard, p. 508.

*Chapter III: Strange Vicissitudes*

1. *Confessions*, p. 544.
2. S. S. B. Taylor, "Rousseau's Contemporary Reputation in France," p. 1555.
3. *Lettre de M. L^xxx à M. D^xxx sur "La Nouvelle Héloïse*," quoted in M. Hervier, *Les Ecrivains français jugés par leurs contemporains*, Vol. II, pp. 157.
4. M. Grimm, *Correspondance littéraire, philosophique et critique*, Vol. IV, pp. 342–6, and A. M. Wilson, "The Unpublished portion of Grimm's Critique of *La Nouvelle Héloïse*," pp. 27–9.
5. Voltaire, *Oeuvres complètes*, ed. Louis Moland, Vol. XXIV, p. 174.
6. Both letters are to d'Argental, January 26; February 11, 1761. Voltaire's letters and letters to him may be found in chronological order in his *Correspondance*, ed. Theodore Besterman, 107 vols.; Geneva, 1953–65. Many are reprinted in R. A. Leigh's edition of Rousseau's *Correspondance*.
7. (February 11, 1761.)
8. (February 3, 1761.)
9. (February 18, 1761.)
10. *Confessions*, p. 547.
11. (To Voltaire, June 25, 1764.)
12. (To Mme. Bourette, March 21, 1761.) Corr., VIII, 245–6.
13. (February 10, 1761.) Corr., VIII, 76.
14. J. L. R. d'Alembert, "Jugement sur *La Nouvelle Héloïse*," *Oeuvres posthumes*, quoted in M. Hervier, *Les Ecrivains français jugés par leurs contemporains*, Vol. II, pp. 155–6.
15. (February 16, 1761.) Corr., VIII, 116.
16. (March 7, 1761.) Corr., VIII, 225–6.
17. (March 29, 1761.) Corr., VIII, 284.
18. (May 26, 1761.) Corr., VIII, 333.
19. (June 24, 1761.) Corr., IX, 27.
20. M. Grimm, *op. cit.*, Vol. IV, pp. 394–8 (May 1, 1761).
21. (April 9, 1761.) Nevertheless, he did mock the work in his "Rescrit de l'empereur de la Chine, à l'occasion du Projet de paix perpétuelle," published in the May 1, 1761, issue of the *Journal encyclopedique*.
22. (To Damilaville, March 19, 1761.)

23. (October 20, 1761.)
24. (February 19, 1761.)
25. *Confessions*, p. 550.
26. *Ibid.*, p. 1545.
27. I. W. Allen, "Thérèse LeVasseur." Ph.D. thesis (unpublished), Western Reserve U., p. 142.
28. (Cornabès to Rousseau, May 28, 1761.) *Corr.*, IX, 335–6.
29. To Roustan, December 23, 1761.) *Corr.*, IX, 344–5.
30. *Confessions*, p. 561.
31. Allen, *op. cit.*, p. 130.
32. C. Guyot, *Plaidoyer pour Thérèse LeVasseur*, p. 74.
33. (October 19, 1761). *Corr.*, IX, 184.
34. *Confessions*, p. 564.
35. *Ibid.*, p. 566.
36. *Ibid.*, p. 1550–1.
37. (December 16, 1761). *Corr.*, IX, 320.
38. (December 17, 1761) *Corr.*, IX, 330–1.
39. (December 22, 1761) *Corr.*, IX, 338–9.
40. (December 23, 1761) *Corr.*, IX, 341.
41. (December 25, 1761) *Corr.*, IX, 354–6.
42. *Confessions*, pp. 564–5.
43. *Ibid.*, p. 569.
44. (To Rey, January 23, 1762). *Corr.*, X, 48–50.
45. *Confessions*, p. 409.
46. R. Grimsley, *Jean-Jacques Rousseau: A Study in Self-awareness.*
47. *Corr.*, V, 60.
48. R. Grimsley, *op. cit.*, p. 167.
49. *Ibid.*, p. 176.
50. (June 1, 1762.) *Corr.*, XI, 2.
51. (June 4, 1762.) *Corr.*, XI, 21.
52. (February 16, 1762.) *Corr.*, X, 102–3.
53. (Ca. February 12, 1762.) *Corr.*, X, 99.
54. (April 29, 1762.) *Corr.*, X, 225–7.
55. *C. G.*, VII, 236.
56. *Confessions*, pp. 575, 1556.
57. *Ibid.*, p. 573.
58. *Ibid.*, p. 574.
59. *Ibid.*, p. 1556 (editor's note).
60. *Ibid.*, p. 575.
61. *Ibid.*, p. 1557.
62. G. Lanson, "Quelques documents inédits sur la condamnation des *Lettres écrites de la montagne*," *AJJR*, pp. 1559–60. Yet it would be pertinent to inquire, suggests F. C. Green, why Malesherbes "consistently ignored the author's objections to a French edition" (*Jean-Jacques Rousseau*; Cambridge, Eng., 1955, p. 312). He had, in fact, assured Rousseau that the *Profession de foi* would be favorably received.
63. See J. Fabre, "Rousseau et le prince de Conti," pp. 7–52.
64. *Ibid.*, p. 16.
65. *Ibid.*, p. 26.
66. P. Grosclaude, *Malesherbes, témoin et interprète de son temps*; Paris, 1961.

*Chapter IV: The Hypothetical Emile,*
*or the Reconstructed Individual*

1. Pléiade, I, 934.
2. *Emile*, ed. F. and P. Richard, p. 65.
3. M. Rang, "Le Dualisme anthropologique dans l'*Emile*," *Jean-Jacques Rousseau et son oeuvre*, pp. 195–203.
4. D. W. Smith, *Helvétius*, pp. 125 ff.

5. See P. H. Meyer, "The Attitude of the Enlightenment Towards the Jew," pp. 1161–1205.
6. W. B. Simon, "The Quest for Subjective Certainty," p. 175.
7. M. Dickstein, "The Faith of a Vicar," pp. 51–2.
8. E. Cassirer, *The Philosophy of the Enlightenment*, p. 106.
9. On Rousseau's sadism and desire for domination, see W. H. Blanchard, *Rousseau and the Spirit of Revolt*, pp. 155, 161.
10. J. Plamenatz, *Man and Society*, Vol. I, p. 382.
11. See L. G. Crocker, "The Problem of Truth and Falsehood in the Enlightenment," pp. 575–603.
12. R. Grimsley, *Rousseau and the Religious Quest*, p. 49.
13. See M. Debesse, "L'Influence pédagogique de l'*Emile* depuis deux siècles. Ses formes, son évolution," pp. 205–17.
14. See P. D. Jimack, "La Genèse et la rédaction de l'*Emile* de Jean-Jacques Rousseau," 3 parts.
15. G. Picon, *Introduction à une esthétique de la littérature*, Vol. I, p. 103.
16. F. C. Green, *Jean-Jacques Rousseau*, p. 268.
17. According to J. Starobinski, the second of these themes may go back to Rousseau's father's separation from his wife and his return (*Jean-Jacques Rousseau, la transparence et l'obstacle*, p. 156n). The history of Sophie's courtship, in the fifth book of *Emile*, is also one of separation and reunion.
18. G. Turbet-Delof, "A propos de l'Emile et Sophie," *Revue d'histoire littéraire de la France*; Lille, 1963, pp. 221–37.
19. *Ibid.*, pp. 53–4. In the second of the *Entretiens sur le fils naturel*, Dorval speaks of founding a utopian colony in Lampedusa, and satirizes Rousseau (or so Rousseau thought) as a hermit who goes from one religion to another.
20. *Ibid.*, p. 55.
21. *Oeuvres complètes*; Hachette, Paris, Vol. III, p. 18. Earlier (p. 4) he confesses that his education was no protection against the temptations of Paris.
22. *Confessions*, pp. 56–7.

## Chapter V: The Reconstructed Society

1. See J. S. Spink, *Jean-Jacques Rousseau et Genève*, pp. 13–29.
2. J. Bronowski and B. Mazlish, *The Western Intellectual Tradition*, p. 280.
3. *Du Contrat social*, ed., Maurice Halbwachs; Paris, 1943, Book I, Ch. VI.
4. L. Gossman, "Rousseau's Idealism," p. 176.
5. C. N. Cochrane, *Christianity and Classical Culture*," p. 179.
6. F. Alexander, *Fundamentals of Psychoanalysis*, pp. 97–8.
7. See S. Cotta, "La Position du problème de la politique chez Rousseau," *Etudes sur le "Contrat Social" de Jean-Jacques Rousseau*, pp. 177–90.
8. A. Schinz, *Etat présent des travaux sur Jean-Jacques Rousseau*, pp. 30–1.
9. J. L. Talmon, *The Rise of Totalitarian Democracy*, pp. 38–9.
10. W. B. Simon, "The Quest for Subjective Certainty," p. 174. Other quotations are from this article.
11. *C.G.*, II, 130–6, translated in R. Grimsley, *Jean-Jacques Rousseau: A Study in Self-awareness*, p. 73.
12. J. Guéhenno, *Jean-Jacques: En marge des "Confessions," 1712–1750*, p. 84.
13. J-J. Rousseau, *Emile*, ed., F. and P. Richard, pp. 438–43.
14. *Lettre à d'Alembert*, ed. M. Fuchs, p. 57.
15. M. R. Stein, A. J. Vidich, and D. M. White, eds., *Identity and Anxiety: Survival of the Person in a Mass Society*, p. 81.
16. J. L. Moreno, "The Creativity Theory of Personality," p. 21–2.

## Chapter VI: The Fugitive

1. "Second Projet de Préface au Lévite d'Ephraïm," Pléiade, II, 1206.
2. *Confessions*, p. 586.

3. J. Starobinski, *Jean-Jacques Rousseau, la transparence et l'obstacle*, p. 297.
4. Pléiade, I, 1041.
5. Pléiade, II, 414.
6. *Confessions*, p. 589.
7. (June 18, 1762). *Corr.*, XI, 108–9.
8. (June 14, 1762). *Corr.*, XI, 73.
9. *Confessions*, p. 591.
10. (June 14, 1762).
11. (June 14, 1762).
12. (June 15, 1762).
13. (End of June 1762). *Corr.*, XI, 167.
14. J. Fabre, "Rousseau et le prince de Conti," p. 33, n. 2.
15. N. L. Torrey, *The Spirit of Voltaire*, p. 127.
16. (D'Alembert to Voltaire, September 25, 1762.)
17. *Corr.*, XI, 308, 311.
18. See G. May, "Voltaire a-t-il fait une offre d'hospitalité à Rousseau?" p. 109, and *Corr.*, XI, 307–11.
19. (July 7, 1762).
20. J. Boswell, *J. Boswell on the Grand Tour*, Vol. I, pp. 260–2.
21. C. Guyot, *Un Ami et défenseur de Rousseau, Pierre-Alexandre Du Peyrou*, p. 83.
22. *Confessions*, p. 594, 1568.
23. (July 9?, 1762). *Corr.*, XII, 3.
24. (Ca. August 18, 1762). *Corr.*, XII, 205–6.
25. *Confessions*, pp. 595–6.
26. *Ibid.*, p. 597–8.
27. (July 21, 1762). *Corr.*, XII, 136–7.
28. (August 20, 1762). *Corr.*, XII, 217–9.
29. (September 10, 1762). *Corr.*, XIII, 48–9.
30. (August 18, 1762). *Corr.*, XII, 207–8.
31. (To the Abbé de Carondolet, March 4, 1764) (*C.G.*, X, 339). He also admits this to Mme. de Boufflers, on October 31, 1762 (*Corr.*, XIII, 279–84).
32. R. Grimsley, *Jean-Jacques Rousseau*, p. 193.
33. *Confessions*, p. 601.
34. (September 4, 1762). *Corr.*, XIII, 9–10.
35. J. Sénelier, "Jean-Jacques Rousseau, ou la désespérance amoureuse," p. 423.
36. Pléiade, II, 1294–5.
37. *Ibid.*, II, 1293–4.
38. Sénelier, *op. cit.*, p. 434.
39. *Ibid.*
40. (To Tscharner, July 27, 1762). *Corr.*, XII, 110.
41. (September 10, 1762). *Corr.*, XIII, 44–5.
42. (Voltaire to Mme. d'Epinay, September 25, 1764).
43. (To Mme. de Boufflers, July 27, 1762). *Corr.*, XII, 112–4.
44. *Ibid.*
45. (July 21, 1762). *Corr.*, XII, 76–7.
46. (September 21, 1762). *Corr.*, XIII, 82–6.
47. (Ca. September 10, 1762). *Corr.*, XIII, 36–40.
48. (August 3, 1762). *Corr.*, XII, 148–9.
49. (September 16, 1762). *Corr.*, XIII, 71–2.
50. *Corr.*, XI, 123.
51. *Ibid.*, XII, 139.
52. *Ibid.*, p. 162.
53. (September 25, 1762). *Corr.*, XIII, 114–8.
54. M. Hervier, *Les Ecrivains français jugés par leurs contemporains*, Vol. II, p. 167.
55. S. S. B. Taylor, "Rousseau's Contemporary Reputation in France," pp. 159–61.
56. (To the Marquis d'Argens, April 22, 1763.)
57. (To d'Argental, July 14, 1766.)
58. (To Damilaville, July 31; October 10, 1762.)
59. (To d'Argental, July 14, 1766.)
60. *Corr.*, XI, 274 (to Julie de Lespinasse).

61. D. Diderot, *Correspondance*, ed. G. Roth, Vol. IV, pp. 71–2 (July 25, 1762).
62. M. Grimm, *Correspondance littéraire, philosophique et critique*, Vol. IV, p. 374.
63. *Ibid.*, V, p. 116.
64. *Ibid.*, V, pp. 121–2.
65. *Ibid.*, V, p. 129.
66. *Corr.*, XI, 34.
67. (To Damilaville, June 25, 1762.)
68. The refutations are analyzed by R. Derathé ("Les Réfutations du *Contrat social* au XVIII° siècle"), pp. 7–54, who does not, however, consider others written after 1789.
69. J. Lough, "The Earliest Refutation of Rousseau's *Contrat social*," p. 28.
70. See J. Godechot, "Le *Contrat social* et la Révolution occidentale de 1762 à 1789," pp. 393–405.
71. P. F. O'Mara, "Jean-Jacques and Geneva. The Petty Bourgeois Milieu of Rousseau's Thought," p. 144.
72. *Ibid.*, p. 152.
73. *Corr.*, XI, 33.
74. R. A. Leigh, "Jean-Jacques Rousseau," pp. 563–4. For Rousseau's relationship to Geneva, the best study is still J. S. Spink, *Jean-Jacques Rousseau et Genève*.
75. See L. G. Crocker, *Rousseau's "Social Contract": An Interpretive Essay*, Chapter 3 and Bibliography.
76. *Corr.*, I, 295.
77. E. Ritter, "La Famille et la jeunesse de Jean-Jacques Rousseau," p. 249.
78. *Confessions*, pp. 619–20. He claims that this was the motive for his not having written her.
79. See R. A. Leigh, "Jean-Jacques Rousseau..." p. 552.
80. J. Starobinski, *L'Oeil vivant*, pp. 180–1.
81. Pléiade, IV, 927.
82. *Ibid.*, IV, 1007
83. F. C. Green, *Jean-Jacques Rousseau*, p. 316.
84. E. Cassirer, *The Question of Jean-Jacques Rousseau*, pp. 74–5.
85. *Ibid.*, p. 1023.
86. *Ibid.*, p. 1024.
87. *Ibid.*, p. 937.
88. *Ibid.*
89. (November 1, 1762). *Corr.*, XIV, 1.
90. (December 7, 1762). *Corr.*, XIV, 165–6.
91. (January 13, 1763). *C.G.*, IX, 3–4.
92. (February 20, 1763). *C.G.*, IX, 106–7.
93. (April 16, 1763). *C.G.*, IX, 231–3.
94. (May 19, 1763). *C.G.*, IX, 301–3.
95. (March 23, 1763). *C.G.*, IX, 183.
96. M. Grimm, *op. cit.*, Vol. V, pp. 290–2 (May 1763).
97. *Ibid.*, Vol. V, 284.
98. (Voltaire to d'Argental, April 25, 1763.)
99. (To Moultou, February 17, 1763). *C.G.*, IX, 93–4.
100. (To Bitaubé, March 3, 1763). *C.G.*, IX, 148.
101. (April 2; April 16, 1763). *C.G.*, IX, 211, 238–9.
102. (De Luc to Rousseau, November 23, 1762). *Corr.*, XIV, 85–6.
103. (February 19, 1763). *C.G.*, IX, 103–4.
104. (February 28, 1763). *C.G.*, IX, 126.
105. (To Mme. Boy de la Tour, May 7, 1763). *C.G.*, IX, 274–7.
106. *Confessions*, pp. 616–8.
107. (Moultou to Rousseau, June 25, 1763.) *C.G.*, IX, 368–70.
108. J. Guéhenno, *Jean-Jacques: En marge des "Confessions," 1712–1750*, Vol. III, p. 133.
109. M. Grimm, *op. cit.*, Vol. V, p. 292.
110. (June 11, 1763.) *C.G.*, IX, 345–7.
111. M. R. Stein, A. J. Vidich, and D. M. White, eds., *Identity and Anxiety: Survival of the Person in Mass Society*, pp. 46, 51.
112. (June 18, 1763.) *C.G.*, IX, 362–3.

113. M. Grimm, *op. cit.*, Vol. V, p. 117.
114. Voltaire, *Oeuvres Complètes*, ed. L. Moland, Vol. XLII, pp. 519–20.
115. See H. Guillemin's Preface to the *Lettres écrites de la montagne*, p. 36.
116. (July [?] 1763.) *C.G.*, X, 7–9.
117. Quoted in P.-P. Plan, ed., *Rousseau raconté par les gazettes*, p. 36.
118. (July 27, 1763.) *C.G.*, X, 51–4.
119. See particularly De Luc's letter of August 28, *C.G.*, X, 105–9.
120. M. Launay, "Les Problèmes politiques dans la correspondance de Rousseau," p. 268.
121. (July 7, 1763.) *C.G.*, X, 17–8.
122. (July 27, 1763.) *C.G.*, X, 48.
123. (July 4, 1763.) *C.G.*, X, 10–11.
124. (September 15, 1763.) *C.G.*, X, 127–8.
125. (August 21, 1763.) *C.G.*, X, 93–5.
126. (September 27, 1763.) *C.G.*, X, 140–1.
127. (December 25, 1763.) *C.G.*, X, 267–9.
128. (September 14, 1763.) *C.G.*, X, 125–6.
129. (September 10, 1763.) *C.G.*, X, 118–20.
130. (September 10, 1764.) *C.G.*, XI, 267–74.
131. (August 5, 1764.) *C.G.*, XI, 218–9.
132. (September 3, 1764.) *C.G.*, XI, 257–8.
133. (January 30, 1764.) *C.G.*, X, 309–11.
134. (February 5, February 9, March 10, 1764.) *C.G.*, X, 317–8, 344.
135. (March 31, 1764.) *C.G.*, X, 377–9.
136. (May 6, 1764.) *C.G.*, XI, 35–7.
137. (To Tscharner, April 29, 1762.) *Corr.*, X, 225–6.
138. (March 25, 1764.) *C.G.*, X, 373.
139. (Ca. May 27, 1764.) *C.G.*, XI, 92.
140. (June 7, 1763.) *C.G.*, XI, 116–8.
141. (June 17, 1764.) *C.G.*, XI, 141–2.
142. (August 26, 1764.) *C.G.*, XI, 239–42.
143. (September 15, 1764.) *C.G.*, XI, 283–4.
144. See H. Buffenoir, *Le Prestige de Jean-Jacques Rousseau*, pp. 283 ff.
145. *Ibid.*, p. 309.
146. To Madame Boy de la Tour (July 7, 1764). *C.G.*, XI, 167.
147. (To Duchesne, September 15, 1764.) *C.G.*, XI, 283.
148. *Corr.*, IX, xxv.
149. (December 8, 1764.) *C.G.*, XII, 127–9.
150. (December 14, 1764.) *C.G.*, XII, 141.
151. J. Boswell, *Boswell on the Grand Tour, Vol. I, Germany and Switzerland, 1764*, ed., F. A. Pottle, pp. 206–16. For a masterful study of Boswell and Rousseau, see R. A. Leigh, "Boswell and Rousseau," p. 189.
152. Boswell, *op. cit.*, p. 229.
153. (December 5, 1764.) *C.G.*, XII, 114–5.
154. Boswell, *op. cit.*, p. 235.
155. *Ibid.*, p. 253–4.
156. *Ibid.*, p. 258.
157. *Ibid.*, p. 264.
158. *Ibid.*, p. 266 and n. 2.
159. *Ibid.*, p. 268.
160. *Ibid.*, p. 302.
161. (To De Luc, July 20, 1764.) *C.G.*, XI, 191–3.
162. (November 11, 1764.) *C.G.*, XII, 53–5.
163. (November 25, 1764.) *C.G.*, XII, 85–7.
164. (December 6, 1764.) *C.G.*, XII, 121.
165. (December 23, 1764.) *C.G.*, XII, 157.
166. (December 23, 1764.) *C.G.*, XII, 158–9.
167. (December 28, 1764.) *C.G.*, XII, 170.
168. (December 31, 1764.) *C.G.*, XII, 182.
169. (December 26, 1764.) *C.G.*, XII, 174–5.

170. *Confessions*, p. 623.
171. (To Du Peyrou, November 4, 1764.) *C.G.*, XII, 24–6.
172. Pléiade, III, 799.
173. See also letter to Damilaville, December 31, 1764.
174. (January 9, 1765.)
175. H. Guillemin, *op. cit.*, p. 43.
176. Voltaire. *Mélanges*, p. 718.
177. *Ibid.*, p. 717.
178. *C.G.*, XII, Appendix, p. 6.
179. (January 15, 1765.)
180. (March 4, 1765.)
181. The first was *Le Sentiment des jurisconsultes* in which, posing as a priest, Voltaire claimed that Geneva had the legal right to demand Rousseau's extradition. The second is *Le Préservatif*, in which Voltaire compares Rousseau to a fanciful wild beast that was terrorizing southern France.
182. *The Political Writings of Rousseau*, ed. C. E. Vaughan, Vol. II, p. 176.
183. *Ibid.*, Vol. II, p. 177.
184. F. C. Green, *op. cit.*, p. 323.
185. Rousseau, *Political Writings*, Vol. II, p. 185.
186. Rousseau, *Political Writings*, Vol. II, pp. 200–1.
187. *Ibid.*, Vol. II, p. 204.
188. *Ibid.*, Vol. II, p. 219.
189. *Ibid.*, Vol. II, p. 274.
190. S. Stelling-Michaud, "Lumières et politique," p. 1543.
191. Irving Babbitt, *Rousseau and Romanticism*, pp. xvii–xviii.
192. *Ibid.*

### Chapter VII: Where Can I Go?

1. J. Starobinski, "The Illness of Rousseau," p. 73.
2. (To Keith, January 26, 1765.) *C.G.*, XII, 255–7.
3. (To Mme. Guyenot la jeune, February 6, 1765.) *C.G.*, XII, 319–20.
4. *C.G.*, XII, 318.
5. (February 11, 1765.) *C.G.*, XII, 359–60.
6. *Confessions*, p. 624.
7. *Ibid.*, p. 626.
8. *Ibid.*, p. 624.
9. (March 18, 1765.) *C.G.*, XIII, 132–6.
10. (To Mme. de Verdelin, February 3, 1765.) *C.G.*, XII, 297–9.
11. (February 8, 1764.) *C.G.*, XII, 331–3.
12. *Confessions*, pp. 627–8.
13. *C.G.*, XIII, 245n.
14. (March 10, 1765.) *C.G.*, XIII, 95.
15. (May 18, 1765.) *C.G.*, XIII, 312–4.
16. See L. G. Crocker, *Jean-Jacques Rousseau: The Quest (1712–1758)*, pp. 303–5.
17. (August 31, 1765.) *C.G.*, XIV, 120.
18. I. W. Allen, "Thérèse LeVasseur," p. 219.
19. (August 25, 1765.) *C.G.*, XIV, 111–3.
20. *Confessions*, pp. 643–4.
21. *Ibid.*, p. 645.
22. *Ibid.*, p. 1602 (comment by Marcel Raymond).
23. *Ibid.*, pp. 639–40.
24. Rousseau, *The Political Writings of Rousseau*, ed., C. E. Vaughan, Vol. II, p. 296.
25. *Ibid.*, Vol. II, p. 250.
26. See *Ibid.*, p. 338.
27. *Ibid.*, p. 240.
28. *Ibid.*, p. 354.

29. *Ibid.*, p. 344.
30. *Ibid.*, p. 349.
31. The preceding discussion is taken largely from the one in L. G. Crocker, *Rousseau's "Social Contract": An Interpretive Essay*, pp. 27–9.
32. *Confessions*, p. 648.
33. (October 13, 1765.) *C.G.*, XIV, 195–6.
34. *Confessions*, p. 646.
35. (To Graffenried, October 20, 1765.) *C.G.*, XIV, 206–8.
36. (October 28, 1765.) *C.G.*, XIV, 227.
37. *Confessions*, p. 655.
38. (Du Peyrou to Rousseau, November 4, 1765.) *C.G.*, XIV, 245.
39. (To d'Ivernois, December 30, 1765.) *C.G.*, XIV, 358.
40. (To Guy, November 4, 1765.) *C.G.*, XIV, 239–42.
41. (To Du Peyrou, December 24, 1765.) *C.G.*, XIV, 349–51.
42. J. Fabre, "Rousseau et le prince de Conti," p. 35.
43. See unsent letter to Malesherbes written at Wooton, May 10, 1766. (*C.G.*, XV, 222–9). For Malesherbes' account, see Pierre Grosclaude, *Malesherbes*, p. 109.
44. Grosclaude, *Ibid.*, pp. 56–8.
45. *Ibid.*, pp. 100–1.
46. (December 24, 1765). *C.G.*, XIV, 347.
47. (December 24, 1765). *C.G.*, XIV, 347–8.

## Chapter VIII: "Cette Affaire infernale"

1. *The Letters of David Hume*, ed., J. Y. T. Greig; Oxford, 1932, Vol. II, p. 8 (hereafter cited as Hume, *Letters*), Vol. II, p. 8 (February 2, 1766).
2. J. Boswell, "Private Papers of James Boswell from Malahide Castle," Vol. VII, pp. 65–7.
3. Hume, *Letters*, Vol. II, p. 3 (January 19, 1766).
4. *C.G.*, XIX, p. 317, 357; Rousseau, *Oeuvres*, Pléiade, I, 229–71.
5. Letter to Blair, March 25, repeated in letter to Mme. de Boufflers, April 3. See Hume, *Letters*, Vol. II, 30, 36.
6. To Mme. de Verdelin, April 9; to Malesherbes, May 10 (not sent); to Hume, July 10. *C.G.*, XV, 154–7, 222–9, 307–9.
7. Hume, *Letters*, Vol. II, pp. 35–6.
8. R. Grimsley, *Jean-Jacques Rousseau*, p. 201.
9. *C.G.*, XV, 196 (editor's note).
10. F. A. Pottle, "The Part Played by Horace Walpole and James Boswell in the Quarrel between Rousseau and Hume," pp. 358–9.
11. Hume, *Letters*, Vol. II, p. 53.
12. E. C. Mossner, *The Life of David Hume*, pp. 528–9.
13. R. Klibansky and E. C. Mossner, *New Letters of David Hume*; Oxford, 1954, p. 140.
14. Hume, *Letters*, Vol. II, p. 76.
15. *C.G.*, XV, 349n.
16. Hume, *Letters*, Vol. II, 73, n. 1.
17. See R. Grimsley, *op. cit.*, pp. 195–9.
18. H. Guillemin, "*Cette Affaire infernale*," *L'Affaire Jean-Jacques Rousseau—David Hume, 1766*.
19. *Ibid.*, p. 344.
20. R. Grimsley, *op. cit.*, pp. 191, 200.
21. *Ibid.*, p. 203.
22. I. W. Allen, "Thérèse LeVasseur," p. 301.
23. (Voltaire to Hume, October 24, 1766.)
24. See especially the letter of September 6 (?) to Davenport. *C.G.*, XVI, 50–1.
25. (October 4.) *C.G.*, XVI, 56.
26. (To Du Peyrou, ca. December 21, 1766.) *C.G.*, XVI, 177.
27. (August [?] 1766.) *C.G.*, XVI, 34.
28. (September 7.) *C.G.*, XVI, 55–6.

29. (February 7, 1767.) *C.G.*, XVI, 275.
30. *C.G.*, XVI, 126.
31. (To Du Peyrou, March 2 [?]; perhaps not sent.) *C.G.*, XVI, 343.
32. H. Blanchard, *Rousseau and the Spirit of Revolt*, pp. 215-6.
33. C. Guyot, *Plaidoyer pour Thérèse LeVasseur*, pp. 107-8.

### Chapter IX: In the Shadow World

1. R. Schiltz, "Rousseau sous le nom de Renou," p. 49.
2. J. Fabre, "Rousseau et le prince de Conti," p. 37.
3. (To Coindet, July 15). *C.G.*, XVII, 138.
4. (August 12). *C.G.*, XII, 204.
5. (July 12). *C.G.*, XVII, 131.
6. (September 3). *C.G.*, XVII, 237.
7. (October 10). *C.G.*, XVII, 307-8.
8. (To Du Peyrou, September 8). *C.G.*, XVII, 251-2.
9. (October 5, 1767). *C.G.*, XVII, 293.
10. (January 20, 1768). *C.G.*, XVIII, 66.
11. R. Schiltz, *op. cit.*, p. 51. Like other scholars, I am indebted to this important article.
12. *Ibid.*, p. 50.
13. *Ibid.*, p. 56.
14. Pléiade, I, 1183-4.
15. C. Guyot, *Plaidoyer pour Thérèse LeVasseur*, pp. 113-4.
16. (To Mme. de Lessert, August [?] 1768.) *C.G.*, XVIII, 278-9.
17. (To Laliaud, December 19, 1768.) *C.G.*, XIX, 27-8.
18. *Oeuvres*, Pléiade, I, 414.
19. *Ibid.*, I, 906.
20. R. Schiltz, *op. cit.*, pp. 59-60.
21. R. Grimsley, *op. cit.*, p. 207.
22. *Ibid.*, p. 211.
23. E. A. Foster, *Le Dernier Séjour de Jean-Jacques Rousseau à Paris, 1770-1778*, p. 180.
24. (March 16, 1770.) *C.G.*, XIX, 310.
25. (March 6, 1770.) *C.G.*, XIX, 275.
26. (October 25, 1770.) *C.G.*, XX, 8.
27. (March 12, 1770.) *C.G.*, XIX, 294.

### Chapter X: Return to Paris

1. *C.G.*, XIX, 375.
2. (September 9, 1770.) *C.G.*, XIX, 365.
3. J. Dusaulx, *De mes rapports avec Jean-Jacques Rousseau*, Paris, An VI (1798).
4. Quoted by E. A. Foster, *Le Dernier Séjour de Jean-Jacques Rousseau à Paris, 1770-1778*, p. 73.
5. Quoted by Allen, p. 417.
6. *Ibid.*, pp. 418-9.
7. (To Laliaud, December 19, 1768.) *C.G.*, XIX, 26-7.
8. D'Escherny, *Mélanges de littérature*, quoted in Allen, *op. cit.*, pp. 408-9.
9. *Confessions*, p. 656.
10. *Dialogues*, pp. 902-3.
11. *Confessions*, pp. 1612-3 (editor's note).
12. Quoted by Leigh, *Corr.*, VII, 124.
13. *Confessions*, p. 175.
14. See L. G. Crocker, *Jean-Jacques Rousseau: The Quest (1712-1758)*, Ch. VIII.
15. R. A. Leigh, "Jean-Jacques Rousseau," p. 553.

16. H. Peyre, *Literature and Sincerity*, p. 38.
17. R. A. Leigh, "Vers une nouvelle édition de la correspondance de Rousseau," p. 277.
18. P. Burgelin, *La Philosophie de l'existence de Jean-Jacques Rousseau*, p. 578.
19. L. Trilling, *Beyond Culture*, pp. 125–6.
20. J. Fabre in the introduction to his invaluable critical edition of the *Considérations*, in the Pléiade III, ccxvi–ccxlv.
21. See C. E. Vaughan's introduction, *Political Writings*, Vol. II, pp. 376–77.
22. *Ibid.*, p. 427.
23. *Ibid.*
24. *Ibid.*, pp. 428–9.
25. *Ibid.*, pp. 491–2.
26. *Ibid.*, p. 434.
27. *Ibid.*, p. 437.
28. *Ibid.*, pp. 437–441.
29. *Ibid.*, p. 445.
30. *Ibid.*, p. 432.
31. (January 15, 1772.) *C.G.*, XX, 122–6.
32. *C.G.*, XX, 248.
33. D'Alembert feigned to have no knowledge of the work. It is not certain that the manuscript which fell into Guy's hands was d'Alembert's. On this question, see E. A. Foster, *op. cit.*, pp. 127–31.
34. I. W. Allen, *op. cit.*, p. 438.
35. *Ibid.*, p. 442.
36. (To Mme. de Saint-Haon, May 23, 1776.) *C.G.*, XX, 317–8.
37. *Ibid.*
38. *Oeuvres*, Pléiade, II, 989.
39. R. Grimsley, *Jean-Jacques Rousseau*, p. 233.
40. *Ibid.*, p. 263.
41. *Ibid.*
42. F. C. Green, *Jean-Jacques Rousseau*, p. 361.
43. R. Grimsley, *Jean-Jacques Rousseau*, pp. 161–2.
44. *Oeuvres*, Pléiade, I, 997.
45. R. Osmont, "Un événement aussi triste qu'imprévu," p. 626.
46. J. Fabre, *op. cit.*, p. 48.
47. *C.G.*, XX, 360.
48. F. C. Green, *op. cit.*, p. 361.
49. (To Mme. de la Tour, September 26, 1762.) *Corr.* XIII, 122.
50. *Oeuvres*, Pléiade, I, 999.
51. Seventh "Promenade."
52. Leigh, *Corr.*, X, 57 (see editor's comment).
53. R. Grimsley, *Jean-Jacques Rousseau*, p. 34.
54. P. Burgelin, *op. cit.*, p. 578.
55. J. Guéhenno, *Jean-Jacques: En marge des "Confessions," 1712–1750*, p. 320.
56. Furne, quoted by Allen, pp. 453–4.
57. *Oeuvres*, Pléiade, I, 1187–8.
58. (February 3, 1778.) *C.G.*, XX, 332–4.
59. J. Guéhenno, *op. cit.*, p. 328.
60. I. W. Allen, *op. cit.*, p. 468, and C. Guyot, *Plaidoyer pour Thérèse LeVasseur*, Ch. 11.
61. *C.G.*, XX, 358.
62. (To Doubrowsky, in V. Olszewicz, "Documents polonais sur Jean-Jacques Rousseau et Thérèse LeVasseur," *AJJR*, VII, 84.)
63. A fuller acount is given in C. Guyot, *op. cit.*, Ch. 11.

# Bibliography[*]

Alexander, Franz, *Fundamentals of Psychoanalysis*; New York, 1963.

Allen, I. W., "Thérèse LeVasseur," Ph.D. thesis (unpublished), Western Reserve U.; Cleveland, 1933.

Anon., "Adresse d'un citoyen très actif, ou Questions preséntées aux États-Généraux du Manège, vulgairement appelés Assemblée Nationale"; n.p., n.d.

[Aubert de Vitry], *Jean-Jacques Rousseau à l'Assemblée Nationale*; Paris, 1789.

Babbit, Irving, *Rousseau and Romanticism*; Boston and New York, 1919.

Bandy, W. T., "Rousseau's Flight from England," *Romanic Review*, 1948, pp. 107–21 (1948).

Barker, Ernest, *Reflections on Government*; Oxford, 1942.

Barth, Hans, "Volonté générale, volonté particulière," in *Rousseau et la philosophie politique, Annales de philosophie politique*, No. 5; Paris, 1965, pp. 35–50.

Bauclair, P. L. de, *Anti-Contrat social*; La Haye, 1765.

Bellenot, J. L., "*La Nouvelle Héloïse*," *AJJR*, XXXIII, 1935–55.

Berlin, Sir Isaiah, "Montesquieu," *Proceedings of the British Academy*, 1955, pp. 267–96.

Besse, Guy, "Marx, Engels et le XVIII⁰ siècle français," *Studies on Voltaire and the Eighteenth Century*, XXIV, 1963, pp. 155–70.

"Observations sur la *Réfutation d'Helvétius* par Diderot," *Diderot Studies VI*; Genève, 1963, pp. 29–46.

Besterman, Theodore, *Voltaire;* New York, 1969.

Blanchard, W. H., *Rousseau and the Spirit of Revolt*; Ann Arbor, Mich., 1967.

Boiteux, L. S., "Le Rôle de d'Alembert dans la querelle Rousseau-Hume," *AJJR*, XXXII, 1950–52, pp. 143–54.

Bonhomme, Henri, *La Société galante et littéraire au XVIIIᵉ siècle*; Paris, 1880.

Boswell, James, *Boswell on the Grand Tour, Vol. I, Germany and Switzerland, 1764*, ed. F. A. Pottle; New York, 1953.

*Boswell on the Grand Tour, Vol. II, Italy, Corsica and France, 1765–1766*, ed. Frank Brady and F. A. Pottle; New York, 1955.

"Private Papers of James Boswell from Malahide Castle," collection of Lt. Col. Ralph Heyward Isham, prepared for the press by Geoffrey Scott and Frederick A. Pottle, *The Journal of James Boswell 1765–1768* 18 vols.; privately printed, Mount Vernon, N.Y. 1930.

Bretonneau, G., *Valeurs humaines de Jean-Jacques Rousseau*; Paris, 1961.

Brody, Jules, "*Don Juan* and *Le Misanthrope*, or the esthetics of individualism in Molière," Publications of the Modern Language Association, LXXXIV, 1969, pp. 559–76.

Bronowski, J., and B. Mazlish, *The Western Intellectual Tradition*; New York, 1960.

Buffenoir, Hippolyte, *Jean-Jacques Rousseau* à Montmorency, discours prononcé par Hippolyte Buffenoir, le 5 juin 1904, à la fête de l'Athénée. Paris, the Author, 1904, p. 189.

*La Maréchale de Luxembourg*; Paris, 1924.

*Le Prestige de Jean-Jacques Rousseau*; Paris, 1909.

Burgelin, Pierre, *La Philosophie de l'existence de Jean-Jacques Rousseau*; Paris, 1952.

* This bibliography is supplementary to the one in *Jean-Jacques Rousseau: The Quest (1712–1758)*; New York, 1968.

"The Second Education of Emile," *Yale French Studies*, No. 28, 1961–62, pp. 106–11.

"Le Social et le politique chez Rousseau," in *Etudes sur le "Contrat social" de Jean-Jacques Rousseau*; Société Les Belles Lettres, Paris, 1964, pp. 165–76.

Casanova de Seingalt, Jacques, *Histoire de ma vie*, 12 vols.; Wiesbaden and Paris, 1960–62.

Casini, Paolo, "Rousseau e Diderot," in *Rivista critica di storia della filosofia*, Vol. III; Florence, 1964, pp. 248–70.

Cassirer, Ernst, *The Philosophy of the Enlightenment*; Princeton, N.J., 1951.

*The Question of Jean-Jacques Rousseau*; New York, 1954.

Champion, Edme, *Jean-Jacques Rousseau et la Révolution Française*; Paris, 1909.

Château, Jean, *Jean-Jacques Rousseau: sa philosophie de l'éducation*; Paris, 1962.

Cobban, Alfred, *In Search of Humanity*; New York, 1960.

(Review of P. Léon, *Le Problème du contrat social chez Rousseau*, *AJJR*, XXV, 1936, p. 287.)

Cochrane, C. N., *Christianity and Classical Culture*; Oxford, 1940.

Cotta, Sergio, "Philosophie et politique dans l'oeuvre de Rousseau," *Archiv für Rechts- und Sozial philosophie*, XLIX; Berlin, 1963, pp. 171–89.

"La position du Problème de la politique chez Rousseau," *Etudes sur le "Contrat social" de Jean-Jacques Rousseau*; Société Les Belles Lettres, Paris, 1964, pp. 177–90.

Crocker, L. G., *Jean-Jacques Rousseau: The Quest (1712–1758)*; New York, 1968.

"Julie ou la nouvelle duplicité," *AJJR*, XXXVI, 1966, pp. 105–52.

"The Problem of Truth and Falsehood in the Age of Enlightenment," *Journal of the History of Ideas*, XIV, 1953, pp. 575–603.

"Rousseau et la voie du totalitarisme," in *Rousseau et la philosophie politique* (*Annales de philosophie politique*, No. 5); Institut international de philosophie politique, Paris, 1965.

*Rousseau's "Social Contract": An Interpretive Essay*; Cleveland, 1968.

Debesse, Maurice, "L'Influence pédagogique de l'*Emile* depuis deux siècles. Ses formes, son évolution," in *Actes et Colloques*; Paris, 1963, pp. 205–17.

Dehaussy, Jacques, "La Dialectique de la souveraine liberté dans le *Contrat social*," in *Etudes sur le "Contrat social" de Jean-Jacques Rousseau*; Société Les Belles Lettres, Paris, 1964, pp. 119–41.

Derathé, Robert, "Les Réfutations du *Contrat social* au XVIII<sup>e</sup> siècle," *AJJR*, XXXII, 1950–52, pp. 7–54.

"La Religion civile selon Rousseau," *AJJR*, XXXV, 1959–62, pp. 161–70.

Dickstein, Morris, "The Faith of a Vicar: Reason and Morality in Rousseau's Religion," *Yale French Studies*, No. 28, 1961–62, pp. 48–54.

Diderot, Denis, *Correspondance*, ed., Georges Roth, 16 vols.; Editions de Minuit, Paris, 1955.

*Oeuvres philosophiques*, ed. Paul Vernière; Paris, 1956.

Dottrens, Robert, "Jean-Jacques Rousseau éducateur," in *Jean-Jacques Rousseau*; Université ouvrière et Faculté des lettres de l'Université de Genève, Neuchâtel, 1962.

Durkheim, Emile, *Montesquieu and Rousseau, Forerunners of Sociology*; Ann Arbor, Mich., 1960.

Dusaulchoy, J. F. N., *La Pelle au cul des Jacobins*; n.p., [1794].

Eisenmann, Charles, "La Cité de Jean-Jacques Rousseau," in *Etudes sur le "Contrat social" de Jean-Jacques Rousseau*; Société Les Belles Lettres, Paris, 1964, pp. 191–201.

Erikson, Erik, "Wholeness and Totality—A Psychiatric Contribution," in *Totalitarianism*, ed. C. J. Friedrich; Cambridge, Mass. 1954, pp. 156–71.

Fabre, Jean, "Rousseau et le prince de Conti," *AJJR*, XXXVI, 1963–65, pp. 7–52.

Feugère, Anatole, "Pourquoi Rousseau a remanié la Préface de la *Lettre à d'Alembert*," *AJJR*, XX, 1931, pp. 127–62.

Foster, Elizabeth A., *Le Dernier Séjour de Jean-Jacques Rousseau à Paris, 1770–1778*; Smith College Studies in Modern Languages, Northampton and Paris, Vol. II, No. 1, October 1970, pp. V + 1–84 + iv.

Francis, Madeleine, "Les Réminiscences spinozistes dans le *Contrat social* de Jean-Jacques Rousseau," *Revue philosophique*, CXLI, 1951, pp. 61–84.

Gallas, K. R., "Autour de Marc-Michel Rey et de Rousseau," *AJJR*, XVII, 1926, pp. 73–90.

Gilliard, François, "Etat de nature et liberté dans la pensée de Jean-Jacques Rousseau," in *Etudes sur le "Contrat social" de Jean-Jacques Rousseau*; Société Les Belles Lettres, Paris, 1964, pp. 393–405.

Godechot, Jacques, "Le *Contrat social* et la Révolution occidentale de 1762 à 1789," in *Etudes sur le "Contrat social" de Jean-Jacques Rousseau*; Société Les Belles Lettres, Paris, 1964, pp. 393–405.

Gossman, Lionel, "Rousseau's Idealism," *Romanic Review*, LVII, 1961, pp. 173–82.

Green, F. C., *Jean-Jacques Rousseau*; Cambridge, Eng., 1955.

"The Letters of Milord Marischal to Rousseau," *French Studies*, X, 1955, pp. 55–9.

Grimm, Melchior, *Correspondance littéraire, philosophique et critique*, 16 vols.; Garnier, Paris, 1877–82.

Grimsley, Ronald, *Jean-Jacques Rousseau: A Study in Self-awareness*; Cardiff, 1961.

*Rousseau and the Religious Quest*; Oxford, 1968.

Grosclaude, Pierre, *Malesherbes, témoin et interprète de son temps*; Paris, 1961.

Grünberg, I., "Rousseau joueur d'échecs," *AJJR*, III, 1907.

Gudin, P. Ph., *Supplément au "Contrat social"*; Paris, 1791.

Guéhenno, Jean, *Jean-Jacques: En marge des "Confessions," 1712–1750*; Paris 1948.

Guillemin, Henri, *"Cette affaire infernale," L'Affaire Jean-Jacques Rousseau–David Hume, 1766*; Paris, 1942.

Guyon, Bernard, "Un Chef-d'oeuvre méconnu: Julie," *Cahiers du Sud*, XLIX, 1962, pp. 335–49.

"La Mémoire et l'oubli dans *La Nouvelle Héloïse*," *AJJR*, XXXV, 1959–62, pp. 49–64.

Guyot, Charly, *Un Ami et défenseur de Rousseau, Pierre-Alexandre Du Peyrou*; Neuchâtel, 1958.

*Plaidoyer pour Thérèse LeVasseur*; Neuchâtel, 1962.

Hegel, G. W. F., *Lectures on the History of Philosophy*, 3 vols.; London, 1955.

Herold, J. Christopher, "The Solitary Wanderer," *Horizon*, 1964, pp. 94–102.

Hervier, Marcel, *Les Ecrivains français jugés par leurs contemporains*, Vol. II, *Le Dix-huitième siècle*; Paris, n.d.

Hocking, W., *Man and the State*; New Haven, 1926.

d'Holbach, P. Th., *La Morale universelle*, 3 vols.; Paris, 1820.

Hume, David, *Hume's Moral and Political Philosophy*, ed. H. D. Aiken; New York, 1948.

*The Letters of David Hume*, ed. J. Y. T. Greig, Vol. II; Oxford, 1932.

*New Letters of David Hume*, ed. R. Klibansky and E. C. Mossner; Oxford, 1954.

James, E. D., "The Political and Social Theory of Pierre Nicole," *French Studies*, 1963, pp. 117–27.

Jimack, P. D., "La Genèse et la rédaction de l'*Emile* de Jean-Jacques Rousseau," *Studies on Voltaire and the Eighteenth Century*, XIII, 1960.

Jouvenel, Bertrand de, "Rousseau évolutionniste pessimiste," in *Rousseau et la philosophie politique, Annales de philosophie politique*, No. 5; Paris, 1965, pp. 1–19.

Kant, I., *Kant's Critique of Practical Reason and Other Works on the Theory of Ethics*, trans., T. K. Abbott; London, 1873.

Kohler, Pierre, review of H. Guillemin, *"Cette Affaire infernale," AJJR*, XXIX, 1941–42, pp. 300–15.

Lacharrière, René de, "Rousseau et le socialisme," in *Etudes sur le "Contrat social" de Jean-Jacques Rousseau*; Société Les Belles Lettres, Paris, 1964.

Lanson, Gustave, "Quelques documents inédits sur la condamnation et la censure de l'*Emile* . . . ," *AJJR*, I, 1905, pp. 95–115.

Launay, Michel, "Les Problèmes politiques dans la correspondance de Rousseau," in *Jean-Jacques Rousseau et son oeuvre: problèmes et recherches*; Colloque de Paris, Paris, 1964.

Leigh, R. A., "Boswell and Rousseau," *Modern Language Review*, XLVII, 1952, p. 189.

"Jean-Jacques Rousseau," review article in *The Historical Journal*, XII, 1969, pp. 549–65.

"Jean-Jacques Rousseau et ses amis anglais," *Revue de littérature comparée*, XXX, 1956, pp. 379–89.

"Vers une nouvelle édition de la correspondance de Rousseau," *AJJR*, XXXV, 1959–62, pp. 263–80.

LeLièvre, Renée, "Julie d'Etange, ou la maternité frustrée," *Revue d'histoire littéraire de la France*, LXII, 1962, pp. 363–70.

[Lenormant, Ch.-Fr.], *Jean-Jacques Rousseau, aristocrate*; Paris, 1790.

Lough, John, "The Earliest Refutation of Rousseau's *Contrat social*," *French Studies*, XXIII, 1969, pp. 23–39.

McAdam, J. I., "Rousseau and the Friends of Despotism," *Ethics*, LXXIV, 1963, pp. 34–43.

McManners, J., *"The Social Contract* and Rousseau's Revolt Against Society," inaugural lecture delivered November 6, 1967, at Leicester University, published in pamphlet form by the Leicester University Press; Leicester, 1968.

MacNeil, G. H., "The Anti-Revolutionary Rousseau," *American Historical Review*, LVIII, 1953, pp. 808–23.

Manuel, F. E. and F. P., "Sketch for a Natural History of Paradise," *Daedalus*, Winter 1972, pp. 83–128.

Marcuse, Herbert, *Reason and Revolution*; London, 1941.

Mauzi, Robert, "La Conversion de Julie dans *La Nouvelle Héloïse*," *AJJR*, XXXV, 1959–62, pp. 29–38.

*L'idée du bonheur en France au XVIII<sup>e</sup> siècle*; Paris, 1960.

"Le Problème religieux dans *La Nouvelle Héloïse*," in *Jean-Jacques Rousseau et son oeuvre: problèmes et recherches*, Paris, 1964, pp. 159–69.

May, Gita, "Voltaire a-t-il fait une offre d'hospitalité à Rousseau?" *Studies on Voltaire and the Eighteenth Century*, XLVII; Genève, 1966, pp. 93–113.

Mazauric, Claude, "Le Rousseauisme de Babeuf," *Annales historiques de la Révolution française*, XXXIV, 1962, pp. 439–64.

Meyer, Paul H., "The Attitude of the Enlightenment Towards the Jew," *Studies in Voltaire and the Eighteenth Century*, XXVI, 1963, pp. 1161–1205.

"The Individual and Society in Rousseau's *Emile*," *Modern Language Quarterly*, XIX, 1958, pp. 99–114.

"Rousseau and the French Language," *Esprit Créateur*, IX, 1969, pp. 187–97.

Moreno, J. L., "The Creativity Theory of Personality," *Arts and Sciences*; New York University Bulletin, New York, 1965, pp. 18–24.

Mossner, E. C., *The Life of David Hume*; Austin, Texas, 1954.

[Naville, Pierre], "Examen du *Contrat social* de Jean-Jacques Rousseau avec des remarques pour servir d'antidote à quelques principes. Publié par Jean Fabre," *AJJR*, XXII, 1933, pp. 9–15.

Neumann, Erich, *The Origins and History of Consciousness*; New York, 1954.

Neumann, Franz, "Anxiety and Politics," in M. R. Stein, A. J. Vidich, and D. M. White, eds., *Identity and Anxiety: Survival of the Person in Mass Society*; Glencoe, Ill., 1960, pp. 269–90.

    *The Democratic and the Authoritarian State*; Glencoe, Ill., 1957.

Nicholas, Jean, "Une lettre inédite de Jean-Jacques Rousseau," in *Jean-Jacques Rousseau (1712–1778) Pour le 250ᵉ anniversaire de sa naissance*; Gap, 1963, p. 208.

Olszewicz, Vencesks, "Documents polonais sur Jean-Jacques Rousseau et Thérèse LeVasseur," *AJJR*, VII, pp. 75–90.

O'Mara, Patrick F., "Jean-Jacques and Geneva. The Petty Bourgeois Milieu of Rousseau's Thought," *The Historian*, XX, 1957–58, pp. 127–52.

Osmont, Robert, "Un événement aussi triste qu'imprévu," *Revue d'histoire littéraire*, LXV, 1965, pp. 614–28.

Peoples, M. H., "La Querelle Rousseau-Hume," *AJJR*, XVIII, 1927–28.

Peyre, Henri, "The Influence of Eighteenth-Century Ideas on the French Revolution," *Journal of the History of Ideas*, X, 1949, pp. 63–87.

    *Literature and Sincerity*; New Haven and London, 1963.

Picon, Gaëtan, *Introduction à une esthétique de la littérature*, 2 vols.; Paris, 1953.

Plamenatz, John, *Man and Society*, 2 vols.; New York, 1963.

    "On le forcera d'être libre," in *Rousseau et la philosophie politique*, *Annales de philosophie politique*, No. 5; Paris, 1965, pp. 137–52.

Plan, P.-P., ed., *Rousseau raconté par les gazettes de son temps*; Paris, 1912.

Politzer, R. L., "Rousseau on the Theatre and the Actors," *Romanic Review*, XLVI, 1955, pp. 250–57.

Pomeau, René, *Politique de Voltaire*; Paris, 1963.

Pottle, F. A., "The Part Played by Horace Walpole and James Boswell in the Quarrel between Rousseau and Hume," *Philosophical Quarterly*, IV, 1925, pp. 351–63.

Rang, M., "Le Dualisme anthropologique dans l'*Emile*," in *Jean-Jacques Rousseau et son temps*; Paris, 1964, pp. 195–203.

Rey, Auguste, *Jean-Jacques Rousseau dans la valée de Montmorency*; Paris, 1909.

Ritter, E., "La Famille et la jeunesse de Jean-Jacques Rousseau," *AJJR*, XVI, 1924–25, pp. 3–250.

Ritter, Gerhard, "Direct Democracy and Totalitarianism," *Diogenes*, No. 7, 1954–55.

Roddier, Henri, "A propos de la querelle Rousseau-Hume. Précisions chronologiques," *Revue de littérature comparée*, XVIII, 1938, pp. 452–77.

    "Education et politique chez Jean-Jacques Rousseau," in *Jean-Jacques Rousseau et son oeuvre*; Colloque de Paris, Paris, 1964, pp. 183–94.

Rousseau, Jean-Jacques, *Du Contrat social*, ed. Maurice Halbwachs; Paris, 1943.

    *Emile, ou de l'education*, ed., F. et P. Richard; Paris, 1951.

    *Lettre à M. d'Alembert sur les spectacles*, critical edition, ed. M. Fuchs; Lille et Genève, 1948.

    *Lettres écrites de la montagne*, with a Preface by Henri Guillemin; Neuchâtel, 1962.

    *The Political Writings of Rousseau*, ed. C. E. Vaughan, 2 vols.; Cambridge, Eng., 1915.

Rousset, Jean, "Rousseau romancier," in *Jean-Jacques Rousseau*; Université ouvrière et Faculté des lettres de l'Université de Genève, Neuchâtel, 1962, pp. 67–80.

Sainte-Beuve, C. A., *Nouveaux lundis*, Vol. IX; Paris, 1884.

Sampson, R. V., *Progress in the Age of Reason*; London, 1956.

Saussure, Hermine de, "Mme. de Créqui et Jean-Jacques Rousseau," *Revue d'Histoire littéraire*, LII, 1952, pp. 330–38.

Schabert, Tilo, "Die Unverstandene metaphysische Revolte," *Philosophische Rundschau*, XVI, 1969, pp. 39–50.

Schiltz, Raymond, "Rousseau sous le nom de Renou," in *Jean-Jacques Rousseau et son oeuvre*; Colloque de Paris; Paris, 1964, pp. 49–61.

Schinz, Albert, *Etat présent des travaux sur Jean-Jacques Rousseau*; New York, 1941.

Sénelier, Jean, "Jean-Jacques Rousseau, ou la désespérance amoureuse, *Mercure de France*, November–December, 1962, pp. 419–42.

Shklar, Judith, "Rousseau's Images of Authority," *American Political Science Review*, LVIII, 1964, pp. 919–32.

Simon, Walter B., "The Quest for Subjective Certainty," *Journal of Social Psychology*, LXVI, 1965, pp. 171–85.

Smith, D. W., *Helvétius: A Study in Persecution*; Oxford, 1965.

Soboul, Albert, "Classes populaires et Rousseauisme sous la Révolution," *Annales historiques de la Révolution Française*, XXXIV, 1962, pp. 421–38.

　　"Jean-Jacques Rousseau et le Jacobinisme," *Etudes sur le "Contrat social" de Jean-Jacques Rousseau*; Société Les Belles Lettres, Paris, 1964, pp. 405–24.

Southworth, M. J., "La Notion de l'île chez Rousseau," *Studies on Voltaire and the Eighteenth Century*, LXX, 1970, pp. 179–93.

Spink, J. S., *Jean-Jacques Rousseau et Genève*; Paris, 1934.

Spinoza, B. de, *Writings on Political Philosophy*, ed., A. G. A. Balz; New York, 1937.

Starobinski, Jean, "Du *Discours de l'inégalité* au *Contrat social*," in *Etudes sur le "Contrat social" de Jean-Jacques Rousseau*; Société Les Belles Lettres, Paris, 1964, pp. 97–110.

　　"The Illness of Rousseau," *Yale French Studies*, No. 28, pp. 64–74.

　　*L'Oeil vivant*; Gallimard, Paris, 1961.

Stein, M. R., Vidich, A. J., and White, D. M., eds., *Identity and Anxiety: Survival of the Person in a Mass Society*; Glencoe, Ill., 1960.

Stelling-Michaud, Sven, "Lumières et politique," *Studies on Voltaire and the Eighteenth Century*, XXVII, 1963, pp. 1519–43.

　　"Rousseau et l'injustice sociale," in *Jean-Jacques Rousseau*; Université ouvrière et Faculté des lettres de l'Université de Genève, Neuchâtel, 1962, pp. 171–86.

Stern, Fritz, *The Politics of Cultural Despair*; Berkeley, Calif., 1961.

Talmon, J. L., *The Rise of Totalitarian Democracy;* Boston, 1952.

Taylor, S. S. B., "Rousseau's Contemporary Reputation in France," *Studies on Voltaire and the Eighteenth Century*, XXIV-XXVII, 1963, pp. 1545–74.

Thomson, D., "The Dream of Unanimity," *Fortnightly Review*, February 1953, pp. 75–80.

Tönnies, Ferdinand, *Community and Society*; East Lansing, Mich., 1957.

Torrey, N. L., *The Spirit of Voltaire*; New York, 1938.

Trilling, Lionel, *Beyond Culture*; New York, 1955.

Van Eerde, J., and Hubbard, A., "The Christian Religion in the *Grande Encyclopédie* and in *The Great Soviet Encyclopedia*," *Saggi filosofici*, XIV; Torino, 1964, pp. 5–22.

Vladchos, Georges, "L'Influence de Rousseau sur la conception du *Contrat social* chez Kant et Fichte," in *Etudes sur le "Contrat social" de Jean-Jacques Rousseau*; Société Les Belles Lettres, Paris, 1964, pp. 459–80.

Volpe, Galvano della, "Critique marxiste de Rousseau," in *Etudes sur le "Contrat social" de Jean-Jacques Rousseau;* Société Les Belles Lettres; Paris, 1964, pp. 503–13.

"Du *Discours sur l'inégalité à l'Etat et la Révolution,"* Europe, No. 391–2, 1961, pp. 181–8.

Voltaire, *Mélanges;* Paris, 1961.

*Oeuvres complètes,* ed. Louis Moland. 52 vols.; Paris, 1877–1885, 1875 ff.

Vyverberg, Henry, *Historical Pessimism in the French Eighteenth Century;* Cambridge, Mass., 1958.

Waisbord, Bernard, "Rousseau et le théâtre," *Europe,* No. 391–2, 1961, pp. 108–20.

Walter, E. B., "The Politics of Decivilization," in M. R. Stein, A. J. Vidich, and D. M. White, eds., *Identity and Anxiety: Survival of the Person in Mass Society;* Glencoe, Ill., 1960, pp. 291–307.

Wilson, A. M., "The Unpublished Portion of Grimm's Critique of *La Nouvelle Héloïse,"* Modern Language Review, LXIX, 1964, pp. 27–9.

Wolpe, Hans, "Psychological Ambiguity in *La Nouvelle Héloïse,"* University of Toronto Quarterly, XXVIII, 1958–59, pp. 279–90.

Wood, M. M., *Paths of Loneliness;* New York, 1953.

# Index

[ 379 ]